A Dictionary of Quotations in Mathematics

ALSO BY ROBERT A. NOWLAN

Born This Day: A Book of Birthdays and Quotations of Prominent People Through the Centuries (1996)

BY ROBERT A. NOWLAN
AND GWENDOLYN W. NOWLAN

A Dictionary of Quotations and Proverbs About Cats and Dogs (2001)

The Films of the Nineties: A Complete, Qualitative Filmography (2001)

Cinema Sequels and Remakes, 1903–1987 (1989/2000)

A Dictionary of Quotations about Communication (2000)

Film Quotations: 11,000 Lines Spoken on Screen, Arranged by Subject, and Indexed (1994)

The Films of the Eighties: A Complete, Qualitative Filmography (1991)

FROM MCFARLAND

A Dictionary of Quotations in Mathematics

Compiled and Edited by

ROBERT A. NOWLAN

McFarland & Company, Inc., Publishers
Jefferson, North Carolina, and London

Library of Congress Cataloguing-in-Publication Data

A dictionary of quotations in mathematics / compiled and edited by
Robert A. Nowlan
p. cm.
Includes bibliographical references and indexes.
ISBN 0-7864-1284-4 (softcover : 50# alkaline paper) ∞
1. Mathematics—Quotations, maxims, etc. I. Nowlan, Robert A.
QA99.D53 2002 510—dc21 2002005268

British Library cataloguing data are available

Manufactured in the United States of America

McFarland & Company, Inc., Publishers
Box 611, Jefferson, North Carolina 28640
www.mcfarlandpub.com

my v

To all th
who

And to the m
who taught

Table of Contents

7 Language, Linguistics and Mathematics

8 Mathematics: Creation, Discovery or Invention?

9 The Sciences and Mathematics I

10 The Sciences and Mathematics II

11 Mathematics and the Arts

12 Mathematics and the Social Sciences

13 Teaching and Learning Mathematics

14 The Nature of Infinity

15 Pure Mathematics and Applied Mathematics

16 Mathematicians

17 Some Mathematical People I

Acknowledgments

My some fifty years as a lover of mathematics has been enhanced by the acquaintance, often all too brief, with many mathematicians, some only through their works; others as long time friends; some my teachers and some my students. The following list is most certainly incomplete, but the individuals named as well as those innocently overlooked are owed my grateful appreciation for assisting me in a lifetime pursuit of the question: "What is mathematics?"

Frank Adams, Carl B. Allendorfer, Laura Altman, Zeki Ararat, William Arroyo, James Aubrey, George Baglini, Linda Bagoly, Mary Bagoly, Thomas Banchoff, Tracy Barber, Frank Bass, Helen Bass, Max Beberman, E.G. Begle, Eric Temple Bell, Jane Berling, William Berlinghoff, Douglas Bey, R.H. Bing, Ralph Boas, Jr., Keith Boucher, Carl B. Boyer, Joseph Brignoli, John Brillante, R. Creighton Buck, David Cady, Cynthia Cafasso, Emil Capatani, Paul Cappello, Roberta Carlson, William Carlson, Constantin Caratheodory, Paul Caron, Jeanne Cavallaro, Eric Ka Sheng Chan, Dan E. Christie, Karen Climis, Edward Connors, Sister Miriam Patrick Cooney, Jim Countryman, Richard Courant, H.S.M. Coxeter.

Charles Davis III, Philip J. Davis, John Derwent, Rich DeCesare, Christopher Decker, Keith Devlin, Leonard Dickson, Jean Dieudonne, Roy Dubisch, William Dunham, W.L. Duren, Jr., Richard Dwyer, Paul Erdos, Vincent Esposito, Joan Evans, Howard W. Eves, Harold P. Fawcett, Sharon Feeley, Howard Fehr, Lucienne Felix, William Feller, Matthew Fitzgerald, John Fraleigh, Hank Franz, Donald Fray, Donna Gagliardi, Martin Gardner, Kathleen Garrison, Henry Gates, Michael Gemignani, Stephen Gilbert, Ross Gingrich, Abraham Goetz, Joanne Gorski, Christine Grabelski, Kerry Grant, Bodh Gulati, Jacques Hadamard, Alexander J. Hahn, Kathleen Halloran, Lawrence Hally, Paul Halmos, G.H. Hardy, Kevin Hart, Nicolle Hartnett, Mary Healy, Thomas Heath, Christopher Hee, Deborah Herbst, I.N. Herstein, David Hilbert, Peter Hilton, Barbara Hoberg, John Hocking, Lancelot Hogben, Alfred Hopper, Gary Hoyt, Anthony Hughes, Witold Hurewicz.

Vicky Jacobson, Milko Jeglic, Donavan A. Johnson, Robert Jones, Mark Kac, Edward Kasner, Nancy Keegan, J.L. Kelley, John G. Kemeny, Mikhail Khlystov, Stephen Kleene, Felix Klein, Morris Kline, Konrad Knopp, Edna Kramer, Barbara Krause, Kyle Kruczek, Leo Kucyznski, Mary Jane Kunde, Kazimierz Kuratowski, Louis Guillou, Jeffrey Lange, Serge Lange, Martha Larkin, Bert Latil, Karen Latil, Walter Lederman, Solomon Lefeschetz, Kevin Lonergan, Cecilia Lowe, Donald Lynch, Dennis Makowski, Benoit Mandelbrot, Susan Mariano, Cecil Mast, Hideeyuki Masui, Kenneth O. May, Hermina Mazeiko, C.T. McCormick, Neal H. McCoy, Thomas McGann, Mark McGuire, Joanne McLoughlin, Michael Meck, Bert Mendelson, Bruce E. Meserve, Richard Miles, C.N. Mills, John W. Milnor, John Misner, Edwin Moise, Christine Moore, E.H. Moore, Jared Moore, John

Moore, Bryan Moran, George D. Mostow, Barbara Mucherino, William Muller.

Joan Nagy, James R. Newman, Carroll V. Newsom, Ivan Niven, Edward Nowlan, Shina Numatsu, Joel Oman, Timothy O'Meara, Oystein Ore, Garry Orlando, Roger Pahl, Walter Petroskey, Jeff Philson, Philip Poffenberger, Michael Pollack, Barth Pollak, Henry O. Pollak, George Polya, Lev Pontryagin, Shalani Prawl, Irene Priess, Willard von Orman Quine, Mina Rees, Constance Reid, Robert Reilly, Kenneth Reynolds, Brien Riedell, T.E. Rine, Herbert Robbins, Julia Robinson, Werner W. Rogosinski, Paul C. Rosenbloom, Arnold Ross, Gian-Carlo Rota, H.L. Royden, Rudy Rucker, Mary Ellen Rudin, Walter Rudin, Karen Ruehling, Arlene Ruff, Andrew Rule, Frank Rush, Bertrand Russell, David Ryan.

Thomas L. Saaty, George Sarton, John Saunders, Nancy Saunders, W.W. Sawyer, William L. Schaaf, Dorothy Schrader, Gerald Schultz, Gary Segal, Waslaw Sierpinski, George F. Simmons, I.M. Singer, Barry Smith, David Eugene Smith, Frank Smith, J. Philip Smith, Max A. Sobel, Susan Spencer, James Stasheff, Lynn A. Steen, Sherman Stein, Hugo Steinhaus, Ian Stewart, Thomas Stewart, Wilhelm Stoll, Marshall Stone, Dirk Struik, Laura Sullivan, Leonard Sulski, Theresa Sutherland, Amy Tavares, Angus Taylor, Mary Terni, Ivo Thomas, Michael Thompson, Heinrich Tietze, E.C. Titchmarsh, Gregory Troughton, A.W. Tucker, Herbert W. Turnbull.

Stanislaw Ulam, Rose Valeriano, Bartel L. van der Waerden, Henry van Engen, Ismat Virani, John von Neumann, Wendy Walker, Robert Washburn, Donald Weidman, Andre Weil, Barry Weiner, Marie J. Weiss, David Wells, Sarah West, Hermann Weyl, Alfred North Whitehead, George Whitehead, Mary Whitman, Helmut Wielandt, Eugene P. Wigner, Raymond L. Wilder, Margaret F. Willerding, Karl Wilson, Robert Wilson, Sharleene Wisniewski, Warren Wong, Xinlan Yang, Joseph Yearsley, Gail Young, J.W. Young, James Young, Hans Zassenhaus, Nancy Zemina, Walter Ziemba.

In addition I owe more than can be repaid to my parents, Robert and Marian Nowlan, to my children and their spouses, Robert and Andy, Philip and Crystal, Edward and Amy, Jennifer and Peter, Evan, Andrew and Melanie, to my grandchildren Alexandra, Thomas, John, Catherine, and to all my brothers and sisters, their spouses, children and grandchildren. I have had many friends not named here, who although not mathematicians, have been so very supportive in my life and career, and I thank them here as well.

R.A.N.

Preface

French mathematician Simeon-Denis Poisson (1781–1840) once remarked "Life is good for only two things, discovering mathematics and teaching mathematics." While a bit of an overstatement, anyone who has spent many years as an active student and teacher of mathematics should find much truth in the assertion. Not everyone agrees as to what it takes to be considered a mathematician. Some assert that there are only a few mathematicians—just those who have made major contributions to the field. Others are more inclusive, numbering among mathematicians all who pursue the subject in any sense in their lives and careers.

The demand that to be considered a mathematician one must be especially ingenious, original and the creator or discoverer of ideas and theories of epoch proportions is harmful. By excluding so many, one reinforces the notion, held by the majority of the excluded, that only a minuscule percentage of human beings can ever understand mathematics or have any need for understanding mathematics. Far preferable is the belief that mathematics is a thing of great beauty and utility, the study of which will be of great benefit intellectually, aesthetically and practically to all who delve into "its unreasonable effectiveness" as Eugene P. Wigner put it in a 1960 article.

It has been asserted that five percent of the mathematicians have produced ninety-five percent of the "important" mathematics, while the other important five percent is the work of the remaining ninety-five percent of mathematicians. As it was early apparent that I would be one of the latter ninety-five percent, I set a goal for myself of contributing to my beloved mathematics by sharing it with others even if I could not excel in creating it. I would be true to Poisson's maxim not by discovering new mathematics, but by playing the role of a middle man who could understand the work of those who did and in turn interpret what was learned to the uninitiated. I would be a teacher.

This book of nearly 3,000 quotations sorted into 38 chapters and 389 sections can serve several audiences, not the least of whom are those seeking appropriate mathematical quotations on particular topics, expecting to find an accurate citation as to its source. But in compiling this book, first from a cache of quotations collected over the years and used in my teaching, and then in an exhaustive search of numerous sources, I have been mindful of my lifelong goal of wanting to share mathematics with other people.

To understand mathematics, one must consider questions of the nature of what, when, where, why, who and how. Sad to say, mathematics is often poorly taught by instructors who give little consideration to such questions. Many believe that mathematics should be taught as "a thing to do" rather that as a way of thinking. It is difficult to fault teachers at the secondary and elementary school levels who do not explore a store of such questions with their students if their college instructors haven't made them aware of the importance and the pleasure in doing so. The latter should know better. One of the most important ways teachers of any subject can help their students is to teach them how to think about the subject. This often is best accomplished if the students can observe how their instructors think.

One of the reasons that mathematics is poorly taught, creating students with an indifference if not a dislike for the subject, is that a disproportionate emphasis is put on learning how to perform certain tasks without enlightening the students with bigger thoughts about what they are doing, when and where it can be done, by whom, and why. Much mathematics is taught as a none-too-useful industrial art, providing students with little insight into distinguishing what is important from what is merely meant to get from here to there, or even what is the underlying idea being studied. These evenhanded presentations leave students with the impression that everything is equally important. Students march through the woods and are shown the trees, but not raised above them so as to see the beauty of the forest.

Frequently, teachers give answers before questions are raised. As mathematics lends itself to being presented in a piecemeal fashion, students learn multiple mathematical bites without ever tasting the scrumptious meal that should be being served. While mathematics is fascinating, many students never get a whiff of this fact. Too much time is spent on ill-explained procedures, treated as if they were the ends, not the means. The mathematics curriculum changes far too slowly. If students of the nineteenth century walked into today's mathematics classrooms, they would feel very much at home. While today's textbooks have more pictures and color, the drill and imitating aspects and the dependence on memory used in teaching the subject would seem all too familiar. These approaches to teaching and learning leave little room for discoveries or acquaintance with advances made in mathematics in the past two centuries. Students are given far too few opportunities to think mathematically as they are busy with the tasks of memorizing techniques and imitating procedures. They are being trained, not educated. It would almost seem that a good student is considered to be one who can jump through hoops rather than ask questions.

Part of the reason for this unfortunate state of affairs, particularly at the elementary and secondary school level, is that those charged with devising the curriculum have decreed that the main goal is to present the tool aspects of mathematics without giving much consideration to the art of mathematics, the language of mathematics, the game of mathematics or the science of mathematics, and certainly not to its beauty and pleasure. This attitude that mathematics is primarily a tool even fails to develop the most significant aspects of mathematics as a tool. There is a widespread misunderstanding as to which life tools are those that mathematics may contribute to.

If properly presented, mathematics assists students in developing the life tools of (1) using language and terminology properly, (2) translating and transforming information from one mode to another, (3) listening effectively, (4) following lines of reasoning, (5) making comparisons, (6) analyzing data and arguments, (7) seeing patterns, (8) employing acquired knowledge in new situations, (9) asking pertinent and impertinent questions, (10) discovering and interpreting relationships, (11) making and validating generalizations, (12) applying general principles to specific cases, (13) drawing and stating inferences, (14) reasoning both deductively and inductively, (15) realizing the relevance of information, (16) developing tenable hypotheses, (17) formulating valid conclusions in making arguments, (18) constructing strategies for learning, (19) making proper use of assumptions and (20) developing critical thinking and problem solving abilities.

Fortunately, there are many in mathematics education who are making great strides in presenting mathematics as the fascinating and useful subject it is. They deserve praise and support. That they exist is a hopeful sign. That their number needs to be greatly increased is obvious. It seems that the beginning of a new century and a new millennium is a perfect time to reconsider the goals, objectives and means of education in all fields, not just mathematics. The gaps between those who know and can do and those who know little and can do little is becoming dangerously great. It is time that all those who are talking about the importance of education in this country should combine their efforts and join a crusade to achieve the goal that all willing students may develop their talents to the fullest extent possible. The first agreement that needs to be made is that there are no easy or unique answers. One size does not fit all.

The French social scientist, mathematician and philosopher Auguste Comte said, "To understand a science it is necessary to know its history." Students can be exposed to many years of mathematical study without learning very much about the history of the subject, and without making the acquaintance of mathematical practitioners who developed the subject over the millenniums. The history of mathematics and the work of those men and women who have created, discovered or developed it should be an integral part of the teaching of the subject, not a rare and passing afterthought or a set of boxes in the textbook with pictures and brief but not very interesting biographies of a few famous mathematicians.

To be fair to those teachers who labor long and hard trying to instill an appreciation of mathematics in the minds and hearts of reluctant students, they themselves may have been exposed to little of the history of mathematics in their own preparation. This book of quotations is meant to be a source of material for teachers who would expand their knowledge of the development and nature of mathematics and learn of those responsible for its creation and discovery. In this way it is possible to reach out to the teachers' pupils and share the exciting news of the fascination of mathematics and its remarkable utility.

What distinguishes this quotations dictionary from many others is that it is designed and arranged in such a way that it may serve as a teaching tool. Each chapter is dedicated to some area of mathematics. Each chapter consists of sections further subdividing the subject. The quotations of each section are arranged alphabetically by the names of the authors of the quotations. Taken as a whole the quotations of the section serve as something of a group discussion of the topic by those who have thought extensively about it. In reading the quotations in the various sections, readers will be privy to something of a conversation among mathematicians and observers of mathematics relating to the topic.

While meant to play a role as a teaching tool, the book of quotations lays no claim to being a mathematics textbook. That is, while mathematical topics are discussed and observations about them are made, they are not provided as instructions in mathematical techniques and theories. The overall goal of the book of quotations is to assist the reader in developing his or her own answers to questions such as "What is mathematics?" "Is mathematics discovered or invented?" "What is the difference between pure mathematics and applied mathematics?" "What is the nature of mathematical proof?" "What is the relationship of mathematics to other branches of learning?" and many others. The following is a brief summary of the chapters.

Chapter **1**, **The God Hypothesis, Religion and Mathematics**, explores the early view of mathematics as the means by which humans could learn of what they believed was their the creator's intentions for the universe and its inhabitants. Is there order and harmony in the workings of the universe? If so, how did it come to be so? God or gods were man's first hypothesis in explaining things. Humans felt a responsibility to seek and discover God's plan.

Chapters **2** and **3**, **The Nature of Mathematics I & II,** is a selection of interpretations of mathematics in the probably futile attempt to definitively answer the question "What is mathematics?" These attempts include descriptions of the essence of mathematics and analogies offered to give one a feeling for mathematics' nature. There are also discussions of mathematics as a tool, an art, a game, a language, and a science. Opinions are given as to what particular talents are needed to understand and appreciate mathematics. Those who have chosen to pursue mathematical careers explain what it is about the subject that drew them to it. Observations are made as to the unfortunate ignorance of the true nature of mathematics by so many otherwise informed and talented individuals.

Chapters 4 and **5, The Development of Mathematics I & II,** offer discussions about the growth of mathematical ideas from their simple beginnings to sophisticated theories. The authors of the quotations comment on the role of intuition, experimentation, induction and deduction in advancing the store of mathematics. The role of undefined terms, definitions, hypotheses, abstractions and generalizations are explored by those who know of such things. The revolutions which have occurred from time to time in mathematics are debated as is the development of what is known as modern mathematics and what makes it modern.

Chapter **6, The Historical Origins of Mathematics,** is a treasure chest of commentary on the contributions of the various civilizations of the world dating back to the ancient nations of Egypt, Sumeria, Babylon, China, Japan, and the Mayan empire. Much attention is given to the Greeks of antiquity who perhaps more than any others of ancient times made mathematics what it has become—a deductive science. The meager contributions of the Romans and the important advances provided by the Hindus and the Arabs while Europe slept through the Dark Ages are highlighted. And yes, attention is given to those who, inspired by their contacts with the achievements in the East, awakened Europe to the study of mathematics.

In Chapter 7, **Language, Linguistics and Mathematics**, the role of mathematics in making convincing arguments and explanations is explored by noting the advances in notation, symbolism and terminology. Chapter **8, Mathematics: Creation, Discovery or Invention?** explores the interesting question of whether mathematical ideas exist, only awaiting those of sufficient cleverness to discover them, or if these are creations and inventions conceived in human minds.

Chapters **9** and **10, The Sciences and Mathematics I & II,** examine the relationships between mathematics and the various sciences. In particular, physics and astronomy are fields of science whose development and history cannot be separated from mathematics. Early mathematicians, physicists and astronomers, right up to at least the eighteenth century, were the same people. They would have seen no sense in identifying themselves as one or another of these seekers of truth, and not the other two. They were seekers of truth about nature and ideas in general. The role of mathematics in other sciences, while perhaps having a shorter history of association and common purpose, has provided rich rewards when it is discovered how to measure ideas that interest practitioners in these fields.

There are many who think of mathematics more as an art than a science. In Chapter **11, Mathematics and the Arts,** much evidence is given to support this view. The authors of the quotations in this chapter discuss the harmony, order, proportion and symmetry common to mathematics and artistic fields such as architecture, painting, and music. The comparisons of mathematics to poetry and literature are expertly made. Those who find it strange to associate beauty with mathematics are most in need of hearing the views of the authors of quotations in this chapter.

Chapter **12, Mathematics and the Social Sciences,** examines relationships of much more recent duration than those with the sciences and the arts. But then disciplines such as sociology, economics and psychology have brief histories by comparison with the arts and sciences. The future relationships between these fields and mathematics looks to be most promising.

Chapter **13**, **Teaching and Learning Mathematics,** concentrates on the ways people learn or do not learn mathematics. Expert recommendations on how to improve things are offered by those who have successfully learned mathematics and in a few cases by those who did not and know why they did not. The quotations stress the importance of proper communication in teaching if learning is to take place. Advice is given on reading and writing mathematics.

Chapter **14**, **The Nature of Infinity,** tackles the perplexing problem of infinity, a concept which does not exist in the world of those who nevertheless have been able to conceive of it. The chapter explores the ever-changing interpretations of infinity and the problems its existence causes in attempting to relate it to mathematical concepts.

In Chapter **15**, **Pure Mathematics and Applied Mathematics**, the proponents of "mathematics for mathematics' sake" and those of "mathematics for solving existing problems" bring out their best arguments. Others abhor the seemingly antagonistic relationships between the two. Perhaps it is the very names "pure" and "applied" which cause the split.

Chapter **16**, **Mathematicians**, looks at those who do mathematics, this being one definition of mathematics, i.e., what mathematicians do. It ends with a brief glance at the role of women in mathematics, a sad commentary on the fact that, as in so many other areas, the mathematical world stood in the way of women by denying that they had any need to learn mathematics or the ability to do mathematics.

Chapters **17**, **18** and **19**, **Some Mathematical People, I, II & III,** offer a few comments on the lives and careers of ninety-three mathematicians. Among these are certainly the greatest mathematicians of all time, but not everyone chosen deserves that designation. The list is representative of mathematicians who have contributed greatly and even modestly to the development of mathematics. A common feature found in these brief glimpses of their lives and careers is to note that these men and women are human—all too human.

Chapter **20**, **Problems and Problem Solving**, provides discussions of some of the more famous problems of mathematics, dating from the three problems of antiquity—that is, the squaring of the circle, the trisection of an angle and the duplication of the cube—to Fermat's last theorem, each of which generated enormous amounts of mathematics during the long history of attempts to solve them. Problem solving is a skill not peculiar to mathematics, but the study of mathematics is a good way of honing the skill.

One of the original uses of mathematics was in the human attempt to understand nature. Chapter **21**, **Mathematics and Nature,** examines this role, concentrating on the various "laws" which have been discovered or deduced over the centuries. Chapter **22**, **Philosophy, Mathematics, Truth and Certainty,** explores the deceptive notions of truth and certainty, and the philosophies which have been developed to explain the concepts. The role of mathematics in this task is paramount.

Is mathematics logical or is it merely that when mathematicians are being illogical they know it? In Chapter **23**, **Logic and Foundations,** there are discussions of the history of attempts to find logic in mathematics or to inject logic into it. It also explores the consequences of these efforts on the foundation of mathematics and the struggles of many great mathematicians to mend the cracks that developed.

How does one know if a mathematical assertion has been proven? It's not an easy question to answer. Chapter **24**, **Proof and Mathematics,** explores the various notions of proof, its nature and the role of rigor in proof. In addition there is commentary by mathematicians on the desire to produce "elegant" proofs.

In Chapter **25**, **Sets, Relations and Functions**, the modern concepts of relations on sets and functions between sets is discussed, with emphasis on the notions of equality and equivalence of ideas.

Chapter **26**, **Space: Real and Idealized,** contrasts the notions of the space in which we reside with spaces created by mathematicians in which their problems are situated and solved.

The examination of the various branches of mathematics begins in earnest with Chapter **27**, **Numbers: The Heart of Mathematics**. Here the authors speak of the nature and development of the number concept, beginning with counting, and describe the uses and meanings attached to whole numbers, fractions, negative numbers, integers, irrational numbers and zero. Chapter **28**, **Numbers and Number Theory,** continues the story of numbers with the introduction into mathematics of real and rational numbers, imaginary and complex numbers, and the algebraic and transcendental numbers, with particular attention paid to the remarkable numbers "e" and "pi." Cantor and others comment on his transfinite numbers. The chapter ends with an examination of topics in number theory, which is what the ancient Greeks meant when they spoke of "arithmetic."

Chapter **29**, **Arithmetic,** differentiates the two notions of arithmetic, that which is concerned with number manipulation and calculations and that which studies the properties of numbers. It ends with some words about the important invention of logarithms by John Napier and others.

In Chapter **30**, **Algebra and Trigonometry**, the discussion ranges from the manipulations and equation solving of elementary algebra on to modern abstract algebras, including linear algebra, group theory and the study of the invariants of transformation groups. These latter notions have led to the modern interpretation of mathematics.

Chapter **31**, **The Art of Measurement,** explores the role mathematics plays in discovering the secrets of nature by taking its measure in many different ways. There is a section on the metric system which has almost everywhere supplanted the old English system of weights and measures, save in the United States.

Chapters **32** and **33**, **Geometry I & II,** explore the long history and development of the branch of mathematics which had its origins in Babylon and Egypt and found its heart and soul with the ancient Greeks. Besides comments on things geometrical in the Euclidean sense, the authors of the quotations tell the fascinating story of the long struggle to prove the parallel postulate as a consequence of the other axioms. This was shown to be impossible independently by three mathematicians, Bolyai, Gauss and Lobachevski, who instead invented new geometries. The sources also discuss the development of projective geometry and the new but still very old notions of chaos and fractal geometry.

In Chapter **34**, **Topology and Graph Theory**, the discussion centers on the absorbing branch of mathematics which deals not with measurements in the usual sense but with position. Topology offers an inquiry into qualitative rather than quantitative properties of figures and spaces. In one sense topological notions are among the very first mathematical concepts with which humans become familiar as very young children. One observer of the subject put it well when he noted that neither an infant nor a topologist can tell a ball from a block. Neither takes the measure of the two items, the child because he cannot, the topologist because he does not choose to do so.

Chapter **35**, **Analysis and Calculus,** offers commentary on the way mathematicians analyze information in order to solve problems and explore the development of the concepts of limits and continuity, as well as both the differential and the integral calculus. The chapter also has a selection of quotations relating to infinite series and differential equations.

In Chapter **36**, **Computers, Algorithms and Mathematical Models**, our commentators focus in on the machines which have come to be so important in many different ways in our daily lives. The advancement of these remarkable tools owes a great debt to Charles Babbage and Ada Byron Lovelace, the former for having developed the first modern conception of a computer and Lord Byron's daughter for being the first to set out the procedures for formulating a computer program.

Chapter 37, **The Theory of Probability**, examines the mathematics of ignorance. The science of probability, if that isn't a contradiction in terms, was inspired by the interests of gamblers, and is employed in the many aspects of life which deal with uncertainty. Chapter **38, Statistics and Statisticians**, details how collections of data can be interpreted as aids to decision making and the analysis of problems—where it may be impossible to find definitive answers, but the search for them is made more convenient.

Each quotation is numbered in a way as to indicate its location in the book. For instance, quotation 11.5.4 is the fourth quotation in section five of chapter eleven. The author of each quotation is cited, as is the source. At the end of the volume is a bibliography of books which are sources of quotations with a few additional ones included for those who wish to read further about a particular topic. The citation of periodicals and journals where some quotations are found are given with the quotations.

There are two indexes. The first is an index of authors, which gives references to their quotations. For instance, 14.6.5 refers the reader to the fifth quote in the sixth section of the fourteenth chapter, where Carl Friedrich Gauss has something to say about infinity. The second is a keyword index, providing references in the same fashion. Among other keywords, there is "thinking."

In deciding which quotations, of some 10,000 collected, to include in this work, one criterion was that each quotation should make a reader think and perhaps even wish to respond—perhaps in agreement, perhaps in disagreement. I hope that the quotations will cause some readers to seek out more of what the particular author or others have had to say on the topic. If those who use this book find the words of the authors as interesting, thought-provoking and fascinating as has your compiler, then my goal is accomplished.

R.A.N.

1

The God Hypothesis, Religion and Mathematics

1.1 In the Beginning: God the Creator

1. Six is a number perfect in itself, and not because God created the world in six days; rather the contrary is true. God created the world in six days because this number is perfect, and it would remain perfect, even if the work of the six days did not exist.

—*St. Augustine:* ***The City of God****, 413–27, R.H. Barrow, tr., 1950*

2. ...indeed what reason may not go to Schoole to the wisdom of Bees, Aunts, and Spiders? what wise hand teacheth them to doe what reason cannot teach us? ruder heads stand amazed at those prodigious pieces of nature, Whales, Elephants, Dromidaires and Camels; these I confess are the Colossus and Majestick pieces of her hand; but in these narrow Engines there is more curious Mathematicks, and the civilities of these little Citizens more neatly sets forth the wisdom of their Maker.

—*Sir Thomas Browne:* ***Certain Miscellany Tracts****, published posthumously, 1690*

3. Many people have an image of God as a sort of pyrotechnic engineer, lighting the blue touchpaper to ignite the Big Bang, and then sitting back to watch the show.

—*Paul Davies:* ***The Mind of God****, 1992*

4. Einstein once remarked that the thing which most interested him was whether God had any choice in creating the world as it is. Einstein was not religious in the conventional sense, but he liked to use God as a metaphor for expressing deep questions of science. This particular question has vexed generations of scientists, philosophers, and theologians. Does the way have to be the way it is, or could it have been otherwise? And if it could have been otherwise, what sort of explanation should we seek for why it is as it is?

—*Paul Davies:* ***The Mind of God****, 1992*

5. Napoleon: "You have written this huge book on the system of the world without once mentioning the author of the universe." Laplace: "Sire, I had no need of that hypothesis." Later when told by Napoleon about the incident, Lagrange commented: "Ah, but that is a fine hypothesis. It explains so many things."

—*Augustus De Morgan:* ***A Budget of Paradoxes****, 1872*

6. God uses beautiful mathematics in creating the world.

—*Paul Adrien Dirac: "Pretty Mathematics";* ***International Journal of Theoretical Physics****, Vol. 21, 1982; quoted in Heinz R. Pagels:* ***The Cosmic Code****, 1982*

7. God created the world and the integers, all in seven days. He then ordered two of his biotechnicians, James and Francis, to construct a genetic code for the fractional numbers. Moreover, they were to give special prominence to His favorite number "π."

—*R.J. Duffin: "The Patron Saint of Mathematics";* ***The Mathematical Intelligencer****, Vol. 15, 1, 1993*

8. If God has created the world, his primary worry was certainly not to make its understanding easy for us.

—*Albert Einstein: Letter to David Bohm, February 10, 1954*

9. In the beginning (if there was such a thing), God created Newton's laws of motion together with the necessary masses and forces. This is all; everything beyond this follows from the development of appropriate mathematics methods by means of deduction.

—*Albert Einstein: Quoted in* ***The Quotable Einstein****, Alice Calaprice, ed., 1996*

10. Geometry existed before the Creation, is co-eternal with the mind of God, is God himself (what exists in God that is not God himself?); geometry provided God with a model for the Creation and was implanted into man, together with God's own likeness—and not merely conveyed to his mind through the eyes.

—Johannes Kepler: ***Harmonies Mundi (The Harmony of the World)****, 1619*

11. Wherefore he [the Creator] made the world in the form of a globe, round as from a lathe, having its extremes in every direction equidistant from the center, the most perfect and the most like itself of all figures; for he considered that the like is infinitely fairer than the unlike.

—Plato: ***Timaeus****, c. 350 B.C.*

12. Just as the author does not write the first chapter, and then leave the others to write themselves, so God's creativity is not to seem as uniquely confined to, or even especially interested in, the event of the Big Bang. Rather, his creativity has to be seen as permeating equally all space and all time: his role as Creator and Sustainer merge.

—Russell Stannard: "Making Sense of God's Time"; ***The Times*** *(London), August 22, 1987*

1.2 The Mathematical Nature of God

1. I think that I shall never c
A # lovelier than 3;
For 3 < 6 or 4,
And than 1 it's slightly more.
.....
Atoms are split by men like me,
But only God is 1 in 3.

—John Atherton: "Threes" (To be Sung by Niels Bohr): ***The New Yorker Magazine****, 1957*

2. The nature of God is a circle whose center is everywhere and its circumference is nowhere.

—St. Augustine: A.D. 354–450; Quoted in Ralph Waldo Emerson: ***Essays: First Series****, "Circles" 1841*

3. God is like a skillful Geometrician.

—Sir Thomas Browne: ***Religio Medici****, 1642*

4. As I picture each planet floating within the geometric perfections of space, I think geometry was implanted in man along with the image of God.
Geometry is indeed God.

—Siv Cedering: ***Letters from the Floating World****, 1984*

5. God does not care about our mathematical difficulties. He integrates empirically.

—Albert Einstein: In L. Infeld: ***Quest****, 1942*

6. God is a child; and when he began to play, he cultivated mathematics. It is the most godly of man's games.

—V. Erath: ***Das blinde Spiel****, 1954*

7. Chance is perhaps the pseudonym of God when He did not want to sign.

—Anatole France (1844–1924): Attributed

8. God does arithmetic.

—Carl Friedrich Gauss: c. 1790s; Attributed

9. God made the universe out of complex numbers.

—R. W. Hamming: "The Unreasonable Effectiveness of Mathematics"; ***The American Mathematical Monthly****, Vol. 87, 2; February, 1980*

10. How orderly philosophical is the landscape, are all the inhabitants of this World! It is the creation of a god who 'ever plays the geometer'.

—Aldous Huxley: "Music at Night"; ***Music at Night and Other Essays****, 1931*

11. The God that reigns in Olympus is Number Eternal.

—Carl Jacobi: c. 1840s; Quoted in Tobias Dantzig: ***Number: The Language of Science****, 1954*

12. God is the tangential point of zero and the infinite.

—Alfred Jarry: ***Gestes et opinions du Docteur Faustroll Pataphysicien****, 1898*

13. All the pictures which science now draws of nature and which alone seem capable of according with observational facts are mathematical pictures.... From the intrinsic evidence of his creation, the Great Architect of the Universe now begins to appear as a pure mathematician.

—Sir James Jeans: ***The Mysterious Universe****, 1930*

14. God made integers, all else is the work of man.

—Leopold Kronecker: ***Jahresbericht der Deutschen Mathematiker Vereinigung****; First published anonymously in the* ***Dublin Nation****, April 1, 1843*

15. As God calculates, so the world is made.

—Gottfried Wilhelm Leibniz: ***Theodicy****, 1710; Quoted in Morris Kline:* ***Mathematics and the Physical World****, 1959*

16. Man knows only these poor mathematical theories about the heavens, and only God knows the real motions of the heavens and their causes.

—Moses Maimonides: ***Guide for the Perplexed****, 1190*

17. Mathematics is the life supreme. The life of God is mathematics. All divine messengers are mathematicians. Pure mathematics is a religion, its attainment requires a theophany. Mathematicians are the only blessed people.

—Novalis [Friedrich Leopold von Hardenberg]: ***Schriften II****, 1802*

18. If God speaks to man, he undoubtedly uses the language of mathematics.

—Henri Poincare (1854–1912): Attributed

1.3 Discovering God's Thoughts

1. The human mind is made so that when we do mathematics, we have the feeling that we are dealing with some reality. There are some parts of mathematics that are more real than others. To me the value of a mathematical theory depends on how much it deals with things made, in some sense, by God and not by man.

*—Lipman Bers: Quoted in Allen L. Hammond: "Mathematics—Our Invisible Culture"; **Mathematics Today—Twelve Informal Essays**, 1978*

2. The mathematical truths which you call eternal have been laid down by God and depend on Him entirely no less than the rest of his creatures.

—Rene Descartes: Letter to Fr. Mersenne, April, 1630

3. God sometimes granteth unto a man to learn and know how to make things the like whereof in his day no other can contrive, and perhaps for a long time none hath been before him, and after him another cometh not soon.

*—Albrecht Durer: Quoted in a review of Erwin Panofsky: "Albrecht Durer" in the [London] **Times Literary Supplement**; February 9, 1946*

4. There's an old debate about whether you create mathematics or just discover it. In other words, are the truths already there, even if you don't yet know them? If you believe in God, the answer is obvious. Mathematical truths are there in the SF's mind, and you just rediscover them.

*—Paul Erdos: Quoted in Paul Hoffman: **The Man Who Loved Only Numbers**, 1998 [SF stands for the "Supreme Fascist," Erdos's way of referring to God.]*

5. If I see a really nice proof, I say it comes straight from the Book ... God has a transfinite Book, which contains all theorems and their best proofs, and if He is well intentioned toward those [mathematicians], He shows them the Book for a moment. And you wouldn't even have to believe in God, but you must believe that the Book exists.

*—Paul Erdos: Quoted in Alexander Soifer: "From Problems of Mathematical Olympiads to Open Problems of Mathematics," **Mathematics Competitions**, vol. 4, 1991*

6. The laws of nature are but the mathematical thoughts of God.

*—Euclid: Quoted in Stanley Gudder: **A Mathematical Journey**, 1976*

7. The mathematicians are the only happy ones. He who does not reach for a mathematical book with devotion and read it as the word of God does not understand it.

*—Friedrich von Hardenberg: In Walter R. Fuchs: **Mathematics for the Modern Mind**, H.A. Holstein, tr., 1967*

8. In God's mind, the difficulties and puzzles in philosophy of mathematics disappear. How do numbers exist? Why do mathematical facts seem certain and timeless? Why does mathematics work in the "real world"? ... In the mind of God, it's no problem.... The trouble with today's Platonism is that it gives up God, but wants to keep mathematics a thought in the mind of God.

*—Reuben Hersh: **What Is Mathematics, Really?**, 1997*

9. ...what is physical is subject to the law of mathematics, and what is spiritual to the laws of God, and the laws of mathematics are but the expression of the thoughts of God.

*—Thomas Hill: "The Uses of Mathesis": **Bibliotheca Sacra**, vol. 32, 1857*

10. Never tell a young person that anything cannot be done. God may have been waiting for centuries for someone ignorant enough of the impossible to do that very thing.

*—John Andrew Holmes: **Wisdom in Small Doses**, 1927*

11. When the first mathematical, logical and natural uniformities, the first laws, were discovered, men were so carried away by the clearness, beauty and simplification that resulted that they believed themselves to have deciphered authentically the eternal thoughts of the Almighty. His mind also thundered and reverberated in syllogisms. He also thought in conic sections, squares and roots and ratios, and geometrized like Euclid. He made Kepler's laws for the planets to follow; he made velocity increase proportional to the time in falling bodies, he made the laws of sines for light to obey when refracted.

*—William James: **The Varieties of Religious Experience**, 1902*

12. Geometry is one and eternal shining in the mind of God. That share in it accorded to men is one of the reasons that Man is the image of God.

*—Johannes Kepler: Open letter to Galileo Galilei: in **Dissertatio cum Nuncio Sidereo**, 1610*

13. Why do I call [Newton] a magician? Because he looked on the whole universe and all that is it as a riddle, as a secret which he could read by applying pure thought to certain evidence, certain mystic clues which God had laid about the world to allow a sort of philosopher's treasure hunt to the esoteric brotherhood. He believed that these clues were to be found partly in the evidence of the heavens and in the constitution of elements ... but also partly in certain papers and traditions handed down by the brethren in an unbroken chain back to the original cryptic revelation in Babylonia. He regarded the universe as a cryptogram set by the Almighty.... By pure thought, by concentration of mind, the riddle, he believed, would be revealed to him.

*—John Maynard Keynes: Address to the Royal Society Club, 1942: "Newton, the Man"; **The World of Mathematics**, James R. Newman, ed., 1956*

14. To understand God's thoughts, we must study statistics, for these are the measure of his purpose.

*—Florence Nightingale: in Karl Pearson: **The Life, Letters and Labors of Francis Galton** 1924*

15. Is mathematics invention or discovery? Or are mathematicians really uncovering truths which are, in fact, already 'there'—truths whose existence is quite independent of the mathematician's activities? ...much more comes out of the structure [of cases such as the Mandelbrot set] than is put in the first place. One may take the view that in such cases the mathematicians have stumbled upon 'works of God.'

*—Roger Penrose: **The Emperor's New Mind: Concerning Computers, Minds and the Laws of Physics**, 1989*

16. The study of infinity is much more than a dry academic game. The intellectual pursuit of the Absolute Infinite is, as Georg Cantor realized, a form of the soul's quest for God. Whether or not the goal is ever reached, an awareness of the process brings enlightenment.

*—Rudy Rucker: **Infinity and the Mind**, 1982*

17. ...the mathematician is entirely free to construct what worlds he pleases; he is not discovering the fundamental principles of the universe nor becoming acquainted with the ideas of God.... Why the external should obey the laws of logic, why, in fact, science should be possible, is not at all an easy question to answer.

*—John W.N. Sullivan: J.R. Newman, ed. in **The World of Mathematics**, 1956*

1.4 Mathematical Evidence of the Existence of God

1. It is at least as certain that God, who is a Being so perfect, is, or exists, as any demonstration of geometry can possibly be.

*—Rene Descartes: **Discourse on Method**, 1637*

2. I could prove God statistically. Take the human body alone—the chance that all the functions of the individual would just happen is a statistical monstrosity.

*—George Gallup: in **Omni**, vol. 2, November, 1979*

3. We still believe that the universe should be logical and beautiful; we just dropped the word "God."

*—Stephen Hawking: "The Breakdown of Physics"; **Nature**, 1975*

4. Science, being human enquiry, can hear no answer except an answer couched somehow in human tones. Primitive man stood in the mountains and shouted against a cliff; the echo brought back his own voice, and he believed in a disembodied spirit. The scientist of today stands counting out loud in the face of the unknown. Numbers come back to him—and he believes in the Great Mathematician.

*—Richard Hughes: in J.R. Newman, ed. **The World of Mathematics**, 1956*

5. It is seemingly paradoxical that Newton could "prove" God's existence on the basis of his mathematical discoveries whereas Laplace with even more marvelous confirmation of the mathematical design of the universe at hand saw no need for God. But this paradox is readily explained by the remark of Pascal that nature proves the existence of God only to those who already believe in Him.

*—Morris Kline: **Mathematics in Western Culture**, 1953*

6. Given for one instance an intelligence which could comprehend all the forces by which nature is animated and the respective positions of the beings which compose it, if moreover, this intelligence were vast enough to submit these data to analysis, it would embrace in the same formula both the movements of the largest bodies in the universe and those of the lightest atom; to it nothing would be uncertain, and the future and the past would be present to its eyes.

—Pierre-Simon de Laplace: "A Philosophical Essay on Probabilities," 1814

7. It is as certain that there is a God, as that the opposite angles made by the intersection of two straight lines are equal.

—John Locke: "An Essay Concerning Human Understanding," 1690

8. Nothing has afforded me so convincing a proof of the unity of the Diety as these purely mental conceptions of numerical and mathematical science which have been by slow degrees vouchsafed to man, and are still granted in these higher times by the Differential Calculus, now superseded by the Higher Algebra, and all of which must have existed in that sublimely omniscient Mind from eternity.

*—Mary Somerville: **Personal Reflections from Early Life to Old Age of Mary Somerville, with Selections from Her Correspondence**, Martha Somerville, ed., 1873*

9. God exists since mathematics is consistent, and the Devil exists since we cannot prove it.

—Andre Weil: Quoted in P. Rosenbloom: ***The Elements of Mathematical Logic,*** *1950*

1.5 God's Universe—Playing Dice or Order and Harmony?

1. Many scientists and philosophers in the 17th and 18th centuries argued that since the universe was created by God, and since God would not do anything unnecessary, everything in the universe must be arranged in the simplest possible way; there is no need to spell out the criticisms to which such an argument might be subjected.

—Robert J. Baum: ***Philosophy and Mathematics,*** *"Introduction," 1973*

2. If God has made the world a perfect mechanism, He has at least conceded so much to our imperfect intellects that in order to predict little parts of it, we need not solve innumerable differential equations, but can use dice with fair success.

—Max Born: in Heinz R. Pagels: ***The Cosmic Code,*** *1982*

3. I cannot believe that God plays dice with the universe.... You believe in the God who plays dice, and I in complete law and order in a world which objectively exists, and which I, in a wildly speculative way, am trying to capture. I firmly believe, but I hope that someone will discover a more realistic way, or rather a more tangible basis than it has been my lot to do. Even the great initial success of the quantum theory does not make me believe in the fundamental dice game, although I am well aware that your younger colleagues interpret this as a consequence of senility.

—Albert Einstein: Letter to Max Born: Quoted in Phillip Frank: ***Einstein, His Life and Times,*** *1947*

4. It therefore seems that Einstein was doubly wrong when he said that God does not play dice. Consideration of particle emission from black holes suggests that God not only plays dice. He also sometimes throws the dice where they cannot be seen.

—Stephen Hawking: "The Breakdown of Physics"; ***Nature,*** *1975*

5. The chief aim of all investigations of the external world should be to discover the rational order and harmony which has been imposed on it by God and which He revealed to us in the language of mathematics.

—Johannes Kepler: ***Harmonies Mundi (The Harmony of the World),*** *1619*

6. Under the assumption that space be something in itself it is impossible to give a reason why God should have put the bodies (without tampering with their mutual distances and relative positions) just at this particular place and not somewhere else; for instance, why He should not have arranged everything in the opposite order by turning East and West about.

—Gottfried Wilhelm Leibniz: ***Leibniz—Basic Writings,*** *George R. Montgomery, tr., 1968*

1.6 Religion, Theology and Mathematics

1. The mathematicians are friends to religion in as much as they charm the passions, restrain the impetuosity of the imagination, and purge the mind from error and prejudice.

—John Arbuthnot: ***The Usefulness of Mathematical Learning,*** *c. 1690; Quoted in Underwood Dudley: "Is Mathematics Necessary?";* ***Mathematics Education Dialogues,*** *March, 1998*

2. If perhaps these [narrow-minded theologians and professors who were tied to literal interpretations of the Bible] are babblers who, although ignorant of mathematics, nevertheless take it upon themselves to pass judgment on mathematical questions and, improperly distorting some passages of the Scriptures to their purpose, dare to find fault with my system and censure it, I disregard them even to the extent of despising their judgment as uninformed.

—Nicolaus Copernicus: ***De Revolutionibus Orbium Coelestium,*** *1543*

3. Suppose we loosely define a religion as any discipline whose foundations rest on an element of faith, irrespective of any element of reason which may be present. Quantum mechanics for example would be a religion under this definition. But mathematics would hold the unique position of being the only branch of theology possessing a rigorous demonstration of the fact that it should be so classified.

—F. De Sua, 1956: Quoted in Howard W. Eves: ***In Mathematical Circles,*** *1969*

[Kurt Goedel proved that a mathematical system cannot be both complete and consistent, which in essence proves that the "truth" of mathematics cannot be proven, and thus must be accepted as a matter of faith.]

4. One of the reasons that was put forward to deny existence to negative numbers was the claim that God would not admit them. This small detail exemplifies a factor in the development of mathematics which historians often ignore: the bearing of belief in religion on the mathematics of its adherents.

—Ivor Grattan-Guinness: ***The Rainbow of Mathematics,*** *1997*

5. Galileo was no idiot. Only an idiot could believe that science requires martyrdom—that may be necessary in religion, but in time a scientific result will establish itself.

—*David Hilbert: in Howard Eves:* ***Mathematical Circles Squared****, 1971*

6. To all of us who hold the Christian belief that God is truth, anything that is true is a fact about God, and mathematics is a branch of theology.

—*Hilda P. Hudson: Quoted in E.T. Bell:* ***The Magic of Numbers****, 1946*

7. The two main divisions of mathematics, analysis and geometry, correspond with some exactness to the two great mysteries of the Christian faith, the Trinity and the Incarnation.

—*Hilda P. Hudson: Quoted in E.T. Bell:* ***The Magic of Numbers****, 1946*

8. The true foundation of theology is to ascertain the character of God. It is by the aid of Statistics that law in the social sphere can be ascertained and codified, and certain aspects of the character of God thereby revealed. The study of statistics is thus a religious service.

—*Florence Nightingale: Quoted in F.N. David:* ***Games, Gods and Gambling****, 1969*

9. Number was born in superstition and reared in mystery, ...numbers were once made the foundation of religion and philosophy, and the tricks of figures have had a marvelous effect on a credulous people.

—*F.W. Parker:* ***Talks on Pedagogics****, 1894*

10. In the common opinion certainty is to be found in two places and only two—religion and mathematics. In religion you believe by faith, in mathematics you prove what you want to prove. Outside these cozy domains, life is full of doubt and uncertainty and that is what people prefer because it is what they are used to. But it is a comfort to feel that, if the doubt and uncertainty become excessive, once can fall back on the eternal verities of religion or mathematics.

—*J.L. Synge:* ***Kandelman's Krim****, 1957*

11. Whatever a man prays for, he prays for a miracle. Every prayer reduces itself to this: "Great God, grant that twice two be not four."

—*Ivan Sergeievich Turgenev: "Prayer"; in* ***Turgenev—The Novels and Tales****, C. Garnett, tr., 1894–9*

12. Kierkegaard once said religion deals with what concerns man unconditionally. In contrast (but with equal exaggeration) one may say that mathematics talks about the things which are of no concern at all to man.

—*Hermann Weyl: "A Half-Century of Mathematics";* ***The American Mathematical Monthly****, 58, 1951*

2

The Nature of Mathematics I

2.1 What Is Mathematics?

1. The existence and nature of mathematics is a more compelling and far deeper problem than any of the problems raised by mathematics itself.

*—David Berlinski: in a review of T.W. Korner: **The Pleasures of Counting**, in **The Sciences**, July/August, 1997*

2. The question "What is mathematics?" cannot be answered meaningfully by philosophical generalities, semantic definitions or journalistic circumlocutions. Such characteristics also fail to do justice to music or painting. No one can form an appreciation of these arts without some experience with rhythm, harmony and structure, or with form, color and composition. For the appreciation of mathematics actual contact with its substance is even more necessary.

*—Richard Courant: "Mathematics in the Modern World," **Scientific American**, September, 1964*

3. ...the word "sophist" applied to Greeks in various disciplines, means "teacher of young men," and indeed "mathematics" itself comes from mathemata, meaning "matters to be taught."

*—Ivor Grattan-Guinness: **The Rainbow of Mathematics**, 1997*

2.2 The Essence of Mathematics

1. The essence of mathematics lies in its freedom.

*—Georg Cantor; **Mathematische Annalen** 46, 1895*

2. Mathematics is the study of what is true of hypothetical states of things. This is its essence and definition. Everything in it, therefore, beyond the first precepts for the construction of the hypotheses, has to be of the nature of apodictic inference.

*—Charles Sanders Peirce: "The Regenerated Logic," **The Monist**, 7, October, 1896*

3. To find the simple in the complex, the finite in the infinite—that is not a bad description of the aim and essence of mathematics.

*—Jacob T. Schwartz: in **Discrete Thoughts: Essays on Mathematics, Science and Philosophy**, Mark Kac, Gian-Carlo Rota, Jacob T. Schwartz; Quoted in **The Mathematical Intelligencer**, vol. 12, 1990*

2.3 Characteristics of Mathematics

1. With even a superficial knowledge of mathematics, it is easy to recognize certain characteristic features: its abstractness, its precision, its logical rigor, the indisputable character of its conclusions, and finally, the exceptionally broad range of its applications.

*—A.D. Aleksandrov: in **Mathematics: Its Content, Methods, and Meanings**, A.D. Aleksandrov, A.N. Kolmogorov & M.A. Lavrentev, eds., 1963*

2. When mathematicians speak of their work, two words carry great importance. Mathematics is a field where a "problem" is not a bad thing. In fact, a good problem is what mathematicians yearn for; it signifies interesting work. The second word is "proof," which strongly suggests the rigor of the discipline.... A proof, once given, is permanent; some have existed since the time of the Greeks. A proof confirms truth for the mathematician the way experiment or observation does for the natural scientist.

*—Phillip A. Griffiths: "Mathematics at the Turn of the Millennium"; **The American Mathematical Monthly**, 107, January, 2000*

3. Mathematics is abstract thought, mathematics is pure logic, mathematics is creative art. All these statements are wrong, but they are all a little right, and they are all nearer the mark than "mathematics is numbers" or "mathematics is geometric shapes."

—Paul R. Halmos: "Mathematics as a Creative Art"; ***American Scientist****, 56, 1968*

4. Among the minor, yet striking characteristics of mathematics, may be mentioned the fleshless and skeletal build of its propositions; the peculiar difficulty, complication, and stress of its reasonings; the perfect exactitude of its results; their broad universality; their practical infallibility.

—Charles Sanders Peirce: "The Essence of Mathematics"; in ***The World of Mathematics****, James R. Newman, ed., 1956*

5. Mathematics occupies a peculiar and a unique role in that it is neither a science nor an art but partakes of both disciplines. Art provides the motivation for most pure mathematicians but science (the term understood in its broadest sense) reaps the harvest.

—H.L. Resnikoff & R.O. Wells, Jr.: ***Mathematics in Civilization****, "Introduction," 1973*

2.4 Mathematics Is...

1. Mathematics is one of the deepest and most powerful expressions of pure human reason, and, at the same time, the most fundamental resource for description and analysis of the experiential world.

—Hyman Bass: in his "Statement" as a candidate for President of the American Mathematical Society, 1999

2. Mathematics is the handwriting on the human consciousness of the very Spirit of Life itself.

—Claude Bragdon: Quoted in Monte Zerger: "A Quote a Day Educates"; ***The Mathematical Intelligencer****, vol. 20, #2, Spring, 1998*

3. Mathematics is the multiplied necessity ... the supreme arbiter. From its decisions there is no appeal.

—Tobias Dantzig: ***Number: The Language of Science****, 1954*

4. Mathematics is the product of real, flesh-and-blood human beings whose lives may reflect the inspiration, the tragic, or the bizarre.

—William Dunham: ***Journey Through Genius****, "Preface," 1990*

5. That is to say [mathematics], the only study which can confer "a just and comprehensive idea of what is meant by science," and at the same time, furnish an exact conception of the general method of scientific investigation, is that which knows nothing of observation, nothing of experiment, nothing of induction, nothing of causation.

—Thomas Henry Huxley: "Scientific Education: Notes of an After-dinner Speech," ***MacMillan's Magazine****, vol. XX, 1869 [See James J. Sylvester's response to Huxley's view of mathematics in item 2.5.6]*

6. Mathematics in general is fundamentally the science of self-evident things.

—Felix Klein: ***Anwendung der Differential-und Integralrechnung auf Geometrie****, 1902*

7. Mathematics is ... a self-realizing infinite field for optional actions, architectural and other labors, for exploration, heroic excursions, daring incursions, surmises.

—Stanislaw Lem: "Non serviam" in ***A Perfect Vacuum: Perfect Reviews of Non-Existent Books****, 1971*

8. Mathematics is not the discoverer of laws, for it is not induction; neither is it the framer of theories, for it is not hypothesis; but it is the judge over both, and it is the arbiter to which each must refer its claims; and neither law can rule nor theory explain without the sanction of mathematics.

—Benjamin Peirce: "Linear Associative Algebra"; ***American Journal of Mathematics*** *vol. 4, 1881*

9. Mathematics is the abstract key which turns the lock of the physical universe.

—John Polkinghorne: in Keith Devlin: ***The Science of Patterns****, 1997*

10. Mathematics is being lazy. Mathematics is letting the principles do the work for you so that you do not have to do the work yourself.

—George Polya: in Marion Walter & Tom O'Brien: "Memories of George Polya"; ***Mathematics Teaching****, vol. 116, 1986*

11. Mathematics is not playing with numbers and doing accounting. Mathematics is dealing with ideas in a creative and yet very precise way.

—Przemyslaw Prusinkiewicz: Quoted in Keith Devlin: ***Life by the Numbers****, 1998*

12. Thus mathematics may be defined as the subject in which we never know what we are talking about, nor whether what we are saying is true.

—Bertrand Russell: "Recent Work on the Principles of Mathematics"; ***International Monthly****, 1901:* ***Mysticism and Logic****, 1917*

13. Mathematics ... is a bit like discovering oil.... But mathematics has one great advantage over oil, in that no one has yet ... found a way that you can keep using the same oil forever.

—Andrew Wiles: ***Notices of the AMS****, May, 1997*

14. [Mathematics] is an independent world Created out of pure intelligence.

—William Wordsworth: in ***The Prelude****, 1850*

2.5 Mathematics as an Intellectual Activity

1. Mathematics as an expression of the human mind reflects the active will, the contemplative reason, and the desire for aesthetic perfection. Its basic elements are logic and intuition, analysis and construction, generality and individuality.

—*Richard Courant & Herbert Robbins:* ***What Is Mathematics?***, *1941*

2. Mathematics is a product—a discovery—of the human mind. It enables us to see the incredible, simple, elegant, beautiful, ordered structure that lies beneath the universe we live in. It is one of the greatest creations of mankind—if it is not indeed the greatest.

—*Keith Devlin:* ***Life by the Numbers***, *1998*

3. Mathematics, like dialectics, is an organ of the higher sense, in its execution it is an art like eloquence. To both nothing but the form is of value; neither cares anything for content. Whether mathematics considers pennies or guineas, whether rhetoric defends truth or error, is perfectly immaterial to either.

—*Johann Wolfgang von Goethe:* ***Proverbs in Prose***, *1819*

4. Mathematics is a world created by the mind of man, and mathematicians are people who devote their lives to what seems to me a wonderful kind of play.

—*Constance Reid: G.L. Alexanderson: "An Interview with Constance Reid";* ***Two-Year College Mathematical Journal***, *vol. 11; September, 1980*

5. Mathematics is concerned exclusively with objects and structures which are creations of the mind, although they may be suggested by or patterned on things that are found in the so-called real world. And since it deals only with creations of the mind, it is cumulative in a way that the other sciences are not.

—*Arte Selberg: "Reflections around the Ramanujan Centenary" in* ***Collected Papers***, *vol. I. 1989*

6. ...we are told [by T.H. Huxley] that "Mathematics is that study which knows nothing of observation, nothing of experiment, nothing of induction, nothing of causation." I think no statement could have been made more opposite to the undoubted facts of the case, that mathematical analysis is continually invoking the aid of new principles, new ideas and new methods, not capable of being defined by any form of words, but springing directly from the inherent powers and activity of the human mind, [...] that it is unceasingly calling forth the faculties of observation and comparison, that one of its principal weapons is induction, that it has frequent resource to experimental trial and error and verification, and that it affords a boundless scope for the exercise of the highest efforts of imagination and invention.

—*James J. Sylvester:* ***Address to The British Association for the Advancement of Science***, *1869*

7. Mathematics is a human activity almost as diverse as the human mind itself.

—*Gabor Szego: in Josef Kurschak:* ***Hungarian Problem Book***, *1963*

8. The question for the ultimate foundation and the ultimate meaning of mathematics remains open; we do not know in which direction it will find its final solution nor even whether a final objective answer can be expected at all. "Mathematizing" may well be a creative activity of man, like language or music, of primary origin, whose historical decisions defy complete objective rationalization.

—*Hermann Weyl:* ***Obituary Notes of Fellows of the Royal Society***, *4, 1944*

2.6 Analogies of Mathematics

1. If science is viewed as an industrial establishment, then mathematics is an associated power plant which feeds a certain kind of indispensable energy into the establishment.

—*Salomon Bochner:* ***The Role of Mathematics in the Rise of Science***, *1966*

2. Mathematics may be likened to a large rock whose interior composition we wish to examine. The older mathematicians appear as perservering stone cutters slowly attempting to demolish the rock from the outside with hammer and chisel. The later mathematicians resemble expert miners who seek vulnerable veins, drill into these strategic places, and then blast the rock apart with well placed internal charges.

—*Howard W. Eves:* ***In Mathematical Circles***, *1969*

3. Mathematics may be compared to a mill of exquisite workmanship, which grinds you stuff of any degree of fineness; but, nevertheless, what you get out depends on what you put in; and as the grandest mill in the world will not extract wheat flour from peascods, so pages of formulae will not get a definite result out of loose data.

—*T.H. Huxley: in* ***Quarterly Journal of the Geological Society***, *vol. 25, 1869*

4. Mathematics is no more the art of reckoning and computation than architecture is the art of making bricks or hewing wood, no more than painting is the art of mixing colors on a palette, no more than the science of geology is the art of breaking rocks, or the science of anatomy the art of butchering.

—*Cassius J. Keyser:* ***Lectures on Science, Philosophy and Art***, *1908*

5. The mathematics of our day seems to be like a great weapons factory in peace time. The show window is filled with parade pieces whose ingenious, skillful, eye-appealing execution attracts the connoisseur. The proper motivation for and purpose of these objects, to battle and conquer the enemy, has receded to the background of consciousness to the extent of having been forgotten.

—Felix Klein: ***Development of Mathematics in the 19th Century****, 1925*

6. Mathematics is removed from this turmoil of human life, but its methods and the relations are a mirror, an incredible pure mirror, of the relations that link the facts of our being.

—Konrad Knopp: "Mathematics as a Cultural Activity"; ***Preusside Jahrbucher****, 1928; Walter Kaufmann-Buhler;* ***The Mathematical Intelligencer****, vol. 7, 1, 1985*

7. Mathematics is like checkers in being suitable for the young, not too difficult, amusing, and without peril to the state.

—Plato: ***The Republic***

8. Mathematics is not just a collection of isolated facts: it is more like a landscape; it has an inherent geography that its users and creators employ to navigate through what would otherwise be an impenetrable jungle.

—Ian Stewart: ***Nature's Numbers****, 1995*

9. I feel mathematics is like this tree that starts from very basic things like space and number, but it has these wonderful branches and flowers that go beyond. I mean, it's too fantastic—the same way that music is too fantastic. It's sort of unbelievable: you start concentrating on one theorem, some really fantastic theorem, and you can't really hold it. It's so amazing.

—Dennis Sullivan: Quoted in Allen L. Hammond: "Mathematics—Our Invisible Culture"; ***Mathematics Today—Twelve Informal Essays****, 1978*

2.7 Mathematics as a Tool

1. Mathematics is the tool specially suited for dealing with abstract concepts of any kind and there is no limit to its power in this field.

—Paul Adrien Maurice Dirac: in P.J. Davis & R. Hersh: ***The Mathematical Experience****, 1981*

2. Mathematics serves as a handmaiden for the explanation of the quantitative situations in other subjects, such as economics, navigation, finance, biology and even the arts.

—H.M. Fehr: "Reorientation in Mathematics Education: ***Teachers College Record****, vol. 54, May, 1953*

3. Mathematics in its pure form, as arithmetic, algebra, geometry, and the applications of the analytic method, as well as mathematics applied to matter and force, or statics and dynamics, furnishes us the peculiar study that gives to us, whether as children or as men, the command of Nature in this its quantitative aspect. Mathematics furnishes the instrument, the tool of thought which we wield in this realm.

—William Toney Harris: ***Psychologic Foundations of Education****, 1898*

4. Once I realized that math was just a tool, it suddenly opened a whole world for me. It allows me to be creative and expressive in whatever domain I want.

—Pattie Maes: Quoted in Keith Devlin: ***Life by the Numbers****, 1998*

5. Mathematics is a process of constructing knowledge, not acquiring it.

—Susan Ohanian: ***Garbage Pizzas, Patchwork Quilts and Math Magic****, 1994*

2.8 The Misunderstanding of the Nature of Mathematics

1. Outside of the closed circle of professional mathematicians, almost nothing is known of the true nature of mathematics research.

—Jerry King: ***The Art of Mathematics****, 1992*

2. Mathematics has this peculiarity, that it is not understood by non-mathematicians.

—Andre Weil: "Organisation et desorganisation en mathematique"; ***Oeuvres Scientifues****, vol. II, 1980*

3. While in other fields brief allusions are met by ready understanding, this is unfortunately seldom the case with mathematical ideas.

—Hermann Weyl: in ***Hermann Weyl****, K. Chandrasekharan, ed., 1986*

2.9 Other Views of the Nature of Mathematics

1. Nor is there much gaiety in mathematics—geometry looks bare and algebra is one more step away from familiar and friendly numbers.

—Jacques Barzun: ***From Dawn to Decadence****, HarperCollins, 2000*

2. A marvelous neutrality have these things Mathematical, and also a strange participation between things supernatural, immortal, intellectual, simple, and indivisible, and things natural, mortal, sensible, compounded and divisible.

—John Dee: "Preface" to his first edition of Euclid's ***Elements****, 1570; Quoted in Stanley Gudder:* ***A Mathematical Journey****, 1976*

3. Mathematics is the one area of human enterprise where the motivation to deceive has been practically eliminated. Not because mathematicians are necessarily virtuous people, but because the nature of mathematical ability is such that deception can be immediately determined by other mathematicians. This requirement of honesty soon affects the character of the conscientious student of mathematics.

*—Howard F. Fehr: "Reorientation in Mathematics Education"; **Teachers College Record**, 54, May, 1953*

4. The word mathematics does not connote a simple entity with a single facet. It relates to a useful art with at least four separate and important aspects. More specifically, mathematics is an art, a language, a tool, and a reckoning.

*—Thornton C. Fry: "Mathematicians in Industry—the First 75 Years": **Science** 143, 1964*

5. Either mathematics is too big for the human mind or the human is more than a machine.

*—Kurt Goedel: in **Collected Works of Kurt Goedel**, Solomon Feferman, John W. Dawson, Jr., Stephen C. Kleene, Gregory H. Moore, Robert M. Solovay & Jean van Heijenoort, 1989*

6. What is exact about mathematics but exactness? And is not this a consequence of the inner sense of truth?

*—Johann Wolfgang von Goethe: **Proverbs in Prose**, 1819*

7. In great mathematics there is a very high degree of unexpectedness, combined with inevitability and economy.

*—G.H. Hardy: **A Mathematician's Apology**, 1941*

8. The best mathematics is serious as well as beautiful—"important" if you like, but the word is very ambiguous, and "serious" expresses what I mean much better.

*—G.H. Hardy: **A Mathematician's Apology**, 1941*

9. In these days of conflict between ancient and modern studies, there must be something to be said for a study which did not begin with Pythagoras, and will not end with Einstein, but is the oldest and youngest of all.

*—G.H. Hardy: "Inaugural Lecture," Oxford, 1920; in **A Mathematician's Apology**, 1941*

10. In mathematics as elsewhere success is the supreme court to whose decisions everyone submits.

*—David Hilbert: "Mathematical Problems"; **Bulletin American Mathematical Society**, vol. 8, 1902*

11. Mathematics knows no races or geographical boundaries; for mathematics, the cultural world is one country.

*—David Hilbert: in Howard Eves, **Mathematical Circles Squared**, 1972*

12. Mathematics is not a topic that one can easily approach with a virgin mind.

*—Wilfrid Hodges: **Building Models by Games**, 1985*

13. Only in mathematics are insights virtually removed from conflicting opinions.

*—Konrad Knopp: "Mathematics as a Cultural Activity"; **Preusside Jahrbucher**, 1928; Walter Kaufmann-Buhler; **The Mathematical Intelligencer**, vol. 7, 1, 1985*

14. Rich in its past, dynamic in the present, prodigious for the future, replete with simple and yet profound ideas and methods, surely mathematics can give something to anyone's culture.

*—Rudolph E. Langer: "The Things I Should Have Done, I Did Not Do"; **American Mathematical Monthly**, vol. 59, September, 1952*

15. A good mathematical joke is better, and better mathematics, than a dozen mediocre papers.

*—J.E. Littlewood: **A Mathematician's Miscellany**, 1953*

16. Mathematics contains much that will neither hurt one if one does not know it nor help one if one does know it.

*—H.L. Mencken: "Minority Reports"; **Notebooks**, 1956*

17. The eternal lesson is that Mathematics is not something static, closed, but living and developing. Try as we may to constrain it into a closed form, it finds an outlet somewhere and escapes alive.

*—Rosza Peter: **Playing with Infinity**, 1962*

18. Not all ideas are mathematics; but all good mathematics must contain an idea.

*—Ian Stewart: **Nature's Numbers**, 1995*

19. If mathematics, including everything that rests on it, were somehow suddenly to be withdrawn from our world, human society would collapse in an instant. And if mathematics were to be frozen, so that it never went a single step farther, our civilization would start to go backward.

*—Ian Stewart: **Nature's Numbers**, 1995*

20. Mathematics begins in bewilderment and ends in bewilderment.

*—John Lighton Synge: **Kandelman's Krim**, 1957*

21. Perhaps the most surprising thing about mathematics is that it is so surprising. The rules which we make up at the beginning seem ordinary and inevitable, but it is impossible to foresee their consequences. These have only been found out by long study, extending over many centuries. Much of our knowledge is due to a comparatively few great mathematicians such as Newton, Euler, Gauss, or Riemann; few careers can have been more satisfying than theirs. They have contributed something to human thought even more lasting than great literature, since it is independent of language.

—*E.C. Titchmarsh:* ***Mathematics for the General Reader****, 1950*

2.10 Mathematics as Art

1. [Mathematics] is also an art—the most intellectual and classical of the arts.

—*Alfred Adler: "Mathematics and Creativity";* ***The New Yorker Magazine****, 1972*

2. We believe that mathematics is an art. The author of a book, the lecturer in a classroom tries to convey the structural beauty of mathematics to his readers, to his listeners. In this attempt he must always fail. Mathematics is logical, to be sure; each conclusion is drawn from previously derived statements. Yet the whole of it, the real piece of art, is not linear; worse than that, its perception should be instantaneous. We all have experienced on some rare occasions the feeling of elation in realizing that we have enabled our listeners to see at a moment's glance the whole of architecture and all its ramifications.

—*Emil Artin: Quoted in John D. Barrow:* ***Pi in the Sky****, 1992*

3. Guided only by their feeling for symmetry, simplicity, and generality, and an indefinable sense of the fitness of things, creative mathematicians now, as in the past, are inspired by the art of mathematics rather than by the prospect of ultimate usefulness.

—*E.T. Bell:* ***The Handmaiden of the Sciences****, 1937*

4. Many arts there are which beautify the mind: of all others none do more garnish and beautify it than the arts which are called mathematical.

—*H. Billinglsey: Quoted in Frank Burk:* ***Lebesque Measure and Integration: An Introduction****, 1998*

5. The mathematician may be compared to a designer of garments, who is utterly oblivious of the creatures whom his garments may fit. To be sure, his art originated in the necessary for clothing such creatures, but this was long ago; to this day a shape will occasionally appear which will fit into the garment as if the garment had been made for it, then there is no end of surprise and delight.

—*Tobias Dantzig:* ***Number, The Language of Science****; 1954*

6. Unlike scientists, who observe nature with all five senses, mathematicians observe nature with the sense of imagination almost exclusively. That is, mathematicians are as specialized, and therefore as well practiced, with this sixth sense as musicians are with sound, gourmets are with tastes and smells, and photographers and filmmakers are with sights. This comparison also suggests that mathematicians are artists of the imagination just as surely as musicians, gourmets, photographers and filmmakers are of their respective sensory domains.

—*Michael Guillen:* ***Bridges to Infinity****, 1999*

7. ...there is a subject called mathematics (mathology?), and that subject is a creative art. It is a creative art because mathematicians live, act, and think like artists; and it is a creative art because mathematicians regard it so.

—*Paul Halmos: "Mathematics as a Creative Art,"* ***American Scientist****, Winter, 1968*

8. I am interested in mathematics only as a creative art.

—*G.H. Hardy:* ***A Mathematician's Apology****, 1941*

9. The mathematician's best work is art, a high perfect art, as daring as the most secret dreams of imagination, clear and limpid. Mathematical genius and artistic genius touch one another.

—*Gosta Mittag-Leffler: Quoted by Havelock Ellis:* ***The Dance of Life****, 1923*

10. Besides the mathematical arts there is no infallible knowledge, except that it be borrowed from them.

—*Robert Recorde:* ***The Ground of Artes****, 1540; Quoted in D. MacHale:* ***Comic Sections****, 1993*

11. Mathematics is too arduous and uninviting a field to appeal to those to whom it does not give great rewards. These rewards are of exactly the same character as those of the artist. To see a difficult, uncompromising material take living shape and meaning is to be Pygmalion, whether the material is stone or hard, stonelike logic. To see meaning and understanding come where there has been no meaning and no understanding is to share the work of a demiurge. No amount of technical correctedness and no amount of labor can replace this creative moment, whether in the life of the mathematician or in that of a painter or musician.

—*Norbert Wiener:* ***Ex-Prodigy****, 1953*

2.11 Mathematics as a Game

1. Mathematics, like Chess, requires too direct and personal a confrontation to allow graceful defeat. There is no element of luck; there are no partners to share the blame for mistakes; the nature of the discipline places it precisely at the center of the intellectual being, where true cerebral power waits to be tested. A loser must admit that in some very important way he is the intellectual inferior of the winner. Both mathematics and chess spread before the participant a vast domain of confrontation of intellect with strong opposition, together with extreme purity, elegance of form, and an infinitude of possibilities.

*—Alfred Adler: "Mathematics and Creativity"; **The New Yorker Magazine**, 1972*

2. To a modern all is fair in war, love and mathematics; to many of the ancients, mathematics was a stulified game to be played according to the prim rules imposed by the philosophy-minded Plato. According to Plato only a straightedge and a pair of compasses were to be permitted as the implements of construction in geometry. No wonder the classical geometers hammered their heads for centuries against "the three problems of antiquity": to trisect an angle; to construct a cube having double the volume of a given cube; to construct a square equal to a circle.

*—E.T. Bell: **Men of Mathematics**, 1937*

3. The mathematician plays a game in which he himself invents the rules while the physicist plays a game in which the rules are provided by Nature, but as time goes on it becomes increasingly evident that the rules which the mathematician finds interesting are the same as those which Nature has chosen.

*—Paul Dirac: "Pretty Mathematics"; **International Journal of Theoretical Physics**, vol. 21, 1982*

4. Reductio ad absurdum, which Euclid loved so much, is one of a mathematician's finest weapons. It is a far finer gambit than any chess play: a chess player may offer the sacrifice of a pawn or even a piece, but a mathematician offers the game.

*—G.H. Hardy: **A Mathematician's Apology**, 1941*

5. Mathematics is a game played according to certain simple rules with meaningless marks on paper.

*—David Hilbert: in N. Rose, **Mathematical Maxims and Minims**, 1988*

6. If mathematics is a game, there is no reason why people should play it if they do not want to. With football, it belongs to those amusements without which life would be endurable.

*—Lancelot Hogben: **Mathematics for the Millions**, 1936*

7. I love mathematics not only for its technical applications, but principally because it is beautiful; because man has breathed his spirit of play into it, and because it has given him his greatest game—the encompassing of the infinite.

*—Rozsa Peter: **Playing with Infinity**, 1962*

8. Pure mathematics is the world's best game. It is more absorbing than chess, more of a gamble than poker, and lasts longer than Monopoly. It's free. It can be played anywhere—Archimedes did it in a bathtub. It is dramatic, challenging, endless, and full of surprises.

*—Richard J. Trudeau: **Dots and Lines**, 1976*

2.12 Mathematics as Language

1. Mathematics is pure language—the language of science. It is unique among languages in its ability to provide precise expression for every thought or concept that can be formulated in its terms.

*—Alfred Adler: "Mathematics and Creativity"; **The New Yorker Magazine**, 1972*

2. Mathematics is in the first place a language in which we discuss those parts of the real world which can be described by numbers or by similar relations of order. But with the workaday business of translating the facts into this language there naturally goes, in those who are good at it, a pleasure in the activity itself. They find the language richer than its bare content; what is translated comes to mean less to them than the logic and the style of saying it; and from these overtones grows mathematics as a literature in its own right.

*—Jacob Bronowski: **Science and Human Values**, 1964*

3. Mathematical language is not only the simplest and most easily understood of any, but the shortest also.

*—H.L. Brougham: **Works**, vol. 7, 1872*

4. Mathematics is the language of high technology. Indeed it is, but I think it is also becoming the eyes of science.

—Tom Bruzustowski: Address to the MITACS NCE annual general meeting; June 6, 2000

5. Mathematics is not so different from other expressions of the human intellectual capacities for communication and imagination. The fact one can learn to say things in mathematical language that cannot be said in other languages is beside the point, as the possibility of different regions of the brain may be used. Mathematics is not the exclusive province of either the gifted or the deranged; it is for all who would seek to be truly educated.

*—James O. Bullock: "Literacy in the Language of Mathematics"; **American Mathematical Monthly**, October, 1994*

6. Mathematics is a way of thinking that can help make muddy relationships clear. It is a language that allows us to translate the complexity of the world into manageable patterns. In a sense, it works like turning off the houselights in a theater the better to see a movie. Certainly, something is lost when the lights go down; you can no longer see the faces of those around you or the inlaid patterns on the ceiling. But you gain a far better view of the subject at hand.

—*K.C. Cole: **The Universe and the Teacup**, 1997*

7. Mathematics, too, is a language, and as concerns its structure and content it is the most perfect language which exists, superior to any vernacular; indeed, since it is understood by every people, mathematics may be called the language of languages. Through it, as it were, nature herself speaks; through it the Creator of the world has spoken, and through it the Preserver of the world continues to speak.

—*C. Dillmann: **Die Mathematik die Fackeltragerin einer neuen Zeit**, 1889*

8. One of the indisputable characteristics of mathematics is that it is a rigorous language with practically no synonyms. If this ideal is not attained in a particular statement or description, that is an indication of imperfection; the corresponding theory is not yet a part of perfected mathematics, though it may very well be a very important chapter of the science in process of formation. Just as mathematics was not created in a day, so its language could not have been fixed from the moment of the work of its construction.

—*Lucienne Felix: **The Modern Aspect of Mathematics**, 1960*

9. Mathematics is a special and subtle language designed to express certain kinds of ideas more briefly, more accurately, and more usefully than ordinary language.

—*Paul R. Halmos: "Mathematics as a Creative Art," **American Scientist**, Vol. 56, 1968*

10. No one would dispute that mathematics is a language. It is the language of the exact sciences. Its "words" are well defined. A serious "essay" expressed in mathematical symbols has a tang of poetry about it for the cognoscenti. The written language of mathematics has evolved in the course of time in an efficient shorthand.

—*H.E. Huntley: **The Divine Proportion**, 1970*

11. It is time that we learned as part of our basic education that mathematics is simply a language, distinguished by its ability for clarity, and particularly well suited to develop logical arguments. The power of mathematics is no more and no less than the power of pure reason.

—*John G. Kemeny: **Random Essays on Mathematics, Education and Computers**, 1964*

12. The sciences of the universe are disciplines whose primary language is mathematics, non-conversational speech, and it's inaccessible even to the reasonably educated nonmathematician.

—*Joyce Carol Oates: Review of E.L. Doctorow's **City of God**; New York Review of Books, March 9, 2000*

13. Without this language [mathematics] most of the intimate analogies of things would have remained forever unknown to us; and we should forever have been ignorant of the internal harmony of the world, which is the only true objective reality....

—*Henri Poincare: "The Value of Science"; **Popular Science Monthly**, 1906*

14. There is nothing that can be said by mathematical symbols and relations which cannot also be said by words. The converse, however, is false. Much that can be and is said by words cannot successfully be put into equations, because it is nonsense.

—*Clifford A. Truesdell: **Six Lectures on Modern Natural Philosophy**, 1966*

3

The Nature of Mathematics II

3.1 Mathematics as Science

1. That mathematics is a theoretical science is evident from those who have pursued that science; they have been lovers of wisdom and have sought to discover eternal truths ... those who have investigated the objects of mathematics have done so not for gain or use but for the sake of truth.

—*H.G. Apostle:* ***Aristotle's Philosophy of Mathematics****, 1952*

2. Mathematics is in many ways the most elaborated and sophisticated of the sciences—or so it seems to me, as a mathematician. So I find both a special pleasure and constraint in describing the progress of mathematics, because it has been part of so much human speculation: a ladder for mystical as well as rational thought in the intellectual ascent of man.

—*Jacob Bronowski: "The Music of the Spheres"* ***The Ascent of Man****, 1973*

3. The science of mathematics performs more than it promises.... The study of the mathematics, like the Nile, begins in minuteness, but ends in magnificence.

—*Charles Caleb Colton:* ***Lacon****, 1820*

4. Mathematics is the science that yields the best opportunity to observe the working of the mind ... and has the advantage that by cultivating it, we may acquire the habit of a method of reasoning which can be applied afterwards to the study of any subject and can guide us in the pursuit of life's object.

—*Marie-Jean Condorcet: Quoted in* ***The Mathematical Intelligencer****, vol. 10, 4, 1988*

5. Mathematics is one of the oldest of the sciences; it is also one of the most active, for its strength is the vigor of perpetual youth.

—*A.R. Forsyth: Presidential Address, British Association for the Advancement of Science, 1897: in* ***Nature****, vol. 56*

6. This science [mathematics] is the work of the human mind, which is destined rather to study than to know, to seek the truth rather than find it.

—*Evariste Galois, 1831; Quoted in Morris Kline:* ***Mathematics: The Loss of Certainty****, 1980*

7. Everything that the greatest minds of all times have accomplished toward the comprehension of forms by means of concepts is gathered into one great science, mathematics.

—*J.F. Herbart: "Pestalozzi's Idee eines A B C der Anschauung";* ***Werke****, 1890*

8. The science of mathematics presents the most brilliant example of the extension of the sphere of pure reason without the aid of experience.

—*Immanuel Kant:* ***Critique of Pure Reason****; "Transcendental Method," 1781*

9. Mathematics is the science which uses easy words for hard ideas.

—*Edward Kasner & James Newman:* ***Mathematics and the Imagination****, 1940*

10. All the mathematical sciences are founded on relations between physical laws and laws of numbers, so that the aim of exact science is to reduce the problems of nature to the determination of quantities by operations with numbers.

—*James Clerk Maxwell: "On Faraday's Lines of Force," 1856*

11. Mathematics is the science which draws necessary conclusions.

—*Benjamin Peirce:* ***Linear Associative Algebra****, 1870 [This is the first sentence of Peirce's book.]*

12. Mathematics is the most abstract of all the sciences. For it makes no external observations, nor asserts anything as a real fact. When the mathematician deals with facts, they become for him mere "hypotheses"; for with the truth he refuses to concern himself. The whole science of mathematics is a science of hypotheses; so that nothing could be more completely abstracted from concrete reality.

*—Charles Sanders Peirce: "The Regenerated Logic"; **The Monist** 7, October, 1896*

13. This science [mathematics] does not have for its unique objective to eternally contemplate its own navel; it touches nature and some day it will make contact with it. On this day it will be necessary to discard the purely verbal definitions and not any more be the dupe of empty words.

*—Henri Poincare: "The Value of Science"; **Popular Science Monthly**, 1906*

14. Mathematics is the cheapest science. Unlike physics or chemistry, it does not require any expensive equipment. All one needs for mathematics is a pencil and paper.

*—George Polya: In D.J. Albers & G.L. Alexanderson: **Mathematical People**, 1985*

15. The mathematical is, so to speak, a superficial science; it builds on a borrowed site, and the principles by aid of which it proceeds, are not its own....

*—Seneca: Quoted in **Edinburgh Review**, vol. 52, January, 1836*

16. Mathematics is a science continually expanding; and its growth, unlike some political and industrial events, is attended by universal acclamation.

*—H.S. White: **Congress of Arts and Sciences** vol. 1, 1905*

17. Mathematics is the science of definiteness, the necessary vocabulary of those who know.

*—William F. White: **A Scrapbook of Elementary Mathematics**, 1908*

18. Mathematics as a science, commenced when first someone, probably a Greek, proved propositions about "any" things or about "some" things, without specifications of definite particular things.

*—Alfred North Whitehead: **An Introduction to Mathematics**, 1911*

19. I would say that mathematics is the science of skillful operations with concepts and rules invented just for this purpose. The principal emphasis is on the invention of concepts. Mathematics would soon run out of interesting theorems if these had to be formulated in terms of the concepts which already appear in the axioms.

*—Eugene P. Wigner: "The Unreasonable Effectiveness of Mathematics in the Natural Sciences"; **Communications in Pure and Applied Mathematics**, 13, 1960*

3.2 Appreciation for Mathematics

1. For the most part, it is true, ordinary men and women regard mathematics with energetic distaste, counting its concepts as rhapsodic as cauliflower. This is a mistake—there is no other word. Where else can the restless human mind find means to tie the infinite in a finite bow? Sometime in the seventeenth century, for example, mathematicians discovered that addition could be extended to infinite sums.

*—David Berlinski: **The Advent of the Algorithm**, "Introduction," 2000*

2. Mathematics plays no role in mass culture, it cannot claim to evoke the sensibilities and inspire the awe that music and sculpture do, it is not a significant companion in the lives of more than a very few. And yet it is worth asking whether mathematics is essentially remote, or merely poorly communicated. Perhaps it is a remediable ignorance, not an inability, that now limits appreciation and enjoyment of mathematics by a wider audience; perhaps our culture is only reaching the stage at which mathematics can begin to penetrate a larger consciousness.

*—Allen L. Hammond: "Mathematics—Our Invisible Culture"; **Mathematics Today—Twelve Informal Essays**, 1978*

3. The fact is that there are few more "popular" subjects than mathematics. Most people have some appreciation of mathematics, just as most people can enjoy a pleasant tune; and there are probably more people really interested in mathematics than music. Appearances may suggest the contrary, but there are easy explanations. Music can be used to stimulate mass emotion, while mathematics cannot; and musical incapacity is recognized ... as mildly discreditable, whereas most people are so frightened of the name of mathematics that they are ready, quite unaffectedly, to exaggerate their own mathematical stupidity.

*—G.H. Hardy: **A Mathematician's Apology**, 1941*

4. ...a presentation of geometry in large brush-strokes, so to speak, and based on the approach through visual intuition, should contribute to a more just appreciation of mathematics by a wider range of people than just the specialists. For it is true, generally speaking, that mathematics is not a popular subject, even though its importance may be generally conceded. The reason for this is to be found in the common superstition that mathematics is but a continuation, a further development, of the fine art of arithmetic, of juggling with numbers.

*—David Hilbert: "Preface" to **Geometry and the Imagination** by Hilbert and S. Cohn-Vossen, tr. by P. Nemenyi, 1952: Quoted in Constance Reid: **Hilbert**, 1970*

5. Mathematics was born and nurtured in a cultural environment. Without the perspective which the cultural background affords, a proper appreciation of the content and state of present-day mathematics is hardly possible.

—*R.L. Wilder: "The Nature of Proof"; **The American Mathematical Monthly**, March, 1994*

3.3 Aptitude for Mathematics

1. In Mathematicks he was greater
Than Tycho Brahe, or Erra Pater:
For he, by Geometrick scale,
Could take the size of Pots of Ale;
Remove by Signs and Tangents streight,
If Bread or Butter wanted weight;
And wisely tell what hour o' th' day
The Clock doth strike, by Algebra.

—*Samuel Butler I: **Hudibras**, 1663*

2. To be a scholar of mathematics you must be born with talent, insight, concentration, taste, luck, drive and the ability to visualize and guess.

—*Paul R. Halmos: **I Want to Be a Mathematician**, 1985*

3. Anyone who cannot cope with mathematics is not fully human. At best he is a tolerable subhuman who has learned to wear shoes, bathe, and not make messes in the house.

—*Robert A. Heinlein; **Time Enough for Love**, 1973*

4. The idea that aptitude for mathematics is rarer than aptitude for other subjects is merely an illusion which is caused by belated or neglected beginners.

—*J.F. Herbart: "Umriss padagogischer Vorlesungen"; **Werke**, 1902: Quoted in Stanley Gudder: **A Mathematical Journey**, 1976*

5. I think ... one does mathematics because one likes to do this sort of thing, and also, much more naturally, because when you have a talent for something, usually you don't have any talent for something else, and you do whatever you have talent for, if you are lucky enough to have it. I must also admit that I do mathematics also because if is difficult, and it is a very beautiful challenge for the mind. I do mathematics to prove to myself that I am capable of meeting this challenge, and win it.

—*Serge Lang: **The Beauty of Doing Mathematics**, 1985*

6. The greatest unsolved theorem in mathematics is why some people are better at it than others.

—*Adrian Mathesis: In Howard Eves: **Return to Mathematical Circles**, 1988*

7. It is with mathematics not otherwise than it is with music, painting or poetry. Anyone can become a lawyer, doctor or chemist, and as such may succeed well, provided he is clever and industrious, but not every one can become a painter or a musician, or a mathematician: general cleverness and industry alone here count for nothing.

—*P.J. Moebius: **Ueber die Anlage zur Mathematik**, 1900*

8. ...there is no more a math mind, than there is a history of an English mind....

—*Gloria Steinem: **Moving Beyond Words**, 1994*

9. There are too many statistics and figures for me. I never could do anything with figures, never had any talent for mathematics, never accomplished anything in my efforts at that rugged study, and today, the only mathematics I know is multiplication, and the minute I get away up in that, as soon as I reach nine times seven—.

—*Mark Twain: Speech in New York City, March 29, 1906*

3.4 The Attraction of Mathematics

1. Those that can readily master the difficulties of Mathematics find a considerable charm in the study, sometimes amounting to fascination. This is far from universal; but the subject contains elements of strong interest of a kind that constitutes the pleasures of knowledge. The marvellous devices for solving problems elate the mind with the feeling of intellectual power; and the innumerable constructions of the science leave us lost in wonder.

—*Alexander Bain: **Education as a Science**, 1898*

2. Somebody came up to me after a talk I had given, and said, "You make mathematics seem like fun." I was inspired to reply, "If it isn't fun, why do it?"

—*Ralph P. Boas: Quoted in Harold a Jacobs: **Mathematics: A Human Endeavor**, 1994*

3. It demeans mathematics to justify it to appeals to work, to getting and spending.... Can you recall why you fell in love with mathematics? It was not, I think, because of its usefulness in controlling inventories.

—*Underwood Dudley: "Is Mathematics Necessary?"; **Mathematics Education Dialogues**, March, 1998*

4. It is, I think, undeniable that a great part of mathematics was born, and lives in respect and admiration, for no other reason than that it is interesting—it is interesting in itself.

—*Paul R. Halmos: "Mathematics as a Creative Art," **American Scientist**, Vol. 56, 1968*

5. Mathematics should be fun.

—Peter J. Hilton: "Avoiding Math Avoidance" in Lynn Arthur Steen: ***Mathematics Tomorrow****, 1981*

6. Someone asked me if I was ever sorry I had chosen mathematics. I said, "I didn't choose. Mathematics is an addiction with me!"

—Marguerite Lehr: in Patricia Kenschraft: "An Interview with Marguerite Lehr: In Memoriam"; ***Association for Women in Math Newsletter****, March–April, 1988*

7. No other field can offer, to such an extent as mathematics, the joy of discovery, which is perhaps the greatest human joy.

—Rosza Peter: "Mathematics is Beautiful"; ***Mathematical Intelligencer****, 12, Winter, 1990*

8. If I feel unhappy, I do mathematics to become happy.
If I am happy, I do mathematics to keep happy.

—Alfred Renyi: "The Work of Alfred Renyi"; ***Matematikai Lapok****, 21, 1970*

9. One of my earliest memories is of arranging pebbles in the shadow of a great saguaro, squinting because the sun was so bright. I think that I have always had a basic liking for the rational numbers. To me they are the one real thing.

—Julia Robinson: in Constance Reid: ***Julia: A Life in Mathematics****, 1997*

10. I like mathematics because it is not human and has nothing particular to do with this planet or with the whole accidental universe—because like Spinoza's God, it won't love us in return.

—Bertrand Russell: Letter to Lady Ottoline Morrell; March, 1912

11. Strange numbers, strange shapes; these are the things that give mathematics its allure, and, even more so, strange connections—topics that seem totally different yet possess a hidden secret unity.

—Ian Stewart: "Mathematical Recreations"; ***Scientific American****, August, 1999*

3.5 Ignorance of Mathematics

1. Mathematics is the gate and key of the sciences.... Neglect of mathematics works injury to all knowledge, since he who is ignorant of it cannot know the other sciences or the things of this world. And what is worse, men who are thus ignorant are unable to perceive their own ignorance and so do not seek a remedy.

—Roger Bacon: ***Opus Majus****, 1265–8*

2. The man ignorant of mathematics will be increasingly limited in his grasp of the main forces of civilization.

—John G. Kemeny: ***Random Essays on Mathematics, Education and Computers****, 1964*

3. And thus many are ignorant of mathematical truths, not out of any imperfection of their faculties, or uncertainty in the things themselves, but for want of application in acquiring, examining, and by due ways comparing those ideas.

—John Locke: ***An Essay Concerning Human Understanding****, Clarendon Press, 1956*

4. For this, is the true source of our ignorance—the fact that our knowledge can only be finite, while or ignorance must necessarily be infinite.

—Sir Karl Rainmund Popper: Lecture to the British Academy, January 20, 1960: in ***Conjectures and Refutations****, 1968*

3.6 Mathematics and Imagination

1. I have often been surprised that Mathematics, the quintessence of Truth, should have found admirers so few and so languid. Frequent consideration and minute scrutiny have at length unraveled the cause: viz. that though Reason is feasted, Imagination is starved; whilst Reason is luxuriating in its proper Paradise, Imagination is wearily travelling on a dreary desert. To assist Reason by the stimulus of Imagination is the design of the following production.

—Samuel Taylor Coleridge: Quoted in ***Mathematical Digest****, John Webb, ed., January, 1980, epigraph [This quote appears in the preface to one of Coleridge's earliest poems in which he rendered the first book of Euclid's* ***Elements*** *into verse.]*

2. The moving power of mathematical invention
is not reasoning but imagination.

—Augustus De Morgan: Quoted in Graves': ***Life of Sir William Rowan Hamilton****, 1889*

3. It is a great mistake to maintain that a high development of the imagination is not essential to progress in mathematical studies as to hold with Ruskin and others that science and poetry are antagonistic pursuits.

—F.S. Hoffman: ***Sphere of Science****, 1898*

4. Many who have never had the occasion to discover more about mathematics confuse it with arithmetic and consider it a dry and arid science. In reality, however, it is a science which demands the greatest imagination.

—Sofia Kovalevsky: in Ann Hibler Koblitz: ***A Convergence of Lives****, 1983*

5. The propensity of the mathematical spirit for escaping physical reality on the wings of its rational imagination often provokes it to fashion concepts in which the uninitiated are prone to see insane nightmares rather than the fruits of logical activity. Of course, in the end one grows accustomed to anything; in short, it is their success which sanctions these innovations, at the same time that it robs them of their charm.

—*Francois Le Lionnais: "Beauty in Mathematics" in* ***Great Currents of Mathematics****, F. Le Lionnais, ed., 1971*

6. Mathematics is not the mystery some people think it is, it's just a way of speaking. It's very imaginative.

—*James Murray: Quoted in Keith Devlin:* ***Life by the Numbers****, 1998*

7. Mathematics, like theology and all free creations of the mind, obeys the inexorable laws of the imagination.

—*Gian-Carlo Rota: in* ***Discrete Thoughts: Essays on Mathematics, Science and Philosophy****, Mark Kac, Gian-Carlo Rota, Jacob T. Schwartz; Quoted in* ***The Mathematical Intelligencer****, vol. 12, 1990*

8. There is an astonishing imagination, even in the science of mathematics.... We repeat, there was far more imagination in the head of Archimedes than in that of Homer.

—*Voltaire:* ***A Philosophical Dictionary****, 1881*

9. The whole of Mathematics consists in the organization of a series of aids to the imagination in the process of reasoning.

—*Alfred North Whitehead:* ***A Treatise on Universal Algebra****, originally published 1898; 1960*

3.7 Mathematical Ideals and Idealization

1. In making ... idealizations, the mathematician deliberately distorts or approximates at least some features of the physical situation. Why does he do it? The reason usually is that he simplifies the problem and yet is quite sure that he has not introduced any gross errors.... To idealize by deliberately introducing a simplification is to lie a little, but the lie is a white one. Using idealizations to study the physical world does impose a limitation on what mathematics accomplishes, but ... even when idealizations are employed, the knowledge gained is of immense value.

—*Morris Kline:* ***Mathematics for the NonMathematician****, 1957*

2. Do you not know also that although they [geometers] make use of the visible forms and reason about them, they are thinking not of these, but of the ideals which they resemble; not of the figures which they draw, but of the absolute square and the absolute diameter ... they are really seeking to behold the things themselves, which can be seen only with the eye of the mind?

—*Plato:* ***The Republic****, c. 371–367 B.C.* ***Dialogues of Plato****, Jowett, 1897*

3. Mathematics is a construct of the human mind: it may model reality, but it is not the same as reality. Mathematics makes use of idealizations, such as 'infinity', that do not have evident counterparts in the real world. If those idealizations had overreached themselves, then mathematics might contain a hidden, fatal flaw. If such a contradiction were ever to be found, mathematics would collapse in ruins. The reason is that, according to the rules of logic, such a contradiction would imply that all statements are true (also false).

—*Ian Stewart:* ***The Magical Maze****, 1997*

4. Mathematics, the science of the ideal, becomes the means of investigating, understanding and making known the world of the real. The complex is expressed in terms of the simple. From one point of view mathematics may be defined as the science of successive substitutions of simpler concepts for more complex.

—*William F. White:* ***A Scrapbook of Elementary Mathematics****, 1908*

4

The Development of Mathematics I

4.1 Growth of New Mathematical Ideas

1. A new mathematical result, entirely new, never before conjectured or understood by anyone, nursed from the first tentative hypothesis through labyrinths of false attempted proofs, wrong approaches, unpromising directions, and months or years of difficult and delicate work—there is nothing, or almost nothing, in the world that can bring a joy and a sense of power and tranquility to equal those of its creator. And a great new mathematical edifice is a triumph that whispers of immortality.

*—Alfred Adler: "Mathematics and Creativity"; **The New Yorker Magazine**, February 19, 1972*

2. Wisdom was not born with us, nor will it perish when we descend into the shadows with a regretful backward glance that other eyes than ours are already lit by the dawn of a new and truer mathematics.

*—Eric Temple Bell: **The Queen of Sciences**, 1931*

3. The advance and perfecting of mathematics are closely joined to the prosperity of the nation.

*—Napoleon Bonaparte: 1815; **Correspondance de Napoleon**, tome 24, 1868*

4. What strikes us first of all, when we compare the mathematics of our times with that of previous epochs, is the extraordinary diversity and the unexpectedness and circuitousness of the paths it has taken; the apparent disorder with which it executes its marches and countermarches; its maneuvers and constant changes of front.

*—Pierre Boutroux: Quoted in Francois Le Lionnais: "Beauty in Mathematics" in **Great Currents of Mathematics**, F. Le Lionnais, ed., 1971*

5. The mathematics is not there till we put it there.

*—Sir Arthur Stanley Eddington: **The Philosophy of Physical Science**, 1958*

6. And perhaps, posterity will thank me for having shown it that the ancients did not know everything.

*—Pierre De Fermat: In D.M. Burton: **Elementary Number Theory**, 1976*

7. From the infinitesimal calculus to the present, it seems to me, the essential progress in mathematics has resulted from successively annexing notions which, for the Greeks or the Renaissance geometers or the predecessors of Riemann, went "outside mathematics" because it was impossible to define them.

*—Jacques Hadamard: Quoted in G.H. Moore: **Zermelo's Axiom of Choice: It's Origins, Development and Influence**, 1982*

8. Who would not lift the veil that hides the future from us, to have a look at the progress of our science [mathematics] and the secrets of its future development in future centuries.

*—David Hilbert: "Sur les problemes futures des mathematiques"; **Proceedings of the Second International Congress of Mathematicians**, Paris, 1902*

9. In fact, mathematics [has] grown like a tree, which does not start at its tiniest rootlets and grow merely upward, but rather sends its roots deeper and deeper at the same time and rate that its branches and leaves are spreading upward.... We see, then, that as regards the fundamental investigation in mathematics, there is no final ending, and therefore on the other hand, no first beginning.

*—Felix Klein: **Elementary Mathematics from an Advanced Standpoint**, 1939*

10. It would appear that the Roman civilization was unproductive in mathematics because it was too much concerned with practical results to see farther than its nose. The medieval period, on the other hand, was unproductive because it was not concerned with the civitas mundi but rather, with the civitas dei and with the preparation for the latter world. One civilization was earth-bound, the other heaven-bound.

—*Morris Kline:* ***Mathematics in Western Culture,*** *1953*

11. The first principle of all things is the One. From the One came an indefinite Two.... From the One and the indefinite Two came numbers; and from numbers points, lines; from lines, plane figures; from plane figures, solid figures, sensible bodies.

—*Diogenes Laertius; 3rd. cent. B.C., in F.M. Cornford;* ***Plato and Parmenides,*** *1957*

12. Informal, quasi-empirical mathematics does not grow through a monotonous increase in the number of indubitably established theorems but through the incessant improvement of guesses by speculation and criticism, by the logic of proofs and refutations.

—*Imre Lakatos:* ***Proofs and Refutations,*** *1976*

13. If I have seen further (than you and Descartes) it is by standing on the shoulders of giants.

—*Isaac Newton: Letter to Robert Hooke; February 5, 1675/1676*

14. Mathematics presented in the Euclidean way appears as a systematic, deductive science; but mathematics in the making appears as an experimental, inductive science. Both aspects are as old as the science of mathematics itself.

—*George Polya:* ***How to Solve It,*** *"Preface," 1945*

15. Mathematics does not shed the old substance as new is added, in the way the natural sciences, for instance, will do. The work of Euclid, Apollonius or Archimedes, to mention some Greek mathematicians from antiquity, is as valid today as when it was done more than two millennia ago. But while the content or substance remains, the form in which it is presented is ever changing. What we may refer to as the landscape of mathematics may change profoundly from one generation to another, and even during shorter time spans, fundamental changes may occur.

—*Arte Selberg: "Reflections around the Ramanujan Centenary" in* ***Collected Papers,*** *vol. I. 1989*

16. It is strange but true that most of the greatest strides in mathematics were made at a time and in an atmosphere when the need for mathematics was the least. Mathematics flourishes when it is free to follow any course it desires and when there is no pressure for practical results limiting its scope and freedom.

—*Margaret F. Willerding: "The Uselessness of Mathematics";* ***School Science and Mathematics,*** *vol. LXVIII, June, 1968*

4.2 The Process of Mathematical Development

1. We can see that the development of mathematics is a process of conflict among the many contrasting elements: the concrete and the abstract, the particular and the general, the formal and the material, the finite and the infinite, the discrete and the continuous, and so forth.

—*A.D. Aleksandrov:* ***Mathematics: Its Content, Methods and Meanings,*** *A.D. Aleksandrov, A.N. Kolmogorov & M.A. Lavrent'ev, eds., 1963*

2. Mathematics is not a careful march down a well-lighted highway, but a journey into a strange wilderness, where the explorers often get lost.

—*W.S. Anglin: "Mathematics and History";* ***The Mathematical Intelligencer,*** *vol.4, no. 4., 1982*

3. There are a lot of fashions in mathematics. Fashions come and go, and it's always a question of what to do. Do you follow the fashion or not? Sometimes I tend not to because I dislike working under intensely competitive conditions.

—*Joan Birman: Quoted in Claudia Henrion:* ***Women in Mathematics: The Addition of Difference,*** *1997*

4. It is clear that originally mathematics arose as a part of the everyday life of man, and if there is validity in the biological principle of the "survival of the fittest," the persistence of the human race probably is not unrelated to the development in man of mathematical concepts.

—*Carl B. Boyer:* ***A History of Mathematics,*** *1968*

5. No mathematician creates a proof by staring at axioms. He draws pictures, measures, experiments, looks at extreme cases, finds analogies, asks authorities, and makes three brilliant but false starts before he finally gets a flash that sets him up for a proof that works. Then he refines the proof, erases unessential steps, and removes the false starts that led him to the true insight. Finally, he has a polished jewel, a tightly-reasoned, correct, but virtually opaque proof ready to frustrate both student and teacher.

—*Douglas Campbell: "The Curse of Euclid";* ***The Whole Craft of Number,*** *1976*

6. Mathematical topics ... do not align themselves in a logical progression so as to mirror the Latin alphabet.

—*William Dunham:* ***The Mathematical Universe,*** *1994*

7. The bottom line for mathematicians is that the architecture has to be right. In all the mathematics that I did, the essential point was to find the right architecture. It's like building a bridge. Once the main lines of the structure are right, then the details miraculously fit. The problem is the overall design.

—*Freeman Dyson: "Freeman Dyson: Mathematician, Physicist, and Writer," Interview with Donald J. Albers,* ***The College Mathematics Journal****, January, 1994*

8. There has been a strong trend in the development of mathematics in the twentieth century to replace seeing with understanding.

—*Nicolas D. Goodman: "Reflections on [Errett] Bishop's Philosophy of Mathematics";* ***Springer Lecture Notes****, No. 873, 1980*

9. The development of mathematics resembles a series of which there is no known first term. For there can be no means of finding out how mathematical thinking developed even in primitive humans, never mind among the animals; but presumably it began as a central part of thought itself, and before any manner or writing or inscription had been conceived.

—*Ivor Grattan-Guinness:* ***The Rainbow of Mathematics****, 1997*

10. A field of mathematics is alive only so long as it continues to ask interesting and worthwhile questions.

—*Paul R. Halmos: "A Glimpse into Hilbert Space";* ***Lectures on Modern Mathematics****, Vol. 1, T.L. Sarty, ed., 1963*

11. The prevalent idea of mathematical works is that you must understand the reason why first, before you proceed to practice. That is fudge and fiddlesticks. I know mathematical processes that I have used with success for a very long time, of which neither I nor anyone else understands the scholastic logic. I have grown into them, and so understand them that way.

—*Oliver Heaviside: Quoted in W.W. Sawyer:* ***Mathematician's Delight****, 1967*

12. When asked what it was like to set about proving something, the mathematician likened proving a theorem to seeing the peak of a mountain and trying to climb to the top. One establishes a base camp and begins scaling the mountain's sheer face, encountering obstacles at every turn, often retracing one's steps and struggling ever foot of the journey. Finally when the top is reached, one stands examining the peak, taking in the view of the surrounding countryside and then noting the automobile road up the other side.

—*Robert J. Kleinhenz: Quoted in Howard W. Eves:* ***Return to Mathematical Circles****, 1988*

13. To understand the development of mathematics, we must have a picture of the men who made the science.

—*Edna Kramer:* ***The Main Stream of Mathematics****, 1955*

14. Mathematics ... would certainly have not come into existence if one had known from the beginning that there was in nature no exactly straight line, no actual circle, no absolute magnitude.

—*Friedrich Nietzsche:* ***Human, All Too Human*** *1886*

15. Mathematical work does not proceed along the narrow logical path of truth to truth, but bravely or gropingly follows deviations through the surrounding marshland of propositions which are neither simply and wholly true nor simply and wholly false.

—*Seymour Papert:* ***Mindstorms****, 1980*

16. The progress of mathematics can be viewed as progress from the infinite to the finite.

—*Gian-Carlo Rota, 1983: Quoted by Xavier G. Viennot: "Opening Plenary Talk,"* ***LACIM 2000****; September 7, 2000*

17. A wood in which trees are planted in rows looks regular when viewed along a row from one end of it, but appear completely higgledy-piggledy when viewed on a slant. The same sort of thing is true of a mathematical subject: if you approach it from the wrong angle, each step will be difficult, you will be entangled in thickets, and you will get no view of the whole; but if you start at the right point and advance in the right direction, the obstacles disappear and progress is easy.

—*Bertrand Russell: "Preface" to W.K. Clifford:* ***The Common Sense of the Exact Sciences****, 1946*

18. I think mathematics is a vast territory. The outskirts of mathematics are the outskirts of mathematical civilization. There are certain subjects that people learn about and gather together. Then there is a sort of inevitable development in those fields, You get to the point where a certain theorem is bound to be proved, independent of any particular individual, because it is just in the path of development.

—*William Thurston: in* ***More Mathematical People****, D.J. Albers G.L. Alexanderson & C. Reid, eds., 1990*

19. In mathematics you don't understand things. You just get used to them.

—*John von Neumann: in Gary Zukav:* ***The Dancing Wu Li Masters****, 1979*

20. Mathematics is as subject to fashions as any other aspect of man's behavior! Sooner or later, however, the so-called speciality is developed to such an extent that either it loses its popularity or achieves immortality through contact with other concepts.

—*Raymond L. Wilder: "The Origin and Growth of Mathematical Concepts";* ***Bulletin of the American Mathematical Society****, 1953*

21. Perhaps I could best describe my experience of doing mathematics in terms of entering a dark mansion. One goes into the first room and it's dark, completely dark. One stumbles around bumping into the furniture and then gradually you learn where each piece of furniture is, and finally after six months or so you find the light switch, you turn it on and suddenly it's all illuminated, you can see where you were.

—Andrew Wiles: From the BBC program "Fermat's Last Theorem" by Simon Singh & John Lynch (broadcast in the U.S. on PBS's ***Nova,*** *as "The Proof," 1990s*

22. In mathematics process and result are equivalent.

—Ludwig Wittgenstein: ***Remarks on the Foundations of Mathematics,*** *1958*

4.3 Mathematical Thinking

1. I am of the opinion that it is possible to develop an art largely on the basis of mathematical thinking.

—Max Bill: Quoted in Eli Maor: ***To Infinity and Beyond,*** *Princeton University Press, 1987*

2. Learning without thinking is useless.
Thinking without learning is dangerous.

—Confucius: ***Analects II***

3. Taught properly, mathematics enables the student to think clearly and independently within the limits of his aptitude.

—Max Dehn: "The Mentality of the Mathematician: A Characterization"; Address at University of Frankfurt; January 18, 1928; Abe Schenitzer, tr., ***The Mathematical Intelligencer,*** *vol. 5, 2, 1983*

4. Cogito Ergo Sum. "I think, therefore I am."

—Rene Descartes: ***Discours de la Methode,*** *1637*

5. If you ask mathematicians what they do, you always get the same answer. They think. They think about difficult and unusual problems. They do not think about ordinary problems: they just write down the answers.

—M. Egrafov: in ***Mathematics Magazine,*** *vol. 65, December, 1992*

6. Practically all of them [the famous mathematicians and scientists he asked to explain what they actually thought while doing their work] ... avoid not only the use of mental words, but also ... the mental use of algebraic or precise signs ... they use vague images ... the mental pictures of the mathematicians whose answers I have received are most frequently visual, but they also may be of another kind—for example kinetic.

—Jacques Hadamard: ***The Psychology of Invention in the Mathematical World,*** *1945*

7. The truth of the matter is that, though mathematics truth may be beauty, it can be only glimpsed after much hard thinking. Mathematics is difficult for many human minds to grasp because of its hierarchical structure: one thing builds on another and depends upon it.

—M. Holt & D.T.E. Marjoram:; ***Mathematics in a Changing World,*** *1973*

8. Mathematics not only demands straight thinking; it grants the student the satisfaction of knowing when he is thinking straight.

—Dunham Jackson: "The Human Significance of Mathematics"; Address of the retiring president of the Mathematical Association of America, December 29, 1927; in ***The American Mathematical Monthly,*** *25, 1928*

9. To think the unthinkable—that's the mathematician's aim.

—Cassius J. Keyser: "The Universe and Beyond"; ***Hilbert Journal,*** *vol. 2, 1903–4*

10. Strange as it may sound, the power of mathematics rests on its evasion of all unnecessary thought and on its wonderful saving of mental operations.

—Ernst Mach: Quoted in E.T. Bell: ***Men of Mathematics,*** *1937*

11. Doubting everything or believing everything are two equally convenient solutions, both of which save us from thinking.

—Henri Poincare: ***Science and Hypothesis,*** *1905*

12. The creative thought processes of a mathematical mind are not easily explained, and it is hard to know what does subconsciously stimulate them.

—Olga Taussky-Todd: in ***Mathematical People,*** *D.J. Albers & G.L. Alexanderson, eds., 1985*

13. You should not expect me to describe the mathematical way of thinking much more clearly than one can describe, say, the democratic way of life.

—Hermann Weyl: in ***Hermann Weyl,*** *K. Chandrasekharan, ed., 1986*

14. It is a profoundly erroneous truism, repeated by all copy books and by eminent people when they are making speeches, that we should cultivate the habit of thinking of what we are doing. The precise Opposite in the case. Civilization advances by extending the number of important operations which we can perform without thinking about them.

—Alfred North Whitehead: ***An Introduction to Mathematics,*** *1911*

4.4 Intuition

1. [Intuition] is founded on a kind of combinatorial playfulness that is only possible when the consequences of error are not overpowering or sinful. Above all, it is a form of activity that depends upon confidence in the worthwhileness of the process of mathematical activity rather than upon the importance of right answers at all times.

—*Jerome Bruner: "On Learning Mathematics"; **Mathematics Teacher**, December, 1960*

2. It was the function of intuition to create new forms; it was the acknowledged right of logic to accept or reject those forms, in whose birth it had no part.

—*Tobias Dantzig: **Number, the Language of Science**, 1939*

3. By intuition I understand, not the fluctuating testimony of the senses, nor the misleading judgment that proceeds from the blundering constructions of imagination, but the conception which an unclouded and attentive mind gives us so readily and distinctly that we are wholly freed from doubt about that which we understand.

—*Rene Descartes: in **The Philosophical Works of Descartes**, E.S. Haldane & G.R. T Ross, tr., 1911*

4. In the process of theory-building, mathematical intuition is indispensable because the "evasion of unnecessary thought" gives freedom to the imagination; mathematical intuition is dangerous, because many sciences demand from this understanding not the evasion of thought, but thought.

—*Freeman J. Dyson: "Mathematics in the Physical Sciences"; **The Mathematical Sciences**, 1969*

5. My intuition was not strong enough in the field of mathematics in order to differentiate clearly the fundamentally important, that which is really basic, from the rest of the more or less dispensable erudition.

—*Albert Einstein: "Autobiographical Notes," in Paul A. Schilpp, **Albert Einstein: Philosopher-Scientist**, 1951*

6. Erdos has great intuition. When I'm trying to prove a theorem he will immediately say "No" that I'm not going in the right direction, and after a while he'll push you in the right direction. Intuition is very important; otherwise you will try so very hard to prove something which is not true. It saves you a lot of energy, and he's great at pushing and pushing. When you finally think you're done, he's asking you another bunch of problems.

—*Fan Chung: Quoted in Claudia Henrion: **Women in Mathematics: The Addition of Difference**, 1997*

7. Some intervention of intuition issuing from the unconscious is necessary at least to initiate the logical work.

—*Jacques Hadamard: **The Psychology of Invention in the Mathematical Field**, 1945*

8. Why then don't we stop earlier, why not say that "the ultimate test whether a method is admissible in arithmetic must of course be whether it is intuitively convincing." ...why not honestly admit mathematical fallibility, and try to defend the dignity of fallible knowledge from cynical skepticism, rather than delude ourselves that we can invisibly mend the latest tear in the fabric of out "ultimate" intuitions?

—*Imre Lakatos: **Proofs and Refutations: The Logic of Mathematical Discovery**, 1976*

9. All mathematicians would then be intuitive if they had clear sight; for they do not reason incorrectly from principles known to them; and intuitive minds would be mathematical if they could turn their eyes to the principles of mathematics to which they are unused.

—*Blaise Pascal: **Pensees**, 1670*

10. Mathematical intuition, like intelligence, is a psychological quality which is ... principally an accumulation of attitudes derived from one's mathematical experience.... The more experienced the mathematician, the more reliable is his intuition.

—*Raymond Wilder: "The Role of Intuition in Mathematics" **Science** 156, May 5, 1967*

4.5 Experiments and Empiricism

1. Experiments test whether or not theories are true. Every time the experiment turns out the way the theory says it should, the theory gains a degree of validity; it gets more and more true. But it cannot ever become completely "true" unless the scientist performs an infinite number of experiments. Laws of nature can be proven untrue, but rarely true. Scientific truths are always provisional.

—*K.C. Cole: **The Universe and the Teacup**, 1997*

2. ...mathematical reality lies outside us ... the theorems which we prove, and which we describe grandiloquently as our "creations," are simply the notes of our observations.

—*G.H. Hardy: **A Mathematician's Apology**, 1940*

3. ...the axioms of any interesting branch of mathematics was originally abstracted more or less directly from empirical facts, and the rules of inference used in it have originally manifested their universal validity in our actual thinking practice.

—*Laszlo Kalmar: "Foundations of Mathematics—Whither now?" in **Problems in the Philosophy of Mathematics**, 1965*

4. The mathematics that existed before Greek times has already been characterized as a collection of empirical conclusions. Its formulas were the accretion of ages of experience much as many medical practices and remedies are today. Though experience is no doubt a good teacher, in many situations it would be a most inefficient way of obtaining knowledge.

—*Morris Kline:* ***Mathematics in Western Culture,*** *1953*

5. A traveler who refuses to pass over a bridge until he has personally tested the soundness of every part of it is not likely to go far; something must be risked, even in mathematics.

—*Sir Horace Lamb: Quoted in Morris Kline:* ***Mathematical Thought from Ancient to Modern Times,*** *1972*

6. ...an experiment can tell you whether a theory is wrong, for you can never be absolutely certain that it's right. You can prove a theorem in mathematics, but you can't prove a theory.

—*Ian Stewart:* ***Does God Play Dice?,*** *1989*

7. As a mathematical discipline travels far from its empirical source, or still more, if it is a second and third generation only indirectly inspired by ideas coming from "reality," it is beset with very grave dangers.... At a great distance from its empirical source, or after much "abstract" inbreeding, a mathematical subject is in danger of degeneration.

—*John von Neumann: Quoted in Serge Lange:* ***The Beauty of Doing Mathematics,*** *1985*

4.6 Induction

1. Induction is the process of generalizing from our known and limited experience, and framing wider rules for the future than we have been able to test fully. At its simplest, then, an induction is a habit or an adaptation—the habit of expecting tomorrow's weather to be like today's, the adaptation to the unwritten conventions of community life.

—*Jacob Bronowski:* ***The Western Intellectual Tradition,*** *1960*

2. Higher arithmetic has this special feature that many of its most beautiful theorems may be easily discovered by induction, while any proof can only be obtained with the utmost difficulty. Thus, it was one of the great merits of Euler to have proved several of Fermat's theorems which he obtained, it appears, by induction.

—*Carl Friedrich Gauss, 1807; Quoted in Paul Ribenboim: "The Early History of Fermat's Last Theorem";* ***Thirteen Lectures on Fermat's Last Theorem,*** *1979*

3. There is in every step of an arithmetical or algebraical calculation a real induction, a real inference from facts to facts, and what disguises the induction is simply its comprehensive nature, and the consequent extreme generality of its language.

—*John Stuart Mill:* ***System of Logic,*** *1843*

4. No one has the faintest idea how the process of scientific induction works, and in calling it a "process" we may already making a dangerous assumption.

—*Gian-Carlo Rota: in* ***Discrete Thoughts: Essays on Mathematics, Science and Philosophy,*** *Mark Kac, Gian-Carlo Rota, Jacob T. Schwartz; Quoted in* ***The Mathematical Intelligencer,*** *vol. 12, 1990*

5. I look upon Induction as a very good Method of Investigation; as that which does very often lead us on to the easy discovery of a General Rule.... And where the Result of such Inquiry affords to the view, an obvious discovery; it needs not (though it may be capable of it) any further Demonstration ... whence there is no ground of suspicion why it should fail....

—*John Wallis:* ***A Treatise of Algebra,*** *1685*

6. There is a tradition of opposition between adherents of induction and deduction. In my view it would be just as sensible for the two ends of a worm to quarrel.

—*Alfred North Whitehead: In N. Rose:* ***Mathematical Maxims and Minims,*** *1988*

7. Induction makes you feel guilty for getting something out of nothing, and it is artificial, but it is one of the greatest ideas of civilization. It is very hard to teach, but WE are TEACHERS.

—*Herbert S. Wilf: Invited MAA address, January 10, 1998*

8. Mathematics in the synthetic finished form is deductive; mathematics in the making is inductive. Not only is the plan for the work inductive, but the theorems or processes themselves are very often discovered inductively, by the consideration of special examples.

—*J.W.A. Young:* ***The Teaching of Mathematics,*** *1907; in* ***The Mathematics Teacher;*** *March, 1968*

4.7 Deduction

1. To be acceptable as scientific knowledge a truth must be a deduction from other truths.

—*Aristotle:* ***Ethics,*** *c. 4th. cent. B.C.*

2. If we possessed a thorough knowledge of all the parts of the seed of any animal (e.g. man), we could from that alone, by reasons entirely mathematical and certain, deduce the whole conformation and figure of each of its members, and, conversely, if we knew several peculiarities of this conformation, we would from those deduce the nature of the seed.

—*Rene Descartes:* ***Discours de la Methode,*** *1637*

3. Deduction is, or ought to be, an exact science and should be treated in the same cold and unemotional manner. You have attempted to tinge it with romanticism, which produces much the same effect as if you worked a love story or an elopement into the fifth proposition of Euclid.

—*Arthur Conan Doyle:* ***The Sign of the Four****, 1890*

4. Gauss replied, when asked how soon he expected to reach certain mathematical conclusions, that he had them long ago, all he was worrying about was how to reach them!

—*Rene J. Dubos: "Mechanisms of Discovery" in I.S. Gordon and S. Sorkin, eds.* ***The Armchair Science Reader****, 1959*

5. Mathematics is not a deductive science—that's a cliche. When you try to prove a theorem, you don't just list the hypothesis, and then start to reason. What you do is trial and error, experimentation, guesswork.

—*Paul R. Halmos:* ***I Want to Be a Mathematician****, MAA Spectrum, 1985*

6. Mathematics as an abstract deductive system is associated with our culture. But people created mathematical ideas long before there were abstract deductive systems. Perhaps mathematical ideas will be here after abstract deductive systems have had their day and passed on

—*Reuben Hersh:* ***What is Mathematics, Really?****, 1997*

7. [Aristotle] and the world at large accepted unquestioningly that ... deductive principles when applied to any premise yielded conclusions as reliable as the premise. Hence if the premises were truths, so would the conclusions be.... Aristotle abstracted the principles of deductive logic from the reasoning already practiced by mathematicians. Deductive logic is, in effect, the child of mathematics.

—*Morris Kline:* ***Mathematics: The Loss of Certainty****, 1980*

8. The mathematician pays not the least regard either to testimony or conjecture, but deduces everything by demonstrative reasoning, from his definitions and axioms. Indeed, whatever is built upon conjecture, is improperly called science; for conjecture may beget opinion, but cannot produce knowledge.

—*Thomas Reid:* ***Essays on the Intellectual Powers of Man****, 1941*

5

The Development of Mathematics II

5.1 Definitions

1. Definition is a "thesis" or a "laying something down," since the arithmetician lays it down that to be a unit is to be quantitatively indivisible; but it is not a hypothesis, for to define what a unit is is not the same as to affirm its existence.

*—Aristotle: "Posterior Analytics" in **The Oxford Translation of Aristotle**, W.D. Ross, ed. and tr., 1928*

2. "There's glory for you!" "I don't know what you mean by 'glory,'" Alice said. "I meant, 'there's a nice knock-down argument for you!'" "But 'glory' doesn't mean 'a nice knock-down argument for you,'" Alice objected. "When I use a word," Humpty Dumpty said in a rather scornful tone, "it means just what I choose it to mean—neither more nor less." "The question is," said Alice, "is can you make a word mean what you want it to?" "The question is," said Humpty Dumpty, "Who's master?, that's all."

*—Lewis Carroll: **Through the Looking-Glass**, 1871*

3. A very important ingredient of mathematical creativity is the ability to formulate useful definitions, ones that lead to interesting results.

*—John B. Fraleigh: **Abstract Algebra**, 1967*

4. If any term be defined in geometry, the mind readily, of itself, substitutes, on all occasions, the definition for the term defined. Or even when no definition is employed, the object itself may be represented to the senses, and by that means be steadily and clearly apprehended.

*—David Hume: **An Enquiry Concerning Human Understanding**, 1748*

5. ...mathematical definitions can never be in error. For since the concept is first given through the definition, it includes nothing except precisely what the definition intends should be understood by it. But although nothing incorrect can be introduced into the content, there may sometimes, though rarely, be a defect in the form in which it is clothed, namely as regards precision.

*—Immanuel Kant: **The Critique of Pure Reason**, 1788*

6. The mathematical "definition" implies more than language because, ... it also implies an operation or a construction of some sort. We note that language grows with the introduction of new words, which must be defined in terms of known words. But mathematicians introduce as few definitions as possible, new mathematical concepts then emerge as the products of pure reasoning, carrying their own meanings with them.

*—Lloyd Motz & Jefferson Hane Weaver: **The Story of Mathematics**, 1993*

7. A definition is no proof.

—William Pinckney: Speech, U.S. Senate, February 15, 1820

8. One of the difficulties in reading, or listening to, mature mathematics is its immense vocabulary and the volume of notions that seem to be required. Nor can one readily discover the meaning of the more popular ideas because all too often they are defined in terms of yet more obscure words. The truth is, unfortunately, that few—perhaps none of us know all the definitions. We rely on a feeling for what must be intended, knowing that we can refine that feeling should needs be. In a sense, these notes should be seen precisely as an attempt to create some useful feelings.

*—Alf van der Poorten: **Notes on Fermat's Last Theorem**, 1996*

5.2 Hypothesis in Mathematics

1. Mathematics may help the naturalists, both to frame hypotheses, and to judge of those that are proposed to them, especially such as relate to mathematical subjects in conjunction with others.

—*Robert Boyle: "Usefulness of Mathematics to Natural Philosophy"; 1772, in* ***Works***

2. The shrewd guess, the fertile hypothesis, the courageous leap to a tentative conclusion—these are the most valuable coin of the thinker at work.... Yet in many classes in school, guessing is heavily penalized and is associated somehow with laziness.

—*Jerome S. Bruner:* ***The Process of Education****, 1960*

3. Therefore let us permit these new hypothesis to make a public appearance among old ones which are themselves no more provable, especially since they are wonderful and easy and bring with them a vast storehouse of learned observations.

—*Nicholaus Copernicus:* ***De Revolutionibus Orbium Coelestium****, 1543*

4. Hypotheses are only the pieces of scaffolding which are erected round a building during the course of construction, and which are taken away as soon as the edifice is completed.

—*Johann Wolfgang von Goethe: Quoted in Anthony M. Ludovici:* ***Introduction to Nietzsche's The Will to Power****, n.d.*

5. The art of discovering the causes of phenomena, or true hypothesis, is like the art of deciphering, in which an ingenious conjecture greatly shortens the road.

—*Gottfried Wilhelm Leibniz:* ***New Essays Concerning Human Understanding****, 1696*

6. But hitherto I have not been able to discover the causes of these properties of gravity from phenomena, and I frame no hypotheses. Hypotheses ... have no place in experimental philosophy ... to us it is enough that gravity does really exist ... and abundantly serves to account for all the motions of the celestial bodies, and of our sea.

—*Isaac Newton: Letter to Robert Hooke; February 5, 1675/1676*

7. We now despise those who, in the Copernican controversy, could not conceive the apparent motion of the sun on the heliocentric hypothesis.... The very essence of these triumphs is that they lead us to regard the views we reject as not only false but inconceivable.

—*William Whewell:* ***Philosophy of the Inductive Sciences and Astronomy and Physics in Reference to Natural Philosophy****, 1833*

5.3 Mathematical Analogies

1. Good mathematicians see analogies between theorems or theories, the very best ones see analogies between analogies.

—*Stefan Banach: Quoted in S.M. Ulam:* ***Adventures of a Mathematician****, 1976*

2. Mathematics compares the most diverse phenomena and discovers the secret analogies that unite them.

—*Joseph Fourier: in James Stewart:* ***Single Variable Calculus****, 1994*

3. Analogy suggests rather than proves.

—*Edward Hodnett:* ***The Art of Problem Solving****, 1955*

4. Analogy pervades all our thinking, our everyday speech and our trivial conclusions as well as artistic ways of expression and the highest scientific achievements. Analogy is used on very different levels. People often use vague, ambiguous, incomplete, or incompletely clarified analogies, but analogy may reach the level of mathematical precision.

—*George Polya:* ***How to Solve It****, 1945*

5. Without appreciation of form, there can be no feeling for analogy. Without perception of analogy, there can be no conception of structure. Without structure, mathematics would only be a collection of techniques, mundanely useful, but ultimately 'without form and void.'

—*David Wells:* ***The Penguin Book of Curious and Interesting Mathematics****, 1997*

6. The first man who noticed the analogy between a group of seven fishes and a group of seven days made a notable advance in the history of thought.

—*Alfred North Whitehead: "Mathematics as an Element in the History of Thought,"* ***Science and the Modern World****, 1925*

7. The only point there can be to elegance in a mathematical proof is to reveal certain analogies in a particularly striking manner when what is wanted; otherwise it is a product of stupidity and its only effect is to obscure what ought to be clear and manifest. The stupid pursuit of elegance is a principal cause of the mathematician's failure to understand their own operations, or perhaps the lack of understanding and the pursuit of elegance have a common origin.

—*Ludwig Wittgenstein:* ***Remarks on the Foundations of Mathematics****, 1956, 1983*

5.4 Abstraction

1. Abstraction, sometimes hurled as a reproach at mathematics, is its chief glory and its surest title to practical usefulness. It is also the source of such beauty as may spring from mathematics.

—*E.T. Bell:* ***The Development of Mathematics****, 1940*

2. The longer mathematics lives the more abstract—and therefore, possibly also the more practical it becomes.

—*E.T. Bell: Quoted in* ***The Mathematical Intelligencer****, vol. 13, #1, 1991*

3. Mathematicians have always been partial to abstraction, and for its own sake—aesthetics, not usefulness, is their criterion. Yet today they are moving to heights of abstraction their forebears hardly dared contemplate.

—*George A.W. Boehm:* ***The New World of Math,*** *1959*

4. My power to follow a long and purely abstract train of thought is very limited; and therefore I could never have succeeded with metaphysics or mathematics.

—*Charles Darwin:* ***The Autobiography of Charles Darwin,*** *1958 reprint*

5. The increased abstraction in mathematics that took place during the early part of this century was paralleled by a similar trend in the arts. In both cases, the increased level of abstraction demands greater effort on the part of anyone who wants to understand the work.

—*Kevin Devlin:* ***Mathematics: The Science of Patterns,*** *1997*

6. VII ABSTRACTION

this power to ABSTRACT is
one of the outstanding characteristics
of human beings as
compared with other animals.
And this power is used not only
by mathematicians,
but also by artists, musicians, poets,
and all other 'human' beings.
Perhaps some day
we shall measure
a person's 'human-ness' by
his power to abstract
rather than by the I.Q.

—*Lillian R. Lieber:* ***Modern Mathematics for T.C. Mits; The Celebrated Man in the Street,*** *1946*

7. To criticize mathematics for its abstraction is to miss the point entirely. Abstraction is what makes mathematics work. If you concentrate too closely on too limited an application of a mathematical idea, you rob the mathematician of his most important tools: analogy, generality and simplicity. Mathematics is the ultimate in technology transfer.

—*Ian Stewart:* ***Does God Play Dice?,*** *2nd ed., 1997*

8. You know of course that a mathematical line, a line of thickness nil, has no real existence. They taught you that? Neither has a mathematical plane. These things are mere abstractions.

—*H.G. Wells:* ***The Time Machine,*** *1895; Ace Books, 1988*

5.5 General Principles and Generalizations

1. The words "generalization" and "abstraction" are often used interchangeably, but there are several particular meanings of the former which should be elucidated.... It should be noticed carefully that while the general includes some aspects of the particular, it cannot include all aspects, for the very particularity grants additional privileges.... One benefit of generalization is a consolidation of information. Several closely related facts are wrapped up neatly and economically in a single package.

—*Philip J. Davis & Reuben Hersh:* ***The Mathematical Experience,*** *1981*

2. The art of doing mathematics consists in finding that special case which contains all the germs of generality.

—*David Hilbert: in N. Rose,* ***Mathematical Maxims and Minims,*** *1988*

3. If we do not succeed in solving a mathematical problem, the reason frequently consists in our failure to recognize the more general standpoint from which the problem before us appears only as a single link in a chain of related problems. After finding this standpoint, not only is this problem frequently more accessible to our investigation, but at the same time we come into possession of a method which is applicable also to related problems.

—*David Hilbert: "Mathematical Problems";* ***Bulletin of the American Mathematical Society,*** *8, 1901–02*

4. One should always generalize.

—*Carl Jacobi: In P. Davis and R. Hersh:* ***The Mathematical Experience,*** *1981*

5. A generalization made not for the vain pleasure of generalizing but in order to solve previously existing problems is always a fruitful generalization.

—*Henri Lebesque: "Sur le developpement de la notion d'integrale,"* ***Matematiska Tidskrift,*** *1926*

6. ...to observe is not enough. We must use our observations, and to do that we must generalize.

—*Henri Poincare:* ***The Foundations of Science,*** *1921*

7. Never rely too much on general principles and routine mechanical methods. Certain classes of problems can be solved by such methods, but they completely lose their interest once the general principle is discovered. It is, of course, good to know these general principles—indeed, science and mathematics couldn't advance without them. But to depend on principles while neglecting intuition is a shame.

*—Raymond Smullyan: "How Kazir Won His Wife"; in **Imaginary Numbers**, William Frucht, ed., 1999*

5.6 Revolutions in Mathematics

1. Revolutions never occur in mathematics.... For this law depends upon at least the minimal stipulation that a necessary characteristic of a revolution is that some previously existing entity (be it king, constitution, or theory) must be overthrown and irrevocably discarded.... Euclid was not disposed by, but reigns along with, the various non-Euclidean geometries.

*—Michael Crowe: "Ten 'laws' concerning patterns of change in the history of mathematics"; **Historia Mathematica**, 1975*

2. ...resistance to new discoveries may be taken as a strong measure of their revolutionary quality.... Perhaps there is no better indication of the revolutionary quality of a new advance in mathematics that the extent to which it meets with opposition. The revolution, then, consists as much in overcoming establishment opposition as it does in the visionary quality of the new ideas themselves.

*—Joseph Dauben: "Conceptual revolutions and the history of mathematics"; **Transformations and Traditions in the Sciences**, E. Mendelsohn, ed., 1984*

3. The secret of the success of modern science was the selection of a new goal for scientific activity. This new goal, set by Galileo and pursued by his successors, is that of obtaining quantitative descriptions of scientific phenomena independently of any physical explanations. The revolutionary character of this new concept of science will be appreciated more if it is compared with the scientific activity of preceding ages.

*—Morris Kline: **Mathematics in Western Culture**, 1953*

4. The Revolution that Comte and the XIXth century historians have seen in Descartes's analytic geometry conceals therefore an illusion. It is neither a question of revolution nor a question of a creation which radically transformed mathematics and renewed science. It is only a matter of normal development, after a return to the Greeks, of the main ideas of their analysis.

*—G. Milhaud: **Descartes savant**, 1921*

5. ...while 'imagination, fancy and invention' are the soul of mathematical research, in mathematics there never has been a revolution.

*—C. Truesdell: **Essays in the History of Mechanics**, "Foreword," 1968*

5.7 Modern Mathematics

1. Modern mathematics does not replace classical mathematics. It generalizes it, supplements it, unifies it. But classical mathematics ... are as important as they ever were.

*—Irving Adler: "The Changes Taking Place in Mathematics"; **Mathematics Teacher**, vol. 55; October, 1962*

2. The primary service of modern mathematics is that it alone enables us to understand the vast abstract permanencies which underlie the flux of things.

*—George Birkhoff: "Mathematics, Quantity and Order"; in **Science Today**, J.G. Crowther, ed., 1934*

3. Because mathematics is generally, and quite incorrectly, categorized with science rather than with philosophy, most people, including our students, tend to think that the mathematics being taught in the present day represents modern developments. In fact, most college students are exposed to very few mathematical ideas which originated since the fifteenth century. The accomplishments of the early Greek, Hindu, and Islamic scholars are of more than historical interest. There were not made obsolete by subsequent developments, but rather formed the basis for those very advances. What is distressing about the present state of education is that so few students have even an inkling of the progress made in mathematics during the last half millennium.

*—James O. Bullock: "Literacy in the Language of Mathematics"; **American Mathematical Monthly**, October, 1994*

4. Modern mathematics, that most astounding of intellectual creations, has projected the mind's eye through infinite time and the mind's hand into boundless space.

*—N.M. Butler: **The Meaning of Education and Other Essays and Addresses**, 1905*

5. It is difficult to give an idea of the vast extent of modern mathematics. The word "extent" is not the right one: I mean extent crowded with beautiful details—not an extent of mere uniformity such as an objectless plain, but of a tract of beautiful country seen at first in the distance, but which will bear to be rambled through and studied in every detail of hillside and valley, stream, rock, wood, and flower....

*—Arthur Cayley: "Presidential Address to the British Association," September, 1883; **The Collected Papers of Arthur Cayley**, 1896*

6. Modern mathematics may be considered to have begun approximately with the seventeenth century. It is well known that the first 1500 years of the Christian era produced, in Western

Europe at least, very little knowledge of value in science.

—*Philip E. B. Jourdain: "The Nature of Mathematics" in* ***The World of Mathematics****, James R. Newman, ed., 1956*

7. To most outsiders, modern mathematics is unknown territory. Its borders are protected by dense thickets of technical terms; its landscapes are a mass of indecipherable equations and incomprehensible concepts. Few realize that the world of modern mathematics is rich with vivid images and provocative ideas.

—*Ivars Peterson: The Mathematical Tourist, 1988*

8. One of the chiefest triumphs of modern mathematics consists in having discovered what mathematics is.

—*Bertrand Russell: International Monthly, vol. 4, 1901*

9. Any part of modern mathematics is the end-product of a long history. It has drawn on many other branches of earlier mathematics, it has extracted various essences from them and has been reformulated again and again in increasingly general and abstract forms. Thus a student may not be able to see what it is all about, in much the same way that a caveman confronted with a vitamin pill would not easily recognize it as food.

—*W. W. Sawyer:* ***A First Look at Numerical Functional Analysis****, 1978*

10. Most, if not all, of the great ideas of modern mathematics have had their origin in observation.

—*J.J. Sylvester: "A Plea for the Mathematician";* ***Nature****, vol. 1, 1869* ***Cambridge Mathematical Papers****, 1908*

11. The anxious precision of modern mathematics is necessary for accuracy, ... it is necessary for research. It makes for clearness of thought and for fertility in trying new combinations of ideas. When the initial statements are vague and slipshod, at every subsequent stage of thought, common sense has to step in to limit applications and to explain meanings. Now in creative thought common sense is a bad master. Its sole criterion for judgment is that the new ideas shall look like the old ones, in other words it can only act by suppressing originality.

—*Alfred North Whitehead:* ***Introduction to Mathematics****, 1911*

6

The Historical Origins of Mathematics

6.1 History of Mathematics

1. An impartial account of Western mathematics, including the award to each man and to each nation of its just share in the intricate development, could be written only by a Chinese historian. He alone would have the patience and detached cynicism necessary for disentangling the curiously perverted pattern to discover whatever truth may be concealed in our variegated Occidental boasting.

—*E.T. Bell: Quoted in Howard W. Eves:* ***Mathematical Circles Revisited****, 1971*

2. For twenty-five centuries mathematicians have been in the habit of correcting their errors—and seeing their science enriched rather than impoverished thereby. This gives them the right to contemplate the future with serenity.

—*Nicolas Bourbaki: "Elements of Mathematics"; Quoted in Lucienne Felix:* ***The Modern Aspect of Mathematics****, 1960*

3. The history of mathematics is important also as a valuable contribution to the history of civilization. Human progress is closely identified with scientific thought. Mathematical and physical researches are a reliable record of intellectual progress.

—*Florian Cajori:* ***A History of Mathematics****, 1897*

4. History shows that those heads of empires who have encouraged the cultivation of mathematics, the common source of all the exact sciences, are those whose reigns have been the most brilliant and whose glory is the most durable.

—*Michael Chasles (1793—1880): Quoted in E.T. Bell:* ***Men of Mathematics****, 1937*

5. It is a curious fact that in the history of mathematics that discoveries of the greatest importance were made simultaneously by different men of genius.

—*J.L. Coolidge:* ***A History of Geometrical Methods****, 1940*

6. The early history of the mind of men with regards to mathematics leads us to point out our own errors; and in this respect it is well to pay attention to the history of mathematics.

—*August De Morgan: Quoted in Florian Cajori:* ***History of Mathematics****, 1897*

7. ...we have no idea who discovered the first mathematic.... We do know that the rudiments of arithmetic and geometry go back a very long way. Before written history, before writing itself, humans had developed some concept of "multitude" or "number," and there are artifacts to support this. A bone from Africa exhibiting what can only be interpreted as tally marks is at least 10,000 years old. In this prehistoric time, our ancestors were counting something, and the scratching of marks into bone provided them—and us—with a permanent record of their counts. It may have had a modest beginning, but mathematics was on its way.

—*William Dunham:* ***The Mathematical Universe****, 1994*

8. Mathematics, like philosophy, is virtually inseparable from its history.

—*Harold M. Edwards: Quoted in Lynn Arthur Steen:* ***Mathematics Tomorrow****, 1981*

9. Biographical history, as taught in our public schools, is still largely a history of boneheads: ridiculous kings and queens, paranoid political leaders, compulsive voyagers, ignorant generals—the flotsam and jetsam of historical currents. The men who radically altered history, the great scientists and mathematicians, are seldom mentioned, if at all.

—*Martin Gardner: Quoted in George F. Simmons:* ***Calculus Gems****, 1992*

10. Like some other commonly used terms in mathematics, the term history of mathematics should probably always remain an undefined term.

—*G.A. Miller:* ***Historical Introduction to Mathematical Literature****, 1921*

11. One can invent mathematics without knowing much of its history. One can use mathematics without knowing much, if any, of its history. But one cannot have a mature appreciation of mathematics without a substantial knowledge of its history.

—*Abe Shenitzer: Quoted in Israel Kleiner: "Thinking the Unthinkable: The Story of Complex Numbers (with a Moral)";* ***The Mathematics Teacher****; October, 1988*

6.2 Oriental Mathematics

1. Among the peoples of the ancient Fertile Crescent only the Babylonians and Egyptians made significant advances in protomathematics. Even so highly cultured a people as the Hebrews got no further than a crude level.

—*Ronald Calinger:* ***Classics of Mathematics****, Ronald Calinger, ed., 1982*

2. ...pre–Hellenic mathematics was empirical. Nowhere do we find in ancient oriental mathematics a single instance of what we today call a logical demonstration. Instead of an argument we find a description of a process explained by means of specific numerical cases. In short, we are instructed to "Do thus and so." It is very interesting to note than although today confirmed students of the scientific method find this "Do thus and so" procedure highly unsatisfactory, it is the procedure employed in much of our elementary teaching.

—*Howard Eves:* ***Foundations and Fundamental Concepts of Mathematics****, 1958*

3. It is commonly accepted that the beginnings of Mathematics as a deductive science go back to the Greek world in the fifth and fourth centuries B.C. It is even more certain that in the course of many hundreds of years before that time people in Egypt and Mesopotamia had accumulated an impressive body of mathematical knowledge, both in Geometry and in Arithmetic. Since this knowledge was recorded in the form of numerical problems and answers it is frequently asserted that pre–Greek Mathematics was purely "empirical."

—*Abraham Robinson: "Some Thoughts on the History of Mathematics";* ***Composito Math****, 20, 1968*

6.3 Egyptian Mathematics

1. Accurate reckoning of entering into things, knowledge of existing things all, mysteries ... secrets all.

—*Ahmes: Rhind Papyrus, 1650 B.C. [A translation of the title page of the Rhind Papyrus.]*

2. When Moses was alive, these pyramids were a thousand years old.... Here began the history of architecture. Here people learned to measure time by a calendar, to plot the stars by astronomy and chart the earth by geometry. And here they developed the most awesome of all ideas—the idea of eternity.

—*Walter Cronkite:* ***Eternal Egypt****, CBS TV, June 28, 1980*

3. Beyond question, Egyptian geometry, such as it was, was eagerly studied by the early Greek philosophers, and was the germ from which in their hands grew that magnificent science to which every Englishman is indebted for his first lessons in right seeing and thinking.

—*James Gow:* ***A Short History of Greek Mathematics****, 1884*

4. The king, moreover (so they say) divided the country among all the Egyptians by giving each an equal parcel of land, and made this his source of revenue, appointing the payment of a yearly tax. And any man who was robbed by the river of a part of his land would come to Sesostris [Pharaoh Ramses II, c. 1300 B.C.] and declare what had befallen him; then the king would send men to look into it and measure the space by which the land was diminished so that thereafter it should pay in proportion to the tax already imposed, from this, to my thinking, the Greeks learned the art of geometry; the sun-clock and the sundial, and the twelve divisions of the day, came to Hellas not from Egypt but from Babylonia.

—*Herodotus:* ***History****, George Rawlinson, tr., Everyman's Library, 1997*

5. The fact that Egyptian mathematics did not contribute positively to the development of mathematical knowledge does not imply that it is of no interest to the historian. On the contrary, the fact that Egyptian mathematics has preserved a relatively primitive level makes it possible to investigate a stage of development which is no longer available in so simple a form, except in the Egyptian documents.

—*Otto Neugebauer:* ***The Exact Sciences in Antiquity****, 1957*

6.4 Sumerian and Babylonian Mathematics

1. Babylonian science has made its impress upon modern civilization. Whenever a surveyor copies the readings from the graduated circle on his theodolite, whenever the modern man notes the time of day, he is, unconsciously perhaps, but unmistakably, doing homage to the ancient astronomers on the banks of the Euphrates.

—*Florian Cajori:* ***History of Elementary Mathematics****, 1896*

2. Astronomy was a central part of Babylonian science, with the Earth placed at the centre of the Universe. The Babylonians seem to have invented the zodiac, the plane in which the heavenly bodies moved, split into 12 divisions of 30 degrees each.

—*Ivor Grattan-Guinness:* ***The Rainbow of Mathematics****, 1997*

3. In all of human history the Sumerians alone invented and made use of a sexagesimal system—that is to say, a system of numbers using 60 as a base. This invention is without doubt one of the great triumphs of Sumerian civilization from a technical point of view, but it is nonetheless one of the greatest unresolved enigmas in the history of arithmetic. Although there have been many attempts to make sense of it since the time of the Greeks, we do not know the reasons which led the Sumerians to choose such a high base.

—*Georges Ifrah:* ***The Universal History of Numbers****, 2000*

4. The Babylonians were prolific makers of mathematical tables, and they have left us some sophisticated tables of reciprocals, squares, cubes and higher powers—such higher powers being useful in calculating interest on loans. The use of mathematical tables is now largely a thing of the past because of the widespread use of calculators, but their importance in facilitating calculations has a long heritage going back to these clay tablets.

—*Richard Mankiewicz:* ***The Story of Mathematics****, Princeton University Press, 2000*

6.5 Chinese Mathematics

1. The origins of Chinese mathematics go back at least to the 3rd. millennium B.C., with some number systems and geometry. Among early instances of more developed theory, the "Book of Changes" (Yi jing) of around the 7th century B.C. draws upon combinations in calculating the number of different forms of trigram and hexagram; that is, stacks of respectively three and six broken lines.

—*Ivor Grattan-Guinness:* ***The Rainbow of Mathematics****, 1997*

2. One of the most influential of all Chinese mathematical treatises was the Chiu-chang suanshu (Nine Chapters on the Mathematical Art). It was probably written by Chang Tsang, about 200 B.C. ... and was based on surviving fragments of a much earlier work. It contains 246 problems on a variety of topics.... The "Nine Chapters" is also the earliest known mathematical work to discuss the significance of negative numbers.

—*Stuart Hollingdale:* ***Makers of Mathematics****, 1989*

3. The origins of mathematical activity in early China are clouded by mysticism and legend. Mythological Emperor Yu is credited with receiving a divine gift from a Lo river tortoise. The gift in the form of a diagram called the Lo shu is believed to be the origin of Chinese mathematics, and pictures of Yu's reception of the Lo shu have adorned Chinese mathematics books for centuries.

—*Frank Swertz: "The Evolution of Mathematics in Ancient China";* ***Mathematics Magazine****, 52, 1979*

6.6 Japanese Mathematics

1. Of the mathematical knowledge possessed by the Japanese in the oldest times we know practically nothing. After the introduction of Buddhism through Korea in the 6th century, something of the Chinese mathematics was brought to Japan and studied for some time by native scholars. But their knowledge must have been exceedingly limited, for they did not even rise to the point of carrying on their work independently.

—*Yoshio Mikami:* ***The Development of Mathematics in China and Japan****, 2nd ed., 1974*

2. ...the Japanese mathematics did not exist as a science but as art. On that account everything studied in Japan had borne the character of speciality, lacking in generality. But the Japanese were by no means wanting in the scientific spirit, they were on the contrary endowed strongly with the zealous yearning after truth or knowledge, which prevailed throughout the whole history of the Japanese mathematics.

—*Yoshio Mikami:* ***The Development of Mathematics in China and Japan****, 2nd ed., 1974*

3. Japan was isolated from western society in the Edo era (1603–1867). During those days Japanese mathematicians created their own mathematical world. Many difficult problems were presented and solved. Most of the answers were dedicated to temples or shrines as beautiful panels which were called "San-Gaku" [mathematical tablet]. Many of them were lost during the tide of modernization after the Meiji revolution. About nine hundred San-Gaku, however, are seen nowadays in rural areas of Japan.

—*Mutsumi Suzuki: "A Brief History of Magic Square in Japan," 2000 [Proofs of the proposed theorems of the San-Gaku were rarely given. Their authors meant them to be challenges to others.]*

6.7 Mayan Mathematics

1. Judging by the Maya calendar, Maya astronomy must have been as good as that of early Egypt, for by the first century A.D. (from which time we have some dated documents), they had developed a remarkably accurate calendar, based on an ingenious intermeshing of the periods of the Sun, the Moon and the Great Star noh ek (Venus). The relationship between the lunar calendar and the day count was highly accurate. The error amounted to less than 5 minutes per year.

—*Petr Beckmann:* ***A History of "π,"*** *1971*

2. The achievements of the Classic Maya in mathematics and calendrical astronomy were remarkable.... Like the ancient Babylonian scribes, their learned men had a number system with a place-value notation that was used in commercial records, taxes or levies of tribute, census, mensuration, eclipse-possible records in astronomy, and other government or religious functions. Their place-value system, which was perhaps seven centuries old even when the Classic period began in the 3rd. century, had a symbol for zero (an ornate shell). The zero symbol was used as it is today.

—*Ronald Calinger:* ***Classics of Mathematics,*** *Ronald Calinger, ed., 1982*

3. ...for numbers [the Mayans] often used a notation known as "dot and dash." In this concise place-value system of numeration, a dot represented "one" and a horizontal dash represented "five," with a symbol for zero that looked like a shell. The system seems to have been used from about 400 B.C

—*Richard Mankiewicz:* ***The Story of Mathematics,*** *2000*

6.8 Greek Mathematics

1. The word "mathematics" is a Greek word, and, by origin, it means "something that has been learned or understood," or perhaps "acquired knowledge," and perhaps even, somewhat against grammar, "acquirable knowledge," that is, "learnable knowledge," that is "knowledge acquirable by learning."

—*Salomon Bochner:* ***The Role of Mathematics in the Rise of Science,*** *1966*

2. The conscious development of mathematical knowledge as well as the recognition of scientific knowledge as such began with the ancient Greeks. With the Greeks as well as the Babylonians before them, the development of mathematical ideas and techniques took place in parallel with the development of the first explicitly rational science—descriptive and predictive astronomy.

—*Felix E. Browder: "Does Pure Mathematics Have a Relation to the Sciences?";* ***American Scientist,*** *64, 1976*

3. It is difficult to give a wholly adequate explanation of just why the Greeks of 600 to 400 B.C. decided to abandon empirical methods of establishing mathematical knowledge and to insist that all mathematical conclusions be established only by deductive reasoning. This completely new viewpoint on mathematical method is usually explained by the peculiar mental bias of the Greeks of classical times toward philosophical inquiries.... Another explanation ... stems from the Hellenic love for beauty. Appreciation of beauty is an intellectual as well as an emotional experience, and conviction found in deductive argument are very satisfying.

—*Howard Eves:* ***Foundations and Fundamental Concepts of Mathematics,*** *1958*

4. Both the Hebrews and the Greeks used the letters of their alphabets to represent numbers, the Greek system being based on that of the Hebrews.... Not having hit on the simple idea of positional values, the Greeks had to use all twenty-four letters of their alphabet, and three other symbols in addition to these, even to represent small numbers. It is easy to be wise after the event, but now that we have our simple positional concept which requires only ten symbols to represent any number, no matter how large, one cannot help marvelling that the great Greek mathematicians whose genius produced the wonderful "Golden Age of Greek Mathematics," ...should not have devised a less complicated and cumbersome method of writing numbers.

—*Alfred Hooper:* ***Makers of Mathematics,*** *1948*

5. Over two thousand years ago, the philosopher-scientists of ancient Greece embarked on a project that was as daunting for those days as exploring the boundaries of the solar system would be today. It was to determine the size and shape of the entire earth.

—*Robert Osserman:* ***Poetry of the Universe,*** *1995*

6. The early Greek study of mathematics had one main goal: the understanding of man's place in the universe according to a rational scheme. Mathematics helped to find order in chaos, to arrange ideas in logical chains, to find fundamental principles. It was the most rational of sciences....

—*Dirk J. Struik:* ***A Concise History of Mathematics,*** *1948*

6.9 Roman Mathematics

1. The Romans' contribution to science was mostly limited to butchering antiquity's greatest mathematician, burning the Library of Alexandria, and slowly stifling the sciences that flourished in the colonies of their Empire.

—*Petr Beckmann:* ***A History of "π,"*** *1970 [It took six months of burning and 4,000 furnaces to destroy the 700,000 scrolls of the Alexandrian library.]*

2. Disliked for their militarism and cruelties, in consequence they [the Romans] are enormously underrated in the history of science in general. Their mathematics must have been wide-ranging to have made possible, for example, map and chart projection on prodigious scales, ... quantity surveying and bookkeeping of similar range, hydraulics for flooding amphitheaters in preparation for games between crocodiles and prisoners, and some naive probability theory when betting on the victores in gladiator bouts.

—*Ivor Grattan-Guinness:* ***The Rainbow of Mathematics,*** *1997*

3. ...we cannot completely dismiss the Roman influence on mathematics, because their great success in engineering projects shows that they were good—though not creative—mathematicians.

—*Lloyd Motz & Jefferson Hane Weaver:* ***The Story of Mathematics,*** *1993*

4. The Roman numerals were commonly used in bookkeeping in European countries until the eighteenth century, although our modern numerals were generally know in Europe at least as early as the year 1000.... The argument was that they [the Hindu-Arabic numerals] were more easily forged or falsified than Roman numerals.... One reason why the Roman numerals were preferred in bookkeeping was that it is easier to add and subtract with them than our modern numerals.

—*David Eugene Smith & Jekuthiel Ginsburg:* ***Numbers and Numerals,*** *1953*

6.10 Hindu Mathematics

1. I can only compare their [The Hindus] astronomical and mathematical literature ... to a mixture of pearl shells and sour dates, or of costly crystals and common pebbles. Both kinds of things are equal in their eyes, since they cannot rise themselves to the methods of strictly scientific deduction.

—*al-Birnui:* ***Hindustan,*** *C.E. Sachau, tr., 1888*

2. The grandest achievement of the Hindus and the one which, of all mathematical investigations, has contributed most to the general process of intelligence, is the invention of the principle of position in writing numbers.

—*Florian Cajori:* ***History of Mathematics,*** *1897*

3. According to an old tale, the Grand Vizier Sissa Ben Dahir was granted a boon for having invented chess of the Indian King, Shirham. Since the game is played on a board with 64 squares, Sissa addressed the king: "Majesty, give me a grain of wheat to place on the first square, and two grains of wheat to place on the second square, and four grains of wheat to place on the third, and eight grains of wheat on the fourth, and so, Oh, King, let me cover each of the 64 squares of the board." "And is that all you wish, Sissa, you fool?" exclaimed the astonished King. "Oh, Sire," Sissa replied, "I have asked for more wheat than you have in your entire kingdom, nay, for more wheat than there is in the whole world, verily, for enough to cover the whole surface of the earth to the depth of the twentieth part of a cubit.

—*Edward Kasner and James Newman:* ***Mathematics and the Imagination,*** *1940*

4. The earliest Vedic literature is mainly religious and ceremonial, the most important for their mathematical content are the appendices of the main Verdas, known as Vedangas. These are set down as sutras—short poetic aphorisms, peculiar to Sanskrit writings, which strive to give the essence of an argument in the most condensed and memorable form.

—*Richard Mankiewicz:* ***The Story of Mathematics,*** *2000*

6.11 Arabic Mathematics

1. The work and responsibility of preserving the great achievements of the Greeks and making further contributions to the sciences and mathematics was carried out by the Arabs, who welcomed scholars of all nationalities into their society.

—*Calvin C. Clawson:* ***Mathematical Mysteries,*** *1996*

2. Among the fine contributions by al-Biruni to trigonometry, outstanding was his solution of the 'gibla' problem. The task is to determine the direction in which the Muslim must face in order to face Mecca when praying at the decreed times; with M as Mecca, L as the location of the worshipper and N as another main point such as the North Pole, the gibla is 'angle' NLM.... Tables were prepared giving this angle for the latitude and longitude of many main locations; other tables provided accurate timings for prayer based upon values of solar parameters such as the altitude and azimuth angles, all measurable by astrolabe or quadrant.

—*Ivor Grattan-Guinness:* ***The Rainbow of Mathematics,*** *1997*

3. The Muslim contribution viewed as a whole exhibits a nice blending of Greek, Babylonian and Hindu influences. The debt of the West is twofold.

First, the Islamic scholars collected, preserved, and translated the Classical Greek mathematical texts. Secondly, they adopted the fully developed Hindu system of numeration, which was in due time transmitted to the West and eventually to the whole world. Although the new system had become known in the West by the year 1000, it took several centuries to displace the Roman number-language in Western Europe and the Ionic Greek number-language in the Byzantine Empire.

—*Stuart Hollingdale: **Makers of Mathematics**, 1989*

4. ...over two thousand years ago the size and shape of the earth were pretty well established. Unfortunately, with the crumbling of the ancient civilizations, a thousand years of accumulated wisdom was lost to the European continent. By good fortune, the decline of the West coincided roughly with the rise of Arabic civilization and culture, and much of ancient knowledge was translated and transferred there.

—*Robert Osserman: **Poetry of the Universe**, 1995*

6.12 Hindu-Arabic Numerals

1. Like us, the Indians use these numerical signs in their arithmetic. I have written a tract which shows, in as much detail as possible, how much more advanced the Indians are than we are in this field.

—*Muhammad ibn Ahmad Abu'l Rayhan al Biruni: **Kitab fi tahgig i ma li'l hind**, c. 1010– 1030*

2. One is hard pressed to think of universal customs that man has successfully established on earth. There is one, however, of which he can boast, the universal adoption of the Hindu-Arabic numerals to record numbers. In this we perhaps have man's unique worldwide victory of an idea.

—*Howard W. Eves: **Mathematical Circles Squared**, 1972*

3. The ingenious number-system, which serves as the basis for modern arithmetic, was used by the Arabs long before it reached Europe. It would be a mistake, however, to believe that this invention is Arabic. There is a great deal of evidence, much of it provided by the Arabs themselves, that this arithmetic originated in India.

—*J.-F. Montucla: **Historie des mathematiques**, 1798; A. Blanchard, tr., 1968*

4. There are only nine figures. These are: 1 2 3 4 5 6 7 8 9 [figures given in their Eastern Arabic form] A sign known as tziphra can be added to these, which, according to the Indians, means "nothing." The nine figures themselves are Indian, and tziphra is written thus: 0.

—*Maximus Planudes: **Logistike Indike** ("Indian Arithmetic"), c. 1252;*

6.13 Decimal System of Numeration

1. The successful propagation of the decimal system throughout so much of the Earth owes much to the vagaries of human language and its concomitant evolution.... The common factor behind all these decimal counting cultures is that their languages belong to the family of related tongues that linguists call "Indo-European," which was spoken over a wide swath of the world from India to Europe.

—*John D. Barrow: **Pi in the Sky**, 1992*

2. Just because primitive man invented the same number of number-sounds as he had fingers, our number-scale today is a decimal one, that is, a scale based on ten, and consisting of endless repetitions of the first ten basic number-sounds.

—*Alfred Hooper: **Makers of Mathematics**, 1948*

3. The decimal notation is not a heritage from the Greeks. As a result, everything dealing with that notation has been superimposed on Greek teaching and not incorporated into it. Our teaching does not yet make full use of that historical event, which is perhaps the most important event in the history of science, namely the invention of the decimal system of numeration.

—*Henri Lebesque: Quoted in Lucienne Felix: **The Modern Aspect of Mathematics**, 1960*

4. One must study the activities and the essence of Number in accordance with the power existing in the Decad (Ten-ness); for it (The Decad) is great, complete, all-achieving, and the origin of divine and human life and its Leader....

—*Philolaus of Tarentum; Quoted by Kathleen Freeman, **Ancilla to the Pre-Socratic Philosophers**, Harvard University Press, 1966*

5. Our modern power of easy reckoning with decimal fractions is the almost miraculous result of the gradual discovery of a perfect notation.

—*Alfred North Whitehead: **An Introduction to Mathematics**, 1911*

6.14 The Rebirth of Mathematics in the West

1. The spread of the Indo-Arab system of numbers into Europe is traditionally credited to the influence of the French scholar Gerbert of Aurillac (945—1003). He spent significant periods of his early life in Spain where he became acquainted with the science and mathematics of the Arabs ... his intellectual influence spread widely throughout Europe.... Elected Pope Sylvester II in 999, [he] is generally credited with the introduction and spread of the Indian-Arab numerals through Europe.

—*John D. Barrow:* ***Pi in the Sky***, *1992*

2. When Alfonso VI of Castile captured Toledo from the Moors in 1085, he did not burn their libraries, containing a wealth of Muslim manuscripts. Under the encouragement of the Archbishop of Toledo, a veritable intelligence evaluation center was set up. A large number of translators, the best known of whom was Gerard of Cremona (1114—1187), translated from Arabic, Greek and Hebrew into Latin, at last acquainting Europe not only with classical Greek mathematics, but also with contemporary algebra, trigonometry and astronomy.

—*Petr Beckmann:* ***A History of "π,"*** *1970*

3. After more than a thousand years of Greek achievement and excellence in science, learning, and mathematics, Justinian I, emperor of the Eastern Roman Empire, in 529 A.D. ordered the famous Academy in Athens ... shut down and its property confiscated, ending the great tradition founded 1100 years earlier by Thales.... From 529 ... until 1500 we encounter no significant European mathematician except Fibonacci, though numerous Eastern and Asian mathematicians were practicing, including Brahmagupta from India, Omar Khayyam from Persia, and Tsu Ch'ung-chi from China.

—*Calvin C. Clawson:* ***Mathematical Mysteries***, *1996*

7

Language, Linguistics and Mathematics

7.1 Rhetoric and Mathematics

1. Mathematics can be shown to sustain a certain relation to rhetoric and may aim in determining its laws.

—*L.A. Sherman:* ***University of Nebraska Studies,*** *Vol. 1*

2. Descartes was led to his analytical geometry by systematically fitting algebraic symbols to the still fashionable rhetorical geometry.

—*Herbert Westren Turnbull:* ***The Great Mathematicians,*** *1940*

3. Mathematics is terribly individual. Any mathematical act, whether of creation or apprehension, takes place in the deepest recesses of the individual mind.... Mathematical thoughts must nevertheless be communicated to other individuals and assimilated into the body of general knowledge. Otherwise they can hardly be said to exist.

—*Oswald Veblen: Opening Address,* ***Proceedings of the International Congress of Mathematicians, American Mathematical Society,*** *vol. I, 1952*

7.2 Making Explanations

1. Knowing something for oneself or for communication to an expert colleague is not the same as knowing it for explanation to a student.

—*Hyman Bass: "Mathematics for Educators";* ***Notices of the American Mathematical Society,*** *Vol. 44, 1; January, 1997*

2. I am master of everything I can explain.

—*Theodore Haeckler:* ***Journal in the Night,*** *tr. 1950*

3. I assume that the job of the philosopher of mathematics is to describe and explain mathematics, not to reform it.

—*Penelope Maddy:* ***Realism in Mathematics,*** *1990*

4. [Presentism is] peeling out what is familiar mathematics and declaring the strange rest to be in need of explanation.

—*Herbert Mehrtens:* ***Social History of Mathematics,*** *1979*

5. As to mathematics, to be imprisoned in an ugly room and set to do sums in algebra without ever having had the meaning of mathematics explained to me, or its relation to science was enough to make me hate mathematics all the rest of my life, as so many literary men do.

—*George Bernard Shaw: Quoted in* ***The Mathematical Intelligencer,*** *vol. 13, Winter, 1991*

7.3 Language and Mathematics

1. Leibniz sought to construct a universal language which would be adequate to represent all human statements and arguments. He foresaw a multitude of benefits flowing from this. Although the procedure would be used primarily to determine indisputable mathematical and scientific truths, its scope was wide enough to include the study of all logical arguments. Human disputes would be amicably resolved without ambiguity and the demonstrable truth would produce harmonious agreement in every case.

—*John D. Barrow:* ***Pi in the Sky,*** *1992*

2. The scientist uses the language of mathematics to construct metaphors which represent insights into the workings of nature. The nature of metaphors is as commonplace in science as it is in poetry.... What distinguishes the mathematical metaphor is the extraordinary power of this language to uncover implications of the underlying idea.

—*James O. Bullock: "Literacy in the Language of Mathematics";* ***American Mathematical Monthly,*** *October, 1994*

3. [The universe] cannot be read until we have learnt the language and become familiar with the characters in which it is written. It is written in mathematical language, and the letters are triangles, circles and other geometrical figures, without which means it is humanly impossible to comprehend a single word.

—Galileo Galilei: ***Opere Il Saggiatore:****, 1623*

4. Such is the advantage of a well constructed language that its simplified notation often becomes the source of profound theories.

—Pierre-Simon de Laplace: In N. Rose ***Mathematical Maxims and Minims****, 1988*

5. ...I do not think that the search for high level programming languages can stop short of anything but a language in which (constructive) mathematics can be adequately expressed.

—Per Martin-lof, 1967; Quoted in E.W. Dijkstra: "On a Cultural Gap"; ***The Mathematical Intelligencer****, vol. 8, 1, 1986*

6. There is in my opinion no important theoretical difference between natural languages and the artificial languages of logicians; indeed, I consider it possible to comprehend the syntax and semantics of both kinds of languages within a single natural and mathematically precise theory.

—Richard Montague: "Universal Grammar"; ***Theoria*** *36, 1970*

7. Because every language has a logical structure (a syntax), we should be able to establish a one-to-one correspondence between any language and logic and, therefore, between any language and mathematics. This correspondence became the basis of information theory and computer software, without which the modern electronic computer would have relatively little value.

—Lloyd Motz and Jefferson Hane Weaver: ***The Story of Mathematics****, 1993*

8. Mathematical language is difficult but imperishable. I do not believe that any Greek scholar today can understand the idiomatic undertones of Plato's dialogues, or the jokes of Aristhophanes, as thoroughly as mathematicians can understand every shade of meaning in Archimedes' works.

—M.H.A. Newman: "What is Mathematics?" ***Mathematics Gazette****, 43, October, 1959*

9. Ordinary language is totally unsuited for expressing what physics really asserts, since the words of everyday life are not sufficiently abstract. Only mathematics and mathematical logic can say as little as the physicist means to say.

—Bertrand Russell: ***The Scientific Outlook****, 1931*

10. [Mathematicians] feel free to use any word we like for any concept, as long as we define the word clearly, but most people learn most words from context and from experience. No wonder, then, that mathematics is viewed as a foreign language by many students—not only is the vocabulary unfamiliar, but even the process by which one learns the vocabulary is different!

—Stephanie Singer: in Kevin Devlin: ***The Language of Mathematics****, 2000*

11. By its geometric and later by its purely symbolic construction, mathematics shook off the fetters of language, and one who knows the enormous work put into this process and its ever recurrent surprising successes can not help feeling that mathematics today is more efficient in its sphere of the intellectual world, than the modern languages in their deplorable state or even music are on their respective fronts.

—Andreas Speiser: Quoted in Hermann Weyl: "The Mathematical Way of Thinking"; ***Philosophy of Mathematics and Natural Science****, 1949*

12. The miracle of the appropriateness of the language of mathematics for the formulation of the laws of physics is a wonderful gift which we neither understand nor deserve. We should be grateful for it, and hope that it will remain valid in future research and that it will extend, for better or for worse, to out pleasure even though perhaps also to our bafflement, to wide branches of learning.

—Eugene P. Wigner: "The Unreasonable Effectiveness of Mathematics," ***Communications on Pure and Applied Mathematics****, 1965*

7.4 The Science of Mathematical Linguistics

1. To say 'this statement if false' is to introduce a confusion between the language of the sentence and its metalanguage because we are talking about statements in some language not merely making them. Without this distinction the linguistic paradoxes are the harbingers of disaster.

—John D. Barrow: ***Pi in the Sky****, 1989*

2. ...linguists must be concerned with the problem of determining the fundamental underlying properties of successful grammars. The ultimate outcome of these investigations should be a theory of linguistic structure in which the descriptive devices utilized in particular grammars are presented and studied abstractly, with no specific reference to particular languages.

—Noam Chomsky: ***Syntactic Structures****, 1957*

3. In the 1950s, the linguist Noam Chomsky surprised everyone by using mathematics to "see" and describe the invisible, abstract patterns of words that we recognize as a grammatical sentence.

—*Keith Devlin:* ***Life by the Numbers****, 1998*

4. It turns out, ... that it is possible to isolate certain structural properties that are common to all languages. These properties are of a formal nature and can be described mathematically. Thus, we may talk about a basic mathematical structure of human language rather than of a particular language.

—*Zellig Harris: "Mathematical Linguistics";* ***The Mathematical Sciences: A Collection of Essays****, Edited by the National Research Council's Committee on Support of Research in the Mathematical Sciences, 1969*

7.5 Mathematical Notation

1. The + and - symbols first appeared in print in Mercantile Arithmetic ... by Johannes Widmann (born c. 1640), published in Leipzig in 1489. However, they referred not to addition or subtraction or to positive or negative numbers, but to surpluses and deficits in business problems.

—*Florian Cajori:* ***A History of Mathematical Notation****, vol. I, 1928*

2. Anyone who understands algebraic notation, reads at a glance in an equation results reached arithmetically only with great labor and pains.

—*Antoine Augustin Cournot:* ***Researches into the Mathematical Principles of the Theory of Wealth****, 1838; N.T. Bacon, tr., 1897*

3. Mathematical notation, like language, has grown up without much looking to, at the dictates of convenience and with the sanction of the majority. Resemblance, real or fancied, has been the first guide, and analogy has succeeded.

—*Augustus De Morgan: "Symbols";* ***Penny Cyclopaedia****, 1842*

4. To study ... abstract patterns, the mathematician has to use an equally abstract notation. Music provides a useful analogy. Musicians use a notation just as abstract as algebra to describe the patterns of music. Why do they do this? Because they are trying to describe on paper a very abstract pattern that exists in the human mind when we listen to music.... To capture an abstract pattern, the musician, like the mathematician, needs an abstract notation.

—*Keith Devlin:* ***Life by the Numbers****, 1998*

5. This difficulty leads very gradually to the recognition of the need for a shorthand to make the sequence of operations easily comprehensible: here we have the problem of notation, which crops up again after every introduction of new objects, and which will probably never cease to torment mathematicians.

—*Jean Dieudonne:* ***Mathematics—The Music of Reason****, 1987*

6. Leibniz's devotion to the advantages of appropriate notation was so wholehearted that one could ask whether he invented the calculus or merely a particularly felicitous system of notation for the calculus. Of course the answer is that he did both; indeed, his differential and integral notation so captured the essence of his calculus as to make notation and concept virtually inseparable. Newton, on the other hand, had little interest in notational matters; neither suggestive nor consistent notation was of great importance to him.

—*C. H. Edwards, Jr.: "The Calculus According to Newton" and "The Calculus According to Leibniz";* ***The Historical Development of the Calculus****, 1979*

7. ...the invention of a convenient and flexible notation is often more seminal than is a proof of even the deepest of theorems. A kind of coarse-grained history of mathematics could even be written which would be devoted entirely to the introduction of significant new notations.

—*John Allen Paulos:* ***Beyond Numeracy****, 1992*

8. A good notation should be unambiguous, pregnant, easy to remember; it should avoid harmful second meanings, and take advantage of useful second meanings; the order and connection of signs should suggest the order and connection of things.

—*George Polya:* ***How to Solve It****, 1945*

9. ...A good notation has a subtlety and suggestiveness which at times makes it seem almost like a live teacher.

—*Bertrand Russell:* ***The Scientific Outlook****, 1931*

10. Any time you are stuck on a problem, introduce more notation.

—*Chris Skinner: Plenary Lecture; August 3, 1997,* ***Topics in Number Theory****, Penn State*

11. By relieving the brain of all unnecessary work, a good notation sets it free to concentrate on more advanced problems, and, in effect, increases the mental power of the race.

—*Alfred North Whitehead:* ***An Introduction to Mathematics****, 1911; in F. Cajori:* ***A History of Mathematical Notation****, 1929*

7.6 Mathematical Symbols and Symbolic Language

1. If a lunatic scribbles a jumble of mathematical symbols it does not follow that the writing means anything merely because to the inexpert eye it is indistinguishable from higher mathematics.

—*E.T. Bell: In J.R. Newman, ed.* ***The World of Mathematics****, 1956*

2. What is the strength of mathematics? What makes mathematics possible? It is symbolic reasoning. It is like "canned thought." You have understood something once. You encode it, and then you go on using it without each time having to think about it. Without symbolic reasoning you cannot make a mathematical argument.

—*Lipman Bers: Donald J. Albers & Constance Reid: "An Interview with Lipman Bers";* ***Coll. Mathematical Journal****, vol. 18, September, 1987*

3. The first printed edition of Euclid's Elements and the earliest translations of Arabic algebra into Latin contained little or no mathematical symbolism. During the Renaissance the need for symbolism disclosed itself more strongly in algebra than in geometry. During the sixteenth century European algebra developed symbolisms for the writing of equations, but the arguments and explanations of the various steps in a solution were written in the ordinary form of verbal expression.

—*Florian Cajori:* ***A History of Mathematical Notation****, vol. I, 1928*

4. "What's the good of **Mercator's**
North Poles and Equators,
Tropics, Zones and Meridian
lines?"
So the Bellman would cry; and
the crew would reply,
"They are merely conventional
signs!"

—*Lewis Carroll:* ***The Hunting of the Snark****, 1876*

5. An idea, in the highest sense of the word, cannot be conveyed but by a symbol.

—*Samuel Taylor Coleridge:* ***Biographia Literaria****, 1817*

6. Every science that has thriven has thriven upon its own symbols: logic, the only science which is admitted to have made no improvements in century after century, is the only one which has grown no symbols.

—*Augustus De Morgan:* ***Transactions Cambridge Philosophical Society****, vol. X, 1864*

7. Mathematics is primarily a symbolic textual activity that uses written inscription and language to create, record, and justify its knowledge.

—*Paul Ernest:* ***Social Constructivism as a Philosophy of Mathematics****, 1998*

8. Behind every symbol is an idea. It is the idea which is important, and it is the familiarity with the idea which puts life in the symbol. It is, therefore, of greatest importance that the idea be developed before it is symbolized....

—*Harold Fawcett: "Reflections of a Retiring Teacher of Mathematics,"* ***The Mathematics Teacher****, November, 1964*

9. Nature's great book is written in mathematical symbols.

—*Galileo Galilei:* ***Il Saggiatore****, 1623*

10. My most nearly immortal contributions are an abbreviation and a typographical symbol. I invented "iff," for "if and only if"—but I could never believe that I was really the first inventor. I am quite prepared to believe that it existed before me, but I don't know that it did, and my invention (re-invention?) of it is what spread it through the mathematical world.

—*Paul R. Halmos:* ***I Want to be a Mathematician: An Automathography****, 1985*

11. Arithmetical symbols are written diagrams and geometrical figures are graphic formulas.

—*David Hilbert: "Mathematical Problems" Lectrue to The International Congress of Mathematicians, Paris, 1900, Mary Winston Newson, tr.,* ***Bulletin of the American Mathematical Society****, 1902*

12. One of Diophantus' major innovations was to introduce some measure of algebraic symbolism into mathematics. His writings occupy an intermediate position between the old rhetorical style, in which everything is written out in words, and the fully symbolic style of modern times.

—*Stuart Hollingdale:* ***Makers of Mathematics****, 1989*

13. A symbolism not interpreted is only a game of signs; it is a language only if it takes on meaning and if one has the use of an interpretation of the symbols and of the symbolic game; ... the problem of the role of intuition cannot be sidestepped.

—*L. Jorgensen: Quoted in Lucienne Felix:* ***The Modern Aspect of Mathematics****, 1960*

14. The symbols of arithmetic have a determinate connection; for instance 4 is always 2 + 2, whatever the things mentioned may be, miles, feet, acres, etc. In algebra we take symbols for numbers which have no determinate connection.

—*Philip E.B. Jourdain: "The Nature of Mathematics," in* ***The World of Mathematics****, James R. Newman, ed., 1956*

15. Why is symbolism used so extensively? Brevity, precision and comprehensibility are the three major reasons.

—*Morris Kline:* ***Mathematics for the Nonmathematician****, 1967*

16. In symbols one observes an advantage in discovery which is greatest when they express the exact nature of a thing briefly and, as it were, picture it; then indeed the labor of thought is wonderfully diminished.

—*Gottfried Wilhelm Leibniz: Letter to Tschirnhaus; in F. Cajori:* ***A History of Mathematical Notations,*** *1929*

17. ...To be sure, mathematics can be extended to any branch of knowledge, including economics, provided the concepts are so clearly defined as to permit accurate symbolic representation. That is only another way of saying that in some branches of discourse it is desirable to know what you are talking about.

—*James R. Newman:* ***The World of Mathematics,*** *1956*

18. If we can approach the Divine only through symbols, then it is the most suitable that we use mathematical symbols, for these have an indestructible certainty.

—*Nicholas of Cusa:* ***Die Kunst der Vermutung,*** *a selection from his works, 1957: Quoted in Stanley Gudder:* ***A Mathematical Journey,*** *1976*

19. [The symbols used in calculus] have been known to so many students only as hostile standards floating above an impregnable citadel.

—*T.P. Nunn: Attributed*

20. In order to translate a sentence from English into French two things are necessary. First, we must understand thoroughly the English sentence. Second, we must be familiar with the forms of expression peculiar to the French language. The situation is very similar when we attempt to express in mathematical symbols a condition proposed in words. First, we must understand thoroughly the condition. Second, we must be familiar with the forms of mathematical expression.

—*George Polya:* ***How to Solve It,*** *1945*

21. Symbolism is useful because it makes things difficult. Obviousness is always the enemy of correctness. Hence we must invent a new and difficult symbolism in which nothing is obvious. The whole of arithmetic and algebra has been shown to require three indefinable notions and five indemonstrable propositions.

—*Bertrand Russell: "Recent Work on the Principles of Mathematics";* ***The International Monthly,*** *vol. 4, July- December, 1901*

22. Mathematics uses symbols, but it no more is those symbols than music is musical notation or language is strings of letters from an alphabet.

—*Ian Stewart:* ***Nature's Numbers,*** *1995*

23. It is the symbolic language of mathematics only which has yet proved sufficiently accurate and comprehensive to demand familiarity with this conception of an inverse process.

—*John Venn:* ***Symbolic Logic,*** *1894*

24. The Numerical Logistic is the one displayed and treated by numbers; the Specific is displayed by kinds of forms of things; or by the letters of the Alphabet.

—*Francois Viete, 1600,* ***In Artem Analyticam Isagore,*** *French ed., 1630*

25. Mathematics is often considered a difficult and mysterious science, because of the numerous symbols which it employs. Of course, nothing is more incomprehensible than a symbolism which we do not understand. Also a symbolism, which we only partially understand and are unaccustomed to use, is difficult to follow. .. in mathematics, granted that we are giving any serious attention to mathematical ideas, the symbolism is invariably an immense simplification.

—*Alfred North Whitehead:* ***An Introduction to Mathematics,*** *1911*

26. The training which mathematics gives in working with symbols is an excellent preparation for other sciences; ... the world's work requires constant mastery of symbols.

—*J.W.A. Young:* ***The Teaching of Mathematics,*** *1907*

7.7 Mathematical Terminology

1. That this subject has hitherto been considered from the wrong point of view and surrounded by a mysterious obscurity, is to be attributed largely to an ill-adapted terminology. If, for instance, +1, -1, and the square root of -1 had been called direct, inverse, and lateral units, instead of positive, negative, and imaginary units, such an obscurity would have been out of the question.

—*Carl Friedrich Gauss:* ***Theoria residiorum biquadraticorum,*** *in Gauss'* ***Werke,*** *1900*

2. Many mathematical terms can be traced to the Pythagoreans. The very word "mathematics" was probably first used by them. The Greek word Mathema simply meant "science."

—*Alfred Hooper:* ***Makers of Mathematics,*** *"Foreword," 1948*

3. Those who favor a more exact terminology in the subjects studied in geometry ... use the term problem to mean an inquiry in which it is proposed to do or to construct something, and the term theorem an inquiry in which the consequences and necessary implications of certain hypotheses are investigated....

—*Pappus: Collection iii, in* ***Greek Mathematical Works, II;*** *Ivor Thomas, tr., 1980*

4. I am intentionally avoiding the standard term which, by the way, did not exist in Euler's time. One of the ugliest outgrowths of the "new math" was the premature introduction of technical terms.

*—George Polya: in P. Hilton & J. Pederson: "The Euler Characteristic and Polya's Dream"; **American Mathematical Monthly**, February, 1996*

5. The knowledge I had in mathematics gave me great assistance in acquiring their phraseology, which depended much upon that science and music; and in the latter I was not unskilled. Their ideas are Perpetually conversant in lines and figures. If they would, for example, praise the beauty of a woman or any other animal, they describe in by rhombs, circles, parallelograms, ellipses, and other geometrical terms, or else by words of art drawn from music, needless here to repeat. I observed in the King's kitchen all sorts of mathematical and musical instruments, after the figures of which they cut up the joints that were served to his Majesty's table.

*—Jonathan Swift: **Gulliver's Travels**, 1726*

8

Mathematics: Creation, Discovery or Invention?

8.1 Creating Mathematics

1. Any idiot can learn anything in mathematics. It requires only patience. Now to create something, that is another matter.

—Alonzo Church: Quoted in David Berlinski: ***A Tour of the Calculus****, 1995*

2. Mathematics is not deductive science, and neither is logic. There is no logical excuse for either mathematics or logic. Mathematics was created by people who generally speaking were much concerned about the durability of their work. They very much needed to know what they were talking about, and they showed a high degree of concern for the truth of their statements.

—Preston C. Hammer: "The Role and Nature of Mathematics"; ***The Mathematics Teacher****, December, 1964*

3. Although the acquisition of skill in mathematics and the sense of increased mathematical power contribute to the enjoyment of mathematical pursuits, neither can exceed the joy of the creation of beauty, remembering that even appreciation is a reenactment of creative activity, so that creating new mathematics and reading old mathematics produced by someone else result in very similar types of aesthetic feeling.

—H.E. Huntley: ***The Divine Proportion, a Study in Mathematical Beauty****, 1970*

4. It would appear as though mathematics is the creation of human fallible minds rather than a fixed, eternally existing body of knowledge. The subject seems very much dependent on the creator.

—Morris Kline: ***Mathematics: A Cultural Approach****, 1962*

5. Students must learn that mathematics is the most human of endeavors. Flesh and blood representatives of their own species engaged in a centuries long creative struggle to uncover and to erect this magnificent edifice. And the struggle goes on today. On the very campuses where mathematics is presented and received as an inhuman discipline, cold and dead, new mathematics is created. As sure as the tides.

—J.D. Philips: "Mathematics as an Aesthetic Discipline"; ***Humanistic Mathematics Network Journal****, #12; October, 1995*

6. The genesis of mathematical creation is a problem which should intensely interest the psychologist. It is the activity in which the human mind seems to take least from the outside world, in which it acts or seems to act only of itself and on itself, so that in studying the procedure of geometric thought we may hope to reach what is most essential in man's mind.

—Henri Poincare: "Science and Method," 1913; in ***The Foundations of Science****, G.B. Halsted, tr., 1929*

7. Of all escapes from reality, mathematics is the most successful ever. It is a fantasy that becomes all the more addictive because it works back to improve the same reality we are trying to evade. All other escapes—sex, drugs, hobbies, whatever—are ephemeral by comparison. The mathematician's feeling of triumph, as he forces the world to obey the laws his imagination has created, feeds on its own success. The world is permanently changed by the workings of his mind, and the certainty that his creations will endure renews his confidence as no other pursuit.

—Gian-Carlo Rota: "The Lost Cafe" in ***From Cardinals to Chaos****, Necia Grant Cooper, ed., 1988 and in* ***Indiscrete Thoughts****, 1997*

8. During the past fifty years, more mathematics has been created than in all previous ages put together.

—Ian Stewart: ***From Here to Infinity****, 1996*

9. Granted an urge to create, one creates with what one has.

—*Norbert Wiener:* ***Ex-Prodigy: My Childhood and Youth,*** *1979*

10. Technical skill is mastery of complexity
while creativity is mastery of simplicity.

—*E. Christopher Zeeman:* ***Catastrophe Theory, Selected Papers 1972–77,*** *1977*

8.2 Discovering Mathematics

1. Standard mathematics has recently been rendered obsolete by the discovery that for years we have been writing the numeral five backward. This has led to reevaluation of counting as a method of getting from one to ten. Students are taught advanced concepts of Boolean algebra, and formerly unsolvable equations are dealt with by threats of reprisal.

—*Woody Allen: In Howard Eves:* ***Return to Mathematical Circles,*** *1988*

2. Coming now to the science of numbers it is clear to the dullest apprehension that his was not created by man, but was discovered by investigation.... Whether, then, numbers are considered in themselves, or as applied to the laws of figures, or of sounds, or of other motions, they have fixed laws which were not made by man, but which the acuteness of ingenious men brought to light.

—*St. Augustine:* ***Christian Doctrine;*** *D.W. Robertson, tr., 1958*

3. It is usually more difficult to discover than to demonstrate any proposition; for the latter process we may have rules, but for the former we have none. The traces of those ideas which, in the mind of the discoverer of any new truth, connect the unknown with the known, are so faint, and his attention is so much more intensely directed to the object, than to the means by which he attains it, that it not unfrequently happens, that while we admire the happiness of the discovery we are totally at a loss to conceive the steps by which its author ascended to it.

—*Charles Babbage:* ***The Mathematical Works of Charles Babbage,*** *1978*

4. "Platonism" is the belief that mathematics exists independently of the human mathematicians who study it. In other words, mathematics is discovered rather than created.

—*E.T. Bell:* ***The Development of Mathematics*** *1940*

5. A working mathematician is always a Platonist. It doesn't matter what he says. He may not be a Platonist at other times. But I think that in mathematics he always has that feeling of discovery.

—*Lipman Bers: Donald J. Albers & Constance Reid: "An Interview with Lipman Bers";* ***Coll. Mathematical Journal,*** *vol. 18, September, 1987*

6. Mathematical discoveries, like springtime violets in the woods, have their season which no human can hasten or retard.

—*Johannes Bolyai: Quoted in Israel Kleiner: "Thinking the Unthinkable: The Story of Complex Numbers (with a Moral)";* ***Mathematics Teacher,*** *vol. 81, no. 7, October, 1988*

7. Every new body of discovery is mathematical in form, because there is no other guidance we can have.

—*C.G. Darwin, 1931: Quoted in E.T. Bell:* ***Men of Mathematics,*** *1937*

8. I hope that posterity will judge me kindly, not only as the the things which I have explained, but also to those which I have intentionally omitted so as to leave to others the pleasure of discovery.

—*Rene Descartes:* ***La Geometrie;*** *1637*

9. In mathematics as in other fields, to find one self lost in wonder at some manifestation is frequently the half of a new discovery.

—*G.L. Dirichlet:* ***Werke,*** *1897*

10. Those who fear muddy feet will never discover new paths.

—*Paul Elridge:* ***Maxims for a Modern Man,*** *1965*

11. The joy of suddenly learning a former secret and the joy of suddenly discovering a hitherto unknown truth are the same to me.—both have the flash of enlightenment, the almost incredibly enhanced vision, and the ecstasy and euphoria of released tension.

—*Paul R. Halmos:* ***I Want to be a Mathematician,*** *MAA Spectrum, 1985*

12. Many of the most beautiful discoveries in mathematics come from the wedding of branches which a priori seem very far apart from each other. One of the characteristics of mathematical genius is the ability to bring together different branches, by what could be called "inbreeding," or to bring together threads going off into many directions.

—*Serge Lang:* ***The Beauty of Doing Mathematics,*** *1985*

13. The art of discovering the causes of phenomena, or true hypothesis, is like the art of decyphering, in which an ingenious conjecture greatly shortens the road.

—*G.W. Leibniz:* ***New Essays Concerning Human Understanding,*** *1696*

14. A good means to discover is to take away certain parts of a system and to find out how the rest behaves.

—*Georg Christoph Lichtenberg:* ***Aphorismen,*** *Albert Leitzmann, ed., 1902–8*

15. So it goes, new mathematics from old, curving back, folding and unfolding, old ideas in new guises, new theorems illuminating old problems. Doing mathematics is like wandering through a new countryside. We see a beautiful valley below us, but the way down is too steep, and so we take another path, which leads us far afield, until, by a sudden and unexpected turning, we find ourselves walking in the valley.

*—Rick Norwood: "In Abstract Domain"; **The Sciences**, Vol. 22, December, 1982*

16. We are usually convinced more easily by reasons we have found ourselves than by those which have occurred to others.

*—Blaise Pascal: **Pensees**, 1670*

17. No other field can offer, to such an extent as mathematics, the joy of discovery, which is perhaps the greatest human joy.

*—Rosza Peter: "Mathematics Is Beautiful" **The Mathematical Intelligencer**, 12, Winter, 1990*

18. Mathematical discoveries, small or great are never born of spontaneous generation. They always presuppose a soil seeded with preliminary knowledge and well prepared by labor, both conscious and subconscious.

*—Henri Poincare: **Science and Hypotheses**, 1905*

19. The first rule of discovery is to have brains and good luck. The second rule of discovery is to sit tight and wait until you have a bright idea.

*—George Polya: **How to Solve It**, 1945*

20. Every mathematician, when they do mathematics, is a Platonist. You have to believe in these subtle cardinals in order to work with them. They're not just marks on a piece of paper. They are real to you. You can see them and turn them around and see different aspects of them. Almost like you move a physical object and you can see different aspects. When you do mathematics, obviously, you do that.

*—Judy Roitman: Quoted in Claudia Henrion: **Women in Mathematics: The Addition of Difference**, 1997*

21. I will be sufficiently rewarded if, when telling it to others, you will not claim the discovery as your own, but will say it is mine.

—Thales of Miletus; c. 6th cent. B.C. [It is the reply of Thales, credited with essentially founding Greek mathematics, when asked what he would take for one of his discoveries.]

8.3 Inventing Mathematics

1. It is the merest truism, evident at once to unsophisticated observation, that mathematics is a human invention.

*—P. W. Bridgman: **The Logic of Modern Physics**, 1972*

2. It is a remarkable fact that the mathematical inventions which have proved to be most accessible to the masses are also those which exercised the greatest influence on the development of pure mathematics.

*—Tobias Dantzig: **Number: The Language of Science**, 1954*

3. Children need to do what "real" mathematicians do— explore and invent for the rest of their lives.

*—Susan Ohanian: **Garbage Pizzas, Patchwork Quilts and Math Magic**, 1994*

4. As the prerogative of Natural Science is to cultivate a taste for observation, so that of Mathematics is, almost from the starting point, to stimulate the faculty of invention.

*—J.J. Sylvester: "A Plea for the Mathematician"; **Nature**, vol. 1, 1869 **Cambridge Mathematical Papers**, 1908*

8.4 Mathematical Existence

1. Mathematical entities exist independently of the activities of mathematicians in much the same way the stars would be there even if there were no astronomers to look at them.

*—Kurt Goedel: in **Collected Works of Kurt Goedel**, Solomon Feferman, John W. Dawson, Jr., Stephen C. Kleene, Gregory H. Moore, Robert M. Solovay & Jean van Heijenoort, 1989*

2. Mathematics exists solely for the honor of the human mind.

*—Carl Jacobi: Quoted in Walter R. Fuchs: **Mathematics for the Modern Mind**, 1967*

3. It is hard for me to believe, as some have tried to maintain, that such SUPERB theories could have arisen merely by some random natural selection of ideas leaving only the good ones as survivors. The good ones are simply much too good to be the survivors of ideas that have arisen in that random way. There must, instead, be some deep underlying reason for the accord between mathematics and physics, i.e. between Plato's world and the physical world.

*—Roger Penrose: **The Emperor's New Mind: Concerning Computers, Minds and the Laws of Physics**, 1989*

8.5 Discovering Mathematical Patterns

1. Looking for patterns trains the mind to search out and discover the similarities that bind seemingly unrelated information together in a whole. A child who expects things to "make sense" looks for the sense in things and from this develops understanding. A child who does not see patterns often does not expect things to make sense and sees all events as discrete, separate and unrelated.

—Mary Baratta-Lorton: in Marilyn Burns: ***About Teaching Mathematics: A K-8 Resource****, 1992*

2. Though the structures and patterns of mathematics reflect the structure of, and resonate in, the human mind every bit as much as do the structures and patterns of music, human beings have developed no mathematical equivalent to a pair of ears. Mathematics can only be "seen" with the "eyes of the mind." It is as if we had no sense of hearing, so that only someone able to sight-read music would be able to appreciate its patterns and harmonies.

—Kevin Devlin: ***Mathematics: The Science of Patterns****, 1997*

3. The mathematician's patterns, like the painter's or the poet's must be beautiful; the ideas, like the colors of the words must fit together in a harmonious way. Beauty is the first test: there is no permanent place in the world for ugly mathematics.

—G.H. Hardy: ***A Mathematician's Apology*** *1941*

4. The mental activity involved in the appreciation of a pattern is that or perceiving relationships.... When one contemplates a pattern, its various parts must be mentally related to the whole and the pattern must be grasped and appreciated as a whole.

—H.E. Huntley: ***The Divine Proportion****, 1970*

5. Nature exhibits not simply a higher degree but an altogether different level of complexity. The number of distinct scales of length or natural patterns is for all practical purposes infinite.

—Benoit Mandelbrot: ***The Fractal Geometry of Nature****, 1982*

6. In other arts, if we see a pattern we can admire its beauty; we may feel that it has significant form, but we cannot say what the significance is. And it is much better not to try.... But in mathematics it is not so. In mathematics, if a pattern occurs, we can go on to ask, Why does it occur? What does it signify? And we can find answers to these questions. In fact, for every pattern that appears, a mathematician feels he ought to know why it appears.

—W.W. Sawyer: ***Prelude to Mathematics****, 1957*

7. What humans do with the language of mathematics is to describe patterns.... To grow mathematically children must be exposed to a rich variety of patterns appropriate to their own lives through which they can see variety, regularity, and interconnections.

—Lynn A. Steen: ***On the Shoulders of Giants*** *Lynn A. Steen, ed., 1990*

8. Each of nature's patterns is a puzzle, nearly always a deep one. Mathematics is brilliant at helping us to solve puzzles. It is a more or less systematic way of digging out the rules and structures that lie behind some observed pattern or regularity, and then using those rules and structures to explain what's going on. Indeed, mathematics has developed alongside our understanding of nature, each reinforcing the other.

—Ian Stewart: ***Nature's Numbers****, 1995*

9. Every art is founded on the study of pattern. The cohesion of social systems depends on the maintenance of patterns of behavior, and advances in civilization depend on the fortunate modification of such behavior patterns. Thus the infusion of patterns into natural occurrences and the stability of such patterns, and the modification of such patterns is the necessary condition for the realization of the Good. Mathematics is the most powerful technique for the understanding of pattern, and for the analysis of the relation of patterns.

—Alfred North Whitehead: "Mathematics as an Element in the History of Thought"; ***The World of Mathematics****, vol. 1; James R. Newman, ed., 1956*

8.6 Principles of Mathematics

1. If I found any new truths in the sciences, I can say that they follow from, or depend on, five or six principal problems which I succeeded in solving and which I regard as so many battles where the fortunes of war were on my side.

—Rene Descartes: ***Discours de la Methode****, 1637*

2. Mathematics is of profound significance in the universe, not because it exhibits principles that we obey, but because it exhibits principles that we impose. It shows us the laws of our own being and the necessary conditions of experience. And is it not true that the other arts do something similar in those regions of experience which are not of the intellect alone?

—John William Navin Sullivan: "Mathematics as an Art": ***Aspects of Science****, 1925*

3. In my own experience ... there were very serious substantive discussions as to what the fundamental principles of mathematics are: as to whether a large chapter of mathematics is really logically binding or not.... It was not at all clear exactly what one means by absolute rigor, and specifically, whether one should limit oneself to use only those parts of mathematics which nobody questioned. Thus, remarkably enough, in a large fraction of mathematics there actually existed differences of opinion!

—John von Neumann: "The Role of Mathematics in the Sciences and Society"; ***Collected Works****, vol. 6, A.H. Taub, ed., 1963*

8.7 Mathematical Structures

1. Structures are the weapons of the mathematician.

—*Nicholas Bourbaki: Quoted in* ***Scientific American,*** *May 1957*

2. Mathematics is the study of structures. We are not born knowing these structures. So it is a relevant question to ask how these structures become built up. At first glance, it is painfully obvious that such structures must in the last resort be built up our of our experiences as we cope with our environment.

—*Zoltan P. Dienes: "On the Learning of Mathematics,"* ***The Arithmetic Teacher,*** *1963*

3. In most sciences one generation tears down what another has built and what one has established another undoes. Only in mathematics does each generation add a new story to the old structure.

—*Herman Hankel:* ***Die Entwickelung der Mathematik in den letzten Jahrhunderten,*** *1884: in R.E. Moritz:* ***On Mathematics and Mathematicians,*** *1942*

4. Mathematics, springing from the soil of basic human experience with numbers and data and space and motion, builds up a far-flung architectural structure composed of theorems which reveal insights into the reasons behind appearances and of concepts which relate totally disparate concrete ideas.

—*Saunders MacLane: "Of Course and Courses";* ***American Mathematical Monthly,*** *vol. 61; March, 1954*

5. Mathematicians study structure independent of context, and their science is a voyage of exploration through all the kinds of structure and order which the human mind is capable of discerning.

—*Charles Pinter:* ***A Book of Abstract Algebra,*** *1990*

6. That mathematics, in common with other art forms, can lead us beyond ordinary existence, and can show us something of the structure in which all creation hangs together, is no new idea. But mathematical texts generally begin the story in the middle, leaving the reader to pick up the thread as best he can.

—*George Spencer-Brown:* ***Laws of Form,*** *1969*

7. As one reads mathematics, one needs to have an active mind, asking questions, forming mental connections between the current topic and other ideas from other contexts, so as to develop a sense of the structure, not just familiarity with a particular tour through the structure.

—*William P. Thurston:* ***Three-Dimensional Geometry and Topology,*** *1997*

8.8 Mathematical Reasoning

1. There are very few things which we know, which are not capable of being reduc'd to a Mathematical Reasoning, and when they cannot it's a sign our knowledge of them is very small and confus'd; and when a Mathematical Reasoning can be had it's as great a folly to make use of any other, as to grope for a thing in the dark, when you have a candle standing by you.

—*John Arbuthnot:* ***Of the Laws of Chance,*** *1692*

2. Although I am not stupid, the mathematical side of my brain is like dumb notes upon a damaged piano.

—*Margot Asquith:* ***More or Less About Myself,*** *1934*

3. We think of Euclid as of fine ice; we admire Newton as we admire the Peak of Teneriffe. Even the intensive labors, the most remote triumphs of the abstract intellect seem to carry us into a region different from our own—to be in a terra incognita of pure reasoning, to cast a chill on human glory.

—*Walter Bagehot: "Mr. Macaulay,"* ***National Review,*** *April, 1856*

4. The reasoning of mathematics is a type of perfect reasoning.

—*P.A. Barnett:* ***Common Sense in Education and Teaching,*** *1905*

5. Since human beings have never encountered actually infinite collections of things in our material existence, all of our attempts to deal with them must involve projecting our finite experience.... Therefore, we must rely on logical reasoning ... and then be prepared to accept the consequences of our reasoning, regardless of whether or not they conform to our intuitive feelings.

—*W.P. Berlinghoff & K.E. Grant:* ***A Mathematical Sampler: Topics for the Liberal Arts,*** *1992*

6. By Political Arithmetick, we mean the Art of Reasoning, by Figures, upon Things relating to Government.

—*Charles Davenant:* ***Discourse on the Publick Revenues,*** *1698*

7. As reason is the substance and original of the mathematics, so by stating and squaring everything by reason, and by making the most rational judgement of things, every man may be in time master of every mechanic art.

—*Daniel Defoe:* ***The Life and Adventures of Robinson Crusoe,*** *1719*

8. In questions of science the authority of a thousand is not worth the humble reasoning of a single individual.

—*Galileo Galilei: Quoted in F. Arago's Eulogy of Laplace; Smithsonian Report, 1874*

9. I implore you, you do not hope to be able to give the reasons for the number of planets, do you? This worthy has been resolved, with the help of God, not badly. Geometrical reasons are co-eternal with God.

*—Johannes Kepler: **Epitome of Copernican Astronomy**, c. 1600*

10. I have hardly ever known a mathematician who was capable of reasoning.

*—Plato: **The Republic; Dialogues of Plato**, Jowett, 1897*

11. All geometrical reasoning is, in the last resort, circular: if we start by assuming points, they can only be defined by the lines or planes which relate them; and if we start by assuming lines or planes, they can only be defined by the points through which they pass.

*—Bertrand Russell: **An Essay on the Foundations of Geometry**, 1897*

12. Mathematical reasoning may be regarded rather schematically as the exercise of a combination of two faculties, which we may call intuition and ingenuity The activity of the intuition consists in making spontaneous judgments which are not the result of conscious trains of reasoning.

*—Alan Turing: in Andrew Hodges: **Alan Turing: The Enigma**, 1983*

13. As an exercise of the reasoning faculty, pure mathematics is an admirable exercise, because it consists of reasoning alone, and does not encumber the student with an exercise of judgment: and it is well to begin with learning one thing at a time, and to defer a combination of mental exercises to a later period.

*—R. Whatley: **Annotations to Bacon's Essays**, 1873*

9

The Sciences and Mathematics I

9.1 The Relationship Between Science and Mathematics

1. ...the vitality of mathematics arises from the fact that its concepts and results, for all their abstractness, originate ... in the actual world and find widely varied application in the other sciences, in engineering, and all the practical affairs of daily life: to realize this is the most important prerequisite for understanding mathematics.

*—A.D. Aleksandrov: Quoted in Allen L. Hammond: "Mathematics—Our Invisible Culture"; **Mathematics Today—Twelve Informal Essays**, 1978*

2. There are four great sciences.... Of these sciences the gate and key is mathematics, which the saints discovered at the beginning of the world. Neglect of mathematics works injury to all knowledge, since he who is ignorant of it cannot know the other sciences or the things of this world. And what is worse, men who are thus ignorant are unable to perceive their own ignorance and so do not seek a remedy.

*—Roger Bacon: **Opus Majus**, 1267; Robert Belle Burke, tr., 1928*

3. Mathematics—the unshaken Foundation of Sciences, and the plentiful Foundation of Advantage to human affairs.

*—Isaac Barrow: **Lectiones Geometricae**, 1670; Quoted in Carl B. Boyer: **A History of Mathematics**, 1968*

4. It is the perennial youth of mathematics itself which marks it off with a disconcerting immortality from the other sciences.

*—E.T. Bell: **Mathematics, Queen and Servant of Science**, 1951*

5. Mathematics: The Handmaiden of the Sciences.

—E.T. Bell: Book title, 1937

6. To isolate mathematics from the practical demands of the sciences is to invite the sterility of a cow shut away from the bulls.

*—Pafnuty Chebyshev: Quoted in G. Simmons: **Calculus Gems**, 1992*

7. It is only through Mathematics that we can thoroughly understand what true science is. Here alone we can find in the highest degree simplicity and severity of scientific law, and such abstraction as the human mind can attain. Any scientific education setting forth from any other point, is faulty in its basis.

*—Auguste Comte: **The Positive Philosophy of Auguste Comte**, Harriet Martineau, tr., 1853*

8. No human investigation can be called a real science if it cannot be demonstrated mathematically.

*—Leonardo da Vinci: **Treatise on Painting**, 1651, J.P. Richter, tr.; **Notebooks**, vol. 1, Edward MacCurdy, tr., 1938*

9. The difference between mathematical science and physical science has never been very clear. There are evidently two extreme tendencies corresponding to opposed mental attitudes—on the one hand, the urge to accumulate observations; on the other, to construct theories logically scaffolded.

*—Lucienne Felix: **The Modern Aspect of Mathematics**, 1960*

10. Mathematics is the queen of the sciences.

*—Carl Friedrich Gauss: In Sartorius von Waltershausen: **Gauss zum Gedachtniss**, 1856*

11. For many generations, mathematics "The Queen of the Sciences" was a much-maligned lady. It was tacitly understood that she reserved her favors exclusively for the select few who had the good fortune to be endowed with a peculiar mental kink that enabled them to penetrate the esoteric halls in which this most attractive lady resided (for such was the description of her dwelling place sedulously spread about by the fortunate few who were lucky enough to have found the key).

—Alfred Hooper: ***Makers of Mathematics,*** *"Foreword," 1948*

12. The essential fact is simply that all the pictures which science now draws of nature, and which alone seem capable of according with observational fact, are mathematics pictures.... We go beyond the mathematics formulas at our own risk.

—Sir James Jeans: ***The Mysterious Universe,*** *1930*

13. Science and mathematics
Run parallel to reality, they symbolize it, they squint at it
They never touch it....

—Robinson Jeffers: "The Silent Shepherds"; ***The Beginning & the End,*** *1954*

14. Theoretical Science is a game of mathematical make-believe.

—Morris Kline: ***Mathematics and the Search for Knowledge,*** *1959*

15. The faith of scientists in the power of mathematics is so implicit that their work has gradually become less and less observation, and more and more calculation. The promiscuous collection and tabulation of data have given way to a process of assigning possible meanings, merely supposed real entities, to mathematical terms, working out the logical results, and then staging certain crucial experiments to check the hypotheses against the actual, empirical results.

—Susanne K. Langer: ***Philosophy in a New Key,*** *1942*

16. The concept of mathematics is the concept of science in general.

—Novalis: ***Schriften,*** *1901*

17. It is a common observation that a science first begins to be exact when it is quantitatively treated. What are called the exact sciences are no other than the mathematical ones.

—Charles Sanders Peirce: ***The Doctrine of Chance,*** *1878*

18. Science was born of a faith in the mathematical interpretation of Nature, held long before it had been empirically verified.

—John Herman Randall, Jr.: ***Making of the Modern Mind,*** *1940*

19. If all the arts aspire to the condition of music, all the sciences aspire to the condition of mathematics.

—George Santayana: ***Some Turns of Thought in Modern Philosophy,*** *1933*

20. The scientist who uses mathematics should be aware that much new mathematical knowledge is being discovered; nearly all of it will be irrelevant to his research, but he should keep his eyes open for the small piece that may be of great value to him.

—W. W. Sawyer: "Algebra," ***Scientific American,*** *September, 1964*

21. Science is reasoning; reasoning is mathematics; and, therefore, science is mathematics.

—Marshall H. Stone: "Mathematics and the Future of Science"; ***Bulletin of the American Mathematical Association,*** *vol. 63, March, 1957*

22. Quantitative science—that is, science with mathematics—has proved effective in altering and controlling nature. The majority of society backs it up for this reason. At the present moment, they want nature altered and controlled—to the extent, of course that we can do it and the results are felicitous.

—William F. Taylor: Quoted in Philip J. Davis & Reuben Hersh: ***The Mathematical Experience,*** *1981*

23. It is undeniable that some of the best inspirations in mathematics—in those parts of it which are as pure mathematics as one can imagine—have come from the natural sciences.... The most vitally characteristic fact about mathematics is, in my opinion, its quite peculiar relationship to the natural sciences, or, more generally, to any science which interprets experience on a higher than purely descriptive level.

—John von Neumann: "The Mathematician," in Robert B. Heywood: ***The Works of the Mind,*** *1947*

24. It is the function of mathematics to be at the service of the natural sciences.

—Hermann Weyl: ***Philosophy of Mathematics and Natural Science,*** *1949*

25. All science as it grows toward perfection becomes mathematical in its ideas.

—Alfred North Whitehead: ***Science and the Modern World,*** *1929*

26. One of the chief duties of the mathematician in acting as an advisor to scientists ... is to discourage them from expecting too much from mathematics.

—Norbert Wiener: Quoted in Richard A. De Millo, Richard J. Lipton & Alan J. Perles: "Social Processes and Proofs of Theorems and Progress"; ***Communications of the ACM,*** *22:5, 1979 & in* ***The Mathematical Intelligencer,*** *vol. 3, 1, 1980*

9.2 Experimentation

1. After all, without the experiment—either a real one or a mathematical model—there would be no reason for a theory of probability.

—Thornton C. Fry: ***Probability and Its Engineering Uses,*** *1965*

2. I know very well that one sole experiment, or concludent demonstration, produced on the contrary part, sufficeth to batter to the ground ... a thousand ... probable Arguments.

*—Galileo Galilei: "Dialogues Concerning the Two Principal Systems of the World," 1636, in **Great Books of the Western World**, Henry Crew & Alfonso de Salvio, trs., 1952*

3. An experiment is a question which science poses to Nature, and a measurement is the recording of Nature's answer.

*—Max Planck: **Scientific Autobiography and Other Papers**, 1949*

4. Examples ... which might be multiplied ad libitum, show how difficult it often is for an experimenter to interpret his results without the aid of mathematics.

*—Lord Rayleigh: Quoted in E.T. Bell: **Men of Mathematics**, 1937*

5. ...mathematics is not a substitute for experiment: neither is mathematics experimental.

*—William R. Thompson: "The Use and Abuse of Mathematics"; **Science and Common Sense** 1937*

9.3 Experience

1. the moderate Aristotelian city
Of darning and the Eight-Fifteen, where Euclid's geometry
And Newton's mechanics would account for our experience,
And the kitchen table exists because I scrub it.

*—W.H. Auden: "For the Time Being: A Christmas Oratorio" **The Oxford Book of American Verse**, F.O. Matthiessen, ed., 1950*

2. Mathematical and physiological researches have shown that the space of experience is simply an actual case of many conceivable cases, about whose peculiar properties experience alone can instruct us.

*—Ernst Mach: **Popular Scientific Lectures**, Chicago, 1910*

3. When we cannot use the compass of mathematics or the torch of experience ... it is certain that we cannot take a single step forward.

*—Voltaire: **Philosophical Dictionary**, "Miscellany," 1764; in **The Portable Voltaire**, 1965*

4. [My thesis is that] much of the best mathematical inspiration comes from experience and that it is hardly possible to believe in the existence of an absolute, immutable concept of mathematical rigor, dissociated from all human experience.

*—John von Neumann: "The Mathematician" in **The Works of the Mind**, Robert B. Heywood, ed., 1947*

9.4 Physics and Mathematics

1. It has come to pass, I know not how, that Mathematics and Logic, which ought to be but the handmaids of Physic, nevertheless presume on the strength of the certainty which they possess to exercise dominion over it.

*—Francis Bacon: **De Augmentis**, 1623*

2. ...it would be better for the true physics if there were no mathematicians on earth.

*—Daniel Bernoulli: in: **The Mathematical Intelligencer**, vol. 13, no. 1, Winter, 1991*

3. The fact is that in the days before calculus and for a long time thereafter much of mathematics was created to facilitate applications in physics. And this may be the reason why before mathematics can become really successful in biology or psychology, mathematics itself will have to be changed. New mathematics will be created.

*—Lipman Bers: Quoted in Allen L. Hammond: "Mathematics—Our Invisible Culture"; **Mathematics Today—Twelve Informal Essays**, 1978*

4. It will probably be the new mathematical discoveries suggested through physics that will always be the most important, for from the beginning Nature has led the way and established the pattern which mathematics, the language of Nature, must follow.

*—George David Birkhoff; "Relativity and Modern Physics"; In **American Scientist**, Vol. 31, # 4, October, 1943*

5. Physics and geometry are one family.
Together and holding hands they roam to the limits of space....
Surprisingly, Math, has earned its rightful place for man and in the sky;
Fondling flowers with a smile—just wish nothing is said!

*—Shiing Shen Chern: in "Interview with Shiing Shen Chern"; **Notices of the American Mathematical Society**, Vol. 45, 7; August, 1998*

6. The domain of physics is no proper field for mathematical pastimes. The best security would be in giving a geometrical training to physicsts, who need not then have recourse to mathematicians, whose tendency is to despise experimental science.

*—Auguste Comte: **Cours de philosophie positive**, 6 vols., 1830—41*

7. Among the mere talkers so far as mathematics are concerned, are to be ranked three out of four of those who apply mathematics to physics, who, wanting a tool only, are very impatient of everything which is not of direct aid to the actual methods which are in their hands.

*—Augustus De Morgan: in Graves' **Life of Sir William Rowan Hamilton**, Vol. 3, 1882–1889*

8. I should consider that I knew nothing about physics if I were able to explain only how things might be, and were unable to demonstrate that they could be otherwise. For having reduced physics to mathematics, the demonstration is now possible, and I think that I can do it within the small compass of my knowledge.

—Rene Descartes: "Geometry," 1637

9. The steady progress of physics requires for its theoretical formulations a mathematics that gets continually more advanced.

*—Paul Dirac: "Quantisized Singularities in the Electromagnetic Field": **Proceedings of the Royal Society**, vol. 133, 1931*

10. I am acutely aware of the fact that the marriage between mathematics and physics, which was so enormously fruitful in past centuries, has recently ended in divorce.

*—Freeman Dyson: **Missed Opportunities**, 1972*

11. Experience, of course, remains the sole criterion for the serviceability of mathematical constructions for physics, but the truly creative principle resides in mathematics.

*—Albert Einstein: in Frank Phillip: **Modern Science and its Philosophy**, 1967*

12. Physics is to mathematics what sex is to masturbation.

*—Richard P. Feynman: Quoted in Lawrence M. Krause: **Fear of Physics**, 1993*

13. A mathematician may say anything he pleases, but a physicist must be at least partially sane.

*—Josiah Willard Gibbs: Quoted by R.B. Lindsay: "On the Relation of Mathematics and Physics"; **The Scientific Monthly**, December, 1944*

14. Of course mathematics works in physics! It is designed to discuss exactly the situation that physics confronts; namely, that there seems to be some order out there—let's find what it is.

*—Andrew Gleason: Quoted in **More Mathematical People**, D.J. Albers, G.L. Alexanderson & C. Reid, eds., 1990*

15. Some laymen confuse mathematics and theoretical physics and speak, for instance, of Einstein as a great mathematician. There is no doubt that Einstein was a great man, but he was no more a great mathematician than he was a great violinist. He used mathematics to find out facts about the universe, and that he successfully used certain parts of differential geometry for that purpose adds a certain piquancy to the appeal of differential geometry. Withal, relativity theory and differential geometry are not the same thing.

*—Paul Halmos: "Mathematics as a Creative Art," **American Scientist**, Vol. 56, 1968*

16. Physics is not applied mathematics. It is a natural science in which mathematics can be applied.

*—Norwood Russell Hanson: **Patterns of Discovery**, 1958*

17. Physics is much too hard for physicists.

*—David Hilbert: Constance Reid; **Hilbert**, 1970*

18. Of one thing we may be sure: physics without mathematics will forever be incomprehensible.

*—R.B. Lindsay: "On the Relation of Mathematics and Physics"; **Scientific Monthly**, vol. 59, December, 1944*

19. Physics is mathematical not because we know so much about the physical world, but because we know so little: it is only its mathematical properties that we can discover.

*—Bertrand Russell: Quoted in John D. Barrow: **The World within the World**, 1988*

20. The present tendency of physics is toward describing the universe in terms of mathematical relations between unimaginable entities.

*—J.W.N. Sullivan: **The Bases of Modern Science**, 1929*

21. The mathematical physicist is one who obtains much prestige from the physicists because they are impressed with the amount of mathematics he knows, and much prestige from the mathematicians, because they are impressed with the amount of physics he knows.

*—W.F.G. Swann: **The Architecture of the Universe**, 1934*

22. Physics is the study of the whole world, while mathematics is the study of all possible worlds.

*—Clifford Taubes: Quoted in Ivars Peterson: **The Mathematical Tourist**, 1988*

23. The branch of physics which is called Elementary Geometry was long ago delivered into the hands of mathematicians for the purposes of instruction. But, while mathematicians are often quite competent in their knowledge of the abstract nature of the subject, they are rarely so in their grasp of its physical meaning.

*—Oswald Veblen: "Geometry and Physics"; **Science**, vol. LVII; February 2, 1923*

24. Freeman Dyson and Harish-Chandra were walking and talking, as mathematicians do, when Harish-Chandra announced, "I am leaving physics for mathematics, I find physics messy, unrigorous, elusive." Freeman Dyson replied, "I am leaving mathematics for physics for exactly the same reasons," and that's what they both did.

*—David Wells: **The Penguin Book of Curious and Interesting Mathematics**, 1997*

25. Whereas physics in its development since the turn of the century resembles a mighty stream running in one direction, mathematics is more like the Nile delta, its water fanning out in all directions.

*—Hermann Weyl: Quoted in **The Mathematical Intelligencer**, vol. 7, 1, 1985*

9.5 Mechanics

1. Mechanics are the paradise of mathematics because here we come to the fruits of mathematics.... There is no certainty in science where one of the mathematical sciences cannot be applied, or which are not in relation with these mathematics.

*—Leonardo Da Vinci: **Notebooks**, vol. 1, Edward MacCurdy, tr., 1938*

2. The application of Newton's mechanics to continuously distributed masses led inevitably to the discovery and application of partial differential equations, which in their turn first provided the language for the laws of the field-theory.

*—Albert Einstein: "The Mechanics of Newton and Their Influence on the Development of Theoretical Physics"; **The World as I See It**, 1934*

3. Mechanics is is the paradise of the mathematical sciences, because by means of it one comes to the fruits of mathematics.

*—Morris Kline: **Mathematics: The Loss of Certainty**, 1980*

4. ...we may regard mechanics as a geometry of four dimensions and analytic mechanics as an extension of analytic geometry.

*—Joseph-Louis Lagrange: **Theorie des fonctions analytiques**, 1797*

5. All that has been accomplished in mechanics since his [Newton's] day has been a deductive, formal and mathematical development of mechanics on the basis of Newton's laws.

*—Ernst Mach: in E.N. Da C. Andrade: "Isaac Newton" in **The World of Mathematics**, vol. 1, James R. Newman, ed., 1956*

6. ...it comes to pass that mechanics is so distinguished from geometry that what is perfectly accurate is called geometrical, what is less so, is called mechanical.

*—Sir Isaac Newton: **Principia Mathematica**, 1687*

7. Eudoxus and Archytas had been the first originators of this far-famed and highly-prized art of mechanics, which they employed as an elegant illustration of geometrical truths, and as a means of sustaining experimentally, to the satisfaction of the senses, conclusions too intricate for proof by words and diagrams.

*—Plutarch: **Parallel Lives: Marcellus**, c. A.D. 100; Quoted in J.L. Coolidge: **The Mathematics of Great Amateurs**, 1963*

8. In modern times the belief that the ultimate explanation of all things was to be found in Newtonian mechanics was an adumbration of the truth that all science, as it grows towards perfection, becomes mathematical in its ideas.

*—Alfred North Whitehead: in N. Rose: **Mathematical Maxims and Minims**, 1988*

10

The Sciences and Mathematics II

10.1 Gravity and Gravitation

1. Were it not for gravity one man might hurl another by a puff of breath into the depths of space, beyond recall for all eternity.

—Ruggero Boscovich: ***Theoria Philosophiae Naturalis****, 1777*

2. It is a mathematical fact that the casting of this pebble from my hand alters the center of gravity of the Universe.

—Thomas Carlyle; "Sartor Resartus III," ***Fraser's Magazine****, 1833–4*

3. Newton was puzzled about why the whole universe does not simply fall together into one great mass. How can the stars hang out there in space forever, unsupported, without being pulled toward each other by their mutual gravitational forces? Newton proposed an ingenious solution. For the universe to collapse to its center of gravity, there has to be a center of gravity. If, however, the universe were infinite in spatial extent, and on average populated uniformly by stars, then there would be no privileged center toward which all the stars could fall. Any star would be tugged similarly in all directions, and there would be no resultant force in any given direction.

—Paul Davies: ***The Mind of God****, 1992*

4. The notion of gravitation was not new, but Newton went on.

—Augustus De Morgan: ***A Budget of Paradoxes*** *1872*

5. It was ... at Woolsthorpe, in 1666 that the well-known legend of Newton and the apple arose. Tradition holds that the idea of gravitation was suggested to Newton by the fall of an apple. Certainly, the supposed tree from which it fell was kept standing until a gale destroyed it in 1820. But the earth's gravitation was an accepted scientific fact long before Newton's time; his genius lay in developing the law of universal gravitation.

—Alfred Hooper: ***Makers of Mathematics****, 1948*

6. Saturn is twice as far from the Sun as Jupiter is, but it takes two and a half times as long to complete one revolution. Saturn is thus not only farther away but travels more slowly. Kepler searches for a physical solution, dismissing the possibility that angels are somehow more tired the farther they are from the Sun. We find here the first discussions of a kind of gravitational force emanating from the Sun, which decreases in strength with distance. [For Kepler] the source of this force was God himself, in the form of the Father emanating the Holy Ghost throughout the universe.

—Richard Mankiewicz: ***The Story of Mathematics****, 2000*

7. ...the closer one looks at Newton's law of gravity the more bizarre it appears: any two objects exert a force of attraction on each other, and that force is somehow transmitted instantaneously across the vastness of empty space, from sun and moon to earth, from star to star, from galaxy to galaxy. Many reputable scientists at the time dismissed the idea as "voodoo physics" and refused to take it seriously.

—Robert Osserman: ***Poetry of the Universe****, 1995*

8. When Newton enunciated the law of gravity he did not say that the sun or the earth had the property of attraction; he said that all bodies from the largest to the smallest have the property of attracting one another, that is, leaving aside the question of the cause of the movement of the bodies, he expressed the property common to all bodies from the infinitely large to the infinitely small.

—Leo Tolstoy: ***War and Peace****, 1863–9; L. & A. Maude, tr., 1922*

9. The law of gravitation is indisputably and incomparably the greatest scientific discovery ever made.

—*William Whewell: **History of the Inductive Sciences**, 1980*

10.2 Relativity

1. In every way in which we live,
Our values are comparative,
Observe the snail who with a sigh,
Says: "See those turtles whizzing by."

—*Anonymous*

2. [Einstein's "The foundations of the General Theory of Relativity"] is the greatest feat of human thinking about Nature, the most amazing combination of philosophical penetration, physical intuition and mathematical skill. But is connections with experience were slender. It appealed to me like a great work of art, to be enjoyed and admired at a distance.

—*Max Born: **Einstein's Theory of Relativity** 1965*

3. Einstein, when discussing an experimental test of the general theory of relativity, was once asked what he would do if the experiment didn't agree with the theory. He was unperturbed at the prospect. "So much the worse for the experiment," he retorted. "The theory is right!"

—*Paul Davies: **The Mind of God**, 1992*

4. General relativity is the prime example of a physical theory built on a mathematical "leap in the dark," It might have remained undiscovered for a century if a man with Einstein's peculiar imagination had not lived.

—*Freeman J. Dyson: "Mathematics in the Physical Sciences"; **Scientific American**, September, 1964*

5. An hour sitting with a pretty girl on a park bench passes like a minute, but a minute sitting on a hot stove seems like an hour.

—*Albert Einstein: Attributed*

6. Since the mathematicians have invaded the theory of relativity, I do not understand it myself anymore.

—*Albert Einstein: In A. Sommerfelt; "To Albert Einstein's Seventieth Birthday," in Paul A. Schlipp, ed. **Albert Einstein, Philosopher-Scientist**, 1949*

7. Relativity is nothing more and nothing less than the admission that a complex state of affairs cannot be described in over-simplified language.

—*Philip Frank: "Einstein, Mach and Logical Positivism" in **Albert Einstein: Philosopher-Scientist**, Paul Arthur Schlipp, ed., 1949*

8. Relativity has taught us to be wary of time.

—*Wolfgang Rindler: **Essential Relativity**, 1977*

9. Since Relativity is a piece of mathematics, popular accounts that try to explain it without mathematics are almost certain to fail.

—*Eric Rogers: **Physics for the Inquiring Mind**, 1960*

10.3 Quantum Theory

1. [In quantum mechanics] we have the paradoxical situation that observable events obey laws of chance, but that the probability for these events itself spreads according to laws which are in all essential features casual laws.

—*Max Born: **Natural Philosophy of Cause and Chance**, 1964*

2. There is a difference between the role of chance in quantum mechanics and the unrestricted chaos of a lawless universe. Although there is generally no certainty about the future states of a quantum system, the relative probabilities of the different possible states are still determined....

—*Paul Davies: **The Mind of God**, 1992*

3. What do we really observe? Relativity theory has returned the answer—we only observe relations. Quantum theory returns another answer—we only observe probabilities.

—*Sir Arthur Eddington, 1959: Quoted in Richard Gregory: **Mind in Science**, 1981*

4. Quantum mechanics is very impressive. But an inner voice tells me that it is not yet the real thing. The theory yields a lot, but it hardly brings us any closer to the secret of the Old One.

—*Albert Einstein: Letter to Max Born; December 4, 1926*

5. It is often stated that of all the theories proposed in this century, the silliest is quantum theory. In fact, some say that the only thing that quantum theory has going for it is that it is unquestionably correct.

—*Michio Kaku: **Hyperspace**, Oxford University Press, 1995*

6. If anybody says he can think about quantum problems without getting giddy, that only shows he has not understood the first thing about them.

—*Max Planck: **The Universe in the Light of Modern Physics**, 1931*

7. In quantum mechanics—at least, as currently formulated—there is a genuine randomness. Just as the rule "shuffle the cards" permits many different outcomes, so the rules of quantum mechanics permit a particle to be in many different states. When we observe its state, we pin it down to a particular value—in the same way turning over the top card of the pack reveals a particular card. But while a quantum system is following its own nose, it has a random choice of possible futures.

—Ian Stewart: ***Does God Play Dice?****, 1989*

10.4 Astronomy and Mathematics

1. Arithmetic and geometry, those wings on which the astronomer soars as high as heaven.

—Robert Boyle: "Usefulness of Mathematics to Natural Philosophy"; 1772, in ***Works***

2. We may therefore define Astronomy as the science by which we discover the laws of the geometrical and mechanical phenomena presented by the heavenly bodies.

—Auguste Comte: ***Cours de philosophie positive****, 6 vols., 1830—41*

3. This art [astronomy] which is as it were the head of all the liberal arts and the one most worthy of a free man leans upon nearly all the other branches of mathematics. Arithmetic, geometry, optics, geodesy, mechanics, and whatever others, all offer themselves in its service.

—Nicolaus Copernicus: ***De Revoluntionibus****, "Introduction"; 1543*

4. The worst of all the historic setbacks of physical science was the definitive adoption by Aristotle and Ptolemy of the earth-centered astronomy in which all heavenly bodies were supposed to move on spheres and circles. The Aristotelian astronomy benighted science almost completely for 1,800 years (250 B.C. to A.D. 1550). There were of course many reasons for this prolonged stagnation, but it must be admitted that the primary reason for the popularity of Aristotle's astronomy was a misguided mathematical intuition that held only spheres and circles to be aesthetically satisfactory.

—Freeman J. Dyson: "Mathematics in the Physical Sciences"; ***Scientific American****, September, 1964*

5. A well-known scientist (some say it was Bertrand Russell) once gave a public lecture on astronomy. He described how the earth orbits around the sun and how the sun, in turn, orbits around the center of a vast collection of stars called our galaxy. At the end of the lecture, a little old lady at the back of the room got up and said: "What you have told us is rubbish. The world is really a flat plate supported on the back of a giant tortoise." The scientist gave a superior smile before replying, "What is the tortoise standing on?" "You're very clever, young man, very clever," said the old lady. "But it's turtle all the way down!"

—Stephen Hawking: ***A Brief History of Time****, 1988*

6. Astronomers work always with the past; because light takes time to move from one place to another, they see things as they were, not as they are.

—Neale E. Howard: ***The Telescope Handbook and Star Atlas****, 1975*

7. The astronomer is severely handicapped as compared with other scientists. He is forced into a comparatively passive role. He cannot invent his own experiments as the physicist, the chemist or the biologist can. He cannot travel about the Universe examining the items that interest him. He cannot, for example, skin a star like an onion and see how it works inside.

—Fred Hoyle: ***The Nature of the Universe****, 1950*

8. The science of celestial bodies, making use of measurements and figures almost as incomprehensible to the average human being as the defense budget.

—Richard Iannelli: ***The Devil's New Dictionary****, 1983*

9. A mind accustomed to mathematical deduction, when confronted with the faulty foundations of astrology, resists a long, long time, like an obstinate mule, until compelled by beating and curses to put its foot into that dirty puddle.

—Johannes Kepler: Quoted in Arthur Koestler: ***The Sleepwalkers****, 1959*

10. Astronomy was the cradle of the natural sciences and the starting point of geometrical theories.

—Cornelius Lanczos: ***Space Through the Ages****, 1961*

11. The discovery in 1846 of the planet Neptune was a dramatic and spectacular achievement of mathematical astronomy. The very existence of this new member of the solar system, and its exact location, were demonstrated with pencil and paper; there was left to observers only the routine task of pointing their telescopes at the spot the mathematicians had marked.

—James R. Newman: ***The World of Mathematics****, 1956*

12. If the earth were flat from east to west, the stars would rise as soon for westerners as for orientals, which is false. Also, if the earth were flat from north to south and vice versa, the stars which were always visible to anyone would continue to be so wherever he went, which is false. But it seems flat to human sight because it is so extensive.

—Ptolemy: ***Almagest****, c. 2nd cent. A.D.*

13. The astronomy ... is surely like a blind man who, with only a staff [mathematics] to guide him, must make a great, endless, hazardous journey that winds through innumerable desolate places.

—*Georg Joachim Rheticus: in O. Neugebauer:* ***The Exact Science of Antiquity****, 1957*

14. The great beauty of astronomy is not what is incomprehensible in it, but its comprehensibility—its geometrical exactitude.

—*William Hale White [Mark Rutherford] in Wilfred Stone:* ***Religion and Art of William Hale White****, 1967*

15. When I heard the learn'd astronomer,
When the proofs, the figures, were ranged in columns before me,
When I was shown the charts and diagrams, to add, divide and measure them,
When I sitting heard the astronomer where he lectured with much applause in the lecture room,
How soon unaccountable I became tired and sick,
Till rising and gliding out I wander'd off by myself,
In the mystical moist night-air, and from time to time,
Look'd up in perfect silence at the stars.

—*Walt Whitman: "When I heard the learn'd astronomer";* ***Nonesuch Edition of Collected Poems****, 1938*

10.5 The Sun and Other Stars

1. ...the first and highest of all is the sphere of the fixed stars, which comprehends itself and all things, and is accordingly immovable.

—*Nicolaus Copernicus:* ***On the Revolutions of the Heavenly Bodies****, Book I, 1543*

2. In the middle of everything is the sun. For in this most beautiful temple, who would place this lamp in another or better position than that from which it can light up the whole thing at the same time? For, the sun is not inappropriately called by some the lantern of the universe, by other, its mind, and, its ruler by still others.... Thus indeed, as though seated on a royal throne, the sun rules the family of planets revolving around it.

—*Nicolaus Copernicus:* ***On the Revolutions of the Heavenly Spheres****, 1543*

3. The sun does not move.

—*Leonardo da Vinci: in J.P. & I.A. Richter:* ***The Literary Works of Leonardo da Vinci****, 1939*

4. The number of fixed stars which observers have been able to see without artificial powers of sight up to this day can be counted. It is therefore decidedly a great feat to add to their number, and to set distinctly before the eyes other stars in myriads, which have never been seen before, and which surpass the old, previously known stars in number more than ten times.

—*Galileo Galilei:* ***Dialogues Concerning Two New Sciences****, 1638*

5. The sun alone appears, by virtue of his dignity and power, suited for this motive duty (of moving the planets) and worthy to become the home of God himself.

—*Johannes Kepler:* ***The Harmonies of the World****, 1619*

6. Why there is one Body in our System qualified to give Light and Heat to all the rest, I know no Reason, but because the Author of the System thought it convenient.

—*Isaac Newton* ***Principia Mathematica****, 1687*

7. The sun is a body of great size and power, the ruler, not only of the seasons and of the different climates, but also of the stars themselves and of the heavens. When we consider his operations, we must regard him as the life, or rather the mind of the universe, the chief regulator and the God of nature; he also lends his light to the other stars. He is the most illustrious and excellent, beholding all things and hearing all things.

—*Pliny the Elder:* ***Historia Naturalis****, A.D. 77*

10.6 Biology, Medicine, Chemistry and Mathematics

1. Mathematical sciences require theories, molecular biology facts.

—*David Berlinski:* ***A Tour of Calculus****, 1995*

2. Graph theory, a special tool borrowed from topology, has now been used to reduce even quite complicated chemical structures to a chain of numbers so that a computer can analyze them.

—*George A.W. Boehm: in* ***The Mathematical Sciences: A Collection of Essays****, Edited by the National Research Council's Committee on Support of Research in the Mathematical Sciences, 1969*

3. ...the idea that we could make biology mathematical, I think, perhaps is not working, but what is happening, strangely enough, is that maybe mathematics will become biological, not that biology will become mathematical, mathematics may go in that direction.

—*Gregory Chaitin: in an interview with Hans-Ulrich Obrist; October, 2000*

4. In mathematics we find the primitive source of rationality, and to mathematics must the biologists resort for means to carry out their researches.

—*Auguste Comte:* ***The Positive Philosophy of Auguste Comte****, Harriet Martineau, tr., 1853*

5. The use if the numerical method in medicine is not essentially new. From the time of Hippocrates to our day any doctor would say that this symptom is rare in a particular disease, but that one common; that this is more common than that one; that this treatment cures more patients than that one. All these expressions rare, common, more etc. are indeterminate numerical expressions and presuppose a count, be it methodical or not.

—Carl Emil Fenger: "About the Numerical Method"; ***Ugeskr Laeger****, 1839*

6. I am convinced that the future progress of chemistry as an exact science depends very much upon the alliance with mathematics.

—A. Frankland: ***American Journal of Mathematics****, 1878*

7. In their everyday work, of course, biologists do make use of mathematics. Like other investigators, biologists must subject their results to statistical tests, ... and they customarily display the relations they discover in the form of he curves of analytic geometry.

—Edward F. Moore: "Mathematics in the Biological Sciences"; ***Scientific American****, September, 1964*

8. Mathematics in the biomedical sciences is like a sophisticated laboratory tool which can be used to suggest other questions or to generate hypotheses.

—James Murray: Quoted in Keith Devlin: ***Life by the Numbers****, 1998*

9. Molecular biologists are starting to use knot theory to understand the different conformations that DNA can take on. They can track the sequence of steps in which one structure is gradually transformed into another during the basic, life-supporting processes that take place within cells. Recent advances are helping them see how the enzymes that do the cutting and gluing must perform their functions.

—Ivars Peterson: ***The Mathematical Tourist****, 1988*

10. Ere long mathematics will be as useful to the chemist as the balance.

—P. Schuttzenberger: in J. W. Mellor: ***Higher Mathematics for Students of Chemistry and Physics****, 1955*

11

Mathematics and the Arts

11.1 Aesthetics: Mathematical Beauty

1. Those who assert that the mathematical sciences say nothing of the beautiful or the good are in error. For these sciences say and prove a great deal about them; if they do not expressly mention them, but prove attributes which are their results or definitions. The chief forms of beauty are order and symmetry and definiteness, which the mathematical sciences demonstrate in a special degree.

—*Aristotle: **Metaphysics**, c. 4th cent. B.C.*

2. I think mathematicians generally agree that simplicity and beauty are important, and there is no trouble in recognizing them when you see them.

—*Lipman Bers: Quoted in Allen L. Hammond: "Mathematics—Our Invisible Culture"; **Mathematics Today—Twelve Informal Essays**, 1978*

3. Many arts there are which beautify the mind of man; of all other none do more garnish and beautify it than those arts which are called mathematical.

—*H. Billingsley: **The Elements of Geometrie of the most ancient Philosopher Euclide of Megara**; "Note to the Reader," 1570*

4. Fundamental aesthetic problem: Within each class of aesthetic objects to define the order O and the complexity C so that the ratio M = O/C yields the aesthetic measure of any object of the class.

—*George David Birkhoff: "Mathematics of Aesthetics," in **The World of Mathematics**, vol. 4, James R. Newman, ed., 1956*

5. No matter how correct a mathematical theorem may appear to be, one ought never to be satisfied that there was not something imperfect about it until it gives the impression of also being beautiful.

—*George Boole: **An Investigation of the Laws of Thought**, 1854*

6. To those who do not know mathematics it is difficult to get across a real feeling as to the beauty, the deepest beauty, of nature.... If you want to learn about nature, to appreciate nature, it is necessary to understand the language that she speaks in.

—*Richard P. Feynman: **The Character of Physical Law**, 1965*

7. When working on a problem, I never think about beauty; I think only of how to solve the problem. But when I have finished, if the solution is not beautiful, I know it is wrong.

—*R. Buckminster Fuller: "In the Outlaw Area"; profile by Calvin Tomkins: **New Yorker**, January 8, 1966*

8. The criterion of quality [in mathematics] is beauty, intricacy, neatness, elegance, satisfaction, appropriateness—all subjective, but all somehow mysteriously shared by all.

—*Paul Halmos: "Mathematics as a Creative Art," in **Mathematics: People, Problems, Results**, vol. 2, Douglas Campbell & John Higgins, ed., 1984*

9. The enjoyment of beauty in mathematics is for the most part an acquired taste. The eye has to be educated to see. How much of beauty the eye misses for lack of training! "Having eyes, they see not." Even the most highly trained mathematician must remain unmoved by much of the splendor because it is hidden from his keenest sight.

—*H.E. Huntley: **The Divine Proportion, a Study in Mathematical Beauty**, 1970*

10. One's intellectual and aesthetic life cannot be complete unless it includes an appreciation of the power and the beauty of mathematics. Simply put, aesthetic and intellectual fulfillment requires that you know about mathematics.

—*Jerry P. King:* ***The Art of Mathematics****, 1992*

11. A peculiar beauty reigns in the realm of mathematics, a beauty which resembles not so much the beauty of art as the beauty of nature and which affects the reflective mind, which has acquired an appreciation of it, very much like the latter.

—*Ernst Eduard Kummer:* ***Berliner Monatsberichte****, 1867*

12. The first essential bond between mathematics and the arts is found in the fact that discovery in mathematics is not a matter of logic. It is rather the result of mysterious powers which no one understands, and in which the unconscious recognition of beauty must play an important part. Out of the infinity of designs a mathematician chooses one pattern for beauty's sake, and pulls it down to earth.

—*Marston Morse:* ***Institute for Advanced Study****: Quoted in George A.W. Boehm:* ***The New World of Math****, 1959*

13. The mathematical passion is an aesthetic passion. I consider myself to be an artist. My motives have been those of any other artist with a passion for beauty.... The mathematical passion seized upon me when I was only nine years of age. I studied with such intensity that I had reached the degree standard in mathematics by the time I was eleven.... Mathematics is still, to me, an aesthetic passion.

—*Paul Painleve: Quoted in J.W.N. Sullivan:* ***Contemporary Mind, Some Modern Answers****, 1934*

14. I love mathematics not only for its technical applications, but principally because it is beautiful; because man has breathed his spirit of play into it, and because it has given him his greatest game—the encompassing of the infinite.

—*Rosza Peter:* ***Playing with Infinity****, 1962*

15. Beauty in mathematics is seeing the truth without effort.

—*George Polya: Quoted in Julian Weissglass:* ***Exploring Elementary Mathematics****, 1990*

16. The essential thing about mathematics is that it gives aesthetic pleasure without coming through the senses.

—*Rudy Rucker: "A New Golden Age"; in* ***Imaginary Numbers****, William Frucht, ed., 1999*

17. Mathematics, rightly viewed, possesses not only truth, but supreme beauty—a beauty cold and austere, like that of sculpture, without appeal to any part of our weaker nature, without the gorgeous trappings of painting or music, yet sublimely pure, and capable of a stern perfection such as only the greatest are can show.

—*Bertrand Russell:* ***The Study of Mathematics****, 1902*

18. The mathematician is fascinated with the marvelous beauty of the forms he constructs, and in their beauty he finds everlasting truth.

—*J.B. Shaw: In N. Rose:* ***Mathematical Maxims and Minims****, 1988*

19. The perfection of mathematical beauty is such ... that whatsoever is most beautiful and regular is also found to be the most useful and excellent.

—*Sir D'Arcy Wentworth Thompson:* ***On Growth and Form****, 1917*

20. In things to be seen at once, much variety makes confusion, another vice of beauty. In things that are not seen at once, and have no respect one to another, great variety is commendable, provided this variety transgress not the rules of optics and geometry.

—*Christopher Wren: Quoted in W.H. Auden & L. Kronenberger:* ***The Viking Book of Aphorisms****, 1966*

11.2 Harmony and Order

1. All things began in order, so shall they end, and so shall they begin again, according to the Ordainer of Order, and the mystical mathematicks of the City of Heaven.

—*Sir Thomas Browne:* ***Hydriotaphia, Urn-burial and The Garden of Cyrus****, 1690; published together in 1896*

2. There is no science which teaches the harmonies of nature more clearly than mathematics....

—*Paul Carus: "Reflections on Magic Squares";* ***The Monist****, vol. 16, 1906*

3. The fundamental importance of the subject of order may be inferred from the fact that all the concepts required in geometry can be expressed in terms of the concept of order alone.

—*E.V. Huntington:* ***The Continuum****, 1917*

4. Then feed on thoughts, that voluntary move Harmonious numbers.

—*John Milton:* ***Paradise Lost****, 1667*

5. Pythagoras, though primarily a pure mathematician, was the first applied mathematician in demonstrating that musical harmony depends on the ratio of the pitches to the sounds we hear. For such combined sounds to be pleasant, the ratio of the pitches must be simple fractions such as $\frac{2}{5}$. Sounds may be defined as atonal if the pitch ratios depart even slightly from these simple fractions.

—*Lloyd Motz & Jefferson Hane Weaver:* ***The Story of Mathematics****, 1993*

6. I see a certain order in the universe and math is one way of making it visible.
—*May Sarton:* ***As We Are Now****, 1973*

7. The Harmony of the world is made manifest in Form and Number, and the heart and soul and all the poetry of Natural Philosophy are embodied in the concept of mathematical beauty.
—*Sir D'Arcy Wentworth Thompson:* ***On Growth and Form****, 1917*

8. ...in the human body the central point is naturally the navel. For if a man be placed flat on his back, with his hands and feet extended, and a pair of compasses is centered at his navel, the fingers and toes of his two hands and feet touch the circumference of a circle described therefrom. And just as the human body yields a circular outline, so too a square figure may be found from it. For if we measure the distance from the soles of the feet to the top of the head, and then apply the measure to the outstretched arms, the breadth will be found to be the same as the height, as in the case of plane surfaces which are perfectly square.
—*Vitruvius:* ***The Ten Books of Architecture****, M.H. Morgan, tr., 1960*

9. There is inherent in nature a hidden harmony that reflects itself in our minds under the image of simple mathematical laws. That then is the reason why events in nature are predictable by a combination of observation and mathematical analysis. Again and again in the history of physics this conviction, or should I say this dream, of harmony in nature had found fulfillments beyond our expectation.
—*Hermann Weyl: Quoted in Morris Kline:* ***Mathematics: The Loss of Certainty****, 1980*

11.3 Proportion

1. ...if one wants to maintain a great giant the same proportion of limb as that found in an ordinary man he must either find harder and stronger material for making the bones, or he must admit a diminution of strength in comparison with men of medium stature; for if his height be increased inordinately he will fall and be crushed under his own weight. Whereas if the size of a body be diminished, the strength of that body is not diminished in proportion; indeed the smaller the body the greater its relative strength.
—*Galileo Galilei:* ***Dialogues Concerning Two New Sciences****, Henry Crew & Alfonso De Salvio, tr., 1914*

2. It is Proportion that beautifies everything, the whole Universe consists of it, and Musicke is measured by it.
—*Orlando Gibbons:* ***The First Set of Madrigals and Mottets, apt for Viols and Voyces****, 1612*

3. In small proportions we just beauties see;
And in short measures, life may perfect be.
—*Ben Jonson: "A Pindaric Ode," 1616*

4. You know, of course, that Lycurgus expelled arithmetical proportion from Lacedaemon, because of its democratic and rabble-rousing character. He introduced geometric proportions.
—*Plutarch:* ***Moralia****, ca. 100 A.D., Loeb, ed.*

5. The doctrine of proportion, as laid down in the fifth book of Euclid, is, probably, still unsurpassed as a masterpiece of exact reasoning; although the cumbrousness of the forms of expression which were adopted in the old geometry has led to the total exclusion of this part of the elements from the ordinary course of geometrical education.
—*H.J.S. Smith: "Presidential Address British Association for the Advancement of Science";* ***Nature****, Vol. 8, 1873*

6. What vexes me most is, that my female friends, who could bear me very well a dozen years ago, have now forsaken me, although I am not so old in proportion to them as I formerly was: which I can prove by arithmetic, for then I was double their age, which now I am not.
—*Jonathan Swift: Letter to Alexander Pope; February 7, 1736*

11.4 Symmetry

1. Tiger, Tiger, burning bright
In the forest of the night;
What immortal hand or eye,
Dare frame thy fearful symmetry?
—*William Blake; "The Tiger";* ***Songs of Experience****, 1794*

2. We find therefore, under this orderly arrangement, a wonderful symmetry in the universe, and a definite relation of harmony in the motion and magnitude of the orbs of a kind that it is not possible to obtain in any other way.
—*Nicolaus Copernicus:* ***On the Revolutions of the Heavenly Spheres****, 1543*

3. Symmetry signifies rest and binding, asymmetry motion and loosening, the one order and law, the other arbitrariness and accident, the one formal rigidity and constraint, the other life, play and freedom.
—*Dagobert Frey: "On the Problem of Symmetry in Art";* ***Studium Generale****, n.d.*

4. My body is all symmetry,
Full of proportions, one limb to another,
And all to all the world besides:
Each part may call the farthest brother:
For head with foot hath private smity,
And both with moon and tides.
—*George Herbert: "The Temple Man";* ***The Works of George Herbert****, 1976*

5. Our notion of symmetry is derived from the human face. Hence, we demand symmetry horizontally and in breadth only, not vertically nor in depth.

*—Blaise Pascal: **Pensees**, 1657; Quoted in W.H. Auden & L. Kronenberger, eds., **The Viking Book of Aphorisms**, 1966*

6. Something in the human mind is attracted to symmetry. Symmetry appeals to our visual sense, and thereby plays a role in our sense of beauty. However, perfect symmetry is repetitive and predictable, and our minds also like surprises, so we often consider imperfect symmetry to be more beautiful than exact mathematical symmetry.

*—Ian Stewart: **Nature's Numbers**, 1995*

7. The universe if built on a plan the profound symmetry of which is somehow present in the inner structure of our intellect.

*—Paul Valery: in Jefferson Hane Weaver: **The World of Physics**, Vol. II, 1987*

8. Symmetry is a vast subject, significant in art and nature. Mathematics lies at its root and it would be hard to find a better one on which to demonstrate the working of the mathematical intellect.

*—Hermann Weyl: **Symmetry**, 1952*

9. Nature seems to take advantage of the simple mathematical representations of the symmetry laws. When one pauses to consider the elegance and the beautiful perfection of the mathematical reasoning involved and contrast it with the complex and far-reaching physical consequences, a deep sense of respect for the power of the symmetry laws never fails to develop.

*—Chen N. Yang; in H.R. Pagels: **The Cosmic Code**, 1982*

11.5 The Arts and Mathematics

1. But when great and ingenious artists behold their so inept performances, not undeservedly do they ridicule the blindness of such men; since sane judgement abhors nothing so much as a picture perpetrated with no technical knowledge, although with plenty of care and diligence. Now the sole reason why painters of this sort are not aware of their own error is that they have not learnt Geometry, without which no one can either be or become an absolute artist; but the blame for this should be laid upon their masters, who are themselves ignorant of the this art.

*—Albrecht Durer: **The Art of Measurement**, 1525*

2. By keenly confronting the enigmas that surround us, and by considering and analyzing the observations that I had made, I ended up in the domain of mathematics. Although I am absolutely without training in the exact sciences, I often seem to have more in common with mathematicians than with my fellow-artists.

*—M.C. Escher: Quoted in C.F. Linn: **The Golden Mean: Mathematics and the Fine Arts**, 1974*

3. The Moors were masters in the filling of a surface with congruent figures and left no gaps over. In the Alhambra, in Spain, especially they decorated the walls by placing congruent multicolored pieces of majolica together without interstices. What a pity it was that Islam forbade the making of "images." In their tessellations they restricted themselves to figures with abstract geometrical shapes....

*—M.C. Escher: Quoted in C.F. Linn: **The Golden Mean: Mathematics and the Fine Arts**, 1974*

4. Basically, art and mathematics speak the same language, expressing the will to form and the general attitude of their times.

*—Konrad Knopp: "Mathematics as a Cultural Activity"; **Preusside Jahrbucher**, 1928; Walter Kaufmann-Buhler; **The Mathematical Intelligencer**, vol. 7, 1, 1985*

5. Mathematical genius and artistic genius touch one another.

—Gosta Mittag-Leffler: Attributed

6. But mathematics is the sister, as well as the servant, of the arts and is touched by the same madness and genius.

*—Marston Morse: "Mathematics and the Arts"; **Bulletin of the Atomic Scientist**, 15, February, 1959*

7. It is a feeling not uncommon amongst artists, that in their greatest works they are revealing eternal truths which have some kind of prior ethereal existence.... I cannot help feeling that, with mathematics, the case for believing in some kind of ethereal, eternal existence ... is a good deal stronger.

*—Roger Penrose: **The Emperor's New Mind: Concerning Computers, Minds and the Laws of Physics**, 1989*

8. A scientist worthy of his name, above all a mathematician, experiences in his work the same impression as an artist; his pleasure is as great and of the same nature.

*—Henri Poincare: **The Value of Science**, 1905; In N. Rose: **Mathematical Maxims and Minims**, 1988*

9. Artists who are interested in four dimensional space are not motivated by a desire to illustrate new physical theories, nor by a desire to solve mathematical problems. We are motivated by a desire to complete our subjective experience by inventing new aesthetic and conceptual capabilities. We are not in the least surprised, however, to find physicists and mathematicians working simultaneously on a metaphor for space in which paradoxical three dimensional experiences are resolved only by a four dimensional space.

—*Tony Robbin: in Linda Dalrymple Henderson:* ***The Fourth Dimension and non-Euclidean Geometry in Modern Art****, 1998*

11.6 Architecture and Mathematics

1. Greek architecture also reveals the emphasis on ideal forms. The simple and austere buildings were always rectangular in shape; even the ratios of the dimensions employed were fixed. The Parthenon at Athens is an example of the style and proportions found in almost all Greek temples.

—*Morris Kline:* ***Mathematics for the Non mathematician****, 1967*

2. Most people associate architecture with built materials: wood, brick, mortar, and stone. The things I do involve building architecture out of information.

—*Marcos Novak: Quoted in Keith Devlin:* ***Life by the Numbers****, 1998*

3. Geometry ... is of much assistance in architecture, and in particular it teaches the use of the rule and compasses.... By means of optics, again, the light in buildings can be drawn from fixed quarters of the sky ... by arithmetic the total cost of the buildings is calculated and measurements computed, but difficult questions involving symmetry are solved by means of geometrical theories and methods....

—*Vitruvius:* ***De Architectura, or, The Ten Books of Architecture****, c. 1st cent. B.C. M. H. Morgan, tr., 1960*

4. So organic architecture is architecture in which you feel and see all this happen as a third dimension ... space alive by way of the third dimension.

—*Frank Lloyd Wright: Quoted in* ***An American Architect****, Edgar Kaufman, ed., 1955*

11.7 Music and Mathematics

1. Mathematics is music for the mind; music is mathematics for the soul.

—*Anonymous*

2. The real difference between the structures of mathematics and music is that, whereas there is no basic condition which tells whether or not something is music, irrespective of whether we happen to like the sound of it, there is such a criterion for mathematics. Inconsistency is sufficient to disqualify a prospective mathematical structure.

—*John D. Barrow:* ***Pi in the Sky****, 1992*

3. A mathematician will recognize Cauchy, Gauss, Jacobi or Helmholtz after reading a few pages, just as musicians recognize, from the first few bars, Mozart, Beethoven or Schubert.

—*Ludwig Boltzmann: Quoted in A. Koestler:* ***The Act of Creation****, 1964*

4. Music is the soul of geometry.

—*Paul Claudel: Attributed*

5. Music is the arithmetic of sounds as optics is the geometry of light.

—*Claude Debussy: Letter to Jacques Durand, September 3, 1907 and in* ***Debussy on Music: The Critical Writings of the Great French Composer****, F. Lesure, ed., Eng. tr., 1977*

6. Bach, Mozart, Schubert—they will never fail you. When you perform their work properly it will have the character of the inevitable, as in great mathematics, which seems always to be made of preexisting truths.

—*E.L. Doctorow;* ***City of God****, Random House, 2000*

7. I see some parallels between the shifts of fashion in mathematics and in music. In music, the popular new styles of jazz and rock became fashionable a little earlier than the new mathematical styles of chaos and complexity theory. Jazz and rock were long despised by classical musicians, but have emerged as art-forms more accessible than classical musicians to a wide section of the public. Jazz and rock are no longer to be despised as passing fads. Neither are chaos and complexity theory. But still, classical music and classical mathematics are not dead. Mozart lives, and so does Euler. When the wheel of fashion turns once more, quantum mechanics and hard analysis will once again be in style.

—*Freeman Dyson: in a review of Ian Stewart:* ***Nature's Numbers; American Mathematical Monthly****, August–September, 1996*

8. Up to the eighteenth century, manuals and textbooks on music were common, music being considered a branch of mathematics.

—*Lucienne Felix:* ***The Modern Aspect of Mathematics****, 1960*

9. Music is architecture translated or transposed from space into time; for in music, besides the deepest feeling, there reigns also a rigorous mathematical intelligence.

—*Georg W.F. Hegel:* ***Logik****, 1812–16*

10. Mathematics and Music, the most sharply contrasted fields of intellectual activity which one can discover, and yet bound together, supporting one another as if they would demonstrate the hidden bond which draws together all activities of our mind and which also in the relations of artistic genius leads us to surmise unconscious expressions of a mysteriously active intelligence.

Hermann Ludwig von Helmholtz: ***On the Sensations of Tone as a Psychological Basis for the Theory of Music****, 1863, A. Ellis, tr., 1875*

11. The comparison of mathematics and music is often partially apt. The most attractive music is spoiled by a bad performance. So it is that many an admirable mathematical thought languishes amid the colorless rigor of a formal exposition.

—Ross Honsberger: ***Mathematical Gems****, 1973*

12. Music is an order of mystic, sensuous mathematics ... a sounding mirror, an aural mode of motion, it addresses itself on the formal side to the intellect, in its content of expression it appeals to the emotions.

—James G. Huneker: ***Chopin: The Man and His Music****, 1900*

13. I like to think of mathematics as a vast musical instrument on which one can play a great variety of beautiful melodies. Many generations of mathematicians have provided us with rich tonal resources that offer limitless possibilities for harmonious combination.

—Donald E. Knuth: "Algorithmic Themes" ***A Century of Mathematics in America, Part I****, Peter Duren, ed., 1988*

14. Music is a hidden exercise in arithmetic, of a mind unconscious of dealing with numbers.

—Gottfried Wilhelm Leibniz: Quoted in R.C. Archibald: "Mathematicians and Music"; Presidential Address, Mathematical Association of America, September 6, 1923; in ***The American Mathematical Monthly****, 31, 1924*

15. ...2500 years ago music was identified with the mathematics of that period: The Pythagorean school created them both on the same principles. Then there was a slackening in the relations between music and mathematics, the tempered scale of 250 years ago being the last important result of their collaboration. There is no reason to conclude that we have seen the last of this collaboration, in fact there are unquestionable possibilities which future musicians will perhaps put to use.

—Henri Martin: "Mathematics and Music" in ***Great Currents of Mathematical Thought****, F. Le Lionnais, ed., 1971*

16. Geometry gives us the sense of equality produced by proportion. It also heals by means of fine music all that is harsh and inharmonious or discordant in the soul, under the influence of rhythm, meter and melody.

—Philo of Megara: ***On the Cherubin****, c. 4th cent. B.C.: in Meleager:* ***The Greek Anthology*** *c. 60 B.C.*

17. There is geometry in the humming of
the strings.
There is music in the spacings of the
spheres.

—Pythagoras; c. 6th cent. B.C.

18. Just as it is possible to appreciate music and to understand its role in civilization in a more than superficial way without being able to play even one instrument nor even to understand the technicalities of how one is played, so also is it possible to attain a serious comprehension of the nature of mathematical achievements and the impact they have on civilization.

—H.L. Resnikoff & R.O. Wells, Jr.: ***Mathematics in Civilization****, "Introduction," 1973*

19. May not Music be described as the Mathematics of sense, Mathematics as Music of the reason? the soul of each the same! Thus the musician feels Mathematic, the mathematician thinks Music,—Music the dream, Mathematic the working life—each to receive its consummation from the other when the human intelligence, elevated to its perfect type, shall shine forth glorified in some future Mozart-Dirichlet or Beethoven-Gauss....

—James Joseph Sylvester: "On a Theorem Connected with Newton's Rule"; ***The Collected Papers of James Joseph Sylvester****, 1908*

20. [Pythagoras] discovered the importance of dealing with abstractions; and in particular directed attention to number as characterizing the periodicities of notes of music. The importance of the abstract idea of periodicity was thus present at the very beginning of mathematics and of European philosophy.

—Alfred North Whitehead: ***Science and the Modern World****, 1925*

11.8 Painting and Mathematics

1. The new painters do not propose, any more than did their predecessors, to be geometers. But it may be said that geometry is to the plastic arts what grammar is to the art of the writer. Today, scholars no longer limit themselves to the three dimensions of Euclid. The painters have been lead quite naturally, one might say by intuition, to preoccupy themselves with the new possibilities of spatial measurement which, in the language of the modern studios, are designated by the term fourth dimension.

—Guillaume Apollinaire: ***Soiress de Paris****, 1912; Quoted in Linda Dalrymple Henderson:* ***The Fourth***

Dimension and non–Euclidean Geometry in Modern Art*, 1998*

2. The principle of the science of painting is the point; second is the line; third is the surface; fourth is the body which is enclosed in these surfaces. And that is just what is to be represented ... since in truth the scope of painting does not extend beyond the representation of the solid body or the shape of all the things that are visible.

—Leonardo da Vinci: 1651, ***Treatise on Painting****, A.P. McMahon, tr., 1956*

3. Geometry is the right foundation of all painting.

—Albrecht Durer: ***Course in the Art of Measurement****, 1525*

4. Perhaps the closest analogy is between mathematics and painting. The origin of painting is physical reality, and so is the origin of mathematics—but the painter is not a camera and the mathematician is not an engineer.

—Paul R. Halmos: "Mathematics as a Creative Art," ***American Scientist****, Vol. 56, 1968*

5. When understood in their original context, however, "the fourth dimension" and non–Euclidean geometry are far from being the "scourge of every history of modern painting," as they have been termed. Instead, these concepts open the door to our understanding more fully the goals of many seminal artists of the early twentieth century.

—Linda Dalrymple Henderson: ***The Fourth Dimension and non–Euclidean Geometry****, 1998*

6. The Renaissance painters went so far in assimilating [mathematical knowledge from the newly recovered Greek works] and in applying mathematics to painting that they produced the first really new mathematics in Europe. In the fifteenth century they were the most accomplished and the most original mathematicians.

—Morris Kline: ***Mathematics for the Nonmathematician****, 1957*

11.9 Perspective

1. Analyze for a moment the method by which a picture is painted. As the artist looks at an object, rays of light enter his eye. When a transparent screen is placed between the eye and the object to be painted, these rays of light will meet the screen in a collection of points. It is this collection of points which the artist must draw if an observer is to receive the same impression from the painting as from the object itself.

—Claire Fisher Adler: ***Modern Geometry****, 1958*

2. Perspective is the bridle and rudder of painting.

—Leonardo da Vinci: Quoted in ***Selections from the Notebooks of Leonardo da Vinci****, Irma A. Richter, ed., 1977*

3. Perspective is the most subtle discovery in mathematical studies, for by the means of lines it causes to appear distant that which is near, and large that which is small.

—Leonardo Da Vinci: 1651, ***Treatise on Painting****, A.P. McMahon, tr., 1956*

4. The advent of linear perspective really mathematized, or probably better geometrized the way we see. The understanding of perspective allows a human being to make a picture of a controlled and confined space. It doesn't have to replicate a real space at all. And perhaps that's the real power of perspective: you're not simply copying nature, you're creating it.

—Sam Edgerton: Quoted in Keith Devlin: ***Life by the Numbers****, 1998*

5. To [Albrecht] Durer, as to many of his contemporaries, perspective meant the crown and keystone of the majestic edifice called Geometry.

—Erwin Panofsky: ***Albrecht Durer****, 2nd edition, 1945*

11.10 Poetry and Mathematics

1. But I think mathematics is very much like poetry. I think that what makes a good poem—a great poem—is that there is a large amount of thought expressed in very few words. In this sense formulas are like poems.

—Lipman Bers; in Donald J. Albers & Constance Reid: "An Interview with Lipman Bers," ***College Mathematics Journal****, 18, September, 1987*

2. Mathematics is a form of poetry which transcends poetry in that it proclaims a truth; a form of reasoning which transcends reasoning in that it wants to bring about the truth it proclaims; a form of action, of ritual behavior, which does not find fulfillment in the act but must proclaim and elaborate a poetic form of truth.

—Salomon Bochner: ***The Role of Mathematics in the Rise of Science****, 1966*

3. Pure mathematics is, in its way, the poetry of logical ideas.

—Albert Einstein: New York Times, May 1, 1935 [The remark was made in reference to the work of Emmy Noether on the occasion of her death.]

4. Here, where we reach the sphere of mathematics, we are among processes which seem to some the most inhuman activities and the most remote from poetry. Yet it is here that the artist has the fullest scope of his imagination.

—Havelock Ellis: ***The Dance of Life****, 1923*

5. We do not listen with the best regard to the

verses of a man who is only a poet, nor to his problems if he is only an algebraist; but if a man is at once acquainted with the geometric foundation of things and with their festal splendor, his poetry is exact and his arithmetic musical.

*—Ralph Waldo Emerson: "Works and Days"; **Society and Solitude**, 1870*

6. Everything you invent is true: you can be sure of that. Poetry is a subject as precise as geometry.

*—Gustave Flaubert: Letter to Louise Colet; August 14, 1853; in **Correspondence 1853–56**, M. Nadeau, ed., 1964*

7. Mathematics and Poetry are ... the utterance of the same power of imagination, only that in the one case it is addressed to the head, in the other to the heart.

*—Thomas Hill: "The Imagination in Mathematics"; **North American Review**, vol. 85, July, 1857*

8. To the aesthetically minded mathematician much mathematics reads like poetry.

*—H.E. Huntley: **The Divine Proportion, a Study in Mathematical Beauty**, 1970*

9. If you don't read poetry how the hell can you solve equations?

*—Harvey Jackins: Quoted in Julian Weissglass **Exploring Elementary Mathematics**,*

10. The union of the mathematician with the poet, fervor with measure, passion with correctedness, this surely is the ideal.

*—William James: "Lectures and Essays," 1879; **Collected Essays and Reviews**, 1920*

11. An elegantly executed proof is a poem in all but the form in which it is written.

*—Morris Kline: **Mathematics in Western Culture**, 1953*

12. It seems to me that the poet has only to perceive that which others do not perceive, to look deeper than others look. And the mathematician must do the same thing.

*—Sonya Kovalevsky: in Lynn M. Osen: **Women in Mathematics**, 1974*

13. Poets in truth are we in mathematics, But our creations also must be proved.

*—Leopold Kronecker: Quoted in Wolfgang Krull: "The Aesthetic Viewpoint in Mathematics"; Betty S. Waterhouse & Willard Waterhouse, trs., **The Mathematical Intelligencer**, vol. 9, 1, 1987*

14. Mathematics and poetry are head-tail of the same coin. Both are an attempt to discern pattern—because you refuse the idea of a chaotic universe—and to develop language which has to be metaphoric, or you'll drown in jargon.

*—Marguerite Lehr: in Patricia Kenschaft: "An Interview with Marguerite Lehr: In Memoriam"; **Association for Women in Mathematics Newsletter**, 18, March–April, 1988*

15. Mathematics is both inductive and deductive, needing, like poetry, persons who are creative and have a sense of the beautiful for its surest progress.

*—Mina Rees: in **Mathematical People**; D.J. Albers & G.L. Alexanderson, eds., 1985*

16. We have heard much about the poetry of mathematics, but very little of it has yet been sung. The ancients had a juster notion of their poetic value than we. The most distinct and beautiful statements of any truth must take at last the mathematical form. We might so simplify the rules of moral philosophy, as well as of arithmetic, that one formula would express them both.

*—Henry David Thoreau: **A Week on the Concord and Merrimac Rivers**, 1889*

17. A mathematician who is not also something of a poet will never be a complete mathematician.

*—Karl Weierstrass: Quoted in Mittag-Leffler: **Compte rendu du deuxieme congres internatinal des mathematiciens**, 1902 and in E.T. Bell: **Men of Mathematics**, 1937*

18. He must be a "practical" man who can see no poetry in mathematics.

*—W.F. White: Quoted in Howard Eves: **Mathematical Circles Squared**, 1972*

11.11 Stories, Myth and Mysticism

1. Every age has its myths and calls them higher truths.

—Anonymous

2. Mysticism generally possesses several features which distinguish it from the practice of mathematics. Most noticeably it is passive in its attitude to reality. It does not seek to improve, or rearrange the Universe. It is a contemplation rather than an exploration.

*—John D. Barrow: **Pi in the Sky**, 1992*

3. In precisely the same way that a novelist invents characters, dialogues, and situations of which he is both author and master, the mathematician devises at will the postulates upon which he bases his mathematical systems. Both the novelist and the mathematician may be conditioned by their environments in the choice and treatment of their material; but neither is compelled by any extrahuman, eternal necessity to create certain characters or invent certain systems.

*—E.T. Bell: **The Development of Mathematics**, 1945*

4. "Fiction" means a "made-up story." And mathematics is a kind of made-up story. But its uniqueness, its difference from other made up stories, is what we care about. Can the literary notion of fiction assist the philosophy of mathematics?

—*Reuben Hersh:* ***What Is Mathematics, Really,*** *1997*

5. The mathematicians and physics men
Have their mythology; they work alongside the truth,
Never touching it; their equations are false
But the things work. Or, when gross error appears,
They invent new ones; they drop the theory of waves
In universal ether and imagined curved space.

—*Robinson Jeffers: "The Great Wound:* ***The Beginning & the End,*** *1954*

6. ...storytelling and informal discourse have given birth over time to the complementary modes of thinking employed in statistics, logic, and mathematics generally. Although the latter skills are perhaps more difficult to come by and may even run counter to our intuitions, we can say that first, we tell stories, and then—in the blink of an eon—we cite statistics.

—*John Allen Paulos:* ***Once Upon a Number,*** *1998*

7. While in scientific thinking number appears as the great instrument of explanation, in mythical thinking it appears as a vehicle of religious significance....

—*T. Zausner:* ***Transformation and Personality and Emergence of Self in Titan's "Presentation of the Virgin to the Temple,"*** *1993*

12

Mathematics and the Social Sciences

12.1 Social Sciences: Sociology, Anthropology and Mathematics

1. Although social scientists still describe more than they measure, they are becoming dependent on mathematics. Some of the techniques they find most useful have been developed in recent years, and in the future their problems will very likely inspire much new mathematics.

*—George A.W. Boehm: in **The Mathematical Sciences: A Collection of Essays**, Edited by the National Research Council's Committee on Support of Research in the Mathematical Sciences, 1969*

2. It is only in the region of mathematics that sociologists, or anybody else, can obtain a true sense of scientific evidence, and form the habit of rational and decisive argumentation; can, in short, learn to fulfill the logical conditions of all positive speculation, by studying universal positivism as its source.

*—Auguste Comte: **The Positive Philosophy of Auguste Comte**, Harriet Martineau, tr., 1853*

3. The patterns identified and studied in the new sciences of mind and language wil involve contexts, which in general can only be partially specified. As a result, the new sciences will involve a mixture of mathematical reasoning and less mathematically formal kinds of reasoning used in the social sciences. A reasonable name for such reasoning would be soft mathematics, by analogy with the existing distinction between the hard sciences, such as physics and chemistry, and the soft sciences, such as sociology and psychology.

*—Keith Devlin: **Goodbye Descartes**, 1997*

4. ...the social scientist who lacks a mathematical mind and regards a mathematical formula as a magic recipe, rather than as the formulation of a supposition, does not hold forth much promise.

*—Bertrand de Jouvenel: **The Art of Conjecture**, 1967*

5. The real difficulty in applying mathematics [in the social sciences] lies in the fact that the social sciences are more complex than the physical sciences. The behavior of a committee of human beings is vastly more complex than the orbits of a planetary system.

*—John G. Kemeny: "The Social Sciences Call on Mathematics"; **The Mathematical Sciences: A Collection of Essays**, Edited by the National Research Council's Committee on Support of Research in the Mathematical Sciences, 1969*

6. A common objection to the use of mathematics in the social sciences is that the information available may be only qualitative, not quantitative. There are, however, several branches of mathematics that deal effectively with qualitative information. A very good example is the theory of graphs.

*—John G. Kemeny: "The Social Sciences Call on Mathematics"; **The Mathematical Sciences: A Collection of Essays**, Edited by the National Research Council's Committee on Support of Research in the Mathematical Sciences, 1969*

7. How can a modern anthropologist embark upon a generalization with any hope of arriving at a satisfactory conclusion? By thinking of the organizational ideas that are present in any society as a mathematical pattern.

*—Edmund Ronald Leach: **Rethinking Anthropology**, 1961*

8. It is notoriously difficult to apply precise mathematical methods in the social sciences, yet the ideas in Nash's thesis are simple and rigorous, and provide a firm background not only for economic theory but also for research in evolutionary biology, and more generally for the study of any situation in which human beings or machines face complexities or conflict.

—John Milnor: "A Nobel Prize for John Forbes Nash,"

The Mathematical Intelligencer*, 17, #3, Summer, 1995*

9. That form of wisdom which is the opposite of single-mindedness, the ability to keep many threads in hand, to draw for an argument from disparate sources, is quite foreign to mathematics. This inability accounts for much of the difficulty which mathematics experiences in attempting to penetrate the social sciences.

—Jacob T. Schwartz: ***Discrete Thoughts: Essays on Mathematics, Science and Philosophy****, 1986*

10. The social sciences mathematically developed are to be the controlling factors in civilization.

—William F. White: ***A Scrapbook of Elementary Mathematics****, 1908*

12.2 Economics and Mathematics

1. Economists are people who work with numbers but who don't have the personality to be accountants.

—Anonymous

2. The effort of the economist is the "see," to picture the interplay of economic elements. The more clearly cut these elements appear in his vision, the better; the more elements he can grasp and hold in his mind at once, the better. The economic world is a misty region. The first explorers used unaided vision. Mathematics is the lantern by which what before was dimly visible now looms up in firm, bold outlines. The old phantasmagoria disappear. We see better. We also see further.

—Irving Fisher: ***Transactions of Connecticut Academy****, 1892*

3. There can be no question, however, that prolonged commitment to mathematical exercise in economics can be damaging. It leads to the atrophy of judgement and intuition....

—John Kenneth Galbraith: ***Economics, Peace, and Laughter****, 1971*

4. Mathematical economics before von Neumann tried to achieve success by imitating the technique of classical mathematical physics. The mathematical tools used were those of analysis (specifically the calculus of variations), and the procedure relied on a not completely reliable analogy between economics and mechanics. The secret of the success of the von Neumann approach was the abandonment of the mechanical analogy and its replacement by a fresh point of view (games of strategy) and new told (the ideas of combinatorics and convexity).

—Paul R. Halmos: "The Legend of John von Neumann"; ***American Mathematical Monthly*** *80, 1973*

5. It is clear that Economics, if it is to be a science at all, must be a mathematical science. There exists much prejudice against attempts to introduce the methods and language of mathematics in any branch of moral sciences. Many persons seem to think that the physical sciences form the proper sphere of mathematical method, and that moral sciences demand some other method,—I know not what. My theory of Economics, however, is purely mathematical in character.

—William Stanley Jevons: ***The Theory of Political Economy****, 1871*

6. ...economics involves optimization, and this is the engine that produces principles of economic analysis. We have either a maximum problem or a minimum problem, which is a compelling reason for the use of mathematics.

—Lawrence R. Klein: "The Role of Mathematics in Economics"; ***The Mathematical Sciences: A Collection of Essays****, Edited by the National Research Council's Committee on Support of Research in the Mathematical Sciences, 1969*

7. Taking the whole earth ... and, supposing the present population equal to a thousand millions, the human species would increase as the numbers 1,2,4,8,16,32,128,256, and substance as 1,2,3,4,5,6,7,8,9. In two centuries the population would be to the means of substance as 256 to 9; in three centuries, as 4096 to 13; and in two thousand years the difference would be almost incalculable.

—Thomas Robert Malthus: "Mathematics of Population and Food"; ***An Essay on the Principle of Population****, 1798*

8. I had a growing feeling in the later years of my work at the subject that a good mathematical theorem dealing with economic hypotheses was very unlikely to be good economics: and I went more and more on the rules—(1) Use mathematics as a shorthand language rather than an engine of inquiry. (2) Keep to them till you are done. (3) Translate into English. (4) Then illustrate by examples that are important in real life. (5) Burn the mathematics. (6) If you can't succeed in 4, burn 3. This last I did often.

—Alfred Marshall: Letter to A.L. Bowley, February, 1906; in ***Memorials of Alfred Marshall****, 1961*

9. ...To be sure, mathematics can be extended to any branch of knowledge, including economics, provided the concepts are so clearly defined as to permit accurate symbolic representation. That is only another way of saying that in some branches of discourse it is desirable to know what you are talking about.

—James R. Newman: "Commentary on Cournot, Jevons, and the Mathematics of Money"; ***The World of Mathematics****, vol. 2, 1956*

10. No law can be laid down respecting quantity, but a tolerably correct one can be laid down respecting proportions. Every day I am more satisfied that the former enquiry is vain and delusive, and the latter only the true objects of the science [of economics].

—*David Ricardo:* ***On the Principles of Political Economy and Taxation****, 1817*

11. There are in the fields of economics no constant relations, and consequently no measurement is possible.

—*Ludwig Elder von Mises:* ***Human Action****, 1949*

12. The mathematical economists ... formulate equations and draw curves which are supposed to describe reality. In fact they describe only a hypothetical and unrealizable state of affairs, in no way similar to the catallactic problems in question.

—*Ludwig von Mises:* ***Positivism: A Study in Human Understanding****, 1951*

13. We hope to obtain a real understanding of the problem of exchange by studying it from an altogether different angle; that is, from the perspective of a "game of strategy."

—*John Von Neumann and Oskar Morgenstern:* ***The Theory of Games and Economic Behavior****, 2nd. ed., 1947*

14. Our federal income tax law defines the tax y to be paid in terms of the income x; it does so in a clumsy enough way by pasting several linear functions together, each valid in another interval or bracket of income. An archeologist who, five thousand years from now, shall unearth some of our income tax returns together with relics of engineering works and mathematical books, will probably date them a couple of centuries earlier, certainly before Galileo and Vieta.

—*Herman Weyl: "The Mathematical Way of Thinking," Address given at the Bicentennial Conference of the University of Pennsylvania, 1940*

12.3 Psychology and Mathematics

1. The manner of [French-born English mathematician Abraham] Demoivre's death has a certain interest for psychologists. Shortly before it, he declared that it was necessary for him to sleep some ten minutes or a quarter of an hour longer each day than the proceeding one: the day after he had thus reached a total of something over twenty-three hours he slept up to the limit of twenty-four hours, and then died in his sleep.

—*W.W. Rouse Ball:* ***History of Mathematics****, 1911 edition*

2. It is not only possible but necessary that mathematics be applied to psychology; the reason for this necessity lies briefly in this: that by no other means can be reached that which is the ultimate aim of all speculation, namely conviction.

—*J.F. Herbart:* ***Werke****, 1890*

3. All more definite knowledge must start with computation; and this is of most important consequences not only for the theory of memory, of imagination, of understanding, but as well for the doctrine of sensations, of desires, and affections.

—*J.F. Herbart:* ***Werke****, 1890*

4. The introduction into geometrical work of conceptions such as the infinite, the imaginary, and the relations of hyperspace, none of which can be directly imagined, has a psychological significance well worthy of examination. It gives a deep insight into the resources and working of the human mind. We arrive at the borderland of mathematics and psychology.

—*J.T. Merz:* ***A History of European Thought in the Nineteenth Century****, 1903*

12.4 Game Theory

1. For a long time, people have accepted this philosophy [the win-at-all-costs strategy] as undeniably true, But for the past two decades, mathematicians have been studying survival strategies to find out which are truly best. To almost everyone's surprise, they have found that nice guys can and frequently do finish first. In tournaments designed to pick out winners in a variety of conflict situations, the top dog turns out to be not the most ferocious but the most cooperative.

—*K.C. Cole:* ***The Universe and the Teacup****, 1997*

2. [John von Neumann in his "Zur Theorie der Gesellschaftspiele"] was the first to show the relations between games and economic behavior and to formulate and prove his now famous minimax theorem which assures the existence of good strategies for certain important classes of games.

—*Herman H. Goldstine:* ***The Computer from Pascal to von Neumann****, 1972*

3. Games constitute an important and rather special part of recreational mathematics [any mathematics which primarily sets a poser with a general cultural and maybe educational purpose]. The mathematical theory includes determining whether a strategy for winning exists, and if so finding an optimal one.

—*Ivor Grattan-Guinness:* ***The Rainbow of Mathematics****, 1997*

4. While the theory of games does not deal with the social process in its full complexity, it is not merely a peripheral aspect of the process which it studies, but its very core. The aim is "to find the mathematically complete principles which define 'rational behavior' for the participants in a social economy, and to derive from the general characteristics of that behavior."

*—Abraham Kaplan: "Sociology Learns the Language of Mathematics"; in **The World of Mathematics**, James R. Newman, ed., 1956*

5. The initial problem in the theory of games was to give precision to the notion of "rational behavior." Qualitative or philosophical arguments have led nowhere; the new quantitative approach may point in the right direction.

*—Oskar Morgenstern: "The Theory of Games"; **Scientific American**, May, 1949*

6. In 1928 John von Neumann reported a curious discovery to the Mathematical Society of Gottingen: he had worked out a rational strategy for matching pennies. This may not strike you as a momentous achievement, but it was the beginning of a new branch of science. The Theory of Games is today regarded as the most promising mathematical tool yet devised for the analysis of man's social relations.

*—James R. Newman: "The Social Application of Mathematics"; **The World of Mathematics**, Vol. 2; James R. Newman, ed., 1956*

7. The value of game theory is not in the specific solutions it offers in highly simplified and idealized situations, which may occur in formalized games but hardly ever do in real life. Rather, the prime value of the theory is that it lays bare the different kinds of reasoning that apply in different kinds of conflict.

*—Anatol Rapoport: "The Use and Misuse of Game Theory"; **Scientific American**, December, 1962*

8. We now try to provide a guide to actions that must be taken under conditions of uncertainty. The aim is to minimize the loss due to our ignorance of the true state of nature. In fact, from the view-point of game theory, statistical inference becomes the best strategy for playing the game called science.

*—Herbert Robbins: Columbia University: Quoted in George A. W. Boehm: **The New World of Mathematics**, 1959*

9. The essential feature of any game is the fact that one has to do with one or more opponents and that, therefore, only some of the relevant variables are under the control of any single player. It is clear that a theory which takes account of this peculiarity can be applied to the analysis of warfare, to economic problems, and even to decisions which must be taken where no specific opponent appears to exist, but where all variables outside one's own control are dependent on 'Chance' or on 'Laws of Nature.'

*—S. Vajda: "Theory of Games" in **The World of Mathematics**, James R. Newman, ed., 1956*

10. [The aim of the theory of games] is to find the mathematically complete principles which define "rational behavior" for the participants in a social economy, and to derive from the general characteristics of that behavior.

*—John von Neumann & Oskar Morgenstern: **Theory of Games and Economic Behavior**, 1944*

11. [Game theorists] are often viewed by the professional students of man as precocious children who, not appreciating the true complexity of man and his works, wander in wide-eyed innocence, expecting that their toy weapons will slay live dragons just as well as they did inanimate ones.

*—John Williams: **The Compleat Strategist**, 1954*

13

Teaching and Learning Mathematics

13.1 The Importance of Examples

1. ...the source of all great mathematics is the special case, the concrete example. It is frequent in mathematics that every instance of a concept of seemingly great generality is in essence the same as a small and concrete special case.

—*Paul R. Halmos:* ***I Want to Be a Mathematician****, 1985*

2. ...it's examples, examples, examples that, for me, all mathematics is based on, and I always look for them. I look for them first, when I begin to study. I keep looking for them, and I cherish them all.

—*Paul R. Halmos:* ***I Want to Be a Mathematician****, 1985*

3. 'For example' is not a proof.

—*Jewish Proverb*

4. ...do examples. Do a million examples. I think there are shameful cases of people making (I'll even say) silly and reckless conjectures just because they didn't take the trouble to look at the first few examples. A well-chosen example can teach you so much.... Sometimes when you work through an example, you suddenly get an insight which you wouldn't have got if you'd just been working with the hypothesis of your future theorem.

—*Irving Kaplansky: D.J. Albers, "Interview with Irving Kaplansky";* ***College Mathematics Journal****, 22, March, 1991*

5. To state a theorem and then to show examples of it is literally to teach backwards.

—*E. Kim Neubuts: In H. Eves:* ***Return to Mathematical Circles****, 1988*

6. For the mathematician doing research, examples are all but indispensable to his work. To begin with, the direction of his research is guided by a thorough examination of all the pertinent examples he can get his hands on. Only after these examples are analyzed does he attempt to formulate their common properties into some form of a theorem, and then attempt to prove the theorem.

—*Michael Weinstein:* ***Examples of Groups****, 1977*

13.2 Learning and Mathematics

1. What I hear I forget;
What I see, I remember;
What I do, I understand.

—*Ancient Chinese Proverb*

2. Our future lawyers, clergy, and statesmen are expected at the University to learn a good deal about curves and angles, and numbers and properties; not because these subjects have the smallest relation to the needs of their lives, but because in the very act of learning them they are likely to acquire that habit of steadfast and accurate thinking, which is indispensable to success in all the pursuits of life.

—*J.C. Fitch:* ***Lectures on Teaching****, 1906*

3. It is not knowledge, but the act of learning, not possession but the act of getting there, which grants the greatest enjoyment, when I have clarified and exhausted a subject, then I turn away from it, in order to go into darkness again; the never-satisfied man is so strange if he has completed a structure, then it is not in order to dwell in it peacefully, but in order to begin another.

—*Carl Friedrich Gauss: Letter to Wolfgang Bolyai, 1808; in Gauss'* ***Werke****, 1900*

4. The best way to learn mathematics is to do mathematics.... The reader is urged to acquire the habit of reading with paper and pencil in hand; in this way mathematics will become increasingly meaningful to him.

—*G. Hajos, G. Neukomm & J. Suranyi:* ***Hungarian Problem Book,*** *Jozsef Kurschak, complier, 1963*

5. The only way to learn mathematics is to do mathematics. That tenet is the foundation of the do-it-yourself, Socratic, or Texas method in which the teacher plays a role of an omniscient but largely uncommutative referee between the learner and the facts.

—*Paul R. Halmos:* ***A Hilbert Space Problem Book,*** *1967*

6. I do have a maxim—I teach it to all the youngsters: "A ship in port is safe, but that's not what ships are built for."

—*Grace Brewster Murray Hopper: In Henry S. Tropp: "Grace Hopper: The Youthful Teacher of Us All";* ***Abacus 2,*** *1984*

7. The resulting ignorance [in using the so-called E.H. Moore method of teaching which emphasizes analogy and the student's intuitive powers] ought to be a hopeless handicap, but in fact it isn't; and the only way that I can see to resolve this paradox is to conclude that mathematics is capable of being learned as an activity, and that knowledge which is acquired in this way has a power which is out of proportion to its quantity.

—*E.E. Moise: "Activity and Motivation in Mathematics";* ***American Mathematical Monthly,*** *vol. 72; April, 1965*

8. Imagine that 90 percent of every course in English up until college was devoted to grammar and the diagramming of sentences. Would graduates have any feeling for literature? Or consider a conservatory which devoted 90 percent of its efforts to the practicing of the scales. Would its students develop an appreciation or understanding of music? The answer, of course, is no, but that, given proper allowance for hyperbole, is what frequently happens in our mathematics classes. Mathematics is identified with a rote recitation of facts and a blind carrying out of procedures.... Countless people feel that if the answer or at least a recipe for finding it doesn't come to them immediately, they'll never get it. The idea of thinking about a problem or discussing it a bit with someone else seems novel to them. Think about a math problem? Discuss it?

—*John Allen Paulos:* ***Beyond Numeracy,*** *1992*

9. Like it or not, mathematics opens career doors, so it's downright practical to be prepared.

—*Eileen L. Poiani: Quoted in Lynn A. Steen:* ***Mathematics Tomorrow,*** *1978*

10. If the learning of mathematics reflects to any degree the invention of mathematics, it must have a place for guessing, for plausible inference.

—*George Polya: Quoted in W.M. Priestley:* ***Calculus: A Liberal Art,*** *1998*

11. There was a footpath leading across fields to New Southgate, and I used to go there alone to watch the sunset and contemplate suicide. I did not, however, commit suicide, because I wished to know more of mathematics.

—*Bertrand Russell:* ***The Autobiography of Bertrand Russell,*** *1951*

12. What one learns about mathematics in primary school corresponds to the alphabet. What one learns in high school corresponds to the sentences of a primer. What one learns in elementary college courses corresponds to simple little stories. Scholars alone are aware of the mathematics that corresponds to literature.

—*Carl Stoermer: Quoted in Francois Le Lionnais: "Beauty in Mathematics" in* ***Great Currents of Mathematics,*** *F. Le Lionnais, ed., 1971*

13. I didn't do very well in math—I could never seem to persuade the teacher that I hadn't meant my answers literally.

—*Calvin Trillin: "Geography Lesson";* ***King Features Syndicate,*** *September 21, 1986*

14. Angling may be said to be so like mathematics that it can never be fully learned.

—*Izaak Walton:* ***The Compleat Angler,*** *1653*

13.3 Lectures and Lecturing

1. Definition of a lecture: a means of transferring information from the notes of the lecturer to the notes of the student without passing through the minds of either.

—*Anonymous*

2. I feel so strongly about the wrongness of reading a lecture that my language may seem immoderate.... The spoken word and the written word are quite different arts ... I feel that to collect an audience and then read one's material is like inviting a friend to go for a walk and asking him not to mind if you go alongside him in a car.

—*Sir Lawrence Bragg:* ***Science,*** *July 5, 1996*

3. Most people tire of a lecture in ten minutes; clever people can do it in five. Sensible people never go to lectures at all. But the people who do go to a lecture and who get tired of it, presently hold it as a sort of grudge against the lecturer personally. In reality his sufferings are worse than theirs.

—*Stephen Leacock:* ***Laugh with Leacock: We Have with Us Tonight,*** *1930*

4. I recall once saying that when I had given

the same lecture several times I couldn't help feeling that they really ought to know it by now.

—*J.E. Littlewood:* ***A Mathematician's Miscellany****, 1953*

5. A mathematical lecture should be, first of all, correct and unambiguous. Still, we know from painful experience that a perfectly unambiguous and correct exposition can be far from satisfactory and may appear uninspiring, tiresome or disappointing, even if the subject-matter is interesting in itself. The most conspicuous blemish of an otherwise acceptable presentation is the "deus ex machina."

—*George Polya: "With, or Without, Motivation?"; Address at the meeting of the Northern California Section of the Mathematical Association of America, January 29, 1949; in* ***The American Mathematical Monthly****, 57, 1950*

13.4 Clarity in Teaching and Learning Mathematics

1. "Then you should say what you mean," the March Hare went on. "I do," Alice hastily replied: "at least I mean what I say, that's the same thing you know." "Not the same thing a bit! said the Hatter. "Why, you might just as well say that 'I see what I eat' is the same thing as 'I eat what I see!'"

—*Lewis Carroll:* ***Alice in Wonderland****, 1865*

2. ..."The name of the song is called 'Haddocks' Eyes.'" "Oh, that's the name of the song is it?" Alice said, trying to feel interested. "No, you don't understand," the Knight said, looking a little vexed. "That's what the name is called. The name really is 'The Aged, Aged Man.'" "Then I ought to have said, 'That's what the song is called'?" Alice corrected herself. "No, you oughtn't; that's quite another thing! The song is called 'Ways and Means'; but's that's only what it's called, you know!" "Well, what is the song, then?" said Alice, who was by this time completely bewildered. "I was coming to that," the Knight said. "The song really is 'A-sitting on a Gate'; and the tune's my own invention."

—*Lewis Carroll:* ***Through the Looking Glass****, 1871*

3. Mathematics is the priestess of definiteness and clearness.

—*J.F. Herbart:* ***Werke****, 1890*

4. Mathematics is the science of what is clear by itself.

—*Carl Jacobi: In J.R. Newman, ed.* ***The World of Mathematics****, 1956*

5. That sometimes clear ... and sometimes vague stuff ... which is ... mathematics.

—*Imre Lakatos:* ***Proofs and Refutation: The Logic of Mathematical Discovery****, 1976*

6. In the study of ideas, it is necessary to remember that insistence on hardheaded clarity issues from sentimental feeling, as it were a mist, cloaking the perplexities of fact. Insistence on clarity at all costs is based on sheer superstition as to the mode in which human intelligence functions Our reasonings grasp at straws for premises and float on gossamers for deductions.

—*Alfred North Whitehead:* ***The World of Mathematics****, James R. Newman, ed., 1956* ***Mathematical Stories***

13.5 On Writing Mathematics

1. This paper contains much that is new and much that is true. Unfortunately, that which is true is not new and that which is new is not true.

—*Anonymous: in Howard Eves:* ***Return to Mathematical Circles****, 1988 [A referee's report on a mathematical paper.]*

2. When writing about transcendental issues, be transcendentally clear.

—*Rene Descartes: In G. Simmons:* ***Calculus Gems****, 1992*

3. If you open a mathematics paper at random, on the pair of pages before you, you will find a mistake.

—*Joseph L. Doob: Quoted in D. MacHale:* ***Comic Sections****, 1993*

4. [S.F. Lacroix] endeavors to take the reader along with him, never to lay down a rule until it begins to be anticipated, never to give a new process, or bring forward a new principle, until its necessity is felt. We are thus enabled to keep pace with him and be present at his discoveries, to divine his reasons and partake of his power.

—*George Barrell Emerson: "Article XVII" (review of the first four books of Farrar's translations of mathematical texts written by French mathematician Lacroix);* ***North American Review****, 1821*

5. As writers, mathematicians are notoriously inept.

—*Martin Gardner: Quoted in Rudy Rucker:* ***The Fourth Dimension: A Guided Tour of the Higher Universes****, 1985*

6. You know that I write slowly. This is chiefly because I am never satisfied until I have said as much as possible in a few words, and writing briefly takes far more time than writing at length.

—*Carl Friedrich Gauss: Quoted in G.F. Simmons:* ***Calculus Gems****, 1992*

7. What then are the rules for good mathematical writing? Answer: local clarity and global organization. In the terminology of another subject; meticulous tactics and sound strategy.

—*Paul Halmos: "Think it gooder"; **The Mathematical Intelligencer**, vol. 4, 1982*

8. If you think that your paper is vacuous,
Use the first-order functional calculus,
It then becomes logic,
And, as if by magic,
The obvious is hailed as miraculous.

—*Paul Halmos: **I Am a Mathematician**, 1985*

9. I cannot fail completely in making the paper interesting, since the subject is so attractive that this would need extravagant incompetence.

—*G.H. Hardy: **Introduction to the Theory of Numbers** (with E. Wright), 1930s; 4th ed., 1960*

10. Mathematicians today have paid too much attention to their beloved specialities and not enough to good writing, good exposition, incisive judgement, and the overall health of the discipline.

—*Steven Krantz: "See No Evil, Hear No Evil, Speak No Evil"; **Notices of the American Mathematical Society**, Vol. 45, 9; October, 1998*

11. In presenting a mathematical argument the great thing is to give the educated reader the chance to catch on at once to the momentary point and take details for granted: his successive mouthfuls should be such as can be swallowed at sight; in case of accidents, or in case he wished for once to check in detail, he should have only a clearly circumscribed little problem to solve (e.g. to check an identity: two trivialities omitted can add up to an impasse). The unpractised writer, even after the dawn of a conscience, gives him no such chance: before he can spot the point he has to tease his way through a maze of symbols of which not the tiniest suffix can be skipped.

—*J.E. Littlewood: **A Mathematician's Miscellany**, 1953*

12. The surprising thing about this paper is that a man who could write it would.

—*John E. Littlewood: **A Mathematician's Miscellany**, 1953*

13. The exponential growth in mathematical publishing has interesting implications. Adding up the numbers in [Mathematical Reviews] or simply extrapolating from the current figure of about 50,000 papers per year and a doubling every 10 years, we come to the conclusion that about 1,000,000 mathematical papers have ever been published. What is much more surprising to most people (but is a simple arithmetic consequence of the growth rate) is that almost half of them have been published in the last 10 years. Even if we imagine to limit the rate of publication to 50,000 papers per year, we will double the size of mathematical literature in another 20 years.

—*Andrew M. Odlyzko: "Tragic Loss or Good Riddance?: The Impending Demise of Traditional Scholarly Journals," July 16, 1994; to appear in the AMS Notices*

14. Since authors seldom, if ever, say what they mean, the following glossary is offered to neophytes in mathematical research to help them understand the language that surrounds the formulas. Since mathematical writing, like mathematics, involves many undefined concepts, it seems best to illustrate the usage by interpretation of examples rather than to attempt definition.

Complete. The proof is now complete.: I can't finish it.

Difficult. The problem is difficult.: I don't know the answer.

Interesting. X's paper is interesting.: I understand it.

New. This was proved by X but the following new proof may present points of interest.: I can't understand X.

Obvious. It is obvious.: I can't prove it.

Reader. The details may be left to the reader.: I can't do it.

Trivial. This problem is trivial.: I know the answer.

Well-Known: This result is well-known.: I can't find the reference.

—*H. Petard: "A Brief Dictionary of Phrases Used in Mathematical Writing," **American Mathematical Monthly**, 1966 [These are among the definitions given by Petard in his article. Petard (H.W.O. Petard, that is, for "Hoist With Own" Petard) is the penname of the imaginary mathematician E.S. Pondiczery, who in fact was Ralph P. Boas, Jr. and Frank Smithies.]*

15. When I read a math paper it's no different than a musician reading a score. In each case the pleasure comes from the play of patterns, the harmonies and contrasts.

—*Rudy Rucker: "A New Golden Age"; in **Imaginary Numbers**, William Frucht, ed., 1999*

16. Neither of us alone [he and Whitehead] could have written the book [The Principles of Mathematics; even together, and with the alleviation brought by mutual discussion, the effort was so severe that at the end we both turned aside from mathematical logic with a kind of nausea. It was, I suppose, inevitable that we would turn aside in different directions, so that collaboration was no longer possible.

—*Bertrand Russell: "Whitehead and Principia Matematica"; **Mind**, April, 1948*

17. This paper gives wrong solutions to trivial problems. The basic error, however, is not new.

—*Clifford Truesdell: **Mathematical Reviews**, 12, n.d.*

18. Math terminology is designed to eliminate extraneous things and focus on fundamental process, but the method of finding results is far different from these fundamental processes. Mathematical writing doesn't permit any indication of the labor behind the result.

—*Donald Weidman: "Emotional Perils of Mathematics"; **Science**, September, 1965*

19. The stringent precision attainable for mathematical thought has led many authors to a mode of writing which must give the reader the impression of being shut up in a brightly illuminated cell where every detail sticks out with the same dazzling clarity, but without relief. I prefer the open landscape under the clear sky with its depth or perspective, where the wealth of sharply defined details gradually fades away toward the horizon.

—*Hermann Weyl: **The Classical Groups: Their Invariants and Representations**, "Preface," 1939*

20. It is a safe rule to apply that, when a mathematical or philosophical author writes with misty profundity, he is talking nonsense.

—*Alfred North Whitehead: **An Introduction to Mathematics**, 1911*

13.6 Reading and Mathematics

1. Every mathematical book that is worth reading must be read "backwards and forwards," if I may use the expression. I would modify Lagrange's advice a little and say, "Go on, but often return to strengthen your faith." When you come on a hard or dreary passage, pass it over; and come back to it after you have seen its importance or found the need for it further on.

—*George Chrystal: **Algebra**, Part 2, "Preface," 1889*

2. ...Either he [Rene Thom] has not read our paper carefully enough or, if he read it, he had not understood it. But then is my experience most mathematicians are intellectually lazy and especially dislike reading experimental papers.

—*Sir Francis Crick: "What Mad Pursuit"; **The Mathematical Intelligencer**, vol. 14, Fall, 1992*

3. I have written elsewhere, in an essay called "Meditations of a Mathematical Moron," of the pleasures of reading about mathematics, pleasures open to anyone who has received a conventional secondary-school education, and is willing to do a little mental work.

—*Clifton Fadiman: **Fantasia Mathematica**, ed. by Fadiman, "Introduction," 1958*

4. Some textbooks claim that they do not expect the reader to have any previous knowledge, only a certain mathematical maturity. This frequently means that they expect the reader to be endowed by nature with the "ability" to take a Euclidean argument without any unnatural interest in the problem background, in the heuristic behind the argument.

—*Imre Lakatos: **Proofs and Refutation: The Logic of Mathematical Discovery**, 1976*

5. This paper is very heavy going, and I should never have read it had I not written it myself.

—*John E. Littlewood: Quoted in D. McHale: **Comic Sections**, 1993*

6. It has been claimed that only three people read the three volumes of Russell and Whitehead's monumental Principia Mathematica in its entirety, namely Russell, Whitehead, and the proofreader. There has been some scepticism, however, about Russell and Whitehead belong to the list.

—*Leo Moser: Quoted in Howard W. Eves: **Mathematical Circles Adieu**, 1977*

7. It is much easier for a mathematician to read a physics book after the physics becomes obsolete, and that is in fact what usually happens.

—*Gian-Carlo Rota: in **Discrete Thoughts: Essays on Mathematics, Science and Philosophy**, Mark Kac, Gian-Carlo Rota, Jacob T. Schwartz; Quoted in **The Mathematical Intelligencer**, vol. 12, 1990*

8. The art of reading mathematics is judicious skipping.

—*William Thomson, Lord Kelvin: Quoted in Andrew Gray: **Lord Kelvin**, 1908*

13.7 The Study of Mathematics

1. It appears to me that if one wants to make progress in mathematics, one should study the masters and not the pupils.

—*Niels H. Abel: Remark found in one of his later mathematical notebooks; Quoted in Oystein Ore: **Niels Henrik Abel: Mathematician Extraordinary**, 1957*

2. There are things which seem incredible to most men who have not studied mathematics.

—*Archimedes: **The Sand-Reckoner**, c. 3rd. cent. B.C.*

3. If a man's wit be wandering, let him study the mathematics.

—*Francis Bacon: "Of Studies"; **Essays**, 1597*

4. I advise my students to listen carefully the moment they decide to take no more mathematics courses. They might be able to hear the sound of closing doors.

—*James Caballero: "Everybody's a Mathematician"; **CAIP Quarterly**, Fall, 1989*

5. Many results must be given of which details are suppressed These must not be taken on trust by the student, but must be worked out by his own pen, which must never be out of his own hand while engaged in any mathematical process.

—*August De Morgan: Quoted in Frank Burk:* ***Lebesque Measure and Integration: An Introduction,*** *1998*

6. When I am violently beset with temptations, or cannot rid myself of evil thoughts, [I resolve] to do some Arithmetic, or Geometry, or some other study, which necessarily engages all my thoughts, and unavoidably keeps them from wandering.

—*Jonathan Edwards:* ***Works,*** *1834; In T. Mallon:* ***A Book of One's Own,*** *1984*

7. The study of mathematics is like climbing up a steep and craggy mountain; when once you reach the top, it fully recompenses your trouble, by opening a fine, clear, and extensive prospect.

—*Tyron Edwards:* ***The New Dictionary of Thoughts,*** *1960*

8. All creative people hate mathematics. It's the most uncreative subject you can study.

—*Alec Issigoinis: Quoted in* ***The Australian*** *October 5, 1988*

9. Mathematics is indeed dangerous in that it absorbs students to such a degree that it dulls their senses to everything else.

—*Prinz Zu Hohlenlohe-Ingelfingen Kraft: In Howard Eves:* ***Mathematical Circles Adieu,*** *1977*

10. I tell them that if they will occupy themselves with the study of mathematics they will find in it the best remedy against the lusts of the flesh.

—*Thomas Mann:* ***The Magic Mountain,*** *1927*

11. Mathematical study and research are very suggestive of mountaineering. Whymper made several efforts before he climbed the Matterhorn in the 1860's and even then it cost the life of four of his party. Now, however, any tourist can be hauled up for a small cost, and perhaps does not appreciate the difficulty of the first ascent. So in mathematics, it may be found hard to realize the great initial difficulty of making a little step which now seems so natural and obvious, and it may not be surprising if such a step has been found and lost again.

—*L.J. Mordell: "Three Lectures on Fermat's Last Theorem"*

12. I know of nothing which acts as such a powerful antidote to that which I ventured to call "opinionatedness," as a study of mathematics.

—*David Eugene Smith:* ***The Poetry of Mathematics and Other Essays,*** *1934*

13. As there is no study which may be so advantageously entered upon with less stock of preparatory knowledge than mathematics, so there is none in which a greater number of uneducated men have raised themselves, by their own exertions, to distinction and eminence Many of the intellectual defects which, in such cases, are commonly placed to the account of mathematical studies, ought to be ascribed to the want of a liberal education in early youth.

—*Dugald Stewart: "Philosophy of the Human Mind"; in* ***Collected Works,*** *Hamilton, ed., 1854*

14. The study of mathematics is apt to commence in disappointment.... We are told that by its aid the stars are weighed and the billions of molecules in a drop of water are counted. Yet, like the ghost of Hamlet's father, this greatest science eludes the efforts of our mental weapons to grasp it.

—*Alfred North Whitehead:* ***An Introduction to Mathematics,*** *1911*

15. I will not go so far as to say that to construct a history of thought without profound study of the mathematical ideas of successive epochs is like omitting Hamlet from the play which is named after him. That would be claiming too much. But is its certainly analogous to cutting out the part of Ophelia. The simile is singularly exact. For Ophelia is quite essential to the play, she is very charming—and a little mad. Let us grant that the pursuit of mathematics is a divine madness of the human spirit, a refuge from the goading urgency of contingent happenings.

—*Alfred North Whitehead: "Mathematics as an Element in the History of Thought,"* ***Science and the Modern World,*** *1925*

16. You can study mathematics all your life and never do a bit of thinking.

—*Frank Lloyd Wright: in* ***The Works of the Mind,*** *Robert B. Heywood, ed., 1947*

13.8 Teaching and Mathematics

1. A mathematics teacher can light the lantern and put it in your hand, but you must walk into the dark.

—*William H. Armstrong: Attributed*

2. Knowing something for oneself or for communication to an expert colleague is not the same as knowing it for explanation to a student.

—*Hyman Bass: "Mathematicians as Educators";* ***Notices of the American Mathematical Society,*** *vol. 44 #1, January, 1997*

3. Teach the student, not just the subject.

—*Ralph Beatley: in Garret Birkhoff, "Mathematics at Harvard, 1836–1944"; in* ***A Century of Mathematics in America, Part II,*** *Peter Duren, ed., 1989*

4. Somewhat related to the notion of discovery in teaching [mathematics] is our insistence that the student become aware of a concept before a name has been assigned to the concept.

—Max Beberman: ***An Emerging Program of Secondary School Mathematics****, 1958*

5. The world of today demands more mathematical knowledge on the part of more people than the world of yesterday, and the world of tomorrow will demand even more. It is therefore important that mathematics be taught in a vital and imaginative way which will make students aware that it is a living, growing subject which plays an increasingly important part in the contemporary world.

—E.G. Begle: "The School Mathematics Study Group"; ***The Mathematics Teacher****, 51; December, 1958*

6. When mathematics is taught, it is presented mainly as a collection of slightly related techniques and manipulations. The profound, yet simple, concepts get little attention. If art appreciation were taught in the same way, it would consist mostly of learning how to chip some stone and mix paints.

—George A.W. Boehm: ***The New World of Mathematics****, 1958*

7. Many teachers and textbook writers have never recognized the power of sheer intellectual curiosity as a motive for the highest type of work in mathematics, and as a consequence they have failed to organize and present the work in a manner designed to stimulate the student's interest through a challenge to his curiosity.

—Charles H. Butler & F. Lynwood Wren: ***The Teaching of Secondary Mathematics****, 1941*

8. Some persons have contended that mathematics ought to be taught by making the illustrations obvious to the senses. Nothing can be more absurd or injurious: it ought to be our never-ceasing effort to make people think, not feel.

—Samuel Taylor Coleridge: ***Lectures on Shakespeare****, 1830*

9. Mathematics is the only instructional material that can be presented in an entirely undogmatic way.

—Max Dehn: in ***The Mathematical Intelligencer****, vol. 5, no. 2, 1983*

10. At the present moment the mathematics taught in our schools corresponds approximately to what was known in 1640.

—Jean Dieudonne: Quoted in Lucienne Felix: ***The Modern Aspect of Mathematics****, 1960*

11. We do not forget that the teacher of mathematics, like his colleagues in other subjects, is also a teacher of ordinary language; his task from that point of view is to teach a correct and logical language which will translate a clear thought exactly.

—Lucienne Felix: ***The Modern Aspect of Mathematics****, 1960*

12. It is the duty of all teachers, and of teachers of mathematics in particular, to expose their students to problems much more than facts.

—Paul R. Halmos: "The Heart of Mathematics"; ***American Mathematical Monthly****, vol. 87; August–September, 1980*

13. Tests tyrannize us—they tyrannize teachers and children. They loom so large that they distort the teaching curriculum and the teacher's natural style; they occur so frequently, and with such dire consequences, that they appear to the child (and, perhaps, to the teacher) to be the very reason for learning mathematics.

—Peter J. Hilton: "Avoiding Math Avoidance" in Lynn Arthur Steen: ***Mathematics Tomorrow****, 1981*

14. Just as any sensitive human being can be brought to appreciate beauty in art, music, or literature, so that person can be educated to recognize the beauty in a piece of mathematics. The rarity of that recognition is not due to the "fact" that most people are not mathematically gifted but to the crassly utilitarian manner of teaching mathematics and of deciding syllabi and curricula, in which tedious, routine calculations, learned as a skill, are emphasized at the expense of genuinely mathematical ideas, and in which students spend almost all their time answering someone else's questions rather than asking their own.

—Peter J. Hilton: "Review: The Pleasures of Counting"; ***The American Mathematical Monthly****, vol. 105, #5; May, 1998*

15. It has been said that we have not had the three R's in America, we had the six R's: remedial readin', remedial ritin' and remedial 'rithmetic.

—Robert M. Hutchins: Attributed

16. The main purpose of professional education is development of skills; the main purpose of education in subjects like mathematics, physics or philosophy is development of attitudes.

—Mark Kac: in ***Discrete Thoughts: Essays on Mathematics, Science and Philosophy****, Mark Kac, Gian-Carlo Rota, Jacob T. Schwartz; Quoted in* ***The Mathematical Intelligencer****, vol. 12, 1990*

17. Unfortunately competitive examinations often encourage deception. The teachers must train their students to answer little fragmentary questions quite well, and they give them model answers that are often veritable masterpieces and that leave no room for criticism. To achieve this, the teachers isolate each question from the whole of mathematics and create for this question alone a perfect language without bothering about its relationships to other questions. Mathematics is no longer a monument but a leap.

—*Henri Leon Lebesque: Quoted in* ***Intersection: NCTM/Exxon Education Foundation Newsletter****, May, 1998*

18. The student of mathematics often finds it hard to throw off the uncomfortable feeling that his science, in the person of his pencil, surpasses him in intelligence,—an impression which the great Euler confessed he often could not get rid of. This feeling finds a sort of justification when we reflect that the majority of the ideas we deal with were conceived by others, often centuries ago. In a great measure it is really the intelligence of other people that confronts us in science.

—*Ernst Mach:* ***Popular Scientific Lectures****, Chicago, 1910*

19. We encourage children to read for enjoyment, yet we never encourage them to "math" for enjoyment. We teach kids that math is done fast, done only one way and if you don't get the answer right, there's something wrong with you. You would never teach reading this way.

—*Rachel McAnallen: "Math? No Problem";* ***The Hartford Courant****; October, 1998*

20. There are two ways to teach mathematics. One is to take real pains toward creating understanding—visual aids, that sort of thing. The other is the old British system of teaching until you're blue in the face.

—*James R. Newman:* ***New York Times****, September 30, 1956*

21. I believe that mathematics education at all levels has more people in it than we care to admit who went into mathematics teaching because it was a way of making a living and avoiding the real world.

—*Henry O. Pollak:* ***Mathematical People****; D.J. Albers & G.L. Alexanderson, eds., 1985*

22. To teach effectively a teacher must develop a feeling for his subject; he cannot make his students sense its vitality if he does not sense it himself. He cannot share his enthusiasm when he has no enthusiasm to share. How he makes his point may be as important as the point he makes; he must personally feel it to be important.

—*George Polya: Quoted in Israel Kleiner: "Thinking the Unthinkable: The Story of Complex Numbers (with a Moral)";* ***The Mathematics Teacher****; October, 1988*

23. ...teaching is like a man struggling with a bear. You don't know how it's going to come out, the result is not preordained. But that can be painful too. Teaching should be like a competition between two antagonists with the outcome really in doubt. And yet you don't want to do a clumsy job. Things are never settled: every answer raises new questions and begins a new cycle in the subject.

—*Herbert Robbins:* ***Mathematical People****; D.J. Albers & G.L. Alexanderson, eds., 1985*

24. Poor teaching leads to the inevitable idea that the subject [mathematics] is only adapted to peculiar minds, when it is the one universal science and the one whose four ground-rules are taught us almost in infancy and reappear in the motions of the universe.

—*T.H. Safford:* ***Mathematical Teaching****, 1907*

25. Giving students a lot of worksheets to fill out is indicative of low expectations. It suggests that you don't think they're capable of deep thinking about mathematics.

—*Midge Siegfried: Quoted in David Ruenzel: "Positive Numbers: Math Equity Programs Unlock the Gate to Algebra and Beyond":* ***Teaching Tolerance****, Spring, 1998*

13.9 Professors, Universities and Mathematics

1. A mathematics professor who talks at length affects both ends of the listener—he makes one end feel numb and the other feel dumb.

—*Howard F. Fehr: Address at Syracuse University. May 11, 1957; reported by Alan Wayne in Howard W. Eves:* ***Mathematical Circles Revisited****, 1971*

2. It is one of the first duties of a professor ... in any subject, to exaggerate the importance of his subject and his own importance in it.

—*G.H. Hardy:* ***A Mathematician's Apology****, 1941*

3. A Ph.D. dissertation is a paper of the professor written under aggravating circumstances.

—*Adolf Hurwitz: Quoted in George Polya: "Some Mathematicians I Have Known";* ***American Mathematical Monthly****, 76, 1969*

4. My occupation is an open question. I was once an assistant professor of mathematics. Since then, I have spent my time living in the woods of Montana.

—*Theodore J. Kaczynski:* ***New York Times****, January 23, 1998*

5. As a professor of mathematics I am practically required by the ethics of the profession to be absentminded, unmethodical, and inconsistent in many ways fatal to bibliographical excellence.

—*L.C. Karpinski:* ***Bibliography of Mathematical Works Printed in America Through 1850****, 1940*

6. Universities hire professors the way some men choose wives—they want the ones the others will admire.

—*Morris Kline:* ***Why the Professor Can't Teach****, 1978*

7. The horse, the mass of human intelligence, draws along the cart of history in which stands the professor, looking backward and explaining the scenery.

—*Stephen Leacock:* ***My Remarkable Uncle: Who Canonizes the Classics?****, 1942*

8. I am what is called a professor emeritus—from the Latin e, "out," and meritus, "so he ought to be."

—*Stephen Leacock:* ***Here Are My lectures****, 1938*

9. The traditional mathematics professor of the popular legend is absentminded. He usually appears in public with a lost umbrella in each hand. He prefers to face the blackboard and to turn his back on the class. He writes a, he says b, he means c, but it should be d.

—*George Polya:* ***How to Solve It****, 1945*

10. Seven pupils, in the class
Of Professor Callias,
Listen silent while he drawls,—
Three are benches, four are walls.

—*Henry Van Dyke: "The Professor";* ***Poems****, 1911*

14

The Nature of Infinity

14.1 Understanding Infinity

1. When the early Christian thinkers such as Plotinus proclaimed that God is infinite, they were primarily concerned to demonstrate that he is not limited in any way. The mathematical concept of infinity was at that time still fairly vague. It was generally believed that infinity is a limit toward which enumeration may proceed, but which is unachievable in reality.

*—Paul Davies: **The Mind of God**, 1992*

2. The infinite is recognizable but not comprehensible.

*—Rene Descartes: in J. Torrey: **The Philosophy of Descartes**, 1892*

3. But how can finite grasp Infinity?

*—John Dryden: **The Hind and the Panther**, 1987*

4. Infinities and indivisibles transcend our finite understanding, the former on account of their magnitude, the latter because of their smallness; Imagine what they are when combined.

*—Galileo Galilei: **Dialogues Concerning Two New Sciences**, 1638*

5. The Cantorian infinite has been one of the main nutrients for the spectacular flowering of mathematics in the twentieth century, and yet it remains mysterious and ill understood.

*—Shaughan Lavine: **Understanding the Infinite**, 1994*

6. We know that there is an infinite, and we are ignorant of its nature.

*—Blaise Pascal: **Pensees**, 1670*

7. Our minds are finite, and yet even in these circumstances of finitude we are surrounded by possibilities that are infinite, and the purpose of life is to grasp as much as we can out of that infinitude.

*—Alfred North Whitehead: **Dialogues of Alfred North Whitehead**, June 28, 1941*

14.2 The Infinite and the Finite

1. As the finite encloses an infinite series
And in the unlimited limits appear,
So the soul of immensity dwells in
minutia
And in narrowest limits no limits inhere.
What joy to discern the minute in infinity!
The vast to perceive in the small, what
divinity!

*—Jakob Bernoulli: in David Eugene Smith: **A Source Book in Mathematics**, 1959 reprint; Quoted in William Dunham: **Journey Through Genius**, 1990*

2. [Paradoxes of the infinite arise] only when we attempt, with our finite minds, to discuss the infinite, assigning to it those properties which we give to the finite and limited; but this I think is wrong, for we cannot speak of infinite quantities as being the one greater or less than or equal to another.

*—Galileo Galilei: Quoted in Rudy Rucker: **Infinity and the Mind**, 1982*

3. If you wish to advance into the infinite, explore the finite in all directions.

*—Johann Wolfgang von Goethe: **Miscellaneous Epigrams**, early 19th century*

4. Since the time of Greek philosophy, men have prided themselves on their ability to understand something about infinity; and it has become traditional in some circles to regard finite things as essentially trivial, too limited to be of any interest. It is hard to debunk such a notion, since there are no accepted standards for demonstrating that something is interesting, especially when something finite is compared with something transcendent. Yet I believe that the climate of thought is changing, since finite processes are proving to be such fascinating objects of study.

*—Donald Knuth: "Mathematics and Computer Science: Coping with Finiteness": **Science**, 194, December 17, 1976*

5. Unity joined to infinity adds nothing to it, no more than one foot to an infinite measure. The finite is annihilated in the presence of the infinite, and becomes a pure nothing.

*—Blaise Pascal: **Pensees**, 1670*

6. God created infinity, and man unable to understand infinity, had to invent finite sets.

*—Gian-Carlo Rota: Quoted in Monte Zerger: "A Quote a Day Educates"; **Mathematical Intelligencer**, Vol. 20, 2; Spring, 1998*

14.3 Numbers and Infinity

1. ...infinity is not a large number or any kind of number at all; at least of the sort we think of when we say "number." It certainly isn't the largest number that could exist, for there is no such thing.

*—Isaac Asimov: **On Numbers**, 1990*

2. I place myself in a certain opposition to widespread views on the mathematical infinite and to oft-defended opinions on the essence of number.

*—Georg Cantor: **Grundlagen einer allgemeinen Mannigfaltigkeitslehre**, 1883*

3. Infinity is the land of mathematical hocus pocus. There Zero the magician is king. When Zero divides any number he changes it without regard to its magnitude into the infinitely small; and inversely, when divided by any number he begets the infinitely great.

*—Paul Carus: "Logical and Mathematical Thought"; **The Monist**, Vol. 20, January 1, 1910*

4. Objects of sense are not unlimited and therefore the Number applying to them cannot be so. Nor is an enumerator able to number to infinity' though we double, multiply over and over again, we still end with a finite number....

*—Plotinus: **The Six Enneads**, c. 3rd. cent. A.D.*

5. We admit, in geometry, not only infinite magnitudes, that is to say, magnitudes greater than any assignable magnitude, but infinite magnitudes infinitely greater, the one than the other. This astonishes our dimension of brains, which is only about six inches long, five broad, and six in depth, in the largest heads.

*—Voltaire: "Infinity"; **A Philosophical Dictionary**, 1881*

6. Tell me, what is the final integer, the one at the very top, the biggest of all?
But that's ridiculous! Since the number of integers is infinite, how can you have a final integer?
Well then how can you have a final revolution?
There is no final revolution. Revolutions are infinite.

*—Yevegny Ivanovich Zamyatin: "We" W.N. Vickery, tr. in P. Blake & M. Hayward: **Dissonant Voices in Soviet Literature**, 1962*

14.4 The Infinitely Large; The Infinitely Small

1. There is no smallest among the small and no largest among the large, But always something still smaller and something still larger.

*—Anaxagoras: Quoted in Eli Maor: **To Infinity and Beyond: A Cultural History of the Infinite**, 1987*

2. Infinity is a floorless room without walls or ceiling.

—Anonymous

3. Great fleas have little fleas upon their back to bite 'em,
And little fleas have lesser fleas, and so on ad infinitum.
And great fleas themselves, in turn, have great fleas to go on,
While these again have greater still, and greater still, and so on.

*—Augustus De Morgan: **A Budget of Paradoxes** 1872*

4. ...infinity and indivisibility are in their very nature incomprehensible to us.

*—Galileo Galilei: **Dialogues Concerning the Two New Sciences**, Henry Crew & Alfonso de Salvio, tr., 1952*

5. The supposition of an infinitely little magnitude [is] too bold a Postulate for such a Science as Geometry.

*—Colin Maclaurin: **A Treatise on Fluxions**, 1742*

14.5 Fear and Loathing of Infinity

1. Another source of the sublime, is infinity. Infinity has a tendency to fill the mind with that sort of delightful horror, which is the most genuine effect, and truest test of the sublime. There are scarce any things which can become the objects of our senses that are really, and in their own nature infinite. But the eye not being able to perceive the bounds of many things, they seem to be infinite, and they produce the same effects as if they really were so.

*—Edmund Burke: **A Philosophical Enquiry into the Origin of Our Ideas of the Sublime and the Beautiful**, 1759*

2. The fear of infinity is a form of myopia that destroys the possibility of seeing the actual infinite, even though it in its highest form has created and sustains us, and in its secondary transfinite forms occurs all around us and even inhabits our minds.

—Georg Cantor: "On the Various Standpoints with Respect to Actual Infinity," 1886

3. The infinite was taboo [to the classical Greeks], it had to be kept out, at any cost; or failing this, camouflaged by arguments ad absurdum and the like.

—Tobias Dantzig: ***Number—The Language of Science****, 1954*

4. That Queer Quantity "infinity" is the very mischief, and no rational physicist should have anything to do with it. Perhaps that is why mathematicians represent it by a sign like a love-knot.

—Sir Arthur Eddington: ***New Pathways in Science****, 1935*

5. The infinite in mathematics is always unruly unless it is properly treated.

—Edward Kasner & James Newman: ***Mathematics and the Imagination****, 1940*

6. I can't help it:—in spite of myself, infinity torments me.

—Alfred de Musset: ***l'Espoir en Dieu****, 1838*

7. The notion of infinity is our greatest friend; it is also the greatest enemy of our peace of mind.... Weierstrass taught us to believe that we had at last thoroughly tamed and domesticated this unruly element. Such however is not the case; it has broken loose again and Hilbert and Brouwer have set out to tame it once more. For how long? We wonder.

—James Pierpont: "Mathematical Rigor, Past and Present"; ***Bulletin of the American Mathematical Society****, January–February, 1928*

8. The infinite normally inspires some feelings of helplessness, futility, and despair that the natural human impulse is to reject it out of hand.

—Rudy Rucker: ***Infinity and the Mind****, 1995*

14.6 Theories of Infinity

1. The fundamental difficulty which the theory of the infinite contains is this: either an outright denial or an outright acknowledgment of the being of the infinite leads to many impossibilities.

—Aristotle: ***Physics****, Book III; in* ***Great Books of the Western World****, Benjamin Jowett, tr., 1952*

2. The toughminded suggest that the theory of the infinite elaborated by the great mathematicians of the Nineteenth and Twentieth Centuries, without which mathematical analysis as it is actually used today is impossible, has been committing suicide in an unnecessarily prolonged and complicated manner for the past half century.

—E. T. Bell, ***Debunking Science****, 1930*

3. Banish the infinite process, and mathematics pure and applied is reduced to the state in which it was known to the pre–Pythagoreans.

—Tobias Dantzig: ***Number, The Language of Science****; 1954*

4. Mathematics, in one view, is the science of infinity.... Significant mathematics is thought to emerge when the universe of its discourse is enlarged so as to embrace the infinite. The contemporary stockpile of mathematical objects is full of infinities.... We have infinities and infinities upon infinities; infinities galore, infinities beyond the dreams of conceptual avarice.

—Philip J. Davis & Reuben Hersh: ***The Mathematical Experience****, 1998*

5. As to your proof, I must protest most vehemently against your use of the infinite as something consummated, as this is never permitted in mathematics. The infinite is but a figure of speech: an abridged form for the statement that limits exist which certain ratios may approach as closely as we desire, while other magnitudes may be permitted to grow beyond all bounds.

—Carl Freidrich Gauss: Letter to Heinrich Schumacher; July 12, 1831; Quoted in Stuart Hollingdale: ***Makers of Mathematics****, 1989*

6. The modern-day theory of the infinite did not begin with an effort to produce a theory of the infinite, and it did not build on a long history of attempts at mathematical theories of the infinite. It began instead with an attempt to clarify the foundations of analysis and specifically of the calculus—that is, it grew out of our theory of rates and of areas under curves.

—Shaughan Lavine: ***Understanding the Infinite****, 1994*

7. The solution of the difficulties which formerly surrounded the mathematical infinite is probably the greatest achievement of which our age has to boast.

—Bertrand Russell: ***The Study of Mathematics; Philosophical Essays****, 1910*

14.7 Nature and Infinity

1. Time and space are fragments of the infinite for the use of finite creatures.

—Henri Frederic Amiel: ***Journal****, November 16, 1865, Mrs. Humphry Ward, tr.*

2. Nature flies from the infinite, for the infinite is unending or imperfect, and Nature ever seeks an end.

—Aristotle: ***Generation of Animals****; c. 4th cent. B.C.*

3. To see a world in a grain of sand
And a heaven in a wild flower
Hold infinity in the palm of your hand
And eternity in an hour.

—William Blake: "The Grey Monk" from ***The Pickering Manuscript****, c. 1803*

4. I am so in favor of the actual infinite that instead of admitting that Nature abhors it, as is commonly said, I hold that Nature makes frequent use of it everywhere, in order to show more effectively the perfections of its Author.

*—Georg Cantor: in Joseph Dauben" **Georg Cantor, His Mathematics and Philosophy of the Infinite,** 1979*

5. There are infinite worlds both like and unlike this world of ours. For the atoms being infinite in number … are borne on far out into space. For these atoms, which are of such nature that a world could be created out of them or made by them, have not been used up either on one world or on a limited number of worlds, nor again on all the worlds which are alike, or on those which are different from these. So that there nowhere exists an obstacle to the infinite number of worlds.

—Epicurus: Letter to Herodotus: c. 3rd. cent. B.C.

14.8 Infinity Is … Definitions, Sort of

1. Infinity is a fathomless gulf, into which all things vanish.

*—Marcus Aurelius: **Meditations,** c. A.D. 2nd cent.*

2. Because I longed
to comprehend the infinite
I drew a line
between the known and the unknown.

*—Elizabeth Barrett Browning: "Because I Longed"; in **The Complete Works of Elizabeth Barrett Browning,** 1900*

3. Infinity is whatever we imagine.

*—Thomas Hobbes: **Leviathan,** 1651*

4. Infinity is a dark illimitable ocean, without bound.

*—John Milton: in Eli Maor: **To Infinity and Beyond,** 1991*

5. Actual infinity does not exist. What we call infinite is only the endless possibility of creating new objects no matter how many objects exist already.

*—Henri Poincare: **Acta Mathematica,** 1909*

6. If any philosopher had been asked for a definition of infinity, he might have produced some unintelligible rigmarole, but he would certainly not have been able to give a definition that had any meaning at all.

*—Bertrand Russell: **A Free Man's Worship and Other Essays,** 1976*

7. If there are many, they must be just as many as they are, neither more nor fewer. But if they are just so many as they are, they must be finite [in number]. If there are many, the existents are infinite [in number] between existents, and again others between these. And thus the existents are infinite [in number].

*—Zeno of Elea; ca. 460 B.C.; Quoted in W.A. Kaufmann, **Philosophic Classics, Thales to St. Thomas,** 1961*

15

Pure Mathematics and Applied Mathematics

15.1 Applied Mathematics and Mathematicians

1. And as for Mixed Mathematics, I may only make this prediction, that there cannot fail to be more kinds of them, as nature grows further disclosed.

—*Sir Francis Bacon:* ***The Advancement of Learning****, 1605*

2. Mathematics is at the core of the most exciting applications today. All of the very dynamic sunrise sectors [of the world's economies] are merging between themselves and altering themselves through the use of mathematical tools.

—*Graciela Chicilnisky: Quoted in Keith Devlin:* ***Life by the Numbers****, 1998*

3. There is a very significant characteristic of the application of the spiral to organic forms; that application invariably results in the discovery that nothing which is alive is ever simply mathematical. In other words, there is in every organic object a factor which baffles mathematics—a factor which we can only describe as Life.

—*Theodore Andrea Cook:* ***The Curves of Life****, 1914*

4. Applied mathematics is not a definable scientific field but a human attitude. The attitude of the applied scientist is directed toward finding clear cut answers which can stand the test of empirical observation. To obtain the answers to theoretically often insuperably difficult problems, he must be willing to make compromises regarding rigorous mathematical completeness; he must supplement theoretical reasoning by numerical work, plausibility considerations and so on.

—*Richard Courant: "Professor Courant's Acceptance Speech for the Association's Distinguished Service Award";* ***American Mathematical Monthly****, vol. 72, April, 1965*

5. Applied mathematics is mathematics for which I happen to know an application. This, I think, includes almost everything in mathematics.

—*Henry O. Pollak:* ***New Directions in Mathematics****, Robert W. Ritchie, ed., 1963*

6. Just as there is an applied mathematics of games, genetics, and mechanics, so there should be an applied mathematics (at least in terms of concepts, perhaps with techniques and operations) of the applications of mathematics. When there is, mathematicians will be able to teach "the applications of mathematics."

—*John W. Tukey: "The Teaching of Concrete Mathematics";* ***American Mathematical Monthly****, vol. 65, January, 1958*

7. There is nothing mysterious, as some have tried to maintain, about the applicability of mathematics. What we get by abstraction from something can be returned.

—*Raymond L. Wilder:* ***Introduction to the Foundations of Mathematics****, 1965*

15.2 Pure Mathematics and Mathematicians

1. Pure mathematics is a sucker's game. It lures the curious and the confident with its seeming simplicity only to make them look like fools.

—*Sharon Begley:* ***Newsweek****, July 5, 1993*

2. Pure mathematicians are often vexed with astonishment to discover that it is very much harder to program the accounts of quite a small company than it is to work out the solutions to a dozen complex partial differential equations.

—*Vivian Bowden: "The Language of Computers";* ***American Scientist*** *58, 1970*

3. Because of this extraordinary position which distinguishes mathematics from all other sciences, and which produces and explanation for the relatively free-and-easy way of pursuing it, it especially deserves the name of free mathematics, a designation which I, if I had the choice, would prefer to the now customary "pure" mathematics.

—Georg Cantor: ***Grundlagen einer allgemeinen Mannigfaltigkeitslehre****, 1883*

4. It may well be doubted whether, in all the range of science, there is any field so fascinating to the explorer—so rich in hidden treasures—so fruitful in delightful surprises—as that of Pure Mathematics. The charm lies chiefly ... in the absolute certainty of its results; for that is what, beyond all mental treasures, the human intellect craves for us. Let us only be more sure of something! More light, more light!.

—Charles Lutwidge Dodgson (Lewis Carroll): ***A New Theory of Parallels****, "Introduction" 1895*

5. Pure mathematics is, in its way, the poetry of logical ideas. One seeks the most general ideas of operation which will bring together in simple, logical and unified form the largest possible circle of formal relationships. In this effort toward logical beauty spiritual formulae are discovered necessary for the deeper penetration into the laws of nature.

—Albert Einstein: "Letter to the Editor"; ***New York Times****, May 5, 1935*

6. ...mathematics (pure mathematics), despite its many subdivisions and their enormous rate of growth ... is an amazingly unified intellectual structure The interplay between widely separated parts of mathematics always shows up. The concepts and methods of each one illuminates all others, and the unity of the structure as a whole is there to be marvelled at.

—Paul Halmos: "Applied Mathematics is Bad Mathematics" in ***Mathematics Tomorrow****, Lynn Arthur Steen, ed., 1990*

7. Here's to pure mathematics! May it never have any use.

—G.H. Hardy: Attributed toast

8. Pure mathematics is the magician's real wand.

—Novalis; ***Schriften****, 1901*

9. The mathematician does not study pure mathematics because it is useful; he studies it because he delights in it and he delights in it because it is beautiful.

—Henri Poincare: Quoted in H.E. Huntley: ***The Divine Proportion****, 1970*

10. ...mathematical knowledge resembles empirical knowledge—that is, the criterion of truth in mathematics just as much in physics it is success of our ideas in practice and that mathematical knowledge is corrigible and not absolute.... What he asserts is that certain things are possible and certain things are impossible—in a strong and uniquely mathematical sense of 'possible' and 'impossible'. In short, mathematics is essentially modal rather than existential.

—Hilary Putnam: "What Is Mathematics Truth?" in ***Mathematics, Matter and Method****, reprinted in* ***New Directions in the Philosophy of Mathematics****, T. Tymoczko, ed., 1986*

11. The nineteenth century which prides itself upon the invention of steam and evolution, might have derived a more legitimate title to fame from the discovery of pure mathematics.

—Bertrand Russell: "Recent Work on the Principles of Mathematics"; ***International Monthly****, vol. 4, July–December, 1901*

12. In pure mathematics the maximum of detachment appears to be reached; the mind moves in an infinitely complicated pattern, which is absolutely free from temporal considerations. Yet this very freedom—the essential condition of the mathematician's activity—perhaps gives him an unfair advantage. He can only be wrong—he can't cheat. But the metaphysician can. The problems with which he deals are of overwhelming importance to himself and the rest of humanity, and it is his business to treat them with an exactitude as if they were some puzzle in the theory of numbers.

—Lytton Strachey: "Hume"; ***Portraits in Miniature and Other Essays****, 1931*

13. The science of Pure mathematics, in its modern developments, may claim to be the most original creation of the human spirit.

—Alfred North Whitehead: ***Science and the Modern World****, 1925*

15.3 Differences Between Applied and Pure Mathematics

1. The pure mathematician judges his work largely by aesthetic standards; the applied mathematician is a pragmatist. His job is to make abstract mathematical models of the real world, and if they work, he is satisfied.

—George A.W. Boehm: ***The New World of Math****, 1959*

2. Outstanding mathematicians have ... sometimes, precisely in the name of applicability within mathematics, termed fruitless, idle, even dangerous, new ideas which later proved fundamental.

The freedom not to consider practical applications, which von Neumann demanded for science as a whole, must also be demanded within mathematics.

—*A. Borel: "Mathematics: Art and Science" Kevin M. Lenzer, tr.,* ***The Mathematical Intelligencer***, *vol. 5, #4, 1983*

3. The reputed superiority of mind over matter finds mathematical expression in the claim that mathematics is at once the noblest and purest form of thought, that it derives from pure mind with little or no assistance from the outer world, and that it need not give anything back to the outer world.... Current terminology distinguishes between "pure" and "applied" mathematics and there is a pervasive unspoken sentiment that there is something ugly about applications.

—*Philip J. Davis and Reuben Hersh:* ***The Mathematical Experience***, *1998*

4. I would like to stress how little recent history has been willing to conform to the pious platitudes of the prophets of doom, who regularly warn us of the dire consequences mathematics is bound to incur by cutting itself off from the applications to other sciences.... Even if mathematics were to be forcibly separated from all other channels of human endeavor, there would remain food for centuries of thought in big problems we still have to solve within our science.

—*Jean Dieudonne: "Modern Axiomatic Methods and the Foundations of Mathematics" in Le Lionnais* ***Great Currents of Mathematical Thought***, *1971*

5. Mathematics, as the word is customary used, consists of at least two distinct subjects, and I propose to call them "mathology" and "mathophysics." Roughly speaking, mathology is what is usually called pure mathematics, and mathophysics is called applied mathematics, but the qualifiers are not emotionally strong enough to disguise that they qualify the same noun.

—*Paul R. Halmos: "Mathematics as a Creative Art,"* ***American Scientist***, *Vol. 56, 1968*

6. Just as pure mathematics can be useful, applied mathematics can be more beautifully useless than is sometimes recognized. Applied mathematics is not engineering; the applied mathematician does not design airplanes or atomic bombs. Applied mathematics is an intellectual discipline, not a part of industrial technology. The ultimate goal of applied mathematics is action, to be sure, but, before that, applied mathematics is a part of theoretical science concerned with the general principles behind what makes planes fly and bombs explode.

—*Paul R. Halmos: "Applied Mathematics Is Bad Mathematics"; in* ***Mathematics Tomorrow***, *Lynn Steen, ed., 1981*

7. Pure mathematics is on the whole distinctly more useful than applied. For what is useful above all is technique, and mathematical technique is taught mainly through pure mathematics.

—*G.H. Hardy:* ***A Mathematician's Apology***, *1941*

8. We are told that pure and applied mathematics are hostile to each other. This is not true. Pure and applied mathematics are not hostile to each other. Pure and applied mathematics have never been hostile to each other. Pure and applied mathematics will never be hostile to each other. Pure and applied mathematics cannot be hostile to each other because, in fact, there is absolutely nothing in common between them.

—*David Hilbert: Address to "Joint Congress of Pure and Applied Mathematics"; quoted in J.R. Oppenheimer* ***Physics in the Contemporary World***

9. It is customary to speak of mathematics, of pure mathematics, and of applied mathematics, as if the first were a genus owning the other two as species. The custom is unfortunate because it is misleading.

—*Cassius J. Keyser:* ***Mole Philosophy and Other Essays***, *1927*

10. This trend [emphasizing applied mathematics over pure mathematics] will make the queen of the sciences into the quean of the sciences.

—*L.M. Passano: In H. Eves:* ***Mathematical Circles Squared***, *1972*

11. While applied mathematics is object-directed, pure mathematics has no outside object; being concerned with objects of its own creation, it may be described as "object creating."

—*Michael Polanyi:* ***Personal Knowledge***, *1958*

12. "Applied mathematics" is an insult directed by those who consider themselves "pure" mathematicians at those whom they take for impure.... But "pure" mathematics as a parricide tantrum denying growth from human sensation, as a shibboleth to cast out the impure, is a disease invented in the last century....

—*Clifford E. Truesdell: Quoted in Morris Kline:* ***Mathematics: The Loss of Certainty***, *1980*

13. Perhaps mathematics is unique among activities of the human mind in being, on the one hand, so much art for art's sake and providing, on the other, so many tangible applications that change to course of the human condition. But in turn these applications mold to a certain extent the development of the abstract art itself.

—*Stanislaw Ulam: "The Applicability of Mathematics";* ***The Mathematical Sciences: A Collection of Essays***, *Edited by the National Research Council's Committee on Support of Research in the Mathematical Sciences, 1969*

15.4 Partnership of Pure and Applied Mathematics

1. We must not accept the old blasphemous nonsense that the ultimate justification of mathematical science is "the glory of the human mind." Mathematics must not be allowed to split and to diverge towards a "pure" and an "applied" variety. It must remain, and be strengthened as, a unified vital strand in the broad stream of science and must be prevented from becoming a little side brook that might disappear in the sand.

—*Richard Courant: Quoted in the* ***SIAM Review****, October, 1962: "Mathematics in the Modern World";* ***Scientific American****, vol. 211, 3, September, 1964*

2. Scientific subjects do not progress necessarily on the lines of direct usefulness. Very many applications of the theories of pure mathematics have come many years, sometimes centuries, after the actual discoveries themselves. The weapons were at hand, but the men were not able to use them.

—*A.R. Forsyth:* ***Perry's Teaching of Mathematics****, 1902*

3. The deepest assertion about the relation between pure and applied mathematics that needs examination is that it is symbiotic, in the sense that neither can survive without the other.

—*Paul R. Halmos: "Applied Mathematics Is Bad Mathematics"; in* ***Mathematics Tomorrow****, Lynn Steed, ed., 1981*

4. Applied mathematics will always need pure mathematics just as anteaters will always need ants.

—*Paul Halmos: "Applied Mathematics Is Bad Mathematics"; in* ***Mathematics Tomorrow****, Lynn Steed, ed., 1981*

5. There is no branch of mathematics, however abstract, which may not some day be applied to phenomena of the real world.

—*Nikolai Lobachevsky: In Stanley Gudder:* ***A Mathematical Journey****, 1976*

6. This is the remarkable paradox of mathematics, no matter how determinably its practitioners ignore the world, they consistently produce the best tools for understanding it. The Greeks decide to study, for no good reason, a curve called an ellipse, and 2,000 years later astronomers discover that it describes the way the planets move around the sun. Again, for no good reason, in 1854 a German mathematician, Bernhard Riemann, wonders what would happen if he discards one of the hallowed postulates of Euclid's plane geometry. He builds a seemingly ridiculous assumption that it's not possible to draw two lines parallel to each other. His non–Euclidean geometry replaces Euclid's plane with a bizarre abstraction called curved space, and then 60 years later, Einstein announces that this is the shape of the universe.

—*John Tierney: "Paul Erdos is in Town. His Brain is Open";* ***Science 84****, Vol. 5, # 8, 1984*

7. It is no paradox to say that in our most theoretical moods we may be nearest to our most practical applications.

—*Alfred North Whitehead:* ***An Introduction to Mathematics****, 1911*

15.5 Uses and Usefulness of Mathematics

1. [Mathematics] is the fruitful Parent of, I had almost said all, Arts, the unshaken Foundation of Sciences, and the plentiful Foundation of Human Affairs. In which last Respect, we may be said to receive from the Mathematics, the principal Delights of Life, Securities of Health, Increase of Fortune, and Conveniences of Labor....

—*Isaac Barrow:* ***Mathematical Lectures****, 1734*

2. Mathematics is the instrument by which the engineer tunnels our mountains, bridges our rivers, constructs our aqueducts, erects our factories and makes them musical by the busy hum of spindles. Take away the results of the reasoning of mathematics, and there would go with it nearly all the material achievements which give convenience and glory to modern civilization.

—*Edward Brooks:* ***Mental Science and Culture*** *1891*

3. Mathematics works for today's society like the fossil fuels worked for industrial society.

—*Graciela Chicilnisky: Quoted in Keith Devlin:* ***Life by the Numbers****, 1998*

4. The composer opens the cage door for arithmetic, the draftsman gives geometry its freedom.

—*Jean Cocteau: Attributed*

5. The usefulness of mathematics, commonly allowed to its elementary parts, not only does not stop in higher mathematics but is in fact so much greater, the further that science is developed.

—*Leonhard Euler:* ***Letters of Euler****, published 1872*

6. I have never done anything "useful." No discovery of mine has made, or is likely to make, directly or indirectly, for good or ill, the least difference to the amenity of the world Judged by all practical standards, the value of my mathematical life is nil; and outside mathematics it is trivial anyhow. I have just one chance of escaping a verdict of complete triviality, that I may be judged to have created something is undeniable; the question is about its value.

—*G.H. Hardy:* ***A Mathematician's Apology****, 1941*

7. ...we cannot get more out of the mathematical mill than we put into it, though we may get it in a form infinitely more useful for our purpose.

—John Hopkinson: James Forrest Lecture, 1894

8. It is true that Fourier has the opinion that the principal object of mathematics is public utility and the explanation of natural phenomena; but a scientist like him ought to know that the unique object of science is the honor of the human spirit and on this basis a question of [the thereof] numbers is worth as much as a question about the planetary system.

—Carl Gustav Jacob Jacobi: Letter to Adrein-Marie Legendre; July 2, 1830

9. There is a strange mixture of attitudes towards the usefulness of mathematics. Men both overestimate and underestimate it. Most men feel that although mathematics is very useful in physics and engineering, it has no place in medicine, sociology, or business (other than business arithmetic). Yet there is no inherent reason why mathematics should, in the long run, be more useful in physics than in medicine. It is only that problems in medicine are more difficult to solve than in physics, and hence the use of mathematics will take longer to develop.

—John G. Kemeny: ***Random Essays on Mathematics, Education and Computers****, 1964*

10. When we learn to drive a car we are able to "go places" easily and pleasantly instead of walking to them with a great deal of effort. And so you will see that the more Mathematics we know the EASIER life becomes, for it is a TOOL, with which we can accomplish things that we could not do at all with our bare hands. Thus Mathematics helps our brains and hands and feet, and can make a race of supermen out of us.

—Lillian R. Lieber: ***The Education of T.C. Mits****, 1944*

11. It is a pleasant surprise to him [the pure mathematician] and an added problem if he finds that the arts can use his calculations, or that the senses can verify them, much as the composer found that sailors could heave better when singing his songs.

—George Santayana: "Realm of Truth"; ***Realms of Reasoning****, 1937*

15.6 Values of Mathematics

1. Mathematical knowledge adds vigor to the mind, frees it from prejudice, credulity, and superstition.

—John Arbuthnot: ***Usefulness of Mathematical Learning****, 1690*

2. Mathematics renders its best service through the immediate furthering of rigorous thought and the spirit of invention.

—J.F. Herbart: "Mathematischer Lehrplan fur Realschulen"; ***Werke****, 1890*

3. In the history of mathematics, values play an important role for the mathematical community as well as for the individual mathematician The community of mathematicians shares values about how research should be done, about how results should be presented, and about the worth of subjects, methods, and problems. One such value of high priority is that mathematical innovations should be fruitful and applicable (in mathematics or outside it).

—Herbert Mehrtens: "T.S. Kuhn's theories and mathematics: a discussion paper on the 'new historiography' of mathematics"; ***Historia Mathematica****, 3, 1976*

4. The value of mathematics is in the fruits of its branches more than in its "roots"; in the great number of surprising and interesting theorems of algebra, analysis, geometry, topology, theory of numbers and theory of chances more than in attempts to get a bit of arithmetic or topology as simply a development of logic itself.

—P.H. Nidditch: ***The Development of Mathematical Logic****, 1962*

5. Mathematical knowledge, therefore, appears to us of value not only in so far as it serves as means to other ends, but for its own sake as well, and we behold, both in its systematic external and internal development, the most complete and purest logical mind-activity, the embodiment of the highest intellect-esthetics.

—Alfred Pringsheim: "Uber Wert und angeblichen Unwert der Mathematik"; ***Jahresbericht der Deutschen Mathematiker Vereinigung****, 1904*

6. I hold ... that utility alone is not a proper measure of value, and would even go so far as to say that it is, when strictly and short-sightedly applied, a dangerously false measure of value. For mathematics which is at once the pure and untrammelled creation of the mind and the indispensable tool of science and modern technology, the adoption of a strictly utilitarian standard could lead only to disaster; it would first bring about the drying up of the sources of new mathematical knowledge and would thereby eventually cause the suspension of significant new activity in applied mathematics as well. In mathematics we need rather to aim at a proper balance between pure theory and practical applications....

—Marshall H. Stone: "Mathematics and the Future of Science"; ***Bulletin of the American Mathematical Association****, vol. 63, March, 1957*

16
Mathematicians

16.1 Mathematicians on Mathematicians

1. Experience has taught most mathematicians that much that looks solid and satisfactory to one mathematical generation stands a fair chance of dissolving into cobwebs under the steadier scrutiny of the next....

—E. T. Bell: in Morris Kline: ***Mathematics: The Lost of Certainty****, 1980*

2. Mathematicians make natural questions precise.

—Richard Bellman: "Eye of the Hurricane"; ***World Scientific****, 1984*

3. Mathematicians are like pilots who maneuver their great lumbering planes in the sky without ever asking how the damn things stay aloft.

—David Berlinski: in a review of T.W. Korner: ***The Pleasures of Counting****, in* ***The Sciences****, July/August, 1997*

4. Mathematics is an exceedingly cruel profession. You notice that if somebody has a bachelor's degree in chemistry, he describes himself as a chemist. But if somebody has been a professor of mathematics for ten years, and you ask him, "Are you a mathematician?" he may say, "I'm trying to be one."

—Lipman Bers: Donald J. Albers & Constance Reid: "An Interview with Lipman Bers"; ***Coll. Mathematical Journal****, vol. 18, September, 1987*

5. The one attribute that virtually all creative mathematicians share is youth. Isaac Newton, for example, said he was at the peak of his mathematical power at the age of twenty-three and twenty-four. Most great mathematicians have made their major contributions by the time they were thirty or forty. After fifty they have generally concentrated on teaching or philosophy or the application of mathematics to other fields.

—George A.W. Boehm: ***The New World of Math****, 1959*

6. All mathematicians live in two different worlds. They live in a crystalline world of perfect platonic forms. An ice palace. But they also live in the common world where things are transient, ambiguous, subject to vicissitudes. Mathematicians move backward and forward from one world to another. They're adults in the crystalline world, infants in the real one.

—S. Cappel; ***Courant Institute of Mathematics****, 1996*

7. A mathematician is a conjurer who gives away his secrets.

—John Horton Conway: ***Open Problems in Communication and Computation****, T.M. Cover and B. Gopinath, eds., Springer-Verlag, 1987*

8. One began to hear it said that World War I was the chemists' war, World War II was the physicists' war, World War III (may it never come) will be the mathematicians's war.

—Philip J. Davis & Reuben Hersh: ***The Mathematical Experience****, 1981*

9. ...contrary to a widespread notion, the mathematician is not an otherworldly eccentric; at any rate; he is not eccentric because of his science.

—Max Dehn: "The Mentality of the Mathematician: A Characterization"; Address at University of Frankfurt; January 18, 1928; Abe Schenitzer, tr., ***The Mathematical Intelligencer****, vol. 5, 2, 1983*

10. ...it is indubitable (and true for the matter of every period) that a 50-year-old mathematician knows the mathematics he learned at 20 or 30, but has only notions, often rather vague, of the mathematics of his epoch, i.e., the period of time when he is 50. It is a fact we have to accept such as it is, we cannot do anything about it.

—Jean Dieudonne: "The Work of Nicholas Bourbaki"; ***American Mathematical Monthly****, 77, 1970*

11. A mathematician is a machine for turning coffee into theorems.

—Paul Erdos: Quoted in Paul Hoffman: ***The Man Who Loved Only Numbers****, 1998 [Although Erdos is*

usually given credit for this comment, it is likely that it originated with his most important collaborator Alfred Renyi. Their long work sessions were sustained by endless cups of coffee. Another collaborator of the two Paul Turan allegedly added "Weak coffee is only fit for lemmas."]

12. Mathematicians are like lovers.... Grant a mathematician the least principle, and he will draw from it a consequence which you must also grant him, and from this consequence another.

—*Bernard le Bovier de Fontenelle: Quoted in E.T. Bell:* ***Men of Mathematics****, 1937*

13. If present trends continue, our country may soon find itself far behind many other nations in both science and technology—nations where, if you inform strangers that you are a mathematician, they respond with admiration and not by telling you how much they hated math in school, and how they sure could use you to balance their checkbooks.

—*Martin Gardner: Quoted in* ***More Mathematical People****, D.J. Albers, G.L. Alexanderson & C. Reid, eds., 1990*

14. It may be true that people who are merely mathematicians have certain specific shortcomings, however, that is not the fault of mathematics, but is true of every exclusive occupation.

—*Carl Freidrich Gauss: Letter to H.C. Schumacher, 1845*

15. The mathematician requires tact and good taste at every step of his work, and he has to learn to trust to his own instinct to distinguish between what is really worthy of his efforts and what is not.

—*J.W. Glaisher: Presidential Address British Association for the Advancement of science, 1890;* ***Nature*** *vol. 42*

16. Ah, you are a mathematician,
they say with admiration or scorn.
Then, they say,
I could use you to balance my
checkbook. I think about checkbooks.
Once in a while
I balance mine,
just like sometimes
I dust high shelves.

—*JoAnne Growney: "Misunderstanding";* ***Intersections****, 1993*

17. Usually when a mathematician lectures, he is a missionary. Whether he is talking over a cup of coffee with a collaborator, lecturing to a graduate class of specialists, teaching a reluctant group of freshmen engineers, or addressing a general audience of laymen—he is still preaching and seeking to make converts.

—*Paul Halmos: in* ***Mathematical People****, D.J. Albers & G.L. Alexanderson, eds., 1985*

18. Do you know any mathematicians—and, if you do, do you know anything about what they do with their time? Most people don't. When I get into conversation with the man next to me in a plane, and he tells me that he is something respectable like a doctor, lawyer, merchant, or dean, I am tempted to say that I am in roofing and siding. If I tell him that I am a mathematician, his most likely reply will be that he himself could never balance his check book, and it must be fun to be a whiz at math. If my neighbor is an astronomer, a biologist, a chemist, or any other kind of natural or social scientist, I am, if anything, worse off—this man "thinks" he knows what a mathematician is, and he is probably wrong.

—*Paul R. Halmos: "Mathematics as a Creative Art,"* ***American Scientist****, Vol. 56, 1968*

19. It is, so to speak, a scientific tact, which must guide mathematicians in their investigations, and guard them from spending their forces on scientifically worthless problems and abstruse realms, a tact which is closely related to esthetic tact and which is the only thing in science which cannot be taught or acquired, and is yet the indispensable endowment of every mathematician.

—*H. Hankel: Quoted in Howard Eves:* ***Mathematical Circles Squared****, 1972*

20. We are servants rather than masters in mathematics.

—*Charles Hermite: in Howard Eves,* ***Mathematical Circles Squared****, 1972*

21. Continue in scientific research, you will experience great joy from it. But you must learn to enjoy it alone. You will be a subject of astonishment to those close to you. You will not be much better understood by the scholarly world. Mathematicians have a place apart there, and even they do not always read each other.

—*Camille Jordan: "Notice sur la Vie et les Travaux de Camile Jordan":* ***L'enseignement Mathematique 3****, April–June, 1957*

22. The mathematician is still regarded as the hermit who knows little of the ways of life outside his cell, who spends his time compounding incredible and incomprehensible theorems in strange, clipped, unintelligible jargon.

—*Edward Kasner & James Newman:* ***Mathematics and the Imagination****, 1940*

23. A mathematician, like everyone else, lives in the real world. But the objects with which he works do not. They live in that other place—the mathematical world. Something else lives here also. It is called truth.

—*Jerry P. King:* ***The Art of Mathematics****, 1992*

24. A mathematician experiments, amasses information, makes a conjecture, finds out that it does not work and then tries to recover. A good mathematician eventually does so—and proves a theorem.

*—Steven Krantz: "Conformal Mappings"; **American Science**, September–October, 1999*

25. It is possible for a mathematician to be "too strong" for a given occasion. He forces through, where another might be driven to a different, and possibly more fruitful approach. (So a rock climber might force a dreadful crack, instead of finding a subtle and delicate route.

*—J.E. Littlewood: **A Mathematician's Miscellany**, 1953*

26. No one will get very far or become a real mathematician without certain indispensable qualities. he must have hope, faith, and curiosity, and prime necessity is curiosity.

*—Louis Joel Mordell: "Reflections of a Mathematician"; **Canadian Mathematical Congress**, 1959*

27. In dealing with academics, it is absolutely superb to be able to say you're a mathematician! Nobody dares to say mathematics is not important or not significant. No discipline surpasses mathematics in purely academic prestige.

*—Mina Rees: in **Mathematical People**, D.J. Albers & G.L. Alexanderson, eds., 1985*

28. Individually [mathematicians] are very different in their mathematical personalities, the kind of mathematics they like, and the way that they do mathematics, but they are alike in one respect. Almost without exception, they love their subject, are happy in their choice of a career, and consider that they are exceptionally lucky in being able to do for a living what they would do for fun.

*—Constance Reid: in **More Mathematical People**, D. Albers, G. Alexanderson & C. Reid, eds., 1990*

29. We often hear that mathematics consists mainly in "proving theorems." Is a writer's job mainly that of "writing sentences?" A mathematician's work is mostly a tangle of guesswork, analogy, wishful thinking and frustration, and proof, far from being the core of discovery, is more often than not a way of making sure that our minds are not playing tricks.

*—Gian-Carlo Rota: "Introduction" to Philip J. Davis & Reuben Hersh: **The Mathematical Experience**, 1981; in **Discrete Thoughts: Essays on Mathematics, Science and Philosophy**, Mark Kac, Gian-Carlo Rota, Jacob T. Schwartz; Quoted in **The Mathematical Intelligencer**, vol. 12, 1990*

30. The desire to explore thus marks out the mathematician. This is one of the forces making for the growth of mathematics. The mathematician enjoys what he already knows; he is eager for new knowledge.

*—W. W. Sawyer: **Prelude to Mathematics**, 1957*

31. I would rather be a dreamer without mathematics, than a mathematician without dreams.

*—David Eugene Smith: **The Poetry of Mathematics and Other Essays**, 1934*

32. The mathematician lives long and lives young; the wings of the soul do not early drop off, nor do the pores become clogged with the earthy particles blown from the dusty highways of vulgar life.

*—James Joseph Sylvester: Presidential Address to the British Association, 1869: **The Collected Mathematical Papers of James Joseph Sylvester**, 1908*

33. The modern mathematician weaves an intricate pattern of microscopic precision. To him, a false statement—an exception to a general statement—is an unforgiven sin. The heroic mathematician, on the other hand, painted with broad splashes of color, with a grand contempt for singular cases until they could no longer be avoided.

*—John L. Synge: "The Life and Early Works of Sir William Rowan Hamilton"; **The Scripta Mathematical Studies Number 2**, 1945*

34. A mathematician does not like to be wrong, and when he is, there is no doubt and no excuse.

*—Clifford Truesdell: **Six Lectures on Modern Natural Philosophy**, 1966*

35. [Mathematicians] are the makers of signs which they hope will fit all contingencies.

*—Stanislaw M. Ulam: **Adventures of a Mathematician**, 1976*

36. Every mathematician worthy of the name has experienced ... the state of lucid exaltation in which one thought succeeds another as if miraculously ... this feeling may last for hours at a time, even for days. Once you have experienced it, you are eager to repeat it but unable to do it at will, unless perhaps by dogged work....

*—Andre Weil: **The Apprenticeship of a Mathematician**, 1992*

16.2 Non-Mathematicians on Mathematicians

1. Mathematicians assume the right to choose, within the limits of logical contradiction, what path they please in reaching their results.

—Henry Adams: Letter to American Teachers of History, 1910

2. Each generation has its few great mathematicians, and mathematics would not even notice the absence of the others. They are useful as teachers, and their research harms no one, but it is of no importance at all. A mathematician is great or he is nothing.

*—Alfred Adler: "Reflections: Mathematics and Creativity," **The New Yorker Magazine**, February 19, 1972*

3. A mathematician is one who is willing to assume everything except responsibility.

—Anonymous

4. Mark all Mathematical heads which be wholly and only bent on these sciences, how solitary they be themselves, how unfit to live with others, how unapt to serve the world.

—Roger Ascham (ca. 1550); Quoted in E.G.R. Taylor: ***The Mathematical Practitioners of Tudor and Stuart England****, 1954*

5. Happy the lot of the pure mathematician. He is judged solely by his peers and the standard is so high that no colleague can ever win a reputation he does not deserve. No cashier writes articles in the *Sunday Times* complaining about the incomprehensibility of Modern Mathematics and comparing it unfavorably with the good old days when mathematicians were content to paper irregularly-shaped rooms or fill bathtubs with the waste-pipe open. Better still, since engineers and physicists have occasionally been able to put his equations to destructive use, he is given a chair....

—W.H. Auden: ***The Dyer's Hand and Other Essays****, 1963*

6. A mathematician is not a man who can readily manipulate figures; often he cannot. He is not even a man who can readily perform the transformations of equations by the use of calculus. He is primarily an individual who is skilled in the use of symbolic logic on a high plane, and especially he is a man of intuitive judgment in the choice of the manipulative processes he employs.

—Vannevar Bush: ***Endless Horizons****, 1946*

7. A mathematician is a blind man in a dark room looking for a black cat which isn't there.

—Charles Darwin: Quoted in Monte Zerger: "A Quote a Day Educates": ***The Mathematical Intelligencer****, vol. 20, #2, Spring, 1998*

8. They say that a mathematician
Once fell to such a passion
For x and y, he locked
His door to keep outside
Whatever might distract
Him from his heavenly bride:
And presently died
In the keenest of blisses
With a dozen untasted dishes
Outside his door.

—Cecil Day Lewis: in ***Collected Poems, 1929–1933****, 1935*

9. After all I am happy about the contact and friendship of mathematicians that resulted from it all. They have often given me new ideas, and sometimes there even is an interaction between us. How playful they can be, those learned ladies and gentlemen!

—M.C. Escher: in Eli Maor: ***To Infinity and Beyond****, 1991*

10. Mathematicians, whose tempers are generally intolerable, are perhaps psychologically excusable, for the constant tension of their mind is, perhaps, the cause of their bad digestion and their state of hypochondria.

—Camille Flammarion: ***Popular Astronomy: A General Description of the Heavens****, 1984*

11. He was absent, no doubt, mathematicians are subject to be so, and we might well advise them to calculate more and write less.

—Stephanie Felicite Genlis: "The Two Reputations"; ***Tales of the Castle****, c. 1793*

12. The mathematicians are distinguished by a peculiar privilege, that, in the course of ages, they may always advance and can never recede.

—Edward Gibbon: ***The History of the Decline and Fall of the Roman Empire****, 1776–1788*

13. Mathematican are a species of Frenchmen: if you say something to them, they translate it into their own language and present it as something entirely different.

—Johann Wolfgang von Goethe; attributed, quoted in R.L. Weber ***A Random Walk in Science****, 1973*

14. A mathematician, it has been suggested, might pray to x^n.

—William R. Inge: ***A Rustic Moralist****, 1937*

15. In the index to the six hundred odd pages of Arnold Toynbee's *A Study of History*, abridged version, the names of Copernicus, Galileo, Descartes and Newton did not occur, yet their cosmic quest destroyed the medieval vision of an immutable social order in a walled-in universe and transformed the European landscape, society, culture, habits and general outlook, as thoroughly as if a new species had arisen on this planet.

—Arthur Koestler: In G. Simmons: ***Calculus Gems****, 1992*

16. Ask a philosopher "What is philosophy?" or a historian "What is history?" and they will have no difficulty in giving an answer. Neither of them, in fact, can pursue his own discipline without knowing what he is searching for. But ask a mathematician "What is mathematics?" and he may justifiably reply that he does not know the answer but that does not stop him from doing mathematics.

—Francois Lasserre: Quoted in John D. Barrow: ***Pi in the Sky****, 1992*

17. So called professional mathematicians have, in their reliance on the relative incapacity of the rest of mankind, acquired for themselves a reputation for profundity very similar to the reputation for sanctity possessed by theologians.

*—G. C. Lichtenberg: **Aphorisms**, "Notebook K," written 1765–99; R.J. Hollingdale, tr. 1990*

18. Mathematics is truly a splendid science, but mathematicians often are not worth a nickel ... very often the so-called mathematician expects to be considered a deep thinker; yet the greatest blockheads are among them, unfit for any kind of occupation which requires contemplation if it cannot be done directly through that easy combination of symbols, which is more the work of routine than of thought.

*—G.C. Lichtenberg: **Aphorisms**; 1770 **Aphorismen**, Albert Leitzmann, ed. 1902—08*

19. Mathematicians boast of their exacting achievements, but in reality they are absorbed in mental acrobatics and contribute nothing to society.

*—Sorai Ogyu: **Complete Works on Japan's Philosophical Thought**, 1956*

20. One of the endearing things about mathematicians is the extent to which they will go to avoid doing any real work.

*—Matthew Pordage: in Howard Eves: **Return yo Mathematical Circles**, 1988*

21. ...a certain impression I had of mathematicians was ... that they spent immoderate amounts of time declaring each other's work trivial.

*—Richard Preston: **New Yorker**, 1992*

22. All my life I have thought of mathematicians as Rosicrucians of some kind, and I always regretted that I never had the opportunity of being initiated into their secrets.

*—Aleksandr Solzhenitsyn: **The First Circle**, 1968*

23. A man or woman obsessed with sex arouses, rightly, a certain feeling of distaste. We must learn to cultivate a similar reaction in the presence of a mathematician. Both types are excessive, and therefore imperfect.

*—J.W.N. Sullivan: **The Contemporary Mind: Some Modern Answers**, 1934*

24. It has been said that the pure mathematician is never as happy as when he does not know what he is talking about.

*—W.F.G. Swann: **The Architecture of the Universe**, 1934*

25. There is a common tendency to consider mathematics so strange, so subtle, rigorous, difficult and deep a subject that if a person is a mathematician he is of course a "great mathematician"—there being, so to speak, no small giants. This is very complimentary, but unfortunately not necessarily true.

*—Warren Weaver: "Lewis Carroll: Mathematician"; **Scientific American**, vol. 194; April, 1956*

16.3 Women and Mathematics

1. The most beautiful woman in the world would not be half so beautiful if she was as great at mathematics as Sir Isaac Newton or as great a mathematician as the noblest and profoundest school man.

*—Anonymous: **The Gentleman's Magazine**, 1738*

2. There is little point in girls of common extraction learning to read as well as young ladies or being taught as fine a pronouncement or knowing what a period is, etc. It is the same thing with writing. All they need is enough to keep their accounts and memoranda; you don't need to teach them fine hand-writing or talk to them of style: a little spelling will do. Arithmetic is different. They need it.

*—Francoise d'Aubigne (Mme. de Maintenon): **Lettres sur l'education des filles**, 1713*

3. Perceiving math as very useful for males does not necessary have a negative consequence for girls, perhaps especially when the stereotype reflects an awareness of the high status jobs that are both male-dominated and math-related. In this case, it may be the status of the job rather than the male domination that elevates the perceived usefulness of advanced math courses for both high ability boys and girls.

*—P. Casserly & D. Rock: "Factors Related to Young Women's Persistence and Achievement in Advanced Placement Mathematics"; **Women in Mathematics: Balancing the Equation**, 1985*

4. All women who have published mathematics hitherto [prior to Lady Byron Lovelace] have shown knowledge, and power of getting it, but no one, except perhaps (I speak doubtfully) Maria Agnesi, has wrestled with difficulties and shows a man's strength in getting over them. The reason is obvious: the very great tension of mind which they require is beyond the strength of a woman's physical power of application.

*—August De Morgan: in Ethel Colburn Mayne: **The Life and Letters of Anne Isabella Lady Noel Byron**, 1929*

5. Women who have left behind a name in mathematics are very few in number—three or four, perhaps five. Does this say, as a common prejudice would tend to persuade us, that mathematics, so very abstract, is not congenial to the feminine disposition? This would be to ignore the true character of mathematics, to forget, as Henri Poincare said, "the feeling of mathematical beauty, of the harmony of numbers and of forms, of geometric elegance. It is a genuinely esthetic feeling, which all mathematicians know. And this is sensitivity." And should not this very sensitivity, contrary to the prejudice, make mathematics a feminine domain?

—*Marie-Louise Dubriel-Jacotin: "Women Mathematicians," in F. Le Lionnais:* ***Great Currents of Mathematical Thought****, 1971*

6. Among the arguments advanced to prove that women cannot do mathematics is that so few have done it. In other words, the absence of women in mathematics is used to confirm their unfitness for the subject. Of course, reasoning along these lines is ridiculous. It is not unlike attributing the absence of African Americans in major league baseball prior to World War II as proof of some fundamental inability to play the game. As Jackie Robinson, Henry Aaron, and so many others have amply demonstrated, the dearth of black major-leaguers reflected not a lack of ability but a lack of opportunity.

—*William Dunham:* ***The Mathematical Universe*** *1994*

7. If a woman's dance
is mathematics,
must she dance alone?

—*JoAnne Growney: "My Dance Is Mathematics";* ***Mathematics Magazine****, December, 1995*

8. Throughout history there has been a recurrent belief that at some fundamental level women were just no good at mathematics. First it was argued that their brains were too small, later that it would compromise their reproductive capacities, still later that their hormones were not compatible with mathematical development. These arguments were buttressed by the underlying belief that mathematics is ultimately a pure meritocracy. Those who have the gift would shine no matter what their background, sex, or race. As a corollary, it was assumed that if women were not excelling in the mathematical realm, they must simply lack the talent to compete. This belief in mathematics as a meritocracy is convenient; it absolves the mathematics community from any responsibility to change, and reduces the underrepresentation of women to a "woman's problem."

—*Claudia Henrion:* ***Women in Mathematics: The Addition of Difference****; "Introduction" 1997*

9. As for Sophie Germain and Sonja Kovalevsky, the collaboration they obtained from first-rate mathematicians [Sophie Germain corresponded with Gauss] prevents us from fixing with precision their mathematical role. Nevertheless what we know allows us to put the finishing touches on a character portrait of any woman mathematician: She is always a child prodigy, who, because of her unusual aptitudes, is admired, encouraged, and strongly aided by her friends and teachers; in childhood she manages to surpass her male fellow-students; in her youth she succeeds only in equalling them; while at the end of her studies, when her comrades of the other sex are progressing, fresh and courageous, she always seeks the support of a teacher, friend or relative; and after a few years, exhausted by efforts beyond her strength, she finally abandons a work which is bringing her no joy....

—*Gino Loria: "Women Mathematicians";* ***Revue Scientifique****, 1904*

10. Many women in our present culture value mathematical ignorance as if it were a social grace, and they perceive mathematics as a series of meaningless technical procedures. They discount the role mathematics has played in determining the direction of philosophic thought, and they ignore its powerful satisfactions and its aesthetic values, which are equal to those offered by any other branch of knowledge.

—*Lynn M. Osen:* ***Women in Mathematics****, 1999*

11. By glamorizing the exceptional cases [i.e. exceptional women, who despite many obstacles became outstanding mathematicians], we often manage to preserve the myth of equality in education and convince ourselves that when women fail to become educated in such disciplines as mathematics or the "hard sciences," the lack of individual enterprize or interest was the important factor, rather than the lack of equal opportunity. Fortunately, we are beginning to have a more sophisticated and sympathetic understanding of the socialization process that shapes the female experience.

—*Lynn M. Osen:* ***Women in Mathematics****, 1999*

12. I looked like any other person, but they had just assumed before they saw me that I would be hunchbacked, or crippled, and would be substituting mathematics for the female attributes I lacked. When it was clear that I was just very ordinary, they couldn't understand why I'd be so interested in mathematics. They would ask, "Why are you here?" And I would say, "Because I like mathematics." For a woman, that was not considered to be sufficient reason.

—*Marion Pour-El: Quoted in Claudia Henrion:* ***Women in Mathematics: The Addition of Difference****, 1997 [Pour-El recalls her reception as a woman in graduate school at Harvard.]*

13. Mathematics is obviously something that

women should be able to do very well. It's very intuitive. You don't need a lot of machinery, and you don't need a lot of physical strength. You just need stamina, and women often have a great deal of stamina. So why do not more women become mathematicians? I think that for some reason, probably sociological, girls are refusing to look—they simply don't try something that they view as a hard problem in mathematics. But boys for some reason are willing and eager to look at the hard problems.

—Mary Ellen Rudin: in D.J. Albers, G.L. Alexanderson & C. Reid: ***More Mathematical People****, 1993*

14. Mathematics is a genderless world.

—Karen Uhlenbeck: Quoted in Claudia Henrion: ***Women in Mathematics: The Addition of Difference****, 1997*

17

Some Mathematical People I

17.1 Niels Henrik Abel (1802–1829)

[Norwegian Mathematician]

1. Abel has left mathematicians enough to keep them busy for 500 years.

—Charles Hermite: Quoted in G.F. Simmons: ***Calculus Gems****, 1992*

2. The best works of Abel are true lyric poems of sublime beauty, whose perfection of form allows the profundity of his thought to show through, while at the same time filling the imagination with dream visions of a remote world of ideas, raised farther above life's commonplaces and emanating more directly from the very soul than any poet, in the ordinary sense of the world, could produce.

—Magnus Mittag-Leffler: Quoted in Francois Le Lionnais: "Beauty in Mathematics" in ***Great Currents of Mathematics****, F. Le Lionnais, ed., 1971*

3. Abel, the lucky fellow! He has done something everlasting! His ideas will always exercise a fertilizing influence on our science.

—Karl Weierstrass: Quoted in E.T. Bell: ***Men of Mathematics****, 1937*

17.2 Maria Gaetana Agnesi (1718–1799)

[Italian Mathematician]

1. The name of Agnesi is most often recalled today in connection with the Curve of Agnesi, known in English texts as the Witch of Agnesi. The last term appears to be John Colson's mistranslation of ***versiera****,* the Italian form of the Latin name *versoria,* both used for this curve by Guido Grandi as early as 1718.

—Hubert Kennedy: "Maria Gaetana Agnesi"; in ***Women of Mathematics****, Louise S. Grinstein and Paul J. Campbell, eds., 1987*

2. Permit me, mademoiselle, to unite my personal homage to the plaudits of the entire Academy. I have the pleasure of making known to my country an extremely useful work which has long been desired, and which has hitherto existed only in outline. I do not know of any work of this kind which is clearer, more methodic, or more comprehensive than your Analytical Institutions. There is none in any language which can guide more surely, lead more quickly, and conduct further those who wish to advance in the mathematical sciences.

—Pope Benedict XIV: Quoted in H.J. Mozans: ***Women in Science****, 1913*

17.3 Ibn Musa al-Khwarizmi [Khowarizmi] (c. 800–c. 850)

[Persian Mathematician]

1. Al-Khwarizimi's text of algebra, named *Al-Jabr Wa-Al-Muqabala* (the science of cancellation and reduction) was written in 820 A.D. A Latin translation of the text became known in Europe under the title *Al-Jabr.* Thus "the Arabic word for reduction, al-Jabr, became the word *algebra.*

—Ali Abdullah Al-Daffa': ***The Muslim Contribution to Mathematics****, 1977*

2. Al-Khwarizmi's algebra is regarded as the foundation and cornerstone of the sciences. In a sense, Al-Khwarizmi is more entitled to be called "the father of algebra" than Diophantus because Al-Khwarizmi is the first to teach algebra in an elementary form and for its own sake. Diophantus is primarily concerned with the theory of numbers.

Solomon Gandz: "The Source of Al-Khwarizmi's Algebra"; ***Osiris****, vol. I, 1936*

3. [Al-Khwarizmi] ...the greatest mathematician of his time, and if one takes all the circumstances into account, one of the greatest of all time....

—*George A. Sarton:* ***The Study of the History of Science****, 1957*

4. [Al-Khwarizmi] ... the great master of the golden age of Baghdad, one of the first of the Muslim writers to collect the mathematical classics of both the East and West, preserving them and finally passing them on to the awakening Europe.

—*David Eugene Smith and Louis Charles Karpinski:* ***The Hindu-Arabic Numbers****, 1911*

17.4 Apollonius of Perga (262–190 B.C.)

[Greek Mathematician]

1. Apollonius so thoroughly investigated the properties of these curves [conics] that he left but little for his successors to add.

—*W. W. Rouse Ball:* ***A Short Account of the History of Mathematics****, 1960 edition*

2. It seems to me that all the evidence points to Apollonius as the founder of Greek mathematical astronomy.

—*Otto Neugebauer:* ***Astronomy and History****, 1983*

17.5 Archimedes of Syracuse (c. 287–212 B.C.)

[Sicilian Greek Mathematican]

1. Archimedes is the second smartest man ever—and the first is not yet born.

—*Anonymous*

2. [The Romans paid homage to Archimedes by erecting a lavish tomb in his honor upon which was engraved] the figure of a sphere inscribed in a cylinder, in commemoration of the proof he had given that the volume of a sphere equals two-thirds that of the circumscribing right cylinder and its surface area equals four times the area of a great circle.

—*W. W. Rouse Ball:* ***A Short Account of the History of Mathematics****, 1960 edition*

3. Who would not rather have the fame of Archimedes than that of his conqueror Marcellus?

—*Sir William Rowan Hamilton: In Howard Eves,* ***Mathematical Circles Revisited****, 1971*

4. Archimedes will be remembered when Aeschylus is forgotten, because languages die and mathematical ideas do not. "Immortality" may be a silly word, but probably a mathematician has the best chance of whatever it may mean.

—*G.H. Hardy:* ***A Mathematician's Apology****, 1941*

5. With one bold stroke
He killed the circle, tangent
And point of intersection in infinity.
  On penalty
Of quartering
He banned numbers
From three up.
  Now in Syracuse
He heads a school of philosophers,
Squats on his halberd
For another thousand years
And writes:
One, two
One, two
One, two
One, two.

—*Miroslav Holub: "The Corporal Who Killed Archimedes";* ***New Scientist****, July 24, 1969 [Continental armies march "one, two," rather than "left, right."]*

6. [Archimedes] ... being perpetually charmed by his familiar siren, that is, by his geometry, he neglected to eat and drink and took no care of his person; that he was often carried by force to the baths, and when there he would trace geometrical figures in the ashes of the fire, and with his finger draws lines upon his body when it was anointed with oil, being in a state of great ecstasy and divinely possessed by his science.

—*Plutarch:* ***The Life of the Noble Grecians and Romans****, c. 100 A.D.; J.& W. Langhorne, trs., 1876*

17.6 Charles Babbage (1792–1871)

[British Mathematician]

1. On two occasions I have been asked [by members of Parliament], "Pray, Mr. Babbage, if you put into the machine wrong figures, will the right answers come out?" I am not able rightly to apprehend the kind of confusion of ideas that could provoke such a question.

—*Charles Babbage:* ***Passages from the Life of a Philosopher****, 1864*

2. Babbage was a forceful, argumentative, and controversial figure, and many of his contemporaries dismissed him as a crank. Nevertheless, he is credited with the invention of, among other things, the speedometer, the ophthalmoscope, the cow-catcher for trains, the overhead cash trolley for stops, and coded flashing for lighthouses.... Babbage's insight into the nature of computational processes led him to speculate that the universe could be regarded as a type of computer, with the laws of nature playing the role of program—a remarkably prescient speculation....

—*Paul Davies:* ***The Mind of God****, 1992*

17.7 Daniel Bernoulli (1700–1782)

[Swiss Mathematician]

1. Daniel Bernoulli has been called the father of mathematical physics.

—*E.T. Bell: Quoted in* ***The World of Mathematics****, vol. 2, James R. Newman, ed., 1956*

2. Daniel won no fewer than ten prizes offered by the French Academy of Sciences, sharing one with his father [Johann], much to the latter's resentment. He was delighted when a stranger once asked him his name, and on replying "I am Daniel Bernoulli" to receive the incredulous and sarcastic reply "And I am Isaac Newton."

—*Alfred Hooper:* ***Makers of Mathematics****, 1948*

17.8 Jacob (James) I Bernoulli (1654–1705)

[Swiss Mathematician]

1. Bernoulli was one of the most significant promoters of the formal methods of higher analysis. Astuteness and elegance are seldom found in his method of presentation and expression, but there is a maximum of integrity.

—*J.E. Hofmann: "Uber Jakob Bernoullis Beitrage zur Infinitesimalmathematik"* ***Enseignement Math****, 2, 1956*

2. Like Archimedes, Jakob Bernoulli requested that a mathematical figure should be engraved on his tombstone. He chose the logarithmic spiral, presumably because it illustrates the inscription he chose to accompany it: *Eadem mutata resurgo*, "I shall arise the same, though changed. The logarithmic spiral frequently reproduces itself under many different conditions.

—*Alfred Hooper:* ***Makers of Mathematics****, 1948*

17.9 Johann (Johannes I) Bernoulli (1667–1748)

[Swiss Mathematician]

1. [Johann Bernoulli] ... played a leading part in developing the ideas and applications of Liebniz's calculus. He was frequently involved in violent quarrels and controversies and he took a leading part in the dispute with English mathematicians regarding the invention of the calculus.

—*Alfred Hooper:* ***Makers of Mathematics****, 1948*

2. Johann Bernoulli ... was known as the "Archimedes of his age" and this is indeed inscribed on his tombstone.

—*J.J. O'Connor & E.F. Robertson: "Johann Bernoulli":* ***The MacTutor History of Mathematics Archive****; University of St. Andrews, 2000*

3. The calculus of variations is generally regarded as originating with the papers of Jean [Johann] Bernoulli on the problem of the brachystochrone [the name of the curve connecting two points not in the same horizontal plane, down which a weighted particle will slide in the "shortest time."]

—*David Eugene Smith:* ***A Source Book in Mathematics****, 1929*

17.10 George David Birkhoff (1884–1944)

[American Mathematician]

1. [Birkhoff] has told us that the formal structure of western music, the riddle of melody, began to interest him in undergraduate days; somewhat intense consideration of the mathematical elements here involved led him to apply his theory also to aesthetic objects such as polygons, tilings, vases, and even poetry.

—*R.C. Archibald:* ***A Semicentennial History of the American Mathematical Society*** *1888–1938, 1980*

2. ...Birkhoff was ... attracted to aesthetics by an interest in the formal structure of Western music, but he later conceived the more ambitious goal of creating a "general mathematical theory of the fine arts, which would do for aesthetics what had been achieved in another philosophical subject, logic, by the symbolisms of Boole, Peano and Russell."

—*James R. Newman:* ***The World of Mathematics****, Vol. IV, 1956*

17.11 Ralph Boas, Jr. (1912–1992)

[American Mathematician]

1. Ralph Boas calls himself a "quasi" mathematician because, although he has been a mathematician throughout his professional career, he has done many things besides mathematical research. He has been an editor (Mathematical Reviews and the American Mathematical Monthly), a translator of Russian mathematics, a longtime department chairperson at Northwestern, as well as a mathematical versifier and humorist.... "Real mathematicians," he says, "do only mathematics."

—*D.J. Albers: "Ralph P. Boas, Jr.";* ***More Mathematical People****; Albers, G. Alexanderson & C. Reid, eds., 1990*

2. In 1938, a famous tongue-in-cheek paper on the mathematical theory of big game hunting was published under the name H. Petard in the American Mathematical Monthly. Although it was once a closely held secret, it is generally known now that the two coconspirators on this paper were my father and Frank Smithies. It is perhaps not generally known that Petard's full initials are H.W.O, standing for "Hoist With Own." Actually H. Petard is the pen name for the imaginary mathematician E.S. Pondiczery, and is thus a second-order pseudonym.

—*Harold P. Boas: "Remarks"; Memorial for Ralph P. Boas; October 9, 1992; in* ***Lion Hunting & Other Mathematical Pursuits;*** *"A Collection of Mathematics, verse and stories by Ralph Boas, Jr., 1995*

17.12 Janos (Johann) Bolyai (1802–1860)

[Hungarian Mathematician]

1. You should detest it [trying to prove Euclid's fifth postulate] just as much as lewd intercourse, it can deprive you of all your leisure, your health, your rest, and the whole happiness of your life. This abysmal darkness might perhaps devour a thousand towering Newtons, it will never be light on earth....

—*Farkas (Wolfgang) Bolyai: Letter to his son Janos; 1820*

2. [Bolyai's Science Absolute of Space]—the most extraordinary two dozen pages in the history of thought! ... Bolyai projected a universal language for speech as we have it for music and mathematics.

—*G.B. Halsted:* ***Bolyai's Science Absolute of Space;*** *"Introduction," 1896*

3. All mathematicians admire the great geometer [Johann] Bolyai, whose eccentricities were of an insane character; thus he provoked thirteen officials to duels and fought with them, and between each duel he played the violin, the only piece of furniture in his house; when pensioned he printed his own funeral card with a blank date, and constructed his own coffin.... Six years later he had a similar funeral card printed, to substitute for the other which he had not been able to use. He imposed on his heir the obligation to plant on his grave an apple-tree, in remembrance of Eve, of Paris, and of Newton. Such was the great reformer of Euclid.

—*Cesare Lombroso:* ***The Man of Genius,*** *1891*

17.13 Bernard Bolzano (1781–1848)

[Czech Mathematician]

1. It is to Bernard Bolzano that the modern concept of continuity is due; he was not like Cauchy a great powerhouse of mathematical thought; his intelligence was delicate but prophetic.... He seems to have had a gentle gift for divining the future of thought, a gift that time bestowed but compromised by depriving Bolzano of the degree of mathematical mastery needed successful to develop his ideas.

—*David Berlinski:* ***A Tour of Calculus,*** *1995*

2. Bernard Bolzano dispelled the clouds that throughout all the foregone centuries had enveloped the notion of Infinitude in darkness, completely sheared the great term of vagueness without shearing it of its strength, and thus rendered it forever available for the purposes of logical discourses.

—*Cassius J. Keyser:* ***Lectures on Science, Philosophy and Art,*** *1908*

17.14 George Boole (1815–1864)

[English Mathematician]

1. George Boole
was nobody's fool:
but never forget—
his mathematical legacy is the empty set.

—*Robin Harte:* ***American Mathematical Monthly,*** *November, 1985*

2. Pure mathematics was discovered by Boole in a work which he called The Laws of Thought.... His work was concerned with formal logic, and this is the same thing as mathematics.

—*Bertrand Russell;* ***International Monthly,*** *1901*

17.15 "Nicolas Bourbaki"

[Nicholas Bourbaki is the collective pseudonym of the Nancy school of mathematics.]

1. The most ambitious movement in mathematical formalism started out as a joke and still has elements of a joke. It consists of a wholly fictitious Frenchman, Nicolas Bourbaki, and it is perhaps the only large-scale collaborative effort in modern mathematics.... Bourbaki was born [in about 1934] in the whimsical imagination of a group of young French mathematicians led by Andre Weil, ... Bourbaki started by writing brief technical notes to the journals. Then about 1940 he set himself an imposing task: to compile a complete and logically rigorous exposition of mathematics....

—*George A.W. Boehm:* ***The New World of Math,*** *1959*

2. Roughly speaking, unfashionable mathematics consists of those parts of mathematics which were declared by the mandarins of Bourbaki not to be mathematics.

—*Freeman J. Dyson: "Unfashionable Pursuits" Address to the Alexander von Humboldt Foundation,*

*August 24, 1981; in **The Mathematical Intelligencer**, vol. 5, 3, 1983*

3. The work of Bourbaki is like a beautiful symphony with too many French horns.

*—Ilan Vardi: **A Classical Reeducation**, 2001*

17.16 Georg Cantor (1845–1918)

[Russian-born German Mathematician]

1. It is tempting to compare him [Georg Cantor] to his contemporary from the world of art, Vincent van Gogh.... Both van Gogh and Cantor were revolutionaries. Just as Vincent in his brief and turbulent career managed to carry art beyond its impressionist boundaries, so too did Cantor move mathematics in profoundly new directions. Whatever is said about this great and troubled man, we cannot help but admire his courage in exploring the nature of the infinite in an absolutely original way.

*—William Dunham: **Journey Through Genius: The Great Theorems of Mathematics**, 1991*

2. No one shall drive us from the paradise which Cantor created for us.

*—David Hilbert: 1926; In O.J. Becker; **Grundlaglen der Mathematik**, 1954*

17.17 Girolamo Cardano (Jerome Cardan) (1501–1576)

[Italian Mathematician]

1. The first of the notable mathematicians to pursue the mathematics of equations of higher degree and certainly the greatest combination of mathematician and rascal is Jerome Cardan.... He was aggressive, high-tempered, disagreeable, and even vindictive.... Because illness continued to harass him from enjoying life, he gambled daily for many years. This experience undoubtedly helped him to write a now famous book *On Games of Chance,* which treats the probabilities in gambling. He even gives advice on how to cheat, which was also gleaned from experience.

*—Morris Kline: **Mathematics for the Nonmathematician**, 1967*

2. Girolamo Cardan [Cardano] was a turbulent man of genius, very unscrupulous, very indiscreet, but of commanding mathematical ability. With strange versatility he was astrologer and philosopher, gambler and algebraist, physician yet father and defender of a murderer, heretic yet receiver of a pension from the Pope.... Yet Cardan combined piracy with a measure of honest toil; and he had enough mathematical genius in him to profit by these spoils.

*—Herbert Westren Turnbull: **The Great Mathematicians**; 1929, 1951*

17.18 "Lewis Carroll"–Charles Lutwidge Dodgson (1832–1898)

[English Mathematician]

1. There is a story that Queen Victoria was so struck with Lewis Carroll's Alice books that she sent out a courtier to bring back a copy of every other book that man had written, and the courtier returned with a bundle of mathematics books that the poor Queen could not read.

*—Howard W. Eves: **In Mathematical Circles**, 1969*

2. The Reverend Charles Lutwidge Dodgson was a mediocre mathematician who taught at Oxford for twenty-seven years without brightening the hour of a single student or producing anything of lasting value to his subject. Making in his own person no claim on men's remembrance, he created an immortal alter ego.... Lewis Carroll.

*—James R. Newman: **The World of Mathematics** 1956*

17.19 Augustin-Louis Cauchy (1789–1857)

[French Mathematician]

1. Cauchy is mad, and there is no way of being on good terms with him, although at present he is the only man who knows how mathematics should be treated. What he does is excellent, but very confused....

*—Niels Abel: **Letters**, vol. 2, 1826*

2. His [Augustin-Louis Cauchy's] scientific production was enormous. For long periods he appeared before the Academy once a week to present a new paper, so that the Academy, largely on his account, was obliged to introduce a rule restricting the number of articles a member could request to be published in a year.

*—Orsten Ore, 1948: Quoted in George F. Simmons: **Calculus Gems**, 1992 [Cauchy's 789 mathematics papers represented research in all of the known areas of mathematics of his day.]*

17.20 Arthur Cayley (1821–1895)

[English Mathematician]

1. During his professorship the higher education of women was a hotly contested issue. Cayley threw all his quiet, persuasive influence on the side of civilization and largely through his efforts women were at last admitted as students (in their own nunneries of course) to the monkish seclusion of medieval Cambridge.

—*Eric Temple Bell:* ***Men of Mathematics****, 1937*

2. Cayley did not start off making a living as a mathematican, but spent fourteen years as a lawyer before accepting the Sadlerian professorship at Cambridge. But he was always careful to restrict his law work so that it would not interfere with his mathematics interests. During his fourteen years in practice of law, Cayley published between two and three hundred papers in mathematics.

—*Howard W. Eves:* ***In Mathematical Circles****, 1969*

17.21 Emilie de Breteuil, Marquise du Chatelet (1706–1749)

[French Mathematician]

1. She pointed out that Newton had been overzealous in condemning hypotheses, while on the other hand, Descartes had excessively stressed the doctrine of intuition. She brought into focus that great thinkers sometimes err in their extremes and abhorred the fact that the doctrines of Descartes and Newton had become polar rallying points for seventeenth century science.

—*Lynn M. Osen:* ***Women in Mathematics****, 1999*

2. [She is] a great man whose only fault was in being a woman. A woman who translated and explained Newton ... in one word, a very great man.

—*Voltaire: Quoted in A. Maurois, "Voltaire," no date. [The French philosopher proudly but not untruthfully speaks of his mistress Emile de Breteuil, Marquise du Chatelet, who published a two-volume French translation and commentary on Newton's* ***Principia*** *and explained works of Leibniz in her* ***Instiutions de physique.****]*

17.22 William Kingdon Clifford (1845–1879)

[English Mathematician]

1. Much of Clifford's best work was actually spoken before it was written. He gave most of his public lectures with no visible preparation beyond very short notes, and the outline seemed to be filled in without effort or hesitation. Afterwards he would revise the lecture from a shorthands report, or sometimes write down from memory almost exactly what he had said. It fell out now and then, however, that neither of these things was done; in such cases there is now no record of the lecture at all.

—*F. Pollock:* ***Clifford's Lectures and Essays****, 1901*

2. [Clifford's gift of clarity] comes of profound and orderly understanding by virtue of which principles become luminous and deductions look easy.

—*Bertrand Russell: Preface to Clifford's* ***The Common Sense of the Exact Sciences****, James R. Newman, ed., 1946*

17.23 Nicolaus Copernicus (1473–1543)

[Polish Mathematician and Astronomer]

1. Copernicus, that learned wight
the glory of his nation,
With draughts of wine refreshed his sight,
and saw the earth's rotation.
Each planet then its orb described
The moon got under way, sir;
There truths from nature he imbibed
for he drank his bottle a day, sir!

—*August De Morgan: "The Astronomer's Drinking Song";* ***A Budget of Paradoxes****, 1872*

2. In 1543 Copernicus lay on his death-bed. Just before he lapsed into complete insensibility a newly printed book was placed in its dying author's hand. It was the book—today world famous—in which he had revived the theory of the movement of the earth [around the sun] that had been laid down by Aristarchus nearly three hundred years before the beginning of the Christian era. During the intervening eighteen centuries men had clung to the opinion held by Aristotle [who held that the earth was the fixed, unmoving center of the universe].

—*Alfred Hooper:* ***Makers of Mathematics****, 1948*

17.24 Jean Le Rond d'Alembert (1717–1783)

[French Mathematician and Philosopher]

1. D'Alembert was always surrounded by controversy.... He was a lightning rod which drew sparks from all foes of the philsophies.... Unfortunately he carried this ... pugnacity into his scientific research and once he had entered a controversy, he argued his cause with vigor and stubbornness. He closed his mind to the possibility that he might be wrong....

—*T.L. Hawkins:* ***Jean d'Alembert 1717–93****, 1963*

2. D'Alembert is on the short list of notable contributors to both mathematics and philosophy. His word of encouragement to a beginner in calculus is often quoted: "Continue, faith will come."

—*Reuben Hersh:* ***What Is Mathematics, Really?****, 1997*

17.25 Julius Wilhelm Richard Dedekind (1831–1916)

[German Mathematician]

1. Dedekind was led to his procedure for introducing the real numbers when he found it difficult in his lectures to give a clear definition of continuity, a property that is possessed by the ordered set of real numbers but that is not possessed by the ordered set of rational numbers.

*—Howard Eves: **Foundations and Fundamental Concepts of Mathematics**, 3rd ed., 1990*

2. Richard Dedekind was not only a great mathematician, but one of the wholly great in the history, now and in the past, the last hero of a great epoch, the last pupil of Gauss, for four decades himself a classic, from whose works not only we, but our teachers and the teachers of our teachers have drawn.

—Edmund Landau: Commemorative Address: Royal Society of Gottingen, 1917

17.26 Rene Descartes (1596–1650)

[French Mathematician and Philosopher]

1. One gets the impression that Descartes wrote *La geometrie* not to explain, but to boast about the power of his method. He built it about a difficult problem and the most important part of his method is presented, all too concisely, in the middle of the treatise for the reason that it was necessary for the solution of this problem.

*—Carl Boyer: **History of Analytic Geometry**, 1956*

2. [Descartes] dared ... to show intelligent minds how to throw off the yoke of scholasticism, of opinion, of authority—in a word, of prejudices and barbarism.... He can be thought of as a leader of conspirators who, before anyone else, had the courage to arise against a despotic and arbitrary power, and who, in preparing a resounding revolution, laid the foundations of a more just and happier government which he himself was not able to see established.

*—Jean Le Rond d'Alembert: Quoted in Reuben Hersh: **What Is Mathematics, Really?**, 1997*

3. Such was the state of Mathematics, and especially of Philosophy, until M. Descartes. This great man, moved by his genius and the superiority he felt inside, abandoned the ancients to follow only this very reason that the ancients had followed. And this happy boldness, which was treated as a revolt, gave us an infinity of new and useful views in Physics and in Geometry.

*—Bernard de Fontenelle: in "Preface" to G.F. l'Hopital: **Analyse des infiniment petits pour l'intelligence des lignes courbes**, 1696*

4. Philosophy students are supposed to read Descartes's *Discourse on Method* (1637). They don't realize that the complete *Discourse* includes Descartes' mathematical masterpiece, the *Geometry*.... On the other hand, mathematics students are also so miseducated. They're supposed to know that Descartes was a founder of analytic geometry, but not that his *Geometry* was part of a great work on philosophy.

*—Reuben Hersh: **What Is Mathematics, Really?**, 1997*

5. Descartes is the completest type which history presents of the purely mathematical type of mind—that in which the tendencies produced by mathematical cultivation reign unbalanced and supreme.

*—John Stuart Mill: **An Examination of Sir William Hamilton's Philosophy**, 1878*

17.27 Diophantus and Diophantine Equations (c. 200–c. 284)

[Greek Mathematician]

1. Diophantus can be considered the inventor of Algebra....

*—Joseph-Louis Lagrange: 1795, **Oeuvres**, Vol. 7*

2. This tomb holds Diophantus. Ah, what a marvel! And the tomb tells scientifically the measure of his life. God vouchsafed that he should be a boy for the sixth part of his life: when a twelfth was added, his cheeks acquired a beard; He kindled for him the light of marriage after a seventh, and in the fifth year after his marriage He granted him a son. Alas! late-begotten and miserable child, when he had reached the measure of half his father's life, the chill grave took him. After consoling his grief by this science of numbers for four years, he reached the end of his life.

*—Metrodorus: **Greek Anthology**, c. A.D. 500: In Ivor Thomas: "Greek Mathematics"; in J.R. Newman, ed. **The World of Mathematics**, 1956 [Can you calculate he number of years Diophantus lived?]*

3. The symbolism that Diophantus introduced for the first time, and undoubtedly devised himself, provided a short and readily comprehensible means of expressing an equation.... Since an abbreviation is also employed for the word "equals," Diophantus took a fundamental step from verbal algebra towards symbolic algebra.

*—K. Vogel: "Diophantus": **Dictionary of Scientific Biography**, 1970—1990*

17.28 Paul Erdos (1913–1996)

[Hungarian Mathematician]

1. To find another life this century as intensely devoted to abstraction, one must reach back to Ludwig Wittgenstein (1889–1951), who stripped his life bare for philosophy. But whereas Wittgenstein discarded his family fortune as a form of self-torture, Mr. Erdos gave away most of the money he earned because he simply did not need it.... And where Wittgenstein was driven by near suicidal compulsions, Mr. Erdos simply constructed his life to extract the maximum amount of happiness.

—Anonymous: "Paul Erdos"; Obituary; ***The Economist****, October 5, 1996*

2. With 485 co-authors, Erdos collaborated with more people than any other mathematician in history. Those lucky 485 are said to have an Erdos number of 1, a coveted code phrase in the mathematical world for having written a paper with the master himself. If your Erdos number is 2, it means you have published with someone who has published with Erdos. If your Erdos number is 3, you have published with someone who has published with someone who has published with Erdos. Einstein had an Erdos number of 2, and the highest number of a working mathematician is 7. The great unwashed who have never written a mathematical paper have an Erdos number of "infinity."

—Paul Hoffman: ***The Man Who Loved Only Numbers****, 1998*

3. His [Paul Erdos] language had a special vocabulary—not just "the SF" (Supreme Fascist; i.e. "God") and "epsilon" (a small child) but also "bosses" (women), "slaves" (men), "captured" (married), "liberated" (divorced), "recaptured" (remarried), "Noise" (music), "Poison" (alcohol), "preaching" (giving a mathematics lecture), "Sam" (the United States), and "Joe" (The Soviet Union). When he said someone had "died," Erdos meant that the person had stopped doing mathematics. When he said someone had "left," the person had died.

—Paul Hoffman: ***The Man Who Loved Only Numbers****, 1998*

4. Paul Erdos was one of those very special geniuses, the kind who comes along only once in a very long while yet he chose, quite consciously I am sure, to share mathematics with mere mortals—like me. And for this, I will always be grateful to him. I will miss the times he prowled my hallways at 4:00 A.M. and came to my bed to ask whether my "brain is open." I will miss the problems and conjectures and the stimulating conversations about anything and everything. But most of all, I will just miss Paul, the human. I loved him dearly.

—Tom Trotter: Quoted in Paul Hoffman: ***The Man Who Loved Only Numbers****, 1998*

17.29 Euclid and His Elements (c. 325–c. 265 B.C.)

[Greek Mathematician]

1. At the age of 12 I experienced a second wonder ... in a little book dealing with Euclidean plane geometry ... [there] were [mathematical] assertions ... which—though by no means evident could nevertheless be proved with such certainty that any doubt appeared to be out of the question. This lucidity and certainty made an indescribable impression on me.

—Albert Einstein: "Autobiographical Notes," in ***Albert Einstein: Philosopher-Scientist*** *Paul A. Schilpp, ed., 1951*

2. This wonderful book, with all its imperfections, which are indeed slight enough when account is taken of the date it appeared, is and will doubtless remain the greatest mathematical textbook of all time....

—T.L. Heath: ***A History of Greek Mathematics****, Part I, 1931*

3. His was the master mind that was able to collect all the muddled, confused pieces of a vast mathematical jigsaw puzzle and put them together in such a way that a clear and beautiful picture suddenly emerged from what had been a welter of odds and ends of mathematical knowledge. This was the reason why his textbook proved to be the world's best-seller.

—Alfred Hooper: ***Makers of Mathematics****, 1948*

4. There is no single book about metaphysics like we have in mathematics. If you want to know what mathematics is, just look at Euclid's Elements.

—Immanuel Kant: ***Prolegomena to any Future Metaphysics****, 1783*

5. The Elements of Euclid is as small a part of mathematics as the Iliad is of literature; or as the sculpture of Phidias is of the world's total art.

—C.J. Keyser: ***Lectures on Science, Philosophy and Art****, 1908*

6. I said, "Lincoln, you can never make a lawyer if you do not understand what demonstrate means"; and I left my situation in Springfield, went home to my father's house, and stayed there till I could give any proposition in the six books of Euclid at sight. I then found out what "demonstrate," means, and went back to my law studies."

—Abraham Lincoln: ***The Face of Lincoln****; James Mellon, ed., 1979*

7. Old Euclid drew a circle
On a sand-beach long ago.
He bounded and enclosed it
With angles thus and so.

—*Vachel Lindsay: "Euclid"; **The Congo and Other Poems**, 1914*

8. When first the shaft into his vision shone
Of light anatomized! Euclid alone
Has looked on Beauty bare. Fortunate
they
Who, though once only and then but far
away,
Have heard her massive sandal set on
stone.

—*Edna St. Vincent Millay: "Euclid Alone Has Looked on Beauty Bare," **Harp-Weaver and Other Poems**, 1923*

9. People who read *The Elements* for the first time often get a feeling that things are missing: it has no preface or introduction, no statement of objectives, and it offers no motivation or commentary. Most strikingly, there is no mention of the scientific and technological uses to which many of the theorems can be put, nor any warning that large sections of the work have no practical use at all.... The theorems are included for their own sake, because they are interesting in themselves. This attitude of self-sufficiency is the hallmark of pure mathematics.

—*Richard J. Trudeau: **Dots and Lines**, 1976*

17.30 Leonhard Euler (1707–1783)

[Swiss Mathematician]

1. Euler could have been called, almost without metaphor and certainly without hyperbole, analysis incarnate.... [He] calculated without apparent effort, as men breathe, or as eagles sustain themselves in the wind.

—*Dominique Francois Jean Arago: **Oeuvres**, 1854; Quoted in E.T. Bell: **Men of Mathematics**, 1937*

2. [Euler] preferred instructing his pupils to the little satisfaction of amazing them.

—*Marquise de Condorcet [Marie Jean Antoine Nicolas Caritat]: c. 1771; Quoted in G.L. Alexanderson "Ars Expositions: Euler as Writer and Teacher"; **Mathematics Magazine**, vol. 56; November, 1983*

3. I have here a geometer (Euler) who is a big Cyclops ... who has only one eye left, and a new curve, which he is presently computing, could render him totally blind.

—*King Frederick II; c. 1760; Quoted in D. Spiers: **Leonhard Euler**, 1929*

4. Read Euler; he is our master in everything.

—*Pierre Simon de Laplace: c. 1790; Quoted in E.T. Bell: **Men of Mathematics**, 1937*

5. Intrigued by the mapmakers' difficulties, [Euler] proved conclusively that what they had been trying to accomplish [develop a map of the world with no distortions] was in fact impossible. There is no map of any portion of the earth's surface which, translated onto a flat sheet of paper has a fixed scale. Every map, in fact, is a compromise.

—*Robert Osserman: **Poetry of the Universe**, 1995*

6. The whole form of mathematical thinking was created by Euler. It is only with the greatest of difficulty that one is able to follow the writings of any author preceding Euler, because it was not yet known how to let the formulas speak for themselves. This art Euler was the first one to teach.

—*Ferdinand Rudio: Quoted in D. MacHale: **Comic Sections**, 1993*

18

Some Mathematical People II

18.1 Pierre Fermat (1601–1665)

[French Mathematician]

1. The conceptual essence of analytic geometry, the "isomorphism" or exact translation between algebra and geometry, was understood more clearly by Fermat than by Descartes. Fermat's analytic geometry predated Descartes's, but it wasn't published until 1679.

—Reuben Hersh: ***What Is Mathematics, Really?****, 1997*

2. A mathematician named Pierre
Thought "I wonder if someone will care
If I say there's a proof
And then (somewhat aloof)
Admit I can't fit it in here.

—Jonathan Matte; in ***Fermat's Last Theorem Poetry Challenge****, 1995–6*

3. A mathematician named Wiles
Came up with a proof for the files
He stretched Fermat's margin
And managed to barge in
Where others lay felled on their trials.

—Matt Perriens: in ***Fermat's Last Theorem Poetry Challenge****, 1995–6*

18.2 Joseph Fourier (1768–1830)

[French Mathematician]

1. It seems that [Fourier] from his experience in Egypt, and maybe his work on heat, became convinced that desert heat is the ideal condition for good health. He accordingly clothed himself in many layers of garments and lived in rooms of unbearably high temperatures. It has been said that this obsession with heat hastened his death, by heart disease, thoroughly cooked, in his sixty-third year.

—Howard Eves: ***An Introduction to the History of Mathematics****, 1976*

2. Fourier is a mathematical poem.

—William [Lord Kelvin] Thomson: Quoted in W. Thompson & P.G. Tait: ***Treatise on Natural Philosophy****, 1890*

18.3 Gottlob Frege (1848–1925)

[German Mathematician]

1. A scientist can hardly meet with anything more undesirable than to have the foundation give way just as the work is finished. A letter from Mr. Bertrand Russell put me in this position at the moment the work [his two-volume *Fundamental Laws of Mathematics*] was nearly through the press.

—Gottlob Frege: Quoted in Morris Kline: ***Mathematics: The Loss of Certainty****, 1980 [Russell warned Frege that his work involved a concept, the set of all sets, that can lead to a contradiction.]*

2. Frege is now a hero to philosophers, but mainly for his interesting insights into language in general. His neglect during his lifetime is normally explained as due to his unusual notation, which used a two-dimensional presentation of symbols in order to reduce substantially the need for brackets....

—Ivor Grattan-Guinness: ***The Rainbow of Mathematics****, 1997*

18.4 Galileo Galilei (1564–1642)

[Italian Astronomer, Physicist and Mathematician]

1. A man does not attain the status of Galileo merely because he is persecuted, he must also be right.

—Stephen Jay Gould: ***Ever Since Darwin****, 1977*

2. If Galileo had said in verse that the world moved, the Inquisition might have let him alone.

—Thomas Hardy: In F.E. Hardy: ***The Later Years of Thomas Hardy****, 1930*

3. Be of good cheer, Galileo, and appear in public. If I am not mistaken, there are only a few among the distinguished mathematicians of Europe who would disassociate themselves from us....

—Johannes Kepler: Letter to Galileo; October 13, 1597; Quoted in Howard Eves: ***In Mathematical Circles****, 1969*

4. Galileo did more than any monarch has done to change the world, and his power immeasurably exceeded that of his persecutors. He had therefore no need to aim at becoming a persecutor in his turn.

—Bertrand Russell: ***In Praise of Idleness****, 1935*

18.5 Evariste Galois (1811–1832)

[French Mathematician]

1. Early in the morning of May 31, 1832, Galois died [killed in a duel], being then in the twenty-first year of his age. He was buried in the common ditch of the South Cemetery, so that today there remains no trace of the grave of Evariste Galois. His enduring monument is his collected works. They fill sixty pages.

—E. T. Bell: ***Men of Mathematics****, 1937*

2. Genius is condemned by a malicious social organization to an eternal denial of justice in favor of fawning mediocrity.

—Eustace Galois: Quoted in E. T. Bell: ***Men of Mathematics****, 1937*

3. In France, about 1830, a new star of unimaginable brightness appeared in the heavens of pure mathematics ... Evariste Galois.

—Felix Klein: Quoted in Leopold Infeld: ***Whom the Gods Love: The Story of Evariste Galois****, 1948*

4. The night before the duel in which Galois was killed he wrote a letter to his friend Auguste Chevalier in which he set forth briefly his discovery of the connection of the theory of groups with the solution of equations by radicals. In this letter, written apparently under the impression that the result of the duel would be fatal to himself, he asked that it be published in the Revue encyclopedique, a wish that was carried out the same year (1832).

—David Eugene Smith: ***A Source Book in Mathematics****, 1959*

18.6 Carl Friedrich Gauss (1777–1855)

[German Mathematician]

1. He [Carl Friedrich Gauss] is like the fox, who effaces his tracks in the sand with his tail.

—Niels H. Abel: c. 1825; Quoted in G.F. Simmons; ***Calculus Gems****, 1992*

2. [Gauss is] the mathematical giant who, from his lofty heights, embraces in one view the stars and the abysses.

—Wolfgang (Farkas) Bolyai; speaking of his very dear friend and fellow-student from 1796 to 1799 at Göttingen University, Carl Friedrich Gauss.

3. All that Gauss has written is first rate; the interesting thing would be to show the influence of his different memoirs in bringing to their present condition the subjects to which they relate, but this is to write a History of Mathematics from the year 1800.

—Arthur Cayley: c. 1883; Quoted in Howard Eves: ***Mathematical Circles Squared****, 1972*

4. Asked by the university [Göttingen] to investigate the administration of the widows and orphans pension fund and work our reform proposals, he fulfilled this assignment so thoroughly that his memorandum served as the beginning of modern actuarial mathematics.

—Richard Courant: "Gauss and the Present Situation of the Exact Sciences" in ***The Spirit and the Uses of the Mathematical Sciences****; Thomas L. Saaty & F. Joachim Weyl, eds., 1969*

5. Thou nature, art my goddess; to thy laws
My services are bound....

—Carl Friedrich Gauss: His motto, adopted from Shakespeare's ***King Lear*** *[Another of his mottos was "Few, but ripe."]*

6. [He was] born in 1777 in Brunswick. He came of a family which for generations had been very humble folk—gardeners, stonecutters, bricklayers. It was only by a fortunate chance that Gauss himself did not become a bricklayer.

—Alfred Hooper: ***Makers of Mathematics****, 1948 [Fortunately, the Duke of Brunswick became aware of young Gauss' mathematical precocity and paid for his education.]*

7. Gauss had the intellectual courage to create non-Euclidean geometry but not the moral courage to face the mobs who would have called the creator mad, for the scientists of the early nineteenth century lived in the shadow of Kant whose pronouncement that there could be no geometry other than Euclidean geometry ruled the intellectual world. Gauss' work on non-Euclidean geometry was found among his papers after his death.

—Morris Kline: ***Mathematics in Western Culture****, 1953*

8. Gauss always strove to give his investigations the form of finished works of art. He did not rest until her had succeeded, and hence he never published a work until it had achieved the form he wanted. He used to say that when a fine building was finished, the scaffolding should no longer be visible.

—*Sartorius von Walterhausen: In E. Worbs,* ***Carl Friedrich Gauss,*** *1955*

18.7 Sophie Germain (1776–1831)

[French Mathematician]

1. [Sophie Germain] never hesitated to compete with her contemporary [mathematical] giants, all male, for the most difficult problems, the harder, the better or the more significant. Her unerring instinct, as it were, would always direct her to such "significant" problems. And, of course, there was always her magnificent talent to solve them somehow or other.

—*J. Fang: "Mathematicians, man or woman: Exercises in a Verstehen-approach";* ***Philosophia Mathematica,*** *1976/77*

2. A taste for the abstract sciences in general and above all the mysteries of numbers is excessively rare: one is not astonished at it; the enchanting charms of this sublime science reveal themselves only to those who have the courage to go deeply into it. But when a person of the sex which, according to our customs and prejudices, must encounter infinitely more difficulties than men to familiarize herself with these thorny researches, succeeds nevertheless in surmounting these obstacles and penetrating the most obscure part of them, then without doubt she must have the noblest courage, quite extraordinary talents and a superior genius.

—*Carl Friedrich Gauss: Letter to Sophie Germain; April 30, 1807; in E.T. Bell:* ***Men of Mathematics,*** *1947; Quoted in John Fauvel & Jeremy Gray:* ***The History of Mathematics: A Reader,*** *1987 [Gauss responds to a letter from Germain in which she reveals that she is in fact the M. Leblanc who had corresponded with him about her mathematical work in number theory.]*

18.8 Kurt Goedel (1906–1978)

[Austrian-American Mathematician and Logician]

1. In [1931] ... Goedel proved a sweeping theorem to the effect that mathematical statements existed for which no systematic procedure could determine whether they are either true or false. This was a no-go theorem with a vengeance, because it provided an irrefutable demonstration that something in mathematics is actually impossible, even in principle. The fact that there exist undecidable propositions in mathematics came as a great shock, because it seemed to undermine the entire logical foundations of the subject.

—*Paul Davies:* ***The Mind of God,*** *1992*

2. Goedel ... mistrusted common sense as a means of discovering truth. It is said that for several years he resisted becoming an American citizen because he found logical contradictions in the Constitution.

—*Howard W. Eves:* ***Return to Mathematical Circles,*** *1988*

3. ...Goedel's Theorem shows that human thought is more complex and less mechanical than anyone had ever believed, but after the initial flurry of the excitement in the 1930s, the result ossified into a piece of technical mathematics ... and became the private property of the mathematical logic establishment, and many of these academics were contemptuous of any suggestion that the theorem could have something to do with the real world.

—*Rudy Rucker:* ***Mind Tools,*** *1987*

4. Speaking of the deductive method, it is a sad reflection on the intellectual level of mathematical education that, unless he takes courses in logic, the mathematics student may get his degree without having heard about Goedel or about his monumental discovery of the intrinsic limitations of the deductive method, a discovery widely recognized as one of the greatest intellectual accomplishments of the 20th century.

—*Abe Shenitzer: "Teaching Mathematics: in* ***Mathematics Tomorrow,*** *L.A. Steen, ed., 1981*

18.9 John Graunt (1620–1674)

[English Shopowner]

1. Statistics was founded by John Graunt of London, a "haberdasher of small-wares" in a tiny book called *Natural and Political Observations made upon the Bills of Mortality* [1662]. It was the first attempt to interpret mass biological phenomena and social behavior from numerical data—in this case, fairly crude figures of births and deaths in London from 1604 to 1661.

—*James R. Newman:* ***The World of Mathematics*** *1956*

2. [John Graunt] not only gave a sound analysis of this problem [the calculation of annuity prices], but he put his results in such a convenient form that this table of mortality has remained the pattern for all subsequent tables, as to its fundamental form of expression.

—*Lowell J. Reed: in "Introduction"; Edmund Halley:* ***Degrees of Mortality of Mankind,*** *1942*

18.10 Sir William Rowan Hamilton (1805–1865)

[Irish Mathematician]

1. ...Hamilton wrestled with the problem of quaternion multiplication for fifteen years, and the story goes that one evening, while walking along the Royal Canal with his wife just before dusk, he was struck by a flash of inspiration. Not having any pencil or paper with him, he took out a pocket knife and scratched the unorthodox multiplication table for quaternions into the stone of the Brougham Bridge. Today there is a cement tablet embedded in the stone and it tells the story.

Here as he walked by
on the 16th of October 1843
Sir William Rowan Hamilton
in a flash of genius discovered
the fundamental formula for
quaternion multiplication
$i^2 = j^2 = k^2 = ijk = -1$
& cut in a stone of this bridge

*—Joseph Ayton: "Historically Speaking Section"; **The Mathematics Teacher**, October, 1969*

2. Hamilton had great confidence in himself. He never seems to have debated as to whether what he was doing was important. He wrote down everything and kept the notes. Most of his notes were coherently and legibly written, and those selected for publication required little editing. He wrote a small clear hand, generally using large notebooks with dated entries. He seldom made an error.... He liked to refer to himself in the words of Ptolemy used of Hipparchus: a lover of labor and a lover of truth.

*—J.L. Synge: "The Life and early Work of Sir William Rowan Hamilton"; **Scripta Mathematica**, 1945*

18.11 Godfrey H. Hardy (1877–1947)

[English Mathematician]

1. G.H. Hardy, one of England's foremost mathematicians and an outstanding expert in analytical number theory, possessed a rebellious spirit. He once listed his four most ardent wishes: (1) to prove the Reimann hypothesis, (2) to make a brilliant play in a critical cricket match, (3) to prove the nonexistence of God, and (4) to assassinate Benito Mussolini.

*—Howard W. Eves: Quoted in Howard Eves: **Return to Mathematical Circles**, 1988*

2. In Hardy's view God had nothing more important to do than frustrate Hardy. This led to a sort of insurance policy for Hardy one time when he was trying to get back to Cambridge after a visit to [Harald] Bohr in Denmark. The weather was bad and there was only a small boat available. Hardy thought there was a real possibility the boat would sink. So he sent a postcard to Bohr saying: "I proved the Riemann Hypothesis. G.H. Hardy." That way if the boat sank, everyone would think that Hardy had proved the Riemann Hypothesis. God could not allow so much glory for Hardy so he could not allow the boat to sink.

*—George Polya: **A Polya Picture Album**; G.L. Alexanderson, ed., 1987*

3. Hardy always referred to God as his personal enemy. This was of course, a joke, but there was something real behind it. He took his disbelief in the doctrines of religion more seriously than most people seem to do. He would not enter a religious building, even for such a purpose as the election of a Warden of New College.

*—E.C. Titchmarsh: "Geoffrey Harold Hardy 1877–1947"; **Collected Papers of G.H. Hardy**, 1966*

18.12 Hermann von Helmholtz (1821–1894)

[German Physicist, Physiologist and Mathematician]

1. Helmholtz—the physiologist who learned physics for the sake of his physiology, and mathematics for the sake of his physics, and is now in the first rank of all three.

*—William Kingdom Clifford: Quoted in **The World of Mathematics**, vol. 1, 1956*

2. [Helmholtz] rejected Kant's view that the properties of space are integral parts of our understanding, determined by the "given form of our capacity of intuition. All we know, he said, is what we have learned from experience.

*—James R. Newman: **The World of Mathematics**, vol. 1, 1956*

18.13 Charles Hermite (1822–1901)

[French Mathematician]

1. Those who have had the good fortune to be students of the great mathematician [Charles Hermite] cannot forget the almost religious accent of his teaching, the shudder of beauty or mystery that he sent through his audience, at some admirable discovery or before the unknown.

*—Paul Painleve: Quoted in Francois Le Lionnais: "Beauty in Mathematics" in **Great Currents of Mathematics**, F. Le Lionnais, ed., 1971*

2. Talk with M. [Charles] Hermite. He never evokes a concrete image, yet you soon perceive that the most abstract entities are to him like living creatures.

*—Henri Poincare: Quoted in G.F. Simmons: **Calculus Gems**, 1992*

18.14 David Hilbert (1862–1943)

[German Mathematician]

1. We are used to the common doctrine according to which [David] Hilbert outlived his friend Minkowski by over thirty years, and was permitted to go on accomplishing important work. But who would care to say if his lonely death in the dark Nazi days was not even more tragic than Minkowski's at the height of his power?

—*Max Born: Quoted in Howard Eves:* ***Mathematical Circles Squared****, 1972*

2. Mathematicians of this century have been singularly fortunate in having a ready-made and inspiring list of problems to work on. It consists of 23 searching questions put together by David Hilbert and presented at the International Congress of Mathematicians in Paris in 1900. Several of the problems have been solved (and have made the reputation of their solvers); many of them are still open.

—*Paul Halmos: "Innovation in Mathematics";* ***Scientific American****, September, 1958*

3. There is a much quoted story about David Hilbert, who one day noticed that a certain student had stopped attending class. When told that the student had decided to drop mathematics to become a poet, Hilbert replied, "Good—he did not have enough imagination to become a mathematician."

—*Robert Osserman:* ***Poetry of the Universe****, 1995*

4. Somebody allegedly asked Hilbert, "If you could revive, like Barbarossa [the emperor Frederick I], after five hundred years, what would you do?" "I would ask," said Hilbert, "Has somebody proved the Riemann hypothesis?"

—*George Polya: "Some Mathematicians I Have Known";* ***The American Mathematical Monthly*** *September, 1969*

18.15 Hipparchus of Rhodes (190 B.C.–120 B.C.)

[Greek Astronomer, Geographer and Mathematician]

1. Even if he did not invent it, Hipparchus is the first person whose systematic use of trigonometry we have documentary evidence.

—*T.L. Heath:* ***A History of Greek Mathematics****, 1931*

2. Hipparchus is also credited with a method to determine latitude and longitude by astronomical means, but antiquity never was able to muster a scientific organization sufficient to do any large-scale mapping.

—*Dirk J. Struik:* ***A Concise History of Mathematics****, 1948*

18.16 Christiaan Huygens (1629–1695)

[Dutch Physicist, Astronomer and Mathematician]

1. ...Huygens was the greatest mechanist of the seventeenth century. He combined Galielo's mathematical treatment of phenomena with Descartes' vision of the ultimate design of nature. Beginning as an ardent Cartesian who sought to correct the more glaring errors of the system, he ended up as one of the sharpest critics....

—*A.E. Bell:* ***Christiaan Huygens and the Development of Science in the Seventeenth Century****, 1947*

2. [Huygens] applied his mathematical discoveries to formulating the theory of a cycloidal pendulum clock, in which the pendulum bob is compelled to move along a cycloidal path instead of a circular path, and in which the period of oscillation is ... exactly the same regardless of the magnitude of the swing, thereby eliminating the circular error.

—*George F. Simmons:* ***Calculus Gems****, 1992 [Huygens discovered that the cycloid was the solution to the* ***tautochrone*** *problem: to find the curve along which a particle moving under the force of gravity will take the same time to reach a given final point, regardless of where the starting point was.]*

18.17 Hypatia (c. 370–415)

[Greek Mathematician and Philosopher]

1. [Hypatia was], among the women of antiquity what Sappho was in poetry and what Aspasia was in philosophy and eloquence—the chiefest glory of her sex. In profundity of knowledge and variety of attainments she had few peers among her contemporaries and she is entitled to a conspicuous place among such luminaries of science as Ptolemy, Euclid, Apollonius, Diophantus and Hipparchus.

—*J.J. Mozans:* ***Women in Science****, 1913 [An intimate friend of Orestes, the prefect of Alexandria, Hypatia incurred the wrath of the Archbishop Cyril. On day during Lent, Christians tore her from her chariot, dragged her to the church, where they brutally butchered her.]*

2. In an era in which the domains of intellect and politics were almost exclusively male. Theron [Hypatia's father] was an unusually liberated person who taught an unusually gifted daughter and encouraged her to achieve things that, as far as we know, no woman before her did or perhaps even dreamed of doing.

—*Ian Mueller:* ***Women of Mathematics****, 1987*

18.18 Johannes Kepler (1571–1630)

[German Astronomer, Mathematician and Physicist]

1. The story of his [Kepler's] persistence in spite of persecution and domestic tragedies that would have broken an ordinary man is one of the most heroic in science.... Undeterred by poverty, failure, domestic tragedy, and persecution, but sustained by the mystical belief in an attainable mathematical harmony and perfection of nature, Kepler persisted for fifteen years before finding the simple regularity [of planetary orbits] he sought....

—*E. T. Bell:* ***The Search for Truth****, 1949*

2. Ardent, restless, burning to distinguish himself by discovery, he attempted everything; and once having obtained a glimpse of a clue, no labor was too hard in following or verifying it. A few of his attempts succeeded—a multitude failed. Those which failed seem to us now fanciful, those which succeeded appear to us sublime.

—*David Brewster: Quoted in Oliver Lodge: "Johann Kepler" in* ***The World of Mathematics****, vol. 1, James R. Newman, ed., 1956*

18.19 Omar Khayyam (c. 1050–c. 1122)

[Persian Poet and Mathematician]

1. Although the English-speaking world primarily knows [Umar] al-Khayyami as the poet Omar Khayyam because of Edward Fitzgerald's translation of the Rubaiyat, to his contemporaries al-Khayyami was primarily a master of the mathematical sciences.

—*Ronald Calinger:* ***Classics of Mathematics****, Ronald Calinger, ed., 1982*

2. By the help of God and with His precious assistance, I say that Algebra is a scientific art.... The perfection of this art consists in the knowledge of the scientific method by which one determines numerical and geometrical unknowns.

—*Omar Khayyam:* ***Algebra****; Quoted in Vivian S. Groza:* ***A Survey of Mathematics****, 1968*

18.20 Felix Klein (1849–1925)

[German Mathematician]

1. There are two kinds of mathematicians at Göttingen—those who do what they want but not what Klein wants, and those who do what Klein wants but not what they want. Klein is clearly of neither kind. Therefore Klein is not a mathematician.

—*Anonymous; Syllogism concerning Felix Klein; Quoted in Howard Eves:* ***Mathematical Circles Squared****, 1972*

2. What Klein was arguing [in his Erlanger Program introduced in 1872] is that it is the group of transformations that gives a geometry its "individuality," not the objects, and that we should focus our attention on how things transform under the elements of some group instead of looking at the things themselves.

—*John L. Casti:* ***Five Golden Rules****, 1996*

3. On his fiftieth birthday, [Felix] Klein was honored in Turin where Grace [Chisholm Young] was then studying. At dinner he was seated next to Grace, said to be his favorite pupil, and he whispered to her: "Ah, I envy you. You are in the happy age of productivity. When everyone begins to speak well of you, you are on the downward road.

—*Sylvia Wiegand: "Grace Chisholm Young";* ***Association for Women in Mathematics Newsletter*** *7, May–June, 1977*

18.21 Sonja Sophia Kovalevsky (Kovalevskaya) (1850–1891)

[Russian Mathematician]

1. Sonja Kovalevsky united a glowing interest for mathematics with a great talent for comprehension and a similar capacity for adaptation. It is to be wondered that she, in spite of her many interests in different fields and in spite of her changeful life, has accomplished so much in mathematics.

—*Felix Klein:* ***Vorlesungen uber die Entwicklung der Mathematik****, 1926*

2. Say what you know, do what you must, come what may.

—*Sonja Kovalevsky: Motto on her paper "On the Problem of the Rotation of a Solid Body About a Fixed Point";* ***Acta Mathematica****, 12; 1888–1889*

3. A female professor of mathematics is a pernicious and unpleasant phenomenon—even, one might say, a monstrosity; and her [Sonja Kovalevsky] invitation to a country where there are so many male mathematicians far superior in learning to her can be explained only by the gallantry of the Swedes toward the female sex.

—*August Strindberg, 1884 [Strindberg refers to the appointment of Sonja Kovalevsky as professor of mathematics at Stockholm University.]*

4. I do not need to tell you how much your success has gladdened the hearts of myself and my sisters, also of your friends here. I particularly experienced a true satisfaction; competent judges have now delivered their verdict that my 'faithful pupil,' my 'weakness' is indeed not a 'frivolous humbug.'

—Karl Weierstrass: Letter to Sonja Kovalevsky; Quoted in E.T. Bell: ***Men of Mathematics****, 1937 [Written on the occasion of Kovalevsky receiving the Bordin Prize of the French Academy of Sciences.]*

18.22 Leopold Kronecker (1823–1891)

[German Mathematician]

1. Kronecker [maintained] that there were actually no mathematical entities other than the natural numbers. He sought to expunge all other quantities from mathematics, believing that fractions, irrationals, and complex numbers were illusory concepts that had arisen merely through some misguided application of mathematical logic to the artifacts of the physical world. Eventually, he believed, a way would be found to recast those subjects into their most natural and elementary form wherein only the natural numbers would appear.

—John D. Barrow: ***Pi in the Sky****, 1992*

2. Kronecker was what is called an "algorist" in most of his works. He aimed to make concise, expressive formulas tell the story and automatically reveal the action from one step to the next so that, when the climax was reached, it was possible to glance back over the whole development and see the apparent inevitability of the conclusion from the premises. Details and accessory aids were ruthlessly pruned away until only the main trunk of the argument stood forth in naked strength and simplicity. In short, Kronecker was an artist who used mathematical formulas as his medium.

—E.T. Bell: ***Men of Mathematics****, 1937*

3. Kronecker too made many discoveries. But if he succeeded it was by forgetting that he was a philosopher and by voluntarily letting go of his principles, which were condemned in advance to sterility.

—Henri Poincare: "L'Oeuvre Mathematique de Weierstrass"; ***Acta Mathematica****, 1899*

18.23 Joseph-Louis Lagrange (1736–1813)

[French Mathematician]

1. Lagrange is the lofty pyramid of the mathematical sciences.

—Napoleon Bonaparte; c. 1800; Quoted in E.T. Bell: ***Men of Mathematics****, 1937*

2. Of all styles, algebraic ones are especially marked for their tenacity. With Lagrange, who wished to algebraize all the main theories of his time, their place is very clear and important.

—Ivor Grattan-Guinness: ***The Rainbow of Mathematics****, 1997*

3. [Antoine] Lavoisier, one of the founders of modern chemistry ... was guillotined in 1794, ... his execution [caused] even the quiet Lagrange to exclaim in protest, "It only took a moment to cause this head to fall; maybe a hundred years will be insufficient to produce one like it."

—Alfred Hooper: ***Makers of Mathematics****, 1948*

18.24 Imre Lakatos (1922–1974)

[Hungarian Mathematician]

1. [Proofs and Refutations is] an overwhelming work. The effect of its polemical brilliance, its complexity of argument and self-conscious sophistication,, its sheer weight of historical learning, is to dazzle the reader.

—Reuben Hersh: "Introducing Imre Lakatos": ***The Mathematical Intelligencer****, vol. 1, 3, 1978*

2. Mathematics develops, according to Lakatos,... —by a process of conjecture, followed by attempts to "prove" the conjecture (i.e. to reduce it to other conjectures) followed by criticism via attempts to produce counterexamples both to the conjectured theorem and to the various steps in the proof.

—J. Worrall: "Imre Lakatos (1922–1974): Philosopher of Mathematics and Philosopher of Science"; ***Z. Algemeine Wissen-schaftstheorie****, vol. 5, 2, 1974*

18.25 Pierre-Simon de Laplace (1749–1827)

[French Mathematician]

1. [J.B.] Biot, who assisted Laplace in revising it [The Mecanique Celeste] for the press, says that Laplace himself was frequently unable to recover the details in the chain of reasoning, and if satisfied that the conclusions were correct, he was content to insert the constantly recurring formula, "Il est aise a voir" (It is easy to see).

—W.W. Rouse Ball: ***History of Mathematics****, 1901*

2. I never come across one of Laplace's 'Thus it plainly appears' without feeling that I have hours of hard work before me to fill up the chasm and find out and show how plainly it appears.

—Nathaniel Bowditch: Quoted in F. Cajori: ***Teaching and History of mathematics in the U.S.****, 1896*

3. What we know is not much. What we do not know is immense.

—Pierre Simon de Laplace: in August De Morgan: ***Budget of Paradoxes****, 1915*

18.26 Henri Lebesque (1875–1941)

[French Mathematician]

1. Lebesque excelled in looking at old things with new eyes. He knew the virtue of attentive examination of an example, of an anomaly, of an exception. He was suspicious of too general theories whose formalism and verbalism repelled him. He had a geometric vision of mathematical facts and preferred synthetic insights which satisfy and nourish the mind to analytic proofs which reassure it.

*—P. Montel: "Notice Necrologique sur M. Henri Lebesque"; **Comptes Rendus**, 215, August 4, 1941*

2. Lebesque introduced his notion of measure: "no more fundamental subject than this," he wrote in 1931, referring to the role this concept has played in man's history. Basing his work upon his now standard notion of measure, Lebesque defined his integration, which definition is now also standard, since it brought unity to the field.

*—Dirk J. Struik: **A Concise History of Mathematics**, 1948*

18.27 Solomon Lefschetz (1884–1972)

[Russian-born American Mathematician]

1. [Lefschetz's] method of organizing seminars on topics in which he was interested and then continually heckling the speaker was typical of the way in which he got things done. It was somewhat harassing for a young man not accustomed to it, but it was kindly meant, and often helpful. Eventually it became so famous that it earned Lefschetz a verse in the song sung by Princeton students about members of the Faculty:

Here's to Lefschetz (Solomon L.)
Who's as argumentative as hell,
When he's at last beneath the sod,
Then he'll start to heckle God.

*—William Hodge: "Solomon Lefschetz" **Bulletin of the London Mathematical Society**, 6, March, 1974*

2. [Lefschetz took Topology] for the title of this first book of his, published in 1930 in the Colloquium Series of the American Mathematical Society. There was an earlier volume in that series, written by [Oswald] Veblen, called Analysis Situs. Lefschetz wanted a distinctive title and also, as he would say, a snappy title, so he decided to borrow the word Topologie from German.... Once he decided on it, he conducted a campaign to get everyone to use it. His campaign succeeded very quickly, mainly I think because of the derivative words: topologist, topologize, topological. That doesn't go so well with analysis situs!

*—Albert W. Tucker: **Mathematical People**: D.J. Albers & G.L. Alexanderson, eds., 1985*

18.28 Adrien-Marie Legendre (1752–1833)

[French Mathematician]

1. The influence of Laplace was steadily exerted against [Legendre's] obtaining office or public recognition, and Legendre, who was a timid student, accepted the obscurity to which the hostility of his colleague condemned him.

*—W.W. Rouse Ball: **A Short Account of the History of Mathematics**, 1960 [Laplace was jealous of Legendre.]*

2. Our colleague has often expressed the desire that, in speaking of him, it would only be the matter of his works, which are, in fact, his entire life.

*—Simeon Denis Poisson: "Discours pronounce aux funerailles de M. Legendre"; **Moniteur universal**, January 20, 1833*

18.29 Gottfried Wilhelm von Leibniz (1646–1716)

[German Mathematician]

1. What is amazing about [Leibniz] is the vast quantity of first-rate contributions to many fields. Although his profession was jurisprudence, his work in mathematics and philosophy rank among the best the world has produced. He also did major work in mechanics, natural science, optics, hydrostatics, logic, philology, and geology, and was a pioneer in historical research. Throughout his life he tried to reconcile the Protestant and Catholic faiths.

*—Morris Kline: **Mathematics for the Nonmathematician**, 1967*

2. It would be difficult to name a man more remarkable for the greatness and universality of his intellectual powers than Leibniz.

*—John Stuart Mill: **System of Logic**, 1843*

3. Anything that happened before Leibniz is not history but paleontology.

*—Gian-Carlo Rota: in **Discrete Thoughts: Essays on Mathematics, Science and Philosophy**, Mark Kac, Gian-Carlo Rota, Jacob T. Schwartz; Quoted in **The Mathematical Intelligencer**, vol. 12, 1990*

4. Leibniz was one of the supreme intellects of all time ... his greatness is more apparent now than it was at any earlier time.

*—Bertrand Russell: **The Principles of Mathematics**, 1936*

5. Leibniz taught us by his principle of continuity to consider rest not as contradictorily opposed to motion, but as a limiting case of motion.

—Hermann Weyl: ***Philosophy of Mathematics and Natural Sciences****, 1949*

18.30 Marius Sophus Lie (1842–1899)

Norwegian Mathematician

1. ...in his lifetime [Sophus] Lie's ideas remained unfashionable, little understood by mathematicians and not at all by physicists.

—Freeman J. Dyson: "Unfashionable Pursuits" Address to the Alexander von Humboldt Foundation, August 24, 1981; in ***The Mathematical Intelligencer****, vol. 5, 3, 1983*

2. Sophus Lie, great comparative anatomist of geometric theories.

—Cassius J. Keyser: ***Lectures on Science, Philosophy and Art****, 1908*

18.31 John Edensor Littlewood (1885–1977)

[English Mathematician]

1. Mathematics is very hard work, and dons tend to be above the average in health and vigor. Below a certain threshold a man cracks up, but above it hard mental work makes for health and vigor (also—on much historical evidence throughout the ages—for longevity).

—J.L. Littlewood: ***The Mathematician's Art of Work****, 1967 [Littlewood remained active in mathematics even at an advanced age: his last paper was published in 1972, when he was 87.]*

2. Littlewood, on Hardy's own estimate, is the finest mathematician he has ever known. He was the man most likely to storm and smash a really deep and formidable problem; there was no one else who could command such a combination of insight, technique and power.

—Royal Society citation when the Sylvester medal was awarded J.E. Littlewood in 1943

18.32 Nikolai Lobachevski (Lobatchevsky) (1795–1856)

[Russian Mathematician]

1. It is no exaggeration to call Lobachevski the Copernicus of Geometry, for geometry is only part of the vaster domain which he renovated; it might even be just to designate him as a Copernicus of all thought.

—E.T. Bell: ***Men of Mathematics****, 1937*

2. Lobatchevsky, too, was attracted to the problem of the parallel axiom. He says that he was struck by the fact that two thousand years of effort by the greatest mathematicians had failed to produce a better axiom. And so, like Saccheri and Gauss, he built a new geometry on the basis of a parallel axiom contradicting Euclid's. The almost unbelievable theorems to which he was led did not discourage him any more than they had Gauss. Sound reasoning had led him to them and sound reasoning was the unquestionable guide. And so, Lobatchevsky, too, affirmed the radical but inescapable conclusion: There are geometries different from Euclid's and just as valid.

—Morris Kline: ***Mathematics in Western Culture****, 1953*

18.33 Gosta Magnus Mittag-Leffler (1846–1927)

[Swedish Mathematician]

1. There is a Nobel prize in several of the great fields of study, but none in mathematics. The reason for this is interesting. At one time the great Swedish mathematician Mittag-Leffler ... antagonized a number of people, in particular Alfred Nobel, who founded the five great prizes for annual award for the best work in Physics, Chemistry, Physiology or Medicine, for Idealistic Literary Work, and for the Cause of Universal Peace. At the time the prizes were set up, mathematics was also under consideration. Nobel asked his advisors, if there should be a prize in mathematics, in their opinion might Mittag-Leffler ever win it? Since Mittag-Leffler was such an able and famous mathematician, they had to admit that such would indeed be a possibility. "Let there be no Nobel Price in Mathematics, then," Alfred Nobel ordered.

—Howard W. Eves: ***In Mathematical Circles****, 1969*

2. His antagonism to his compatriot Alfred Nobel has been asserted since the 1910s to be the reason why mathematics does not have a Nobel prize; however, Nobel offered them for inventions, so that mathematics was not an obvious candidate subject anyway.

—Ivor Grattan-Guinness: ***The Rainbow of Mathematics****, 1997*

18.34 Gaspard Monge (1746–1818)

[French Mathematician]

1. Without Monge's geometry—originally invented for use in military engineering—the wholesale spawning of machinery in the nineteenth century would probably have been impossible. Descriptive geometry is the root of all the mechanical drawing and graphical methods that help to make mechanical engineering a fact.

—*E. T. Bell:* ***Men of Mathematics**, 1937*

2. Monge was one of the first modern mathematicians whom we recognize as a specialist: a geometer—.... In Monge's descriptive geometry lay the nucleus of projective geometry and his mastery of algebraic and analytical methods in their application to curves and surfaces contributed greatly to analytical and differential geometry.

—*Dirk J. Struik:* ***A Concise History of Mathematics**, 1948*

18.35 John Napier (1550–1617)

[English Astronomer and Mathematician]

1. "Napier's Rule of circular parts" is perhaps the happiest example of artificial memory that is known.

—*Florian Cajori:* ***History of Mathematics**, 1897*

2. It is probably true that no great mathematical invention, with one solitary exception, has resulted from the work of any one individual. One mathematician sows a seed which starts a train of thought in the minds of others. Eventually, it may be after years and even centuries have elapsed, the seed develops into full and vigorous life, and, as a consequence, mathematical knowledge and power are advanced another step. This is the normal course of events. The one solitary exception is the invention of [Napier's] logarithms.

—*Alfred Hooper:* ***Makers of Mathematics**, 1948*

3. [Napier's logarithms] ... by shortening the labors doubled the life of the astronomer.

—*Pierre-Simon de Laplace: In Howard Eves:* ***In Mathematical Circles**, 1969*

4. Many mathematicians had been struck by the relationship between arithmetic and geometric series, and that the product of two powers could be reduced to the sum of the powers. Napier's insight was that this could apply to any power, and he compiled a table of Napierian logarithms which appeared in his 1614 book *Mirifici logarithmorum canonis descriptio* ("A Description of the Marvelous Rule of Logarithms.")

—*Richard Mankiewicz:* ***The Story of Mathematics**, 2000*

19

Some Mathematical People III

19.1 Sir Isaac Newton (1642–1727)

[English Physicist and Mathematician]

1. The efforts of the great philosopher [Newton] were always superhuman; the questions which he did not solve were incapable of solution in his time.

*—Francois Arago: "Eulogy on Laplace"; **Smithsonian Report**, 1874*

2. And make us as Newton was, who in his garden watching
The apple falling toward England, became aware
Between himself and her of an eternal tie.

*—W.H. Auden: "Look Stranger," No. 1, 1936 **Collected Poems, 1933–1938***

3. When Newton saw an apple fall, he found....
A mode of proving that the earth turned round
In a most natural whirl, called gravitation;
And thus is the sole mortal who could grapple
Since Adam, with a fall or with an apple.

*—Lord Byron: **Don Juan**, 1819–1824*

4. Every discovery of Newton had two aspects. Newton had to make it and then you had to find out that he had done so.

*—Augustus De Morgan: **A Budget of Paradoxes** 1915 [De Morgan alludes to Newton's long-lasting aversion to publication of his works.]*

5. Nature to him was an open book, whose letters he could read without effort.... In one person he combined the experimenter, the theorist, the mechanic and, not least, the artist in exposition. He stands before us strong, certain and alone; his joy in creation and his minute precision are evident in every word and in every figure.

*—Albert Einstein: "Preface" to Sir Issac Newton: **The Opticks, or a Treatise on the Reflections, Refractions, Inflections and Colors of Light**, 1931*

6. Silly! A stupid, officious man asked Newton how he discovered the law of gravitation. Seeing that he had to deal with a child intellect, and wanting to get rid of the bore, Newton answered that an apple fell and hit him on the nose. The man went away fully satisfied and completely enlightened.

*—Carl Freidrich Gauss: Quoted in E.T. Bell: **Men of Mathematics**, 1937*

7. It is not permitted to any mortal to approach nearer to divinity than Newton.

*—Edmund Halley: in a Review of Newton's "Principia"; **Philosophical Transactions**, 1687*

8. Isaac Newton was not a pleasant man. His relations with other academics were notorious, with most of his later life spent embroiled in heated disputes.... A serious dispute arose with the German philosopher Gottfried Leibniz. Both Leibniz and Newton had independently developed a branch of mathematics called calculus, which underlies most of modern physics.... Following the death of Leibniz, Newton is reported to have declared that he had taken great satisfaction in "breaking Leibniz's heart."

*—Stephen W. Hawking: **A Brief History of Time**, 1988*

9. The discoveries of Newton has done more for England and for the race, than has been done by whole dynasties of British monarchs.

*—Thomas Hill: "Imagination in Mathematics"; **North American Review**, vol. 85, July, 1857*

10. In the eighteenth century and since, Newton came to be thought of as the first and greatest of the modern age of scientists, a rationalist, one who taught us to think on the lines of cold and untinctured reason. I do not see him in this light.... He was the last of the magicians, the last of the Babylonians and Sumerians, the last great mind which looked with the same eyes as those who began to build our intellectual inheritance rather less than 10,000 years ago. Isaac Newton, a posthumous child born with no father on Christmas Day, 1642, was the last wonder-child to whom the Magi could do sincere and appropriate homage.

*—John Maynard Keynes: "Newton, the Man"; **The World of Mathematics**, James R. Newman, ed., 1956*

11. Taking mathematics from the beginning of the world to the time of Newton, what he has done is the better half.

*—Gottfried Wilhelm Leibniz: Quoted in F.R. Moulton: **Introduction to Astronomy**, 1906*

12. Nature and nature's laws lay hid in
night;
God said, Let Newton be! and all was
light.

*—Alexander Pope: "Epitaph Intended for Sir Isaac Newton in Westminster Abbey," 1730; Quoted in **The Faber Book of Epigrams and Epitaphs**, Geoffrey Grigson, ed. 1977*

13. One had to be a Newton to notice that the moon is falling, when everyone sees that it doesn't fall.

*—Paul Valery: **Analects; Collected Works**, vol. 14, J. Matthews, ed., 1970*

14. Mortals, congratulate yourselves that so great a man has lived for the honor of the human race.

—Epitaph for Sir Isaac Newton; Westminster Abbey

15. The antechapel where the statue stood
Of Newton with his prism and silent
face,
The marble index of a mind for ever
Voyaging through strange seas of
thought alone.

*—William Wordsworth: in **The Prelude**, 1850*

19.2 Emmy Noether (1882–1935)

[German Mathematician]

1. When the sagacious Nazis expelled Fraulein Noether from Germany because she was a Jewess, Bryn Mawr College, Pennsylvania, took her in. She was the most creative abstract algebraist in the world. In less than a week of the new German enlightenment, Göttingen lost the liberality which Gauss cherished and which he strove all his life to maintain.

*—E.T. Bell: **Men of Mathematics**, 1937*

2. Emmy Noether was the chief creator of modern abstract algebra, the greatest woman mathematician of all time, and one of the greatest mathematicians of the twentieth century of either sex. Her brother, Fritz Noether, was also a mathematics professor, and her father was the distinguished mathematician Max Noether. Max once heard Emmy referred to as his daughter. Not so, he explained, "Emmy Noether is the origin of coordinates in the Noether family.

*—John Bowers: **Invitation to Mathematics**, 1988*

3. In the judgement of the most competent living mathematicians, Fraulein Noether was the most significant creative mathematical genius thus far produced since the higher education of women began. In the realm of algebra, in which the most gifted mathematicians have been busy for centuries, she discovered methods which have proved of enormous importance in the development of the present-day younger generation of mathematicians.

*—Albert Einstein: **New York Times**, May 4, 1935 [The quote is part of a "Letter to the Editor" from Einstein, praising Noether who had died shortly before it appeared in the New York Times.]*

4. They called you der Noether, as if mathematics
was only for men. In 1964, nearly thirty
years
past your death, at last I saw you in a
spotlight,
in a World's Fair mural, "Men of Modern
Mathematics."

*—JoAnne Growney: "My Dance Is Mathematics" **Mathematics Magazine**, December, 1995*

5. She was not clay, pressed by the artistic hands of God into a harmonious form, but rather a chunk of primary rock into which he had blown his creative breath of life.

*—Hermann Weyl: Address at Bryn Mawr College, April 26, 1935; **Scripta Mathematica**, Vol. 3, 1935 [Weyl speaks of Emmy Noether twelve days after her death.]*

6. ...Miss Noether is a great personality, the greatest woman mathematician who has ever lived; and the greatest woman scientist of any sort now living and a scholar at least on the plane of Madame Curie. Leaving all questions of sex aside, she is one of the ten or twelve leading mathematicians of the present generation in the entire world and has founded what is certain to be the most important close-knit group of mathematicians in Germany—the Modern School of Algebraists.

—Norbert Wiener: Letter to Jacob Billikopf, January 2, 1935; found in the Einstein papers at Princeton

19.3 Pappus (Lived c. A.D. 300)

[Greek Mathematician]

1. In what must be one of the most anthropomorphic statements ever made, Pappas asserted that bees "Believ[e] themselves, no doubt, to be entrusted with the task of bringing from the gods to the more cultured part of mankind a share of ambrosia." Having thus suggested that bees made honey primarily for human consumption, Pappas noted that they naturally would want to store it without waste, by depositing it in cells arranged so that "nothing else might fall into the interstices" and thus be lost. The cells of the honeycomb, in other words, must be constructed so as to leave no gaps [i.e., identical regular polygons].

—*William Dunham: **The Mathematical Universe**, 1994*

2. Although Pappus wrote a number of mathematical commentaries, his really great work is his *Mathematical Collection,* a combined commentary and guidebook of the existing geometrical works of his time.... It is a veritable mine of rich geometrical nuggets and may be called a swan song, or requiem, of Greek geometry, for after Pappus Greek mathematics ceased to be a living study and we find merely its memory perpetuated by minor writers and commentators.

—*Howard W. Eves: **In Mathematical Circles**, 1969*

19.4 BLAISE PASCAL (1623–1662)

[French Mathematician, Physicist and Philosopher]

1. [Pascal] is to France what Plato is to Greece, Dante to Italy, Cervantes and St. Theresa to Spain, Shakespeare to England.'

—*Claude Chevalier: Quoted in Ernest Mortimer: **Pascal**, 1959*

2. Had [Blaise Pascal] confined his attention to mathematics he might have enriched the subject with many remarkable discoveries. But after his early youth he devoted most of his small measure of strength to theological questions.

—*J.L. Coolidge: **A History of the Conic Sections and Quadric Surfaces**, 1945*

19.5 BENJAMIN PEIRCE (1809–1880)

[American Mathematician]

1. ...To [Benjamin Peirce] mathematics not the handmaid of philosophy. It was not a humanly devised instrument of investigation, it was Philosophy itself, the divine revealer of TRUTH.

—*W.E. Byerly: "Benjamin Peirce, Reminiscences"; **The American Mathematical Monthly**, 32; January, 1925*

2. [Benjamin Peirce's] fame today seems to rest chiefly on the fact that it was he who first caused the powers-that-be to recognize that mathematical research is one of the reasons for the existence of departments of mathematics in America.

—*Howard Eves: **Return to Mathematical Circles**, 1988*

19.6 CHARLES SANDERS PEIRCE (1839–1914)

[American Mathematician and Philosopher]

1. Even to the most unsympathetic, Peirce's thought cannot fail to convey something of lasting value. It has a peculiar property, like that of the Lernean hydra: discover a weak point, and two strong ones spring up beside it. Despite the elaborate architectonic planning of its creator, it is everywhere uncompleted, and no doubt what they value is much to be valued. In his quest for magnificent array, in his design for a mighty temple that should house his ideas, Peirce failed. He succeeded only in advancing philosophy.

—*Justus Buchler: **The Philosophy of Charles Sanders Peirce**, 1940*

2. But he [Charles Sanders Peirce] was always somewhat proud of his ancestry and connections, overbearing towards those who stood in his way, indifferent to the consequences of his acts, quick to take affront, highly emotional, easily duped, and with, as he puts it, "a reputation for not finding things."

—*Paul Weiss: "Charles Sanders Peirce"; **Dictionary of American Biography**, 1928–44*

19.7 JULES HENRI POINCARE (1854–1912)

[French Mathematician]

1. Poincare was the last man to take practically all mathematics, both pure and applied, as his province.

—*E.T. Bell: **Men of Mathematics**, 1937*

2. A story is told that during the days of the War (WWI) someone asked Bertrand Russell who he regarded as the greatest man produced by France in modern times. Without hesitation, Russell replied, "Poincare," "What! That man?" exclaimed the astonished questioner in surprise, believing that Russell meant Raymond Poincare (Henri's cousin), the President of the French Republic.

—*Howard W. Eves: **Mathematical Circles Squared**, 1972*

3. The record of [Poincare's] life shows that he was not one of those who sit by the roadside waiting for inspiration. He was always at work, ever acquiring fresh knowledge by assimilating the work of others, and constantly giving verbal expression to the form in which it stood to the things he had known before.... All this knowledge and much besides he could bring to bear upon any matter to which it could be applied....

—*A.E.H. Love: "Jules Henri Poincare"*; ***Proceedings of the London Mathematical Society****, 11, 1913*

4. For Bourbaki, Poincare was the devil incarnate. For students of chaos and fractals, Poincare is of course God on Earth.

—*Marshall Stone: Quoted in Desmond MacHale:* ***Comic Sections****, 1993*

19.8 George Polya (1887–1985)

[Hungarian-American Mathematician]

1. Polya believes that there is a craft of discovery. He believes that the ability to discover and ability to invent can be enhanced by skillful teaching which alerts the student to the principles of discovery and which gives him an opportunity to practice these principles....

—*Philip J. Davis & Reuben Hersh:* ***The Mathematical Experience****, 1981*

2. All his work radiates the cheerfulness of his personality, wonderful taste, crystal clear methodology, simple means, powerful results. If I would be asked who I would have liked to be myself, I have my answer ready: Polya.

—*N.G. de Bruijnin:* ***The Polya Picture Album****, G.L. Alexanderson, ed., 1987*

3. Polya has become the Marx and Lenin of mathematical problem solving: a few words of obeisance need to be offered in his name before an author can get down to the topic at hand.

—*Jeremy Kilpatrick: "George Polya's Influence on Mathematics Education";* ***Mathematics Magazine****, 60; December, 1987*

19.9 Ptolemy [Claudius Ptolemaeus] (fl. 127–145)

[Egyptian-Greek Astronomer and Mathematician]

1. ...the Geography of Ptolemy introduced the systems of latitudes and longitudes as used today, described methods of cartographic projection, and catalogued some 8000 cities, rivers and other important features of the earth.

—*Carl B. Boyer:* ***A History of Mathematics****, 1985*

2. Ptolemy's Almagest shares with Euclid's Elements the glory of being the scientific text longest in use. From its conception in the second century up to the late Renaissance, this work determined astronomy as a science. During this time the Almagest was not only a work on astronomy; the subject was defined as what is described in the Almagest.

—*G. Grasshoff:* ***The History of Ptolemy's Star Catalogue****, 1990*

19.10 Pythagoras and the Pythagoreans (c. 580–500 B.C.)

[Greek Mathematician and Astronomer]

1. The so-called Pythagoreans, who were the first to take up mathematics, not only advanced the subject, but saturated with it, they fancied that the principles of mathematics were the principles of all things.

—*Aristotle:* ***Metaphysics****, ca. 330 B.C.*

2. The Pythagoreans and Plato noted that the conclusions they reached deductively agreed to a remarkable extent with the results of observation and inductive inference. Unable to account otherwise for this agreement, they were led to regard mathematics as the study of ultimate, eternal reality, immanent in nature and the universe, rather than as a branch of logic or a tool of science and technology. An understanding of mathematical principles, they decided, must precede any valid interpretation of the experience.

—*Carl B. Boyer:* ***The Concepts of Calculus****, 1949*

3. It is hard for us today, familiar as we are with pure mathematical abstraction and with the mental act of generalization, to appreciate the originality of this Pythagorean contribution [the abstract idea of a proof].

—*R.S. Brumbaugh:* ***The Philosophers of Greece****, 1981*

4. The Pythagoreans applied their numerology to astronomy. They devised a system of 9 concentric spherical shells to convey the known heavenly bodies as they turned, and invented a mystical "counter–Earth" to make up the tetraktus number 10. This connection between musical and heavenly harmony was epitomized by the assertion that the astronomical spheres gave forth music as they turned—the music of the spheres.

—*Paul Davies:* ***The Mind of God****, 1992*

5. Pythagoras was intellectually one of the most important men that ever lived.... The influence of mathematics on philosophy, partly owing to him, has, ever since his time, been both profound and unfortunate.... He may be described, briefly, as a combination of Einstein and Mary Baker Eddy. He founded a religion, of which the main tenets were the transmigration of souls and the sinfulness of eating beans.

—*Bertrand Russell:* ***A History of Western Philosophy****, 1945*

6. To Pythagoras we owe the very word mathematics and its doubly twofold branches—the discrete and the continued.

*—Herbert Westren Turnbull: "The Great Mathematicians" in **The World of Mathematics**, vol. 1, James R. Newman, ed., 1956*

19.11 Srinivasa Ramanujan (1887–1920)

[Indian Mathematician]

1. Whenever I am angry or depressed, I pull down [Ramanujan's] collected papers from the shelf and take a quiet stroll in Ramanujan's garden. I recommend this therapy to all of you who suffer from headaches or jangled nerves. They also are full of beautiful ideas which may help you to do more interesting mathematics.

—Freeman Dyson: "A Walk Through Ramanujan's Garden," Conference celebrating the centenary of Ramanujan's birth, 1887

2. I have often been asked whether Ramanujan had any special secret; whether his methods differed in kind from those of other mathematicians; whether there was anything really abnormal in his mode of thought. I cannot answer these questions with any confidence or conviction; but I do not believe it. My belief is that all Mathematicians think, at bottom, in the same way, and that Ramanujan was no exception. He had, of course, an extraordinary memory. He could remember the idiosyncrasies of numbers in an almost uncanny way. It was Mr. Littlewood (I believe) who remarked that 'every positive integer was one of his personal friends.'

*—G.H. Hardy: **A Mathematician's Apology**, 1940*

3. His intuition worked in analogies [...] and [...] by empirical induction from particular numerical cases [...] The clear-cut idea of what is meant by a proof [...] he perhaps did not possess at all. If a significant piece of reasoning occurred somewhere, and the total mixture of evidence and intuition gave him certainty, he looked no further.

*—J.E. Littlewood: "Review of Ramanujan's Collected Papers"; **A Mathematician's Miscellany**, 1963*

19.12 Robert Recorde (1510?–1558)

[English Mathematician]

1. In Recorde's algebra, *The Whetstone of Witte* (1557), the most original and historically important is the sign of equality (=).... Also the plus (+) and minus (-) signs ... make here their first appearance in an English book.

*—Florian Cajori: **A History of Mathematical Notations**, 1928–29*

2. The last of the great Oxford mathematicians was Robert Recorde (1510?—1558).... The earliest use of the word "algebra" in English occurs in his *Pathway of Knowledge* in 1551. He wrote an arithmetic, The Grounde of Arts; a geometry *The Pathway of Knowledge;* and an algebra, *The Whetstone of Witte.*

*—Dorothy V. Schrader: "The Arithmetic of the Medieval Universities"; **The Mathematics Teacher**, vol. LX, no. 3, March, 1967*

19.13 Georg Friedrich Bernhard Riemann (1826–1866)

[German Mathematician]

1. A geometer like Riemann might almost have foreseen the more important features of the actual world.

*—A.S. Eddington: **Space, Time and Gravitation**, 1920*

2. Only the genius of Riemann, solitary and uncomprehended, had already won its way by the middle of the last century to a new conception of space, in which space was deprived of its rigidity, and in which its power to take part in physical events was recognized as possible.

*—Albert Einstein: **The Evolution of Physics** (with Leopold Infeld), 1938*

3. The general theory of relativity splendidly justified his work. In the mathematical apparatus developed from Riemann's address [his 1854 lecture "On the Hypotheses that Lie at the Foundations of Geometry"], Einstein found the frame to fit his physical ideas, his cosmology, and cosmogony: and the spirit of Riemann's address was just what physics needed: the metric system determined by data.

*—Hans Freudenthal: "Riemann"; **Dictionary of Scientific Biography**, 1970—1990*

4. Although Riemann's collected papers fill only one single volume of 539 pages, this volume weighs tons if measured intellectually. Every one of his many discoveries was destined to change the course of mathematical science.

*—Cornelius Lanczos: **Space Through the Ages**, 1965*

19.14 Lord Bertrand Russell (1872–1970)

[English Mathematician and Philosopher]

1. I believe that it can be shown that all Russell's philosophy has been based on this quest for reassurance. It is sceptical in the sense that it questions all claims, but it also tries to find a solid base for them. The reason why Russell was always attempting to reduce things was to give fewer hostages to fortune.

—*A.J. Ayer:* ***Language, Truth and Logic,*** *1936*

2. I can remember Bertrand Russell telling me of a horrible dream. He was in the top floor of the University Library, about A.D. 2100. A library assistant was going round the shelves carrying an enormous bucket, taking down book after book, glancing at them, restoring them to the shelves or dumping them into the bucket. At last he came to three large volumes which Russell could recognize as the last surviving copy of *Principia Mathematica.* He took down one of the volumes, turned over a few pages, seemed puzzled for a moment by the curious symbolism, closed the volume, balanced it in his hand and hesitated....

—*G.H. Hardy:* ***A Mathematician's Apology,*** *1941*

3. Bertrand Russell was most mortified,
When a box was washed up by the tide,
For he said with regret
"Why, the set of all sets
Which belong to themselves is inside."

—*Paul Ritger:* ***Rome Press 1956 Calendar***

19.15 Takakazu Seki (Kowa) (1642–1708)

[Japanese Mathematician]

1. Seki Kowa was the creator of the yenri, or circle principle. Thus Seki Kowa probably invented the calculus of the East just as Newton invented the calculus of the West.

—*Howard W. Eves:* ***In Mathematical Circles,*** *1969*

2. ...there appeared a great genius who is called the Japanese Newton. Seki Kowa was his name. Seki was born in the same year in which Galileo died and Newton was born, namely in 1642. If Seki did not surpass Newton in his achievements, yet he was no inferior of the two. The same uplift Newton gave the mathematics of his country, Seki was also able to render for Japan. The Japanese mathematics properly so called had waited his genius for its sound establishment. No doubt was Seki the father of Japanese mathematics.

—*Yoshio Mikami:* ***The Development of Mathematics in China and Japan,*** *2nd ed., 1974*

19.16 Mary Somerville (1780–1872)

[Scottish Mathematician]

1. [Mary Somerville]'s scientific friends persuaded her to translate Laplace's formidable treatise *Mecanique celeste* and her version was published as *The Mechanism of the Heavens* in 1831, when she was nearly 51 years old. Unexpectedly the book became very popular—it was reprinted many times and it was used as a textbook of mathematical astronomy for nearly a century.

—*G.T. Lee: "The Pioneering Women Mathematicians"; Invited Address, First Australian Mathematics Convention, May, 1978; in* ***The Mathematical Intelligencer,*** *vol. 5, 4, 1983*

2. Her grasp of scientific truth in all branches of knowledge, combined with an exceptional power of exposition, made her the most remarkable woman of her generation.

—*Unknown: "Mary Somerville";* ***Dictionary of National Biography,*** *1897*

19.17 Hugo Steinhaus (1887–1972)

[Polish Mathematician]

1. In the preface to the first edition of *Mathematical Snapshots,* [Steinhaus] stated that the book's gimmicks and haphazard arrangements were designed to appeal "to the scientist in the child and the child in the scientist." "Perhaps," he concluded, "I have succeeded only in amusing myself."

—*Martin Gardner: in Hugo Steinhaus:* ***One Hundred Problems in Elementary Mathematics,*** *1964*

2. ...to understand and appreciate Steinhaus' mathematical style, one must read (or rather look at [*Mathematical Snapshots* (1937)].... It expresses, not always explicitly and at times even unconsciously, what Steinhaus thought mathematics is and should be. To Steinhaus mathematics was a mirror of reality and life much in the same way as poetry is a mirror, and he liked to "play" with numbers, sets, and curves, the way a poet plays with words, phrases, and sounds.

—*Mark Kac: "Hugo Steinhaus—A Reminiscence and a Tribute";* ***The American Mathematical Monthly,*** *Vol. 81, 1974*

19.18 James Joseph Sylvester (1814–1897)

[British Mathematician]

1. Sylvester's *Methods*! He had none. Statements like the following were not infrequent in his lectures: "I haven't proved this, but I am as sure as I can be of anything that it must be so. From this it will follow, etc." At the next lecture it turned out that what he was so sure of was false. Never mind, he kept on forever guessing and trying, and presently a wonderful discovery followed, then another and another. Afterward he would go back and work it all over again, and surprise us with all sorts of side lights. He then made another leap in the dark, more treasures were discovered, and so on forever.

—E.W. Davis: Quoted in ***Teaching and History of Mathematics in the U.S.****, F. Cajori, ed., 1890*

2. [Sylvester] was twice in America, the first time as a professor at the University of Virginia (1841–42), the second time as a professor at Johns Hopkins University in Baltimore (1877–83). During this second period he was one of the first to establish graduate work in mathematics in American universities. With the teaching of Sylvester, mathematics began to flourish in the United States.

—Dirk J. Struik: ***A Concise History of Mathematics****, 1948*

19.19 Thales (640–547 B.C.)

[Greek Mathematician and Philosopher]

1. Around 600 B.C. in the town of Miletus on the western coast of Asia Minor, there lived the great Thales (ca. 640—ca. 546 B.C.), one of the so-called "Seven Wise Men" of antiquity. Thales of Miletus is generally credited with being the father of demonstrative mathematics, the first scholar who supplied the "why" along with the "how." As such, he is the earliest known mathematician.

—William Dunham: ***Journey Through Genius****, 1990*

2. When Thales was asked what was difficult, he said, "To know one's self." And what was easy, "To advise another."

—Diogenes Laertius: ***The Lives of Eminent Philosophers****, c. 200 A.D.*

3. Thales who had travelled to Egypt was the first to introduce this science [geometry] into Greece.

—Proclus: ***A Commentary on the First Book of Euclid's Elements****, Glenn R. Morrow, tr., 1970*

19.20 Alan Turing (1912–1954)

[British Mathematician and Computer Scientist]

1. [Alan Turing] disdained to conceal his homosexuality, imagining, perhaps, that his own sexuality as an adult would fall behind the sturdy defenses of his talent and so come to be treated by other men as an indiscretion or an idiosyncrasy, something personal and so something helpless. In this he was mistaken. He never quite understood that like all men marked by a high and unusual talent, he lived in a world of enemies, and by proudly failing to conceal his homosexuality, he opened the fatal chink in the armor that his talent provided and he learned too late that without his armor he was destined to live life other men and so was doomed by his destiny.

—David Berlinski: ***The Advent of the Algorithm****, "Introduction," 2000 [Officials in the British government forced Turning to accept a course of hormone treatment designed to suppress his "gayness." Instead it changed him physically, causing him to become more and more despondent. He took his own life by eating an apple laced with cyanide.]*

2. Many people have acclaimed von Neumann as the "father of the computer" (in a modern sense of the term), but I am sure that he would never have made that mistake himself. He might well be called the midwife, perhaps, but he firmly emphasized to me, and to others I am sure, that the fundamental conception is owed to [Alan] Turing—insofar as not anticipated by Babbage, Lovelace, and others.

—S. Frankel: Quoted by B. Randell in Michael Shub: "Mysteries of Mathematics"; ***The Mathematical Intelligencer****, vol. 16, Winter, 1994*

3. L.J. Good, a wartime colleague and friend, has aptly remarked that it is fortunate that the authorities did not know during the war that [Alan] Turing was a homosexual; otherwise, the Allies might have lost the war.

—Peter J. Hilton: "Cryptanalysis in World War II—and Mathematics Education"; ***The Mathematics Teacher****, October, 1984*

4. [Turing] proved that there was no "miraculous machine" that could solve all mathematical problems, but in the process he had discovered something almost equally miraculous, the idea of a universal machine that could take over the work of any machine. He argued that anything performed by the human computer could be done by a machine.

—Andrew Hodges: ***Alan Turing: The Enigma****, 1983*

19.21 Stanislaw Ulam (1909–1984)

[Polish-American Mathematician]

1. The Germans have aptly called *Sitzfleisch* the ability to spend endless hours at a desk, doing gruesome work. *Sitzfleisch* is considered by mathematicians to be a better gauge of success than any of the attractive definitions of talent with which psychologists regale us from time to time. Stan Ulam, however, was able to get by without any *Sitzfleisch* whatsoever. After his bout with encephalitis, he came to lean on his unimpaired imagination for his ideas, and on the *Sitzfleisch* of others for technical support. The beauty of his insights and the promise of his proposals kept him amply supplied with young collaborators, willing to lend (and risking to waste) their time.

—Gian-Carlo Rota: "The Lost Cafe" in ***Contention****, vol. 2, Winter 1993 [The Lost Cafe, located in Stanislaw Ulam's native Poland, is where many prominent mathematicians used to meet prior to WWII.]*

2. Stan Ulam's best work is a game played in the farthest reaches of abstraction, where the cares of the world cannot intrude: in set theory, in measure theory, and in the foundations of mathematics. He used to refer to his volume of collected papers as a slim volume of poems. It is just that.

—Gian-Carlo Rota: "The Lost Cafe" in ***Contention****, vol. 2, Winter 1993*

19.22 John von Neumann (1903–1957)

[Hungarian-American Mathematician]

1. Perhaps one reason for von Neumann's attention to detail was that he found it quicker to hack through the underbrush himself than to trace references and see what others had done. The result was that sometimes he appeared ignorant of the standard literature. If he needed facts, well-known facts, ... he waded in, defined the basic notions, and developed the theory to the point where he could use it. If, in a later paper, he needed [the] ... theory again, he would go back to the beginning and do the same thing over again.

—Paul R. Halmos: "The Legend of John von Neumann"; ***American Mathematical Monthly*** *80, 1973*

2. Preparing a problem for an electronic computer, he said, would be something comparable to the presentation of instructions to a not overly bright human being with a desk computer, who would be locked up incommunicado for a period of years and expected to emerge thereafter with all the answers.

—A.S. Householder: "Numerical Analysis"; ***Lectures on Modern Mathematics****, Vol. 1, T.L. Sarty, ed., 1963*

3. John, with whom I had many conversations, could not separate mathematics from life; he saw mathematics wherever he looked. His feel for nature inspired him to be a better mathematician and his mathematics inspired him to better understand nature.

—Carroll V. Newsom: "The Image of the Mathematician"; ***American Mathematical Monthly****, 79; October, 1972*

4. Johnny was the only student I was ever afraid of. If in the course of a lecture I stated an unsolved problem, the chances were he'd come to me as soon as the lecture was over, with the complete solution in a few scribbles on a slip of paper.

—George Polya:: Quoted in Paul R. Halmos: "The Legend of John von Neumann"; ***American Mathematical Monthly*** *80, 1973*

19.23 Karl Weierstrass (1815–1897)

[German Mathematician]

1. For the analysts, Weierstrass was the leader; his followers were proud to be known as Weierstrassains, and they constitute a school in the strict sense.

—Ivor Grattan-Guinness: ***The Rainbow of Mathematics****, 1997*

2. You have made a mistake, sir, you should follow Weierstrass's course at Berlin. He is the master of all of us.

—Charles Hermite: Quoted in E.T. Bell: ***Men of Mathematics****, 1937 [Hermite offers a recommendation to a young G.M. Mittag-Leffler who was set to study analysis with Hermite in Paris]*

3. His lectures were carefully prepared and continually revised. Each lecture was a creative adventure for himself and his students alike, for his courses were always important new mathematics in the process of being born. The student notes of his lectures, and copies of these notes, and copies of copies, were passed from hand to hand throughout Europe and even America.

—George F. Simmons: ***Calculus Gems****, 1992*

19.24 Alfred North Whitehead (1861–1947)

[British Mathematician and Philosopher]

1. It is often desperately difficult to understand what it is that Whitehead is asserting. When one is fairly certain of this, it is often equally hard to discover what he considers to be the reason for asserting it; for he seems often to be 'not arguing but just telling you.' And, finally, when one thinks that one knows what he is asserting and what he is alleging as the ground for it, one often fails to see how the latter proves or makes probable the former....

—C. D. Broad: "Obituary of Alfred North Whitehead"; ***Mind****, April, 1948*

2. At Oxford University, when a professor concludes a course, it is custom for the students to pound the floor with their feet as a "tribute" to the teacher for his fine teaching. On one occasion, when A.N. Whitehead had finished his last lecture, the pounding of the feet was so enthusiastic that in the room below, where a professor of logic was lecturing, the ceiling began to fall. The professor of logic remarked: "I am afraid that the premises will not support Dr. Whitehead's conclusion!"

—*Howard W. Eves:* ***Mathematical Circles Revisited****, 1971*

19.25 Norbert Wiener (1894–1964)

[American Mathematician]

1. Norbert Wiener
Was very much keener
On Fourier transforms
Than on acrobatic dance forms.

—*Ralph P. Boas, Jr.: Quoted in* ***Lion Hunting & Other Mathematical Pursuits****, Gerald L. Alexanderson & Dale H. Mugler, eds., 1995*

2. For Wiener, mathematical notation and language was an encumbrance. He could get an insight and he would be wanting to say it and he would fumble with the notation ... because he was not thinking about the notation he was working in, he was thinking about the problem behind it....

—*S.J. Heims: "John Von Neumann and Norbert Wiener";* ***From Mathematics to the Technologies of Life and Death****, 1980*

3. After the publication of his Cybernetics, Wiener was often embarrassed by the enthusiasm of some of his followers, who saw in it a kind of universal panacea. Remembering that Marx had exclaimed that he was not a Marxian, Wiener said to one of his friends, "I am not a Wienerian." Answered his friend, "Yes, but there are plenty with Wienerian disease.

—*Dirk J. Struik: Quoted in Howard W. Eves:* ***Mathematical Circles Squared****, 1972*

19.26 Christopher Wren 1632–1723)

[English Architect and Mathematician]

1. Sir Christopher Wren
said, "I am going to dine with some men.
If anyone calls
Say I am designing St. Paul's"

—*Edmund Clerihew Bentley:* ***Biography for Beginners****, 1905*

2. ...it seems that but for London's Great Fire of 1666, Wren would have been known as a mathematician instead of an architect. He was Savilian professor of astronomy at Oxford from 1661 to 1673, and, for a time, president of the Royal Society.... But after the Great Fire, Wren took such a prominent part in the rebuilding of St. Paul's Cathedral and some fifty or more other churches and public buildings that his fame as an architect overshadowed his reputation as a mathematician.

—*Howard W. Eves:* ***In Mathematical Circles****, 1969*

19.27 Zeno of Elea (c. 5th century B.C.)

[Greek Philosopher and Mathematician]

1. When Zeno was still a young man
Impressed with the way turtles ran
He challenged Achilles
And some say that still he's
Not certain which one's in the van.

—*Paul Ritger:* ***Rome Press 1985 Mathematical Calendar***

2. In this capricious world nothing is more capricious than posthumous fame. One of the most notable victim's of posterity's lack of judgement is the Eleatic Zeno. Having invented four arguments all immeasurably subtle and profound, the grossness of subsequent philosophers pronounced him a mere ingenious juggler, and his arguments to be one and all sophisms. After two thousand years of continual refutation, these sophisms were reinstated, and made the foundation of a mathematical renaissance.

—*Bertrand Russell:* ***The Principles of Mathematics****, 1903*

20

Problems and Problem Solving

20.1 The Three Problems of Antiquity

1. With the straight ruler I set to work
To make the circle four-cornered.

—*Aristophanes:* ***The Birds****, 414 B.C.*

2. [The proof of the irrationality of "π"] definitely disposed of the problem of squaring the circle, without, of course, dampering in the least the ardor of the circle-squarers. For it is characteristic of these people that their ignorance equals their capacity for self-deception.

—*Tobias Dantzig:* ***Number: The Language of Science****, 1954*

3. He [circle-squarer James Smith] is beyond a doubt the ablest head at unreasoning, and the greatest hand at writing it, of all who have tried in our day to attach their names to an error. Common cyclometers sink into puny orthodoxy by his side.... We can only say this: he is not mad. Madmen reason rightly upon wrong premises. Mr. Smith reasons wrongly upon no premises at all.

—*Augustus De Morgan: Quoted in David Blatner:* ***The Joy of "π,"*** *1997 [De Morgan coined the phrase* ***morbus cyclometricus****—the circle-squaring disease in* ***A Budget of Paradoxes****, 1872]*

4. For, in the first place, it is against the geometer's style to put forward problems that they cannot solve themselves. Moreover, some problems are impossible, like the quadrature of the circle, etc.

—*Rene Descartes: Letter to Father Mersenne; March 31, 1638 in the Adam and Tannery edition of* ***Geometrie****, 1897–1910*

5. Archimedes knew the impossibility of trisecting an angle. But he also knew that proving this proposition was not for his time, and so he concentrated his energies on problems that he could solve.

—*Paul Erdos: Lecture at University of Minnesota; Quoted in Ian Richards: "Impossibility";* ***Mathematics Magazine****, 48, 1975*

6. There is evidence that the [duplication-of-the-cube] problem may have originated in the words of some mathematically unschooled and obscure ancient Greek poet who represented the mythical King Minos as dissatisfied with the size of a tomb erected to his son Glaucus. Minos ordered that the tomb be doubled in size. The poet then had Minos add, incorrectly, that this can be accomplished by doubling each dimension of the tomb. This faulty mathematics on the part of the poet led the geometers to take up the problem of finding how one can double a given solid while keeping the same shape.

—*Howard W. Eves:* ***In Mathematical Circles****, 1969*

7. ...people puzzled their heads vainly for hundreds of years, trying to divide any angle into three equal parts, using only ruler and compasses. They also tried in vain to draw a square equal to a given circle, and to draw a line equal to the edge of a cube that would double the volume of a given cube. They did not know that none of these three constructions can be done if only a ruler and compasses are allowed to be used. The long, unsuccessful search for their solution was not all wasted time, for it led to the development of very important mathematical processes and concepts.

—*Alfred Hooper:* ***Makers of Mathematics****, 1948*

8. One would almost fancy that amongst circle-squarers there prevails an idea that some kind of ban or magic prohibition has been laid upon this problem; that like the hidden treasures of the pirates of old, it is protected from the attacks of ordinary mortals by some spirit or demoniac influence, which paralyses the mind of the would-be solver and frustrates his efforts.

—John Phin: ***The Seven Follies of Science****, 1912*

9. Circles to squares and cubes to double
Would give a man excessive trouble.

—Matthew Prior: in ***Matthew Prior: Literary Works****, H.B. Wright & M.K. Spears, eds., 1959*

10. The British Association for the Advancement of Science may assume infallibility, and authoritatively proclaim that the solution of the problem is impossible, and may consequently decline to permit the consideration of the subject to be introduced in their deliberations.... And yet, the solution of the problem is extremely simple after all. It would almost appear as if its very simplicity has been the grand obstacle which had hitherto stood in the way of its discovery.... I have subjected my theory to every conceivable test, both mathematical and mechanical, with an honest determination to find a flaw if possible, and having failed to do so, I now unhesitatingly propound it, as the true theory on this important question.

—James Smith: ***The Quadrature and Geometry of the Circle Demonstrated****, 1872 [Circle-squarer Smith is a true believer. Finding nothing in his mind wrong with his arguments, he stands alone against the world which dismisses his attempt to do the impossible.]*

20.2 Fermat's Last Theorem

1. To divide a cube into two cubes, a fourth power, or in general any power whatever above the second, into two powers of the same denomination, is impossible, and I have assuredly found an admirable proof of this, but the margin is too narrow to contain it.

—Pierre de Fermat: In the margin of his copy of Bachet's edition of the complete works of Diophantus; in the works of Fermat, Samuel de Fermat, ed., 1670 ["Fermat's Last Theorem" may be stated as follows: there does not exist positive integers x, y, z, n such that $x^n + y^n = z^n$ *when* $n > 2$.*]*

2. I am very much obliged for your news concerning the Paris prize. But I confess that Fermat's theorem as an isolated proposition has very little interest for me, because I could easily lay down a multitude of such propositions, which one could neither prove nor dispose of.

—Carl Freidrich Gauss: Letter to Olbers, March 21, 1816 [Gauss declines to enter into the mathematical contest of the Paris Academy on Fermat's last theorem.]

3. Mathematics often owes more to those who ask questions than to those who answer them. The solution of a problem may stifle interest in the area around it. But "Fermat's Last Theorem," because it is not yet a theorem, has generated a great deal of "good" mathematics, whether goodness is judged by beauty, by depth or by applicability.

—Richard K. Guy: ***Unsolved Problems in Number Theory****, 1994*

4. There is no problem that will mean the same to me [as Fermat's Last Theorem]. I had this very rare privilege of being able to pursue in my adult life what had been my childhood dream. I know it's a rare privilege but, if one can do this it's more rewarding than anything I could imagine.

—Andrew Wiles: From the BBC program "Fermat's Last Theorem" by Simon Singh & John Lynch (broadcast in the U.S. on PBS's ***Nova****, as "The Proof," 1990s*

20.3 Other Mathematical Problems

1. An estate consisted of seven houses; each house had seven cats; each cat had seven mice; each mouse ate seven heads of wheat; and each head of wheat was capable of yielding seven hekat measures of grain, how many of these in all were in the estate?

—Ahmes: ***Rhind Papyrus****, c. 1650 B.C.*

2. As I was going to St. Ives,
I met a man with seven wives,
Each wife had seven sacks,
Each sack had seven cats,
Each cat had seven kits;
kits, cats, sacks, and wives,
How many were there going to St. Ives?

—Anonymous; c. Anonymous 18th cent. [This riddle with the surprising (to some) answer probably has its origins the Rhind Papyrus problem stated above.]

3. I was x years old in the year x^2.

—Augustus De Morgan, sometime in the 19th century. [The problem was given as an answer when De Morgan was asked the year of his birth. When was he born? Hint De Morgan was born in the 19th century, so $1800 < x^2 < 1900$.*]*

4. Since you are now studying geometry and trigonometry, I will give you a problem. A ship sails the ocean. It left Boston with a cargo of wool. It grosses 200 tons. It is bound for Le Havre. The mainmast is broken, the cabin boy is on deck, there are 12 passengers aboard, the wind is blowing East-North-East, the clock points to a quarter past three in the afternoon. It is the month of May. How old is the captain?

—Gustave Flaubert: Quoted in Edward Kasner and James R. Newman: "Pastimes of Past and Present Times"; in ***The World of Mathematics****, vol. 4, James R. Newman, ed., 1956*

5. It would be very discouraging if somewhere down the line you could ask a computer if the

Riemann hypothesis is correct and it said, "Yes, it is true, but you won't be able to understand the proof."

*—Ronald Graham: Quoted by John Horgan in **Scientific American**, October, 1993*

6. The circumferential arrows are eighteen in number. How many in all are the arrows to be found in the bundle?

*—Mahavira; c. A.D. 850: in G.G. Joseph, **The Crest of the Peacock**, 1991*

7. If you are told: A truncated pyramid of 6 for the vertical height by 4 on the base by 2 on the top. You are to square this 4, result 16. You are to double 4, result 8. You are to square 2, result 4. You are to add the 16, the 8, and the 4, result 28. You are to take one third of 6, result 2. You are to take 28 twice, result 56. See, it is 56. You will find it right.

—Moscow papyrus; c. 1850 B.C.

8. Zeno was concerned with three problems.... These are the problem of the infinitesimal, the infinite, and continuity.... From his to our own day, the finest intellects of each generation in turn attacked these problems, but achieved broadly speaking, nothing ... Weierstrass, Dedekind, and Cantor, ... have completely solved them. Their solutions ... are so clear as to leave no longer the slightest doubt or difficulty. This achievement is probably the greatest of which the age can boast.... The problem of the infinitesimal was solved by Weierstrass, the solution of the other two was begun by Dedekind and definitely accomplished by Cantor.

*—Bertrand Russell: in **International Monthly**, vol. 4, 1901*

20.4 Posing Mathematical Problems and Questions

1. In other sciences the essential problems are forced upon the subject from external sources, and the scientist has no control over the ultimate end. The mathematician, however, is free to prescribe not only the means of realizing the end, but also the end itself.

*—Raymond G. Ayoub: in a book review of Morris Kline's **Mathematics: The Loss of Certainty** in **MAA Monthly**, Vol. 89, # 9, 1982*

2. The greatest single feat of problem posing was that of the great German mathematician David Hilbert. In 1900 he stated not less than twenty-three problems and challenged his fellow mathematicians to solve them in the new century. For years mathematicians used the status of the Hilbert problems as a barometer of progress.

*—George A.W. Boehm: **The New World of Math**, 1959*

3. These problems are proposed simply for pleasure; the wise man can invent a thousand others, or he can solve the problems of others by the rules given here. As the sun eclipses the stars by his brilliancy, so the man of knowledge will eclipse the fame of others in assemblies of the people if he proposes algebraic problems, and still more if he solves them.

*—Brahmagupta; ca. 628; Quoted in F. Cajori: **History of Mathematics**, 1897*

4. The art of asking the right questions in mathematics, is more important than the art of solving them.

*—Georg Cantor: In **Mathematische Annalen**, 1895*

5. There is a distinction between what may be called a problem and what may be considered an exercise. The latter serves to drill a student in some technique or procedure, and requires little if any, original thought.... An exercise, then, can always be done with reasonable dispatch and with a minimum of creative thinking. In contrast to an exercise, a problem, if it is a good one for its level, should require thought on the part of the student.

*—Howard Eves: **A Survey of Geometry**, 1963*

6. Often, half the battle in trying to solve a difficult problem is knowing the right question to ask. If you know what it is you are trying to look for, you can often be very far along in finding the solution.

*—Ronald Graham: in **For All Practical Purposes**, Lynn A. Steed, ed., 1988*

7. As long as a branch of science offers an abundance of problems, so long is it alive; a lack of problems foreshadows extinction or the cessation of independent development.

—David Hilbert: Address to International Congress of Mathematics, Paris, 1900

8. Our appetite for calculation [computational problems for computers] has caused us to deal with finite numbers much larger than those we considered before, and this has opened up a rich vein of challenging problems, just as exciting as the problems about infinity which have inspired mathematicians for so many centuries.

*—Donald Knuth: "Mathematics and Computer Science: Coping with Finiteness": **Science**, 194, December 17, 1976*

9. The wealth of your practical experience with sane and interesting problems will give to mathematicians a new direction and a new impetus.... One-sided and introspective mathematical speculations lead into sterile fields.

—Leopold Kronecker: Letter to Herman von Helmholtz, 1888

10. It's a person's taste in problems that decides what kind of mathematics he does.

*—Peter Lax: in **More Mathematical People**, D. Albers, G. Alexanderson & C. Reid, eds., 1990*

11. Mystery is an inescapable ingredient of mathematics. Mathematics is full of unanswered questions, which far outnumber known theorems and results. It's the nature of mathematics to pose more problems than it can solve. Indeed, mathematics itself may be built on small islands of truth comprising the pieces of mathematics that can be validated by relatively short proofs. All else is speculation.

*—Ivars Peterson: **Islands of Truth: A Mathematical Mystery Cruise**, 1990*

12. In a perfectly stated mathematical problem all data and all clauses of the condition are essential and must be taken into account. In practical problems we have a multitude of data and conditions; we take into account as many as we can but we are obliged to neglect some.

*—George Polya: **How to Solve It**, 1945*

13. But, if logic is the hygiene of the mathematician, it is not his source of food; the great problems furnish his daily bread on which he thrives.

*—Andre Weil: "The Future of Mathematics"; **American Mathematical Monthly**, vol. 57, May, 1950*

20.5 Complicated and Unsolved Problems

1. If a problem is too difficult to solve, one cannot claim that it is solved by pointing at all the efforts made to solve it.

*—Hannes Alfven; Quoted by Lord Flowers in 1976; in A. Sampson: **The Changing Anatomy of Britain**, 1982*

2. I have yet to see any problem, however complicated, which, when you looked at it in the right way, did not become still more complicated.

*—Poul Anderson: **New Scientist**, September 25, 1969*

3. Problems worthy of attack,
Prove their worth by fighting back.

*—Anonymous: Quoted in Paul Hoffman: **The Man Who Loved Only Numbers**, 1998*

4. Among professional mathematicians, asking questions rates almost as high as answering them. Mathematics abounds with problems that have remained unsolved for decades or even centuries and yet have stimulated whole new branches of the science.

*—George A. W. Boehm: **The New World of Math**, 1959*

5. Maybe people don't realize that mathematics is not dead. There are a lot of unsolved problems in mathematics. And there are a lot of things about the world we don't know, and it seems that maybe the only way we'll ever know them is through the application of mathematics.

*—Nate Dean: Quoted in Keith Devlin: **Life by the Numbers**, 1998*

6. When a mathematician meets a problem he cannot solve, like any other scientist he tries to solve instead some related problem which seems to contain only part of the difficulties of the original. But the mathematician has far more alternatives in choosing a simpler problem than does the chemist or biologist. Other scientists are restricted by nature, whereas the mathematician is restricted only by logical coherence and somewhat vague considerations of taste.

*—Andrew Gleason: "Evolution of an Active Mathematical Theory"; **Science**, 145; July, 1964*

7. A mathematical problem should be difficult in order to entice us, yet not completely inaccessible, lest it mock at our efforts.

*—David Hilbert: "Mathematical Problems"; **Bulletin American Mathematical Society**, vol. 8*

8. Try a hard problem. You may not solve it, but you will prove something else.

*—John Edensor Littlewood: Quoted in J.C. Burkill: "John Edensor Littlewood"; **Bulletin of the London Mathematical Society**, 11, 1979*

9. Theorems are fun especially when you are the prover, but then the pleasure fades. What keeps us going are the unsolved problems.

—Carl Pomerance: MAA invited talk; January 21, 2000

10. It has been said that unsolved problems form the very life of mathematics; certainly they can illuminate and, in the best cases, crystallize and summarize the essence of the difficulties inherent in the various fields.

*—S.M. Ulam: **A Collection of Mathematical Problems**, 1960*

11. If we concentrate our attention on trying to solve a problem in geometry, and if at the end of an hour we are no nearer to doing so than at the beginning, we have nevertheless been making progress each minute of that hour in another more mysterious dimension. Without our knowing or feeling it, this apparently barren effort has brought more light into the soul.

*—Simone Weil: "Reflections on the Right Use of School Studies with a View to the Love of God"; **A Simone Weil Reader**, George A. Panichas, ed., 1977*

20.6 Solving Problems

1. When working towards the solution of a problem, it always helps if you know the answer.
—*Anonymous*

2. Most problems have either many answers or no answer. Only a few problems have a single answer.
—*Edmund C. Berkeley: "Right Answers—A Short Guide for Obtaining Them"; **Computers and Automation**, September, 1969*

3. To use an industrial metaphor, mathematics (and especially pure mathematics) is the machine-tool industry of the sciences, and we cannot use only the tools manufactured in the past unless we believe that science will never again have significantly new problems to solve—a belief that is clearly false.
—*Felix E. Browder: "Does Pure Mathematics Have a Relation to the Sciences?"; **American Scientist**, 64, 1976*

4. We must make it our goal to find a method of solutions of all problems ... by means of a single simple method.
—*Jean-le-Rond D'Alembert: Quoted in V.M. Tikhomirov: **Stories About Maxima and Minima**, Abe Schenitzer, tr., 1990*

5. Each problem that I solved became a rule which served afterwards to solve other problems.
—*Rene Descartes: **Discours de la Methode**, 1637*

6. The life of a mathematician is dominated by an insatiable curiosity, a desire bordering on passion to solve the problems he is studying.
—*Jean Dieudonne: **Mathematics—The Music of Reason**, 1992*

7. 'It is quite a three-pipe problem.'
—*Arthur Conan Doyle: **The Adventures of Sherlock Holmes**, 1892*

8. An expert problem solver must be endowed with two incompatible qualities, a restless imagination and a patient pertinacity.
—*Howard W. Eves: **In Mathematical Circles**, 1969*

9. If we want to solve a problem that we have never solved before, we must leave the door to the unknown ajar.
—*Richard Feynman: **The Feynman Lectures on Physics**, 1963*

10. There is not much difference between the delight a novice experiences in cracking a clever brain teaser and the delight a mathematician experiences in mastering a more advanced problem. Both look on beauty bare—that clean, sharply defined, mysterious, entrancing order that underlies all structure.
—*Martin Gardner: **Mathematical Puzzles and Diversions**, 1959*

11. New mathematics often comes from plain curiosity. The right kind of mathematical curiosity is a precious possession that usually belongs only to professionals of the highest rank. The hardest problem of a young mathematician is to find a problem.
—*Paul Halmos: "Innovation in Mathematics"; **Scientific American**, September, 1958*

12. There are many things you can do with problems besides solving them. First you must define them, pose them. But then of course you can also refine them, depose them, or expose them, even dissolve them! A given problem may send you looking for analogies, and some of these may lead you astray, suggesting new and different problems, related or not to the original. Ends and means can get reversed. You had a goal, but the means you found didn't lead to it, so you found a new goal they did lead to. It's called play. Creative mathematicians play a lot; around any problem really interesting they develop a whole cluster of analogies, of playthings.
—*David Hawkins: "The Spirit of Play" in **From Cardinals to Chaos**, Necia Grant Cooper, ed., 1988*

13. We shall have to evolve
problem-solvers galore—
Since each problem they solve
creates ten problems more.
—*Piet Hein: "The Only Solution"; Quoted in **The Mathematical Intelligencer**, vol. 13, Summer 1991*

14. The value of a problem is not so much coming up with the answer as in the ideas and attempted ideas it forces on the would be solver.
—*I.N. Herstein: **Topics in Algebra**, 1964,*

15. It is hard to convince a high-school student that he will encounter a lot of problems more difficult than those of algebra and geometry.
—*Edgar W. Howe: **Country Time Sayings**, 1911*

16. If we really understand the problem, the answer will come out of it, because the answer is not separate from the problem.
—*Krishnamurti: **The Penguin Krishnamurti Reader: Questions and Answers**, 1970*

17. In mathematics if I find a new approach to a problem, another mathematician might claim he has a better, more elegant solution. In chess, if anyone claims he is better than I, I can checkmate him!
—*Emmanuel Laskar: Quoted in **Chess: Quotations from the Masters**, H. Hunrold, compiler, 1972 [World chess champion Laskar (1894–1920) had a Ph.D. in mathematics.]*

18. It is the man not the method that solves the problem.

*—H. Maschke: **Present Problems of Algebra and Analysis**, 1905*

19. There are no solved problems, there are only more-or-less solved problems.

—Henri Poincare: Address to the International Congress of Mathematicians, Rome, 1908

20. A great discovery solves a great problem but there is a grain of discovery in the solution of any problem.

*—George Polya: **How to Solve It**, "Preface," 1945*

21. You propound a complicated mathematical problem: give me a slate and half an hour's time, and I can produce a wrong answer.

—George Bernard Shaw: Attributed

22. An elegant solution is generally considered to be one characterized by clarity, conciseness, logic and surprise.

*—C.W. Trigg, ed. **Mathematical Quickies**, 1985*

23. The mathematician must be capable of total involvement in a specific problem. To do mathematics, you must immerse yourself completely in a situation, studying it from all aspects, toying with it day and night, and devoting every scrap of available energy to understanding it. You can permit yourself occasional breaks, and probably should; nevertheless the state of immersion must go on for somewhat extended periods, usually several days or weeks.

*—Donald Weidman: "Emotional Perils of Mathematics"; **Science**, September, 1965*

20.7 Learning and Teaching Problem Solving

1. The best way to conduct a problem seminar is, of course, to present problems, but it is just as bad for an omniscient teacher to do all the asking in a problem seminar as it is for an omniscient teacher to do all the talking in a lecture course.... Just as you would not tell your students all the answers, you should also not ask them all the questions. One of the hardest parts of problem solving is to ask the right question and the only way to do so is to practice.

*—Paul Halmos: "The Heart of Mathematics"; **The American mathematical Monthly**, 87; August–September, 1980*

2. The student of arithmetic who has mastered the first four rules of his art, and successfully striven with money sums and fractions, finds himself confronted by an unspoken expanse of questions known as problems.

*—Stephen B. Leacock: **Literary Lapses**, 1910*

3. Teach to the problems, not to the text.

*—E. Kim Neubuts: In H. Eves: **Return to Mathematical Circles**, 1988*

4. Teaching to solve problems is education of the will. Solving problems which are not too easy for him, the student learns to persevere through success, to appreciate small advance, to wait for the essential idea, to concentrate with all his might when it appears. If the student had no opportunity in school to familiarize himself with the varying emotions of the struggle for the solution his mathematical education failed in the most vital point.

*—George Polya: **How to Solve It**, 1945*

5. Solving problems is a practical art, like swimming, or skiing, or playing the piano; you can learn it only by imitation and practice ... if you wish to learn swimming you have to go into the water, and if you want to become a problem solver you have to solve problems.

*—George Polya: **Mathematical Discovery, Vol. I**, 1962*

6. A student who has merely done mathematical exercises but has never solved a mathematical problem may be likened to a person who has learned the moves of the chess pieces but has never played a game of chess. The real thing in mathematics is to play the game.

*—Stephen J. Turner: Quoted in Howard Eves: **Mathematical Circles Adieu**, 1977*

20.8 Puzzles

1. A good puzzle should demand the exercise of our best with and ingenuity, and although a knowledge of mathematics ... and ... of logic are often of great service in the solution of these things, yet it sometimes happens that a kind of natural cunning and sagacity is of considerable value.

*—Henry E. Dudeney: **Amusements in Mathematics**, 1917*

2. When a man says, "I have never solved a puzzle in my life," it is difficult to know exactly what he means, for every intelligent individual is doing it every day. The unfortunate inmates of our lunatic asylums are sent there expressly because they cannot solve puzzles—because they have lost their powers of reason. If there were no puzzles to solve, there would be no questions to ask; and if there were no questions to be asked, what a world it would be! We should all be equally omniscient, and conversation would be useless and idle.

*—Henry E. Dudeney: **Amusements in Mathematics**, 1917*

3. Puzzles are made of the things that the mathematician, no less than the child, plays with, and dreams and wonders about, for they are made of things and circumstances of the world he [or she] live in.

—Edward Kasner: Quoted in Harold Jacobs: ***Mathematics: A Human Endeavor****, 1994*

4. [My criterion for a good puzzle is:] Does its statement involve, not only the labor of working out the answer (which for many has a very slight appeal) but also the excitement of first discovering how the answer is to be arrived at? My main pleasure, in constructing puzzles, lies in seeking to provide just this 'kick'.

—Hubert Phillips: ***Question Time****; "Introduction," 1937*

5. I'm primarily interested in puzzles related to deep ideas in mathematics.—My favorite puzzles are those in which it seems there's no possibility of a solution.

—Raymond Smullyan: ***What Is the Name of this Book?****, 1979*

21

Mathematics and Nature

21.1 Nature Interpreted by Mathematics

1. Mathematical metaphors are not different from other forms of human understanding. They may provide some significant insights, but are not a holy grail of ultimate truth.... Despite our desires to the contrary, nature is not obliged to limit its complexity to the confines of the human imagination.

*—James O. Bullock: "Literacy in the Language of Mathematics"; **American Mathematical Monthly**, October, 1994*

2. Countless laws of construction and constitution penetrate matter like secret flashes of mathematical lightning. To equal nature it is necessary to be mathematically and geometrically exact. Number and fantasy, law and quantity, these are the living creative strengths of nature; not to sit under a green tree but to create crystals and to form ideas, that is what it means to be at one with nature.

*—Karel Capek: **R.U.R.**, 1920*

3. Treat nature in terms of the cylinder, the sphere, the cone, all in perspective.... Nature, for us, lies more in depth than on the surface.

*—Paul Cezanne: in Emile Bernard: **Paul Cezanne**, 1925*

4. In the study of the sciences which depend upon mathematics, those who do not consult nature but authors, are not children of nature but only her grandchildren.

*—Leonardo Da Vinci: **The Notebooks of Leonardo Da Vinci**, Edward MacCurdy, tr., 1938*

5. Our experience hitherto justifies us in believing that nature is the realization of the simplest conceivable mathematical ideas.

*—Albert Einstein: **The World As I See It**, 1934*

6. Nature seems very conversant with the rules of pure mathematics, as our mathematicians have formulated them in their studies, out of their own inner consciousness and without drawing to any appreciable extent on their experience of the outer world.... In any event, it can hardly be disputed that nature and our conscious mathematical minds work according to the same laws.

*—Sir James Jeans: **The Mysterious Universe**, 1930*

7. All the effects of nature are only the mathematical consequences of a small number of immutable laws.

—Pierre-Simon de Laplace: "A Philosophical Essay on Probabilities," 1814

8. Why is geometry often described as "cold" and "dry"? One reason lies in its inability to describe the shape of a cloud, a mountain, a coastline, or a tree. Clouds are not spheres, mountains are not cones, coastlines are not circles, and bark is not smooth, nor does lightning travel in a straight line.... I claim that many patterns of Nature are so irregular and fragmented, that compared with Euclid, ... nature exhibits not simply a higher degree but an altogether different level of complexity....

*—Benoit Mandelbrot: **The Fractal Geometry of Nature**, 1982*

9. It would be necessary to have completely forgotten the history of science not to remember that the desire to understand nature has had on the development of mathematics the most important and happiest influence....

*—Henri Poincare: "The Value of Science"; **Popular Science Monthly**, 1906*

10. Minds conceived of strange monsters without counterpart in nature. Having once discovered these monsters (and congratulated themselves on a creativity superior to nature), mathematicians banished the pathological beasts, mostly unseen, to a mathematical zoo. They could imagine no use for, nor interest in, their creations by natural scientists. Nature, however, was not so easily outdone.

—Richard Voss: in Benoit Mandelbrot: ***The Fractal Geometry of Nature****, 1982*

11. Mathematics is found to be the special, necessary lens through which nature must be observed since nature is defined as being exactly a structure of mathematical entities and relations....

—Will Wright: ***Wild Knowledge: Science, Language and Social Life in a Fragile Environment****; University of Minnesota Press, 1992*

21.2 Laws of Mathematics

1. As far as the laws of mathematics refer to reality, they are not certain; and as far as they are certain, they do not refer to reality.

—Albert Einstein: In J.R. Newman, ed. ***The World of Mathematics****, 1956*

2. The laws of mathematics are not merely human inventions or creations. They simply are; they exist quite independently of the human intellect. The most that any ... with a keen intellect can do is find out that they are there and take cognizance of them.

—M.C. Escher: Quoted in Theoni Pappas: ***The Music of Reason****, 1995*

3. All mathematical laws which we find in Nature are always suspect to me, in spite of their beauty. They give me no pleasure. They are merely auxiliaries. At close range it is all not true.

—Georg Christoph Lichtenberg: ***Aphorisms****, c. 1791; in J.P. Stern:* ***Lichtenberg****, 1959*

4. The latest authors, like the most ancient, strove to subordinate the phenomena of nature to the laws of mathematics.

—Isaac Newton: ***Principia Mathematica****, 1687*

5. Conterminous with space and coeval with time is the kingdom of Mathematics; within this range her dominion is supreme; otherwise than according to her order nothing can exist, and nothing takes place in contradiction to her laws.

—William Spottiswoode: Presidential Address to the British Association, 1878

21.3 Laws of Motion

1. Give me a place to stand on and I will move the earth.

—Archimedes: Quoted by Pappus of Alexandria: ***Collection****, c. 4th. cent. A.D.;* ***Synagogue****, F. Hultsch, ed., 1868*

2. The mathematics of instantaneous motion was invented by two superb minds of the late seventeenth century—Isaac Newton and Gottfried Leibniz. It is now so familiar to us that we think of time as a natural element in a description of nature; but that was not always so.

—Jacob Bronowski: "The Music of the Spheres" ***The Ascent of Man****, 1973*

3. Alice looked round in great surprise. "Why, I do believe we've been under this tree all the time! Everything's just as it was!" "Of course it is," said the Queen, "what would you have it?" "Well, in our country," said Alice, "you'd generally get to somewhere else if you ran very fast for a long time, as we've been doing." "A slow sort of country!" said the Queen. "Now here, you see, it takes all the running you can do to keep in the same place. If you want to get somewhere else, you must run at least twice as fast as that!"

—Lewis Carroll: ***Alice's Adventures in Wonderland****, 1865*

4. Since nothing stands in the way of the movability of the earth, I believe we must now investigate whether it also has several motions, so that it can be considered one of the planets. That it is not the center of all the revolutions is proven by the irregular motions of the planets, and in their varying distances from the earth, which cannot be explained as concentric circles with the earth as the center.

—Nicolaus Copernicus: ***De Revolutionibus Orbium Coelestium****, 1530, published at his death, 1543*

5. I should think that anyone who considered it more reasonable for the whole universe to move in order to let the Earth remain fixed would be more irrational than one who should climb to the top of a cupola just to get a view of the city and its environs, and then demand that the whole countryside should revolve around him so that he would not take the trouble to turn his head.

—Galileo Galilei: ***Dialogue on the Two Chief World Systems****, 1632*

6. Now computer calculations, based on observations from the Voyager satellites and ground-based telescopes, show that just about every moon—except the earth's—has experienced millions of years chaotic tumbling. A tumbling moon falls end over end, twists sideways, speeds up, slows down, all the time obeying Newton's completely deterministic laws of motion, yet defy prediction in a way that scientists used to consider impossible.

—James Gleick, 1987; Quoted in Isaac Asimov: ***Book of Science and Nature****, 1988*

7. A body at rest remains at rest and a body in motion remains in uniform motion in a straight line unless acted upon by an external force; the acceleration of a body is directly proportioned to the applied force and is the direction of the straight line in which the force acts; and for every force there is an equal and opposite force in reaction.

—*Isaac Newton: "Laws of Motion"; **The Mathematical Principles of Natural Philosophy**, 1687; Andrew Motte, tr., 1729*

8. Geometry supposes ... that we know what thing is meant by words: motion, number, space; and without stopping uselessly to define them it penetrates their nature and lays bare their marvelous properties.... These three things, which comprise the entire universe ... are reciprocally and necessarily related. For we cannot imagine a motion without something that moves, and this thing being one, that unity is the origin of all number. Finally, since motion is impossible without space, we see that these three things are contained in the first. Even time is included there too, for motion and time are correlative (fast and slow, which differentiate motion, having a necessary reference to time.)

—*Blaise Pascal: **Geometrical Demonstration**, c. 1640s*

9. So, I for one, think it is gratuitous for anyone to enquire into the causes of the motion towards the center when once the fact that the Earth occupies the middle place in the universe, and that all weights move towards it, is made so patent by the observed phenomena themselves.

—*Ptolemy: **Almagest**, c. 2nd cent. A.D.*

21.4 Laws of Nature

1. If all events from now through eternity were continually observed (whereby probability would ultimately become certainty), it would be found that everything in the world occurs for definite reasons and in definite conformity with law, and that hence we are constrained, even for things that may seem quite accidental, to assume a certain necessity and, as it were, fatefulness.

—*Jacob I Bernoulli: **Ars Conjectandi**, 1713*

2. Every one of our laws is a purely mathematical statement in rather complex and abstruse mathematics.... Why? I have not the slightest idea.

—*Richard Feynman: **The Character of Physical Laws**, 1967*

3. If you do something once, people will call it an accident. If you do it twice, they call it a coincidence. But do it a third time and you've just proven a natural law.

—*Grace Murray Hopper: in Ethlie Ann Vare and Greg Ptacek: **Mothers of Invention**, 1988*

4. The chess board is the world, the pieces are the phenomena of the universe, the rules of the game are what we call the laws of Nature. The player on the other side of the board is hidden from us. We know that his play is always fair, just, and patient. But also we know, to our cost, that he never overlooks a mistake, or makes the smallest allowance for ignorance.

—*T.H. Huxley: **A Liberal Education**, 1868*

5. It seems self-evident that mathematics is not likely to be of much help in discovering laws of nature.

—*Mark Kac: Quoted in **The Mathematical Intelligencer**, vol. 1, 1978*

6. All events, even those which on account of their insignificance do not seem to follow the great laws of nature, are a result of it just as necessarily as the revolutions of the sun.

—*Pierre-Simon de Laplace: **A Philosophical Essay on Probabilities**, 1814, F.W. Truscott & F.L. Emory, tr., 1951*

7. Although the idea that the universe has an order that is governed by natural laws that are not immediately apparent to the senses is very ancient, it is only in the last three hundred years that we have discovered a method for uncovering the hidden order—the scientific-experimental method. So powerful is the method that virtually everything scientists know about the natural world comes from it. What they find is that the architecture of the universe is indeed built according to invisible universal rules, what I call the cosmic code—the building code of the Demiurge.

—*Heinz Pagels: **The Cosmic Code**, 1983*

8. ...we have no right to assume that any physical laws exist, or if they have existed up to now, that they will continue to exist in a similar manner in future.

—*Max Planck: **Universe in the Light of Modern Physics**, 1931*

9. Scientific laws, when we have reason to think them accurate, are different in form from the common-sense rules which have exceptions: they are always, at least in physics, either differential equations, or statistical averages.

—*Bertrand Russell: **The Analysis of Matter**, 1954*

22

Philosopy, Mathematics, Truth and Certainty

22.1 Philosophy and Mathematics

1. Those who occupy themselves with Mathematics to the neglect of Philosophy, are like the wooers of Penelope, who, unable to attain the mistress, contend themselves with the maids.

—Chian Aristo: in ***Edinburgh Review****, Vol. 52, January, 1836*

2. Mathematics has come to be identical with philosophy for modern thinkers, though they say that it should be studied for the sake of other things.

—Aristotle: ***Metaphysics****; c. 4th cent. B.C.*

3. There is a crisis in contemporary mathematics, and nobody who has not noticed it is being willfully blind. The crisis is due to our neglect of philosophical issues....

—Errett Bishop: "The Crisis in Contemporary Mathematics"; ***Historica Mathematica****, 2, 1975*

4. Without mathematics one cannot fathom the depths of philosophy; without philosophy one cannot fathom the depths of mathematics; without the two one cannot fathom anything.

—Bordas-Demoulins: Quoted in A. Rebiere: ***Mathematiques et Mathematiciens****, 1898*

5. The real finisher of our education is philosophy, but it is the office of mathematics to ward off the dangers of philosophy.

—J.F. Herbart: "Pestalozzi's Idee eines A B C der Anschauung"; ***Werke****, 1890*

6. In the end mathematics is but simple philosophy, and philosophy, higher mathematics in general.

—Novalis: ***Schriften****, 1901*

7. The only practical direction to the philosopher is a course in mathematics to train him in abstract thought, and in a faith in the unembodied.

—Plotinus (A.D. c. 203–262): Quoted in P.V. Pistorius: ***Plotinus and Neoplatonism****, 1952*

8. Plato caused mathematics in general and geometry in particular to make a very great advance, by reason of his enthusiasm for them, which of course is obvious from the way he filled his books with mathematical illustrations, and everywhere tries to kindle admiration for these subjects, in those who make a pursuit of philosophy.

—Proclus: ***Commentary on Euclid, Book I****, c. 5th cent. A.D., published in Europe, 1533*

9. To create a healthy philosophy you should renounce metaphysics but be a good mathematician.

—Bertrand Russell: "The Problems of Philosophy," 1912: Lecture, 1935: Quoted in E.T. Bell: ***Men of Mathematics****, 1937*

10. Philosophy is an attempt to express the infinity of the universe in terms of the limitations of language.

—Alfred North Whitehead: "Autobiographical Notes" in Paul Schilpp: ***The Philosophy of Alfred North Whitehead****, 1941*

11. Someone once said that philosophy is the misuse of a terminology which was invented just for this purpose. In the same vein, I would say that mathematics is the science of skillful operations with concepts and rules invented just for this purpose.

—Eugene Wigner: "The Unreasonable Effectiveness of Mathematics in the Natural Sciences"; ***Comm. on Pure and Applied Mathematics****, 13; February, 1960*

12. With my full philosophical rucksack I can only climb slowly up the mountain of mathematics.

—Ludwig Wittgenstein: ***Culture and Value****, 1959*

22.2 Philosophy of Mathematics

1. Of Aristotle's extant work no one treats of mathematics systematically.... However, numerous passages on mathematics are distributed throughout the works we possess and indicate a definite philosophy of mathematics.

—*H.G. Apostle:* ***Aristotle's Philosophy of Mathematics****, 1952*

2. Hilbert returned to Greece for the beginning of his philosophy of mathematics. Resuming the Pythagorean program of a rigidly and fully stated set of postulates from which a mathematical argument must proceed by strict and deductive reasoning, Hilbert made the program of the postulational development of mathematics more precise that it had been with the Greeks, and in 1899 issued the first edition of his classic on the foundations of geometry.

—*E.T. Bell:* ***Men of Mathematics****, 1937*

3. ...there are still real controversies in the philosophy of mathematics over whether the history of mathematics has any bearing on its philosophy, and whether the experiences and practices of working mathematicians can shed any light on questions of mathematical knowledge.

—*Paul Ernest:* ***Social Constructivism as a Philosophy of Mathematics****; "Introduction," 1998*

4. It is reasonable to propose a new task for mathematical philosophy: not to seek indubitable truth but to give an account of mathematical knowledge as it really is—fallible, corrigible, tentative and evolving, as is every other kind of human knowledge.

—*Reuben Hersh: "Some Proposals for Reviving the Philosophy of Mathematics";* ***Advances in Mathematics****, 1979*

5. A distinguishing characteristic of mathematics is its universality, its independence of time, place, and circumstance. The philosophers have made a great deal of this. They have ascribed to mathematical truth an absolute quality, transcending human experience and human existence. Perhaps they are right; nobody can prove the contrary. The alleged absoluteness of mathematics has always made it a refuge for souls who wanted to shut themselves away from the world.

—*Dunham Jackson: "The Human Significance of Mathematics"; Address of the retiring president of the Mathematical Association of America, December 29, 1927; in* ***The American Mathematical Monthly****, 25, 1928*

6. As the philosophy of law does not legislate, or the philosophy of science devise or test scientific hypotheses—the philosophy of mathematics does not add to the number of mathematical theorems and theories. It is not mathematics. It is a reflection upon mathematics, giving rise to its own particular questions and answers.

—*Stephen Korner:* ***The Philosophy of Mathematics****, 1960*

7. Under the present dominance of formalism, one is tempted to paraphrase Kant: the history of mathematics, lacking the guidance of philosophy, has become blind, while the philosophy of mathematics, turning its back on the most intriguing phenomena in the history of mathematics, has become empty.

—*Imre Lakatos:* ***Proofs and Refutations: The Logic of Mathematical Discovery****, 1976*

8. I assume that the job of the philosopher of mathematics is to describe and explain mathematics, not to reform it.

—*Penelope Maddy:* ***Realism in Mathematics****, 1990*

9. [Auguste Comte] may truly be said to have created the philosophy of higher mathematics.

—*John Stuart Mill:* ***System of Logic****, 1846*

10. The philosophy of mathematics begins when we ask for a general account of mathematics, a synoptic vision of the discipline that reveals its essential features and explains just how it is that human beings are able to do mathematics.

—*T. Tymoczko:* ***New Directions in the Philosophy of Mathematics****, Tymoczko, ed., 1996*

11. Philosophy ... can in the end only describe ... it cannot give any foundation ... [it] leaves mathematics as it is....

—*Ludwig Wittgenstein:* ***Philosophical Investigations****, G.E.M. Anscombe, tr., 1953*

22.3 Metaphysics and Metamathematics

1. The right method of philosophy is to wait till somebody says something metaphysical, then show him that it is nonsense.

—*A.J. Ayer:* ***Language, Truth and Logic****, 1936*

2. In Greek philosophy, the term "metaphysics" originally meant "that which comes after physics." It refers to the fact that Aristotle's metaphysics was found, untitled, placed after his treatise on physics. But metaphysics soon came to mean those topics that lie beyond physics (we would today say beyond science) and yet may have a bearing on the nature of scientific inquiry. So metaphysics means the study of topics about physics (or science generally), as opposed to the scientific study of the subject itself.

—*Paul Davies:* ***The Mind of God****, 1992*

3. A man who could give a convincing account of mathematical reality would have solved very many of the most difficult problems of metaphysics. If he could include physical reality in his account, he would have solve them all.

—*G.H. Hardy:* ***A Mathematician's Apology****, 1941*

4. The metaphysical philosopher from his point of view recognizes mathematics as an instrument of education, which strengthens the power of attention, develops the sense of order and the faculty of construction, and enables the mind to grasp under the simple formulae the quantitative differences of physical phenomena.

—*Benjamin Jowett:* ***Dialogues of Plato****, 1897*

5. Metamathematics must study the formal system as a system of symbols, etc., which are considered wholly objectively. This means simply that those symbols, etc. are themselves the ultimate objects, and are not being used to refer to something other than themselves. The metamathematician looks at them, not through and beyond them; thus they are objects without interpretation or meaning.

—*Stephen Cole Kleene:* ***Introduction to Metamathematics****, 1952*

6. The basic idea of metamathematics may be understood through an analogy. If one wished to study the effectiveness of comprehensiveness of the Japanese language, to do so in Japanese would handicap the analysis because it might be subject to the limitations of Japanese. However, if English is an effective language, one might use English to study Japanese.

—*Morris Kline:* ***Mathematics: The Loss of Certainty****, 1980*

7. ...we have to admit that meta-mathematics does not stop the infinite regress in proofs which now appears in the infinite hierarchy of ever richer meta-theories.

—*Imre Lakatos: "Mathematics, Science, and Epistemology";* ***Philosophical Papers****, Vol. 2, 1978*

8. Mathematics is the only true metaphysics.

—*William Thomson, Lord Kelvin: in S.P. Thompson:* ***The Life of William Thomson, Baron Kelvin of Larp****, 1910*

9. There is no religious denomination in which the misuse of metaphysical expressions has been responsible for so much sin as it has in mathematics.

—*Ludwig Wittgenstein:* ***Remarks on the Foundations of Mathematics****, 1956, 1983 G.E.M. Anscombe & B. Blackwell, tr.*

22.4 The Nature of Mathematical Truth

1. There are and can exist but two ways of investigating and discovering truth. The one hurries on rapidly from the senses and particulars to the most general axioms, and from them, as principles and their supposed indisputable truth, derives and discovers the intermediate axioms.... The other constructs its axioms from the senses and particulars, by ascending continually and gradually, till it finally arrives at the most general axioms, which is the true but unattempted way.

—*Francis Bacon:* ***Novum Organum****, 1620*

2. Mathematicians have loved mathematics because, like the graces of which Sappho wrote, the subject has wrists like wild roses. If it is beauty that governs the mathematician's souls, it is truth and certainty that remind them of their duty. At the end of the nineteenth century, mathematicians anxious about the foundations of their subject asked themselves why mathematics was true and whether it was certain and to their alarm discovered that they could not say and did not know.

—*David Berlinski:* ***The Advent of the Algorithm****, "Introduction," 2000*

3. Mathematics is neither a description of nature nor an explanation of its operation; it is not concerned with physical motion or with the metaphysical generation of quantities. It is merely the symbolic logic of possible relations, and as such is concerned with neither approximate nor absolute truth, but only with hypothetical truth.

—*Carl B. Boyer:* ***The History of the Calculus and Its Conceptual Development****, 1949*

4. He who gives a portion of his time and talent to the investigation of mathematical truth will come to all other questions with a decided advantage over his opponents. He will be in argument what the ancient Romans were in the field: to them the day of battle was a day of comparative recreation, because they were ever accustomed to exercise with arms much heavier than they fought; and reviews differed from a real battle in two respects: they encountered more fatigue, but the victory was bloodless.

—*Charles Caleb Colton:* ***Lacon****, 1866*

5. Geometrical truths are in a way asymptotes to physical truths; that is to say, the latter approach the former indefinitely near without ever reaching them exactly.

—*Jean le Rond D'Alembert: Quoted in Alphonse Rebiere:* ***Mathematiques et Mathematiciens: Pensees et Curiosites****, 1889*

6. But in our opinion such truths [arithmetical] should be derived from notions rather than notations.

—*Richard Dedekind: Quoted in E.T. Bell:* ***Men of Mathematics****, 1937*

7. If you would be a real seeker after truth, you

must at least once in your life doubt, as far as possible, all things.

—Rene Descartes: ***Discourse on the Method of Rightly Conducting the Reason and Seeking for Truth in the Sciences****, 1637*

8. Social constructivism views mathematics as a social construction. It draws on conventionalism, in accepting that human language, rules and agreement play a key role in establishing and justifying the truths of mathematics....

—Paul Ernest: ***The Philosophy of Mathematics Education****, 1991*

9. A mind that had the power to perceive at once the totality of mathematical truths—not just those known to us but all the truths possible—would be able to deduce them regularly and, as it were mechanically ... but it does not happen like that.

—Evariste Galois: ***Ecrits et memoires mathematiques d'Evariste Galois****, R. Bourgne & J.P. Azra, eds., 1962*

10. If others would but reflect on mathematical truths as deeply and as continuously as I have, they would make my discoveries.

—Carl Friedrich Gauss: In J.R. Newman, ed. ***The World of Mathematics****, 1956*

11. The shortest path between two truths in the real domain passes through the complex domain.

—Jacques Hadamard: In Jean-Pierre Kahane: "Jacques Hadamard" ***The Mathematical Intelligencer****, vol. 13, Winter, 1991*

12. It seems hardly credible at first sight that the whole of mathematics with its hard-earned theorems and its frequently surprising results could be dissolved into tautologies. But this argument overlooks just a minor detail, namely the circumstance that we are not omniscient.

—Hans Hahn: ***The Collected Works of Hans Hahn****, L. Schmetterer & K. Sigmund, eds., 1995*

13. The joy of suddenly learning a former secret and the joy of suddenly discovering a hitherto unknown truth are the same to me—both have the flash of enlightenment, the almost incredibly enhanced vision, and the ecstasy and euphoria of released tension.

—Paul R. Halmos: ***I Want to Be a Mathematician****, 1985*

14. The truths of geometry exist and are verified in every part of space, as the statue in the marble. They may not depend on the thinking mind for their conception and discovery, but they cannot be contradictory to that which forms their subject-matter, and in which they are realized, in every place and at every instant of time.

—John Herschel: Review of William Whewell: "History of the Inductive Sciences," 1837; ***Philosophy of Inductive Sciences****, 1840; in* ***The Quarterly Review****, 68; June and September, 1841*

15. For how would it be above all with the truth of our knowledge and with the existence and progress of science if there were no truth in mathematics? Indeed there often appears today in professional writings and public lectures skepticism and despondency about knowledge; this is a certain kind of occultism which I regard as damaging.

—David Hilbert: Address at the International Congress in Bologna, 1928

16. If the rules of mathematics are rules of grammar, there is no stupidity involved when we fail to see that a mathematical truth is obvious.

—Lancelot Hogben: ***Mathematics for the Million****, 1964*

17. ...we have overcome the notion that mathematical truths have an existence independent and apart from our own minds. It is even strange to us that such a notion could ever have existed.

—Edward Kasner & James R. Newman: ***Mathematics and the Imagination****, 1940*

18. There are ... two kinds of truth, those of reasoning and those of fact. Truths of reasoning are necessary and their opposite is impossible: truths of fact are contingent and their opposite is possible. When a truth is necessary, its reason can be found by analysis, resolving it into more simple ideas and truths, until we come to those which are primary.

—Gottfried Wilhelm Leibniz: ***Monadology****, Robert Latta, tr.*

19. A mathematical truth is neither simple nor complicated in itself, it is.

—Emile Lemoine: Quoted in E.T. Bell: ***Men of Mathematics****, 1937*

20. The peculiarity of the evidence of mathematical truths is that all the argument is on one side. There are no objections, and no answers to objections.

—John Stuart Mill: ***On Liberty****, 1859*

21. I do not know what I may appear to the world; but to myself I seem to have been only like a boy playing on the seashore, and diverting myself in now and then finding a smoother pebble or a prettier shell than ordinary, whilst the great ocean of truth lay all undiscovered before me.

—Isaac Newton: Quoted by David Brewster, ***Memoirs of the Life, Writings, and Discoveries of Sir Isaac Newton****, 1855*

22. The real nature of what exists, which constitutes its truth, is therefore never entirely attainable. It has been sought by all the philosophers, but never really found. The further we penetrate into informed ignorance, the closer we come to the truth itself.

—Nicholas of Cusa: ***Die Kunst der Vermutung****, a selection from his works, 1957*

23. ...what do we think of that question: Is the Euclidean geometry true? It has no meaning. As well ask whether the metric system is true and the old measures false; whether Cartesian coordinates are true and polar coordinates false. One geometry can not be more true than another; it can only be more convenient.

—Henri Poincare: ***Science and Hypothesis****, 1905*

24. ...the mathematician feels compelled to accept mathematics as true, even though he is today deprived of the belief in its logical necessity and doomed to admit forever the conceivable possibility that its whole fabric may suddenly collapse by revealing a decisive self-contradiction.

—M. Polanyi: ***Knowing and Being****, 1969*

25. Yes, these are reflections, negative images
Tossing themselves about like a motionless object
Throwing their active multitude into the nothingness
And composing a counterpart for every truth.

—Raymond Queneau: Quoted in Francois Le Lionnais: "Beauty in Mathematics" in ***Great Currents of Mathematics****, F. Le Lionnais, ed., 1971*

26. Whereas the facts of mathematics, once discovered, will never change, the method by which these facts are verified has changed many times in the past, and it would be foolhardy to expect that it will not change again at some future date.

—Gian-Carlo Rota: "The Concept of Mathematical Proof" in ***Essays in Humanistic Mathematics****, Alvin White, ed., 1993*

27. Who does not know the works of the mathematicians and scientists dies without knowing truth.

—Karl Schellbach: Quoted in Howard W. Eves: ***Mathematical Circles Adieu****, 1977*

28. Where else do you have absolute truth? You have it in mathematics and you have it in religion, at least for some people. But in mathematics you can really argue that this is as close to absolute truth as you can get. When Euclid showed that there were an infinite number of primes, that's it! There are an infinite number of primes, no ifs, ands, or buts! That's as close to absolute truth as I can see getting.

—Joel Spencer: Quoted in a film about Erdos: ***N Is a Number****, Paul Csicery, producer; in Reuben Hersh:* ***What Is Mathematics, Really?****, 1997*

29. Mathematics is the most exact science, and its conclusions are capable of absolute proof. But this is so only because mathematics does not attempt to draw absolute conclusions. All mathematical truths are relative, conditional.

—Charles P. Steinmetz: In E.T. Bell: ***Men of Mathematics****, 1937*

30. Doubt is faith in the main;
But faith, on the whole is doubt;
We cannot believe by proof;
But could we believe without?

One and two are not one;
But one and nothing is two;
Truth can hardly be false,
If falsehood cannot be true.

—Algernon Swinburne (Faith, Truth, False): "The Heptalogia," ***Parodies: An Anthropology from Chaucer to Beerbohm—and After****, Dwight Macdonald, ed., 1960*

31. The investigation of mathematical truths accustoms the mind to method and correctness in reasoning, and is an employment peculiarly worthy of rational beings.... From the high ground of mathematical and philosophical demonstration, we are insensibly led to far nobler and sublime medications.

—George Washington: in Edmund Ingalls: "George Washington and Mathematics Education"; ***Mathematics Teacher****, vol. 47; 1954*

32. Apart from blunt truth, our lives sink decadently amid the perfume of hints and suggestions.

—Alfred North Whitehead: In ***The Viking Book of Aphorisms****, W.H. Auden & L. Kronenberger, eds., 1966*

33. Of the many varieties of truth, mathematical truth does not stand the lowest.

—Norbert Wiener: Quoted in Arcadii Z. Grinshpan, Mourad E.H. Ismail and David L. Milligan: "Complete Monotonicity and Diesel Fuel Spray"; ***The Mathematical Intelligencer****, Vol. 22, 2, Spring, 2000*

22.5 The Certainty of Mathematics?

1. If a man begin with certainties, he shall end in doubts; but if he will be content to begin with doubts, he shall end in certainties.

—Francis Bacon: ***Advancement of Learning***

2. I shall preserve until I find something that is certain—or, at least, until I find for certain that nothing is certain.

—Rene Descartes: ***Discourse on Methods****, 1637*

3. And for mathematical science, he that doubts their certainty hath need of a dose of hellebore.

—Joseph Glanvill: ***The Vanity of Dogmatizing****, 1661; 1931 ed.*

4. The most distinctive characteristic which differentiates mathematics from the various branches of empirical science, and which accounts for its fame as the queen of the sciences, is no doubt the peculiar certainty and necessity of its results.

—Carl G. Hempel: "Geometry and Empirical Science" in J.R. Newman, ed. ***The World of Mathematics,*** *1956*

5. We ought not to believe those who today, adopting a philosophical air and a tone of superiority, prophecy the decline of culture and are content with the "unknowable" in a self-satisfied way. For us there is no unknowable, and in my opinion there is none whatsoever for the natural sciences. In place of the foolish "unknowable," let our watchword on the contrary be: Wir mussen wissen—wir werden wissen (We must know—we shall know).

—David Hilbert: "Natural Philosophy and Logic"; Address to Society of German Scientists and Physicians, September 8, 1930

6. Though there never were a circle or triangle in nature, the truths demonstrated by Euclid would for ever retain their certainty and evidence.

—David Hume: ***Treatise Concerning Human Understanding,*** *1748*

7. It is ... of the highest importance for us to know whether the method of arriving at demonstrative certainty, which is termed mathematical, be identical with that by which we endeavor to attain the same degree of certainty in philosophy, and which is termed in that science dogmatical.

—Immanuel Kant: ***Critique of Pure Reason;*** *"Transcendental Method," 1781*

8. The highest probability amounts not to certainty, without which there can be no true knowledge.

—John Locke: "Essay concerning Concerning Human Understanding," 1690

9. To explain all nature is too difficult a task for any one man or even for any one age. 'Tis much better to do a little with certainty, and leave the rest for others that come after you, than to explain all things.

—Isaac Newton: Quoted in G.F. Simmons: ***Calculus Gems,*** *1992*

10. It is not certain that everything is uncertain.

—Blaise Pascal: ***Pensees,*** *1670*

11. A habit of basing convictions upon evidence, and of giving to them only that degree of certainty which the evidence warrants, would, if it became general, cure most of the ills from which the world suffers.

—Bertrand Russell: In G. Simmons: ***Calculus Gems,*** *1992*

12. There is no more common error than to assume that, because prolonged and accurate mathematical calculations have been made, the application of the result to some fact of nature is absolutely certain.

—Alfred North Whitehead: ***Introduction to Mathematical Science,***

23

Logic and Foundations

23.1 The Nature of Logic

1. O Logic: born gatekeeper to the Temple of Science, victim of capricious destiny: doomed hitherto to be the drudge of pedants: come to the aid of thy master.

—*Jeremy Bentham: In* ***Works,*** *J. Browning, ed., 1838–43*

2. Logic, n. The art of thinking and reasoning in strict accordance with the limitations and incapacities of the human misunderstanding.

—*Ambrose Bierce:* ***The Devil's Dictionary,*** *1906*

3. "I know what you're thinking about," said Tweedledum, "but it ain't so, nohow." "Contrariwise," continued Tweedledee, "if it was so, it might be, and if it were so, it might be; and if it were so, it would be, but if it isn't, it ain't. That's logic."

—*Lewis Carroll:* ***Through the Looking Glass,*** *1871*

4. Logic is a large drawer, containing some useful instruments, and many more that are superfluous. A wise man will look into it for two purposes, to avail himself of those instruments that are really useful, and to admire the ingenuity with which those are not so, are assorted and arranged.

—*Charles Caleb Colton:* ***Lacon,*** *1825*

5. When one of those who were present said [to Epictetus], "Persuade me that logic is necessary," he replied: "Do you wish me to prove this to you." The answer was, "Yes." "Then I must use a demonstrative form of speech." This was granted. "How then will you know if I am cheating you by argument?" The man was silent. "Do you see," said Epictetus, "that you yourself are admitting that logic is necessary, if without it you cannot know so much as this, whether logic is necessary or not necessary?"

—*Epicteus:* ***Discourses,*** *C. A.D. 100*

6. Just as "beautiful" points the way for aesthetics and "good" for ethics, so do words like "true" for logic. All sciences have truth as their goals; but logic is also concerned with it in quite a different way: logic has much the same relation to truth as physics has to weight and heat. To discover truths is the task of all sciences; it falls to logic to discern the laws of truth.

—*Gottlog Frege: "Logical Investigations";* ***Collected Papers on Mathematics, Logic and Philosophy,*** *Brian McGuinness, ed., 1984*

7. While, traditionally, logic has corrected or avoided it, fuzzy logic compromises with vagueness; it is not just a logic of vagueness, it is—from what Frege's point of view could have been a contradiction in terms—a vague logic.

—*Susan Haack:* ***Deviant Logic, Fuzzy Logic,*** *1996*

8. Logic is invincible because one must use Logic to defeat Logic.

—*Oliver Heaviside: Quoted in Morris Kline:* ***Mathematics: The Loss of Certainty,*** *1980*

9. Logic is not satisfied with assertion. It cares nothing for the opinions of the great—nothing for the prejudices of the many, and least of all for the superstitions of the dead.

—*Robert G. Ingersoll:* ***Prose-Poems and Selections,*** *1884*

10. So the logicians entered the picture in their usual style, as spoilers.

—*Yiannis Moshovekias:* ***Descriptive Set Theory,*** *1980*

11. Few persons care to study logic, because everybody conceives himself to be proficient enough in the art of reasoning already. But I observe that this satisfaction is limited to one's own ratiocination, and does not extend to that of other men.

—*C.S. Peirce:* ***Fixation in Belief,*** *in* ***Writings of C.S. Peirce,*** *1872–78*

12. Logic, properly used, does not shackle thought. It gives freedom, and above all, boldness. Illogical thought hesitates to draw conclusions, because it never knows what it means, or what it assumes, or how far it trusts its own assumptions, or what will be the effect of any modification of assumptions.

—Alfred North Whitehead: ***The Organization of Thought****, 1917*

13. There can be no surprises in logic.

—Ludwig Wittgenstein: In ***The World of Mathematics****, James R. Newman, ed., 1956*

23.2 Symbolic Logic

1. It is upon the foundation of this general principle [of symbolic logic], that I propose to establish the Calculus of Logic, and that I claim for it a place among the acknowledged forms of Mathematical Analysis, regardless that in its objects and in its instruments it must at present stand alone.

—George Boole: ***Mathematical Analysis of Logic****, 1847*

2. ...the two great components of the critical movement, though distinct in origin and following separate paths, are found to converge at last in the thesis: Symbolic Logic is Mathematics. Mathematics is Symbolic Logic, the twain are one.

—Cassius J. Keyser: ***Lectures on Science, Philosophy and Art****, 1908*

3. Mathematics is but the higher development of symbolic logic.

—W.C.D. Whetman: ***The Recent Development of Physical Science****, 1904*

23.3 Logic and Mathematics

1. It is commonly considered that mathematics owes its certainty to its reliance on the immutable principles of formal logic. This ... is only half the truth imperfectly expressed. The other half would be that the principles of logic owe such a degree of permanence as they have largely to the fact that they have been tempered by long and varied use by mathematicians. "A vicious circle!" you will perhaps say. I should rather describe it as an example of the process known by mathematicians as the method of successive approximation.

—Maxime Bochner" ***Bulletin of the American Mathematical Society****, vol. 11, 1906*

2. In other words, logic, so far as we mathematicians are concerned, is no more and no less than the grammar of the language which we use, a language which had to exist before the grammar could be constructed.

—Nicolas Bourbaki: ***Journal for Symbolic Logic****, 1949*

3. We know that mathematicians care no more for logic than logicians for mathematics. The two eyes of exact science are mathematics and logic. The mathematical sect puts out the logical eye, the logical sect puts ut the mathematical eye; each believing that it sees better with one eye than with two.

—Augustus De Morgan: Quoted in Adrian Rice "Augustus De Morgan (1860–1871)"; ***The Mathematical Intelligencer****, vol. 18, Summer, 1996*

4. A mathematician's ultimate concern is that his or her inventions be logical, not realistic.

—Michael Guillen: ***Bridges to Infinity****, 1999*

5. Mathematics, that giant pincers of scientific logic....

—G.B. Halsted: ***Science****, 1905*

6. The emancipation of logic from the yoke of Aristotle very much resembles the emancipation of geometry from the bondage of Euclid; and, by its subsequent growth and diversification, logic, less abundantly perhaps but not less certainly than geometry, has illustrated the blessings of freedom.

—Cassius J. Keyser: Quoted in ***Science****, vol. 35, 1912*

7. The science of logic was founded by Aristotle in his Organon (Instrument [of reasoning], c. 300 B.C.). He said explicitly that he noted the principles of reasoning used by the mathematicians, abstracted them, and recognized them to be principles applicable to all reasoning. Thus one of the fundamental principles is the law of the excluded middle, which states that every meaningful statement is either true or false.

—Morris Kline: ***Mathematics: The Loss of Certainty****, 1980*

8. The rules of logic are to mathematics what those of structure are to architecture. In the most beautiful work, a chain of argument is presented in which every line is important on its own account, in which there is an air of ease and lucidity throughout, and the premises achieve more than would have been thought possible, by means which appear natural and inevitable.

—Bertrand Russell: "The Study of Mathematics," ***Mysticism and Logic and Other Essays****, 1917*

9. Logic is the railway track along which the mind glides easily. It is the axioms that determine our destination by setting us on this track or the other, and it is in the matter of choice of axioms that applied mathematics differs most fundamentally from pure. Pure mathematics is controlled (or should we say "uncontrolled"?) by a principle of ideological isotropy: any line of thought is as good as another, provided that it is logically smooth. Applied mathematics on the other hand follows only those tracks which offer a view of natural scenery; if sometimes the track dives into a tunnel it is because there is prospect of scenery at the far end.

*—J.L. Synge: "Postcards on Applied Mathematics"; **American Mathematical Monthly**, vol. 46, March, 1939*

10. The conclusion seems inescapable: that formal logic has to be taken over by the mathematicians. The fact is that there does not exist an adequate logic at the present time, and unless the mathematicians create one, no one else is likely to do so.

*—Oswald Veblen: Retiring Address, American mathematical Society, 1924; in **A Century of Mathematics in America***

11. It cannot be denied, however, that in advancing to higher and more general theories the inapplicability of the simple laws of classical logic eventually results in an almost unbearable awkwardness. And the mathematician watches with pain the larger part of the towering edifice which he believed to be built of concrete dissolve into mist before his eyes.

*—Hermann Weyl: **Philosophy of Mathematics and Natural Science**, 1949*

23.4 Common Sense

1. Common sense is the measure of the possible; it is composed of experience and prevision; it is calculation applied to life.

*—Henri Friedric Amiel: **Journal**, December, 26, 1852*

2. Common sense is not really so common.

*—Antoine Arnauld: **The Art of Thinking: Port-Royal Logic**, 1662*

3. Common sense is the most widely shared commodity in the world, for every man is convinced that he is well supplied with it.

*—Rene Descartes: **Discourse on Method**, 1637*

4. Common sense is the collection of prejudices acquired by age eighteen.

*—Albert Einstein: In E.T. Bell: **Mathematics, Queen and Servant of the Sciences**, 1952*

5. Mathematics is often erroneously referred to as the science of common sense. Actually, it may transcend common sense and go beyond either imagination or intuition. It has become a very strange and perhaps frightening subject from the ordinary point of view, but anyone who penetrates into it will find a veritable fairyland, a fairyland which is strange, but makes sense, if not common sense.

*—E. Kasner & J. Newman: **Mathematics and the Imagination**, 1940*

6. Do not imagine that mathematics is hard and crabbed, and repulsive to common sense. It is merely the etherialization of common sense.

*—William Thomson [Lord Kelvin]: In S.P. Thompson: **Life of Lord Kelvin**, 1910 in Morris Kline: **Mathematics in Western Culture**, 1953*

23.5 Postulates, Axioms and the Axiomatic Method

1. It cannot be that axioms established by argumentation can suffice for the discovery of new works, since the subtlety of nature is greater many times over than the subtlety of argument.

*—Francis Bacon: **Novum Organum**, 1620*

2. Before Pythagoras it had not been clearly realized that proof must proceed from assumptions. Pythagoras, according to persistent tradition, was the first European to insist that the axioms, the postulates, be set down first in developing geometry and that the entire development thereafter shall proceed by application of close deductive reasoning to the axioms.

*—E.T. Bell: **Men of Mathematics**, 1937*

3. Euclid's axiomatic procedure is a breakthrough; it is a procedure for the unification of material. It allows key assumptions to stand out. It allows for systematic procedures of verification. But as long as students are misled into believing that the polished jewels are the actual reasoning rather than the end product of reasoning, just so long will it be that Euclidean geometry will remain a curse rather than a blessing to the teaching of reasoning.

*—Douglas Campbell: "The Curse of Euclid"; **The Whole Craft of Number**, 1976*

4. The unproved postulates with which we start are purely arbitrary. They must be consistent, but they had better lead to something interesting.

*—Julian Coolidge: Quoted in D. MacHale: **Comic Sections**, 1993*

5. Goedel's theorem warns us that the axiomatic method of making logical deductions from given assumptions cannot in general provide a system which is both provably complete and consistent. There will always be truth that lies beyond, that cannot be reached from a finite collection of axioms.

*—Paul Davies: **The Mind of God**, 1992*

6. Mathematical axioms have the reputation of being self-evident, but it might seem that the axioms of infinity and that of God have the same character as far as self-evidence is concerned. Which is mathematics and which is theology? Does this, then, lead us to the idea that an axiom is merely a dialectical position on which to base further argumentation, the opening move of a game without which the game cannot get started?

—Philip J. Davis & Reuben Hersh: ***The Mathematical Experience****, 1981*

7. Taking the principle of excluded middle from the mathematician would be the same, say, as proscribing the telescope to the astronomer or to the boxer the use of his fists. To deny existence theorems derived by using the principle of excluded middle is tantamount to relinquishing the science of mathematics altogether.

—David Hilbert, 1927 [The principle of excluded middle can be stated as either a proposition or its negation is true but not both. The principle is employed in pure existence proofs and indirect proofs. The Intuitionists reject such proofs, demanding constructive proofs.]

8. To the Greeks the premises on which mathematics was to be built were self-evident truths, and they called these premises axioms. Socrates and Plato believed, as did many later philosophers, that these truths were already in our minds at birth and that we had but to recall them.

—Morris Kline: ***Mathematics for the Nonmathematician****, 1967*

9. The terms, about which the axioms say something, signify nothing concrete but rather arbitrary things that possess the basic properties stated in the axiom. However, everyone who deals with them secretly thinks about concrete things.

—Rosza Peter: "Mathematics is Beautiful"; Address to high school teachers and students, 1963; Leon Harklerond, tr. ***The Mathematical Intelligencer****, vol. 12, Winter, 1990*

10. The facts of mathematics are verified and presented by the axiomatic method. One must guard, however, against confusing the presentation of mathematics with the content of mathematics. As axiomatic presentation of a mathematical fact differs from the fact that is being presented as medicine differs from food. It is true that this popular medicine is necessary to keep the mathematician at a safe distance from the self-delusions of the mind. Nonetheless, understanding mathematics means being able to forget the medicine and enjoy the food.

—Gian-Carlo Rota: ***Indiscrete Thoughts****, 1997*

11. The method of postulating what we want has many advantages; they are the same as the advantages of theft over honest toil.

—Bertrand Russell: ***Introduction to Mathematical Philosophy****, 1919*

12. Just as independence assures that an axiom system does not say too much, the property of completeness assures us that the system says enough. A set of axioms is said to be complete if it is impossible to add a new independent axiom which is consistent with the given set and which does not contain any new undefined terms.

—Annita Tuller: ***A Modern Introduction to Geometries****, 1967*

13. There can be no formal proofs of the consistency of the logical premises themselves.

—Alfred North Whitehead, 1907

23.6 The Possible and the Impossible

1. Probable impossibilities are always to be preferred to improbable possibilities.

—Aristotle: ***Poetics****, c. 4th cent. B.C.*

2. Intellect distinguishes between the possible and the impossible; reason distinguishes between the sensible and senseless. Even the possible can be senseless.

—Max Born: ***My Life and My Views****, 1968*

3. Alice laughed: "There's no use trying," she said; "one can't believe impossible things." "I daresay you haven't had much practice," said the Queen. "When I was younger, I always did it for half an hour a day. Why sometimes I've believed as many as six impossible things before breakfast.

—Lewis Carroll: ***Through the Looking-Glass****, 1871*

4. The question of proving the impossibility of certain geometrical constructions provides one of the simplest examples of this trend in algebra. By the use of algebraic concepts we shall be able ... to prove the impossibility of trisecting the angle, constructing the regular heptagon, or doubling the cube, by ruler and compass alone.

—Richard Courant & Herbert Robbins; ***What Is Mathematics?****, 1941*

5. Today we know that possibility and impossibility have each only a relative meaning; that neither is an intrinsic property of the operation but merely a restriction which human tradition has imposed on the field of the operand. Remove the barrier, extend the field, and the impossible becomes possible.

—Tobias Dantzig: ***Number the Language of Science****, 1939*

6. When you have eliminated the impossible, what ever remains, however improbable. must be the truth.

—Arthur Conan Doyle: ***The Sign of the Four****, 1890*

7. ...when a mathematician says that something is impossible, he doesn't mean that it is very very difficult, beyond his powers, and probably beyond the powers of all humanity for the foreseeable future.... The mathematical impossible is the logical impossible.

—*Paul R. Halmos: "Mathematics as a Creative Art,"* ***American Scientist****, Vol. 56, 1968*

23.7 CONTRADICTIONS AND PARADOXES

1. How wonderful that we have met with a paradox. Now we have some hope of making progress.

—*Niels Bohr: in L.I. Ponomarev:* ***The Quantum Dice****, 1993*

2. Paradoxes are useful to attract attention to ideas.

—*Mandell Creighton:* ***Life and Letters****, 1904*

3. Mathematicians have always possessed a vast repertoire of techniques for dissolving or avoiding the problems produced by apparent logical contradictions, and thereby preventing crises in mathematics.

—*Michael Crowe: "Ten 'laws' concerning patterns of change in the history of mathematics";* ***Historia Mathematica****, 1975*

4. One of the most alluring aspects of mathematics is that its thorniest paradoxes have a way of blooming into beautiful theories.

—*P.J. Davis: Quoted in I. Kleiner & N. Movshovitz-Hadar: "The Role of Paradoxes in the Evolution of Mathematics";* ***American Mathematical Monthly****, vol. 101, #10, December, 1994*

5. He who confronts the paradoxical exposes himself to reality.

—*Friedrich Durrenmatt: "21 Points";* ***The Physicists****, James Kirkup, tr., 1962*

6. How quaint the ways of paradox—
At common sense she gaily mocks.

—*W.S. Gilbert:* ***The Pirates of Penzance****, 1879*

7. The set-theoretical paradoxes are hardly any more troublesome for mathematics than deceptions of the senses are for the physics.

—*Kurt Goedel: in Shaughan Lavine:* ***Understanding the Infinite****, 1994*

8. If you can prove two contradictory theorems then you can prove anything.

—*G.H. Hardy: in Ian Stewart:* ***Concepts of Modern Mathematics****, 1975*

9. Perhaps the greatest paradox of all is that there are paradoxes in mathematics.

—*E. Kasner & J. Newman:* ***Mathematics and the Imagination****, 1940*

10. The results obtained by Cantor had already [toward 1900] so transformed thinking that these contradictions were called paradoxes—which sounds ever so much less disturbing.

—*Henri Lebesque; 1938: Quoted in Lucienne Felix:* ***The Modern Aspect of Mathematics****, 1960*

11. After the paradoxes come the anomalies, the irregularities. They arouse some people's indignation and to others bring delight.

—*Francois Le Lionnais: Quoted in David Wells:* ***You Are a Mathematician****, 1995*

12. Contradiction is not a sign of falsity, nor the lack of contradiction a sign of truth.

—*Blaise Pascal: Quoted in* ***The Viking Book of Aphorisms****, W.H. Auden & L. Kronenberger, eds., 1966*

13. Logistic is not sterile; it engenders antinomies.

—*Henri Poincare: Attributed*

14. May we say in general ... a paradox is just any conclusion that at first sounds absurd but that has an argument to sustain it? In the end I think this account stands up pretty well. But it leaves much unsaid. The argument that sustains a paradox may expose the absurdity of a buried premise or to some preconception previously reckoned as central to physical theory, to mathematics or to the thinking process. Catastrophe may lurk, therefore, in the most innocent-seeming paradox. More than once in the history the discovery of paradox has been the occasion for major reconstruction at the foundations of thought.

—*W.V. Quine: "Paradox";* ***Scientific American****, April, 1962*

15. I felt about the contradictions much as an earnest Catholic must feel about wicked Popes.

—*Bertrand Russell:* ***The Basic Writings of Bertrand Russell****; Robert E. Egner & Lester E. Denonn, eds., 1961 [Russell is dismayed to discover paradoxes in the foundations of mathematics.]*

16. Truth consists of paradoxes and a paradox is two facts that stand on opposite hilltops and across the intervening valley call each other liars.

—*Carl Sandburg:* ***Incidentals****, 1904*

17. As lightning clears the air of impalpable vapors, so an incisive paradox frees the human intelligence from the lethargic influence of latent and unsuspected assumptions. Paradox is the slayer of Prejudice.

—*James Joseph Sylvester:* ***The Collected Mathematical Papers of James Joseph Sylvester****, Vol. 3, 1908*

18. In formal logic, a contradiction is the signal of a defeat; but in the evolution of real knowledge it marks the first step in progress towards a victory. This is one great reason for the utmost toleration of variety of opinion.... A clash of doctrines is not a disaster— it is an opportunity.

*—Alfred North Whitehead: **Science and the Modern World**, 1925*

23.8 Syllogisms and Validity

1. I have found that, as for Logic, its syllogisms and the majority of its precepts are useful rather in the communication of what we already know or ... in speaking without judgement about things of which one is ignorant.

*—Rene Descartes: **Discourse on Methods**, 1637*

2. What eludes logic is the most precious element in us, and one can draw nothing from a syllogism that the mind has not put there in advance.

*—Andre Gide: **Journals**, June, 1927*

3. ...the validity of mathematics rests neither on its alleged self-evidential character nor on any empirical basis, but derives from the stipulations which determine the meaning of mathematical concepts, and that the propositions of mathematics are therefore essentially "true by definition."

*—Carl G. Hempel: "On the Nature of Mathematical Truth"; in **The World of Mathematics**, vol. 3, James R. Newman, ed., 1956*

4. But even while this creative activity of pure thought is going on, the external world once again reasserts its validity, and by thrusting new questions upon us through the phenomena that occur, it opens up new domains of mathematical knowledge; and as we strive to bring these new domains under the dominion of pure thought we often find answers to outstanding unsolved problems, and thus at the same time we advance in the most effective way the earlier theories.

—David Hilbert: Address to Second International Congress of Mathematics, 1900

5. The validity of mathematical propositions is independent of the actual world—the world of existing subject-matters—is logically prior to it, and would remain unaffected were it to vanish from being.

*—Cassius J. Keyser: **The Pastures of Wonder**, 1929*

6. It is hard to know what you are talking about in mathematics, yet no one questions the validity of what you say. There is no other realm of discourse half so queer.

*—James R. Newman: "Commentary on The Foundations of Mathematics"; **The World of Mathematics**, 1956*

7. Formal logic, as every schoolboy knows, began with the syllogisms of Aristotle, the most famous of which is: "All men are mortal; all heroes are men; therefore all heroes are mortal." The Greek philosopher set forth 14 such syllogisms and believed that they summed up most of the operations of reasoning. Medieval theologians added 5 syllogisms to Aristotle's 14. For hundreds of years these 19 syllogisms were the foundation of the teaching of logic.

*—John E. Pfeiffer: "Symbolic Logic"; **Scientific American**, December, 1950*

8. For when one's proofs are aptly chosen,
Four are as valid as four dozen.

—Matthew Prior: "Alma: or, The Progress of Mind," 1718

23.9 Foundations of Mathematics

1. On these foundations I state that I can build up the whole of the mathematics of the present day; and if there is nothing original in my procedure, it lies solely in the fact that, instead of being content with such a statement, I proceed to prove it in the same way as Diogenes proved the existence of motion; and my proof will become more and more complete as my treatise grows.

*—Nicolas Bourbaki: "Foundations of Mathematics for the Working Mathematician"; **The Journal of Symbolic Logic**, 1949*

2. We come now to the question: what is a priori certain or necessary, respectively in geometry (doctrine of space) or its foundations? Formerly we thought everything; nowadays, we think—nothing. Already the distance-concept is logically arbitrary; there need be no things that correspond to it, even approximately.

*—Albert Einstein: "Space-Time" article; **Encyclopedia Britannica**, 14th ed.*

3. The mathematician at work relies on surprisingly vague intuitions and proceeds by fumbling fits and starts with all too frequent reversals. Clearly logic as it stands fails to give a direct account of either the historical growth of mathematics or the day-to-day experience of its practitioners. It is also clear that the search for ultimate foundations via formal systems has failed to arrive at any convincing conclusion.

*—Solomon Feferman: "The Logic of Mathematical Discovery vs. the Logical Structure of Mathematics," **Departure of Mathematics**, 1976*

4. It is difficult today to realize how bold an innovation it was to introduce talk about paper tapes and patterns punched in them into the discussions of the foundations of mathematics.

*—Max Newmann: Quoted in Charles & Ray Eames: **A Computer Perspective**, 1990 [Newmann comments on the Universal Turing Machine, a computer envisioned in 1945 by Alan Turing.]*

5. Questions that pertain to the foundations of mathematics, although treated by many in recent times, still lack a satisfactory solution. The difficulty has its main source in the ambiguity of language.

—Giuseppe Peano: ***Arithmetices principia, nova methode exposita,*** *1889: English translation in* ***Selected Works of Giuseppe Peano,*** *H. C. Kennedy, ed., 1973*

6. As mathematical logic becomes even more central within mathematics, its contributions to the philosophical understanding of foundations wane to the point of irrelevance.

—Gian-Carlo Rota: in ***Discrete Thoughts: Essays on Mathematics, Science and Philosophy,*** *Mark Kac, Gian-Carlo Rota, Jacob T. Schwartz; Quoted in* ***The Mathematical Intelligencer,*** *vol. 12, 1990*

7. For us, whose shoulders sag under the weight of the heritage of Greek thought and who walk in the paths traced out by the heroes of the Renaissance, a civilization without mathematics is unthinkable. Like the parallel postulate, the postulate that mathematics will survive has been stripped of its "evidence;" but, while the former is no longer necessary, we would not be able to get on without the latter.

—Andre Weil: "The Future of Mathematics," ***The American Mathematical Monthly,*** *1950*

8. Mathematics, like all other subjects, has now to take its turn under the microscope and reveal to the world any weaknesses there may be in its foundations.

—F. W. Westaway: in E. T. Bell: ***Men of Mathematics,*** *1956*

24

Proof and Mathematics

24.1 Mathematical Arguments

1. For hundreds of pages the closely-reasoned arguments unroll, axioms and theorems. And what remains with us in the end? A general sense that the world can be expressed in closely-reasoned arguments, in interlocking axioms and theorems.

—Michael Frayn: ***Constructions****, 1974*

2. When a somewhat long argument leads us to a simple and striking result, we are not satisfied until we have shown that we could have foreseen, if not the entire result, at least its principal features.

—Henri Poincare: Quoted in Morris Kline: ***Mathematics: The Loss of Certainty****, 1980*

3. The Euclidean way of exposition can be highly recommended, without reservation, if the purpose is to examine the argument in detail.... The Euclidean way of exposition, however, cannot be recommended without reservation if the purpose is to convey an argument to a reader or a listener who has never heard of it before.

—George Polya: ***How to Solve It****, 1945*

4. A classical example [of making arguments based on pictures or diagrams] may be found in the well-known "proof" that all triangles are isosceles, which is based on a diagram that deceives the eye by placing a certain point within and angle instead of outside, where rigorous reasoning about the situation would place it.

—Raymond L. Wilder: ***Introduction to the Foundations of Mathematics****, 1965*

24.2 Mathematical Demonstrations

1. ...I have not demonstrated here most of what I have said, because the demonstrations seem to me so simple that, provided you take the pains to see methodically whether I have been mistaken, they will present themselves to you; and it will be of much more value to you to learn them this way than by reading them.

—Rene Descartes: Quoted in ***History of Analytic Geometry****, 1956*

2. For, in the first place, his [Fermat] method is such that without intelligence and by chance, one can easily fall upon the path that one has to follow in order to find it, which is nothing else than a false position, based on the way of demonstrating which reduces to absurdity, and which is the least esteemed and the least ingenious of all those of which use is made in mathematics.

—Rene Descartes: 1638; in the Adam and Tannery edition of ***Geometrie****, 1897–1910 [Descartes dismisses Fermat's use of proofs by contradiction.]*

3. The force of rigid demonstrations such as occur only in mathematics fills me with wonder and delight. From accounts given by gunners, I was already aware of the fact the in the use of cannon and mortars, the maximum range, that is the one in which the shot goes farthest, is obtained when the elevation is 45 degrees or, as they say, at the sixth point of the quadrant; but to understand why this happens far outweighs the mere information obtained by the testimony of others or even be repeated experiment.

—Galileo Galilei: ***Dialogues Concerning Two New Sciences****, Henry Crew & Alfonso De Salvio, 1914*

4. In this proposition, that "the three angles of a triangle are equal to two right ones," one who has seen and clearly perceived the demonstration of this truth knows it to be true, when that demonstration is gone out of his mind; so that at present it is not actually in view, and possibly cannot be recollected: but he knows it in a different way from what he did before.

—*John Locke: "Essay Concerning Human Understanding," 1690*

5. Rules for Demonstration: I. Do not attempt to demonstrate any of those things so self-evident that we have nothing clearer to prove them by.

—*Blaise Pascal: "On geometrical demonstration"; in "The Provincial Letters, Pensees, Scientific Treatise" R.M. Hutchins, ed.,* ***Encyclopedia Britannica,*** *1952*

6. Thus, be it understood, to demonstrate a theorem, it is neither necessary nor even advantageous to know what it means. The geometer might be replaced by the "logic piano" imagined by Stanley Jevons; or, if you choose, a machine might be imagined where the assumptions were put in at one end, while the theorems came out the other, like the legendary Chicago machine where the pigs go in alive and come out transformed into hams and sausages. No more that these machines need the mathematician know what he does.

—*Henri Poincare:* ***The Foundations of Science,*** *1946*

24.3 Cause and Effect

1. In all disciplines in which there is systematic knowledge of things with principles, causes, or elements, it arises from a grasp of those: we think we have knowledge of a thing when we have found its primary causes and principles, and followed it back to its elements. Clearly, then, systematic knowledge of nature must start with an attempt to settle questions about principles.

—*Aristotle:* ***Posterior Analytics,*** *c. 4th cent. B.C.*

2. There is no correlation between the cause and the effect. The events reveal only an aleatory determination, connected not so much with the imperfection of our knowledge as with the structure of the human world.

—*Raymond Aron:* ***The Opium of the Intellectuals,*** *Terrence Kilmartin, tr., 1955*

3. It is the job of the astronomer to use painstaking and skilled observation in gathering together the history of the celestial movements, and then—since he cannot by any line of reasoning reach the true cause of these movements—to think up or construct whatever causes of hypothesis he pleases such that, by the assumption of these causes, those same movements can be calculated from the principles of geometry for the past and the future too.

—*Nicolaus Copernicus:* ***De Revolutionibus,*** *"Introduction to the Reader"; 1543*

4. The idea that everything in the world has a meaning is an exact analogue of the principle that everything has a cause, on which rests all science.

—*Kurt Goedel: Letter to his Mother, Quoted in John D. Barrow:* ***π in the Sky,*** *1992*

5. From (cause and effect reasoning) is derived all philosophy excepting only geometry and arithmetic.

—*David Hume:* ***A Treatise of Human Nature,*** *1739*

24.4 The Role of Assumptions in Mathematics

1. Euclid taught me that without assumptions there is no proof.
Therefore, in any argument, examine the assumptions.

—*Eric Temple Bell: In Howard Eves:* ***Return to Mathematical Circles,*** *1988*

2. We must never assume that which is incapable of proof.

—*G.H. Lewes:* ***Physiology of Common Life,*** *1859*

3. In mathematics, the "cold war" of conflicting sets of assumptions has proved fruitful and exciting. Mathematicians realize that the conflicting sets of assumptions are incompatible, but they are willing to let the proponents of the conflicting sets develop the theorems which follow from each set of assumptions.

—*Harriet F. Montague and Mabel D. Montgomery: "How Mathematicians Develop a Branch of Pure Mathematics";* ***The Significance of Mathematics,*** *1963*

4. First principles, even it they appear certain, should be carefully considered; and when they are satisfactorily ascertained, then, with a sort of hesitating confidence in human reason, you may, I think follow the course of the argument.

—*Socrates: Plato:* ***The Republic,*** *c. 380 B.C.*

24.5 That Which Is Obvious

1. "Obvious" is the most dangerous word in mathematics.

—*E.T. Bell:* ***The Handmaiden of the Sciences*** *1937*

2. A thing is obvious mathematically after you see it.

—*R.D. Carmichael:* ***The Logic of Discovery,*** *1930*

3. We decided that 'trivial' means 'proved'. So we joked with the mathematicians: "We have a new theorem—that mathematicians can prove only trivial theorems, because ever theorem that is proved is trivial."

—*Richard Feynman:* ***Surely You're Joking Mr. Feynman,*** *1985*

4. The Epicureans are wont to ridicule this theorem [the one which claims that in any triangle the sum of two sides is always greater than the remaining one], saying it is evident even to an ass and needs no proof; it is as much the mark of an ignorant man, they say, to require persuasion of evident truths as to believe what is obscure without question.... That the present theorem is known to an ass they make our from the observations that, if straw is placed at one extremity of the sides, an ass in quest of provender will make his way along the one side and not by way of the two others.

—Proclus: ***A Commentary on the First Book of Euclid's Elements****, Glenn R. Morrow, tr., 1970*

5. The proof of self-evident propositions may seem to the uninitiated, a somewhat frivolous occupation. To this we might reply that it is often by no means self-evident that one obvious proposition follows from another obvious proposition; so that we are really discovering new truths when we prove what is evident by a method which is not evident. But a more interesting retort is, that since people have tried to prove obvious propositions, they have found that many of them are false. Self-evidence is often a mere will-o'-the-wisp, which is sure to lead us astray if we take it as our guide.

—Bertrand Russell: "Mathematics and the Metaphysicians"; ***Mysticism and Logic****, 1963*

6. Not seldom did he [Sir William Thomson], in his writings, set down some mathematical statement with the prefacing remark "it is obvious that" to the perplexity of mathematical readers, to whom the statement was anything but obvious from such mathematics as preceded it on the page. To him it was obvious for physical reasons that might not suggest themselves at all to the mathematician, however competent.

—S.P. Thompson: ***Life of Lord Kelvin****, 1910*

24.6 The Nature of Proof

1. ...other things being equal, that proof is the better which proceeds from the fewest postulates, or hypotheses, or propositions.

—Aristotle: ***Analytica posteriora****; in* ***The Works of Aristotle****, W.D. Ross, ed., 1931*

2. There is a sharp disagreement among competent men as to what can be proved and what cannot be proved, as well as an irreconcilable divergence of opinions as to what is sense and what is nonsense.

—Eric Temple Bell; ***Debunking Science****, 1930*

3. What is now proved was once only imagin'd.

—William Blake: ***The Marriage of Heaven and Hell****, 1790–3*

4. Proof requires a person who can give and a person who can receive....

—Augustus De Morgan: Quoted in Howard Eves: ***In Mathematical Circles****, 1969*

5. Another roof, another proof.

—Paul Erdos: In Paul Hoffman: ***The Man Who Loved Only Numbers: The Story of Paul Eros and the Search for Mathematical Truth****, 1998*

6. Q.E.D. [Quod erat demonstrandum: Which was to be proved.]

—Euclid: ***Elements****, ca. 300 B.C.; Sir Thomas L. Heath, tr.,* ***The Thirteen Books of Euclid's Elements*** *[These letters once appeared at the end of a proof to mark its ending. A more modern means of marking the end of proofs is E.M.D.W.—"Elementary, My Dear Watson."]*

7. I mean the word proof not in the sense of the lawyers, who set two half proofs equal to a whole one, but in the sense of the mathematician, where ½ proof = 0 and it is demanded for proof that every doubt becomes impossible.

—Carl Friedrich Gauss: Quoted in G.F. Simmons: ***Calculus Gems****, 1992*

8. Proofs really aren't there to convince you that something is true—they're there to show you why it is true.

—Andrew Gleason: in ***More Mathematical People****, D. Albers, G. Alexanderson & C. Reid, eds., 1990*

9. Prepare your proof before you argue.

—Samuel HaNagid: ***Ben Mishle****, 11th cent.*

10. For centuries before the time of Cantor mathematicians simply assumed that anyone who was properly educated in their subject could distinguish a correct proof from an incorrect one. Those who had trouble in making this distinction were simply "weeded out" in the course of their training and were turned from mathematics to lesser fields of study. And no one took up seriously the question of setting forth, in explicit and mathematical terms, exactly what was meant by a correct proof.

—Leon Henkin: "Are Logic and Mathematics Identical?" ***Science****, 138, November 16, 1962*

11. The notion of proof is not absolute. Mathematicians' view of what constitutes an acceptable proof have evolved.... The validity of a proof is a reflection of the overall mathematical climate at any given time.

—Israel Kleiner: "Rigor and Proof in Mathematics: A Historical Perspective"; ***Mathematics Magazine****, December, 1991*

12. A proof becomes a proof after the social act of "accepting it as a proof." This is as true of mathematics as it is of physics, linguistics and biology.

—Y.I. Manin: ***A Course in Mathematical Logic****, 1977*

13. There are three levels of understanding of a proof. The lowest is the pleasant feeling of having grasped the argument; the second is the ability to repeat it; and the third or top is that of being able to refute it.

—*Karl Popper:* ***The Logic of Scientific Discovery,*** *1959*

14. It is one of the chief merits of proofs that they instill a certain skepticism about the result proved.

—*Bertrand Russell:* ***Principles of Mathematics,*** *1903*

15. Everything is trivial when you know the proof.

—*D.V. Widder: Quoted by Ralph P. Boas, Jr.: in* ***More Mathematical People,*** *D.J. Albers et al, ed., 1990*

16. [Proof is no more than the] testing of our intuition.... Obviously we don't possess, and probably will never possess, any standard of proof that is independent of time, the thing to be proved, or the person of school of thought using it. And under these conditions, the sensible thing to do seems to admit that there is no such thing, generally, an absolute truth [proof] in mathematics, whatever the public may think.

—*Raymond L. Wilder: "The Nature of Mathematical Proof,"* ***The American Mathematical Monthly,*** *1944*

17. ...till, demanding proof,
And seeking it in everything, I lost
All feeling of conviction, and, in fine,
Sick, wearied out with contradictions,
Yielded up moral questions in despair,
And for my future studies, as the sole
Employment of the engulfing faculty,
Turn'd towards mathematics, and then clear
And solid evidence....

—*William Wordsworth: "The Prelude"; Quoted in* ***The Mathematical Intelligencer,*** *Vol., 22, 2, Spring, 2000*

24.7 Mathematical Proofs

1. ...the mathematician learns to accept no fact, to believe no statement, however apparently reasonable or obvious or trivial, until it has been proved, rigorously and totally by a series of steps proceeding from universally accepted first principles.

—*Alfred Adler: "Mathematics and Creativity";* ***The New Yorker Magazine,*** *1972*

2. Proof is the glue that holds mathematics together.

—*Michael Atiyah: Comment: "A Mathematical Mystery Tour";* ***Nova;*** *PBS Television*

3. Pythagoras ... imported proof into mathematics. This is his greatest achievement. Before him geometry had been largely a collection of rules of thumb empirically arrived at without any clear indication of the mutual connections of the rules, and without the slightest suspicion that all were deducible from a comparatively small number of postulates.

—*E.T. Bell:* ***Men of Mathematics,*** *1937*

4. A mathematician's reputation rests on the number of bad proofs he has given.

—*A.S. Besicovitch: In J.E. Littlewood:* ***A Mathematician's Miscellany,*** *1953*

5. Only professional mathematicians learn anything from proofs. Other people learn from explanations. I'm not sure that even mathematicians learn much from proofs in fields with which they are not familiar. A great deal can be accomplished with arguments that fall short of being formal proofs.

—*Ralph P. Boas, Jr.: "Can We Make Mathematics Intelligible?";* ***American Mathematical Monthly*** *88, 1981*

6. The first proof in the history of mathematics is said to have been given by Thales of Miletus (600 B.C.). He proved that the diameter divides a circle into two equal parts. Now this is a statement which is so simple that it appears self-evident. The genius of the act was to understand that a proof is possible and necessary.

—*Philip J. Davis & Reuben Hersh:* ***The Mathematical Experience,*** *1981*

7. Proof, in its best instances, increases understanding by revealing the heart of the matter. Proof suggests new mathematics. The novice who studies proofs gets closer to the creation of new mathematics Proof is mathematical power, the electric voltage of the subject which vitalizes the static assertions of the theorems.

—*Philip J. Davis & Reuben Hersh:* ***The Mathematical Experience,*** *1981*

8. Considering that, among all those who up to this time made discoveries in the sciences, it was the mathematicians alone who had been able to arrive at demonstrations—that is to say, at proofs certain and evident—I did not doubt that I should begin with the same truths that they have investigated, although I had looked for no other advantage from them than to accustom my mind to nourish itself upon truths and not to be satisfied with false reasons.

—*Rene Descartes:* ***Philosophy of Descartes,*** *J. Torrey, tr., 1892*

9. Whoever ... proves his point and demonstrates the prime truth geometrically should be believed by all the world, for there we are captured.

—Albrecht Durer: ***Von menschlicher Proportion,*** *1525*

10. Proof is the idol before whom the pure mathematician tortures himself.

—Sir Arthur Eddington: ***The Nature of the Physical World,*** *1928*

11. The Great Bear is looking so geometrical One would think that something or other could be proved.

—Christopher Fry: ***The Lady's Not for Burning,*** *1949*

12. Anyone, anywhere along the line, can fill in the details and check them. The fact that a computer can run through more details in a few hours than a human could ever hope to do in a lifetime does not change the basic concept of mathematical proof. What has changed is not the theory but the practice of mathematics.

—Wolfgang Haken: in Ian Stewart: ***From Here to Eternity,*** *1996*

13. A mathematical proof should resemble a simple and clear-cut constellation, not a scattered cluster in the Milky Way.

—G.H. Hardy: ***A Mathematician's Apology,*** *1941*

14. There is strictly speaking no such things as mathematical proof.... We can, in the last analysis, do nothing but point; ... proofs are what Littlewood and I call gas, rhetorical flourishes designed to affect psychology, pictures in the board in lectures, devices to stimulate the imagination of pupils.

—G.H. Hardy, "Mathematical Proof," ***Mind,*** *1928*

15. There are different versions of proof or rigor, depending on time, place, and other things. The use of computers in proofs is a nontraditional rigor. Empirical evidence, numerical experimentation, probabilistic proof all help us decide what to believe in mathematics. Aristotelian logic isn't always the only way to decide.

—Reuben Hersh: ***What Is Mathematics, Really?,*** *1997*

16. The trouble is, "mathematical proof" has two meanings. In practice, it's one thing. In principle, it's another. We show students what proof is in practice. We tell them what it is in principle. The two meanings aren't identical. That's O.K. But we never acknowledge the discrepancy. How can that be O.K.?

—Reuben Hersh: ***What Is Mathematics, Really?,*** *1997*

17. If Gauss says he has proved something, it seems very probable to me; if Cauchy says so, it is about as likely as not; if Dirichlet says so, it is certain. I would gladly not get involved in such delicacies.

—Carl Gustav Jacob Jacobi: Letter to Alexander von Humboldt; Quoted in H. Pieper: "Gegen die Schmach des Belagerungszustands"; ***Spectrum,*** *1980*

18. ...mathematical proofs, like diamonds, are hard and clear, and will be touched with nothing but strict reasoning.

—John Locke: D. Burton: ***Elementary Number Theory,*** *1980*

19. The purpose of a legal proof is to remove a doubt, but this is also the most obvious and natural purpose of a mathematical proof. We are in doubt about a clearly stated mathematical assertion, we do not know whether it is true or false. Then we have a problem: to remove the doubt, we should either prove that assertion or disprove it.

—George Polya: ***Mathematical Discovery: On Understanding, Learning, and Teaching Problem Solving,*** *1981*

20. Irrefragability, thy name is mathematics. Let natural scientists accept evidence; the mathematician demands proof.

—W.V. Quine: "The Foundations of Mathematics"; ***Scientific American,*** *September, 1964*

21. Some proofs command assent. Others woo and charm the intellect. They evoke a delight and an overpowering desire to say "Amen, Amen."

—Lord Rayleigh: Quoted in H.E. Huntley: ***The Divine Proportion,*** *1970*

22. Proof is beautiful when it gives away the secret of the theorem, when it leads us to perceive the actual and not the logical inevitability of the statement that is proved.

—Gian-Carlo Rota: "The Phenomenology of Mathematical Beauty"; ***Synthese,*** *Vol. III, 2; May, 1997*

23. Even the very best mathematicians have on occasion claimed to have proved something that later turned out not to be so—their proof had a subtle gap, or there was a simple error in calculation, or they inadvertently assumed something that was not as rock-solid as they had imagined. So over the centuries, mathematicians have learned to be extremely critical of proofs. Proofs knit the fabric of mathematics together, and if a single thread is weak, the entire fabric may unravel.

—Ian Stewart: ***Nature's Numbers,*** *1995*

24. When a theorem has been proved with the help of a computer, it is impossible to give an exposition of the proof which meets the traditional test—that a sufficiently patient reader should be able to work through the proof and verify that it is correct. Even if one were to print all the programs and all the sets of data used ... there can be no assurance that a data tape has not been mispunched or misread. Moreover, every modern computer has obscure faults in its software and hardware—which so seldom causes errors that they go undetected for years—and every computer is liable to transient faults. Such errors are rare, but a few of them have probably occurred in the course of the calculations reported here.

—*H.P.F. Swinnerton-Dyer: in* ***Acta Mathematica,*** *1971; Quoted in Y.I. Manin:* ***Introduction to Mathematical Logic,*** *1977*

25. It always seems to me absurd to speak of a complete proof, or of a theorem being rigorously demonstrated. An incomplete proof is no proof, and a mathematical truth not rigorously demonstrated is not demonstrated at all.

—*J.J. Sylvester: in* ***The Collected Papers of James Joseph Sylvester*** *1908*

26. A mathematical proof must be perspicuous.

—*Ludwig Wittgenstein:* ***Remarks on the Foundations of Mathematics,*** *1956, 1983 G.E.M. Anscombe & B. Blackwell, tr.*

24.8 Rigor in Mathematical Proofs

1. Rigor should be a signal to the historian that the maps have been made, and the real explorers have gone elsewhere.

—*W.S. Anglin: "Mathematics and History,"* ***The Mathematical Intelligencer,*** *vol. 4, no. 4, 1982*

2. Modern mathematics is indebted to Cauchy for ... the introduction of rigor into mathematical analysis. It is difficult to find an adequate simile for the magnitude of this advance; perhaps the following will do. Suppose that for centuries an entire people had been worshipping false gods and suddenly their error was revealed to them. Before the introduction of rigor mathematical analysis was a whole pantheon of false gods.

—*E.T. Bell:* ***Men of Mathematics,*** *1937*

3. Rigor is the concern of philosophy not of geometry.

—*Bonaventura Cavalieri:* ***Exercitationes geometricae sex,*** *1647: Quoted in Morris Kline:* ***Mathematics: The Loss of Certainty*** *1980*

4. The only way in which to treat the elements of an exact and rigorous science is to apply to them all the rigor and exactness possible.

—*Jean Le Rond D'Alembert: Quoted in August De Morgan:* ***Trigonometry and Double Algebra,*** *1849*

5. While we must admit that mathematics has not always met reasonable standards of rigor, we must also concede that the layman is entirely right when he thinks that mathematical knowledge is more seriously based than all other knowledge.

—*Max Dehn: "The Mentality of the Mathematician: A Characterization"; Address at University of Frankfurt; January 18, 1928; Abe Schenitzer, tr.,* ***The Mathematical Intelligencer,*** *vol. 5, 2, 1983*

6. The object of mathematical rigor has been only to sanction and legitimatize the conquests of intuition.

—*Jacques Hadamard:* ***Psychology of Invention in the Mathematical Field,*** *1945*

7. Mathematics renders its best service through the immediate furthering of rigorous thought and the spirit of invention.

—*J.F. Herbart; "Mathematischer Lehrplan fur Realschulen";* ***Werke,*** *1890*

8. It is an error to believe that rigor in proof is an enemy of simplicity. On the contrary we find it confirmed by numerous examples that the rigorous method is at the same time the simpler and the most easily comprehended. The very effort for rigor forces us to find out simpler methods of proof.

—*David Hilbert: "Mathematical Problems" Lectrue to The International Congress of Mathematicians, Paris, 1900, Mary Winston Newson, tr.,* ***Bulletin of the American Mathematical Society,*** *1902*

9. The axiomatic method in Greece did not come without costs.... Too much rigor may lead to rigor mortis.

—*Israel Kleiner: "Rigor and Proof in Mathematics: A Historical Perspective";* ***Mathematics Magazine,*** *December, 1991*

10. We are inclined to believe that the literature and arts of our time have ignored two aspects of the civilizing function of mathematics. They have sacrificed the rigor which represents the part that clear consciousness plays in anything creative; and they have ignored one of the most original sources of lyricism.

—*Francois Le Lionnais: in Charles-Edouard Le Corbusier: "Architecture and the Mathematical Spirit"; in* ***Great Currents of Mathematical Thought,*** *F. Le Lionnais, ed., 1971*

11. All science, logic and mathematics included, is a function of the epoch—all science in the ideals as well as its achievements.... Sufficient unto the day is the rigor thereof.

—*E.H. Moore, 1903: Quoted in Morris Kline:* ***Mathematics: The Loss of Certainty,*** *1980*

12. True rigor is productive, being distinguished in this from another rigor which is purely formal and tiresome, casting a shadow over the problem it touches.

—*Emile Picard:* ***Bulletin American Mathematical Society,*** *Vol. 2, 1905*

13. Should we teach mathematical proofs in the high school? In my opinion, the answer is yes.... Rigorous proofs are the hallmark of mathematics, they are an essential part of mathematics' contribution to general culture.

*—George Polya: **Mathematical Discovery: On Understanding, Learning, and Teaching Problem Solving**, 1981*

14. Purity, ... is more fundamental a criterion than mathematical rigor. Indeed, rigor is basically a tool for purity, for penetrating to an insight as to just what is really going on. Historically, its meaning has varied, and the notion of a correct proof has usually changed in response to a crisis in understanding.

*—Tim Poston: "Purity in Applications"; in **Mathematics Tomorrow**, Lynn Steed, ed., 1981*

15. Mathematical rigor is like clothing; in its style it ought to suit the occasion, and it diminishes comfort and restricts freedom of movement if it is either too loose or too tight.

*—G.F. Simmons: Quoted in **The Mathematical Intelligencer**, vol. 13, Winter, 1991*

16. Rigor is no longer considered a kind of cramping formal dress which one wears for state occasions and takes off with relief upon returning home. We no longer ask whether a theorem has been rigorously proved, but whether it has been proved.

*—Andre Weil: Quoted in Lucienne Felix: **The Modern Aspect of Mathematics**, 1960*

17. Rigor is to the mathematician what morality is to man. It does not consist in proving everything, but in maintaining a sharp distinction between what is assumed and what is proved, and in endeavoring to assume as little as possible at every stage.

*—Andre Weil: "Mathematical Teaching in Universities"; **The American Mathematical Monthly**, Vol. 61, 1954*

18. A teacher once, having some fun,
In presenting that two equals one,
Remained quite aloof
From his rigorous proof;
But his class was convinced and undone.

*—Arthur White: in **Mathematics Magazine**, vol. 64; April, 1991*

24.9 Elegant Mathematical Proofs

1. One of the highest compliments one mathematician can pay another's work is to call it "elegant," for if one thing sets pure mathematics from all other sciences, it is the aesthetic standard mathematicians apply to their subject.

*—George A.W. Boehm: **The New World of Math**, 1959*

2. The best proofs in mathematics are short and crisp like epigrams, and the longest have swings and rhythms that are like music.

*—Scott Buchanan: **Poetry and Mathematics**, 1962*

3. A large part of the activity of professional mathematicians is a search for new proofs of old facts. One reason for this is pure pleasure: there is esthetic enjoyment in getting a fresh point of view on a familiar landmark. Another is that the original creator hardly ever reached his goal by the shortest, neatest, most efficient route, nor fully appreciated the connections between his brainchild and other fields of mathematics. This is connected with a third and very practical motive. Mathematics has grown so luxuriantly in the past 2,000 years that it must be continually polished, simplified, systematized, unified, and condensed.

*—Paul Halmos: "Innovation in Mathematics"; **Scientific American**, September, 1958*

4. [In a good proof] there is a high degree of unexpectedness, combined with inevitability and economy. The argument takes so odd and surprising a form; the weapons used seem so childishly simple when compared with the far-reaching consequences; but there is no escape from the conclusions.

*—G.H. Hardy: **A Mathematician's Apology**, 1940*

5. ...the feeling of mathematical elegance is only the satisfaction due to any adaptation of the solution to the needs of our mind, and it is because of this very adaptation that this solution can be for us an instrument. Consequently this esthetic satisfaction is bound up with the economy of thought.

*—Henri Poincare: "The Future of Mathematics" **Monist**, vol. 20; 1910*

6. Mathematics consists of proving the most obvious thing in the least obvious way.

*—George Polya: **How to Solve It**, 1948*

7. The elegance of a theorem is directly proportional to the number of ideas you can see in it and inversely proportional to the effort it takes to see them.

*—George Polya: **How to Solve It**, 1957, Quoted in George A.W. Boehm: **The New World of Math**, 1959*

8. I was struck by the art with which mathematicians remove, reject, and little by little eliminate everything that is not necessary for expressing the absolute with the least possible number of terms, while preserving in the arrangement of these terms a discrimination, a parallelism, a symmetry which seems to be the visible elegance of an eternal idea.

*—Edgar Quinet: Quoted in Francois Le Lionnais: "Beauty in Mathematics" in **Great Currents of Mathematics**, F. Le Lionnais, ed., 1971*

9. One expects a mathematical theorem or a mathematical theory not only to describe and to classify in a simple and elegant way numerous and a priori disparate cases. One also expects "elegance" in its "Architectural" structural makeup ... if the deductions are lengthy or complicated, there should be some simple, general principle involved, which "explains" the complications and detours, reduces the apparent arbitrariness to a few simple guiding motivations. These criteria are clearly those of any creative art....

—John von Neumann: "The Mathematician" in ***Works of the Mind****, R.B. Heywood, ed., 1947*

10. The only point there can be to elegance in a mathematical proof is to reveal certain analogies in a particularly striking manner when that is what is wanted; otherwise it is a product of stupidity and its only effect is to obscure what ought to be clear and manifest. The stupid pursuit of elegance is a principal cause of the mathematicians' failure to understand their own operations, or perhaps the lack of understanding and the pursuit of elegance have a common origin.

—Ludwig Wittgenstein: ***Tractatus Logico-Philosophicus****, 1921*

24.10 Mathematical Propositions and Theorems

1. The inner circle of creative mathematicians have a well-kept trade secret than in a great many cases theorems come first and axioms second. This process of justifying a belief by finding premises from which it can be deduced is shockingly similar to much reasoning in our daily lives, and it is somewhat embarrassing to me to realize that mathematicians are experts at this art.

—Carl Allendoerfer: "The Narrow Mathematician," ***American Mathematical Monthly****, June–July, 1962*

2. If the number of theorems is larger than one can possibly survey, who can be trusted to judge what is "important"? One cannot have survival of the fittest if there is no interaction.

—Philip Davis & Reuben Hersh: ***The Mathematical Experience****, 1982*

3. A theorem a day
Means promotion and pay!
A theorem a year And you're out on your ear!

—Paul Erdos: Quoted in Howard Eves: ***Mathematical Circles Revisited****, 1971*

4. The assumption that the angle sum [of a triangle] is less than 180 degrees leads to a curious geometry, quite different from ours [Euclidean] but thoroughly consistent, which I have developed to my entire satisfaction. The theorems of this geometry appear to be paradoxical, and, to the uninitiated, absurd, but calm, steady reflection reveals that they contain nothing at all impossible.

—Carl Freidrich Gauss: Letter to Franz Adolf Taurinus; November 8, 1824

5. ...there are no deep theorems—only theorems that we have not understood very well. That is the constructive impulse.

—Nicolas D. Goodman: "Reflections on [Errett] Bishop's Philosophy of Mathematics"; ***Springer Lecture Notes****, No. 873, 1980*

6. We throw out intuitive reasoning in the name of rigor—and then we leave out the rigorous reasoning and tell the students to accept the theorem on our authority.

—Seymour Haber: "The Axiom of Choice and Calculus Revision: A Dialogue"; ***The Mathematical Intelligencer****, vol. 13, Winter 1991*

7. A theorem is not a pyramid; inspiration has never been known to descend on a committee. A great theorem can no more be obtained by a "project" approach than a great painting.

—Paul R. Halmos: "Mathematics as a Creative Art," ***American Scientist****, Vol. 56, 1968*

8. The "seriousness" of a mathematical theorem lies, not in its practical consequences, which are usually negligible, but in the significance of the mathematical ideas which it connects.

—G.H. Hardy: ***A Mathematician's Apology****, 1941*

9. How thoroughly it is ingrained in mathematical science that every real advance goes hand in hand with the invention of sharper tools and simpler methods which, at the same time, assist in understanding earlier theories and in casting aside some more complicated developments.

—David Hilbert: in N. Rose, ***Mathematical Maxims and Minims****, 1988*

10. Everyone knows that mathematics is about Miracles, only mathematicians have a name for them: Theorems.

—Roger Howe: Invited MAA address, January 9, 1998

11. Mathematicians are not concerned merely with finding and proving theorems; they also strive to arrange and assemble the theorems so that they appear not only correct but evident and compelling. Such a goal, I feel, is aesthetic rather than epistemological.

—Wolfgang Krull: "The Aesthetic Viewpoint in Mathematics"; Betty S. Waterhouse & Willard Waterhouse, trs., ***The Mathematical Intelligencer****, vol. 9, 1, 1987*

12. It gives me the same pleasure when someone else proves a good theorem as when I do it myself.

—Edmund Landau: Quoted in D. McHale: ***Comic Sections****, 1993*

13. All great theorems were discovered after midnight.

—Adrian Mathesis: In Howard Eves: ***Return to Mathematical Circles****, 1988*

14. For what is important when we give children a theorem to use is not that they should memorize it. What matters most is that by growing up with a few very powerful theorems one comes to appreciate how certain ideas can be used as tools to think over a lifetime. One learns to enjoy and to respect the power of powerful ideas. One learns that the most powerful idea of all is the idea of powerful ideas.

—Seymour Papert: ***Mindstorms****, 1999*

15. We must remember that because a proposition has not yet been proved, we have no right to infer that its converse must be true.

—Karl Pearson: ***The Grammar of Science****, 1937*

16. Mathematics is purely hypothetical: it produces nothing but conditional propositions.

—Charles Sanders Peirce: in Carl Boyer: ***A History of Mathematics****, 1989*

17. If I only had the theorems! Then I should find the proofs easily enough.

—Bernard Riemann: Quoted in Imre Lakatos: ***Proof and Refutation****, 1976*

18. Theorems are not to mathematics what successful courses are to a meal. The nutritional analogy is misleading.

—Gian-Carlo Rota: in Philip J. Davis & Reuben Hersh: ***The Mathematical Experience****, 1981*

19. No mathematician nowadays sets any store on the discovery of isolated theorems, except as affording hints of an unsuspected new sphere of thought, like meteorites detached from some undiscovered planetary orb of speculation.

—J.J. Sylvester: Notes to the Exeter Association Address; ***Collected Mathematical Papers****, 1908*

20. It is more important that a proposition be interesting than that it be true. This statement is almost a tautology:,

—Alfred North Whitehead: ***Adventures of Ideas****, 1933*

21. If you know a mathematical proposition, that's not to say you yet know anything.

—Ludwig Wittgenstein: ***Remarks on the Foundations of Mathematics****, 1956, 1983 G.E.M. Anscombe & B. Blackwell, tr.*

25

Sets, Relations and Functions

25.1 Sets and Set Theory

1. A set is a Many that allows itself to be thought of as a One.

—Georg Cantor: in Rudy Rucker: ***Infinity and the Mind****, 1995*

2. It can be argued that the mathematics behind these images [of the orbit diagram for quadratic functions and the Mandelbrot set] is even prettier than the pictures themselves.

—Robert L. Devaney: "The Orbit Diagram and the Mandelbrot Set"; ***College Mathematics Journal****, vol. 22, #1, January, 1991*

3. A linguist would be disturbed to learn that "set E is closed" does not mean "set E' is open," and that "E is dense in E" does not have the same meaning as "E is dense in itself." On the other hand, the phrases "there is more than one" and "there are fewer than two" can sound queer to a mathematician.

—Howard W. Eves: ***Mathematical Circles Squared****, 1972*

4. If the entire Mandelbrot set were placed on an ordinary sheet of paper, the tiny sections of boundary we examine would not fill the width of a hydrogen atom. Physicists think about such tiny objects: only mathematicians have microscopes fine enough to actually observe them.

—John Ewing: "Can We See the Madelbrot Set?" ***The College Mathematics Journal****, March, 195*

5. Set theory was introduced by Georg Cantor as a fundamental new branch of mathematics. The idea of set—any collection of distinct objects—was so simple and fundamental, it looked like a brick out of which all mathematics could be constructed. Even arithmetic could be downgraded (or upgraded) from primary to secondary rank, for the natural numbers could be constructed ... from nothing—i.e., the empty set—by operations of set theory.

—Reuben Hersh: ***What Is Mathematics, Really?****, 1997*

6. I think it [set theory] is the highest manifestation of mathematical genius and one of the greatest achievements of man's purely spiritual activities.

—David Hilbert: Quoted in V.M. Tikhomirov: ***Stories About Maxima and Minima****, Abe Schenitzer, tr., 1990*

7. The platonic notion that there is somewhere the ideal realm of sets, not yet fully described, is a glorious illusion.

—Saunders MacLane: ***Mathematics: Form and Function****, 1986*

8. Dedekind expressed his opinion about the concept of set. He imagined a set as a closed sack containing definite objects which are not seen, and of which nothing is known except that they are existing and definite. Some time later Cantor made known his idea of a set. He raised his colossal figure, with lifted arm he made an imposing gesture, and with a glance in an indefinite direction he said, "I imagine a set to be like an abyss."

—Emmy Noether: Quoted in Dedekind's ***Gesammelte Werke****, 1932*

9. Later generations will regard Mengenlehre [set theory] as a disease from which one has recovered.

—Henri Poincare: Attributed; "Did Poincare say 'Set Theory is a Disease'?" in ***The Mathematical Intelligencer****, vol. 13, 1, 1991*

25.2 Equality and Equivalence

1. A manuscript, kept in the Library of the University of Bologna, contains data regarding the sign of equality (=). These data ... tend to show that (=) as a sign of equality was developed at Bologna independently or Robert Recorde and perhaps earlier.

—Florian Cajori: ***A History of Mathematical Notation****, vol. I., 1928*

2. ...we do not need to be able to count objects in sets in order to determine whether or not the sets are equinumerous. On the contrary, the notion of being equally numerous, seen in the light of one-to-one correspondences, becomes the more primitive, fundamental concept; counting, by contrast is the more sophisticated, advanced one.

—William Dunham: ***Journey Through Genius****, 1990*

3. Mathematics is the science of the connection of magnitudes. Magnitude is anything that can be put equal or unequal to another thing. Two things are equal when in every assertion each may be replaced by the other.

—Hermann Grassman: ***Stucke aus dem Lehrbuche der Arithmetik****, 1904*

4. In 1638 Galileo remarked that the squares of the positive integers can be placed in a 1–1 correspondence with the positive integers themselves, thus

$$\begin{matrix} 1, & 4, & 9, & 16, & \ldots, & n^2, & \ldots \\ 1, & 2, & 3, & 4, & \ldots, & n, & \ldots \end{matrix}$$

despite the ancient axiom that the whole is greater than any of its parts.

—Stephen Cole Kleene" ***Introduction to Metamathematics****, 1952*

5. I will sette as I doe often in woorke use, a paire of parallels, or Gemone [twin] lines of one length, thus: =, bicause noe 2 thynges can be moare equalle.

—Robert Recorde: ***The Whetstone of Witte****, 1557*

25.3 Mathematical Relations

1. Mathematics deals exclusively with the relations of concepts to each other without consideration of the relation of the experience.

—Albert Einstein: In Phillip Frank: ***Einstein, His Life and Times****, 1947*

2. It is because the mathematician is expert in analyzing relations, in distinguishing what is essential from what is superficial in the statement of these relations, and in formulating broad and meaningful problems, that he has come to be an important figure in industrial research teams.

—Thornton C. Fry: "Mathematics as a Profession Today in Industry"; ***American Mathematical Monthly****, 63; February, 1956*

3. We may say, roughly, that a mathematical idea is "significant" if it can be connected, in a natural and illuminating way, with a large complex of other mathematical ideas.

—G.H. Hardy: Quoted in Richard A. De Millo, Richard J. Lipton & Alan J. Perlis: "Social Processes and Proofs of Theorems and Programs"; ***Communications of the ACM****, 22:5, 1979*

4. To imagine geometrical relationships visually means to imagine the experiences which we would have if we lived in a world where those relations hold.

—Herman von Helmholtz: Quoted in H. Reichenbach: ***The Rise of Scientific Philosophy****, 1951*

5. Nobody before the Pythagoreans had thought that mathematical relations held the secret of the universe. Twenty-five centuries later, Europe is still blessed and cursed with their heritage. To non–European civilizations, the idea that numbers are the key to both wisdom and power, seems never to have occurred.

—Arthur Koestler: ***The Sleepwalkers****, 1959*

6. Higher Mathematics is the art of reasoning about numerical relations between natural phenomena; and the several sections of Higher Mathematics are different modes of viewing these relations.

—J. W. Mellor: ***Higher Mathematics for Students of Chemistry and Physics****, 1902; 1955*

7. Mathematicians do not study objects, but relations among objects; they are indifferent to the replacement of objects by others as long as the relations don't change. Matter is not important, only form interests them.

—Henri Poincare: Quoted in Tobias Dantzig: ***Number: The Language of Science****, 1954*

8. It is upon the exactness with which we follow phenomena into the infinitely small that our knowledge of their casual relations essentially depends.

—George Friedrich Bernhard Riemann: ***Uber die Hypothesen welche der Geometrie zu Grunde liegen****, read in 1854 to the Philosophical Faculty at Gottingen; Quoted in a translation by W.K. Clifford:* ***Nature****, Vol. VIII, 1973*

9. It's remarkable to discover how many connections mathematics makes, how many lightbulbs it suddenly turns on.

—Sylvia Spengler: Quoted in Keith Devlin: ***Life by the Numbers****, 1998*

10. The progress of Science consists in observing interconnections and in showing with a patient ingenuity that the events of this ever-shifting world are but examples of a few general relations, called laws. To see what is general is what is particular, and what is permanent in what is transitory, to the aim of scientific thought.

—*Alfred North Whitehead:* ***An Introduction to Mathematics****, 1911*

25.4 Functions and Function Theory

1. We call here Function of a variable magnitude, a quantity that is composed in any possible manner of this variable magnitude and of constants.

—*John Bernoulli: 1718; in* ***Opera Omnia II****, 1968*

2. The question of what properties, such as angle or area, are reproduced on a map without distortion is of prime interest to mathematicians. The question extends far beyond the confines of geometry, for all mathematics can be considered broadly as a study of maps and mapping.

—*George A.W. Boehm:* ***The New World of Math****, 1959*

3. If you want to understand function, study structure.

—*Francis Harry Compton Crick:* ***What Mad Pursuit****, 1988*

4. One of the most important concepts in all mathematics is that of function.

—*T.P. Dick & C.M. Patton:* ***Calculus of a Single Variable****, 1994*

5. [Function] theory was, in effect, founded by Cauchy; but, outside his own investigations, it at first made slow and hesitating progress. At the present day, its fundamental ideas may be said almost to govern most departments of the analysis of continuous quantity. On many of them, it has shed a completely new light; it has educed relations between them before unknown. It may be doubted whether any subject is at the present day so richly endowed with variety of method and fertility of resources; its activity is prodigious, and no less remarkable than its activity is its freshness.

—*A.R. Forsyth: Presidential Address British Association for the Advancement of Science, 1897: in* ***Nature****, vol. 56*

6. A function has a curve as its graph; and a curve (subject to mild restrictions) is the graph of a function. Today we teach the function as primary. The graph is derived from the function. Until a hundred years ago, it was the other way around. As a geometric object, the curve was part of the best understood branch of mathematics. Functions leaned on geometry. Mathematicians were upset when, late in the nineteenth century, they learned of functions with wild graphs impossible to visualize.

—*Reuben Hersh:* ***What Is Mathematics, Really?****, 1997*

7. The Modern Theory of Functions—that stateliest of all the pure creations of the human intellect.

—*C.J. Keyser:* ***Lectures on Science, Philosophy and Art****, 1908*

8. To express the physical principles in the manner he regarded as significant, Galileo introduced a new mathematical concept, the extremely important concept of a function. For the next two centuries mathematicians devoted themselves to the construction of functions and to the study of their properties.

—*Morris Kline:* ***Mathematics for the Nonmathematician****, 1967*

9. That flower of modern mathematical thought—the notion of a function.

—*Thomas J. McCormack: "On the Nature of Scientific Law and Scientific Explanation";* ***Monist****, vol. 10, 1899–1900*

10. Nature herself exhibits to us measurable and observable quantities in definite mathematical dependence; the conception of a function is suggested by all the processes of nature where we observe natural phenomena varying according to distance or to time. Nearly all the "known" functions have presented themselves in the attempt to solve geometrical, mechanical, or physical problems.

—*J.T. Merz:* ***A History of European Thought in the Nineteenth Century****, 1903*

11. When earlier, new functions were introduced, the purpose was to apply them. Today, on the contrary, one constructs functions to contradict the conclusion of our predecessors and one will never be able to apply them for any other purpose.

—*Henri Poincare: Second International Congress of Mathematics, Paris, 1900*

12. The continuous function is the only workable and usable function. It alone is subject to law and the laws of calculation. It is a loyal subject of the mathematical kingdom. Other so-called or miscalled functions are freaks, anarchists, disturbers of the peace, malformed curiosities which one and all are of no use to anyone, least of all to the loyal and burden-bearing subjects who by keeping the laws maintain the kingdom and make its advance possible.

—*E.D. Roe, Jr. "A Generalized Definition of Limit";* ***The Mathematics Teacher****, vol. III, Number 1, September, 1910*

13. The theory that has the greatest development in recent times is without any doubt the theory of functions.

—*Vito Volterra: in Stanley Gudder:* ***A Mathematical Journey****, 1976*

14. ...the more I ponder the principles of function theory—and I do this constantly—the firmness becomes the conviction that the latter must be built on the basis of algebraic facts, and that it is therefore not the right way to proceed when contrariwise the "transcendental"—to use a short expression—is used to establish simple and basic algebraic theorems....

*—Karl Weierstrass: Letter to H.A. Schwarz, October 3, 1875; in **Werke II**, 1870*

25.5 Special Functions

1. The greatest shortcoming of the human race is our inability to understand the exponential function.

*—Albert A. Bartlett: "The Exponential Function" (series); **The Physics Teacher**, 1976–1996*

2. The theory of elliptic functions is the fairyland of mathematics. The mathematician who once gazes upon this enchanting and wondrous domain crowded with the most beautiful relations and concepts is forever captivated.

*—Richard Bellman: **A Brief Introduction to Theta Functions**, 1961*

3. The principal advantage arising from the use of hyperbolic functions is that they bring to light some curious analogies between the integrals of certain irrational functions.

*—W.E. Byerly: **Integral Calculus**, 1890*

4. After exponential quantities the circular functions, sine and cosine, should be considered because they arise when imaginary quantities are involved in the exponential.

*—Leonhard Euler: in Reinhold Remmert: **Theory of Complex Functions**, 1991*

5. It is well known that the central problem of the whole of modern mathematics is the study of the transcendental functions defined by differential equations.

*—Felix Klein: **Lectures on Mathematics**, 1911*

6. Who has not been amazed to learn that the function $y = e^x$, like a Phoenix rising from its own ashes, is its own derivative.

*—Francois Le Lionnais: **Great Currents of Mathematical Thought**, 1971*

26

Space: Real and Idealized

26.1 Real and Mathematical Space

1. I felt myself rising through space. It was even as the Sphere had said. The further we receded from the object we beheld, the larger became the field of vision. My native city, with the interior of every house and every creature therein, lay open to my view in miniature. We mounted higher, and lo, the secrets of the earth, the depths of mines, and inmost caverns of the hills, were bared before me.

*—Edwin A. Abbott: **Flatland**, 1884*

2. It is fairly certain that our space is finite though unbound. Infinite space is simply a scandal in human thought.

*—Bishop Barnes: Quoted in Eli Maor: **To Infinity and Beyond**, 1987*

3. There is a single general space, a single vast immensity which we may freely call Void; in it are innumerable globes like this on which we live and grow. This space we declare to be infinite; since neither reason, convenience, possibility, sense-perception nor nature assign to it a limit. In it are an infinity of worlds of the same kind as our own. For there is no reason nor defect of nature's gifts, either of active or of passive power, to hinder the existence of other worlds throughout space, which is identical in natural character with our own space.

*—Giordano Bruno: **On the Infinite Universe and Worlds**, 1584*

4. In Euclid's comfortably flat space, you could assume that the space a million light-years away was just like the space next door, that space 15 million years ago was the same as space 15 million years from now. The idea that space has shape, however, means it is no longer possible to say with any certainty what is happening everywhere at any time. It could be flat here, but curled up over there. Or flat now, but curled up previously.

*—K.C. Cole: **The Universe and the Teacup**, 1997*

5. A mathematician ... can study flat space or curved space, according to interest. This is because the mathematical universe is an abstract idealization of the real universe, a what-if idealization where the mathematician can postulate, say, a particular curvature, and then investigate the properties of such a space. Or maybe the mathematician decides to investigate a space of four or more dimensions. Again, such freedom is not available to the physicist, but there is nothing to prevent the mathematician from heading off—mathematically speaking—into four dimensions.

*—Keith Devlin: **Life by the Numbers**, 1998*

6. To put the conclusion rather crudely—space is not a lot of points close together; it is a lot of distances interlocked.

*—Sir Arthur Stanley Eddington: **The Mathematical Theory of Relativity**, 1954*

7. Whereas at the outset geometry is reported to have concerned herself with the measurement of muddy land, she now handles celestial as well as terrestrial problems: she has extended her domain to the furthest bounds of space.

*—W.B. Frankland: In Hodder and Stoughton: **The Story of Euclid**, 1901*

8. We must confess in all humility that, while number is a product of our mind alone, space has a reality beyond the mind whose rules we cannot completely prescribe.

*—Carl Friedrich Gauss: Letter to Freidrich Wilhelm Bessel; October 9, 1830; Quoted in Charles W. Misner, Kip Thorne & John A. Wheeler: **Gravitation**, 1973*

9. Among the splendid generalizations effected by modern mathematics, there is none more brilliant or more inspiring or more fruitful, and none more commensurate with the limitless immensity of being itself, than that which produced the great concept designated ... hyperspace or multidimensional space.

*—C.J. Keyser: "Mathematical Emancipations"; **Monist**, Vol. 16, 1906*

10. ...when we analyze the highly refined concept of space used by mathematicians we find it to be quite similar to the concept of number.

*—Gilbert Newton Lewis: **The Anatomy of Science**, 1926*

11. From now on space by itself, and time by itself, are destined to sink completely into shadows, and only a kind of union of both to retain an independent existence.

*—Hermann Minkowski: "Four-dimensional space-time continuum," Lecture at University of Gottingen, 1907; Quoted in Stuart Hollingdale: **Makers of Mathematics**, 1989*

12. Space acts on matter, telling it how to move. In turn, matter reacts back on space telling it how to curve. Or: Geometry tells matter how to move, and matter tells geometry how to curve.

*—Charles W. Misner, Kip S. Thorne & John Archibald Wheeler: **Gravitation**, 1972*

13. Space extends infinitely in all directions. For we cannot imagine any limit anywhere without at the same time imagining that there is space beyond it.

*—Sir Isaac Newton: "De Gravitatione et Aequipondio Fluidorum," A. Rupert Hall & Marie Boas Hall, tr. In **Unpublished Scientific Papers of Isaac Newton**, 1962*

14. [I feel] engulfed in the infinite immensity of spaces whereof I know nothing, and which know nothing of me, I am terrified the eternal silence of these infinite spaces alarm me.

*—Blaise Pascal: **Pensees**, 1670*

15. Space is only a word that we have believed a thing.

*—Henri Poincare: **The Foundations of Science**, "Preface," 1921*

16. The clear possession of the Idea of Space is the first requisite for all geometrical reasoning; and this clearness of idea may be tested by examining whether the axioms offer themselves to the mind as evident.

*—William Whewell: **The Philosophy of the Inductive Sciences**, Part 1, Book 2, 1858*

26.2 Curvature of Space

1. [Small portions of space are] analogous to little hills on a surface which is on the average flat ... that this property of being curved or distorted is continually being passed on from one portion of space to another after the manner of a wave; that this variation of the curvature of space is what really happens in the motion of matter ... that in the physical world nothing else takes place but this variation, subject (possibly) to the laws of continuity....

*—William Kingdon Clifford: "On the Space Theory of Matter," contribution to the Cambridge Philosophical Society, 1876 In **Lectures and Essays**, L. Stephen & F. Pollock, eds., 1879*

2. The idea of curved space started with the nineteenth-century mathematician Georg Friedrich Riemann. In effect, what Riemann said to himself was this: The surface of the earth is a two-dimensional object that curves around and comes back on itself. If you start on a journey from anywhere on the earth and keep traveling (on the surface) in exactly the same direction, then eventually you will circumvent the globe and come back to your starting point. Maybe if you set off on a journey through space and keep going in the same direction, you will eventually come back to your starting point. This would mean that space itself is "curved," though the idea of a curved space is hard to visualize.

*—Keith Devlin: **Life by the Numbers**, 1998*

3. To the pure geometer the radius of curvature is an incidental characteristic—like the grin of the Cheshire cat. To the physicist it is an indispensable characteristic. It would be going too far to say that to the physicist the cat is merely incidental to the grin. Physics is concerned with interrelatedness such as the interrelatedness of cats and grins. In this case the "cat without a grin" and the "grin without a cat" are equally set aside as purely mathematical phantasies.

*—Sir Arthur Eddington: **The Expanding Universe**, 1933*

4. There are few Problems concerning Curves more elegant than this (i.e. Curvature), or that give a greater Insight into their Nature.

*—Isaac Newton: **Methodus Fluxionum et Serierum Infinitarum**, 1671*

5. There is nothing in the world except empty curved space. Matter, charge, electromagnetism and other fields are only manifestations of the curvature of space.

*—John Archibald Wheeler: **The New Scientist** September 26, 1974*

26.3 The Universe

1. There is a theory which states that if ever anyone discovers exactly what the Universe is for and why it is here, it will instantly disappear and be replaced by something even more bizarre and inexplicable. There is another theory that this has already happened.

—Douglas Adams: ***The Hitch-hiker's Guide to the Galaxy****, 1979*

2. The first question concerning the Celestial Bodies is whether there be a system, that is whether the world or universe compose together one globe, with a center, or whether the particular globes of earth and stars be scattered dispersedly, each on its own roots, without any system or common center.

—Francis Bacon: ***Novum Organum****, 1620*

3. The most extreme example of this direct observation of the past arises from our understanding of what occurred in the Universe during the brief interval of time between one second and three minutes after it began its present state of expansion from some unknown state that we usually call the "beginning of the universe" (although it may have been nothing of the sort). Our mathematical theory allows us to determine the ambient conditions of the Universe during those first few minutes of cosmic history from what we observe at present, some fifteen billion years later.

—John D. Barrow: ***Pi in the Sky****, 1992*

4. There is in the universe neither center nor circumference.

—Giordano Bruno: ***On the Infinite Universe and Worlds****, 1584*

5. In the first place we must observe that the universe is spherical. This is either because that figure is the most perfect, as not being articulated, but whole and complete in itself; or because it is the most capacious and therefore best suited for that which is to contain and preserve all things....

—Nicolaus Copernicus: Quoted in V.M. Tikhomirov: ***Stories About Maxima and Minima****; Abe Schenitzer, tr., 1990*

6. A man said to the universe:
"Sir, I exist."
"However," replied the universe,
"The fact has not created in me
A sense of obligation."

—Stephen Crane: ***War Is Kind and Other Lines****, 1899*

7. Since the start of the twentieth century, scientists have known that the universe is expanding. All the stars and galaxies we see in the sky are rushing away from us. This is thought to be the result of the universe beginning with the Big Bang many billions of years ago, a cosmic explosion that simultaneously created matter and sent it hurtling outward, a process that is still going on.

—Keith Devlin: ***Life by the Numbers****, 1998*

8. Our feeble attempts at mathematics enable us to understand a bit of the universe, and as we proceed to develop higher and higher mathematics we can hope to understand the universe better.

—P.A.M. Dirac: "The Evolution of the Physicist's Picture of Nature"; in ***Scientific American****, May, 1963*

9. I will give you a "celestial multiplication table." We start with a star as the unit most familiar to us, a globe comparable to the sun. Then—A hundred thousand million Stars make one Galaxy; A hundred thousand million Galaxies make one Universe.

—Sir Arthur Eddington: ***The Expanding Universe****, Cambridge University Press, 1933*

10. Man is not born to solve the problems of the universe, but to find out where the problems begin, and then to take his stand within the limits of the intelligible.

—Johann Wolfgang von Goethe: in Louis Berman: ***Exploring the Cosmos****, 1973*

11. The universe is not only queerer than we suppose but queerer than we can suppose.

—J.B.S. Haldane: Quoted in Manfred Schroder: ***Fractals, Chaos, Power Laws: Minutes from an Infinite Paradise****, 1992*

12. "Imaginary" universes are so much more beautiful that the stupidly constructed "real" one; and most of the finest products of applied mathematicians' fancy must be rejected, as soon as they have been created, for the brutal but sufficient reason that they do not fit the facts.

—G.H. Hardy: ***A Mathematician's Apology****, 1940*

13. The boundary condition of the universe is that it has no boundary.

—Stephen W. Hawking: ***A Brief History of Time****, 1988*

14. Even if there is only one possible unified theory, it is just a set of rules and equations. What is it that breathes fire into the equations and makes a universe for them to describe? The usual approach of science of constructing a mathematical model cannot answer the questions of why there should be a universe for the model to describe. Why does the universe go to the bother of existing?

—Stephen Hawking: ***A Brief History of Time****, 1988*

15. There is no absolute scale of size in the Universe, for it is boundless towards the great and also boundless towards the small.

—Oliver Heaviside: Quoted in D'Arcy Wentworth Thompson: ***On Growth and Form****, 1917*

16. Is the universe finite? If a voyager of the skies travels deep into the inter-stellar spaces, past the great blue helium stars of Orion, past Betelgeuse and Antares, beyond the white variable Cepheids, the gaseous red and yellow giant-stars, the faintest of the super-nebulae, "lying like silver snails in the garden of the stars" but whirling in fiery spirals in the dim void of remote space—will he ever reach any limit to the universe?

—Archibald Henderson: "Is the Universe Finite" Paper delivered to the joint meeting of the American Mathematical Society, the Mathematical Association of America and the American Association for the Advancement of Science, January 1, 1925 in ***The American Mathematical Monthly****, 32, 1925*

17. We discover that the universe shows evidence of a designing or controlling power that has something in common with our own individual minds—not, so far as we have discovered, emotion, morality, or aesthetic appreciation, but the tendency to think in the way which, for want of a better word, we describe as mathematical.

—James Jeans: ***The Mysterious Universe****, 1931*

18. We find, therefore, under this orderly arrangement, a wonderful symmetry in the universe, and a definite relation of harmony in the motion and magnitude of the orbs, of a kind that is not possible to obtain in any other way.

—Johannes Kepler: ***The Harmonies of the World****, 1619*

19. The whole universe is one mathematical and harmonic expression, made up of finite representations of the infinite.

—F.L. Kunz: in Renee Weber: ***Dialogues with Scientists and Sages****, 1986*

20. In the very beginning, there was a void, a curious form of vacuum, a nothingness containing no space, no time, no matter, no light, no sound. Yet the laws of nature were in place and this curious vacuum held potential. A story logically begins at the beginning, but this story is about the universe and unfortunately there are no data for the very beginnings—none, zero. We don't know anything about the universe until it reaches the mature age of a billion of a trillionth of a second. That is, some very short time after creation in the big bang. When you read or hear anything about the birth of the universe, someone is making it up—we are in the realm of philosophy. Only God knows what happened at the very beginning.

—Leon Lederman: ***The God Particles****; 1996*

21. ...the existing universe is bounded by none of its dimensions; for then it must have an outside.

—Lucretius: ***On the Nature of Things****, Book I, c. 1st cent. B.C.*

22. The universe is a disymmetrical whole.

—Louis Pasteur: Comptes Rendus de l'Academie des Sciences; June 1, 1874

23. The universe ought to be presumed too vast to have any character.

—C.S. Peirce: ***Collected Papers****, late 19th—early 20th century*

24. Mathematics is the abstract key which turns the lock of the physical universe.

—John Polkinghorne: Quoted in Keith Devlin: ***Mathematics: The Science of Patterns****, 1997*

25. The universe forces those who live in it to understand it.

—Carl Sagan: ***Cosmos****, 1980*

26. A genuine theory of everything must explain not only how our universe came into being, but also why it is the only type of universe that there could have been—why there could only be one set of physical laws.... This goal I believe to be illusory.

—Russell Standard: "No Faith in the Grand Theory"; ***The Times*** *(London), November 13, 1989*

27. The universe is built on a plan the profound symmetry of which is somehow present in the inner structure of the intellect.

—Paul Valery: in Jefferson Hane Weaver: ***The World of Physics****, 1987*

28. Real nature is beautiful, you can go out and look at a flower or look off into space. It's a miracle that we have this physical universe to explore. I think it is no less a miracle that we also have this mathematical universe to explore, a universe full of beautiful, intricate patterns lying there, waiting to be discovered.

—Jeff Weeks: Quoted in Keith Devlin: ***Life by the Numbers****, 1998*

26.4 The World

1. It is enigma enough that the world is described by mathematics, but by simple mathematics, of the sort that a few years energetic study now produces familiarity with, this is a mystery within an enigma.

—John Barrow: ***Theories of Everything: The Quest for Ultimate Explanation****, 1991*

2. All the magnificent achievements of mathematical and physical science ... proceed from our indomitable desire to cast the world into a more rational shape in our minds than the shape into which it is thrown there by the crude order of our experience.

—William James: ***Principles of Psychology****, 1890*

3. Mathematics is a study independent of the actual world.

—Cassius J. Keyser: ***Mathematical Philosophy****, 1922*

4. Science provides the understanding of the universe in which we live. Mathematics provides the dies by which science is molded. Our world is to a large extent what mathematics says it is.

*—Morris Kline: "The Meaning of Mathematics," **The Saturday Evening Post**, 1960*

5. I think we can never know enough mathematics. Mathematics is not about numbers, That's what arithmetic is about. Mathematics is about structures—possible structures. And virtual reality is about visiting possible worlds.

*—Marcos Novak: Quoted in Keith Devlin: **Life by the Numbers**, 1998*

6. In Geography one must contemplate the extent of the entire earth, as well as its shape, and its position under the heavens, in order that one may rightly state what are the peculiarities and proportions of the part with which one is dealing.... It is the great and exquisite accomplishment of mathematics to show all these things to human intelligence....

*—Ptolemy: **Geography**, 2nd cent. A.D. translated and printed about 1472*

7. Mathematics takes us ... into the region of absolute necessity, to which not only the actual world, but every possible world must conform.

*—Bertrand Russell: **The Study of Mathematics**, 1902*

8. Every man's world picture is and always remains a construct of his mind and cannot be proved to have any other existence.

*—Erwin Schrodinger: **From Mind and Matter**, 1992*

9. According to Leibniz our world is the best possible. That is why its laws can be described by external principles.

*—C.L. Siegel: Quoted in V.M. Tikhomirov: **Stories About Maxima and Minima**, Abe Schenitzer, tr., 1990*

10. Given some particular subsystem of the real world, is it best modeled by a deterministic mathematical system of a random one?

*—Ian Stewart: **Does God Play Dice?: The New Mathematics of Chaos**, 1989*

11. The earth is veiled in geometry as far back as we can see. It crystallizes. But not completely.

*—Pierre Teilhard de Chardin: **The Phenomenon of Man**, 1955*

27

Numbers: The Heart of Mathematics

27.1 THE NATURE AND DEVELOPMENT OF NUMBERS

1. Familiarity with numbers, acquired by innate faculty sharpened by assiduous practice, does give insight into the profoundest theorems of algebra and analysis.

—*R.G. Aitken: Quoted in Robert M. Young:* ***Excursions in Calculus****, 1992*

2. To be a Greek was to seek to know, to know the primordial substance of matter; to know the meaning of number, to know the world as a rational whole.

—*Anonymous; Quoted in T.L. Heath,* ***The Legacy of Greece****, 1963*

3. Human beings are very conservative in some ways and virtually never change numerical conventions once they grow used to them. They even come to mistake them for laws of nature.

—*Isaac Asimov:* ***Foundation and Earth****, 1986*

4. Numbers are intellectual witnesses that belong only to mankind, and by whose means we can achieve an understanding of words.

—*Honore de Balzac:* ***Louis Lambert****, 1827–47*

5. If "Number rules the universe" as Pythagoras asserted, Number is merely our delegate to the throne, for we rule Number.

—*E.T. Bell: Quoted in Howard W. Eves:* ***Mathematical Circles Revisited****, 1971*

6. Mathematics arises when the subject of twoness, which results from the passage of time, is abstracted from all special occurrences. The remaining empty form of the common content of all these twoness becomes the original intuition of mathematics and repeated unlimitedly creates new mathematical subjects.

—*Luitzen E.J. Brouwer:* ***On the Foundations of Mathematics****, 1907*

7. There is no inquiry which is not finally reducible to a question of Numbers; for there is none which may not be conceived of as consisting in the determination of quantities by each other, according to certain relations.

—*Auguste Comte:* ***The Positive Philosophy of Auguste Comte****, Harriet Martineau, tr., 1853*

8. The complexity of a civilization is mirrored in the complexity of its numbers.

—*Philip J. Davis: "Number,"* ***Scientific American****, September, 1964*

9. The numbers are a catalyst that can help turn raving madmen into polite humans.

—*Philip J. Davis and Reuben Hersh:* ***The Mathematical Experience****, 1981*

10. Numbers are the free creation of the human mind.

—*Richard Dedekind: Quoted in J. Henle & T. Tymoczko:* ***Sweet Reason****, 1994*

11. Why are numbers beautiful? It's like asking why is Beethoven's Ninth Symphony beautiful. If you don't see why, someone can't tell you. I know numbers are beautiful. If they aren't beautiful, nothing is.

—*Paul Erdos: Quoted in Paul Hoffman:* ***The Man Who Loved Only Numbers****, 1999*

12. ...Numbers as realities misbehave. However, there is an ancient and innate sense in people that numbers ought not to misbehave. There is something clean and pure in the abstract notion of number ... and there ought to be a way of talking about numbers without always having the silliness of reality come in and intrude. The hard-edged rules that govern "ideal" numbers constitute arithmetic, and their more advanced consequences constitute another theory.

—*Douglas R. Hofstader:* ***Goedel, Escher, Bach: An Eternal Golden Braid****, 1979*

13. If you wanted to schematize the history of numbering systems, you could say that if fills the space between One and Zero, the two concepts which have become the symbols of modern technological society.... Nowadays we step with careless ease from Zero to One, so confident are we, thanks to computer scientists and our mathematical masters, that the Void always comes before the Unit. We never stop to think for a moment that in terms of time it is a huge step from the invention of the number "one," the first of all numbers even in the chronological sense, to the invention of the number "zero," the last major invention in the story of numbers.

—Georges Ifrah: ***The Universal History of Numbers****, 2000*

14. Take from all things their number and all shall perish.

—Isidore of Seville: ***Origines****, ca. 600 A.D.*

15. Number is another name for diversity.

—William Stanley Jevons: ***The Principles of Science****, 1887*

16. Words of wisdom are spoken by children at least as often as scientists. The name "googol" was invented by a child (Dr. Kasner's nine-year-old nephew) who was asked to think up a name for a very big number, namely, 1 with a hundred zeros after it.... At the same time that he suggested "googol" he gave a name for a still larger number "Googolplex." [1 with a googol zeros after it.]

—Edward Kasner & James Newman: ***Mathematics and the Imagination****, 1940*

17. Perhaps in some far distant century they may say, "Strange that those ingenious investigators into the secrets of the number system had so little conception of the fundamental discoveries that would later develop from them.

—D.H. Lehmer: "Hunting Big Game in the Theory of Numbers"; ***Scripta Mathematica****, vol. 1, 1932*

18. With the help of the accomplished holy sages, who are worthy to be worshipped by the lords of the world ... I glean from the great ocean of the knowledge of numbers a little of its essence, in the manner in which gems are [picked] from the sea, gold from the stony rock and the pearl from the oyster shell; and I give out according to the power of my intelligence, the *Sara Samgraha*, a small work of arithmetic, which is [however] not small in importance.

—Mahavira; c. A.D. 850: in G.G. Joseph, ***The Crest of the Peacock****, 1991*

19. ...abstraction of numbers was the beginning of mathematics, for men could now deal with numbers or symbols rather than actual objects. Addition and subtraction could be carried out without physically increasing or diminishing a quantity of objects.

—Jane Muir: ***Of Men and Numbers****, 1996*

20. Were it not for number and its nature, nothing that exists would be clear to anybody either in itself or in its relation to other things.... You can observe the power of number exercising itself ... in all the acts and the thoughts of men, in all handcrafts and music.

—Philolaus of Croton: In H. Diels: ***Die Fragmente der Vorsokratiker****, 1957*

21. Number is the ruler of forms and ideas, and the cause of gods and demons.

—Pythagoras: From ***Iamblichus****; Robert Graves:* ***The White Goddess****, 1952*

22. Numbers are the heart of mathematics, an all-pervading influence, the raw materials out of which a great deal of mathematics is forged. But numbers on their own form only a tiny part of mathematics.

—Ian Stewart: ***Nature's Numbers****, 1995*

27.2 Number in Verse

1. Give me to learn each secret clause;
Let number's, figure's motion's laws
Revealed before me stand;
These to great Nature's scene apply,
And round the Globe, and through the
sky,
Disclose her working hand.

—Mark Akenside: "Hymn to Science"; ***Works of the English Poets****, vol. 55, S. Johnson, ed., 1779*

2. From a number that's odd,
cut off the head,
It then will even be;
Its tail I pray now take away,
Your mother then you'll see.

—Anonymous [This is a riddle whose solution is "SEVEN -> EVEN -> EVE.]

3. The Binary Gray code is fun,
For in it strange things can be done.
Fifteen, as you know,
Is one, oh, oh, oh,
And ten is one, one, one, and one.

—Anonymous: in Martin Gardner's "Mathematical Games" column; ***Scientific American****, August, 1972*

4. Five hundred begins it. Five hundred
ends it.
Five in the middle is seen.
The first of all the letters, the first of all
the numbers,
Have taken their places between.
And if you correctly this medley can
spell

The Name of an eminent king it will
tell.

—The Bible: King James Version [The answer to this riddle is DAVID.]

5. numbers
supposedly
direct us
in a precise way
yet in certain combinations
numbers become
elusive
and their only answer
in the many answers
to our search
is
a question

—Ilse Bing: "Indeterminate Numbers"; in E. Robson & J. Wimp: ***Against Infinity****, 1979*

6. Taking Three as the subject to reason about—
A convenient number to state—
We add Seven, and Ten, and then multiply out
By One Thousand diminished by Eight.
The result we proceed to divide, as you see,
By Nine Hundred and Ninety and Two:
Then subtract Seventeen, and the answer must be
Exactly and perfectly true.

—Lewis Carroll: "The Hunting of the Snark," 1876 [The Butcher explains to the Beaver how to count the number of times the Butcher warned the Beaver "The proof is complete, if only I've stated it thrice."]

7. One thousand two hundred and sixty–
Four million eight hundred and fifty–
Three thousand nine hun–
Dred and seventy-one
Point two seven five eight four six three.

—Leigh Mercer: in Martin Gardner's "Mathematical Games" column; ***Scientific American****, April, 1963 [The puzzle was how to read the number 1,264,853,971.2758463 as a limerick.]*

8. As yet a child, nor yet a fool to fame,
I lisp'd in numbers, for the numbers came....
Hark! the numbers soft and clear
Gently steal upon the ear.

—Alexander Pope: "Epistle to Dr. Arbuthnot," 1733; ***The Complete Poetical Works of Alexander Pope****, 1903*

27.3 The Notion of Quantity

1. Quantity is either discrete or continuous. Moreover, some quantities are such that each part of the whole has a relative position to the other parts: others have within them no such relation of part to part.

—Aristotle: ***Categories, 6****, c. 4th cent. B.C.*

2. There are those who are so impressed by the notion that "quantification" is the only form of scientific knowledge, that they see no danger in the distorted, misleading, or simply ineffective picture that a statistical description of events may give. To such people the statistical picture is always to be preferred as the most meaningful and objective. It is indeed because this view is so widespread, that an argument stated in statistical terms has such a powerful influence in policy decision, and induces everyone to try to impress their case on public attention by peppering it with statistics.

—Ely Devons: ***Essays on Economics****, 1961*

3. Quantity is that which is signified by what we answer to him that asketh, how much anything is? and thereby determines the magnitude thereof. And because for the computing of the magnitudes of bodies, it is not necessary that the bodies themselves be present, the ideas and memory of them supplying their presence, we reckon upon those imaginary bodies, which are the quantities themselves.... So also is number quantity; but in no other sense than as a line is quantity divided into equal parts.

—Thomas Hobbes: "Six Lessons to the Professors of Mathematics," ***The English Works of Thomas Hobbes****, W. Molesworth, ed., 1839–45*

4. Every statement in physics has to state relations between observable quantities.

—Ernst Mach: ***The Economical Nature of Physical Inquiry****, 1882*

5. The passion between the sexes ... in every age ... is so nearly the same that it may be considered in algebraic language as a given quantity.

—Thomas Robert Malthus: ***An Essay on the Principles of Population****, 1798*

6. If ... we regard quantity (as we do very often and easily) as it exists in the imagination, we find it to be finite, divisible, and composed of parts; but if we regard it as it exists in the intellect, and conceive it insofar as it is substance, which is very difficult, than, as we have already sufficiently demonstrated, we find it to be infinite, one, and indivisible.

—Benedict (Baruch) Spinoza: ***Ethics****, 1665, published 1667*

7. The lure of quantity is the most dangerous of all.

—Simone Weil; ***First and Last Notebooks****, 1970*

27.4 Cardinal and Ordinal Numbers

1. We have learned to pass with great facility from cardinal to ordinal number that the two aspects appear to us as one. To determine the plurality of a collection, i.e. its cardinal number, ... —we count it. And to this fact we have learned to identify the two aspects of number is due to our progress in mathematics. For whereas in practice we are really interested in the cardinal number, this latter is incapable of creating an arithmetic. The operations of arithmetic are based on the tacit assumption that we can always pass from any number to its successor, and this is the essence of the ordinal concept....

—*Tobias Dantzig:* ***Number: The Language of Science****, 1930*

2. ...the ordinal aspect of number—its ordering property as distinct from its cardinal or quantitative property—was introduced in mathematics because this ordinal aspect is the bridge that connects arithmetic to geometry.

—*Lloyd Motz & Jefferson Hane Weaver:* ***The Story of Mathematics****, 1993*

27.5 Counting

1. There was a young fellow named Ben
Who could only count modulo ten.
He said, "When I go
Past my little toe,
I shall have to start over again.

—*Anonymous: in Martin Gardner's "Mathematical Games" column;* ***Scientific American****, February, 1981*

2. Let him who has understanding count the number of the beast: for it is the number of a man; and his number is Six hundred threescore and six.

—*The Bible, Old Testament; Revelations*

3. Sir, allow me to ask you one question. If the church should say to you, "Two and three make ten," what would you do? "Sir," said he, "I should believe it, and I would count like this: one, two, three, four, ten." I was now fully satisfied.

—*James Boswell:* ***The Life of Samuel Johnson*** *1791*

4. Arithmetic sat in the shade,
Where she says, and where she figures,
That ten and two and one make thirteen,
And three more make sixteen;
Four and three and nine to boot
Again make sixteen in their way;
Thirteen and twenty-seven make forty,
And three times twenty by themselves make sixty;
Five twenties make hundred and ten hundred a thousand.
Does counting involve anything further? No.
One can easily count a thousand thousands
In the foregoing manner,
From the number which increases and diminishes
And which in counting goes from one to hundred.
The dame makes from this her tale,
That usurer, print, and count
Today love the countess better
Than the chanting of High Mass.
Arithmetic then mounted
Her horse and proceeded to count
All the knights of the army....

—*Henri d'Andeli:* ***Battle of the Seven Arts****; c. 15th cent., published, 1927 [Medieval author d'Andeli portrays a battle among the liberal arts. Arithmetic is portrayed as a maiden sitting under a tree, placidly counting and figuring.]*

5. Whenever a counting technique, worthy of the name, exists at all, finger counting has been found to either precede it or accompany it.

—*Tobias Dantzig:* ***Number, The Language of Science****, 1954*

6. Although I am almost illiterate mathematically, I grasped very early in life that any one who can count to ten can count upward indefinitely if he is fool enough to do so.

—*Robertson Davies:* ***The Table Talk of Samuel Marchbanks****, 1949*

7. It does not follow that because something can be counted it therefore should be counted.

—*Harold L. Enarson: Speech to Society for College and University Planning, September, 1975*

8. Whenever you can, count.

—*Sir Francis Galton: In J.R. Newman, ed.* ***The World of Mathematics****, 1956*

9. One has to be able to count if only so that at fifty he doesn't marry a girl of twenty.

—*Maxim Gorky:* ***The Zykrovs****, 1914*

10. She was a crazy mathematics major from the Wharton School of Business who could not count to twenty-eight each month without getting into trouble.

—*Joseph Heller:* ***Catch-22****, 1955*

11. To count is a modern practice, the ancient method was to guess; and when numbers are guessed they are always magnified.

—*Samuel Johnson: In James Boswell,* ***Life of Samuel Johnson****, 1775*

12. There is no problem in all mathematics that cannot be solved by direct counting. But with the present implements of mathematics many operations can be performed in a few minutes which without mathematical methods would take a lifetime.

—*Ernst Mach:* ***Popular Scientific Lectures****, Chicago, 1910*

13. 'Counting': Ounce, dice, trice, quartz, quince, sago, serpent, oxygen, nitrogen, denim.

—*Alastair Reid:* ***Ounce, dice, trice****, 1956*

14. Counting is the religion of this generation it is its hope and its salvation.

—*Gertrude Stein:* ***Everybody's Autobiography****, 1937*

15. Counting is a symbolic process employed only by man, the sole symbol-creating animal.

—*R.L. Wilder:* ***the Evolution of Mathematical Concepts****, 1974*

16. If mathematics teaches us to count, then why doesn't it also teach us to compare colors?

—*Ludwig Wittgenstein:* ***Remarks on the Foundations of Mathematics****, 1956, 1983 G.E.M. Anscombe & B. Blackwell, tr.*

27.6 Whole Numbers—Natural Numbers

1. I've dealt with numbers all my life, of course, and after a while you begin to feel that each number has a personality of its own. A twelve is very different from a thirteen, for example. Twelve is upright, conscientious, intelligent, whereas thirteen is a loner, a shady character who won't think twice about breaking the law to get what he wants. Eleven is tough, an outdoorsman who likes tramping through woods and scaling mountains; ten is rather simpleminded, a bland figure who always does what he's told; nine is deep and mystical, a Buddha of contemplation.... Numbers have souls, and you can't help but get involved with them in a personal way.

—*Paul Auster:* ***The Music of Chance****, 1990*

2. It was the Greeks who first recognized the natural (or counting numbers) 1,2,3, ... as forming an infinite collection on which the basic arithmetic operations of addition and multiplication could be performed.

—*Keith Devlin:* ***Mathematics: The New Golden Age****, 1988*

3. The Pythagoreans were impressed with numbers and, because they were mystics, attached to the whole numbers meanings and significances which we now regard as childish. Thus, they considered the number "one" as the essence or very nature of reason, for reason could produce only one consistent body of doctrines. The number "two" was identified with opinion, clearly because the very meaning of opinion implies the possibility of an opposing opinion, and thus of at least two. "Four" was identified with justice because it is the first number which is the product of equals.... "Five" signified marriage because it was the union of the first masculine number, three, and the first feminine number, two. (Odd numbers were masculine and even numbers feminine.) The number "seven" represented health and "eight," friendship or love.

—*Morris Kline:* ***Mathematics for the Nonmathematician****, 1967*

4. I doubt whether anyone could adequately celebrate the properties of the number 7, for they are beyond all words.... So august is the dignity inherent by nature in the number 7, that it has a unique relation distinguishing it from all the other numbers, for of these some beget without being begotten, some are begotten but do not beget, some do both these, both beget and are begotten: 7 alone is found in no such category.

—*Philo Judacus of Alexandria (c. 20 B.C.—c. A.D. 54); In* ***Greek & Roman Philosophy After Aristotle****, J.L. Saunders, ed., 1966 [The begetting and begotten can be explained as follows: the only number which has neither a multiple between 1 and 10 or a factor between 1 and 10 is 7.]*

27.7 Fractions

1. I though about this mathematical need to reduce fractions to their minimum. I thought of all the energy that students put out on reducing thirty four divided by sixty eight to one half. And I was reminded of the feeling of relief in the discovery that some fraction is actually one fifth. No I though that this was all baloney. As though that one fifth is clearer. They gave a semblance of clarity to something that is not necessarily clearer and they idiotized people. They idiotized me. What is clear in the fraction "one fifth?" Same thing with logarithms.

—*Orly Castel-Bloom: "The New Book of Orly Castel-Bloom";* ***Taking the Trend****, 1998*

2. Stating amounts in sounding fractional sums conveys a much fuller notion of their magnitude than by disguising their immensity in such aggregations of value as doubloons, sovereigns and dollars. Who would not rather be worth 125,000 francs in Paris than only 5000 pounds in London.

—*Herman Melville:* ***Redburn****, 1849*

3. The only way I can distinguish proper from improper fractions Is by their actions.

—*Ogden Nash:* ***Ask Daddy—He Won't Know****, 1968*

4. That is, indeed, the precise and only use or significance of these fractions termed probabilities: they give security in the long run.

*—Charles Sanders Peirce: Review of John Venn's **The Logic of Chance**, 1867; in **Collected Papers of C.S. Peirce**, vol. 8, 1966*

5. Fractions cannot be arranged in an order of magnitude. At first this sounds extremely interesting. One would like to say of it, e.g., "It introduces us to the mysteries of the mathematical world." This is the aspect against which I want to give a warning. When ... I form the picture of an unending row of things, and between each of these things and its neighbor new things appear, and more new ones between each of these and its neighbor, and so on without end, then certainly there is something here to make one dizzy. But once we see that this picture, though very exciting, is all the same not appropriate, that we ought not to let ourselves be trapped by the words "series," "order," "exist," and others, we shall fall back on the technique of calculating fractions about which there is no longer anything queer.

*—Ludwig Wittgenstein: **Philosophical Grammar**, 1974*

27.8 Negative Numbers

1. ...a problem leading to a negative solution means that some part of the hypothesis was false but assumed to be true.... Arriving at a negative solution means that the opposition of the number [the corresponding positive] is the desired solution.

*—Jean Le Rond D'Alembert: **Encyclopedia**, "Negative"; 1751–65*

2. The terms positive and negative, as used in the mathematics, are merely relative. They imply that there is, either in the nature of quantities, or in their circumstances, or in the purposes which they are to answer in calculation, some such opposition as requires that one should be subtracted from the other.

*—Jeremiah Day: **An Introduction to Algebra**, 1857*

3. The number is like human life. First you have the natural numbers. The ones that are whole and positive. Like the numbers of a small child. But human consciousness expands. The child discovers longing. Do you know the mathematical expression for longing? The negative numbers. The formalization of the feeling that you're missing something.

*—Peter Hoeg: **Smilla's Sense of Snow**; Tina Nunnally, tr., 1994*

4. The Hindus added to the logical woes of mathematicians by introducing negative numbers to represent debts. In such uses positive number represented assets. The first known use was by Brahmagupta about A.D. 628, who merely stated rules for the four operations with negative numbers. No definitions, axioms, or theorems appeared.

*—Morris Kline: **Mathematics: The Loss of Certainty**, 1980*

5. It were to be wished ... that negative numbers had never been admitted into algebra or were again discarded from it: for if this were done, there is good reason to imagine, the objections which many learned and ingenious men now make to algebraic computations, as being obscure and perplexed with almost unintelligible notions, would be thereby removed.

*—Baron Francis Maseres: in Morris Kline: **Mathematical Thought**, 1972*

6. Will anyone seriously assert that the existence of negative numbers is guaranteed by the fact that there exist in the world hot and cold, assets and debts? Shall we refer to these things in the structure of arithmetic? Who does not see that thereby an entirely foreign element enters into arithmetic, which endangers the pureness and clarity of its concepts?

*—Friedrich Waismann: **Introduction to Mathematical Thinking**, 1951*

27.9 Integers

1. Of the integers, so we are told,
No matter how many are bought or sold,
Or how many you give away or lend,
Of the rest there is no end.

—Anonymous

2. Nature does not count nor do integers occur in nature. Man made them all, integers and all the rest, Kronecker to the contrary nothwithstanding.

*—P.W. Bridgman: **The Way Things Are**, 1959*

3. The trouble with integers is that we have examined only the very small ones. Maybe all the exciting stuff happens at really big numbers, ones we can't even begin to think about in any very definite way. Our brains have evolved to get us out of the rain, find where the berries are, and keep us from getting killed. Our brains did not evolve to help us grasp really large numbers or to look at things in a hundred thousand dimensions.

*—Ronald L. Graham: Quoted in Clifford A. Pickover: **Keys to Infinity**, 1995*

4. Integers are the fountainhead of all mathematics.

*—Hermann Minkowski: **Diophantische Approximationen: eine Einfuhrung in die Zahlentheorie, von Hermann Minkowski**, 1907*

5. Today there remains in analysis only integers and finite and infinite systems of integers, interrelated by a net of relations of equality or inequality. Mathematics, as we say has been arithmetized.

—Henri Poincare: Second International Congress of Mathematics, Paris, 1900

27.10 Irrational Numbers

1. Now as to what pertains to these Surd numbers (which, as it were by way of reproach and calumny, having no merit of their own are also styled Irrational, Irregular, and Inexplicable) they are by many denied to be numbers properly speaking, and are wont to be banished from arithmetic to another Science, (which yet is no science) viz. algebra.

—Isaac Barrow: ***Mathematical Lectures,*** *1734*

2. Yet what are all such gaieties to me Whose thoughts are full on indices and surds?

—Lewis Carroll; ***Four Riddles,*** *1869*

3. To attempt to apply rational arithmetic to a problem in geometry resulted in the first crisis in the history of mathematics. The two relatively simple problems—the determination of the diagonal of a square and that of the circumference of a circle—revealed the existence of new mathematical beings for which no place could be found within the rational domain.

—Tobias Dantzig: Quoted in Eli Maor: ***To Infinity and Beyond: A Cultural History of the Infinite,*** *1987*

4. Every attempt to treat the irrational numbers formally and without the concept of [geometric] magnitude must lead to the most abstruse and troublesome artificialities, which, even if they can be carried through with complete, rigor, as we have every right to doubt, do not have a higher scientific value.

—Hermann Hankel: ***Theorie der complexen Zahlensystem,*** *1867*

5. There is an interesting story connected with the name given by Greek mathematicians to numbers like "square root of 2," square root of 3, square root of 5, and so on. Greek mathematicians used the word logos, which meant "a word" and also "the mind behind the word" for any number that could be expressed as a ratio, such a number being one that their minds could grasp. In fact, the Greek word for "ratio" was logos. Any number like "square root of 2, which ... cannot be expressed as ratio between two numbers, was called a-logos, that is, "not logos," "not a ratio number." We must now jump ahead about 1000 years in order to follow up the story of a-logos. The Arab mathematician al-Khowarizmi made use of an Arabic translation of the work of some Greek mathematician, who naturally used the word a-logos in its technical sense, as indicating "not ratio-nal." Whoever translated the work into Arabic took the word a-logos, in its primary instead of its technical sense, as meaning "without a word," and translated it by the Arabic word meaning "deaf." So al-Khowarizmi came to call numbers like "square root of 2," "square root of 3," etc. by this Arabic word. Some three hundred years later the European translator Gherado rendered into, Latin a book written by al-Khowarizmi. He found certain numbers described in the Arabic as "deaf," so he translated this by the Latin surdus, "deaf." To this day we sometimes call a number like "square root of 2" a "surd," with its meaningless reference to deafness.

—Alfred Hooper: ***Makers of Mathematics,*** *1948*

6. It is well known that the man who first made public the theory of irrationals perished in a shipwreck in order that the inexpressible and unimaginable should ever remain veiled. And so the guilty man, who fortuitously touched on and revealed this aspect of living things, was taken to the place where he began and there is for ever beaten by the waves.

—Proclus Diadochus: ***Commentary on Euclid,*** *c. 5th cent. A.D.*

27.11 Zero

1. ...it took men about five thousand years, counting from the beginning of number symbols, to think of a symbol for nothing.

—Isaac Asimov: ***On Numbers,*** *1990*

2. ...the optimist who treats a problem in algebra or analytic geometry will say, if he stops to reflect on what he is doing: "I know that I have no right to divide by zero; but there are so many other values which the expression by which I am dividing might have that I will assume that the Evil One has not thrown a zero in my denominator this time.

—Maxime Bochner: "The Fundamental Conceptions and Methods in Mathematics"; ***Bulletin of the American Mathematical Society,*** *vol. 9 1904*

3. The most important innovation that the eager, inquisitive, and tolerant Arab scholars brought from afar was in writing numbers. The European notation for numbers which was still the clumsy Roman style, in which the number is put together from its parts by simple addition.... However, a system that describes magnitude by place must provide for the possibility of empty places.

The Arabic notation requires the invention of a zero.... The words zero and cipher are Arab words....

—*Jacob Bronowski: "The Music of the Spheres"* ***The Ascent of Man****, 1973*

4. "Take some more tea," the March Hare said to Alice, very earnestly. "I've had nothing yet," Alice replied in an offended tone: "so I can't take more." "You mean you can't take less," said the Hatter" "it's very easy to take more than nothing."

—*Lewis Carroll:* ***Alice's Adventures in Wonderland****, 1865*

5. Infinity is the land of mathematical hocus pocus, There Zero the magician is king. When Zero divides any number he changes it without regard to its magnitude into the infinitely small; and inversely, when divided by any number he begets the infinitely great.

—*Paul Carus: "The Nature of Logical and Mathematical Thought";* ***Monist****, Vol. 20, 1; January, 1910*

6. Every number is zero in the presence of the infinite.

—*Victor Hugo:* ***The Toilers of the Sea****, 1866; M.W. Artosi, tr., 1892*

7. If you look at zero you see nothing; but look through it and you will see the world. For zero brings into focus the great, organic sprawl of mathematics, and mathematics in turn the complex nature of things.

—*Robert Kaplan:* ***The Nothing That Is****, 1999*

8. I don't agree with mathematics; the sum total of zeros is a frightening figure.

—*Stanislaw J. Lec:* ***More Unkempt Thoughts****, 1968*

9. When One made love to Zero spheres embraced their arches and prime numbers caught their breath....

—*Raymond Queneau: "Sines";* ***Pounding the Pavement, Beating the Bush, and Other Pataphysical Poems****, 1985*

10. From generation to generation skepticism increases, and probability diminishes; and soon probability is reduced to zero.

—*Voltaire:* ***Philosophical Dictionary****, "Miscellany," 1764; in* ***The Portable Voltaire****, 1965*

28

Numbers and Number Theory

28.1 Even and Odd Numbers

1. The next fundamental assumption of the Pythagoreans lies much deeper, so deep in fact that civilized man can scarcely hope to fetch it up to the full light of reason. Odd numbers are male; even numbers, female. We can only ask why, expecting no answer except possibly a hesitant allusion to a vestigial phallicisms of a forgotten Orphism.

—Eric Temple Bell: ***The Magic of Numbers****, 1946*

2. Round numbers are always false.

—Samuel Johnson: Quoted in Hester Piozzi, ***Anecdotes of Samuel Johnson****, 1786; in* ***Johnsoniana: Apothegms, Sentiment, etc.***

3. One ... is reason, 2 is opinion; 4, justice.... Odd numbers are masculine and even numbers feminine. Therefore, reasoned Pythagoras, even number represent evil; and odd, or masculine numbers, good. Five, the first sum of an odd and even number (1 was not counted) symbolizes marriage.

—Jane Muir: ***Of Men and Numbers****, 1996*

4. The Pooka MacPhellimey, a member of the devil class, sat in his hut in the middle of a firewood meditating on the nature of the numerals and segregating in his mind the odd ones from the even.

—Flann O'Brien: ***At Swim-Two-Birds****, 1939*

5. The gods below ... should receive everything in even numbers, and of the second choice, and ill omen; while the odd numbers, and of the first choice, and the things of lucky omen, are given to the gods above.

—Plato: ***Republic****, c. 360 B.C.*

6. Why is it that we entertain the belief that for every purpose odd numbers are the most effectual?

—Pliny the Elder: ***Natural History****, c. 1st cent. A.D.*

7. This is the third time; I hope good luck lies in odd numbers.... They say there is divinity in odd numbers, either in nativity, chance or death.

—William Shakespeare: ***The Merry Wives of Windsor****, 1597*

8. The god delights in an odd number.

—Virgil: ***Aeneid****, c. 1st cent. B.C.*

28.2 Real and Rational Numbers

1. It is worthy of note that Cassiordorius was the first writer to use the terms "rational" and "irrational" in the sense now current in arithmetic and algebra.

—Florian Cajori: ***A History of Mathematics****, 1919*

2. For all practical purposes the rational numbers are more than sufficient. Indeed, in the real world (as opposed to the mathematics one) these are the only numbers that are used, with answers to problems being given to at most a few decimal points.

—Keith Devlin: Mathematics: The New Golden Age, 1988

3. It is customary to say that a digital computer is one that performs the arithmetic operations on numbers that are represented in the machine in terms of some radix, formerly the radix 10, now quite often the radix 2. But the fact is that the numbers represented in any machine are only those of some subset of the real numbers. This subset is indeed large, but it is finite, and apart from trivial exceptions, no finite subset of the real numbers is closed under any one of the four arithmetic operations. Consequently the operations performed by any digital machine are only pseudo-arithmetic.

—A.S. Householder: "Numerical Analysis"; ***Lectures on Modern Mathematics****, Vol. 1, T.L. Sarty, ed., 1963*

4. It is far easier to go from the real numbers to the complex numbers than ... from the rationals to the reals.

—*Jerry P. King:* ***The Art of Mathematics****, 1992*

5. ...it seems only natural to conclude—as the Greeks did—that the entire number line is populated by rational points. But in mathematics, what seems to be a natural conclusion often turns out to be false. One of the most momentous events in the history of mathematics was the discovery that the rational numbers, despite their density, leave "holes" along the number line—points that do not correspond to rational numbers.

—*Eli Maor:* ***e: The Story of a Number****, 1994*

28.3 Imaginary Numbers

1. The number you have dialed is imaginary. Please multiply by i and dial again.

—*Anonymous: MIT telephone exchange; attributed.*

2. ...neither the true roots nor the false are always real; sometimes they are, however, imaginary; namely, whereas we can always imagine as many roots for each equation as I have predicted, there is still not always a quantity which corresponds to each root so imagined.

—*Rene Descartes: "La Geometrie," 1637 [Descartes thus introduces the terms "imaginary" and "real."]*

3. During the sixteenth century, European mathematicians—and in particular the Italian Rafaello Bombelli—began to realize that in the solution of algebraic problems it was often useful to assume that negative numbers have square root. It is perhaps understandable when we consider the climate of the time that such 'numbers' were referred to as imaginary numbers, though to the present-day mathematician all numbers are 'imaginary' concepts, the square root of negative quantities no more or no less than any others.

—*Keith Devlin:* ***Mathematics: The New Golden Age****, 1988*

4. The square roots of negative numbers are neither zero, nor less than zero, nor greater than zero. Then it is clear that the square roots of negative numbers cannot be included among the possible numbers [real numbers]. Consequently we must say that these are impossible numbers. And this circumstance leads us to the concept of such numbers, which by their nature are impossible, and ordinarily are called imaginary or fancied numbers, because they exist only in the imagination.

—*Leonhard Euler:* ***Algebra****, 1770*

5. How poor were we? Why, we were so poor we only had imaginary numbers to play with.

—*Kenneth Kaminsky: "Professor Fogelfroe,"* ***Mathematics Magazine****, Vol. 69, October, 1996*

6. The imaginary number is a fine and wonderful resource of the divine spirit, almost an amphibian between being and not being.

—*Gottfried Wilhelm Leibniz:* ***New Essays Concerning Human Understanding****, 1696; in* ***Philosophical Papers and Letters****, 1956*

7. A carpenter named Charlie Bratticks,
Who had a taste for mathematics,
One summer Tuesday, just for fun,
Made a wooden cube side minus one

—*J.A. Lindon "A Positive Reminder"; in* ***Imaginary Numbers****, William Frucht, ed., 1999*

8. There are certainly people who regard the square root of two as something perfectly obvious, but jib at the square root of negative one. This is because they think they can visualize the former as something in physical space, but not the latter. Actually the square root of negative one is a much simpler concept.

—*E.C. Titchmarsh: Quoted in Gabor Toth:* ***Glimpses of Algebra and Geometry****, 1998*

9. I met a man once who told me that far from believing in the square root of minus one, he didn't believe in minus one. This is at any rate a consistent attitude.

—*Edward Titchmarsh:* ***Mathematics for the General Reader****, 1950*

28.4 Complex Numbers

1. We have shown the symbol 'square root of -a' to be void of meaning, or rather self-contradictory and absurd. Nevertheless, by means of such symbols, a part of algebra is established which is of great utility. It depends upon the fact, which may be verified by experience that the common rules of algebra may be applied to these expressions [complex numbers] without leading to any false results.

—*Augustus De Morgan:* ***On the Study and Difficulties of Mathematics****, 1831*

2. There can be very little of present-day science and technology that is not dependent on complex numbers in one way or another.... Indeed, nowadays no electrical engineer could get along without complex numbers, and neither could anyone working in aerodynamics or fluid dynamics.

—*Kevin Devlin:* ***Mathematics: The New Golden Age****, 1991*

3. [Leonhard] Euler deserves much of the credit for popularizing complex numbers. He showed how to find their powers and roots and even defined such things as their logarithms. In a sense, he established their arithmetic and algebraic legitimacy.

—*William Dunham:* ***The Mathematical Universe****, 1994*

4. One could say: What are these impossible solutions [complex roots]? I answer: For three things, for the certitude of the general rules, that there are no other solutions, and for their utility.

—*Albert Girard:* ***New Invention in Algebra;*** *1595–1632*

5. The first mathematician who really developed the geometric concept of complex numbers—and gave them their name, ... was Gauss....

—*Alfred Hooper:* ***Makers of Mathematics,*** *1948*

6. [Complex numbers are] a fine and wonderful refuge of the divine spirit—almost an amphibian between being and non-being.

—*Gottfried Leibniz: in Israel Kleiner: "Thinking the Unthinkable: The Story of Complex Numbers (with a Moral)";* ***Mathematics teacher,*** *October, 1988*

28.5 Algebraic and Transcendental Numbers

1. π vs e

π goes on and on and on....
And e is just as cursed.
I wonder: Which is larger
When their digits are reversed?

—*Anonymous*

2. The algebraic numbers are spotted over the plane like stars against a black sky; the dense blackness is the firmament of the transcendentals.

—*Eric Temple Bell:* ***Men of Mathematics,*** *1937*

3. It is frankly, difficult to imagine a non-algebraic number, one that is not the solution of any polynomial equations with integral coefficients.... It was Euler who first speculated that such numbers exist. A real number that is not algebraic he called transcendental because it transcends the operations of algebra. Transcendentals were thus introduced not by saying what they are but by saying what they are not: They are not algebraic.

—*William Dunham:* ***The Mathematical Universe,*** *1994*

4. The work of the great Swiss mathematician Leonhard Euler represents the outstanding example of eighteenth-century formal manipulation in analysis. it was by purely formal devices that Euler discovered the remarkable formula

$$e^{ix} = \cos x + i \sin x,$$

which, for $x = \pi$, yields

$$e^{i\pi} + 1 = 0$$

a relation connecting five of the most important numbers of mathematics.

—*Howard W. Eves:* ***In Mathematical Circles,*** *1969*

5. No one had ever knowingly seen a transcendental number; their actual existence was proved in 1851 by Joseph Liouville. It was only in 1882 that our old friend π was proved to be transcendental, by Ferdinand Lindemann, thereby answering in the negative the centuries-old question of whether it was possible to square the circle using ruler and compass method.

—*Richard Mankiewicz:* ***The Story of Mathematics,*** *2000*

6. In contrast to the irrational numbers, whose discovery arose from a mundane problem in geometry, the first transcendental numbers were created specifically for the purpose of demonstrating that such numbers exist....

—*Eli Maor:* ***e: The Story of a Number,*** *1994*

7. Hiding between all the ordinary numbers was an infinity of transcendental numbers whose presence you would never have guessed until you looked deeply into mathematics.

—*Carl Sagan:* ***Contact,*** *1985*

8. It is not known if the number π^e is rational or irrational.

—*David Wells:* ***The Penguin Dictionary of Curious and Interesting Numbers,*** *1986*

28.6 "e"

1. If (1 + x) (real close to 1)
Is raised to the power of 1
Over x, you will find
Here's the value defined:
2.718281....

—*Anonymous*

2. "e" is the fifth letter of the English alphabet, but the mathematician's e is a real number with decimal expansion 2.718281828459045.... Whereas everyone knows that "e," the most frequently used letter in the English language, is indispensable, it may come as a surprise to nonmathematicians that e is likewise indispensable.

—*William Dunham:* ***The Mathematical Universe,*** *1994*

3. The definition of e is usually, in imitation of the French models, placed at the very beginning of the great text books of analysis, and entirely unmotivated, whereby the really valuable element is missed, the one which mediates the understanding, namely, an explanation why precisely this remarkable limit is used as base and why the resulting logarithms are called natural.

—*Felix Klein:* ***Elementary Mathematics From an Advanced Standpoint,*** *1953*

4. The letter e may now no longer be used to denote anything other than this positive universal constant [the solution of the equation $\ln x = 1$].

—*Edmund Landau:* ***Differential and Integral Calculus,*** *1934*

5. Why did he [Euler] chose the letter e? There is no general consensus. According to one view, Euler chose it because it is the first letter of the word exponential. More likely, the choice came to him naturally as the first "unused" letter of the alphabet, since the letters a,b,c, and d frequently appeared elsewhere in mathematics. It seems unlikely that Euler chose the letter because it is the initial of his own name, as occasionally has been suggested: he was an extremely modest man and often delayed publication of his own work so that a colleague or student of his would get due credit. In any event, his choice of the symbol e, like so many other symbols of his, became universally accepted.
—Eli Maor: ***e: The Story of a Number****, 1994*

6. The irrationality of e was proved in 1737 by Euler. Charles Hermite in 1873 proved that e is transcendental; that is, it cannot be a solution of a polynomial equation with integer coefficients.
—Eli Maor: ***e: The story of a Number****, 1994*

7. ...well shuffling two packs of cards, and turning up pairs of cards, one from each pack. The probability that there will be no match among the 52 pairs is approximately 1/e.
—David Wells: ***The Penguin Dictionary of Curious and Interesting Numbers****, 1986*

28.7 "Pi"

1. ...in the Old Testament (I Kings ...), we find the following verse: "Also, he made a molten sea of ten cubits from brim to brim, round in compass, and five cubits the height thereof; and a line of thirty cubits did compass it round about." The molten sea, we are told, is round; it measures 30 cubits round about (in circumference) and 10 cubits from brim to brim (in diameter); thus the biblical value of π is 30/10 = 3.
—Petr Beckmann: ***The History of π****, 1971*

2. The digits beyond the first few decimal places are of no practical or scientific value. Four decimal places are sufficient for the design of the finest engines; ten decimals are sufficient to obtain the circumference of the earth to within a fraction of an inch if the earth were a smooth sphere....
—Petr Beckmann: ***The History of π****, 1971*

3. There's a beauty to π that keeps us looking at it.... The digits of π are extremely random. They really have no pattern, and in mathematics that's really the same as saying they have every pattern.
—Peter Borwein: Quoted in David Blatner: ***The Joy of π****, 1997*

4. It was in that year (1706) that William Jones made himself noted, without being aware that he was doing anything noteworthy, through his designation of the ratio of the length of the circle to its diameter by the letter π. He took this step without ostentation No length introduction prepares the reader for the bringing upon the stage of mathematical history this distinguished visitor from the field of Greek letters. It simply came, unheralded....
—Florian Cajori: ***A History of Mathematical Notation****, 1928 [The first use of the Greek letter π in its modern understanding was found in William Jones :****Synopsis palmariorum matheseos****, 1706, when he denoted 3.14159 by π.]*

5. 'Tis a favorite project of mine A new value of π to assign. I would fix it at 3 For its simpler, you see, Than 3 point 14159.
—Harvey L. Carter: in William S. Baring-Gould: ***The Lure of the Limerick: An Uninhibited History****, 1963*

6. The mysterious and wonderful π is reduced to a gargle that helps computing machines clear their throats.
—Philip J. Davis: ***The Lore of Large Numbers,***

7. The mysterious 3.14159 ... which comes in at every door and window, and down every chimney.
—Augustus de Morgan: ***A Budget of Paradoxes*** *1872*

8. ...the Pendulum ... governed by the square root of the length of the wire and by π, that number which, however irrational to sublunar minds, through a higher rationality binds the circumference and diameter of all possible circles.
—Umberto Eco: ***Foucault's Pendulum****, 1990*

9. [Hugo] Steinhaus, with his predilection for metaphors, used to quote a Polish proverb: "Luck runs in circles," to explain why π, so intimately connected with circles, keeps cropping up in probability theory and statistics, the two disciplines which deal with randomness and luck.
—Mark Kac: ***Enigmas of Chance****, 1985*

10. What good is your beautiful investigation regarding π? Why study such problems, since irrational numbers do not exist?
—Leopold Kronecker: Commenting to Ferdinand von Lindemann who had just proved the the transcendence of π.; 1882: Quoted in E.T. Bell; ***Men of Mathematics****, 1937*

11. The ratio of the diameter of a circle to its circumference cannot be known ... but it is possible to approximate it ... and the approximation used by scientists is the ratio of one to three and one seventh.... Since it is impossible to arrive at a perfectly accurate ratio ... they assumed a round number and said "any [circle] which has a circumference of three fists has a diameter of one fist." And they relied on this for all the measurements they needed.
—Maimondies (Rabbi Moshe ben Maimon, 1135–1204); ***Guide for the Perplexed****, 1190*

12. π is not the solution to any question built upon a less than infinite series of whole numbers. If equations are trains threading the landscape of numbers, then no train stops at π.

—*Richard Preston: in Clifford A. Pickover:* ***Keys to Infinity****, 1995*

13. Seven hundred seven, Shanks did state, Digits of π he would calculate. And none can deny It was a good try. But he had erred in five twenty eight.

—*Nicholas J. Rose:* ***Rome Press 1985 Mathematical Calendar*** *[The reference is to William Shanks, who in 1873 first published his computation of π to 707 digits. An error was found in the 528th digit.]*

14. Probably no symbol in mathematics has evoked as much mystery, romanticism, misconception and human interest as the number π.

—*William L. Schaff:* ***Natural History of π.****, in David Blatner:* ***The Joy of π.*** *1997*

15. It can be of no practical use to know that π is irrational, but if we can know, it sure would be intolerable not to know.

—*E.C. Titchmarsh: In N. Rose:* ***Mathematical Maxims and Minims****, 1988*

28.8 Quaternions

1. Hamilton's development [of the quaternions] marked the beginning of a period in which mathematicians freely created systems of symbols using prescribed self-consistent rules governing their combination one with another giving no thought for whether such systems described anything in the real world.

—*John D. Barrow:* ***Pi in the Sky****, 1992*

2. Quaternions have found considerable use in modern physics, as has an even more bizarre number system—the octonions, an eight-dimensional number system in which not only the commutative law of multiplication but the associative law too is lost.

—*Kevin Devlin:* ***Mathematics: The New Golden Age****, 1988*

3. The eminent algebraist Frobenius showed, in 1878, that no numbers exist beyond the ordinary complex numbers, which could satisfy all the postulates of ordinary algebra. The hyper-complex numbers as originally envisaged by Hamilton, simply did not exist.... In 1878, Frobenius had shown that Hamilton's quaternion algebra is entirely unique inasmuch as there exists no higher algebra which preserves all the postulates of algebra, with the exception of the commutative law.

—*C. Lanczos: "William Rowan Hamilton—An Appreciation";* ***American Scientist*** *55, 1967*

4. It is true that, in the eyes of the pure mathematician, Quaternions have one grand and fatal defect. They cannot be applied to space of n dimensions, they are contented to deal with those poor three dimensions in which mere mortals are doomed to dwell, but which cannot bound the limitless aspirations of a Cayley or a Sylvester. From the physical point of view this, instead of a defect, is to be regarded as the greatest possible recommendation. It shows, in fact, Quaternions to be the special instrument so constructed for application to the Actual as to have thrown overboard everything which is not absolutely necessary, without the slightest consideration whether or no it was thereby being rendered useless for application to the Inconceivable.

—*P.G. Tait: "Presidential Address British Association for the Advancement of Science"* ***Nature****, vol. 4, 1871*

5. Quaternions came from Hamilton ... and have been an unmixed evil to those who have touched them in any way. Vector is a useless survival ... and has never been of the slightest use to any creature.

—*William Thomson, Lord Kelvin; in J.E. Mardsen & A.J. Tromba:* ***Vector Calculus****, 1981*

28.9 Transfinite Numbers

1. What [Georg] Cantor ... set out to do was create exact notions of what it means for an infinity to be equal to, greater than, or less than another infinity. The resulting arithmetic of the infinite, or transfinite arithmetic, was a dramatic and controversial departure from the past attitudes to actual infinities by mathematicians who had regarded them as a concept for the theologians.

—*John D. Barrow:* ***Pi in the Sky****, 1988*

2. The transfinite with its plenty of figures and shapes refers with necessity to an absolute, to the true infinity, from which we cannot subtract anything and to which we cannot add anything. Therefore the absolute must be regarded as being the absolute maximum. It exceeds the human intellect and, in particular, cannot be determined mathematically.

—*Georg Cantor:* ***Contributions to the Founding of the Theory of Transfinite Numbers****, 1955*

3. Georg Cantor's creation of transfinite numbers in the nineteenth century transformed mathematics by enlarging its domain from finite to infinite numbers. Above all, the conceptual ship from transfinite sets to transfinite numbers represents a shift that was in many ways the same at the shift from irrational magnitudes to irrational numbers. From the concrete to the abstract, the transformation in both cases revolutionized mathematics.

—*Joseph Dauben: "Conceptual revolutions and the history of mathematics"; **Transformations and Traditions in the Sciences**, E. Mendelsohn, ed., 1984*

4. [Cantor's transfinite numbers are] the most beautiful realizations of human activity in the domain of the purely intelligible.

—*David Hilbert: "Sur l'infinit"; **Acta Mathematica**, 1926*

5. Cantor's transfinite numbers, then, are impossible and self-contradictory; ... the exhaustion of continua remains a pious belief. Cantor hopes to prove that the second class of numbers will exhaust continua, and there seems as yet no reason to suppose the contrary. But the proof is not yet forthcoming.

—*Bertrand Russell: "On Some Difficulties of Continuous Quantity"; unpublished article written in June, 1896*

28.10 Number Theory

1. That subject [number theory] is in itself one of peculiar interest and elegance, but its conclusions have little practical importance.

—*W.W. Rouse Ball: **History of Mathematics**, 1896*

2. [Number theory] is a field of almost pristine irrelevance to everything except the wondrous demonstration that pure numbers, no more substantial than Plato's shadows, conceal magical laws and orders that the mind can discover after all.

—*Sharon Begley: **Newsweek**; July 5, 1993*

3. [Number theory remains] the last great uncivilized continent of mathematics.]

—*Eric Temple Bell: "The Queen of Mathematics": in **The World of Mathematics**, James R. Newman, ed., 1956*

4. The science of numbers ought to be preferred as an acquisition before all others, because of its necessity and because of the great secrets and other mysteries which there are in the properties of numbers. All sciences partake of it, and it has need of none.

—*Boethius: Quoted in J. Fauvel & J. Gray: **The History of Mathematics: A Reader**, 1987*

5. A peculiarity of the higher arithmetic is the great difficulty which has often been experienced in proving simple general theorems which have been suggested quite naturally by numerical evidence.

—*Harold Davenport: **The Higher Arithmetic**, 1952*

6. Thank God that number theory is unsullied by any applications.

—*Leonard Eugene Dickson: Favored expression*

7. Mathematics is the Queen of the Sciences, and Arithmetic is the Queen of Mathematics.

—*Carl Freidrich Gauss: Quoted in E.T. Bell: **Men of Mathematics**, 1937 [Gauss refers to number theory not ordinary arithmetic.]*

8. I have always thought of number theory as an experimental science.

—*Richard K. Guy: **Unsolved Problems in Number Theory**, 1994*

9. It is certain that the Theory of Numbers originated in the school of Pythagoras; and with regard to Pythagoras himself, we are told by Aristoxenus that "he seems to have attached supreme importance to the study of arithmetic, which he advanced and took out of the region of commercial utility."

—*Sir T.L. Heath: **A History of Greek Mathematics**, 1981*

10. ...while writing a book on computer arithmetic, I found that virtually every theorem in elementary number theory arises in a natural, motivated way in connection with the problem of making computers do high-speed calculations. Therefore I believe that the traditional courses in elementary number theory might well be changed to adopt this point of view, adding a practical motivation to the already beautiful theory.

—*Donald E. Knuth: "Computer Science and Its Relation to Mathematics"; **The American Mathematical Monthly**, 81; April, 1974*

11. Number-theorists are like lotus-eaters—having once tasted of this food they can never give it up.

—*Leopold Kronecker: In Howard Eves: **Mathematical Circles Squared**, 1972*

12. The theory of numbers is particularly liable to the accusation that some of the problems are the wrong sort of questions to ask. I do not myself think the danger is serious; either a reasonable amount of concentration leads to new ideas or methods of obvious interest, or else one just leaves the problem alone. "Perfect numbers" certainly never did any good, but then they never did any particular harm.

—*J.E. Littlewood: **A Mathematician's Miscellany**, 1953*

13. A lady of 80 named Gertie
Had a boyfriend of 60 named Bertie.
She told him emphatically
That viewed mathematically
By modulo 50 she's30.

—*John McClellan: in Martin Gardner's "Mathematical Games" column; **Scientific American**, February, 1981*

14. Here's a toast to L.J. Mordell,
young in spirit, most active as well,
He'll never grow weary,
of his love, number theory,
The results he obtains are just swell.

*—L. Moser: In L.J. Mordell: "Reminiscences of an Octogenarian Mathematician"; **American Mathematical Monthly**, November, 1971*

15. The importance of number theory in cryptography vividly demonstrates how esoteric, playful mathematics developed with no particular application in mind, can flower into an indispensable element of modern society.

*—Ivars Peterson: **The Mathematical Tourist**, 1998*

16. Two centuries ago Carl Freidrich Gauss, one of the greatest mathematicians and a founder of number theory, described his brainchild as "the queen of mathematics." Queens are regal, but they are also largely decorative, and this nuance was not lost on Gauss.

*—Ian Stewart: "Proof of Purchase on the Internet"; **Scientific American**, February, 1996*

17. In terms of the common division of mathematics into 'pure' and 'applied', number theory is about as pure as you can get; poles apart from traditional applied topics, such as dynamics.... Not any more.... What not long ago was generally held to be the most useless branch of mathematics—as regards practical applications—has suddenly acquired new importance in dynamical systems theory.

*—Ian Stewart: **Does God Play Dice?**, 1989*

28.11 Continued Fractions

1. Helmut Hasse spoke yesterday on continued fractions. But, of course, he didn't finish.

*—Clayton W. Dodge: Quoted in Howard Eves: **Mathematical Circles Adieu**, 1977*

2. The theory of continued fractions is one of the most useful theorems in Arithmetic ... since it is absent from most works on Arithmetic and Algebra, it may not be well known among geometers. I would be satisfied if I were able to contribute to make it slightly more familiar.

*—Joseph-Louis Lagrange: **Oeuvres**, vol. 7, 1793*

3. [Leonhard] Euler proved that every rational number can be written as a finite continued fraction, whereas an irrational number is represented by an infinite continued fraction, where the chain of fractions never end.

*—Eli Maor: **e: The Story of Number**, 1994*

28.12 Divisibility

1. No priestly dogmas, invented on purpose to tame and subdue the rebellious reason of mankind, every shocked common sense more than the doctrine of the infinite divisibility of extension, with its consequences; as they are pompously displayed by all geometricians and metaphysicians, with a kind of triumph and exultation. A real quantity, infinitely less than any finite quantity, containing quantities infinitely less than itself, and so on in infinitum; this is an edifice so bold and prodigious, that it is too weighty for any pretended demonstration to support, because it shocks the clearest and most natural principles of human reason.

*—David Hume: **An Enquiry into Human Understanding**, 1748*

2. Sir, lay aside your fears about the tortoise that the Pyrrhonian sceptics have made to move as fast as Achilles. You are right in saying that all magnitudes may be infinitely subdivided. There is none so small in which we cannot conceive an inexhaustible infinity of subdivisions. But I see no harm in that or any necessity to exhaust them. A space infinitely divisible is traversed in a time also infinitely divisible. I conceive no physical indivisibles short of a miracle, and I believe nature can reduce bodies to the smallness Geometry can consider.

*—G.W. Leibniz: Letter to Canon Foucher, 1692; in **Leibniz Selections**, P.P. Wiener, ed., 1951*

28.13 Perfect Numbers

1. It is the greatest that will be discovered, for, as they are merely curious without being useful, it is not likely that any person will attempt to find one beyond it.

*—Peter Barlow; **The Theory of Numbers**, 1811 [Barlow refers to the ninth perfect number (i.e. a whole number which is the sum of its proper divisors, such as 6 = 1 + 2 + 3 and 28 = 1 + 2 + 4 + 7 + 14). He was mistaken. In 1963. with the help of a computer, the University of Illinois was able to announce finding a perfect number consisting of 6751 digits and 22,425 divisors.]*

2. Perfect numbers, like perfect men are very rare.

*—Rene Descartes: In Howard Eves: **Mathematical Circles Squared**,*

3. One would be hard put to find a set of whole numbers with a more fascinating history and more elegant properties surrounded by greater depths of mystery—and more totally useless—than the perfect numbers.

*—Martin Gardner: Quoted in S. Bezuszka & M. Kenney: "Even Perfect Numbers"; **The Mathematics Teacher**, vol. 90. #8; November, 1997*

4. The whole idea of mathematics is high-level doodling. I got involved with perfect numbers our of idle curiosity, because it is probably the oldest unsolved problem. It is, perhaps, a trivial pursuit, yet the problem is so old that it is not considered a complete waste of time to work on it. If the problem had first been brought up five years ago, it would be totally uninteresting.

—*Peter Hagis, Jr.: Quoted in Paul Hoffman:* ***Archimedes' Revenge****, 1988*

5. Among simple even numbers, some are superabundant, others are deficient: these two classes are as two extremes to one another; as for those that occupy the middle position between the two, they are said to be perfect.

—*Nicomachus:* ***Introductio Arithmetica****, c. A.D. 100*

6. [Six], the first perfect number, as defined by Euclid. Its factors are 1,2,3 and 6 = 1+2+3. It is the only perfect number that is not the sum of successive cubes.

—*David Wells:* ***The Penguin Dictionary of Curious and Interesting Numbers****, 1986*

28.14 Prime Numbers

1. Prime numbers. It was all so neat and elegant. Numbers that refuse to cooperate, that don't change or divide, numbers that remain themselves for all eternity.

—*Paul Auster:* ***The Music of Chance****, 1990*

2. Prime numbers have always fascinated mathematicians. They appear among the integers seemingly at random, and yet not quite. There seems to some order or pattern, just a little below the surface, just a little out of reach.

—*Underwood Dudley: Quoted in Ivars Peterson:* ***The Mathematical Tourist****, 1998*

3. Prime numbers may lie at the heart of the higher arithmetic, but they also are responsible for its greatest mathematical snarls. The reason is simple: Whereas the whole numbers are literally created by the operation of addition, questions about primes and composites thrust multiplication into the picture. Number theory is so difficult, albeit so fascinating, because mathematicians try to examine additive creations under a multiplicative light.

—*William Dunham:* ***The Mathematical Universe****, 1994*

4. It will be another million years, at least, before we understand primes.

—*Paul Erdos: in Monte Zerger: "A Quote a Day Educates";* ***The Mathematical Intelligencer****, vol. 20, #2, Spring, 1998*

5. The problem of distinguishing prime numbers from composite numbers and of resolving the latter into their prime factors is known to be one of the most important and useful in arithmetic.... The dignity of the science itself seems to require that every possible means be explored for the solution of a problem so elegant and so celebrated.

—*Carl Friedrich Gauss:* ***Disquistiones Arithmeticae****, 1801*

6. In September 1985, when the Chevron Geosciences Company in Huston was checking out a new supercomputer, called a Cray X-MP, it identified the largest prime number known to man (or machine) after more than three hours of doing 400 million calculations per second.... The record-setting prime that Chevron's computer hit upon weighs in at 65,050 digits. This 65,050-digit whopper is a Mersenne number; it is equal to the number 2 raised to the 216,091st power minus 1. To list all the digits would require 30 pages of this book.

—*Paul Hoffman:* ***Archimedes' Revenge****, 1988*

7. In number theory, Euclid, like most mathematicians of his day, studied primes, searching for a test to determine whether any given number is a prime or not. Needless to say, he never found it, but he did settle one question about primes: whether or not they are infinite in number.

—*Jane Muir:* ***Of Men and Numbers****, 1996*

8. The infinitude of primes
Is the subject of plenty of rhymes
But we cannot begin
To prove there's a twin
An infinite number of times.

—*Peter Rosenthal:* ***The American Mathematical Monthly****, May, 1999*

9. Let us now praise prime numbers
With our fathers who begat us:
The power, the peculiar glory of prime
  numbers
Is that nothing begat them,
No ancestors, no factors,
Adams among the multiplied generations.

—*Helen Spalding: "Prime Numbers" in Martin Gardner's "Mathematical Games" column:* ***Scientific American****, December, 1980*

10. ...upon looking at prime numbers, one has the feeling of being in the presence of one of the inexplicable secrets of creation.

—*Don Zaiger: Quoted in Ivars Peterson:* ***The Mathematical Tourist****, 1998*

28.15 Magic Squares

1. The peculiar interest of magic squares ... lies in the fact that they possess the charm of mystery. They appear to betray some hidden intelligence which by a preconceived plan produces the impression of intelligent design, a phenomenon which finds its close analogue in nature.

—*Paul Carus: "Reflections on Magic Squares";* ***The Monist****, vol. 16, 1906*

2. The Chinese were fascinated by magic squares, which are square arrays of whole numbers each of whose rows, columns and main diagonals has the same sum. As with all ancient mathematics, it is difficult to assign a precise date to the origins of the subject, but there is a legend that Emperor Yu of 5,000 years ago copied a magic square from the shell of a mystical turtle.

—*William Dunham:* ***The Mathematical Universe,*** *1994*

3. The magical squares, how wonderful soever they may seem, are what I cannot value myself upon, but am ashamed to have it known I spent any part of time in an employment that cannot possibly be of any use to myself or others.

—*Benjamin Franklin:* ***The Works of Benjamin Franklin,*** *Jared Sparks, ed. Hilliard, Gray & Co., 1836–1840.*

28.16 BISTROMATHICS

1. Bistromathics itself is simply a revolutionary new way of understanding the behavior of numbers. Just as Einstein observed that space was not an absolute but depended on the observer's movement in space, and that time was not an absolute, but depended upon the observer's movement in time, so it is not realized that numbers are not absolute, but depend on the observer's movement in restaurants. The first nonabsolute number is the number of people for whom the table is reserved. This will vary during the course of the first three telephone calls to the restaurant, and then bear no apparent relation to the number of people who actually turn up, or to the number of people who subsequently join them after the show/match/party/gig, or to the number of people who leave when they see who else has turned up.

—*Douglas Adams:* ***Life, the Universe and Everything,*** *1982*

2. Numbers written on restaurant bills within the confines of restaurants do not follow the same mathematical laws as numbers written on any other piece of paper in other parts of the Universe. This simple statement took the scientific world by storm. It completely revolutionized it. So many mathematical conferences got held in such good restaurants that many of the finest minds of a generation died of obesity and heart failure and the science of math was put back by years.

—*Douglas Adams:* ***Life, the Universe and Everything,*** *1982*

29

Arithmetic

29.1 The Nature of Arithmetic

1. Arithmetic is the first of the sciences and the mother of safety.

—*Louis D. Brandeis: Quoted in Alpheus Mason:* ***Brandeis: A Free Man's Life****, 1946*

2. ...there is no place and no moment in history where I could stand and say "Arithmetic begins here, now." People have been counting, as they have been talking, in ever culture. Arithmetic, like language, begins in legend. But mathematics in our sense, reasoning with numbers, is another matter. And it is to look for the origin of that, at the hinge of legend and history, that I went sailing to the island of Samos.

—*Jacob Bronowski: "The Music of the Spheres"* ***The Ascent of Man****, 1973*

3. If scientific reasoning were limited to the logical processes of arithmetic, we should not get very far in our understanding of the physical world. One might as well attempt to grasp the game of poker entirely by the use of the mathematics of probability.

—*Vannevar Bush:* ***Science Is Not Enough****, 1967*

4. The way to enable a student to apprehend the instrumental value of arithmetic is not to lecture him on the benefit it will be to him in some remote and uncertain future, but to let him discover that success is something he is interested in doing depends on ability to use number.

—*John Dewey:* ***Democracy and Education****, 1916*

5. [Arithmetic] is another of the great master-keys of life. With it the astronomer opens the depths of the heavens; the engineer, the gates of the mountains; the navigator, the pathways of the deep. The skillful arrangement, the rapid handling of figures, is a perfect magician's wand.

—*Edward Everett:* ***Orations and Speeches****, 1870*

6. An intellectual is a highly educated man who can't do arithmetic with his shoes on, and is proud of his lack.

—*Robert A. Heinlein:* ***The Cat Who Walks Through Walls****, 1985*

7. Greek mathematics gave their Science of Numbers the Greek word arithmetike, since arithmos meant "number," techne, "science. We must not be misled by our present use of the word "arithmetic" into supposing that this arithmetike had any connection originally with the simple number-reckoning we now call by this name. Such number-reckoning was known as logistic by the Greeks and was considered by mathematicians as unworthy of their study and attention, being connected with the everyday calculations that were made on an abacus.

—*Alfred Hooper:* ***Makers of Mathematics****, 1948*

8. The truths of arithmetic are inductions from experience.

—*John Stuart Mill:* ***A System of Logic****, 1869*

9. At the beginning of the nineteenth century elementary arithmetic was a Freshman subject in our best colleges. In 1802 the standard of admission to Harvard College was raised so as to include a knowledge of arithmetic to the "Rule of Three." A boy could enter the oldest college in America prior to 1803 without a knowledge of a multiplication table. From that time on the entrance requirements in mathematics were rapidly increased, but it was not until after the founding of Johns Hopkins University that the spirit of mathematical investigation took deep root in this country.

—*G.A. Miller: "A Popular Account of Some New Fields of Thought in Mathematics";* ***The American Mathematical Monthly****, 7, 1900*

10. ...arithmetic ... existed before all the others [of the quadrivium: music, geometry and astronomy] in the mind of the creating God like some universal and exemplary plan, relying upon which as a design and archetypal example the creator of the universe sets in order his material creations and makes them attain to their proper ends.

—Nicomachus of Gerasa: ***Introduction to Arithmetic****, Martin Luther D'Orge, tr., 1946*

11. The science of arithmetic may be called the science of exact limitation of matter and things in space, force, and time.

—F.W. Parker: ***Talks on Pedagogics****, 1894*

12. Arithmetic has a very great and elevating effect, compelling the soul to reason about abstract number, and if visible or tangible objects are obtruding upon the argument, refusing to be satisfied.

—Plato: ***The Republic****; In* ***The Dialogues of Plato****, Benjamin Jowett, tr., 1953*

13. Arithmetic is where numbers fly like pigeons in and out of your head.

—Carl Sandburg: ***Complete Poems****, "Arithmetic," 1950*

14. Arithmetic is numbers you squeeze from your head to your hand to your pencil till you get the answer.

—Carl Sandburg: ***Complete Poems****, "Arithmetic," 1950*

15. That arithmetic is the basest of all mental activities is proven by the fact that it is the only one that can be accomplished by a machine.

—Arthur Schopenhauer: Quoted in David Singmaster: ***Chronology of Computing, Version 4****, 1994*

16. [Arithmetic] is one of the oldest branches, perhaps the very oldest branch, of human knowledge; and yet some of its most abstruse secrets lie close to its tritest truths.

—H.J.S. Smith: Quoted in E.T. Bell: ***Men of Mathematics****, 1937*

17. Lucy, dear child, mind your arithmetic. You know, in the first sum of yours I ever saw, there was a mistake. You had carried two (as a cab is licensed to do) and you ought, dear Lucy, to have carried but one. Is this a trifle? What would life be without arithmetic but a sense of horrors?

—Sydney Smith: Letter to his niece, Miss Lucie Austen, July 22, 1835: Quoted by Clifton Fadiman: ***Any Number Can Play****, 1957*

18. Are there not two kinds of arithmetic, that of the people and that of the philosophers...? And how about the arts of reckoning and measuring as they are used in building and trade when compared with philosophical geometry and elaborate computations—shall we speak of each of these as one or two?

—Socrates: in Plato: ***Philebus****, c. 4th cent. B.C.*

19. And so the development of the new arithmetic consists of a long, secret, and finally victorious battle against the notion of magnitude.

—Oswald Spengler: "Meaning of Numbers"; ***The Decline of the West: Form and Actuality****, 1926*

20. The first acquaintance which most people have with mathematics is through arithmetic.... Arithmetic, therefore, will be a good subject to consider in order to discover, if possible, the most obvious characteristic of the science. Now, the first noticeable fact about arithmetic is that it applies to everything, to tastes and to sounds, to apples and to angels, to the ideas of the mind and to the bones of the body.

—Alfred North Whitehead: ***An Introduction to Mathematics****, 1911*

21. Edgar to Pleasaunce: "Now I kiss you three times on one cheek, and for times on your mouth. How many did that make altogether?" "Seven," whispered the girl, disengaging herself to breathe more freely. "That is arithmetic," said the youth triumphantly. "Dear me," said Pleasaunce, "I should not have thought it."

—Ellen Wood: ***The Channings****, 1862*

29.2 The Fundamental Operations of Arithmetic

1. Here tells (th)at (th)er ben .7. spices of partes of (th)is craft. The first is called addiction, (th)e secunde is called subtraccion. The thyrd is called duplacion. The 4. is called dimydicion. The 5. is called multiplicacion. The 6. is called diuision. The 7. is called extraccion of (th)e rote.

—Anonymous: "The crafte of nombrynge"; ca. 1300; included in "The Earliest arithmeticis in English," Robert Steele, ed., 1922

2. Multiplication is vexation;
Division is as bad;
The Rule of Three perplexes me,
And fractions drive me mad.

—Anonymous; possibly 16th cent. appeared in ***Lean's Collectanea****, 1904*

3. There was an old man who said, "do
Tell me how I should add two and two?
I think more and more
That it makes about four—
But I fear that is almost too few."

—Anonymous

4. Minus times minus is plus,
The reason for this we need not discuss.

—W.H. Auden; ***Poems****, 1933*

5. I know that two and two make four—& should be glad to prove it too if I could—though I must say if by any sort of process I could convert

2 & 2 into five it would give me much greater pleasure.

—*Lord Byron: Letter to Annabella Milbanke, 1813, published in* ***Byron's Letters and Journals****, Leslie A. Marchand, ed. 1973–81*

6. Four times five is twelve, and four times six is thirteen, and four times seven is—oh dear! I shall never get to twenty at that rate!

—*Lewis Carroll:* ***Alice's Adventures in Wonderland****, 1865*

7. Can you do Division? Divide a loaf by a knife—what's the answer to that?

—*Lewis Carroll:* ***Through the Looking Glass****, 1871*

8. "Can you do Addition?" the White Queen asked. "What is one and one and one and one and one and one and one and one and one and one?" "I don't know," said Alice, "I lost count." "She can't do Addition," the Red Queen interrupted.

—*Lewis Carroll:* ***Through the Looking Glass****, 1871*

9. "I only took the regular course."
"What was that?" inquired Alice.
"Reeling and Writhing, of course, to
begin with," the Mock Turtle replied:
"and then the different branches of
Arithmetic—Ambition, Distraction,
Uglification, and Derision.

—*Lewis Carroll:* ***Alice's Adventures in Wonderland****, 1865*

10. I admit that twice two makes four is an excellent thing, but if we are to give everything its due, twice two makes five is sometimes a very charming thing too.

—*Feodor Dostoyevsky:* ***Notes from the Underground****, 1864*

11. We used to think that if we knew one, we knew two, because one and one is two. We are finding that we must learn a great deal more about 'and.'

—*Sir Arthur Eddington: In N. Rose,* ***Mathematical Maxims and Minims****, 1988*

12. It is not uncommon in histories of mathematics to read that Egyptian multiplication was clumsy and awkward, and that this clumsiness and awkwardness was due to the Egyptian's very poor arithmetical notation.

—*Richard J. Gillings:* ***Mathematics in the Time of the Pharaohs****, 1972*

13. To begin with, mathematicians have very little to do with numbers. You can no more expect a mathematician to be able to add a column of figures rapidly and correctly than you can expect a painter to draw a straight line or a surgeon to carve a turkey—popular legend attributes such skills to these professions, but popular legend is wrong.

—*Paul Halmos: in* ***Mathematical People****, D.J. Albers & G.L. Alexanderson, eds., 1985*

14. A child of the new generation
Refused to learn multiplication.
He said, "Don't conclude
That I'm stupid or rude;
I am simply without motivation."

—*John Henry Hildebrand:* ***Perspectives in Biology and Medicine****, 1970*

15. To think that two and two are four
And neither five nor three,
The heart of man has long been sore
And long 'tis like to be.

—*A.E. Housman: "To Think That Two and Two are Four,"* ***The Collected Poems of A.E. Housman****, 1940*

16. An old man insisted on referring to mathematical fleas. He explained that they subtracted from his happiness, divided his attention, added to his misery, and multiplied rapidly.

—*C.W. Kimmins:* ***The Springs of Laughter****, 1928*

17. I do hate sums. There is no greater mistake than to call arithmetic an exact science. There are permutations and aberrations discernible to minds entirely noble like mine; subtle variations which ordinary accountants fail to discover; hidden laws of number which it requires a mind like mine to perceive. For instance, if you add a sum from the bottom up, and then again from the top down, the result is always different.

—*Mrs. La Touche (19th century):* ***Mathematical Gazette****, vol. 12, May, 1924*

18. The object of all arithmetical operations is to save direct enumeration, by utilizing the results of our old operations of counting. Our endeavor is, having done a sum once, to preserve the answer for future use.... Such, too, is the purpose of algebra, which substitutes relations for values, symbolizes and definitely fixes all numerical operations which follow the same rule.

—*Ernst Mach:* ***The Science of Mechanics****, 1942*

19. Thus numbers may be said to rule the whole of quantity, and the four rules of arithmetic may be regarded as the complete equipment of the mathematician.

—*James Clerk Maxwell: in E.T. Bell:* ***Men of mathematics****, 1937*

20. July 4, 1662.... Up by 5 o'clock.... Comes M. Cooper of whom I intend to learn mathematics, and do, being with him today. After an hours being with him at arithmetic, my first attempt to learn the multiplication table.

—*Samuel Pepys: in Charles J. Finger:* ***Pepys' Diary***
[It is interesting to note that the famous diarist, who in

his 30th year was trying to learn the multiplication table, was a graduate of Cambridge University; a successful businessman, and secretary to the British Admiralty.]

21. Arithmetic is where you have to multiply—and you carry the multiplication table in your head and hope you won't lose it.

—*Carl Sandburg: "Arithmetic"* ***Complete Poems****, 1950*

22. If you take a number and double it and double it again and then double it a few more times, the number gets bigger and bigger and goes higher and higher and only arithmetic can tell you what the number is when you decide to quit doubling.

—*Carl Sandburg: "Arithmetic"* ***Complete Poems****, 1950*

23. A Dozen, a Gross and a Score,
Plus three times the square root of four,
Divided by seven,
Plus five times eleven,
Equals nine squared and not a bit more.

—*Jon Saxton; no date*

24. In a manuscript of 1456. written in Germany, the word *et* is used for addition and is generally written so that it closely resembles the symbol +. The et is also found in many other manuscripts, as in "5 et 7" for 5 + 7, written in the same contracted form, as when we write the ligature & rapidly. There seems, therefore, little doubt that this sign is merely a ligature for *et.*

—*David Eugene Smith:* ***History of Mathematics****, vol. II, 1925*

25. It is impossible to fix an exact date for the origin of our present arrangement of figures in long division, partly because it developed gradually.

—*David Eugene Smith:* ***History of Mathematics****, vol. II, 1925*

26. That odious and confusing and unvanquishable and unlearnable and shameless invention, the multiplication table.

—*Mark Twain: "Marjorie Fleming, the Wonder Child";* ***Europe and Elsewhere****, Albert Bigelow Paine, ed., 1923*

27. During the morning I thought about thought, and decided it would be easier to believe in Divinity and Christ than in twice two making four.

—*Sylvia Townsend Warner:* ***The Diaries of Sylvia Townsend Warner****, Clare Harman, ed., 1994*

28. I learned that two and two are four and five will get you ten if you know how to work it.

—*Mae West:* ***The Wit and Wisdom of Mae West****, 1967*

29. A man has one hundred dollars and you leave him with two dollars, that's subtraction.

—*Mae West: In* ***My Little Chickadee****, 1940; in* ***The Wit and Wisdom of Mae West****, 1967*

30. Entities should not be multiplied unnecessarily.

—*William of Occam:* ***Quodlibeta***

31. The multiplication table is wiser and more absolute than the ancient God: it never—do you realize the full meaning of the words?—it never errs.

—*Yevegny Ivanovich Zamyatin: "We" W.N. Vickery, tr. in P. Blake & M. Hayward:* ***Dissonant Voices in Soviet Literature****, 1962*

29.3 Calculation and Computation

1. [The abacus] is also called the "geometrical radius" since it permits so many operations. In particular, thanks to it the subtleties of geometry become perfectly clear and comprehensible.

—*Adelard of Bath (c. 1095—c. 1160): Quoted in B. Boncompani:* ***Trattati d'aritmetica****, 1857*

2. The fondness for science, ... that affability and condescension which God shows to the learned, that promptitude with which he protects and supports them in the elucidation of obscurities and in the removal of difficulties, has encouraged me to compose a short work on calculating by al-jabr and al-muqabala, confining it to what is easiest and most useful in arithmetic. [al-jabr means "restoring," referring to the process of moving a subtracted quantity to the other side of an equation; al muqabala is "comparing" and refers to subtracting equal quantities from both sides of an equation.]

—*Musa al-Khowarizmi:* ***Hisab, al-jabr w'al-muquabala****, c. 780—850*

3. Mathematics is not the art of computation but the art of minimal computation.

—*Anonymous*

4. I wish to God these calculations had been executed by steam.

—*Charles Babbage: In Howard Eves:* ***Mathematical Circles****, 1969*

5. Several ... phenomenal calculating prodigies have been known, and though their power is little understood, it is clear that they share with the computer its two basic abilities: the rapid execution of arithmetical operations, and the storage (memory) of vast amounts of information. Some of them also have an additional gift: They can recognize large number of objects without counting them.

—*Petr Beckmann:* ***A History of π****, 1971*

6. The miraculous powers of modern calculation are due to three inventions: the Arabic Notation, Decimal Fractions and Logarithms.

—*Florian Cajori:* ***History of Mathematics,*** *1897*

7. For the examination of the rules of mathematical thought and of the numbers which are at the base of musical modulations, and for the calculations of which, thanks to the skillful industry of the astrologers, explain the various trajectories of the moving stars, the abacus shows itself absolutely indispensable.

—*Radulph de Laon (c. 1125): Quoted in David Eugene Smith & L.C. Karpinski:* ***The Hindu-Arabic Numerals,*** *1911*

8. I must emphasize that the amount of computing done for applied mathematics is an almost invisible fraction of the total amount of computing today.

—*George E. Forsythe: "What to Do till the Computer Scientist Comes";* ***American Mathematical Monthly,*** *75, April, 1968*

9. Jump on calculations with both feet: group the operations, classify them according to their difficulty and not according to their form; such, according to me, is the task of future geometers; such is the path I have embarked upon in this work ... here one makes an analysis of analysis.

—*E. Galois: "Preface" in* ***Galois,*** *1962; English tr. by Fauvel and Gray, 1987*

10. Because the true perfection of a practical occupation consists not only in knowing the actual performance of the occupation but also in its explanation, why the work is done in a particular way, and because the art of calculating is a practical occupation, it is clear that it is pertinent to concern ourself with the theory.

—*Levi ben Gerson:* ***Book of Numbers,*** *1321*

11. The purpose of computing is insight, not numbers!

—*R.W. Hamming: Quoted in R.S. Pinkham: "Mathematics in Modern Technology";* ***The American Mathematical Monthly,*** *vol. 103, #7; August–September, 1996*

12. [The Egyptians] calculate with pebbles by moving the hand from right to left, while the Hellenes (Greeks) move it from left to right.

—*Herodotus:* ***History,*** *c. 1650 B.C.*

13. Before and during the time of the Roman Empire, very simple calculations, such as the counting of votes, were often made on a tray covered with sand. Marks were made in the sand with a pointed stick. Afterwards, the sand would be smoothed out by hand. Euclid and other mathematicians used such sand-trays for drawing geometrical figures. Practically all the geometry learned in school today was first worked out by figures drawn on such sand-trays more than twenty-two centuries ago. The Greek word for a flat board or tray was abax, and the sand-tray used for making calculations was called an abacus.

—*Alfred Hooper:* ***Makers of Mathematics,*** *1948*

14. It is wonderful when a calculation is made, how little the mind is actually employed in the discharge of any profession.

—*Samuel Johnson: in James Boswell;* ***The Life of Johnson,*** *1775*

15. Human decisions affecting the future, whether personal or political or economic, cannot depend on strict mathematical expectation, since the basis for making such calculations does not exist; and that it is our innate urge to activity which makes the wheels go round, our rational selves choosing between the alternatives as best we are able, calculating where we can, but often falling back for our motive on whim or sentiment or chance.

—*John Maynard Keynes:* ***Treatise on Probability,*** *1912*

16. A good calculator does not need artificial aids.

—*Lao Tze:* ***Tao Te Ching,*** *6th cent. B.C.*

17. Truth ... and if mine eyes
Can bear its blaze, and trace its symmetries,
Measure its distance, and its advent wait,
I am no prophet—I but calculate.

—*Charles MacKay: "The Prospects of the Future,"* ***The Poetical Works of Charles MacKay,*** *1876*

18. Whatever there is at all in the three worlds, which are possessed of moving and non-moving beings, cannot exist apart from Ganita (calculation).

—*Mahavira; c. A.D. 850: Quoted in Shakuntala Devi:* ***Figuring, the Joy of Numbers,*** *1977*

19. Seeing there is nothing (right well-beloved Students of Mathematics) that is so troublesome to mathematical practice, nor doth more molest and hinder calculations, than the multiplications, divisions, square and cubical extractions of great numbers, which beside the tedious expense of time are for the most part subject to many slippery errors, I began therefore to consider in my mind by what certain and ready art I might remove these hindrances.

—*John Napier:* ***Mirifici lgarithmorum canonis constructio,*** *(The Construction of the Wonderful Canon of Logarithms), 1614; W.R. MacDonald, tr., 1889*

20. Mathematics is much more than computation with pencil and a paper and getting answers to routine exercises. In fact, it can easily be argued that computation, such as doing long division, is not mathematics at all. Calculators can do the same thing and calculators can only calculate—they cannot do mathematics at all.

—*John A. Van de Walle:* ***Elementary School Mathematics: Teaching Developmentally****, 1997*

21. The process of calculating brings about just this intuition. Calculation is not an experiment.

—*Ludwig Wittgenstein:* ***Tractus Logico-Philosophicus****, 1921; Peats & McGuinness, tr.*

29.4 LOGARITHMS

1. When he had a few moments for diversion, [Napoleon Bonaparte] not unfrequently employed them over a book of logarithms, in which he always found recreation.

—*J.S.C. Abbott:* ***Napoleon Bonaparte****, 1904*

2. My lord, I have undertaken this long journey purposedly to see your person, and to know by what engine of wit or ingenuity you came first to think of this most excellent help in astronomy, namely, the logarithms, but, my lord, being by you found out, I wonder nobody found it out before, when now know it is so easy.

—*Henry Briggs: Quoted in Howard W. Eves:* ***In Mathematical Circles****, 1969*

3. The logarithm function approaches infinity with the argument, but very reluctantly.

—*Julian Lowell Coolidge: Quoted in Howard W. Eves:* ***Return to Mathematical Circles****, 1988*

4. The word logarithm means "ratio number," and was adopted by Napier after first using the expression artificial number.

—*Howard W. Eves:* ***In Mathematical Circles****, 1969*

5. The invention of logarithms and the calculation of the earlier tables form a very striking episode in the history of exact science, and, with the exception of the Principia of Newton, there is no mathematical work published in the country which has produced such important consequences, or to which so much interest attaches as to Napier's *Descripto.*

—*J.W.L. Glaisher: "Logarithms,"* ***Encyclopedia Britannica****, 9th edition*

6. Everybody knows (or at least knew, before they all had pocket calculators) that with logarithms one can reduce the odious task of multiplying two long numbers to the merely distasteful one of adding two others, and a little hunting through tables. by having many sunny hours of our adolescence filled with such pursuits, some of us have acquired a deep hatred of logarithms.

—*N. David Mermin: "Logarithms";* ***American Mathematical Monthly****, January, 1980*

7. ...this concept [the logarithm of a number] was introduced into arithmetic by the Scottish nobleman and mathematician John Napier (1550–1617) in the seventeenth century. The discovery of the concept of logarithms came at a very propitious time for astronomy because it coincided with Johannes Kepler's calculations of the positions of the planet Mars which led to the discovery of the laws of planetary motions. These laws, in turn, led Newton to the discovery of the law of gravity.

—*Lloyd Motz and Jefferson Haven Weaver:* ***The Story of Mathematics****, 1993*

8. The invention of logarithms came to the world as a bolt from the blue. No previous work had led up to it; nothing had foreshadowed it or heralded its arrival. It stands isolated, breaking in upon human thought abruptly, without borrowing from the work of other intellects or following known lines of mathematical thought. It reminds one of those islands in the ocean which rise suddenly from great depths and which stand solitary, with deep water close around all their shores.

—*Lord Moulton: Inaugural address to an international congress held to commemorate the publication of John Napier's* ***Descriptio****, Edinburgh, July, 1914*

9. Nothing is perfect at birth. I await the judgement and criticism of the learned on this [his logarithmic tables], before unadvisedly publishing of the others and exposing them to the detraction of the envious.

—*John Napier: Quoted in Herbert Westren Turnbull: "The Great Mathematicians"; in* ***The World of Mathematics****, James R. Newman, ed., 1956*

10. What logarithms are to mathematics that mathematics are to the other sciences.

—*Novalis:* ***Schriften****, 1901*

11. Students usually find the concepts of logarithms very difficult to understand.

—*B.L. van der Waerden: "Uber die Einfuhrung des Logarithmus un Schuluntsrricht";* ***Elemente der Math.****, Vol. 12, 1957*

30

Algebra and Trigonomentry

30.1 Elementary Algebra

1. The Muslims not only created algebra, which was to become the indispensable instrument of scientific analysis, but they laid the foundations for methods in modern experimental research by the use of mathematical models.

*—Ali Abdullah Al-Daffa': **The Muslim Contribution to Mathematics**, 1977*

2. When you long for the good old days of your youth, just think of algebra.

—Anonymous

3. Algebra begins with the unknown and ends with the unknowable.

—Anonymous

4. Miss Susan: What is algebra exactly; is it those three-cornered things? Phoebe: It is x minus y equals z plus y and things like that. And all the time you are saying they are equal, you feel in your heart, why should they be?

*—J.M. Barrie: **Quality Street**, 1901*

5. As the sun eclipses the stars by his brilliancy, so the man of knowledge will eclipse the fame of others in assemblies of the people if he proposes algebraic problems, and still more if he solves them.

*—Brahmagupta: in Florian Cajori: **History of Mathematics**, 1897*

6. You may always depend on it that algebra, which cannot be translated into good English and sound common sense, is bad algebra.

*—William Kingston Clifford: **Common Sense in the Exact Sciences**, 1885*

7. The science of algebra, independently of any of its uses, has all the advantages which belong to mathematics in general as an object of study, and which it is not necessary to enumerate. Viewed either as a science of quantity, or as a language of symbols, it may be made of the greatest service to those who are sufficiently acquainted with arithmetic, and who have sufficient power of comprehension to enter fairly upon its difficulties.

*—August De Morgan: **Elements of Algebra**, 1837*

8. Algebra exists only for the elucidation of geometry.

*—William Edge: Quoted in D. MacHale: **Comic Sections**, 1993*

9. This Araby word Algebra sygnifyeth as well fractures of bones as sometyme the restauration of the same.

*—J. Halle, 1565: Quoted in Alfred Hooper: **Makers of Mathematics**, 1948*

10. Factoring a quadratic becomes confused with genuine mathematical talent.

*—I.N. Herstein: **Topics in Algebra**, 1964*

11. It is interesting to see how this Arabic word "al-jabr" also found its way into Europe through the Moors who conquered Spain. There, for centuries, it was used in a distinctly unmathematical connection. Mathematics certainly plays a very essential part in every day life, but even the most ardent mathematician would hesitate before declaring that it could mend broken bones! Yet in Spain during the Middle Ages it was usual for a barber to call himself a "algebrista," or bone-setter, since medieval barbers undertook bone-setting (and blood-letting) as a sideline to their regular business.

*—Alfred Hooper: **Makers of Mathematics**, 1948*

12. ...the science of calculation also is indispensable as far as the extraction of the square and cube roots: Algebra as far as the quadratic equation and the use of logarithms are often of value in ordinary cases: but all beyond these is but a luxury; a delicious luxury, indeed: but not be in indulged in by one who is to have a profession to follow for his subsistence.

—*Thomas Jefferson: In J. Robert Oppenheimer "The Encouragement of Science," in I. Gordon and S. Sorkin, eds.,* ***The Armchair Science Reader****, 1959*

13. I would advise you Sir, to study algebra, if you are not already an adept in it: your head would be less muddy, and you will leave off tormenting your neighbors about paper and packthread, while we all live together in a world that is bursting with sin and sorrow.

—*Samuel Johnson; Quoted in Hester Piozzi,* ***Anecdotes of Samuel Johnson****, 1786 [Dr. Johnson made the remark to a warehouse packer.]*

14. Whoever thinks algebra is a trick in obtaining unknowns has thought it in vain. No attention should be paid to the fact that algebra and geometry are different in appearance. Algebras are geometric facts which are proved.

—*Omar Khayyam:* ***Algebra****. c. 1050–1123; Quoted in Stuart Hollingdale:* ***Makers of Mathematics****, 1989*

15. Stand firm in your refusal to remain conscious during algebra. In real life, I assure you, there is no such thing as algebra.

—*Fran Lebowitz;* ***Social Studies****, "Tips for Teens," 1981*

16. Marriage is the square of a plus b
In other words
$a^2 + b^2 + 2ab$
Where 2ab (of course)
Are twins.

—*Christopher Morley: "$(a + b)^2$";* ***Translations from the Chinese****, 1927*

17. I wrote emotional algebra.

—*Anais Nin:* ***The Diary of Anais Nin****, 1974*

18. Algebra is poetry.

—*Novalis: Quoted in Francois Le Lionnais: "Beauty in Mathematics" in* ***Great Currents of Mathematics****, F. Le Lionnais, ed., 1971*

19. Algebra and money are essentially levelers; the first intellectually, the second effectively.

—*Simone Weil:* ***La Peasanteur et la Grace****, 1967*

20. Algebra is the intellectual instrument which has been created for rendering clear the quantitative aspects of the world.

—*Alfred North Whitehead:* ***Universal Algebra****, 1898*

30.2 Exponents

1. In 1636 James Hume brought out an edition of the algebra of Vieta, in which he introduced a superior notation, writing down the base and elevating the exponent to a position above the regular line and a little to the right. The exponent was expressed in Roman numerals. Thus he wrote A^{iii} for A^3. Except for the use of Roman numerals, one has here our modern notation. Thus, this Scotsman, residing in Paris, had almost hit upon the exponential symbolism which has become universal through the writings of Descartes.

—*Florian Cajori:* ***A History of Mathematical Notation****, vol. I., 1928*

2. ...we can use exponents to change a multiplication problem, which can be tedious and difficult, into a simpler addition problem. Our hero of the moment is John Napier, who realized the great need to simplify calculations. He worked for 20 years to invent a system called logarithms, which is based on this idea of exponents.

—*Calvin C. Clawson:* ***Mathematical Mysteries****, 1996*

3. [Napier's] line of thought was this: If we could write any positive number as a power of some given, fixed number (later to be called a base), then multiplication and division of numbers would be equivalent to addition and subtraction of their exponents.

—*Eli Maor:* ***e: the Story of a Number****, 1994*

30.3 Formulas

1. If I am given a formula, and I am ignorant of its meaning, it cannot teach me anything, but if I already know it what does the formula teach me?

—*St. Augustine:* ***De Magistro****, c. 400*

2. ...from the time of Kepler to that of Newton, and from Newton to Hartley, not only all things in external nature, but the subtlest mysteries of life and organization, and even of the intellect and moral being, were conjured within the magic circle of mathematical formulas.

—*Samuel Taylor Coleridge: "The Theory of Life," 1836*

3. Authors who discover formulas should not rush into print. Even as in business and marriage, in mathematics not all that is true needs to be published.

—*Underwood Dudley: "Formulas for Primes";* ***Mathematics Magazine****, Vol. 56, January, 1983*

4. One cannot escape the feeling that these mathematical formulas have an independent existence and an intelligence of their own, that they are wiser than we, wiser even than their discoverers, that we get more out of them than was originally put into them.

—*Heinrich Hertz: Quoted by E.T. Bell in* ***Men of Mathematics****, 1937; Quoted in R.L. Wilder:* ***Evolution of Mathematical Concepts****, 1974*

5. It is utterly implausible that a mathematical formula should make the future known to us, and those who think it can would once have believed in witchcraft.

—Bertrand de Jouvenel: ***The Art of Conjecture****, 1970*

6. If you see a formula in the Physical Review that extends over a quarter of a page, forget it. It's wrong. Nature isn't that complicated.

—Bernd T. Matthias: Attributed

7. ...She knew only that if she did or said thus-and-so, men would unerringly respond with the complimentary thus-and-so. It was like a mathematical formula and no more difficult, for mathematics was the one subject that had come easy to Scarlett in her schooldays.

—Margaret Mitchell: ***Gone with the Wind****, 1936*

30.4 Unknowns and Variables

1. Given any problem containing n equations, there will be n + 1 unknowns.

—Anonymous

2. We have found that where science has progressed the farthest, the mind has but regained from nature that which the mind has put into nature. We have found a strange footprint on the shores of the unknown. We have discovered profound theories, one after another, to account for its origin. At last we have succeeded in reconstructing the creature that made the footprint. And Lo! It is our own.

—Sir Arthur Eddington: ***Time and Gravitation****, 1920*

4. The predominant use of the letter x to represent an unknown value came about in an interesting way. During the printing of La Geometrie and its appendix, Discours de la Methode, which introduced coordinate geometry, the printer reached a dilemma. While the text was being typeset, the printer began to run short of the last letters of the alphabet. He asked Descartes if it mattered whether x, y, or z was used in each of the book's many equations. Descartes replied that it made no difference which of the three letters was used to designate an unknown quantity. The printer selected x for most of the unknowns, since the letters y and z are used in the French language more frequently than is x.

—Art Johnson: "History of Mathematical Terms": ***Classic Math: History Topics for the Classroom****, 1994*

5. It is a maxim universally admitted in geometry, and indeed in every branch of knowledge, that, in the progress of investigation, we should proceed from known facts to what is unknown.

—Antoine Laurent Lavoisier: ***Elements of Chemistry****; Robert Kerr, tr.*

6. In a time when much of the world's geography has been explored, and space exploration is restricted to astronauts, mathematics offers fertile ground for exploring the unknown.

—Walter Meyer: "Missing Dimensions of Mathematics"; ***Humanistic Mathematics Network Journal****, No. 11' February, 1995*

7. To be is to be the value of a variable.

—Willard Van Ormand Quine: Quoted in Reuben Hersh: ***What is Mathematics, Really?****, 1997*

30.5 Equations and Their Solutions

1. I swear to you by the Sacred Gospel, and on my faith as a gentleman, not only never to publish your discoveries [Niccolo Tartaglia's secret of solving cubic equations], if you tell them to me, but I also promise and pledge my faith as a true Christian to put them down in cipher so that after my death no one shall be able to understand them.

—Girolamo Cardano: March 25, 1539; in Oystein Ore: ***Cardano: The Gambling Scholar****, 1965*

2. Scipio Ferro of Bologna well-nigh thirty years ago discovered this rule and handed it on to Antonio Maria Fior of Venice, whose contest with Niccolo Tartaglia of Brescia gave Niccolo occasion to discover it. He gave it to me in response to my entreaties, though withholding the demonstration. Armed with this assistance, I sought out its demonstration in [various] forms. This was very difficult.

—Girolamo Cardano: ***Ars Magna****, 1545 [Cardano had received the secret of the depressed cubic in cipher form from Tartaglia, but when he discovered the solution in the papers of del Ferro, he felt he was no longer prohibited from publishing the result, giving credit where credit was due.]*

3. The business of concrete mathematics is to discover the equations which express the mathematical laws of the phenomenon under consideration; and these equations are the starting points of the calculus, which must obtain from them certain quantities by means of others.

—Auguste Comte: ***Cours de philosophie positive****, 6 vols., 1830—41*

4. It was not until early in the nineteenth century that the Italian Ruffini and the Norwegian genius N.H. Abel conceived of the then revolutionary idea of proving the impossibility of the solution of the general algebraic equation of degree n by means of radicals.

—Richard Courant & Herbert Robbins; ***What Is Mathematics?****, 1941*

5. One must divide one's time between politics and equations. Equations are more important to me, because politics is for the present, but an equation is something for eternity.

—Albert Einstein: in Stephen Hawking: ***A Brief History of Time****, 1988*

6. The designation "Diophantine equations," commonly applied to indeterminate equations of the first degree when investigated for integral solutions, is a striking misnomer. Diophantus nowhere considers such equations, and, on the other hand allows fractional solutions of indeterminate equations of the second degree.

—Henry B. Fine: ***The Number System of Algebra****, 1902*

7. There is a current professional joke which states that the way to distinguish a mathematician from an engineer or physicist is to give the suspect an equation to solve. The engineer or physicist will proceed to seek a solution; the mathematician will first try to prove that a solution exists. The joke is usually told at the expense of mathematicians. The history of mathematics is replete, however, with tales of hours of wasted efforts attempting to solve problems ultimately proven to be unsolvable. The mathematician knows by now that problems of existence are not to be taken lightly!

—W.T. Fishback: ***Projective and Euclidean Geometry****, 1962*

8. I'm very well acquainted too with
matters mathematical,
I understand equations, both simple and
quadradical....

—W.S. Gilbert: ***The Pirates Of Penzance****, 1879*

9. Someone told me that each equation I included in the book would halve the sales.

—Stephen Hawking: ***A Brief History of Time****, 1988*

10. To equations simultaneously Pellian
My approach is Machiavellian.
Anything goes, rather than resort to such
actions
As covering the walls with continued
fractions.

—J.A. Lindon: in Martin Gardner's "Mathematical Games" column; ***Scientific American****, July, 1974*

11. Setting up equations is like translation from one language into another.

—George Polya: ***How to Solve It****, 1945*

12. Now the seriousness of mathematics comes precisely of its remarkable and exact relevance to material facts, both familiar and remote; so that mathematical equations, besides being essentially necessary in themselves, are often also true of the world we live in. And this is a surprising measure....

—George Santayana: "Realm of Truth"; ***Realms of Being****, 1937*

13. I have discovered the general rule [for solving equations of degree 3], but for the moment I want to keep it secret for several reasons.

—Tartaglia, 1530: Quoted in M. Cantor: ***Vorlesungen uber Geschichte der Mathematik****, Vol. II, 1891*

14. Cardano was ... the first, as it happened, to consider the possibility of finding approximate solutions of equations. This was not a serious practical problem in his day, but it became one in due course, for a variety of reasons. Once it became apparent that equations of the fifth degree and higher could not generally be solved by a formula, it was natural to consider how their roots, which certainly existed, might be found by other means, as approximations.

—David Wells: ***You Are a Mathematician****, 1995*

30.6 Fundamental Theorem of Algebra

1. The fundamental theorem of algebra is just one of several reasons why the complex-number system is such a "nice" one. Another important reason is that the field of complex numbers supports the development of a powerful differential calculus, leading to the rich theory of functions of a complex variable.

—Keith Devlin: ***Mathematics: The New Golden Age****, 1988*

2. A New Proof of the Theorem That Every Integral Rational Algebraic Function [that is, every polynomial with real coefficients] Can Be Decomposed into Real Factors of the First or Second Degree.

—Carl Friedrich Gauss: in John Fauvel & Jeremy Gray: ***The History of Mathematics: A Reader****, 1987 [This is the title of Gauss' doctoral dissertation of 1799, the University of Helmstadt, which provided the first reasonably complete proof of what has come to be known as the Fundamental Theorem of Algebra, which essentially says that every algebraic equation of degree n has exactly n solutions. In France, it was known as d'Alembert's theorem.]*

30.7 Trigonometry

1. ...the trigometric functions ... exhibit an utterly characteristic periodic face, repeating their behavior again and again and again. Periodic phenomena in nature range from menstrual cycles to the cycles of the moon, and the trigonometric functions embody in their regularity some essential rhythm of the universe.

—David Berlinski: ***A Tour of the Calculus****, 1995*

2. A straight line is straight
And a square mile is flat:

But you learn in trigonometrics a trick
worth two of that.

—*Gilbert Keith Chesterton: "The Higher Mathematics": **The Collected Poems of G.K. Chesterton**, 1932*

3. The tangent and cotangent functions were introduced by Arabs such as Abu'l Wafa in the 10th century, and rather slowly made their way into European trigonometry via translators such as Adelard of Bath. They rose largely in connection with lengths of shapes made by shadows....

—*Ivor Grattan-Guinness: **The Rainbow of Mathematics**, 1997*

4. Trigonometry, as we know the subject today, is a branch of mathematics that is linked with algebra. As such, it dates back only to the eighteenth century.... When treated purely as a development of geometry, however, it goes back to the time of the great Greek mathematician-astronomers who flourished some two hundred years before and after the commencement of the Christian era.

—*Alfred Hooper: **Makers of Mathematics**, 1948*

5. A considerable portion of my high school trigonometry course was devoted to the solution of oblique triangles ... I have still not had an excuse for using my talents for solving oblique triangles. If a professional mathematician never uses these dull techniques in a highly varied career, why must all high school students devote several weeks to the subject?

—*John Kemeny: **Random Essays on Mathematics, Education and Computers**, 1964*

6. Perhaps to the student there is no part of elementary mathematics so repulsive as is spherical trigonometry.

—*Peter Guthrie Tait: "Quaternions," **Encyclopedia Britannica**, 11th ed., 1911*

30.8 Abstract Algebra

1. Algebra is generous; it often gives more than one demands of it.

—*Jean Le Rond D'Alembert: **Encyclopedia**, 1751–65; Quoted in R.E. Moritz: **On Mathematics**, 1942*

2. Algebra is the cornerstone of modern mathematics.

—*Tobias Dantzig: **Number: The Language of Science**, 1954*

3. Nothing proves more clearly that the mind seeks truth, and nothing reflects more glory upon it, than the delight it takes, sometimes in spite of itself, in the driest and thorniest researches of algebra.

—*Bernard de Fontenelle: **Historie du Renouvellement de l'Academie des Sciences**, 1719*

4. Algebra is but written geometry and geometry is but figured algebra.

—*Sophie Germain: "Memoire sur l'emploi de l'epaisseur dans la theorie des surfaces elastiques"; **Journal de mathematiques pures et appliques 6**, 1880*

5. Modern algebra cannot long endure separation from concrete mathematical theories, and thesis, in turn, cannot long flourish without the systematizing and furthering of abstract algebra.

—*Helmut Hasse: "The Modern Algebraic Method," 1930; Abe Schenitzer, tr.; **The Mathematical Intelligencer**, vol. 8, 2, 1986*

6. In mathematics itself abstract algebra plays a dual role: that of a unifying link between disparate parts of mathematics and that of a research subject with a highly active life of its own.... A subject that was once regarded as esoteric has become considered as fairly down-to-earth for a large cross section of scholars.

—*I.N. Herstein: **Abstract Algebra**, 1986*

7. The branch of mathematics known as abstract algebra was born and reared ... in the nineteenth century; it came to maturity in the twentieth. Its subject matter is collections of discrete objects, such as sets, vectors, quaternions or matrices, as well as real or complex numbers, or some prescribed subset of them.

—*Stuart Hollingdale: **Makers of Mathematics**, 1989*

8. ...all of modern abstract algebra owes its origins to Hamilton's creation of quaternions.

—*Morris Kline: **Mathematics: The Loss of Certainty**, 1980*

9. That a formal science like algebra, the creation of our abstract thought, should thus, in a sense, dictate the laws of its own being, is very remarkable. It has required the experience of centuries for us to realize the full force of this appeal.

—*G.B. Mathews: Quoted in F. Spencer: **Chapters on Aims and Practice of Teaching** 1899*

10. As long as algebra was used only as a mathematical tool in daily activities, its growth was limited. Once it threw off these constraints and became the intellectual toy of the pure mathematician, however, it grew phenomenally, sending out shoots into every realm of mathematics from which new branches of algebra grew.

—*Lloyd Motz and Jefferson Hane Weaver: **The Story of Mathematics**, 1993*

11. Algebra is the analysis of bunglers in mathematics.

—*Sir Isaac Newton: Letter to David Gregory*

12. Algebra ... is essentially a written language, and it endeavors to exemplify in its written structures the patterns which it is its purpose to convey.... The algebraic method is our best approach to the expression of necessity, by reason of its reduction of accident to the ghostlike character of the real variable.

—*Alfred North Whitehead:* ***The Organization of Thought****, 1917*

30.9 LINEAR ALGEBRA

1. Come gather round me and I'll show you how
We're solving simultaneous equations now;
Just write them out in a matrix way,
Set to work and row reduce—you cannot go astray.

Row reduction: add 'em and subtract 'em;
Row reduction: make the zeros grow;
Row reduction: it's the perfect system;
Get a lot of zeros and the rank will show.

—*Ralph P. Boas, Jr. "The Row-Reduction Song" (sung to the tune of "Casey Jones");* ***Lion Hunting & Other Pursuits****, Gerald L. Alexanderson & Dale H. Mugler, eds., 1995*

2. We (he and Paul Halmos) share a philosophy about linear algebra: we think basis-free, we write basis-free, but when the chips are down we close the office door and compute with matrices like fury.

—*Irving Kaplansky: Quoted in Paul Halmos:* ***Celebrating 50 Years of Mathematics***

3. The development of the theory of simultaneous equations led to the vast subject of linear algebra and, in particular to the algebra of matrices, two branches of algebra which owe a great debt to the British mathematicians Cayley and Sylvester as well as the Irish mathematical physicist William Hamilton.

—*Lloyd Motz and Jefferson Hane Weaver:* ***The Story of Mathematics****, 1993*

4. For what is the theory of determinants? It is an algebra upon algebra; a calculus which enables us to combine and foretell the results of algebraical operations, in the same way as algebra itself enables us to dispense with the performance of the special operations of arithmetic. All analysis must ultimately clothe itself under this form.

—*James J. Sylvester:* ***Philosophical Magazine****, vol. 1, 1851:* ***Collected Papers****, 1908*

5. What if angry vectors veer
Round your sleeping head, and form.
There is never need to fear
Violence of the poor world's abstract storm.

—*Robert Penn Warren: "Lullaby in Encounter": May, 1957*

30.10 GROUPS AND GROUP THEORY

1. And now we can solve the problem without any mathematics at all: just group theory.

—*Anonymous Cambridge Professor*

2. Wherever groups disclosed themselves, or could be introduced, simplicity crystallized out of comparative chaos.

—*Eric Temple Bell:* ***Mathematics, Queen and Servant of Science****, 1951*

3. A group has been compared to the grin that remains when Lewis Carroll's Cheshire cat fades away.

—*George A.W. Boehm:* ***The New World of Math****, 1959*

4. Who would have thought in 1831, when Galois introduced the concept of the group into the study of the solvability properties of algebraic equations in terms of radicals, that a century and more later the fundamental principles of physics would be formulated in terms of concepts from group theory?

—*Felix E. Browder: "Does Pure Mathematics Have a Relation to the Sciences?";* ***American Scientist****, 64, 1976*

5. Physicists who try to answer the question of why there is something rather than nothing in the universe study symmetries. Indeed, much of particle physics these days is based on a mathematical notion called group theory—where a group is the collection of all transformations of an object that leave that object invariant.

—*K.C. Cole:* ***The Universe and the Teacup****, 1997*

6. A "group" is an abstract mathematical structure, one of the simplest and the most pervasive in the whole of mathematics. The notion finds applications, for example, to the theory of equations, to number theory, to differential geometry, to crystallography, to atomic and particle physics. The latter applications are particularly interesting in view of the fact that in 1910 a board of experts including Oswald Veblen and Sir James Jeans, upon reviewing the mathematics curriculum at Princeton, concluded that group theory ought to be thrown out as useless. So much for the crystal ball of experts.

—*Philip J. Davis and Reuben Hersh:* ***The Mathematical Experience****, 1981*

7. The great notion of Group, ... though it had barely merged into consciousness a hundred years ago, has meanwhile become a concept of fundamental importance and prodigious fertility, not only according the basis of an imposing doctrine—the Theory of Groups—but therewith serving also as a bond of union, a kind of connective tissue, or rather as an an immense cerebrospinal system, uniting together a large number of widely dissimilar doctrines as organs of a single body.

*—Cassius J. Keyser: **Lectures on Science, Philosophy and Art**, 1908*

8. ...the theory of groups is, so to say, the whole of mathematics divested of its matter and reduced to pure form.

*—Henri Poincare: **Acta Math.**, 38, 1921*

9. The notion of a "group" viewed only 30 years ago as the epitome of sophistication, is today the one mathematical concept most widely used in physics, chemistry, biochemistry and mathematics itself.

*—Alexey Sosinsky: Quoted in J. Gallian: **Contemporary Abstract Algebra**, 1998*

30.11 Transformation Groups

1. If I only knew how to get the mathematicians interested in transformation groups and their applications to differential equations, I am certain, absolutely certain in any case, that these theorems in the future will be recognized as fundamental.

*—Sophus Lie: Letter to A. Meyer; Quoted in Nils A, Baas: "Sophus Lie"; **The Mathematical Intelligencer**, vol. 16, Winter, 1994*

2. What is geometry in fact? It is the study of the group of operations formed by the motions one can apply to a figure without deforming it. In Euclidean geometry this group is reduced to rotations and translations. In the pseudogeometry of Lobachevsky the group is more complicated.

*—Henri Poincare: "Sur les fonctions fuchsiennes"; **Acta Mathematica**, 1882*

3. If one figure is derived from another be a continuous change and the latter is as general as the former, then any property of the first figure can be asserted at once for the second figure.

*—Jean-Victor Poncelot: **Treatise on the Projective Properties of Figures**, 1822*

4. A transformation which preserves the structure of space—and if we define this structure in the Helmholtz way, that would mean that it carries any two congruent figures into two congruent ones—is called an automorphism by the mathematicians. Leibniz recognized that this is the idea underlying the geometric concept of similarity. Au automorphism carries a figure into one that in Leibniz's words is "indiscernible from it if each of the two figures is considered by itself."

*—Hermann Weyl: **Symmetry**, 1952*

30.12 Invariants of Groups

1. In the language of math, invariants are usually referred to as symmetries. They are not limited to the same kind of symmetries we admire in snowflakes and butterfly wings. Something has symmetry to the extent that it is invariant to certain kinds of change. For example, a circle is perfectly symmetrical because it is invariant to any rotation about its center. A square is less symmetrical because only rotations through right angles leave it unchanged. The letter A is symmetrical under reflection because its mirror image is unchanged from the original.

*—K.C. Cole: **The Universe and the Teacup**, 1997*

2. This [David Hilbert's work in invariant theory] is not mathematics, it is theology.

*—Paul Gordon: Quoted in P. Davis and R. Hersh: **The Mathematical Experience**, 1981*

3. ...the doctrine of Invariants, a theory filling the heavens like a light-bearing ether, penetrating all the branches of geometry and analysis, revealing everywhere abiding configurations in the midst of change, everywhere disclosing the eternal reign of the law of form.

*—Cassius J. Keyser: **Lectures on Science, Philosophy and Art**, 1908*

4. In recent times the view becomes more and more prevalent that many branches of mathematics are nothing but the theory of invariants of special groups.

*—Sophus Lie: **Continuierliche Gruppen**, 1893*

5. The theory of invariants sprang into existence under the strong hand of (Arthur) Cayley, but that it emerged finally a complete work of art, for the admiration of future generations of mathematicians, was largely owing to the flashes of inspiration with which (James) Sylvester's intellect illuminated it.

*—P. A. MacMahon: Presidential Address British Association for the Advancement of Science, 1901; **Nature***

6. As all roads are said to lead to Rome, so I find, in my own case at least, that all algebraic inquiries sooner or later end at the Capitol of Modern Algebra over whose shining portal is inscribed "Theory of Invariants."

*—James Joseph Sylvester: "On a Theorem Connected with Newton's Rule"; **The Collected Papers of James Joseph Sylvester**, 1908*

31
The Art of Measurement

31.1 Measure and Measurement

1. One accurate measurement is worth a thousand expert opinions.
—*Anonymous*

2. Who was it who measured the water of the sea in the hollow of his hand and calculated the dimensions of the heavens, gauged the whole earth to the bushel, weighed the mountains in scales, the hills in a balance?
—*The Bible, Old Testament; Isaiah*

3. Measurement is one of the notions which modern science has taken over from common sense. Measurement does not appear as part of common sense until a comparatively high stage of civilization is reached; and even the common-sense conception has changed and developed enormously in historic times. When I say that measurement belongs to common sense, I only mean that it is something with which every civilized person today is entirely familiar. It may be defined, in general, as the assignment of numbers to represent properties.
—*Norman Campbell:* ***What Is Science****, 1921*

4. Perhaps the most insidious obstacle to accurate measurement is the normally unacknowledged fact that you can only measure the stuff that you know (or suspect) is actually there. Astronomy is a humbling science in this regard, because it seems as if every time astronomers find a new way to measure the universe, they find an entirely new and unexpected category of species.
—*K.C. Cole:* ***The Universe and the Teacup****, 1997*

5. It is important to realize that it is not the one measurement, alone, but its relation to the rest of the sequence that is of interest.
—*William Edwards Deming:* ***Statistical Adjustment of Data****, 1943*

6. We measure shadows, and we search among ghostly errors of measurement for landmarks that are scarcely more substantial.
—*Edwin Powell Hubble: Quoted in Dennis Overbye:* ***Lonely Hearts of the Cosmos****, 1991*

7. I used to measure the Heavens, now I measure the shadows of Earth. The mind belonged to Heaven, the body's shadow lies here.
—*Johannes Kepler: Epitaph for himself;*

8. To measure is to know.
—*Ernst Werner von Siemens: Attributed*

9. All space measurement is from stuff in space to stuff in space.
—*Alfred North Whitehead:* ***The Aims of Education****, 1929*

31.2 Measurement and Mathematics

1. ...nature in creating the want, and in furnishing to man within himself the means of its supply, has established a system of numbers and or proportions between the man, the measure [the unit], and the objects measured.
—*John Quincy Adams: "Report of the Secretary of State upon Weights and Measures";* ***State Papers, Sixteenth Congress of the United States****, 1821*

2. Measurement, it's probably fair to say, is the cornerstone of knowledge. It allows us to compare things with other things and to quantify relationships.... We put numerical measures onto everything from public opinion to fat content, from wealth to waistlines, from nuclear reactions to success. Can all these disparate things be measured? Can quality be boiled down to quantity?
—*K.C. Cole:* ***The Universe and the Teacup****, 1997*

3. We can now define Mathematical science with precision. It has for its object the indirect measurement of magnitudes, and it purposes to determine magnitudes by each other, according to the precise relations which exist between them.

—Auguste Comte: ***The Positive Philosophy of Auguste Comte****, Harriet Martineau, tr., 1853*

4. Mathematics and measurement are not to be unduly worshipped, nor can they be neglected by even the lay observer.

—James B. Conant: ***Science and Common Sense*** *1951*

5. I remember one occasion when I tried to add a little seasoning to a review, but I wasn't allowed to. The paper was by Dorothy Maharam, and it was a perfectly sound contribution to abstract measure theory. The domains of the underlying measures were not sets but elements of more general Boolean algebras, and their range consisted not of positive numbers, but of certain abstract equivalence classes. My proposed first sentence was: "The author discusses valueless measure in pointless spaces."

—Paul R. Halmos: ***I Want to Be a Mathematician****, MAA Spectrum, 1985*

6. ...that, in a few years, all great physical constants will have been approximately estimated, and that the only occupation which will be left to men of science will be to carry these measurements to another place of decimals.

—James Clerk Maxwell: ***Scientific Papers****, October, 1871*

7. ...geometry is founded in mechanical practice, and is nothing but that part of universal mechanics which accurately proposes and demonstrates the art of measuring.

—Sir Isaac Newton: ***Mathematical Principles of Natural Philosophy****, 1687*

8. When you can measure what you are speaking about, and express it in numbers, you know something about it, when you cannot express it in numbers, your knowledge is of a meager and unsatisfactory kind; it may be the beginning of knowledge, but you have scarcely, in your thoughts, advanced to the stage of science.

—William Thomson, Lord Kelvin: ***Popular Lectures and Addresses****, 1891–1894*

31.3 Weights and Measures

1. A thing cannot be weighed in a scale incapable of containing it.

—Thomas Bailey Aldrich: ***The Stillwater Tragedy****, 1880*

2. There shall be standard measures of wine, beer, and corn—the London quarter—throughout the whole of our kingdom, and a standard width of dyed, russet and halberject cloth—two ells within the selvedges; and there shall be standard weights also.

—Magna Charta; June 15, 1215

3. The scientists had another idea which was completely at odds with the benefits to be derived from the standardization of weights and measures; they imposed the decimal system, taking the meter as a unit, and suppressed all complicated numbers. Nothing is more contrary to the organization of the mind, the memory, and the imagination.... The new system of weights and measures will be a stumbling block and a source of difficulties for several generations to come.... It is just tormenting the people with trivialities!

—Napoleon I (Bonaparte): ***Memories ... ecrits a Ste-Helene****, 1823–25*

4. Nobody knows what they mean. When You buy a pound of a drug and the man asks you which you want, troy or avoirdupois, it is best to say "Yes," and shift the subject.

—Mark Twain; ***Following the Equator****, 1897*

5. The early races of Babylon worked out the original system of weights and measures in use among mankind—a system on which all other systems in use in the world until the end of the eighteenth century are founded.

—Sir Charles Warren: ***The Ancient Cubit****, 1903*

6. The word "troy" [used in troy pound] did not originally mean a particular kind of pound nor did it refer to the original articles weighed, but to the manner of weighing. "Troy" is probably derived from the Old English word "troi" signifying a balance.... From time immemorial articles of value were weighed by the balance and in the process of time weighing by the balance came to be called "troy weight."

—C.M. Watson: ***British Weights and Measures*** *1910*

7. Unfortunately, 10 is not an ideal base for a system in which merchants and dealers have to measure small quantities, fractions of a whole, because only halves and fifths can be represented by whole numbers. Even a simple fraction like a quarter has to be represented by a fraction of 10ths. Consequently, although using a number system based on 10, an extraordinary variety of systems of weights and measures was used throughout Europe in historical times based on mixtures of units. They all agreed in using 8ths, 12ths, 20ths, 24ths, 60ths, anything but the awkward 10th.

—David Wells: ***The Penguin Dictionary of Curious and Interesting Numbers****, 1986*

31.4 The Measurable and the Unmeasurable

1. The [intelligence] scale, properly speaking, does not permit the measure of intelligence, because intellectual qualities are not superposable, and therefore cannot be measured as linear surfaces are measured.

—Alfred Binet: Quoted in Stephen Jay Gould: ***The Measurement of Man****, 1996*

2. The measure of our intellectual capacity is the capacity to feel less and less satisfied with our answers to better and better problems.

—C.W. Churchman: In J.E. Littlewood: ***A Mathematician's Miscellany****, 1953*

3. The wonder is, not that the field of the stars is so vast, but that man has measured it.

—Anatole France: ***The Garden of Epicurus****, 1894*

4. Measure what is measurable, and make measurable what is not so.

—Galileo Galilei: Quoted in H. Weyl: "Mathematics and the Laws of Nature" in I. Gordon and S. Sorkin, eds.; ***The Armchair Science Reader****, 1959*

5. Measurement of life should be proportioned rather to the intensity of the experience than to its actual length.

—Thomas Hardy: ***A Pair of Blue Eyes****, 1873*

31.5 Measurement in Verse

1. He made an instrument to know
If the moon shine at full or no;
That would, as soon as e'er she shone straight,
Whether 'twere day or night demonstrate;
Tell what her d'ameter to an inch is,
And prove that she's not made of green cheese.

—Samuel Butler I: ***Hudibras****, 1663*

2. In Xanadu did Kubla Khan
A stately pleasure-dome decree:
Where Alph, the sacred river, ran
Through caverns measureless to man
Down to a sunless sea.

—Samuel Taylor Coleridge: "Kubla Khan: or, A Vision in a Dream," ***The Harper Anthropology of Poetry****, John Frederick Nims, ed., 1981*

3. I have measured out my life with coffee spoons.

—T.S. Eliot: "The Love Song of J. Alfred Prufrock," ***The Harper Anthropology of Poetry****, John Frederick Nims, ed., 1981*

4. thou mayest know,
That flesh is but the glass, which holds the dust
That measures all our time.

—George Herbert: "Church Monuments," ***The New Oxford Book of American Verse****, Richard Ellmann, ed., 1976*

5. Four seasons fill the measure of the year;
There are four seasons in the mind of man.

—John Keats: "The Human Seasons," ***English Romantic Poetry and Prose****, Russell Noyes, ed., 1956*

6. Our souls, whose faculties can comprehend
The wondrous Architecture of the world:
And measure ever wand'ring planet's course,
Still climbing after knowledge infinite.

—Christopher Marlowe: ***Tamburlaine****, c. 1857–8*

7. But just a pound of flesh. If thou tak'st more
Or less than just a pound—be it by but so much
As makes it light or heavy in the substance
Or the division of the twentieth part
Or one poor scruple; nay, if the scale do turn
But in the estimation of a hair—
Thou diest, and all thy goods are confiscate.

—William Shakespeare: ***The Merchant of Venice****, 1596–7 [Portia bids Shylock to take his pound of fresh but no more or less than a pound from Antonio's chest.]*

31.6 Length, Area and Volume

1. If it is possible to have a linear unit that depends on no other quantity, it would seem natural to prefer it. Moreover, a mensural unit taken from the earth offers another advantage, that of being perfectly analogous to all the real measurements that inordinary usage are also made upon the earth, such as the distance between two places or the area of some tract, for example. It is far more natural in practice to refer geographical distances to a quadrant of a great circle than to the length of a pendulum....

—Marie-Jean de Condorcet: ***Sketch for a Historical Picture of the Human Mind****, 1794*

2. In Gulliver's Travels the Lilliputians were about six inches high, their tallest trees about seven feet, their cattle, houses, cities in corresponding proportion. In Brobdingnag the folk appeared as tall as an ordinary spire steeple; the cat seemed three times larger than an ox; the corn grew forty feet high. Intrinsically Lilliput and Brobdingnag were just the same; that indeed was the principle on which Swift worked out his story. It needed an intruding Gulliver— an extraneous standard of length—to create a difference.

*—Sir Arthur Stanley Eddington: "The Constants of Nature"; **Space, Time and Gravitation**, 1920*

3. Who wishes correctly to learn the ways to measure surfaces and to divide them, must necessarily thoroughly understand the general theorems of geometry and arithmetic, on which the teaching of measurement ... rests. If he has completely mastered these ideas, he ... can never deviate from the truth.

*—Abraham bar Hiyya: **Treatise on Mensuration***

4. To understand this [that a solid can have finite volume even though it has infinite extent] for sense, it is not required that a man should be a geometrician or a logician, but that he should be mad.

*—Thomas Hobbes: 1672, in **The English Works of Thomas Hobbes**, Sir William Molesworth, ed., 1939–45 [In 1643 Evangelista Torricelli proved that the hyperbolic solid generated by revolving y = 1/x about the x axis from x = 1 to x = infinity has finite volume.]*

5. [Socrates] said that the study of geometry should be pursued until the student was competent to measure a parcel of land accurately in case he wanted to take it over, convey or divide it, or to compare the yield; and this knowledge was so easy to acquire, that everyone who gave his mind to mensuration knew the size of the piece and carried away a knowledge of the principles of land measurement.

*—Xenophon: **Memorobilia**, c. 4th cent. B.C.*

31.7 Measuring Devices and Techniques

1. It is not the barometer which has a great effect on the weather; rather the weather has a great effect on it.

*—Anonymous: **The Adventures of Sylvia Hughes**, 1761*

2. The moon and its phases gave man his first calendar. Trying to match that calendar with the seasons helped give him mathematics. The usefulness of the calendar helped give rise to the thought of beneficent gods. And with all that the moon is beautiful too.

*—Isaac Asimov: **Book of Science and Nature**, 1988*

3. The question of what properties, such as angle or area, are reproduced on a map without distortion is of prime interest to mathematicians. The question extends far beyond the confines of geometry, for all mathematics can be considered broadly as a study of maps and mapping.

*—George A.W. Boehm: **The New World of Math**, 1959*

4. Scientific cartography was born in France in the reign of Louis XIV (1638—1715), the offspring of astronomy and mathematics. The principles and methods which had been used and talked about for over two thousand years were unchanged; the ideal of Hipparchus and Ptolemy, to locate each place on earth scientifically, according to its latitude and longitude, was still current. But something new had been introduced into the picture in the form of two pieces of apparatus—a telescope and a timekeeper. The result was a revolution in map making and a start towards an accurate picture of the earth. With the aid of these two mechanical contrivances it was possible, for the first time, to solve the problem of how to determine longitude, both on land and at sea.

*—Lloyd Brown: "The Longitude," **The Story of Maps**, 1949*

5. The next important phase in the development of a timekeeper was the attachment of a pendulum as a driving force. This clock was developed by Christiaan Huygens.... He built the first one in 1656 in order to increase the accuracy of his astronomical observations, and later presented it to the States General of Holland on the 16th of June, 1657.

*—Lloyd A. Brown; "The Longitude" in **The World of Mathematics**, vol.2, 1956*

6. Nothing tends so much to the advancement of knowledge as the application of a new instrument. The native intellectual powers of men in different times are not so much the causes of the different success of their labors, as the peculiar nature of the means and artificial resources in their possession.

*—Sir Humphrey Davy: Quoted in Thomas Hager; **Forces of Nature**, Simon & Schuster, 1995*

7. Since the measuring device has been constructed by the observer ... we have to remember that what we observe is not nature in itself but nature exposed to our method of questioning.

*—Werner Karl Heisenberg: **Physics and Philosophy**, 1958*

8. We still call the "rod" on a sundial the gnomon. This word has had a long and varied history. It was given by the Greeks to the "rod" on a sundial because it "gave them knowledge" about the passing of time. Gnomon is derived from the Greek word meaning "to know," which is also found ion our word "agnostic," "one who does not know (whether God exists)." Then the word came to be applied to an instrument used by mathematicians for drawing lines at right angles to each other—this time, a reference to the relative position of a sundial's gnomon and its shadow.

—*Alfred Hooper:* ***Makers of Mathematics****, 1948*

9. The inhabitants of Mesopotamia, first the Sumerians and then the Babylonians, are credited with the first calendar. In the 14th century B.C., the Chinese established the year as 365¼ days and the lunar month as 29½ days. The works of Hesoid and Homer established the Greeks as using lunar calendars in the 13th century B.C. In the late 10th century there is reference to the Hebrew lunar calendar and the lunar-solar Hindu calendar. But the Mayan calendar was the most advanced. It was a calendar that kept track of various astronomical cycles—of days (24 hours of the Earth's rotation), of lunar months, and of the solar year....

—*Theoni Pappas:* ***More Joy of Mathematics****, 1991*

10. Since the Star [Sirius] advances one day every four years, and in order that the holidays celebrated in the summer shall not fall in the winter, as has been and will be the case if the year continues to have 300 and 5 additional days, it is hereby decreed that henceforth every four years there shall be celebrated the holidays of the Gods of Euergetes after the 5 additional days and before the new year, so that everyone might know that the former shortcomings in reckoning the seasons of the year have henceforth been truly corrected by King Euergetes.

—*Ptolemy III Euergetes: Decree, 238 B.C. [This ruler of Egypt, a mathematician, adjusted the calendar to account that a year is something less that 365 and ¼ days.]*

11. Time is a wealth of change, but the clock in its parody makes it mere change and no wealth.

—*Rabindranath Tagore:* ***Stray Birds****, 1916*

31.8 Approximations

1. I have always observed that graduate mathematicians and physicists are very well acquainted with theoretical results, but have no knowledge of the simplest approximate results.

—*L. Collatz:* ***Numb. Beh. Diffgl.****, 1951; English tr., 1960*

2. Examples of rational approximations [of irrational numbers] are to be found in Greek writings from the fourth century B.C. onwards. It seems likely that a number of techniques were available at various times, but there is no agreement among scholars as to exactly what they were.

—*Stuart Hollingdale:* ***Makers of Mathematics****, 1989*

3. Measurement ... always has an element of error in it. The most exact description or prediction that a scientist can make is still only approximate. If, as sometimes happens, a perfect correspondence with observation does appear, it must be regarded as accidental, and, as Jevons [in The Principles of Science] ... remarks, it "should give rise to suspicion rather than to satisfaction."

—*Abraham Kaplan:* ***The Conduct of Inquiry****, 1964*

4. Although this may seem a paradox, all exact science is dominated by the idea of approximation.

—*Bertrand Russell: In* ***The Viking Book of Aphorisms****, W.H. Auden & L. Kronenberger, eds., 1966*

5. Far better an approximate answer to the right question, which is often vague, than the exact answer to the wrong question, which can always be made precise.

—*J. W. Tuckey:* ***Annals of Mathematical Statistics****, Volume 33, 1962*

6. Truth is much too complicated to allow anything but approximations.

—*John von Neumann: Quoted in Manfred Schroder:* ***Fractals, Chaos, Power Laws: Minutes from an Infinite Paradise****, 1992*

31.9 Longitude and Latitude

1. ...the *Geography* of Ptolemy introduced the systems of latitudes and longitudes as used to day, described methods of cartographic projection, and catalogued some 8000 cities, rivers, and other important features of the earth.

—*Carl B. Boyer:* ***A History of Mathematics****, 1968*

2. Sometimes a cyclometer persuades a skipper, who has made land in the wrong place, that the astronomers are in fault for using a wrong measure of the circle; and the skipper thinks it is a very comfortable solution! And this is the utmost that the problem ever has to do with longitude.

—*Augustus de Morgan:* ***A Budget of Paradoxes*** *1872*

3. Some do understand that the Knowledge of the Longitude myght be founde, a thynge doubtless greatly to be desyred, and hytherto not certaynly knowen, although Sebastian Cabot, on his death-bed told me that he had knowledge thereof by divine revelation, yet so, that he myght not teache any man. But, I thinke that the good olde man, in that extreme age, somewhat doted, and had not yet even in the article of death, utterly shaken off all worldly vayne glorie.

—*Richard Eden: "Epistle Dedicatory" in his translation of John Taisnier:* ***A Very Necessarie and Profitable Book Concerning Navigation****, 1579 (?)*

4. As, in spite of seeming discouragement, some mathematicians are yet in hopes of hitting upon an exact method of determining the longitude, the more earnest psychologists may, in the face of previous failures, still cherish expectations with regard to some mode of infallibly discovering the heart of man.

—Herman Melville: ***The Confidence Man****, 1857*

5. ...I do not know if the Devil will succeed in making a longitude timekeeper but it is folly for man to try.

—Jean-Baptiste Morin; in S. Chapin: "A Survey of the Efforts to Determine Longitude at Sea, 1600–1760," ***Navigation****, 3 (7), 1953*

6. There isn't a Parallel of Latitude but thinks it would have been the Equator if it had had its rights.

—Mark Twain: "Pudd'nhead Wilson's New Calendar"; ***Following the Equator****, 1897*

7. The Art of Navigation is to be perfected by the Solution of this Problem. To find, at any Time, the Longitude of a Place at Sea. A Public Reward is promised for the Discovery. Let him obtain it who is able.

—Bernhard Varenius: ***Geographica Generalis****, 1650*

31.10 The Metric System

1. The rest of the world is probably right to bully us into adopting the metric system since it's convenient for everybody to tell the same lies. But let us not give it the benediction of the scientific community.

—Kenneth E. Boulding: Quoted in Howard W. Eves: ***Return to Mathematical Circles****, 1988*

2. By the Act of November 24, 1793 (decreed by the Revolutionary government in France) a radically new calendar and an almost equally new system of measuring time were proclaimed.... The following, in tabular form, is the system of units which was then set up (note the desperate attempt to decimalize time):

100 seconds = 1 minute
100 minutes = 1 hour
10 hours = 1 day
10 days = 1 week or decad
3 weeks = 30 days = 1 month
12 months plus 5 or 6 carnival days = 1 year

—Burdette R. Buckingham: ***Elementary Arithmetic: Its Meaning and Practice****, 1947*

3. One mathematical effect of the [French] Revolution was the adoption of the metric system, in which the subdivision of money, weights and measures is strictly based on the number ten. When someone objected to the number, naturally preferring twelve, because it has more factors, Lagrange unexpectedly remarked, what a pity it was that the number eleven had not been chosen as base, because it was prime.

—Herbert Westren Turnbull: "The Great Mathematicians"; in ***The World of Mathematics****, James R. Newman, ed., 1956*

4. It shall be lawful throughout the United States of America to employ the weights and measures of the metric system, and no contract or dealing or pleading in any court shall be deemed invalid or liable to objection because the weights and measures expressed or referred to therein are weights and measures of the metric system.

—U.S. Congress; "Act of Congress," July 28, 1866 [This is an enabling act not an establishment the metric system as the sole system of weights and measures, but gave it as much legitimacy as the more familiar and still more popular English system of weights and measures in the U.S.]

5. If Parliament were ever so unwise as to pass a law making the Metric system compulsory in the United Kingdom, the certain result would be that the law would not be obeyed. A new kind of crime would have been created, but no government, and no courts of justice could compel a free people, like the British nation, to adopt a system of weights and measures to which they were not accustomed and which they did not want.

—C.M. Watson: ***British Weights and Measures****, 1910*

6. Not until 1791 when the Paris Academy of Sciences recommended a new metric system did any generally acceptable and uniform system start to emerge. 1 meter was defined to be 1/40,000,000 part of a circumference of the earth through the poles. The ratios between units were to be always powers of 10. Greek and Latin Prefixes were used for larger and smaller units, respectively.

—David Wells: ***The Penguin Dictionary of Curious and Interesting Numbers****, 1986*

31.11 Time

1. As we look ahead, time is interminable.
As we look back, it is infinitesimal.

—Anonymous

2. In time there is something indivisible—namely, the instant; and there is something else which endures—namely, time. But in eternity the indivisible now stands always still.

—Thomas Aquinas: ***Summa Theologica****, c. 1260; Fathers of Dominion Province, tr. 1911–25*

3. Where does time come from, and by what way does it pass, and where does it go, while we are measuring it? Where is it from?—obviously from the future. But what way does it pass?—by the present. Where does it go?—into the past. In other words it passes from that which does not exist, by way of that which lacks extension, into that which is no longer.

—St. Augustine: ***Confessions****, 397–401*

4. Because Mathematicians frequently make use of Time, they ought to have a distinct idea of the meaning of that Word, otherwise they are Quacks.

—Issac Barrow; Quoted in Paul Davies: ***About Time,*** *1995*

5. The ignorant suppose that infinite number of drawings require an infinite amount of time; in reality it is quite enough that time be infinitely subdivisible, as is the case in the famous parable of the Tortoise and the Hare. This infinitude harmonizes in an admirable manner with the sinuous numbers of Chance and of the Celestial Archetype of the Lottery adored by the Platonists.

—Jorge Luis Borges: ***Ficiones,*** *1962*

6. The measurement of time is essentially the process of counting.

—G.M. Clemence: "Time and Measurement"; ***The American Scientist,*** *Vol. 40, 2; April, 1952*

7. Space and time, ... are inseparable partners. You can talk about here and now, and there and then. But it makes no sense to talk about there and now. Even if you stand in one place on Earth and measure the time now, and again two seconds from now, you have also measured motion in space—for the simple reason that the Earth moves. If it didn't, we wouldn't have such a thing as a day to be divided into hours and minutes and seconds in the first place. In a way, measuring the distance that a point on the surface of Earth moves in a given moment of time can be viewed as a tautology, since a movement of time is defined by the rotation of Earth through space. If nothing ever happened in the universe, there would be no conceivable concept of time.

—K.C. Cole: ***The Universe and the Teacup,*** *1997*

8. Time is really nothing but a huge circle. You divide a circle of three hundred and sixty degrees into twenty-four hours, and you get fifteen degrees of arc that is equivalent to each hour.

—Erle Stanley Gardner: ***The Case of the Buried Clock,*** *1943*

9. The laws of science do not distinguish between the past and the future.

—Stephen W. Hawking: ***A Brief History of Time,*** *1988*

10. Absolute, true, and mathematical time, of itself, and from its own nature, flows equably without relation to anything external, and by another name is called duration: relative, apparent, and common time, is some sensible and external (whether accurate or unequable) measure of duration by the means of motion, which is commonly used instead of true time; such as an hour, a day, a month, a year.

—Sir Isaac Newton: ***Principia Mathematica;*** *"Definitions, Scholium," 1687*

11. Unlike the divisions of time into days and years, which correspond to natural phenomena, such as the rotation of the earth on its axis and the orbit of the earth around the sun, the concept of century has no physical basis. Rather, it derives from an arithmetical artifact built upon an anatomical accident. If human beings came equipped with four fingers on each hand, then we would undoubtedly have developed a number system with base eight rather than base ten, leading to divisions of time into octads rather than decades and intervals of eight octads—or sixty-four years—instead of a century.

—Robert Osserman: ***Poetry of the Universe,*** *1995*

12. Time is infinite motion without a moment of rest and is unthinkable otherwise.

—Leo Tolstoy: ***War and Peace,*** *1863–9*

13. Time is defined so that motion looks simple.

—John Archibald Wheeler: ***Gravitation,*** *1973*

14. Time is the longest distance between two places.

—Tennessee Williams: ***The Glass Menagerie,*** *1945*

32

Geometry I

32.1 The History of Geometry

1. Let no one enter who does not know geometry [mathematics].

—Anonymous: Inscription on Plato's Academy of Athens, Elias Philosophus: ***Aristotelis Categorias Commentaria***

2. [Thomas Hobbes] was 40 years old before he looked on geometry; which happened accidently. Being in a gentleman's library, Euclid's Elements lay open [to Pythagoras' Theorem]. He read the proposition. "By God, said he, "this is impossible." So he reads the demonstration of it, which referred him back to another proposition; which proposition he read. That referred him back to another, which he also read ... at last he was demonstratively convinced of that truth. This made him in love with geometry.

—John Aubrey: In O.L. Dick, ed. ***Brief Lives****, 1960*

3. I am the most travelled of my contemporaries; I have extended my field of enquiry wider than anyone else; I have seen more countries and climes, and have heard more speeches of learned men. No one has surpassed me in the composition of lines according to demonstration, not even the Egyptian knotters of ropes, or geometers.

—Democritus of Abdera: ***Diogenes Laertius****, c. 5th cent. B.C.*

4. How is it that the Church produced no geometers in her autocratic reign of twelve hundred years?

—John William Draper: ***The Conflict Between Science and Religion****, 1890*

5. Oh King, in the real world there are two kinds of roads, roads for the common people to travel upon and roads reserved for the King to travel upon. In geometry there is no royal road.

—Euclid: Quoted in Proclus: ***Eudemian Summary****, c. A.D. 5th cent. [This comment by Euclid to his student Ptolemy Soter, the first King of Egypt, who finding the study of geometry difficult, asked his teacher if there weren't some easier way to learn the subject is likely apocryphal.]*

6. Descartes indeed understood thoroughly the significance of what he had done, and he was right when he boasted that he had so far surpassed all geometry before him as Cicero's rhetoric surpasses the ABC.

—Jacques Hadamard: Quoted in E.T. Bell: ***Men of Mathematics****, 1937*

7. The Golden Age of Greek geometry ended with the time of Apollonius of Perga. The beginning of the Christian era sees quite a different state of things.... Production was limited to elementary textbooks of decidedly feeble quality.... The study of higher geometry languished or was completely in abeyance until Pappus arose to revive interest in the subject.... The great task which he set himself was the reestablishment of geometry on its former high plane of achievement.

—Sir Thomas Heath: ***A History of Greek Mathematics****, 1921*

8. Geometry, which is the only science that it hath pleased God hitherto to bestow on mankind.

—Thomas Hobbes: ***Leviathan****, 1651*

9. The whole science of geometry may be said to owe its being to the [Lagrange's] *Analytical Mechanics* is a book you have to be rather cautious about, as some of its content is more supernatural than based on strict demonstration. You therefore have to be prudent about it, if you don't want to be deceived or come to the delusive belief that something is proved which is actually not. There are only a few points which do not entail major difficulties; I find students who understood Analytical Mechanics better than I did, but sometimes it is not a good sign if you understand something.

—Carl Gustav Jacob Jacobi: "Lectures on Analytical Mechanics, 1847–8"; Quoted in Helmut Pulte: "After 150 Years: News from Jacobi about Lagrange's ***Analytical Mechanics****";* ***The Mathematical Intelligencer****, vol. 19, Summer, 1997*

10. Geometry has two great treasures: one is the theorem of Pythagoras; the other, the division of a line in extreme and mean ratio. The first we may name as a measure of gold, the second we may name a precious jewel.

—Johannes Kepler: Quoted in Stuart Hollingdale: ***Makers of Mathematics,*** *1989*

11. In geometry I find certain imperfections which I hold to be the reason why this science, apart from the transition into analytics, can as yet make no advance from that state in which it has come to us from Euclid.

—Nikolai Ivanovich Lobachevsky: ***Geometrical Researches on the Theory of Parallels,*** *1840; George B. Halsted, tr., 1914*

12. ...geometry was first discovered among the Egyptians and originated in the remeasuring of their lands. This was necessary for them because the Nile overflows and obliterates the boundary lines between their properties.

—Proclus: ***A Commentary on the First Book of Euclid's Elements,*** *Glenn R. Morrow, tr., 1970*

13. Geometry was the major part of ancient mathematics. It is, with several of its ramifications, still one of the main divisions of modern mathematics. There can be no doubt that its origin in antiquity was empirical and that it began as a discipline not unlike theoretical physics today. Apart from all other evidence, the very name "geometry" indicates this.

—John von Neumann: "The Mathematician" in Robert B. Heywood: ***The Works of the Mind,*** *1947*

14. We are only geometricians of matter; the Greeks were, first of all, geometricians in the apprenticeship to virtue.

—Simone Weil: "The Iliad of the Poem of Force" in ***Cahiers du Sud,*** *December, 1940*

32.2 The Science of Geometry

1. ...there is an independent science of geometry just as there is an independent science of physics, and ... either of these may be treated by mathematical methods. Thus geometry becomes the simplest of the natural sciences, and its axioms are of the nature of physical laws, to be tested by experience and to be regarded as true only within the limits of the errors of observation.

—Maxime Bochner: "The Fundamental Conceptions and Methods in Mathematics"; ***Bulletin of the American Mathematical Society,*** *vol. 9 1904*

2. The goal of geometry is to study those properties of bodies which can be considered independent of their matter, but only with respect to their dimensions and their forms. Geometry measures the surface of a field without bothering to find out whether the soil is good or bad.

—Emile Borel: ***Geometrie, premier et second cycles,*** *2nd. ed., 1908*

3. The doctrines of pure geometry often, and in many questions, give a simple and natural way to penetrate to the origin of truths, to lay bare the mysterious chain which unites them, and to make them known individually, luminously and completely.

—Michael Chasles: Quoted in Morris Kline: ***Mathematical Thoughts from Ancient to Modern Times,*** *1972*

4. Geometry is a true natural science;—only more simple, and therefore more perfect than any other. We must not suppose that, because it admits the application of mathematical analysis, it is therefore a purely logical science, independent of observation. Every body studied by geometers presents some primitive phenomena which, not being discoverable by reasoning, must be due to observation alone.

—Auguste Comte: ***Cours de philosophie positive,*** *6 vols., 1830—41*

5. Geometry was the midwife of science.

—Paul Davies: ***Superforce,*** *1984*

6. Geometry, of course, is based on spatial intuition, hence is of physical origin. But to trace the "applied" aspect back this far is surely to beg the question: almost all of mathematics is based on geometry or number, so is "rooted in reality" in some sense.

—Albert Einstein: Quoted in Ian Stewart: "The Science of Significant Form," ***The Mathematical Intelligencer,*** *vol. 3, 2, 1981*

7. Geometry, that is to say, the science of harmony in space, presides over everything. We find it in the arrangement of the scales of a fir-cone, as in the arrangement of an Epeira's lime-snare; we find it in the spiral of a Snail-shell, in the chaplet of a Spider's thread, as in the orbit of a planet; it is everywhere, as perfect in the world of atoms as in the world of immensities.

—Henri Fabre: ***The Life of the Spider,*** *1921*

8. I have no fault to find with those who teach geometry. That science is the only one which has not produced sects; if is founded on analysis and on synthesis and on the calculus; it does not occupy itself with probable truth; moreover it has the same method in every country.

—Frederick the Great [King of Prussia]: ***Oeuvres,*** *Decker, ed.; Quoted in A.L. Mackay:* ***The Harvest of a Quite Eye,*** *1977*

9. To construct a geometry is to state a system of axioms and to deduce all possible consequences from them. All systems of pure geometry ... are constructed in just this way. Their differences ... are differences not of principle or of method, but merely of richness of content and variety of application.... You must naturally be prepared to sacrifice simplicity to some extent if you wish to be interesting.

—G.H. Hardy: "What Is Geometry?" ***Mathematical Gazette****, 1925*

10. ...to characterize the import of pure geometry, we might use the standard form of a movie-disclaimer: No portrayal of the characteristics of geometrical figures or of the spatial properties of relationships of actual bodies is intended, and any similarities between the primitive concepts and the customary geometrical connotations are purely coincidental.

—Carl G. Hempel: "Geometry and Empirical Science," in ***The World of Mathematics****, James R. Newman, ed., 1956*

11. Geometry enlightens the intellect and sets one's mind right. All of its proofs are very clear and orderly. It is hardly possible for errors to enter into geometrical reasoning, because it is well arranged and orderly. Thus, the mind that constantly applies itself to geometry is not likely to fall into error. In this convenient way, the person who knows geometry acquires intelligence.

—Ibn Khaldun: ***The Muqaddimah. An Introduction to History*** *c. 14th cent A.D. N.J. Dawood's abridgment of F. Rosenthal, tr., 1967*

12. Where there is matter, there is geometry.

—Johannes Kepler: Quoted in J. Koenderink: ***Solid Shape****, 1990*

13. I constantly meet people who are doubtful, generally without due reason, about their potential capacity [as mathematicians]. The first test is whether you got anything out of geometry. To have disliked or failed to get on with other [mathematical] subjects need mean nothing; much drill and drudgery is unavoidable before they can get started, and bad teaching can make them unintelligible even to a born mathematician.

—J.E. Littlewood: ***A Mathematician's Miscellany****, 1953*

14. ...geometry is founded in mechanical practice, and is nothing but that part of universal mechanics which proposes and demonstrates the art of measuring.... It is the glory of geometry that from so few principles, fetched from without, it is able to produce so many things.

—Isaac Newton: ***The Mathematical Principles of Natural Philosophy****, 1687; Andrew Motte, tr., 1729*

15. Geometry may sometimes appear to take the lead over analysis but in fact precedes it only as a servant goes before the master to clear the path and light him on his way.

—James J. Sylvester: ***Philosophic Magazine****, vol. 31, 1866:* ***Collected Papers****, 1908*

32.3 Geometry and Art

1. One can say that geometry is to the plastic arts what grammar is to the writer.

—G. Appollinaire: ***Soiress de Paris****, 1912*

2. Inspiration is needed in geometry, just as much as in poetry.

—Aleksandr Sergeyevich Pushkin: ***Likhtenshtein****; in* ***The Complete Prose Tales****, G. Aitken, tr., 1962*

3. I have come to know that Geometry is at the very heart of feeling, and that every expression of feeling is made by a movement governed by Geometry. Geometry is everywhere in Nature. This is the Concert of Nature.

—Auguste Rodin: Quoted on ***Omnibus****; BBC, 1986*

4. Geometry is a mountain. Vigor is needed for its ascent. The views all along the paths are magnificent. The effort of climbing is stimulating. A guide who points out the beauties, the grandeur, and the special places of interest commands the admiration of a group of pilgrims.

—David Eugene Smith: ***The Teaching of Geometry****, 1911*

32.4 Points, Lines and Planes

1. The straight line of the geometers does not exist in the natural universe. It is a pure abstraction, an invention of the imagination or, if one prefers, and idea of the Eternal Mind.

—E.T. Bell: ***The Magic of Numbers****, 1946*

2. A point therefore is considered a triangle, or a triangle is supposed to be formed in a point. Which to conceive seems quite impossible. Yet some there are who, though they shrink at all other mysteries, make no difficulty of their own, who strain at a gnat and swallow a camel.

—Bishop G. Berkeley: ***The Analyst: or a Discourse addressed to an Infidel Mathematician****, 1734*

3. A vertical line is dignity. The horizontal line is peaceful. The obtuse angle is action. That's universal, it is primary.

—Janet Collins: ***I Dream a World****, 1989*

4. The principle of the science of painting is the point; second is the line; third is the surface; fourth is the body which is enclosed by these surfaces. And this is just what is to be represented ... since in truth the scope of painting does not extend beyond the representation of the solid body or the shape of all the things that are visible.

—Leonardo da Vinci: in ***Leonardo on Painting****, M. Kemp, ed., 1989*

5. There are lines that are monsters.

—Ferdinand Delacroix: Quoted in Francois Le Lionnais: "Beauty in Mathematics" in ***Great Currents of Mathematics****, F. Le Lionnais, ed., 1971*

6. Geometry should not include lines that are like strings, in that they are sometimes straight and sometimes curved, since the ratios between straight and curved lines are not known, and I believe cannot be discovered by human minds.

—Rene Descartes: ***Geometry****, 1637*

7. A mathematical point is the most indivisible and unique thing which art can present.

—John Donne: ***Letters****, 1635*

8. The number of measurements necessary to give the position of a point, is equal to the number of dimensions of the space in question. In a line the distance from one fixed point is sufficient, that is to say, one quantity; in a surface the distance from two fixed points must be given; in space, the distances from three; or we require, as on the earth, longitude, latitude, and height above the sea, or, as is usual in analytical geometry, the distances from three co-ordinate planes.

—Herman von Helmholtz: "On the Origin and Significance of Geometrical Axioms," lecture at Heidelberg, 1870

9. The whole science of geometry may be said to owe its being to the exorbitant interest which the human mind takes in lines. We cut up space in every direction in order to manufacture them.

—William James: ***Principles of Psychology****, 1890*

10. Points
Have no parts or joints.
How can they combine
To form a line?

—J.A. Lindon: in Martin Gardner's "Mathematical games"; ***Scientific American****, March, 1971*

11. One of the most curious of these games [geometrical paradoxes] was that of a student, I am not sure but a graduate, of the University of Virginia, who claimed that geometers were in error in assuming that a line had no thickness. He published a school geometry based on his views, which received the endorsement of a well-known New York school official and, on the basis if this, was actually endorsed, or came very near being endorsed, as a textbook in the public schools of New York.

—Simon Newcomb: ***The Reminiscences of an Astronomer****, 1903*

12. Everyone makes for himself a clear idea of the motion of a point, that is to say, of the motion of a corpuscle which one supposes to be infinitely small, and which one reduces by thought in some way to a mathematical point.

—Louis Poinsot: ***Theorie nouvelle de la rotation des corps****, 1834*

32.5 Commensurability

1. For all men begin, ... by wondering that things are as they are, ... about the incommensurability of the diagonal of a square with the side; for it seems wonderful to all who have not yet seen the reason, that there is a thing which cannot be measured even by the smallest unit. But we must end in the contrary and, according to the proverb, the better state, as is the case in these instances too when men learn the cause; for there is nothing which would surprise a geometer so much as if the diagonal turned not to be commensurable.

—Aristotle: ***Metaphysics***

2. [Hippasus, a student of Pythagoras, was] the first to betray the nature of commensurability and incommensurability to the unworthy.

—Iamblichus: ***On the Philosophy of the Pythagoreans****, ca. 283—330 A.D. [For his transgression, Hippasus was expelled from the Pythagorean order, and a grave was prepared for him, as though he were going to disappear completely.]*

3. As for Euclid he set himself to give rigorous rules, which he established, relative to commensurability and incommensurability in general; he made precise the definitions and the distinctions between rational and irrational magnitudes, he set out a great number of orders of irrational magnitudes, and finally he clearly showed their whole extent.

—Pappus: ***Mathematical Collection****, c. 4th cent. A.D.*

4. He is unworthy of the name of man who is ignorant of the fact that the diagonal of a square is incommensurable with its side.

—Plato: Quoted in Sophie Germain: "Memoire sur les surfaces elastiques": ***Journal de Mathematique pures et appliques****, 6; 1880*

32.6 Curves

1. A curve, though it cannot exist except in sensible matter, does not, however, include sensible matter in its definition. This is the way that all mathematicals are, for instance, number, size, and figure....

—St. Thomas Aquinas (c. 1225—1274): "Exposition of Aristotle's Physics"; ***The Pocket Aquinas****, Vernon J. Bourke, ed.,1960*

2. The efforts of my brother were without success; for my part, I was more fortunate, for I found the skill (I say it without boasting, why should I conceal the truth?) to solve it in full.... It is true that it cost me study that robbed me of rest for an entire night ... but the next morning, filled with joy, I ran to my brother (Jakob), who was still struggling miserably with this Gordian knot without getting anywhere, always thinking, like Galileo, that the catenary was a parabola. Stop! Stop! I say to him, don't torture yourself any more to try to prove the identity of the catenary with thc parabola, since it is entirely false.

—Johann Bernoulli: in Morris Kline: ***Mathematical Thought from Ancient to Modern Times****, 1972; Quoted in William Dunham:* ***Journey Through Genius****, 1990 [The catenary is the shape assumed by a chain, fixed at two points, hanging under its own weight]*

3. While it is true that every curve which can be described by a continuous motion should be accepted in geometry, this does not mean that we should use at random the first one that we meet in the construction of a given problem. We should always choose with care the simplest curve that can be used in the solution of the problem.

—Rene Descartes: ***Geometrie****, 1637; appendix to* ***Discours de la methode****; Smith and Latham edition, 1952*

4. The investigations about the curved surfaces deeply affect many other things; I would go so far as to say they are involved in the metaphysics of the geometry of space.

—Carl Friedrich Gauss: Letter to Hansen, December 11, 1825; ***Werke****, 1929*

5. At the very threshold of geometry lies the concept of the curve; everyone believes that he has an intuitively clear notion of what a curve is, and since ancient times it has been held that this idea could be expressed by the following definition: Curves are geometric figures generated by the motion of point [i.e., a continuous motion]. But, attend! In the year 1890 the Italian mathematician Giuseppe Peano ... proved that the geometric figures that can be generated by a moving point also include entire plane surfaces. For instance, it is possible to imagine a point moving in such a way that in a finite time it will pass through all the points of a square—and yet no one would consider the entire area of a square as simply a curve.

—Hans Hahn: "The Crisis in Intuition" in ***The World of Mathematics****, James R. Newman, ed., 1956*

6. ...he seemed to approach the grave as a hyperbolic curve approaches a line, less directly as he got nearer, till it was doubtful if he would ever reach it at all.

—Thomas Hardy: ***Far From the Madding Crowd****, 1874*

7. The curves treated by the calculus are normal and healthy; they possess no idiosyncrasies. But mathematicians would not be happy merely with simple, lusty configurations. Beyond these their curiosity extends to psychopathic patients, each of whom has an individual case history resembling no other; these are the pathological curves in mathematics.

—E. Kasner & J. Newman: ***Mathematics and the Imagination****, 1940*

8. Everyone knows what a curve is, until he has studied enough mathematics to become confused through the countless number of possible exceptions.

—Felix Klein: in ***On Mathematics****, Robert Moritz, ed., 1958*

9. The study of curves in classical and analytic geometry is equally blessed with harmony. Has not the cycloid, found in so many natural phenomena, been called the "Helen of Geometry"?

—Francois Le Lionnais: "Beauty in Mathematics" in ***Great Currents of Mathematics****, F. Le Lionnais, ed., 1971*

10. The catenary or "hanging string" as it was called in old Japan was another curve that was deeply studied. Its study happened to arise some time later than the problem of the center of gravity. The very complexity of treatment strongly reminds us of its unindebtedness to any foreign source of knowledge....

—Yoshio Mikami: ***The Development of Mathematics in China and Japan****, 1974*

11. A single curve, drawn in the manner of the curve of prices of cotton, describes all that the ear can possibly hear as the result of the most complicated musical performance.... That to my mind is a wonderful proof of the potency of mathematics.

—William Thomson, Lord Kelvin: Quoted in E.T. Bell: ***Men of Mathematics****, 1937*

12. A curved line is the loveliest distance between two points.

—Mae West: ***The Wit and Wisdom of Mae West****, 1967*

32.7 Size and Shapes

1. There is no smallest among the small and no largest among the large; but always something still smaller and something still larger.

—Anaxagoras: Quoted in Eli Maor: ***To Infinity and Beyond: A Cultural History of the Infinite****, 1987*

2. I do not suppose there is anyone in this room who has not occasionally blown a common soap bubble, and while admiring the perfection of its form, and the marvelous brilliancy of its colors, wondered how it is that such a magnificent object can be so easily produced. I hope that none of you are yet tried of playing with bubbles, because, as I hope we shall see, there is more in a common bubble that those who have only played with them generally imagine.

—Sir Charles Vernon Boys: ***Soap-Bubbles: Their Colors and the Forces That Mold Them****, 1931*

3. Until a person has thought out the stars and their interspaces, he has hardly learnt that there are things much more terrible than monsters of shape, namely, monsters of magnitude without known shape. Such monsters are the voids and waste places of the sky.

—Thomas Hardy: ***Two on a Towner****, 1882*

4. There is no absolute scale of size in the Universe, for it is boundless towards the great and also boundless towards the small.

—Oliver Heaviside: Quoted in D'Arcy W. Thompson: ***On Growth and Form****, 1917*

5. [Of Quartz] Why it is formed with hexagonal faces cannot be readily explained; and any explanation is complicated by the fact that, on the one hand, its terminal points are not symmetrical and that, on the other hand, its faces are so perfectly smooth that no craftsmanship could achieve the same effect.

—Pliny the Elder: ***Natural History Book***

6. Questions about the very large are idle questions for the explanation of nature. But such is not the case with questions about the very small. They are of paramount importance to natural science, for our knowledge of the casual connection of phenomena rests essentially upon the exactness with which we pursue such matters down to the very small. Questions concerning the metrical relations of space in the very small are therefore not idle ... it is ... quite conceivable that the metrical relations of space in the infinitely small do not agree with the assumptions of geometry; and indeed we ought to hold that this is so if phenomena can thereby be explained in a simpler fashion.

—Bernard Riemann: "Uber die Hypothesen, welche der Geometrie zu Grunde liegen," 1854; ***Werke****, 1876*

7. In the physical world, one cannot increase the size or quantity of anything without changing its quality. Similar figures exist only in pure geometry.

—Paul Valery: ***Collected Works****, J, Matthews, ed., 1970*

32.8 Geometric Constructions

1. In Euclidean geometry, constructions are made with the ruler and compass. Projective geometry is simpler; its constructions require only the ruler.

—H.S.M. Coxeter: ***Projective Geometry****, 1964*

2. It is well known that for every beginner in Geometry that various regular polygons can be constructed geometrically, namely the triangle, pentagon, 15-gon, and those which arise from these be repeatedly doubling the number of sides, One had already got this far in Euclid's time, and it seems that one has persuaded oneself ever since that the domain of elementary geometry could not be extended.... It seems to me then to be all the more remarkable that besides the usual polygons there is a collection of others which are constructible geometrically, e.g., the 17-gon.

—Carl Friedrich Gauss: in John Fauvel & Jeremy Gray: ***The History of Mathematics: A Reader****, 1987*

3. From a man and a woman make a circle, then a square, then a triangle, finally a circle and you will obtain the Philosophers's Stone.

—Michael Maier: 17th century, in ***Scrutinium Chymicum****, 1867*

4. The compass and square produce perfect circles and squares. By the sages, the human relations are perfectly exhibited.

—Mencius: ***Discourses****, 3rd. cent. B.C.*

5. The cubic root of 2 is not constructible by ruler and compass, but the cubic root of 2 plus the square root of 5, which looks more complicated, is, (since it equals the golden ratio). Things like that make it fun to be a mathematician.

—Tom Osler: ***Temple Talk****; March 25, 1998*

6. One type of problem which the ancient Greek geometers were fond of setting themselves was that of constructing a length with given properties. For example, they asked how to construct the side of a square which should be equal in area to a given triangle. "Construction" here had a special meaning. They were only allowed to use ruler and compasses; that is, a straight line through two given points could be constructed, and a circle with a given center and a radius of a given length could be constructed. Anything else must be made by some combination of these processes. One might imagine the existence of other curves, but as they could not be so easily drawn in practice, it was not regarded as playing the game to use them in constructions.

—Edward Charles Titchmarsh: "π and e" ***Mathematics for the General Reader****, 1959*

7. The Geometer has the special privilege to carry out, by abstraction, all constructions by means of the intellect. Who, then, would wish to prevent me from freely considering figures hanging on a balance imagined to be an infinite distance beyond the confines of the world?

—*Evangelista Torricelli: in P. Mancosu & E. Vailati: "Torricelli's Infinitely Long Solid and Its Philosophical Reception in the Seventeenth Century"; **Isis**, 82, 1991*

32.9 Angles and Triangles

1. In Flatland, the birth of a true equilateral triangle from isosceles parents is the subject of rejoicing from many miles around.

—*Edwin A. Abbott: **Flatland**, 1884*

2. ...to form a right angle, the Egyptians took a closed circle of rope and divided it by means of three knots into three parts whose lengths were in the ratio 3:4:5. Then three men, each holding a knot, stretched the rope tight, thus forming a triangular figure.

—*Claire Fisher Adler: **Modern Geometry**, 1958*

3. I imagine a triangle, although perhaps such a figure does not exist and never has existed anywhere in the world outside my thought. Nevertheless this figure has a certain nature, or form, or determinate essence which is immutable or eternal, which I have not invented and which in no way depends on my mind. This is evident from the fact that I can demonstrate various properties of this triangle.... Whether I desire to or not, I recognize very clearly and convincingly that these properties are in the triangle although I have never thought about them before, and even if this is the first time I have imagined a triangle. Nevertheless no one can say that I have invented or imagined them.

—*Charles Hermite: Quoted in E.T. Bell: **Men of Mathematics**, 1937*

4. There is a very good saying that if triangles invented a god, they would make him three-sided.

—*Charles-Louis de Secondat Montesquieu: Quoted in John Barrow: **Pi in the Sky**, 1992*

5. The proposition [5 of Book I of Euclid] represented substantially the limit of instruction in many courses in the Middle Ages. It formed a bridge across which fools could not hope to pass, and was therefore known as the pons asinorum, or bridge of fools. It has also been suggested that the figure given by Euclid resembles the simplest form of a truss bridge, one that even a fool could make. The name seems to be medieval.

—*David Eugene Smith: **History of Mathematics**, 4th ed., 1906*

6. ...a few days ago a German geometrician proposed to send a scientific expedition to the steppes of Siberia. There, on those vast plains; they were to describe enormous geometric forms, drawn in characters of reflecting luminosity, among which was the proposition regarding "the square of the hypotenuse" commonly called the "Ass's Bridge" by the French. "Every intelligent being," said the geometrician, "must understand the scientific meaning of the figure. The Selenites [moon inhabitants], do they exist, will respond by a similar figure; and, a communication being at once established, it will be easy to form an alphabet which shall enable us to converse with the inhabitants of the moon.

—*Jules Verne: **From the Earth to the Moon***

32.10 Polygons and Polyhedrons

1. A little thought shows that, while an infinite number of polygons may be drawn on a plane surface, it is not possible to construct more than five regular polyhedra in three-dimensional space. The surface of a regular polyhedron is bounded by congruent regular polygons. The simplest polygons that can form the surface are the equilateral triangle, the square, and the pentagon.

—*H.E. Huntley: **The Divine Proportion**, 1970*

2. Oh, but it's like this, look you. I've no grounds to be dissatisfied with my polyhedra; they breed every six weeks, they're worse than rabbits. And its also quite true to say that the regular polyhedra are the most faithful and most devoted to their master, except that this morning the icosahedron was a little fractious, so that I was compelled, look you, to give it a smack on each of its twenty faces, and that's the kind of language they understand. And my thesis, look you, on the habits of polyhedra—it's getting along nicely, thank you, only another twenty-five volumes.

—*Alfred Jarry: "Ubu Cuckolded" in **Achras**, 1896, published 1944*

3. The landlady of a boarding house is a parallelogram—that is, an oblong angular figure, which cannot be described, but which is equal to anything.

—*Stephen B. Leacock: "Boarding House Geometry," **Literary Lapses**, 1910*

4. In the "commentatio" (note presented to the Russian Academy) in which his theorem on polyhedra [that the number of faces, edges and vertices satisfy the formula $V + F = E + 2$]) was first published, Euler gives no proof. In place of a proof, he offers an inductive argument: he writes the relation in a variety of special cases. There is little doubt that he also discovered the theorem, as many of his other results, inductively.

—*George Polya: in P. Hilton & J. Pederson: "The Euler Characteristic and Polya's Dream"; **American Mathematical Monthly**, February, 1996*

32.11 Circles

1. Continuous as an endless circle.
—Anonymous

2. If inside a circle a line
Hits the center and goes spine to spine
And the line's length is "d"
The circumference will be
d times 3.14159.
—Anonymous

3. Do not disturb my circles.
*—Archimedes: 212, B.C.: **Valerius Maximus** [Said to a Roman soldier who during the siege of Syracuse burst into Archimedes' study to find him figuring some circles, and being unable to obtain a satisfactory reply to his questions, put him to death.]*

4. It is the physician's business to know that circular wounds heal more slowly, the geometer's to know the reason why.
*—Aristotle: **Posterior Analytics**; c. 4th cent. B.C.*

5. Everything tries to be round.
*—Black Elk: in Monte Zerger: "A Quote a Day Educates"; **The Mathematical Intelligencer**, Vol. 20, 2; Spring, 1998*

6. Circles and right lines limit and close all bodies, and the mortal right-lined circle must conclude and shut up.
*—Sir Thomas Browne: **Hydriotaphia**, 1650s [The mortal red-lined circle is the character of death.]*

7. A small circle is quite as infinite as a large circle.
*—G.K. Chesterton: **Orthodoxy**, 1909*

8. The circle is one of the noblest representations of Diety, in his noble works of human nature. It bounds, determines, governs, and dictates space, bounds latitude and longitude, refers to the sun, moon and all planets, in direction, brings to the mind thoughts of eternity, and concentrates the mind to imagine for itself the distance and space it comprehends. It rectifies all boundaries; is the key to information of the knowledge of God.
*—John Davis: **The Measure of the Circle**, 1854*

9. A circle may be small, yet it may be as mathematically beautiful and perfect as a large one.
*—Isaac D'Israeli: **Miscellanies**, 1834*

10. Then, soul, to thy first pitch up again;
Know that all lines which circles do contain,
For once they the centre touch, do touch
Twice the circumference; and be thou such;
Double on heaven thy thoughts on earth employed.
—John Donne: "Of the Progress of the Soul. The Second Anniversary," 1601

11. The eye is the first circle; the horizon which it forms is the second; and throughout nature this primary figure is repeated without end. It is the highest emblem in the cipher of the world.
*—Ralph Waldo Emerson: **Essays: First Series**, "Circles" 1841*

12. Every man is the center of a circle, whose fatal circumference he cannot pass.
—John James Ingalls: Eulogy on Benjamin Hill given in the U.S. Senate; January 23, 1882

13. Take a perfect circle, caress it and you'll have a vicious circle.
*—Eugene Ionesco: **The Bald Soprano**, 1950*

14. He drew a circle that shut me out—
Heretic, rebel, a thing to flout.
But Love and I had the wit to win:
We drew a circle that took him in!
—Edwin Markham: "Outwitted," 1915

15. He took the golden compasses, prepared
In God's eternal store, to circumscribe
This universe, and all created things:
One foot he centered, and the other turned
Round through the vast profundity obscure,
And said, "Thus far extended, thus far thy bounds
This be thy circumference, O world."
*—John Milton: **Paradise Lost**, 1967*

16. A circle is a happy thing to be—
Think how the joyful perpendicular
Erected at the kiss of tangency
Must meet my central point, my avatar.
And lovely as I am, yet only 3
Points are needed to determine me.
*—Christopher Morley: "The Circle" Quoted in **Fantasia Mathematica**, Clifton Fadiman, ed., 1958*

17. And on the smooth expanse of crystal lakes,
The sinking stone at first a circle makes;
The trembling surface by the motion stirr'd,
Spread in a second circle, then a third;
Wide, and more wide, the floating rings advance,
Fill all the wat'ry plain, and to the margin dance.
*—Alexander Pope: "Temple of Fame"; **The Poetry of Alexander Pope**, J. Butt, ed., 1940–69*

18. The universe was made on purpose, the circle said. In whatever galaxy you happen to find yourself, you take the circumference of a circle, divide it by its diameter, measure closely enough, and uncover a miracle, drawn kilometers downstream of the decimal point.... As long as you live in this universe, and have a modest talent for mathematics, sooner or later you'll find it.

*—Carl Sagan: **Contact**, 1985*

19. Four circles to the kissing come,
The smaller are the benter.
The bend is just the inverse of
The distance from the center.
Though their intrigue left Euclid dumb
There's now no need for rule of thumb,
Since zero bend's a dead straight line
And concave bends have minus sign,
The sum of squares of all four bends
Is half the square of their sum.

*—Frederick Soddy: "The Problem of Apollonius," **Nature**, 137, 1936*

32.12 The Other Conic Sections

1. They are worthy of acceptance for the sake of the demonstrations themselves, in the same way as we accept many other things in mathematics for this and no other reason.

*—Apollonius: **Conics**; c. 260–190 B.C., Quoted in Stuart Hollingdale: **Makers of Mathematics**, 1989 [It is Apollonius reply when questioned as to the practical value of his study of the Conic sections.]*

2. A circle no doubt has a certain appealing simplicity at the first glance, but one look at a healthy ellipse should have convinced even the most mystical of astronomers that the perfect simplicity of the circle is akin to the vacant smile of complete idiocy. Compared to what an ellipse can tell us, a circle has nothing to say.

*—E. T. Bell: **The Handmaiden of the Sciences**, 1937*

3. What mathematician has never pondered over an hyperbola, mangling the unfortunate curve with lines of intersection here and there, in his efforts to prove some property that perhaps after all is mere calumny, who has not fancied at last that the ill-used locus was spreading out its asymptotes as a silent rebuke, or winking one focus at him with contemptuous pity?

*—Lewis Carroll: "The Dynamics of a Parti-cle"; **The Compete Works of Lewis Carroll**, 1936*

4. "What," [Edmund] Halley asked Newton, "would be the curve described by the planets on the supposition that gravity diminished as the square of the distance?" Newton answered without hesitation: "An ellipse." How did he know that? "Why," replied Newton, "I have calculated it." These four words informed Halley that Newton had worked out one of the most fundamental laws of the universe—the law of gravity.

*—J. Bernard Cohen: "Isaac Newton" **Scientific American**, December, 1955*

5. And first, the fair PARABOLA behold,
Her timid arms, with virgin blush, unfold!
Though, on one focus fixed, her eyes betray
A heart that glows with love's resistless sway.

*—C. Frere & B. Canning: in Charles Edmonds: **Poetry of the Anti-Jacobian**, 1890*

6. ...these [the conics] are not spring flowers, at the mercy of the changing seasons, but rather never-fading amaranths, gathered from the most beautiful flower-beds of geometry.

*—Blaise Pascal: Letter to M. De Sluse: Quoted in Francois Le Lionnais: "Beauty in Mathematics" in **Great Currents of Mathematics**, F. Le Lionnais, ed., 1971*

7. Along a parabola life like a rocket flies,
Mainly in darkness, now and then on a rainbow.

—Andrei Voznesenski: "Parabolic Ballad," 1960, W.H. Auden, tr.

8. If the Greeks had not cultivated Conic Sections, Kepler could not have superseded Ptolemy; if the Greeks had cultivated Dynamics, Kepler might have anticipated Newton.

*—William Whewell: **History of the Inductive Sciences**, 1980*

9. An ellipse is fine for as far as it goes,
But modesty, away!
If I'm going to see
Beauty without her clothes Give me hyperbolas any old day.

*—Roger Zelazny: in William L. Burke: **Spacetime, Geometry, Cosmology**, 1980*

32.13 Spheres

1. Now it is quite clear to me that there are no solid spheres in the heavens, and those that have been devised by the authors to save the appearances, exist only in the imagination, for the purpose of permitting the mind to conceive the motion which the heavenly bodies trace in their courses.

*—Tycho Brahe: c. 1597; in Isaac Asimov: **Book of Science and Nature Quotations**, 1988*

2. Nature centers into balls,
And her proud ephemerals,
Fast to surface and outside
Scan the profile of the sphere.

*—Ralph Waldo Emerson: **Essays: First Series**, "Circles" 1841*

3. ...the axiom of there being only one shortest line between two points would not hold without a certain exception for the dwellers on a sphere.

*—Herman von Helmholtz: **The Axioms of Geometry**, 1870*

4. The Pythagoreans were the first to discover that the earth is a sphere. This they did by observing the shadow cast by the earth on the moon. Although this fact became an accepted commonplace to later Greek mathematicians, it was not until the time of the great navigations of the fifteenth and sixteenth centuries that the average man was convinced that the earth was not flat.

—Alfred Hooper: ***Makers of Mathematics****, 1948*

5. Not being able to go to the moon to look at the earth, men [of early civilizations] could not see its true shape. How, then, did Greek astronomers come to the conclusion that the earth was round? By observing that the North Star was higher in the sky in Greece than in Egypt. Thus it is evident that we can recognize that a sphere is round either by observing it from a distance or, if we stand on it, by observing objects far away.

—P. Le Corbeiller: "The Curvature of Space"; ***Scientific American****, November, 1954*

6. Also the earth is not spherical, as some have said, although it tends towards sphericity, for the shape of the universe is limited in its parts as well as its movement.... The movement which is more perfect than others is, therefore, circular, and the corporeal form which is the most perfect is the sphere.

—Nicholas of Cusa:: ***Die Kunst der Vermutung****, a selection from his works, 1957*

7. The perfection of the heavenly spheres does not depend upon the order of their relative position as to whether one is higher than another.

—Nicole Oresme: "The Latitude of Forms"; in ***Nicole Oresme and the Medieval Geometry****, Marshall Cladgett, tr., 1968*

8. The most beautiful solid is the sphere, and the most beautiful plane figure—the circle.

—Pythagoras: Quoted in V.M. Tikhomirov: ***Stories About Maxima and Minima****; Abe Schenitzer, tr., 1990*

32.14 Solid Geometry

1. Considerable obstacles generally present themselves to the beginner, in studying the elements of Solid Geometry, from the practice which has hitherto prevailed in this country, of never submitting to the eye of the student, the figure on whose properties he is reasoning, but of drawing perspective representations of them upon a plane.... I hope that I shall never be obliged to have recourse to a perspective drawing of any figure whose parts are not in the same plane.

—Augustus De Morgan: An Introductory Lecture delivered at the opening of the mathematical classes at the University of London, November 5, 1828

2. [This book, Euclid's Elements] will treat of the so-called Platonic solids, incorrectly named, because three of them, the tetrahedron, cube, and dodecahedron are due to the Pythagoreans, while the octrahedron and icosahedron are due to Theaeteus.

—Euclid: ***Elements****, ca. 300 B.C.*

3. Each of us carries in his mind a phantom cube, by which to estimate the orthodoxy of whatever we encounter in the world of space.

—Hugh Kenner: ***Bucky****, 1973*

4. The orbit of the Earth is a circle: round the sphere to which this circle belongs, describes a dodecahedron; the sphere including this will give the orbit of Mars. Round Mars describe a tetrahedron; the circle including this will be the orbit of Jupiter. Describe a cube round Jupiter's orbit; the circle including this will be the orbit of Saturn. Now inscribe in the Earth's orbit an icosahedron; the circle inscribed in it will be the orbit of Venus. Inscribe an octrahedron in the orbit of Venus; the circle inscribed in it will be Mercury's orbit. This is the reason of the number of the planets.

—Johannes Kepler: ***Mysterium cosmographicum****, 1596*

5. So their [the five Platonic Solids] combination with themselves and with each other give rise to endless complexities, which anyone who is to give a likely account of reality must survey.

—Plato: ***The Timaeus****, c. 350 B.C.*

33
Geometry II

33.1 Pythagorean Theorem

1. To this day, the theorem of Pythagoras remains the most important single theorem in the whole of mathematics. That seems a bold and extraordinary thing to say, yet it is not extravagant; because what Pythagoras established is a fundamental characterization of the space in which we move, and it is the first time that it is translated into numbers. And the exact fit of the numbers describes the exact laws that bind the universe. In fact, the numbers that compose right-angled triangles have been proposed as messages which we might send out to planets in other star systems as a test for the existence of rational life there.

—Jacob Bronowski: "The Music of the Spheres" ***The Ascent of Man****, 1973*

2. But neither thirty years, nor thirty centuries, affect the clearness, of the charm, of Geometrical truths. Such a theorem as "the square of the hypotenuse of a right-angled triangle is equal to the sum of the squares of the sides" is as dazzlingly beautiful now as it was in the day when Pythagoras first discovered it, and celebrated is advent, it is said, by sacrificing a hecatomb of oxen—a method of doing honor to Science that has always seemed to me slightly exaggerated and uncalled for.

—Charles L. Dodgson (Lewis Carroll): ***A New Theory of Parallels****, 1895 [It is unlikely that Pythagoras sacrificed a hecatomb of oxen in honor of the discovery of the theorem that bears his name as the Pythagoreans were vegetarians and preached respect for all life.]*

3. One of the most fascinating Babylonian mathematical artifacts is the tablet now known as Plimpton 322, kept at the University of Columbia, New York. It bears four columns and fifteen rows of numbers, and appears to be incomplete; it may well be part of a larger tablet which became broken. It is now generally accepted that this tablet presents derivations of fractional Pythagorean triples. Such a sophisticated procedure must mean that the Babylonians understood the Pythagorean theorem as early as 1800–1650 B.C., more than a thousand years before Pythagoras.

—Richard Mankiewicz: ***The Story of Mathematics****, 2000*

33.2 Flatland

1. I call our world Flatland, not because we call it so, but to make its nature clearer to you, my happy readers, who are privileged to live in Space.... Imagine a vast sheet of paper on which straight Lines, Triangles, Squares, Pentagons, Hexagons, and other figures, instead of remaining fixed in their places, move freely about, on or in the surface, but without the power of rising above or sinking below it, very much like shadows—and you will then have a pretty correct notion of our country and countrymen.

—Edwin A. Abbott: ***Flatland****, 1884*

2. [In Flatland] Abbott challenged his readers to imagine trying to understand the nature of phenomena in higher dimensions if all they could see directly were lower-dimensional slices. That is precisely the situation that radiologists face today as they analyze the slices produced by CAT scans or magnetic resonance imaging.

—Thomas Banchoff" "Introduction"; Edwin A. Abbott: ***Flatland****, 1991*

3. Flatland, first published in 1884, is the story of a square who takes a trip into higher dimensions.... The author of Flatland was a Victorian schoolmaster names Edwin Abbott Abbott. Given the curious fact that his middle and last names were identical, it seems possible that Abbott might have been nicknamed Abbott Squared or A Squared. Thus, it may be that Abbott felt a considerable degree of identification with A Square, the hero of Flatland

—Rudy Rucker: ***The Fourth Dimension****, 1984*

33.3 Dimensions and Dimension Theory

1. Yet I exist in the hope that these memoirs ... may find their ways to the minds of humanity in Some Dimension, and may stir up a race of rebels who shall refuse to be confined to limited Dimensionality.

*—Edwin A. Abbott; **Flatland**, 1884*

2. People ask me, "Can you show us this fourth dimension?" And I reply, "Can you show me the first, second, and third?"

—Anonymous

3. The slicing technique from Flatland stil remains one of the most powerful tools for dealing with aggregates in higher dimensions.

*—Thomas Banchoff" "Introduction"; Edwin A. Abbott: **Flatland**, 1991*

4. All of us are slaves to the prejudices of our own dimension.

*—Thomas Banchoff" "Introduction"; Edwin A. Abbott: **Flatland**, 1991*

5. Since I found that one could make a case shadow from a three-dimensional thing, any object whatsoever—just as the projecting of the sun on the earth makes two dimensions—I thought that by simple intellectual analogy, the fourth dimension could project an object of three dimensions, or, to put it another way, any three-dimensional object, which we see dispassionately, is a projection of something four-dimensional, something we are not familiar with.

*—Marcel Duchamp: Quoted in Linda Dalrymple Henderson: **The Fourth Dimension and non-Euclidean Geometry in Modern Art***

6. ...however successful the theory of a four-dimensional world may be, it is difficult to ignore a voice inside us which whispers: "At the back of your mind, you know a fourth dimension is all nonsense."

*—Sir Arthur Eddington: **Space, Time and Gravitation**, 1920*

7. The nonmathematician is seized by a mysterious shuddering when he hears of "four-dimensional" things, by a feeling not unlike that awakened by thoughts of the occult. And yet there is no more commonplace statement than that the world in which we live is a four-dimensional space-time continuum.

*—Albert Einstein: "Relativity" in **Albert Einstein: Philosopher-Scientist**, Paul A. Schilpp, ed. 1949*

8. I take the plane upon which my shadow-man is, and move it through three dimensions. Thus the shadow-man perceives this third dimension. The man himself may be changed, and. at the end of the trip be pale and rumpled, when he had started the trip rosy and flat.

—Gustave Theodor Fechner: "Why Space Has Four Dimensions," 1846

9. Our cosmos—the world we see, hear, feel—is the three-dimensional "surface" of a vast, four-dimensional sea.... What lies outside the sea's surface? The wholly other world of God! No longer is theology embarrassed by the contradiction between God's immanence and transcendence. Hyperspace touches every point of three-space. God is closer to us that our breathing. He can see every portion of our world, touch every particle without moving a finger through our space. Yet the Kingdom of God is completely "outside" of three-space, in a direction in which we cannot even point.

—Martin Gardner: "The Church of the Fourth Dimension," 1962

10. He had greatly enjoyed this dinner, "thanks to the delectable company of the young lady on my right and the young lady on my left. Now in a three-dimensional world one can have only two ladies sitting next to one. Heaven, I believe, might be conceived to be, a place in N-dimensional space, where one could therefore expect dinner to enjoy the company of N—1 young ladies.

*—John Burdon Sanderson Haldane: After-dinner speech in E. Ashby, **Nature**, April 28, 1977*

11. Time is said to have only one dimension, and space to have three dimensions.... The mathematical quaternion partakes of both of these elements; in technical language it may be said to be "time plus space," or "space plus time": and in this sense it has, or at least involves a reference to, four dimensions....

*—William Rowan Hamilton: in Robert Percival Graves: **Life of Sir William Rowan Hamilton**, 1882–89*

12. ...the fourth dimension was primarily a symbol of liberation for artists.... Specifically, belief in a fourth dimension encouraged artists to depart from visual reality and to reject completely the one-point perspective system that for centuries had portrayed the world as three-dimensional.

*—Linda Dalrymple Henderson: **The Fourth Dimension and Non-Euclidean Geometry in Modern Art**, 1983*

13. The greatest advantage to be derived from the study of geometry of more than three dimensions is a real understanding of the great science of geometry. Our plane and solid geometries are but the beginning of this science. The four-dimensional geometry is far more extensive than the three-dimensional, and all the higher geometries are more extensive than the lower.

—*Henry Parker Manning:* ***Geometry of Four Dimensions,*** *1960*

14. Without dimension, where length,
breath, and height,
And time and place are lost; where eldest
night
And chaos, ancestors of nature, hold
Eternal anarchy.

—*John Milton:* ***Paradise Lost,*** *1663*

15. And when we shall see or feel ourselves in the world of four dimensions we shall see that the world of three dimensions does not really exist and has never existed; that it was the creation of our own fantasy, a phantom host, and optical illusion, a delusion—anything one pleases excepting only reality.

—*P.D. Ouspensky:* ***Tertium Organum,*** *1912*

16. Dimension is not easy to understand. At the turn of the century it was one of the major problems in mathematics to determine what dimension means and which properties it has. And since then the situation has become somewhat worse because mathematicians have come up with some ten different notions of dimension.... They are all related. Some of them, however, make sense in certain situations, but not at all in others, where alternate definitions are more helpful. Sometimes they all make sense and are the same. Sometimes several make sense but do not agree. The details can be confusing even to a research mathematician.

—*Heinz-Otto Peitgen, Hartmut Jurgens & Dietmar Sa:* ***Fractals in the Classroom,*** *1992*

17. Let us assume that the three dimensions of space are visualized in the customary fashion, and let us substitute a color for the fourth dimension. Every physical object is liable to changes in color as well as in position. An object might, for example, be capable of going through all shades of red through violet to blue. A physical interaction between any two bodies is possible only if they are close to each other in space as well as in color. Bodies of different colors would penetrate each other without interference.

—*Hans Reichenbach:* ***The Philosophy of Space and Time,*** *1927*

18. We conclude, therefore, that a higher world than ours is not only conceivably possible, but probable; secondly, that such a world may be considered as a world of four dimensions; and thirdly, that the spiritual world agrees largely in its mysterious laws, in its language which is foolishness to us, in its miraculous appearances and interpositions, in its high and lofty claims of omniscience, omnividence, etc., and in other particulars, with what by analogy would be the laws, languages, and claims of a fourth dimension....

—*A.T. Schofield:* ***Another World,*** *1888*

19. Whereas Nature does not admit of more than three dimensions ... it may justly seem very improper to talk of a solid ... drawn into a fourth, fifth, sixth, or further dimension.

—*John Wallis:* ***Algebra,*** *1685*

20. The great man was used to say, as we can conceive beings (like infinitely attenuated bookworms in an infinitely thin sheet of paper) which possess only the notion of space of two dimensions, so may we imagine beings capable of realizing space of four or greater number of dimensions.

—*Sartorius von Walterhausen:* ***Biography of Carl Friedrich Gauss,*** *1860*

21. Things, objects, mutely cry to us, "Touch us, taste us, feel us, see us, understand us, learn us, make us more than we are through your association, through your tactile and spiritual intimacy." The use then that we make of matter is gauged by our power, our quality or our energy, to wield it, to adopt it, to share it, to urge in on into the fourth dimension.

—*Max Weber: in Linda Dalrymple Henderson:* ***The Fourth Dimension and non-Euclidean Geometry in Modern Art,*** *1998*

22. There are really four dimensions, three of which we call the three planes of Space, and a fourth, Time. There is, however, a tendency to draw an unreal distinction between the former three dimensions and the latter, because it happens that out consciousness moves intermittently in one direction along the latter from the beginning to the end of our lives.

—*H.G. Wells: "The Time Machine," 1895; reissue edition, 1967*

33.4 Analytic or Analytical Geometry

1. The opinion is currently held among mathematicians that analytic geometry sprang full-armed from the head of Descartes as did Athene from that of Zeus.... There is much to be said in favor of this thesis, but ... another opinion is certainly possible. The fact that in inquiring into the origin of analytic geometry we run into a difficulty that lies at the bottom of a good proportion of our disputes in this Vale of Tears. What do we mean by the words "analytic geometry"? Till that is settled, it is futile to inquire as to who discovered it.

—*J.L. Coolidge:* ***A History of Geometrical Methods,*** *1940*

2. [I have developed] an entirely new science which will allow of a general solution of all problems that can be proposed in any and every kind of quantity, continuous or discontinuous, each in accordance with its nature ... so that almost nothing will remain to be discovered in geometry.

—Rene Descartes: Letter to Isaac Beeckman; March 26, 1619; ***Correspondence: Rene Descartes;*** *C. Adam & G. Milhaud, eds., 1935–56*

3. The analytical equations, unknown to the ancient geometers, which Descartes was the first to introduce into the study of curves and surfaces, are not restricted to the properties of figures, and to those properties which are the object of rational mechanics; they extend to all general phenomena. There cannot be a language more universal and more simple, more free from errors and from obscurities, that is to say more worthy to express the invariable relations of natural things.

—Jean-Baptiste-Joseph Fourier: ***Analytical Theory of Heat;*** *"Preliminary Discourse," Alexander Freeman, tr., 1878*

4. The value of analytic geometry is that it reveals a connection between two branches of mathematics—algebra and geometry—which had been thought to be entirely separate.

—Paul Halmos: "Innovation in Mathematics"; ***Scientific American,*** *September, 1958*

5. If a mathematician of the past, an Archimedes or even a Descartes, could view the field of geometry in its present condition, the first feature to impress him would be its lack of concreteness. There are whole classes of geometric theories which proceed not only without models and diagrams, but without the slightest (apparent) use of spatial intuition. In the main this is due, to the power of the analytic instruments of investigations as compared with the purely geometric.

—Edward Kasner: "The Present Problems in Geometry"; ***Bulletin American Mathematical Society,*** *1905*

6. As long as algebra and geometry proceeded along separate paths, their advance was slow and their applications were limited. But when these sciences joined company, they drew from each other fresh vitality and thenceforward marched on at a rapid pace towards perfection.

—Joseph-Louis Lagrange: ***Lecons Elementaries sur les Mathematiques, Lecon cinquieme,*** *1767*

7. There are relationships even more monumental, such as the bridging the gap between algebra and geometry: this striking dualism, which associates a figure with every equation and vice versa, each of them holding a mirror wherein the other is reflected, is one of the most distinctive in all of mathematics; truth, utility and beauty, joined in intimate marriage, give birth to the most glorious and vital perfection.

—Francois Le Lionnais: "Beauty in Mathematics" in ***Great Currents of Mathematics,*** *F. Le Lionnais, ed., 1971*

8. Neither Descartes, nor Fermat, nor Roberval, nor Mersenne, nor Pascal, nor any one of those who would have had as a matter of course a judgement to express remarks by a single word the important fact that Descartes's analytic geometry was already clearly defined in its principles and its applications in some writings of Fermat which predate the Geometry.

—G. Milhaud: ***Descartes savant,*** *1921*

9. When school children study analytic geometry, they should be made aware that this seemingly trivial and esoteric subject exists to us only because of the heroic efforts of a succession of brilliant minds, culminating in the work of Descartes. Its depth, originality, and profundity are lost on students. It has been carefully polished and refined so exquisitely, presented so elegantly and simply, that students myopically receive it as a trifle.

—J.D. Philips: "Mathematics as an Aesthetic Discipline"; ***The Humanistic Mathematics Network Journal,*** *12; October, 1995*

10. If I was smitten by algebra, I was dazzled by the application of algebra to geometry.... The idea, the possibility of expressing a line, a curve, in algebraic terms, by an equation, seemed to me as beautiful as the Iliad. When I saw this equation function and solve itself, so to speak, in my hands, and burst into an infinity of truths, all equally indisputable, equally eternal, equally resplendent, I believed I had in my possession the talisman which would open the door of every mystery.

—Edgar Quintet: Quoted in Francois Le Lionnais: "Beauty in Mathematics" in ***Great Currents of Mathematics,*** *F. Le Lionnais, ed., 1971*

11. In analytical geometry the subject-matter is geometry while the language is algebraic. For progress and pleasure it is of primary importance that the language be properly adjusted to the subject; elasticity must be preserved and unnecessary restrictions cast aside.

—Charlotte Angus Scott: ***Projective Methods in Plane Analytical Geometry,*** *1894*

33.5 Algebraic Geometry

1. Modern algebraic geometry has deservedly been considered for a long time as an exceedingly complex part of mathematics, drawing practically on every other part to build up its concepts and methods and increasingly becoming an indispensable tool in many seemingly remote theories. It shares with number theory the distinction of having one of the longest and most intricate histories among all branches of our science, of having attracted the efforts of the best mathematicians in each generation, and of still being one of the most active areas of research.

*—Jean Dieudonne: "The Historical Development of Algebraic Geometry"; **American Mathematical Monthly**, vol. 79; October, 1972*

2. A systematic mathematics does not exist, but I believe it could be created—based on algebraic geometry, which is usually thought of as the most abstract and "useless" part of mathematics.

*—R. Hermann: "A View of Applied Mathematics" **The Mathematical Intelligencer**, vol. 1, 1978*

3. Algebra introduced the concepts of "imaginary point, imaginary line" into geometry. The word imaginary is here, as always, to be translated as unconceived rather than inconceivable. Geometry has not dismissed these ideas, but reasons with them, using them as an intermediary tool for propositions concerning conceived geometric entities. This reasoning is algebraic. One has searched for a representation of the imaginary in geometry, that is, one has searched for higher viewpoints and more comprehensive definitions under which the imaginary entities would also exist.

—Sophus Lie: Handwritten notes reproduced in the "Anmerkungen zum ersten Bande," 18602

33.6 Differential Geometry

1. Riemann in 1854 produced his classic dissertation on the hypothesis which lie at the foundations of geometry, which in its turn, began the second great period of differential geometry, that which is today of use in mathematical physics, particularly in the theory of general relativity.

*—Eric Temple Bell: **Men of Mathematics**, 1937*

2. Differential geometry is probably as old as any mathematical discipline and certainly was well launched after Newton and Leibniz had laid the foundations of calculus. Many results concerning surfaces in 3-space were obtained by Gauss in the first half of the nineteenth century, and in 1854 Riemann laid the foundations for a more abstract approach.

*—Noel J. Hicks: **Notes on Differential Geometry**, 1965*

3. Another branch of mathematics which was virtually founded by Euler is differential geometry: the study of those properties of curves and surfaces that vary from point to point (e.g. over the surface of an egg) and do need the techniques of the calculus for their investigation.

*—Stuart Hollingdale: **Makers of Mathematics**, 1989*

33.7 Distance—Metric Geometry

1. Euclidean geometry is based upon the fundamental notion of distance, or length; distance is never defined, but is regarded as an intuitive concept which underlies every geometrical theorem. Euclidean geometry is metrical, for it assumes that every segment or angle can be measured and expressed in terms of a standard distance or standard angle.

*—T. Ewan Faulkner: **Projective Geometry**, 1949*

2. Could a spectator exist unsustained by the earth, or any solid support, he would see around him at one view the whole contents of space—the visible constituents of the universe: and in the absence of any means of judging their distances from him, would refer them, in the directions in which they were seen from his station, to the concave surface of an imaginary sphere, having his eye for a center, and its surface at some vast indeterminate distance.

*—John Herschel: **A Preliminary Discourse on the Study of Natural Philosophy**, 1830*

3. Distances are only the relation of space to time and vary with that relation.

*—Marcel Proust: **Cities of the Plain**, 1896*

33.8 Parallel Lines and the Parallel Postulate

1. It is now my definite plan to publish a work on parallels as soon as I can complete and arrange the material and an opportunity presents itself; ... I have discovered such wonderful things that I was amazed and it would be an everlasting piece of bad fortune if they were lost. When you see, my dear Father, see them, you will understand; at present I can say nothing except this: that out of nothing I have created a strange new universe. All that I have sent you previously is like a house of cards in comparison with a tower. I am no less convinced that these discoveries will bring me honor, that I would be if they were completed.

*—Johann (Janos) Bolyai: In a letter to his father Wolfgang Bolyai, November 3, 1823: quoted in Paul Stackel: **Wolfgang and Johann Bolyai, Geomtrische Untersuchungen**, 1913*

2. It is inconceivable that this inevitable darkness, this eternal eclipse, this blot on geometry, was allowed—this eternal cloud on virgin truth.

*—Wolfgang Bolyai: Quoted in J. Kopency: **Euclid's***

Fifth Postulate, *1933 [The elder Bolyai expresses frustration with his fruitless efforts and those of other mathematicians over a period of two thousand years who unsuccessfully tried to prove Euclid's fifth postulate.]*

3. During the long period from the time of Euclid to the nineteenth century, many professional and amateur mathematicians ... tried to deduce the disquieting Fifth Postulate from the others by the indirect method" They hoped that its denial would lead to a contradiction. The most prominent of these pioneers was the Jesuit Gerolamo Saccheri (Italian, 1667–1773), who discovered, for the sole purpose of demolishing them, many theorems of what we now call hyperbolic geometry.

—H.S.M. Coxeter: "Non-Euclidean Geometry" ***The Mathematical Sciences: A Collection of Essays,*** *Edited by the National Research Council's Committee on Support of Research in the Mathematical Sciences, 1969*

4. [The impossibility of proving Euclid's parallel postulate is] the scandal of geometry and the despair of geometers.

—Jean-le-Rond D'Alembert; Quoted in ***Great Currents of Mathematics,*** *F. Le Lionnais, ed., 1971*

5. Lagrange, in one of the later years of his life, imagined that he had overcome the difficulty (of the parallel axiom). He went so far as to write a paper which he took with him to the Institute, and began to read it. But in the first paragraph something struck him which he had not observed; he muttered: "I must think about it again.," and put the paper in his pocket.

—Augustus De Morgan: ***Budget of Paradoxes,*** *1878*

6. Detection is, or ought to be, an exact science and should be treated in the same cold and unemotional manner. You have attempted to tinge it with romanticism, which produces much the same effect as if you worked a love story or an elopement into the fifth proposition of Euclid.

—Sir Arthur Conan Doyle: ***The Sign of the Four,*** *1890*

7. "Lines that are parallel
meet at infinity!"
Euclid repeatedly,
heatedly,
urged
Until he died.
and so reached that vicinity:
in it he
found that the damned things
diverged.

—Piet Hein: "Parallelism"; in ***Imaginary Numbers,*** *William Frucht, ed., 1999*

8. One of Euclid's postulates—his postulate 5—has the fortune to be an epoch-making statement—perhaps the most famous single utterance in the history of science.

—Cassius J. Keyser: ***Mathematical Philosophy,***

9. Proofs of the Euclidean [parallel] postulate can be developed to such an extent that apparently a mere trifle remains. But a careful analysis shows that in this seeming trifle lies the crux of the matter; usually it contains either the proposition that is being proved or a postulate equivalent to it.

—Johann H. Lambert: Quoted in Carl B. Boyer: ***A History of Mathematics,*** *1968*

10. As lines, so loves oblique, may well
Themselves in every angle greet
But ours, so truly parallel,
Though infinite, can never meet.

—Andrew Marvell: From ***The Definition of Love***

11. Anomalies are phenomena that do not follow the expectations from the accepted disciplinary matrix. A prominent example in mathematics is Euclid's fifth postulate, which eventually led to new geometries and to the overthrow of the "metaphysics" of geometry.

—Herbert Mehrtens: "T.S. Kuhn's theories and mathematics: a discussion paper on the 'new historiography' of mathematics"; ***Historia Mathematica,*** *3, 1976*

12. It appears that the first mathematician to realize that the parallel axiom could be denied and yet a perfectly self-consistent geometry constructed was Gauss. But Gauss quite realized how staggering, how shocking, a thing he had done, and was afraid to publish his researches. It was reserved for a Russian, Lobachevsky, and a Hungarian, Bolyai, to publish the first non-Euclidean geometry.

—John William Navin Sullivan: "Mathematics as an Art": ***Aspects of Science,*** *1925*

13. The problem [of Euclid's Parallel Axiom] is now at a par with the squaring of the circle and the trisection of an angle by means of ruler and compass. So far as the mathematical public is concerned, the famous problem of the parallel is settled for all time.

—John Wesley Young: ***Fundamental Concepts of Algebra and Geometry,*** *1911*

33.9 NON-EUCLIDEAN GEOMETRY

1. When we came to the theory of parallel lines, Eiges began with amazing pedagogical tact and skill to tell us about Lobachevskii's geometry. The very statement of the problem astonished me. Never before had anything aroused my interest and enthusiasm to that extent. Geometry became an enchanted kingdom for me, and I dreamed of that alone.

—Pavel Sergeevich Aleksandrov: "P.S. Aleksandrov"; ***Russian Mathematical Surveys,*** *31, 1976*

2. Gauss introduced the term "non–Euclidean geometry" to describe a type of geometry which is in effect that of Sacchieri's acute-angle hypothesis. The Russian mathematician Lobachevsky and the Hungarian Bolyai independently published accounts of the same type of geometry. Unlike Saccheri, who had regarded his acute-angle hypothesis as absurd, these mathematicians were consciously developing what they regarded as a new type of logically consistent geometry.

—Stephen F. Barker: "Non-Euclidean Geometry" in ***Philosophy of Mathematics****, 1964*

3. The most remarkable thing about non–Euclidean geometry is that it turned out to be an essential prerequisite for Einstein's general theory of relativity. Riemann created Riemannian geometry for the purely abstract purpose of unifying, clarifying and deepening the non–Euclidean geometry of Lobachevsky, Bolyai and Gauss. The geometry turned out to be the indispensable tool for Einstein's revolutionary reinterpretation of the gravitational force.

—Paul J. Cohen & Reuben Hersh: "Non-Cantorian Set Theory"; ***Scientific American****, December, 1967*

4. Hyperbolic geometry resulted from denial of Euclid's Fifth Postulate. Elliptic geometry results from denial of his Second Postulate. The Second Postulate says that a straight line can be extended indefinitely; this statement clearly means that a line is infinite and not closed. But in elliptic geometry every line is finite though unbounded; that is to say, it has a finite length and is closed like a circle. On the surface of a sphere (such as the geographical globe or the earth itself), the shortest distance between two points is an arc of a great circle.

—H.S.M. Coxeter: "Non-Euclidean Geometry" ***The Mathematical Sciences: A Collection of Essays****, Edited by the National Research Council's Committee on Support of Research in the Mathematical Sciences, 1969*

5. Nobody can serve two masters. One cannot serve truth and untruth at the same time. If Euclidean geometry is true, then Non-Euclidean geometry is false, and if Non-Euclidean geometry is true, then Euclidean geometry is false.

—Gottlob Frege: ***Begriffsschrift****, 1879 [Frege did not consider another possibility: neither is true and neither false.]*

6. If I begin with the statement that I dare not praise such a work, you will of course be startled for a moment: but I cannot do other-wise; to praise it would amount to praising myself; for the entire content of the work, the path which your son has taken, the results to which he is led, coincide almost exactly with my own meditations which have occupied my mind for from thirty to thirty-five years.

—Carl Friedrich Gauss: Letter to Wolfgang Bolyai; March 6, 1832: quoted in Paul Stackel: ***Wolfgang and Johann Bolyai, Geomtrische Untersuchungen****, 1913 [The letter is Gauss' response to his university classmate Wolfgang Bolyai who had sent Gauss an advance cop of the* ***Appendix*** *to his book* ***Tentamen****, which contained the work of Johann Bolyai, essentially creating a non–Euclidean geometry.]*

7. Non-Euclidean geometry makes Kant's philosophy of space untenable. But mathematicians avoid philosophical disputation by not mentioning the issue. To this day, texts on non–Euclidean geometry ignore its revolutionary philosophical implications.

—Reuben Hersh: ***What Is Mathematics, Really?****, 1997*

8. The most suggestive and notable achievement of the last century is the discovery of Non-Euclidean geometry.

—David Hilbert: Quoted by G.D. Fitch in P. Manning" ***The Fourth Dimension Simply Explained,****" 1910*

9. ...non–Euclidean geometry is proof that mathematics ... is man's own handiwork, subject only to the limitations imposed by the laws of thought.

—Edward Kasner & James R. Newman: ***Mathematics and the Imagination****, 1940*

10. In respect of soundness—inner consistency—self-compatiability—logical concordance among the parts of each—the three geometries are on exactly the same level, and the level is the highest that man has attained. The three doctrines are equally legitimate children of one spirit—the geometrizing spirit, which Plato though divine,—and they are immortal. Work inspired and approved by the muse of intellectual harmony cannot perish.

—Cassius J. Keyser: ***Mathematical Philosophy****, 1922 [Keyser speaks of Euclidean geometry, hyperbolic geometry and elliptic geometry.]*

11. The creation of non–Euclidean geometry was the most consequential and revolutionary step in mathematics since Greek times.

—Morris Kline: ***Mathematical Thought from Ancient to Modern Times****, 1972*

12. Should we ever live in an environment whose geometrical structure is noticeably different from Euclidean geometry, we would get adjusted to this environment and learn to see non–Euclidean triangles and laws in the same way that we now see Euclidean structures.... The philosophers had committed the mistake of regarding as a vision of ideas, or as laws of reason, what is actually the product of habit. It took more that two thousand years to uncover this fact; without the work of the mathematician and all its technicalities we would never have been able to break away from established habits and free our minds from alleged laws of reason.

—*Hans Reichenbach:* ***The Rise of Scientific Philosophy****, 1951*

13. The discovery of the non–Euclidean geometries also brought about a revolution in philosophic thought. It gave new significance to the whole question of the nature of truth. Before this the postulates of Euclid were viewed as absolute truths, not as mere assumptions no more "true" than other assumptions which might contradict them. All we can say about the truth of a geometry, considered as a mathematical system, is that if the postulates are true then the theorems are true.

—*Annita Tuller:* ***A Modern Introduction to Geometries****, 1967*

14. M. Princet has studied at length non–Euclidean geometry and the theorems of Riemann, ... M. Princet one day met M. Max Jacob and confided him one or two of his discoveries relating the the fourth dimension. M. Jacob informed the ingenious M. Picasso of it, and M. Picasso saw there a possibility of new ornamental schemes. M. Picasso explained his intentions to M. Appollinaire, who hastened to write them up in formularies and codify them. The thing spread and propagated ... Cubism, the child of M. Princet, was born.

—*Louis Vauxcelles: in Linda Dalrymple Henderson:* ***The Fourth Dimension and non–Euclidean Geometry in Modern Art****, 1998*

33.10 Projection

1. If Desargues, the daring pioneer of the seventeenth century, could have foreseen what his ingenious method of projection was to lead to, he might well have been astonished. He knew that he had done something good, but he probably had no conception of just how good it was to prove.

—*E. T. Bell:* ***Men of Mathematics****, 1937*

2. I mentally conceived of some movable projected on a horizontal plane all impediments being put aside. Now it is evident ... that the equable motion on this plane would be perpetual if the plane were of infinite extent; but if we assume it to be ended, and [situated] on high, the movable, ... driven to the end of the plane and going on further, adds on to its previous equable and indelible motion that downward tendency which it has from its own heaviness. Thus there emerges a certain motion, compounded from equable horizontal and from naturally downward [motion], which I call projection.

—*Galileo Galilei:* ***Two New Sciences****, 1638*

3. In 1883 Schlegel solved Picasso's problem (how to paint a cow showing all features at the same time) by his construction of Schlegel projections.

—*Rudolf Hoppe: "Abstract 6.2," Paul Niggli Symposium in* ***ETH****, August, 1984*

4. The use of projection and section raised a geometrical question, first voiced by the painters and alter taken up by mathematicians. What geometrical properties do an original figure and its section have in common that enable them to create the same impression on the eye?

—*Morris Kline: "Geometry";* ***Scientific American****, September, 1964*

33.11 Projective Geometry

1. On November 18, 1812, the exhausted remnant of the French army ... was overwhelmed at Krasnoi. Among those left for dead on the frozen battlefield was young Poncelot.... A searching party, discovering that he still breathed, took him before the Russian staff for questioning. As a prisoner of war ... at Saratoff on the Volga, ... he remembered that he had received a good mathematical education, and to soften the rigors of his exile he resolved to reproduce as much as he could of what he had learned. It was thus that he created projective geometry.

—*E. T. Bell:* ***Men of Mathematics****, 1937*

2. Projective geometry is all geometry.

—*Arthur Cayley: Quoted in Morris Kline: "Projective Geometry";* ***Mathematics in Western Culture****, 1953*

3. ...Projective Geometry: a boundless domain of countless fields where reals and imaginaries, finites and infinities, enter on equal terms, where the spirit delights in the artistic balance and symmetric interplay of a kind of conceptual and logical counterpoint,—an enchanted realm where thought is double and flows throughout in parallel streams.

—*Cassius J. Keyser:* ***Lectures on Science, Philosophy and Art****, 1908*

4. Projective geometry has opened up for us with the greatest facility new territories in our science, and has rightly been called a royal road to its own particular field of knowledge.

—*Felix Klein: Quoted in E. T. Bell:* ***Men of Mathematics****, 1937*

5. In the house of mathematics there are many mansions and of these the most elegant is projective geometry.... The science born of art proved to be an art.

—*Morris Kline: "Projective Geometry";* ***Scientific American****, January, 1955*

6. This work is the result of researches which I began as early as the spring of 1813 in the prisons of Russia. Deprived of books and comforts of all sorts, distressed above all by the misfortunes of my country and my own lot, I was not able to bring these studies to a proper perfection. I discovered the fundamental theorems, however, that is to say, the principles of the central projection of figures in general and of conic sections in particular....

—Jean-Victor Poncelot: ***Traite des proprietes projectives des figures****, 1822*

7. At the present time it is a common practice to adjoin to the ordinary Euclidean plane ideal or infinitely remote points which form an ideal or infinitely remote line. In this way uniformity in the statements and proof of a succession of theorems in analytic geometry and in several other branches of geometry is achieved.... This procedure leads to the construction of classical projective geometry. With the development of the axiomatic method various descriptions of projective spaces were constructed....

—L.A. Skornyakov: "Projective Planes"; in ***Translations****, Series One, Vol. 1,* ***Algebra****, 1962*

33.12 Duality

1. ...a very striking feature of this part of geometry that does not depend at all on metrical relationships between parts of the figures, is that, except for some theorems which are symmetrical of themselves, ... all the theorems there are double, that is to say, in plane geometry to each theorem always corresponds necessarily another one which can be deduced from it by merely exchanging two words points and lines with one another, whereas in space geometry points and planes are the words that have to be exchanged with one another to pass from one theorem to its correlate.

—Joseph Diaz Gergonne: "considerations philosophiques sur les elemens de la science de l'etendue"; ***Annales de Mathematiques Pures et Appliquees****, vol. XVI, 1826 [Gergonne comments on the concept of "duality" in certain parts of plane and solid geometry.]*

2. One of the most surprising phenomena of projective geometry is the point-line dualism. Let us imagine that somebody studies projective geometry from a textbook written in a foreign tongue. Owing to an oversight he translates two words wrongly. What is meant by the word "point" is translated as "line," and vice versa. Then the peculiar fact holds that he is not able to discover his mistake because all statements remain correct, in spite of the different interpretation given to them.

—Cornelius Lanczos: ***Space Through the Ages****, 1961*

33.13 Modern Geometry

1. ...today perhaps geometry more properly describes a point of view—a way of looking at a subject—that it does any one part of mathematics.

—L.M. Blumenthal: ***A Modern View of Mathematics****, 1961*

2. In our times, geometers are still exploring those new Wonderlands, partly for the sake of their applications to cosmology and other branches of science but much more for the sheer joy of passing through the looking glass into a land where the familiar lines, planes, triangles, circles and spheres are seen to behave in strange but precisely determined ways.

—H.S.M. Coxeter: "Non-Euclidean Geometry" in ***COSRIMS, The Mathematical Sciences****, 1969*

3. Geometry as conceived today, is fundamentally the study of spatial structure. But space in the modern sense is only weakly related to the space of ordinary experience. It is an abstract set of unspecified things which may be referred to a system of labels which possess a certain mathematical structure.

—J.C. H. Gerretsen: ***Lectures on Tensor Calculus and Differential Geometry****, 1962*

4. Modern pure geometry differs from the geometry of earlier times not so much in the subjects dealt with as the processes employed and the generality of the results obtained. Much of the material is old, but by utilizing the principle of projection and the theory of transversals, facts which were thought of as in no way related, prove to be simply different aspects of the same general truth. This generalizing tendency is the chief characteristic of modern geometry.

—Thomas F. Holgate: "Modern Pure Geometry"; ***Monographs on the Topics of Modern Mathematics Relevant to the Elementary Field****, J.W.A. Young, ed., 1911*

5. We are just beginning to understand how geometry rules the universe.

—Frank Morgan: "Review: The Parsimonious Universe"; ***American Mathematical Monthly****, April, 1997*

6. It has often been said that if individual experience could not create geometry the same is not true of ancestral experience. But what does that mean? Is it meant that we could not experimentally demonstrate Euclid's postulate, but that our ancestors have been able to do it? Not in the least. It is meant that by natural selection our mind has adapted itself to the conditions of the external world, that it has adopted the geometry most advantageous to the species: or in other words the most convenient. This is entirely in conformity with our conclusions; geometry is not true, it is advantageous.

—*Henri Poincare:* ***Science and Hypothesis****, 1905*

7. It was formerly supposed that Geometry was the study of the nature of space in which we live, and accordingly it was urged, by those who held that what exists can only be known empirically, that Geometry should really be regarded as belonging to applied mathematics. But it has gradually appeared, by the increase of non-Euclidean systems, that Geometry throws no more light upon the nature of space than Arithmetic throws upon the population of the United States.

—*Bertrand Russell:* ***Mysticism and Logic and Other Essays****, 1918*

33.14 Chaos

1. In plain words, Chaos was the law of nature; Order was the dreams of man.

—*Henry Adams:* ***The Education of Henry Adams****, 1946*

2. For the mass of practicing scientists ... the change did not matter immediately.... But they were aware of something called chaos.... More and more of them realized that chaos offered a fresh way to proceed with old data ... chaos was the end of the reductionist program in science.

—*James Gleick:* ***Chaos: Making a New Science****, 1987*

3. Over the last decade, physicists, biologists, astronomers and economists have created a new way of understanding the growth of complexity in nature. This new science, called chaos, offers a way of seeing order and pattern where formerly only the random, erratic, the unpredictable—in short, the chaotic—had been observed.

—*James Gleick:* ***Chaos: Making a New Science*** *1987*

4. Lo! thy dread empire, Chaos! is restor'd;
Light dies before thy uncreating word;
Thy hand, great Anarch! lets the curtain fall,
And universal darkness buries all.

—*Alexander Pope:* ***The Dunciad****, 1728*

5. "Chaos" is not just a trendy word for random. In the sense now prevalent in science, it is an entirely new and different concept. Chaos occurs when a deterministic (that is, non-random) system behaves in an apparently random manner. It may sound paradoxical, but "apparently" hides many sins. The big discovery of the last decade is that chaos is just as common as traditional types of regular behavior, such as steady states and periodic cycles.

—*Ian Stewart:* ***Does God Play Dice?****, 2nd ed., "Preface," 1997*

6. Chaos is lawless behavior governed entirely by law.

—*Ian Stewart:* ***Does God Play Dice? The Mathematics of Chaos****, 1990*

7. Chaos is a growth industry. Every week sees new discoveries about the underlying mathematics of chaos, new applications of chaos to our understanding of the natural world, or new technological uses of chaos—including the chaotic dishwasher, a Japanese invention that uses two rotating arms, spinning chaotically, to get dishes cleaner using less energy; and a British machine that uses chaotic-theoretic data analysis to improve quality control in spring manufacture.

—*Ian Stewart:* ***Nature's Numbers****, 1995*

33.15 Fractal Geometry

1. A fractal set generally contains infinitely many points whose organization is so complicated that it is not possible to describe the set by specifying directly where each point lies. Instead the set may be defined by "the relations between the pieces."

—*Michael Barnsley:* ***Fractals Everywhere****, 1993*

2. While fractal geometry can indeed take us into the far reaches of high-tech science, its patterns are surprisingly common in traditional African designs, and some of its basic concepts are fundamental to African knowledge systems.

—*Ron Eglash:* ***African Fractals****, 1999*

3. In the mind's eye, a fractal is a way of seeing infinity.

—*James Gleick:* ***Chaos****, 1987*

4. There is not even a universally accepted definition of the term "fractal." It seems that if one does not prove theorems (as evidently, fractal geometers do not), then one does not need definitions. One notable difference between fractal geometry and calculus is that fractal geometry has not solved any problems. It is not even clear that it has created any new ones.

—*Steven Krantz: "Fractal Geometry";* ***The Mathematical Intelligencer****, vol. 11, #4, 1989*

5. Many important spatial patterns of Nature are either irregular or fragmented to such an extreme degree that ... classical geometry ... is hardly of any help in describing their form ... I hope to show that it is possible in many cases to remedy this absence of geometrical representation by using a family of shapes I propose to call fractals—or fractal sets.

—*Benoit Mandelbrot:* ***The Fractal Geometry of Nature****, 1977*

6. I coined fractal from the Latin adjective fractus. The corresponding Latin verb frangere means "to break": to create irregular fragments. It is therefore sensible and how appropriate for our needs!—That, in addition to "fragmented" (as in fraction or refraction) fractus should also mean "irregular," both meanings preserved in fragment.

—Benoit Mandelbrot: ***The Fractal Geometry of Nature****, 1982*

7. Fractal geometry reveals that some of the most austerely formal chapters of mathematics had a hidden face: a world of beauty unsuspected until now.

—Benoit Mandelbrot: ***The Fractal Geometry of Nature****, 1982*

8. In 1918, the year after Einstein presented his model of the universe as a positively curved four-dimensional space-time, the German mathematician Felix Hausdorff suggested a possibility never before considered: fractional dimension. The importance of Hausdorff's new notion was not immediately apparent. As the usefulness of his ideas grew, however, they gained gradual acceptance and finally an enthusiastic embrace as an integral part of mathematics. But it was not until 1975 that Hausdorff's notion of fractional dimension became known outside the world of mathematics. Benoit Mandelbrot, a mathematician working at IBM, wrote a book on objects with fractional dimension in which he coined the word "fractal" to refer to them, and made the key observation that fractals were not just a figment of mathematicians' overheated imaginations, but in fact were more the rule than the exception in nature. During the past twenty years, applications of fractals have ranged from chemistry and metallurgy to the design of imaginary landscapes in films.

—Robert Osserman: ***Poetry of the Universe****, 1995*

9. The simple equations that generate the convoluted Mandelbrot fractal have been called the wittiest remarks ever made.

—John Allen Paulos: ***Once Upon a Number****, 1998*

10. Perhaps the most convincing argument in favor of the study of fractals is their sheer beauty.

—Heinz-Otto Peitgen & Peter H. Richter: ***The Beauty of Fractals****, 1986*

11. Fractals have been used in the movie *Star Trek II: The Wrath of Khan*, for the landscape of the Genesis planet; and in *Return of the Jedi* to create the geography of the moons of Endor and the outlines of the Death Star.

—Ian Stewart: ***Does God Play Dice?****, 2nd ed., 1997*

34
Topology and Graph Theory

34.1 Origins of Analysis Situs [Topology]

1. In addition to that branch of geometry which is concerned with magnitudes, and which has always received the greatest attention, there is another branch, previously almost unknown, which Leibniz first mentioned, calling it the geometry of position. This branch is concerned only with the determination of position and its properties; it does not involve measurements, nor calculations made with them.

*—Leonhard Euler: "The Problem of the Seven Bridges of Konigsburg," **Commentari** of the St. Petersberg Academy, 1736; Quoted in N.L. Biggs, E.K. Lloyd & R.J. Wilson, **Graph Theory, 1736–1936**, 1976*

2. Analysis situs ... constitutes a revenge of geometry on analysis. Since Descartes, we have been accustomed to replace each geometric relation by a corresponding relation between numbers, and this has created a sort of predominance of analysis.

*—Jacques Hadamard: Lectures at Columbia University, 1911; Quoted in **The History of Modern mathematics**, vol. I, David E. Rowe & John McCleary, eds., 1989*

3. One of the most difficult branches of mathematics, analysis situs, that spring whose waters lose themselves in the ocean of modern topology, abounds in spells and charms. Certain of these, like the one-sided Moebius strip, are as amusing to children as conjuring tricks, even though arising from serious problems.

*—Francois Le Lionnais: "Beauty in Mathematics" in **Great Currents of Mathematics**, F. Le Lionnais, ed., 1971*

4. Topology got under way as a full-fledged branch of geometry in the nineteenth century, *Vorstudien zur Topologie*, published in 1847 by the German mathematician Listing, was the first systematic treatise in the field. Its origins, however, go back to the major discoveries made by Descartes and Euler.

*—James R. Newman: **The World of Mathematics** "A Famous Problem," vol. 1, 1956*

5. Leibniz ... was led by purely metaphysical speculations about the divine principle and its relation to infinite extent to conceive and develop the notion of an analysis situs [topology]—probably the most inspired of all interpretations of pure and emancipated space....

*—Oswald Spengler: **The Decline of the West**, 1934*

34.2 The Nature of Topology

1. A topologist: isn't that someone who stuffs monkeys?

—Anonymous

2. In a certain sense topology takes a downright primitive view of space, striping geometry to its bare essentials. Some seemingly basic notions, such as straightness and size, often turn out to be irrelevant in topology, which is generally concerned with the way in which parts of geometric figures are connected.

*—George A.W. Boehm: in **The Mathematical Sciences: A Collection of Essays**, Edited by the National Research Council's Committee on Support of Research in the Mathematical Sciences, 1969*

3. Topology is more than a free-wheeling species of geometry. Like logic and set theory, it is so fundamental that it infiltrates nearly all of mathematics.

*—Dan E. Christie: **Basic Topology**, 1976*

4. Topology is an abstraction of geometry; it deals with sets having a structure which permits the definition of continuity for functions and a concept of "closeness" of points and sets. This structure, called the "topology" on the set, was originally determined from the properties of open sets in Euclidean spaces, particularly the Euclidean plane.

—*Fred H. Croom:* ***Basic Concepts of Algebraic Topology****, 1941*

5. Topology is the study of badly drawn figures.

—*Howard W. Eves:* ***Mathematical Circles Squared****, 1972*

6. What he says is a topological map of the truth.

—*Lipot Fejer: Quoted in D. MacHale:* ***Comic Sections****, 1993*

7. Topologists do not distinguish between a square and a circle, because the one can be deformed into the other by stretching. The curves and surfaces which arise in analysis are smooth, like the circle, the sphere, or the torus; they have no corners or edges. Differential topology focuses entirely on these smooth curves and surfaces.

—*Andrew M. Gleason: "The Evolution of Differential Topology";* ***The Mathematical Sciences: A Collection of Essays****, Edited by the National Research Council's Committee on Support of Research in the Mathematical Sciences, 1969*

8. A topologist is one who doesn't know the difference between a doughnut and a coffee cup.

—*John Kelley: In N. Rose:* ***Mathematical Maxims and Minims****, 1988*

9. Topology seems a queer subject; it delves into strange implausible shapes and its propositions are either childishly obvious (that is, until you try to prove them) or so difficult and abstract that not even a topologist can explain their intuitive meaning.

—*James R. Newman:* ***The World of Mathematics*** *vol. 1, 1956*

10. A child's ... first geometrical discoveries are topological.... If you ask him to copy a square or a triangle, he draws a closed circle.

—*Jean Philips: "How Children Form Mathematical Concepts"*

11. Many of the simpler topological concepts are used every day by people who have never heard of topology. The basic ideas of topology are so fundamental that we learn many of them as infants. The concepts of insideness and outsideness, of right-handedness and left-handedness, of linkedness and unlinkedness are forced on us at an early age.

—*Albert W. Tucker and Herbert S. Bailey, Jr.: "Topology";* ***Scientific American****, January, 1950*

34.3 Rubber Sheet Geometry

1. A topologist is interested in those properties of a thing that while they are in a sense geometrical are the most permanent—the ones that will survive distortion and stretching.

—*Stephen Barr:* ***Experiments in Topology****, 1964*

2. Topology is the branch of mathematics that lies behind those sequences in movies and television advertisements where a character or object having one shape is transformed in a fluid fashion into a quite different shape. The movie term for such a transformation is "morphing." The name comes from the mathematical term for such a transformation: a morphism.

—*Keith Devlin:* ***Life by the Numbers****, 1998*

3. Mathematicians, with their hyperactive imaginations, pretend that surfaces are made of superflexible rubber. If one of these surfaces can be deformed into another by stretching, shrinking, twisting, or any other manipulation that does not involve ripping, puncturing, or filing holes, the two surfaces are said to have the same topology.

—*Paul Hoffman:* ***Archimedes' Revenge: The Joys and Perils of Mathematics****, 1988*

4. Topology is often called "rubber sheet geometry," because it studies those features of a geometric shape that are unchanged if the shape is stretched, compressed, bent, or twisted—but not cut or torn. It is what geometry would be like if you drew the diagrams on a sheet of rubber: no fixed angles, no parallels, no straight lines.... Topology deals with geometrical features such as holes, knots, links, and boundaries.

—*Ian Stewart:* ***Life's Other Secret****, 1998*

34.4 Set-Theoretic Topology

1. I would formulate the basic problem of set-theoretic topology as follows: to determine which set-theoretic structures have a connection with the intuitively given material of elementary polyhedral topology and hence deserve to be considered as geometrical figures—even if very general ones.

—*Paul Alexandroff: 1932; in Stephen Watson's "Ask a Topologist" feature, December 15, 1997*

2. The object whose intrinsic qualitative properties are to be studied can be virtually anything: a geometric figure, a rubber band, a doughnut, a collection of functions, an "abstract space." A property common to all objects of a topological study is that they are sets. The elements of the sets will be referred to as points, although, as the above examples indicate, the geometric notion of a point is not the only applicable one. A point may be a function, a book, a dog on Main Street, a point in the sense of Euclidean geometry, or just about anything else.

—M.J. Mansfield: ***Introduction to Topology*** *1963*

34.5 Topology, Algebra and Algebraic Topology

1. Topology and algebra could be said to be symbiotic organisms in the sea of mathematics: Each is partially responsible for the remarkable growth of the other.

—Dan E. Christie: ***Basic Topology****, 1976*

2. ...the main fact about our time which will be emphasized by future historians of mathematics is the extraordinary upheaval which has taken place in an around what was earlier called algebraic topology.

—Jean Dieudonne: "Recent Developments in Mathematics"; ***American Mathematical Monthly****, Vol. 71, # 3, 1964*

3. Progress in algebraic topology is usually not achieved by going forward and applying the already existing tools to new problems, but by constantly going back and forging new, more refined tools which are necessary to achieve further results.

—Samuel Eilenberg: "Algebraic Topology"; ***Lectures on Modern Mathematics****, Vol. 1, T.L. Sarty, ed., 1963*

4. The geometry of Algebraic Topology is so pretty, it would seem a pity to slight it and miss all the intuition which it provides. At deeper levels, algebra becomes increasingly important, so for the sake of balance it seems only fair to emphasize geometry at the beginning.

—Allen Hatcher: ***Algebraic Topology****, 2000*

5. If it's just turning the crank, it's algebra; but if there is an idea present then it's topology.

—Solomon Lefschetz: Attributed; Quoted in ***The Mathematical Intelligencer****, vol. 13, Winter, 1991*

6. It was my lot to plant the harpoon of algebraic topology into the body of the whale of algebraic geometry.

—Solomon Lefschetz: ***Some Mathematical People****; D.J. Albers & G.L. Alexanderson, eds., 1985*

7. In these days the angel of topology and the devil of abstract algebra fight for the soul of each individual mathematical domain.

—Hermann Weyl: "Invariants"; ***Duke Mathematical Journal****, 1939*

34.6 Königsberg Bridge Problem

1. The city of Königsberg (now called Kaliningrad) in Western Russia stands where the New Pregel and Old Pregel Rivers join to form the Pregel River; there is an island formed at the point of confluence. In the eighteenth century there were seven bridges (two more bridges have since been built). It was asked whether or not it would be possible to make a walking tour of Königsberg and cross each of the bridges exactly one.

—B.H. Arnold: ***Intuitive Concepts in Elementary Topology****, 1962*

2. Leonhard Euler was feeling the urge,
To sing a lamentable dirge,
For he knew he was lost,
By the third time he crossed,
The Same bridge in old Köingsberg.

—Jennifer Austin, Cormac O'Sullivan & Richard Carr: Attributed

3. As concerns the Königsberg problem of the seven bridges, it could be solved by a complete enumeration of all walks possible; then we would know if one of them fulfills the condition or none. This method, however, is, because of the great number of combinations, too difficult and cumbersome. Moreover, it could not be applied to other questions where still more bridges exist.

—Leonhard Euler: "From the Problem of the Seven Bridges of Königsberg," 1736; in ***A Source Book in Mathematics, 1200–1800****, D.J. Struik, ed., 1969*

4. ...there cannot be an ultimate or "most trivial" piece of mathematical trivia, so we merely claim that this is very trivial indeed: the names of the seven bridges over the Pregel river which feature in Euler's problem of the Bridges of Königsberg were the Kramer, Schmiede, Holz, Hohe, Honig, Kottel and Grune.

—H. Steinhaus: ***Mathematical Snapshots****, 1969*

34.7 Graph Theory

1. The Jordan curve theorem is important and frequently used in topology.... It states, roughly, that there is an inside and an outside of a simple closed curve in a plane.

—B.H. Arnold: ***Intuitive Concepts in Elementary Topology****, 1962*

2. A graph is a good way to mathematically represent a physical situation in which there is a flow of something—materials, people, money, information—from one place to another.

—John L. Casti: ***Five Golden Rules****, 1996*

3. As early as the nineteenth century, the physicist Kirchhoff recognized the importance of investigations in topology in order to aid in the solution of problems connected with the branching out and intertwining of wires or other conductors carrying an electric current.

—Edward Kasner & James Newman: ***Mathematics and the Imagination****, 1940*

4. The mathematical tool for translating chemical structures into a form that a computer can handle digitally is a concept that topologists call a graph. This kind of graph has little relation to the curves and bar charts used to display data; rather, it a formal diagram for analyzing connections among a number of entities, [for instance] the individual atoms that make up an organic molecule.

—*Joshua Lederberg: "Topology of Molecules"; **The Mathematical Sciences: A Collection of Essays,** Edited by the National Research Council's Committee on Support of Research in the Mathematical Sciences, 1969*

5. It pays to keep wide awake in studying any graph. The thing looks so simple, so frank, and so appealing that the careless are easily fooled.

—*M.J. Moroney: **Facts from Figures,** 1951*

6. Despite the prevailing use of graphs as metaphors for communicating and reasoning about dependencies, the task of capturing informational dependencies by graphs is not at all trivial.

—*Judea Pearl: **Probabilistic Reasoning in Intelligent Systems,** 1988*

34.8 The Moebius Strip

1. A mathematician confided
That a Moebius strip is one-sided,
And you'll get quite a laugh
If you cut one in half,
For it stays in one piece when divided.

—*Anonymous*

2. Narcissus achieved his ambition:
He was taught by a mathematician
To perform with great ease
A Moebius-strip tease,
With an auto-erotic emission.

—*Anonymous: in **The New Limerick,** G. Legman, ed., 1977*

3. I created a single-sided object by searching for a solution of a hanging sculpture, turning in the rising air. My search was neither scientific nor mathematical, but purely aesthetic ... I named my sculpture *Endless Ribbon*.... Sometimes later I was informed that my creation, which I thought I had discovered or invented, was only an artistic interpretation of the so-called Moebius strip, and theoretically identical to it ... I was shocked by the fact that I was not the first one to discover this object. I therefore stopped all further research in this direction for a while.

—*Max Bill: Quoted in Eli Maor: **To Infinity and Beyond,** Princeton University Press, 1987*

4. One version [of the true discovery of the Moebius strip] is that the mathematician August Ferdinand Moebius once took a vacation at a seashore. He found himself so pestered at night with flies that he secured a strip of paper sticky on both sides. Giving the strip a half-turn and pasting the two ends together, he hung the resulting loop from a rafter in the bedroom of his vacation cottage. His improvised flycatcher worked well and he slept undisturbed by flies. Awakening one morning after a fine night's rest, his eye fell upon the flycatcher hanging over his bed and he noticed, to his surprise, that the strip had only one side and only one edge. Thus was born the famous Moebius strip.

—*Howard W. Eves: **Return to Mathematical Circles,** 1988*

5. ...the Moebius strip is of service not only to chemists but to industrialists as well. The B.F. Goodrich Company has a patent on a Moebius-strip conveyor belt. In an ordinary conveyor belt, one side is subject to more wear and tear. In a Moebius belt, however, the stress of spread out over "both sides," so that the belt lasts twice as long.

—*Paul Hoffman: **Archimedes' Revenge: The Joys and Perils of Mathematics,** 1988*

6. A burleycue dancer, a pip
Named Virginia, could peel in a zip;
But she read science fiction
And died of constriction
Attempting a Moebius strip.

—*Cyril Kornbluth "The Unfortunate Topologist": **The Magazine of Fantasy and Science Fiction** Quoted in **Fantasia Mathematica,** Clifton Fadiman, ed., 1958*

7. A mathematician confided
That a Moebius strip is one-sided.
You'd get quite a laugh
If you cut it in half,
For it stays in one piece when divided.

—*Cyril Kornbluth: in William S. Baring-Gould; **The Lure of the Limerick,** 1967*

34.9 The Klein Bottle

1. A mathematician named Klein
Thought a Moebius strip was divine.
Said he, "If you glue
The edges of two
You'll get a weird bottle like mine."

—*Anonymous*

2. A topologist, rather well known in his line,
Quite liked a drink at the right time.
His reason was clear enough:
With a little of the stuff
Every body is just like Klein's.

—*Anonymous: "A Topologist"*

3. Three jolly sailors from Blaydon-on-Tyne
They went to sea in a bottle by Klein.
Since the sea was entirely inside the hull
The scenery seen was exceedingly dull.

*—Frederick Winsor: in **The Space Child's Mother Goose**; in Martin Gardner's "Mathematical Games" column; **Scientific American**, July, 1963*

34.10 Four Color Problem

1. The domain of maths is the mind,
But now we're in a bit of a bind.
For Appel & Haken
The distinction did darken
With a proof of a mechanical kind.

—Jennifer Austin, Cormac O'Sullivan & Richard Carr

2. Our pursuit is not the accumulation of facts about the world or even facts about mathematical objects. The mission of mathematics is understanding. The Appel and Haken work on the Four Color Problem amounts to a confirmation that a map-maker with only four paint pots will not be driven out of business. This is not really what mathematicians were worried about in the first place. Admitting the computer shenanigans of Appel and Haken to the ranks of mathematics would only leave us intellectually unfulfilled.

*—Daniel Cohen: "The Superfluous Paradigm" in **The Mathematical Revolution in Computing**; J.H. Johnson & M.J. Loomis, eds., 1991*

3. My first reaction was, "Wonderful! How did they do it [prove the four-color problem]?" I expected some brilliant new insight, a proof which had in its kernel an idea whose beauty would transform my day. But when I received the answer, "They did it by breaking it down into thousands of cases, and then running them all on the computer, one after another," I felt disheartened. My reaction was, "So it just goes to show it wasn't a good problem after all."

*—Philip F. Davis & Reuben Hersh; in **From Here to Infinity**, 1996*

4. A student of mine asked me today to give him a reason for a fact which I did not know was a fact—and do not yet. He says that if a figure be anyhow divided and the compartments differently colored so that the figures with any portion of common boundary line are differently colored—four colors may be wanted, but not more—the following is the case in which four colors are wanted. Query cannot a necessity for five or more be invented.... If you report with some very simple case which makes me out a stupid animal, I think I must do as the Sphinx did....

—Augustus de Morgan: Letter to William Rowan Hamilton; October 23, 1852 [In London in 1852. Francis Guthrie had been trying to color a map of England subdivided into counties. After much trial and error he wrote to his younger brother, a mathematician, asking if 'every map drawn on the plane [can] be colored with four (or fewer) colors so that no two regions having a common border have the same color.' Unsuccessful in attempts to answer his brother the young mathematican passed the problem on to de Morgan.]

5. I'm not an expert on the four-color problem, but I assume the proof is true. However, it's not beautiful. I'd prefer to see a proof that gives insight into why four colors are sufficient.

*—Paul Erdos: Quoted in Paul Hoffman: **The Man Who Loved Only Numbers**, 1998*

6. I do not find it easy to say what we learned from all that [the Haken-Appel computer-based proof of the Four Color Problem]. We are still far from having a good proof of the Four Color Theorem. I hope as an article of faith that the computer missed the right concept and the right approach. 100 years from not the map theorem will be, I think, an exercise in a first-year graduate course, provable in a couple of pages by means of the appropriate concepts, which will be completely familiar by then. The present proof relies in an effect on an Oracle, and I say down with Oracles! They are not mathematics.

—Paul Halmos: Address to the 75th Annual summer meeting of the Mathematical Association of America, 1990

7. If we accept the four-colored theorem as a theorem, then we are committed to changing the sense of "theorem," or more to the point, to changing the sense of the underlying concept of proof.

*—Thomas Tymoczko: "The Four-Color Problem and Its Philosophical Significance"; **Journal of Philosophy**, 1979*

34.11 Knot Theory

1. Knot theory for a long time was a little backwater of topology. It's now been recognized as a very deep phenomenon in many areas of mathematics.

*—Joan Birman: Quoted in Ivars Peterson: **The Mathematical Tourist**, 1998*

2. ...the study of knots presents difficult mathematical problems of a topological nature. A knot is formed by first looping and inter-lacing a piece of string and then joining the ends together. The resulting closed curve represents a geometrical figure that remains essentially the same even if it is deformed by pulling or twisting without breaking the string.

*—Richard Courant and Herbert Robbins: **What Is Mathematics?**, 1941*

3. Round and round the circle
Completing the charm
So the knot be unknotted
The cross be uncrossed
The crooked be made straight
And the curse be ended.
—*T.S. Eliot: "The Family Reunion," 1939*

4. Molecular biologists are starting to use knot theory to understand the different conformations that DNA can take on. They can track the sequence of steps in which one structure is gradually transformed into another during the basic, life-supporting processes that take place within cells. Recent advances are helping them see how the enzymes that do the cutting and gluing must perform these functions.
—*Ivars Peterson:* ***The Mathematical Tourist****, 1998*

5. Chemists interested in synthesizing new compounds are also beginning to pay attention to topology and knot theory. In general, they try to create new, unusual molecules by changing the way atoms are connected. In this way, they hope to increase their understanding of how the chemical process of building compounds works. Geometry and especially topology suggest a range of targets for this effort.
—*Ivars Peterson:* ***The Mathematical Tourist****, 1998*

6. Knot theory began as applied mathematics and now, in its second century, is enjoying new applications in science that go back to its beginnings.
—*DeWitt Sumners: "Untangling DNA";* ***The Mathematical Intelligencer****, vol. 12, Summer, 1990*

7. You need no more or less than three dimensions to make a knot, a knot that tightens on itself and won't pull apart, and that's what the ultimate particles are—knots in space-time. You can't make a knot in two dimensions because there's no over or under.
—*John Updike:* ***Roger's Version****, 1986*

35
Analysis and Calculus

35.1 Analytical Methods in Mathematics

1. I shall devote all my efforts to bring light into the tremendous obscurity which one unquestionably finds in analysis. It lacks so completely any plan and system that it is peculiar that so many men have studied it. The worst of it is, it has never been treated stringently. There are very few theorems in advanced analysis which have been demonstrated in a logically tenable manner. Everywhere one finds this miserable way of concluding from the special to the general and it is extremely peculiar that such a procedure has led to so few of the so-called paradoxes.

—*Niels Henrik Abel: Letter to Professor Christopher Hansteen;* ***Oeuvres****, Vol. 2, 1826: Quoted in Shaughan Lavine:* ***Understanding the Infinite****, 1994*

2. Wherin It Is Examined Whether the Object, principles, and Inferences of the Modern Analysis Are More Distinctly Conceived, or More Evidently Deduced, than Religious Mysteries and Points of Faith. "First Cast the Beam Out of Thine Own Eye; and Then Shalt Thou See Clearly to Cast Out the Mote of Thy Brother's Eye."

—*Bishop George Berkeley:* ***The Analyst Or a Discourse Addressed to an Infidel Mathematician****, 1734 [The above is the alternate title to philosopher Berkeley's attack on the soundness of the efforts to make calculus rigorous. The infidel of the title is Edmund Halley.]*

3. Mathematical Analysis is ... the true rational basis of the whole system of our positive knowledge.

—*Auguste Comte:* ***The Positive Philosophy of Auguste Comte****, Harriet Martineau, tr., 1853*

4. We have sufficient evidence that the ancient geometers made use of a certain "analysis" which they applied in the resolution of all their problems, although, as we find, they grudged to their successors knowledge of this method. There is now flourishing a certain kind of arithmetic, called algebra, which endeavors to determine in regard to numbers what the ancients achieved in respect of geometrical shapes.

—*Rene Descartes: "Regulae":* ***Descartes' Philosophical Writings****, Norman Kemp Smith, ed. & tr., 1952*

5. The astronomer, the geometer, rely on their irrefragable analysis, and disdain the results of observation.

—*Ralph Waldo Emerson: "Nature";* ***The Works of Ralph Waldo Emerson****, 1903*

6. Nature is not embarrassed by difficulties of analysis.

—*Augustin Fresnel: in Morris Kline:* ***Mathematical Thought****, 1972*

7. It is a nontrivial mathematical enterprise ... to find the actual facts hidden behind the logical double-talk of the classical analyst.

—*Nicolas D. Goodman: "Reflections on [Errett] Bishop's Philosophy of Mathematics";* ***Springer Lecture Notes****, No. 873, 1980*

8. I believe that the numbers and functions of analysis are not the arbitrary product of our spirits; I believe that they exist outside of us with the same character of necessity as the objects of objective reality; and we find or discover them and study them as do the physicists, chemists, and zoologists.

—*Charles Hermite: Letter to Thomas Jan Stieltjes; May 30, 1893: In I. Kleiner: "Rigor and Proof in Mathematics";* ***Mathematics Magazine****, vol. 64, December 5, 1991*

9. If time and strength are granted me, I myself will show the mathematical world that not only geometry, but also arithmetic can point the way to analysis, and certainly a more rigorous way. If I cannot do it myself those who come after me will

... and they will recognize the incorrectness of all those conclusions with which so-called analysis works at present.

—*Leopold Kronecker: Quoted by Weierstrass in a letter to Sonja Kovalevsky, 1855; in E.T. Bell:* ***Men of Mathematics****, 1937*

10. When, still a boy, I knew only the propositions of ordinary logic, and mathematics was strange to me, the thought occurred to me (I know not through what impulse) that an analysis of concepts could be invented with the help of which in combination truths could be expressed and by the same means numbers could be calculated. It is a delight now to recollect by what reasons, even if childish, I came to the notion of so great a thing.

—*Gottfried Leibniz:* ***Schopferische Vernunft****, published 1955*

11. In analysis, we start from what is required, we take it for granted, and we draw consequences from it, and consequences from the consequences till we reach a point that we can use as starting point in synthesis. For in analysis we assume what is required to be done as already done (what is sought as already found, what we have to prove as true). We inquire from what antecedent the desired result could be derived; then we inquire again what could be the antecedent of that antecedent, and so on, until passing from antecedent to antecedent, we come eventually upon something already known or admittedly true. This procedure we call analysis, or solution backwards, or regressive reasoning.

—*Pappus:* ***Collectiones****, A.D. 300: in T.L. Heath,* ***The Thirteen Books of Euclid's Elements****, 1908*

12. ...the progress of analysis has in no way affected the philosophical status of our notions of space and time, and that, consequently, metaphysicians need feel no alarm at what is going on behind the veil of mathematical symbolism.... Mathematics are neutral in Philosophy.

—*Samuel Roberts: "Remarks on Mathematical Terminology, and the Philosophic Bearing on recent Mathematical Speculations concerning the Realities of Space";* ***Proceedings of the London Mathematical Society****, vol. 14, 1882–83*

13. [Around 1590] the French mathematician [Francois] Vieta [in *In Artem analyticem isagore*,] opted for the term analysis rather than algebra, claiming that algebra doesn't mean anything in any European language. He didn't succeed in driving out the word algebra, but he did popularize analysis to the point where it has stayed with us.

—*Steven Schwartzman:* ***The Words of Mathematics: An Etymological Dictionary of Mathematical Terms Used in English****, 1994*

35.2 Calculus of Variations

1. According to classical mythology, Princess Dido, whose murderous brother Pygmalion was king of Tyre, fled her homeland, sailed the Mediterranean with a band of followers, and landed on the northern coast of Africa.... Dido's acquisition of land for a great new city was to be limited to the area she could enclose with the hide of a bull.... Dido first cut the hide into a number of long thin strips.... She placed these rawhide strands in the shape of a great semi-circle whose diameter ran along the seashore. Within this large area was built the city of Carthage.

—*William Dunham:* ***The Mathematical Universe****, 1994*

2. The calculus of variations is ... the bridge that connects pure geometry with the most sophisticated branch of physics. Lagrange and Euler knew nothing about the theory of relativity or the quantum theory, but their work in mathematical dynamics, particularly their concepts of the Lagrangian and action, are of fundamental importance in both of these remarkable physical theories which enable scientists to probe the universe from quarks to galaxies.

—*Lloyd Motz and Jefferson Hane Weaver:* ***The Story of Mathematics****, 1993*

3. Here they bought ground; they used to
call it Byrsa,
That being a word for a bull's hide; they
bought only
What a bull's hide could cover.

—*Virgil:* ***Aeneid****, Rolfe Humphries, tr., 1951*

35.3 Continuity

1. Between every two points there are infinite intermediate points, since "no two points follow one another without a middle...." And the same must be said of divisible places, and this is shown from the continuous motion of a body. For a body in not moved from place to place except in time. But in the whole time which measures the motion of a body, there are not two nows in which the body moved is not in one place and in another; for if it were in one and the same place in two nows, it would follow that it would be at rest there, since to be at rest is nothing else than to be in the same place now and previously. Therefore, since there are infinite nows between the first and the last now of the time which measures the motion, there must be infinite places between the first from which the motion begins, and the last where the motion ceases.

—*St. Thomas Aquinas: "Summa Theologia"; In* ***Basic Writings of St. Thomas Aquinas****, Anton C. Pegis, ed., 1945*

2. The sovereign wisdom which is the source of all things, acts like a perfect Geometer, in accordance with a complete harmony. That is why this principle [the "law of continuity"] often serves as a proof or test, enabling one to see from the start and from outside the flaw in an opinion badly put together, even before entering into an internal discussion of it.

—G.W. Leibniz: Letter to P. Bayle, 1687; in ***Leibniz Selections****, P.P. Wiener, ed., 1951*

3. ...the fact that the continuity of space and time is a natural belief is perhaps evidence that it is true. Better evidence is that it explains the personal identity of consciousness in time, which is almost if not quite incomprehensible otherwise.

—C.S. Peirce: Quoted in ***The New Elements of Mathematics****, Vol. III, Carolyn Eisele, ed., 1976*

4. Calculus required continuity, and continuity was supposed to require the infinitely little; but nobody could discover what the infinitely little might be.

—Bertrand Russell: ***The Study of Mathematics****, 1910*

5. This modern branch of mathematics, unknown to the ancients, when dealing with problems of motion admits the conception of the infinitely small, and so conforms to the chief condition of motion (absolute continuity) and thereby corrects the inevitable error which the human mind cannot avoid when it deals with separate elements of motion instead of examining continuous motion.

—Leo Tolstoy: ***War and Peace****, 1863–9; L. & A. Maude, tr., 1922*

35.4 Infinitesimals

1. And what are these fluxions? The velocities of evanescent increments. And what are these evanescent increments? They are neither finite quantities, nor quantities infinitely small, nor yet nothing. May we not call them ghosts of departed quantities?

—Bishop George Berkeley; ***The Analyst****, 1734 [Berkeley scoffs at Isaac Newton's fluxions.]*

2. Infinitesimal is the nearest to zero
infinitesimal is so small
that it is no longer something
but it is not yet nothing.

—Ilse Bing: "Infinitesimal"; in E. Robson & J. Wimp: ***Against Infinity****, 1979*

3. The objections which have been raised against the infinitesimal method are based on the false proposition that the errors due to neglecting infinitely small quantities during the actual calculation will continue to exist in the result of the calculation.

—L. Carnot: ***Reflections sur la Metaphysique du Calcul Infinitestimal****, 1813*

4. Fluxions are, as near as we please, as the increments of fluents [variables] generated in times, equal and small as possible, and to speak accurately, they are in the prime ratio of nascent increments....

—Sir Isaac Newton: "Quadrature of Curves," 1676

5. The idea of an infinitesimal involves no contradiction.... As a mathematician, I prefer the method of infinitesimals to that of limits, as far easier and less infested with snares.

—C.F. Pierce: "The Law of Mind"; ***Monist****, Vol. 2, 1891–1982*

6. [The infinitesimals] neither have nor can have theory; in practice it is a dangerous instrument in the hands of beginners ... anticipating, for my part, the judgement of posterity, I would predict that this method will be accused one day, and rightly, of having retarded the progress of the mathematical sciences.

—Francois Servois: in J.D. Gergonne: ***Annales de mathematiques****, Tome V, 1815*

35.5 The Limit Concept

1. Throughout the 1960s and 1970s devoted [Samuel] Beckett readers greeted each successively shorter volume from the master with a mixture of awe and apprehensiveness. It was like watching a great mathematician wielding an infinitesimal calculus, his equations approaching nearer and still nearer to the null point.

—John Banville: Quoted in a review of Samuel Beckett's ***Nohow On: Ill Seen Ill Said, Worstword Ho****, in the* ***New York Review of Books****; August 13, 1992*

2. The definition of limit is essential his [Cauchy's] creation and is as much of a miracle as those fantastic Swiss clocks of the period in which hundreds of gleaming cogs are made to celebrate not only the time and date but the phases of the moon.

—David Berlinski: ***A Tour of Calculus****, 1997*

3. A limiting ratio is neither more nor less difficult to define than an infinitely small quantity.

—L. Carnot: ***Reflections sur la Metaphysique du Calcul Infinitesimal****, 1813*

4. The average duration of human life is destined to increase continually, if physical revolutions do not oppose themselves thereto; but we do not know what limit it is that it can never pass; we do not even know if the general laws of nature have fixed such a limit.

—Marie-Jean de Condorcet: ***Sketch for a Historical Picture of the Human Mind****, 1794*

5. The theory of limits is the base of the true metaphysics of the differential calculus....

—Jean Le Rond D'Alembert: ***Encyclopedia****, "Limit,"*

1761–65; Quoted in Stuart Hollingdale: ***Makers of Mathematics****, 1989*

6. Sure, some [teachers] could give the standard limit definitions, but they [the students] clearly did not understand the definitions—and it would be a remarkable student who did, since it took mathematicians a couple of thousands years to sort out the notion of a limit, and I think most of us who call ourselves professional mathematicians really only understand it when we start to teach the stuff, either in graduate school or beyond.

—Kevin Devlin: "The Calculus Ultrafilter"; ***Focus****, December, 1994*

7. It will be sufficient if, when we speak of ... infinitely small quantities (i.e., the very least of those within our knowledge), it is understood that we mean quantities that are ... indefinitely small, as the ultimate things, ... it can be done, ... aye even though he think that such things are utterly impossible, it will be sufficient simply to make use of them as a tool that has advantages for the purpose of calculation, just as the algebraists retain imaginary roots with great profit.

—Gottfried Wilhelm von Leibniz: Letter to Pierre Bayle, 1687; in C.H. Edwards, Jr. ***The Historical Development of the Calculus****, 1979*

8. The concept of the limit of a function was probably first defined with sufficient rigor by Weierstrass.

—A. Pringsheim; ***Grundlagen der Allgemeinen Funktionenlehre****, 1899*

9. It is thought that Hippocrates reached his conclusions [concerning the ratio of the circles] by looking upon a circle as the limiting form of a regular polygon, either inscribed or circumscribed. This was an early instance of the 'method of exhaustion'—a particular use of approximation from below and above to a desired limit.

—Herbert Westren Turnbull: "The Great Mathematicians"; in ***The World o Mathematics****, James R. Newman, ed., 1956*

35.6 The Calculus

1. Foreshadowings of the principles and even of the language of [the infinitesimal] calculus can be found in the writings of Napier, Kepler, Cavalieri, Pascal, Fermat, Wallis, and Barrow. It was Newton's good luck to come at a time when everything was ripe for the discovery, and his ability enabled him to construct almost a complete calculus.

—W.W. Rouse Ball: ***History of Mathematics****, 1901*

2. The calculus is the story this [the Western] world first told itself as it became the modern world.

—David Berlinski: ***A Tour of Calculus****, 1997*

3. When I was teaching mathematics to future naval officers during the war, I was told that the Navy had found that men who had studied calculus made better line officers than men who had not studied calculus. Nothing is clearer (it was even clear to the Navy) than that a line officer never has the slightest need for calculus.

—Ralph P. Boas, Jr. "If This Be Treason... " ***American Mathematical Monthly****, 1957*

4. I am going to be accused by my colleagues of advocating a cookbook approach to calculus. This I deny. There was once a really cookbook approach to calculus, in which the student had to listen to incomprehensible nonsense until he developed a sound intuition (if he ever did). The approach that some of my colleagues favor makes the student listen to incomprehensible sense instead.

—Ralph P. Boas, Jr.: "Calculus as an Experimental Science," ***American Mathematical Monthly****, 1971*

5. [I]t might be far better to speak of the evolution of the calculus. Nevertheless, inasmuch as Newton and Leibniz, apparently independently, invented algorithmic procedures which were universally applicable and which were essentially the same as those employed at the present time in the calculus, ... there will be no inconsistency involved in thinking of these two men as the inventors of the subject.

—Carl B. Boyer: ***The History of the Calculus and Its Conceptual Development****, 1949*

6. Algebra is the Calculus of Functions, and Arithmetic is the Calculus of Values.

—Auguste Comte: ***The Positive Philosophy of Auguste Comte****, Harriet Martineau, tr., 1853*

7. With an absurd oversimplification, the "invention" of the calculus is sometimes ascribed to two men, Newton and Leibniz. In reality, the calculus is the product of a long evolution that was neither initiated nor terminated by Newton and Leibniz, but in which both played a decisive part.

—Richard Courant & Herbert Robbins: ***What Is Mathematics?****, 1941*

8. One good thing about teaching calculus is that you develop a hardened attitude towards repeating yourself.

—Phil Hanlon: Attributed

9. That the calculus is regarded as dry and uninteresting by many students, and that its value is occasionally doubted, is the strongest proof possible that its significance is not grasped. Here the connection with realities is so easy and so abundant that it is actually a skillful feat to conceal the fact. Yet it is done, I know personally of courses in the calculus (and so may you) in which the pressure to obtain and enforce a memory of formal algebraic rules has resulted in absolute neglect of the idea that a derivative represents a rate of change!

—*E.R. Hedrick: "The Significance of Mathematics"; Retiring Presidential Address at the second annual summer meeting of the Mathematical Association of America, September 6, 1917; in* ***The American Mathematical Monthly****, 24, 1917*

10. Every one who understands the subject will agree that even the basis on which the scientific explanation of nature rests, is intelligible only to those who have learned at least the elements of the differential and integral calculus, as well as of analytical geometry.

—*Felix Klein:* ***Jahresbericht der Deutschen Mathematiker Vereinigung****, Vol. 11, 1902*

11. My new calculus, ... offers truth by a kind of analysis and without any effort of imagination—which often succeeds only by accident; and it gives us all the advantages over Archimedes that Vieta and Descartes have given us over Apollonius.

—*Gottfried Wilhelm Leibniz:* ***A New Method for Determining Maxima and Minima****, 1684*

12. The calculus is the greatest aid we have to the application of physical truth in the broadest sense of the word.

—*W.F. Osgood: Quoted in N. Rose:* ***Bulletin American Mathematical Society****, vol. 13, 1907*

13. But so great is the average person's fear of the infinite that to this day calculus all over the world is being taught as a study of limit processes instead of what it really is: infinitesimal analysis.

—*Rudy Rucker:* ***Infinity and the Mind****, 1995*

14. One should not forget that our term calculus is derived from calcule, "pebble," a reference to counting with pebbles.

—*Annemarie Schimmel:* ***The Mystery of Numbers****, 1993*

15. The famed Newton-Leibniz controversy concerning the discovery of the calculus involves more than merely the question of priority of time. Mutual accusations of plagiarism, secrecy which manifested itself in cryptograms, letters published anonymously, treatises withheld from publication, assertions of friends and supporters of the two men, national jealousies, and the efforts of would-be peacemakers, all serve to complicate the situation and make such a tangle of truth and falsehood, information and misinformation, that it can probably never be solved conclusively.

—*Dorothy V. Schrader: "The Newton-Leibniz Controversy Concerning the Discovery of the Calculus";* ***The Mathematics Teacher****, vol. LV, No. 5; May, 1962*

16. The story of calculus brings out two of the main things that mathematics is for: providing tools that let scientists calculate what nature is doing, and providing new questions for mathematicians to sort out to their own satisfaction. These are the external and internal aspects of mathematics, often referred to as applied and pure mathematics (I dislike both adjectives, and I dislike the implied separation even more).

—*Ian Stewart:* ***Nature's Numbers****, 1995*

17. [Calculus is] the art of numbering and measuring exactly a Thing whose Existence cannot be conceived.

—*Voltaire:* ***Letters on the English****, 1910*

35.7 Derivatives and Differentiation

1. He who can digest a second and third fluxion, a second or third difference, need not, methinks, be squeamish about any point in Divinity.

—*George Berkeley:* ***The Analyst****, 1734*

2. I turn aside in horror from the lamentable plague of functions which do not have derivatives.

—*C. Hermite: Letter to Thomas Jan Stieltjes; May 20, 1893; Quoted in Lucienne Felix:* ***The Modern Aspect of Mathematics****, 1960*

3. The differential calculus has all the exactitude of other algebraic operations.

—*Pierre-Simon de Laplace:* ***Theorie Analytique des Probabilities****; "Introduction" in* ***Oeuvres****, tome 7, 1886*

4. To many mathematicians, I became the man of the functions without derivatives, although I never at any time gave myself completely to the study or consideration of such functions. And since the fear and fear which Hermite showed was felt by almost everybody, whenever I tries to take part in a mathematical discussion there would always be an analyst who would say, 'This won't interest you; we're discussing functions having derivatives.'

—*Henri Lebesque: Quoted in Lucienne Felix:* ***The Modern Aspect of Mathematics****, 1960*

5. ...the differential calculus could be employed with diagrams in an even more wonderfully simple manner than it was with numbers, because with diagrams the differences were not comparable with the things which differed; and as often as they were connected together by addition or subtraction, being incomparable with one another, the less vanished in comparison with the greater.

—*G.W. Leibniz:* ***Historia et origo calculi differentialis****, 1714;* ***Mathematische Schriften****, C.I. Gerhardt, ed., 1971*

6. He said—very seriously, I think—that functions have everything to gain by having derivatives!

—*Emile Picard: 1875, Quoted in Lucienne Felix:* ***The***

Modern Aspect of Mathematics, *1960 [Picard quotes physicist Valentin Boussinesq's astonishment when he learns that their exist continuous functions without derivatives.]*

7. If Newton and Leibniz had known that continuous functions need not necessarily have a derivative, the differential calculus would never have been created.

—*Emile Picard:* ***Bulletin American Mathematical Society***, *Vol. 2, 1905*

8. In the fall of 1972 President Nixon announced that the rate of increase of inflation was decreasing. This was the first time a sitting president used the third derivative to advance his case for re-election.

—*Hugo Rossi: "Mathematics is an Edifice, Not a Toolbox";* ***Notices of the AMS***, *vol. 43, 10, October, 1996*

35.8 Maximum and Minimum Values

1. Most practical questions can be reduced to problems of largest and smallest magnitudes ... and it is only by solving these problems that we can satisfy the requirements of practice which always seeks the best, the most convenient.

—*P.L. Cebysev: Quoted in V.M. Tikhomirov:* ***Stories About Maxima and Minima***; *Abe Schenitzer, tr., 1990*

2. Starting in the seventeenth century, the general theory of extreme values—maxima and minima—has become one of the systematic integrating principles of science.

—*Richard Courant & Herbert Robbins:* ***What Is Mathematics?***, *1941*

3. For since the fabric of the Universe is most perfect and the work of a most wise Creator, nothing at all takes place in the Universe in which some rule or maximum or minimum does not appear.

—*Leonhard Euler:* ***Methodus inveniendi lineas curvas maximi minimive proprietate gaudentes***, *1744*

4. A quadratic function, ambitious,
Said, "It's not only wrong, but it's vicious.
It's surely no sin
To have max. and min.;
To limit me so is malicious."

—*Leo Moser "Theory and Practice";* ***The Penguin Book of Limericks***, *E.O. Parrott, ed., 1983*

35.9 Mean Value Theorem

1. This [rigor] was supplied by the mean value theorem; and it was Cauchy's great service to have recognized its fundamental importance.... Because of this we adjudge Cauchy as the founder of exact infinitesimal calculus.

—*Felix Klein:* ***Elementary Mathematics from and Advanced Standpoint***, *1908, English tr., 1924*

2. The Mean Value Theorem is the midwife of calculus—not very important of glamorous by itself, but often helping to deliver other theorems that are of major significance.

—*E. Purcell & D. Varberg:* ***Calculus with Analytic Geometry***, *1991*

35.10 Integrals and Integration

1. At one time Leibniz and Johann Bernoulli discussed in their letters both the name and the principal symbol of the integral calculus. Leibniz favored the name *calculus summatorius* and the long letter [long S symbol] as the symbol. Bernoulli favored the name *calculus integralis* and the capital letter I as the sign of integration.... Leibniz and Johann Bernoulli finally reached a happy compromise, adopting Bernoulli's name "integral calculus," and Leibniz's symbol of integration.

—*Florian Cajori:* ***A History of Mathematics***, *1919*

2. Common integration is only the memory of differentiation ... the different artifices by which integration is effected are changes, not from the known to the unknown, but from forms in which memory will not serve us to those in which it will.

—*Augustus De Morgan: Quoted in Howard Eves:* ***In Mathematical Circles***, *1969*

3. Perhaps the most clear-cut example in the history of calculus, between discovery and the recognition of significance, is provided by the "fundamental theorem of calculus," which explicitly states the inverse relationship between tangent and area problems (or, in modern terminology between differentiation and integration).

—*C. H. Edwards, Jr.: "The Calculus According to Newton" and "The Calculus According to Leibniz";* ***The Historical Development of the Calculus***, *1979*

4. Does anyone believe that the difference between the Lebesque and Riemann integrals can have physical significance, and that whether say, an airplane would or would not fly could depend on this difference? If such were claimed, I should not care to fly in that plane.

—*Richard W. Hamming: In N. Rose;* ***Mathematical Maxims and Minims***, *1988*

5. In our universe, matter is arranged in a hierarchy of structures by successive integrations.

—*Francois Jacob:* ***The Possible and the Actual***, *1982*

6. Nature laughs at the difficulties of integration.

—*Pierre-Simon de Laplace: In J.W. Krutch "The*

Colloid and the Crystal," In I. Gordon and S. Sorkin, eds., ***The Armchair Science Reader****, 1959*

7. There are in this world optimists who feel that any symbol that starts off with an integral sign must necessarily denote something that will have every property that they should like an integral to possess. This of course is quite annoying to us rigorous mathematicians: what is even more annoying is that by doing so they often come up with the right answer.

—E.J. McShane: ***Bulletin of the American Mathematical Society****, vol. 69, 1963*

8. The experimental verification of a theory concerning any natural phenomenon generally rests on the result of an integration.

—J.W. Mellor: ***Higher Mathematics for Students of Chemistry and Physics****, 1902; 1955*

9. Integration keeps pace with differentiation

—Herbert Spencer: In C.G. Phillips: ***PRS****, 1977*

10. This new integral of Lebesque is proving itself a wonderful tool. I might compare it with a modern Krupp gun, so easily does it penetrate barriers which were impregnable.

—Edward Van Vleck: ***Bulletin of the American Mathematical Society****, vol. 23, 1916*

35.11 Series

1. Until now the theory of infinite series in general has been very badly grounded. One applies all the operations to infinite series as if they were finite; but is that permissible? I think not. Where is it demonstrated that one obtains the differential of an infinite series by taking the differential of each term? Nothing is easier that to give instances where this is not so.

—Niels Henrik Abel: ***Oeuvres****, 1826: Quoted in Reinhold Remmert:* ***Theory of Complex Functions****, Leslie Kay, tr., 1998*

2. The divergent series are the invention of the devil, and it is a shame to base on them any demonstration whatsoever. By using them one may draw any conclusion he pleases and that is why these series have produced so many fallacies and so many paradoxes.... I have become prodigiously attentive to all this, for with the exception of the geometrical series, their does not exist in all of mathematics a single infinite series the sum of which has been determined rigorously. In other words, the things which are the most important in mathematics are also those which have the least foundation. That most of these things are correct in spite of that is extraordinarily surprising. I am trying to find the reason for this; it is an exceedingly interesting question.

—Niels Henrik Abel: Letter to Berndt Holmboe: January, ***Oeuvres****, 1826; Quoted in Lucienne Felix:* ***The Modern Aspect of Mathematics****, 1960*

3. Learn the particular strength
of the Fibonacci series,
a balanced spiraling
outward of shapes,
those golden numbers
which describe dimensions
of sea shells, rams' horns,
collections of petals
and generations of bees.

—Judith Baumel: "Fibonacci"; ***The Weight of Numbers****, 1988*

4. Even as the finite encloses an infinite series
And in the unlimited limits appear,
So the soul of immensity dwells in minutia
And in narrowest limits no limits inhere.
What joy to discern the minute in infinity!
The vast to perceive in the small, what divinity!

—Jacob Bernoulli I: "On Infinite Series"; ***Ars Conjectandi****, 1713; Helen M. Walker, tr., in D.E. Smith:* ***A Source Book of Mathematics***

5. We must admit that many series are such as we cannot at present safely use, except as a means of discovery, the results of which are to be subsequently verified and the most determined rejector of all divergent series doubtless makes this use of them in his closet....

—Augustus De Morgan: ***Transactions of the Cambridge Philosophical Society****, 8, 1849*

6. A man has one pair of rabbits at a certain place entirely surrounded by a wall. We wish to know how many pairs can be bred from it in one year, if the nature of these rabbits is such that they breed every month one other pair and begin to breed in the second month after their birth. Let the first pair breed a pair in the first month, then duplicate it and there will be 2 pairs in a month, from these pairs one, namely the first, breeds a pair in the second month, and thus there are 3 pairs in the second month. From these in one month two will become pregnant, so that in the third month 2 pairs of rabbits will be born. Thus there are 5 pairs in this month. From these in the same month 3 will be pregnant, so that in the fourth month there will be 8 pairs. From these pairs 5 will breed 5 other pairs, which added to the 8 pairs gives 13 pairs in the fifth month....

—Leonardo Fibonacci (Leonardo of Pisa): ***Liber abbaci****; in* ***A Source Book of Mathematics, 1200–1800****, D.J. Struik, ed., 1969 [Fibonacci explains the origin of his famous number series, named for him, 1, 1, 2, 3, 5, 8, 13, 21, 34, 55, 89, 144, 233, 377....]*

7. Pick up a pinecone and count the spiral

rows of scales. You may find eight spirals winding up the left and 13 spirals winding up to the right, or 13 left and 21 right spirals, or other pairs of numbers. The striking fact is that these pairs of numbers are adjacent numbers in the famous Fibonacci series: 1, 1, 2, 3, 5, 8, 13, 21.... Here each term is the sum of the previous two terms. The phenomenon is well known and called phyllotaxis. Many are the efforts of biologists to understand why pinecones, sunflowers, and many other plants exhibit this remarkable pattern.

—*Stuart Kauffman:* ***At Home in the Universe****, 1995*

8. Population when unchecked, increases in a geometrical ratio. Subsistence increases only in an arithmetical ratio. A slight acquaintance with numbers will show the immensity of the first power in comparison with the second.

—*Thomas Robert Malthus:* ***An Essay on the Principle of Population****, 1798*

9. No part of Mathematics suffers more from the triviality of its initial presentation than the great subject of series.... The general ideas are never disclosed and thus the examples, which exemplify nothing, are reduced to silly trivialities

—*Alfred North Whitehead:* ***An Introduction to Mathematics****, Oxford University Press, 1958*

35.12 Differential Equations

1. Thus the partial differential equation entered theoretical physics as a handmaid, but has gradually become a mistress.

—*Albert Einstein:* ***The World As I See It****, 1934*

2. Among all the mathematical disciplines the theory of differential equations is the most important.... It furnishes the explanation of all those elementary manifestations of nature which involve time....

—*Sophus Lie:* ***Leipziger Berichte 47****, 1895*

3. In order to solve a differential equation you look at it till a solution occurs to you.

—*George Polya:* ***How To Solve It****, 1948*

4. The successes of the differential equation paradigm were impressive and extensive. Many problems, including basic and important ones, led to equations that could be solved. A process of self-selection set in, whereby equations that could not be solved were automatically of less interest than those that could.

—*Ian Stewart:* ***Does God Play Dice? The Mathematics of Chaos****, 1989*

5. ...that Cinderella of pure mathematics—the study of differential equations. The closely guarded secret of this subject is that it has not yet attained the status and dignity of a science, but still enjoys the freedom and freshness of such a prescientific study as natural history compared with botany. The student of differential equations—significantly he has no name or title to rank with the geometer or analyst—is still living at the stage when his main tasks are to collect specimens, to describe them with loving care, and to cultivate them for study under laboratory conditions. The work of classification and systematization has hardly begun. This is true even of differential equations which belong to the genus technically described as "ordinary, linear equations." ...In the case of non-linear equations.... An inviting flora of rare equations and exotic problems lies before a botanical excursion into the non-linear field.

—*George Temple: "Linearization and delinearization" in* ***Proceedings of the International Congress of Mathematicians****, J.A. Todd, ed., 1958*

6. Science is a differential equation. Religion is a boundary condition.

—*Alan M. Turing: in John D. Barrow:* ***Theories of Everything****, 1991*

7. Knowing what is big and what is small is more important than being able to solve partial differential equations.

—*Stan Ulam:* ***Adventures of a Mathematician****, 1976*

8. Matter-of-fact is an abstraction, arrived at by confining thought to purely formal relations which then masquerade as the final reality. This is why science, in its perfection, relapses into the study of differential equations. The concrete world has slipped through the meshes of the scientific net.

—*Alfred North Whitehead:* ***Modes of Thought****, 1938*

36

Computers, Algorithms and Mathematical Models

36.1 The History and Development of Computers

1. Computers are composed of nothing more than logic gates stretched out to the horizon in a vast numerical irrigation system.

—*Stan Augarten: **State of the Art: A Photographic History of the Integrated Circuit**, 1984*

2. The whole of the developments and operations of analysis are now capable of being executed by machinery.... As soon as an Analytical Engine exists, it will necessarily guide the future course of science. Whenever any result is sought by its aid, the question will then arise—By what course of calculation can these results be arrived at by the machine in the shortest time?

—*Charles Babbage: **Passages from the Life of a Philosopher**, 1864*

3. The idea that the human mind is essentially a computational device commends itself by virtue of an unanswerable question: What else could it be? But whatever the rhetorical merits of the claim, the idea that the mind is nothing more than a computational device subordinates itself to an unavoidable challenge: If that is so, what precisely are the computations (and so the algorithms) involved?

—*David Berlinski: **The Advent of the Algorithm**, "Introduction," 2000*

4. In a classic article published over forty years ago, A.M. Turing has argued that no computer could ever be programmed to solve the problem of detecting infinite loops in computer programs.

—*Arthur Charlesworth: "Infinite Loops in Computer Programs"; **Mathematics Magazine**, 52, 1979*

5. ...the limitations of mathematics, some mathematicians say may be the main reason we don't yet have fully intelligent computers, like Hal in Arthur Clarke's 2001. Traditional approaches to artificial intelligence assumed that thought could be programmed into computers in part because thought itself was logical, But increasingly, evidence suggests that the road to intelligence is not reason—or, at least not logical rules.

—*K.C. Cole: **The Universe and the Teacup**, 1997*

6. An area is ... developing in computer science to provide "proofs of programs." As one might expect it takes much longer to produce a proof of correctedness of the program than to produce the program itself.

—*Philip J. Davis and Reuben Hersh: **The Mathematical Experience**, 1981*

7. He said, as soon as we have good computers we shall be able to divide the phenomena of meteorology into two categories, the stable and the unstable. The unstable phenomena are those which are upset by small disturbances, the stable phenomena are those which are resilient to small disturbances. He said, as soon as we have some large computers working, the problems of meteorology will be solved. All processes that are stable we shall predict. All processes that are unstable we shall control.... This was John von Neumann's dream.

—*Freeman Dyson: **Infinite in All Directions**, 1988*

8. Things were going badly [with a Harvard computer one night in 1945]. There was something wrong in one of the circuits. Finally, someone located the trouble spot, and using ordinary tweezers, removed the problem, a two-inch moth. From then on, when anything went wrong with a computer, we said it had bugs in it.

—*Grace M. Hopper: "Grace M. Hopper, 1906–1992"; **Mathematical Digest**, July, 1992*

9. The Analytical Engine [of Charles Babbage] has no pretensions whatever to originate anything. It can do whatever we know how to order it to perform. It can follow analysis; but it has no power of anticipating any analytical relations or truths. Its province is to assist us in making available what we are already acquired.

*—Agusta Ada Lovelace: "Sketch of the Analytical Engine invented by Charles Babbage, Esq., by L.F. Menabrea of Turin, officer of the Military Engineers"; **Taylor's Scientific Memoirs**, 1843*

10. Computing "π" is the ultimate stress test for a computer—a kind of digital cardiogram.

*—Ivars Peterson: **Islands of Truth**, 1990*

11. The computer is really very much more than a super slide rule. Our whole intellectual horizons are going to increase a great deal because computers exist and they are going to imply something like a new way of life in many respects. You could, of course, go back and look at some historical analogues. An automobile is not just a super horse. It is true that, given enough time and given enough horses, you can get a group of horses to do just about everything that an automobile can do, but still the automobile has changed our entire way of life. I think that a computer may well do the same.

*—Henry O. Pollak: in **New Directions in Mathematics**, Robert W. Ritchie, ed., 1963*

12. We tend to think of computer calculations as being the pinnacle of accuracy. Actually, they're not. The limitations of memory mean that numbers can be held in the computer to a very limited accuracy, say eight or ten decimal places. Furthermore, the 'private' internal code that the computer uses to represent its numbers and the 'public' one that gets printed on the screen are different. This introduces two sources of error: rounding error in internal calculations and translation error from private code to public.

*—Ian Stewart: **Does God Play Dice?**, 1989*

36.2 Computers and Mathematics

1. At this point the program began to surprise us.... It would work out compound strategies based on all the tricks it had been "taught," and often these approaches were far more clever than those we would have tried. Thus it began to teach us things about how to proceed that we never expected. In a sense it had surpassed its creators in some aspects of the "intellectual" as well as the mechanical parts of the task.

*—Kenneth Appel & Wolfgang Haken: "The Four Color Problem"; **Mathematics Today: Twelve Informal Essays**, 1978*

2. Most mathematicians who were educated prior to the development of fast computers tend not to think of the computer as a routine tool to be used in conjunction with other older and more theoretical tools in advancing mathematical knowledge. Thus they intuitively feel that if an argument contains parts that are not verifiable by hand calculations it is on rather insecure ground. There is a tendency to feel that verification of computer results by independent computer programs is not as certain to be correct as independent hand checking of the proof of theorems proved in the standard way.

*—Kenneth Appel & Wolfgang Haken: "The Four-Color Problem" in **Mathematics Today**, L.A. Steen, ed., 1978*

3. I cannot see that the machines [electronic computers] have dethroned the Queen. Mathematicians who would dispense entirely with brains possibly have no need of any.

*—E.T. Bell: Quoted in Howard W. Eves: **Mathematical Circles Adieu**, 1977*

4. The computer has in turn changed the very nature of mathematical experience, suggesting for the first time that mathematics, like physics, may yet become an empirical discipline, a place where things are discovered because they are seen.

*—David Berlinski: in a review of T.W. Korner: **The Pleasures of Counting**, in **The Sciences**, July/August, 1997*

5. I must admit that for a number of my friends, mostly number theorists and topologists, who fool around with small numbers and low dimensional spaces, the computer is a tremendous sketch pad. But those same friends, perhaps in other bodies, got along just fine twenty-five years ago, before the computer became a scratch pad, using a different scratch pad. Maybe they weren't as efficient but mathematics isn't in a hurry. Efficiency is meaningless. Understanding is what counts. So, is the computer important to mathematics? My answer is no. It is important, but not to mathematics.

*—Paul Halmos: in Donald Albers, "Paul Halmos: Maverick Mathologist"; **Two-Year College Mathematics Journal**, 13; September, 1982*

6. Many of the most able people in computing were attracted there from mathematics and probably represent a loss to mathematics. On the other hand, the glamor and money in computing probably have attracted more people to mathematics. The net balance would be hard to measure.

*—R.W. Hamming: "Impact of Computers"; **American Mathematical Monthly**, vol. 72; February, 1965*

7. It is impossible to exaggerate the extent to which modern applied mathematics has been shaped and fueled by the general availability of fast computers with large memories. Their impact on mathematics, both applied and pure is comparable to the role of telescopes in astronomy and microscopes in biology.

—Peter Lax: "The Flowering of Applied Mathematics

*in America"; **A Century of Mathematics in America, Part II**, Peter Duren, ed., 1989*

8. I think everyone would agree that the computer just makes the mathematician all the more necessary, because it can't decide what to do, and can't think out what the problem should be. As a result the more computing help is available, the more we'll need the mathematician to tell us what to do.

—Donald C. May: "Professional Mathematicians in Government and Industry"; SIAM Review 2, January, 1960

9. ...my hunch is that the number of people caught up by computers will be vastly more than the number of people who become mathematicians. I think that most of the people who are driven towards mathematics are driven towards mathematics, and they are not going to be diverted by the practical aspects of computers. They may be absorbed by the mathematical problems in computing or by the use of computers in mathematics—that's quite different. But there will be many, many more people using computers for practical purposes than would have gone into mathematics.

*—Mina Rees: Interview in **Mathematical People**, D.J. Albers & G.L. Alexanderson, eds., 1985*

10. In the quest for simplification, mathematics stands to computer science as diamond mining to coal mining. The former is a search for gems.... The latter is permanently involved with bulldozing large masses of ore—extremely useful bulk material.

*—Jacob T. Schwartz: **Discrete Thoughts: Essays on Mathematics, Science and Philosophy**, 1986*

36.3 Humans and Machines

1. Probability of human error is considerably higher than that of machine error.

*—Ken Appel and Wolfgang Haken: "The Four-Color Problem" in **Mathematics Today**, L. Steen, ed., 1978*

2. One machine can do the work of fifty ordinary men. No machine can do the work of one extraordinary man.

*—Elbert Hubbard: **The Roycroft Dictionary and Book of Epigrams**, 1923*

3. Not until a machine can write a sonnet or compose a concerto because of thoughts and emotions felt, and not by the chance fall of symbols, could we agree that machine equals brain—that is, not only write it but know that it had written it. No mechanism could feel (and not merely artificially signal, an easy contrivance) pleasure at its successes, grief when its valves fuse, be warmed by flattery, be made miserable by its mistakes, be charmed by sex, be angry or depressed when it cannot get what it wants.

*—G. Jefferson: "The Mind of Mechanical Man," Lister Oration for 1949; **British Medical Journal**, 1949*

4. It is unworthy of excellent men to lose hours like slaves in the labor of calculation which could safely be relegated to anyone else if machines were used.

*—Gottfried Wilhelm Leibniz: in **The Magic of Mathematics**, 1994*

5. To the theoretical question, Can you design a machine to do whatever a brain can do? the answer is this: If you will specify in a finite and unambiguous way what you think a brain does do with information, then we can design a brain to do it. Pitts and I have prove this constructively. But can you say what you think brains do?

*—Warren S. McCullough: In Stafford Beer; **Platform for Change**, 1975*

6. The arithmetical machine produces effects which approach nearer to thought than all the actions of animals. But it does nothing which would enable us to attribute will to it, as to the animals.

*—Blaise Pascal: **Pensees**, 1670; tr. 1688*

7. The computer is just and instrument for doing faster what we already know how to do slower. All pretensions to computer intelligence and paradise-tomorrow promises should be toned down before the public turns away in disgust. And if that should happen, our civilization might not survive.

*—Gian-Carlo Rota: **Indiscrete Thoughts**, 1996*

8. It is not my aim to surprise or shock you.... But the simplest way I can summarize is to say that there are now in the world machines that think, that learn and create. Moreover, their ability to do these things is going to increase rapidly until—in a visible future—the range of problems they can handle will be coextensive with the range to which the human mind has been applied.

*—Herbert Simon: "Heuristic Problem Solving: The Next Advance in Operations Research"; **Operations Research**, vol. 6, January, 1958.*

9. In considering the functions of the mind or the brain we find certain operations which we can explain in purely mechanical terms. This we say does not correspond to the real mind: it is a sort of skin which we must strip off if we are to find the real mind. But then in what remains we find a further skin to be stripped off, and so on. Proceeding in this way do we ever come to the "real" mind, or do we eventually come to the skin which has nothing in it? In the latter case the whole mind is mechanical.

*—Alan Turing: "Can a Machine Think?" in **The World of Mathematics**, James R. Newman, ed., 1956*

10. The ... question, "Can machines think?" I believe to be too meaningless to deserve discussion. Nevertheless I believe that at the end of he century the use of words and general educated opinion will have altered so much that one will be able to speak of machines thinking without expecting to be contradicted.

*—Alan Turing: "Computing Machinery and Intelligence" in **Computers and Thought**, E.A. Feigenbaum & J. Feldman, eds., 1963*

11. The claim that "machines cannot make mistakes" seems a curious one. One is tempted to retort, "Are they the worst for that?"

*—Alan M. Turing: "Can a Machine Think?" in **The World of Mathematics**, James R. Newman, ed., 1956*

12. Machines take me by surprise with great frequency.

*—Alan M. Turing: "Can a Machine Think?" in **The World of Mathematics**, James R. Newman, ed., 1956*

13. It is my thesis that machines can and do transcend some of the limitations of their designers, and that in doing so they may be both effective and dangerous. It may well be that in principle we cannot make any machine the elements of whose behavior we cannot comprehend sooner or later

*—Norbert Wiener: "Some Moral and Technical Consequences of Automation"; **Science** 131, 1960*

36.4 Miscellaneous Views of Computers

1. The great supercomputer, asked what is the answer to the great problem of life, the universe and everything replied, after many years of computation 42.

*—Douglas Adams; **The Hitch-hiker's Guide to the Galaxy**, 1979*

2. The difference between us and a computer is that, the computer is blindly stupid, but it is capable of being stupid many million times a second.

*—Douglas Adams: SCO Forum 97, **Review It**, July, 1999*

3. To err is human, but to really foul things up requires a computer.

—Anonymous: Quoted n "Quote Unquote," Feb. 22, 1982, BBC Radio 4

4. What I shall say about these marvelous aids to the feeble human intelligence [electronic computers] will be little indeed, for two reasons: I have always hated machinery, and the only machine I ever understood was a wheelbarrow, and that but imperfectly.

*—E.T. Bell: Quoted in Howard W. Eves: **Mathematical Circles Adieu**, 1977*

5. A Modern computer hovers between the obsolescent and the nonexistent.

*—Sydney Brenner: attributed in **Science**, January 5, 1990*

6. Nature might be somehow more powerful than a digital computer.

*—Aviezri S. Fraenkel: Quoted in the **New York Times**, March 25, 1997*

7. Everyone knows putting ideas into words is difficult—the computer types call it "documentation" and avoid doing it at all costs.

*—Seymour Haber: "The Axiom of Choice and Calculus Revision: A Dialogue"; **The Mathematical Intelligencer**, vol. 13, Winter 1991*

36.5 Cybernetics

1. The future science of government should be called "la cybernetique."

*—Andre-Marie Ampere, 1843: Quoted in A.L. Mackay: **Dictionary of Scientific Quotations**, 1944*

2. Cybernetics is mappable to Marxist
theory.
Liberty must be a computable function.

*—Stafford Beer: **Brain of the Firm**, 1972*

3. Cybernetics is a word invented to define a new field in science. It combines under one heading the study of what in a human context is sometimes loosely described as thinking and in engineering is known as control and communication. In other words, cybernetics attempts to find the common elements in the functioning of automatic machines and of the human nervous system, and to develop a theory which will cover the entire field of control and communication in machines and in living organisms.

*—Norbert Wiener: "Cybernetics"; **Scientific American**, November, 1948*

4. The study of cybernetics is likely to have fruitful applications in many fields, from the design of control mechanisms for artificial limbs to the almost complete mechanization of industry. But in our view it encompasses much wider horizons. If the 17th and early 18th centuries were the age of clocks, and the latter 18th and 19th centuries the age of steam engines, the present time is the age of communication and control.

*—Norbert Wiener: "Cybernetics"; **Scientific American**, November, 1948*

36.6 Combinatorics and Combinatorial Analysis

1. The recent development of combinatorics is somewhat like a Cinderella story. It used to be looked down on by "mainstream" mathematicians as being somehow less respectable than other areas.... Then along came the prince of computer science with its many mathematical problems and needs—and it was combinatorics that best fitted the glass slipper held out.

—*Anders Bjorner and Richard Stanley; "A Combinatorial Miscellany," to appear 2001*

2. Most popular mathematics puzzles and games, such as Rubik's cube and jigsaw puzzles, are essentially problems in combinatorics.

—*Anders Bjorner and Richard Stanley; "A Combinatorial Miscellany," to appear 2001*

3. Combinatorics without Algebra and Topology is like Sex without Love.

—*Anthony Joseph: Attributed*

4. Combinatorial problems are found nowadays in increasing numbers in every branch of science, even in those where mathematics is rarely used. It is now becoming clear that, once the life sciences develop to the stage at which mathematical apparatus becomes indispensable, their main support will come from combinatorial theory.

—*Gian-Carlo Rota: "Combinatorial Analysis"* ***The Mathematical Sciences: A Collection of Essays****, Edited by the National Research Council's Committee on Support of Research in the Mathematical Sciences, 1969*

5. The earliest glimmers of mathematical understanding in civilized man were combinatorial. The most backward civilization, whenever it let fantasy roam as far as the world of numbers and geometric figures, would promptly come up with binomial coefficients, magic squares, or some rudimentary classification of solid polyhedra.

—*Gian-Carlo Rota: "Combinatorial Analysis"* ***The Mathematical Sciences: A Collection of Essays****, Edited by the National Research Council's Committee on Support of Research in the Mathematical Sciences, 1969*

6. The very term "combinatorial methods" has an oxymoronic character.

—*Joel Spencer:* ***Handbook of Combinatorics****, 1991*

7. ...combinatorial analysis deals with the properties of arrangements and patterns defined by means of a finite class of "points." Familiar examples are the problems on permutations and combinations studied in high school algebra.... In the broadest sense one could say that combinatorial analysis deals with relations and patterns, their classification and morphology.

—*Stanislaw M. Ulam: "Computers";* ***Scientific American****, September, 1964*

8. The difficulty of counting has given rise to a whole branch of mathematics, called combinatorics, sometimes described as the art of advanced counting. Fortunately, an amazing number of problems in combinatorics are exact analogues of each other. Solve one, and you solve both, or all of them.

—*David Wells:* ***You Are a Mathematician****, 1995*

36.7 ALGORITHMS

1. Years ago, in grade school,
Teachers used to say,
"For every problem there's a rule,
So do it just that way."
But when I got to college
They said I always must
Apply my basic knowledge,
Since rules are to distrust.
The New Math thought that every kid
Should give real thought a try.
It didn't matter what you did
Just so you told them why.
Then the computers came along,
And algorithms, too,
Constructed so you can't go wrong
No matter what you do.

—*Anonymous*

2. An algorithm is a scheme for the manipulation of symbols, but to say this is only to say what an algorithm does. Symbols do more than suffer themselves to be hustled around; they are there to offer their reflections of the world. They are instruments that convey information.

—*David Berlinski:* ***The Advent of the Algorithm****, "Introduction," 2000*

3. Some time around A.D. 825, a Persian mathematician called al-Khowarizmi wrote a book outlining the rules for performing basic arithmetic using numbers expressed in the Hindu decimal form that we use today.... From his name comes the modern word 'algorithm.' ... An algorithm is a step-by-step method for performing some kind of calculation.

—*Keith Devlin:* ***Mathematics: The New Golden Age****, 1988*

4. [The Turing machine, a] hypothetical computing device was invented by the English mathematician Alan Turing in the 1930s to provide an abstract framework for the study of computation. Despite its simplicity, it can be shown that any computation, no matter how complicated, can be carried out using a Turing machine. The Turing machine concept allows a precise definition of an 'algorithm' as a Turing machine program.

—*Keith Devlin:* ***Mathematics: The New Golden Age****, 1988*

5. [The Euclidean algorithm is] the granddaddy of all algorithms, because it is the oldest nontrivial algorithm that has survived to the present day.

—*Donald Knuth: in "Media Highlights"; **The College Mathematics Journal**, March, 1996*

6. One of my mathematician friends told me he would be willing to recognize computer science as a worthwhile field of study as soon as it contains 1,000 deep theorems. This criterion should obviously changed to include algorithms as well as theorems—say, 500 deep theorems and 500 deep algorithms.

—*Donald Knuth: "Algorithm and Program: Information and Data"; **Comm. ACM**, 9;654, 1966*

7. Mathematicians have set a great stock in abstract mathematics in which concepts and rigor have been the dominant things. But now algorithms are really important. There have been algorithms around from Euclid's algorithm on, but they have been regarded as rather unusual. I think that mathematics will have to become more algorithmic if it is going to be active and vital in the creative life.

—*Albert W. Tucker: in **Mathematical People**; D.J. Albers & G.L. Alexanderson, eds., 1985*

8. Mathematics consists entirely of calculations. In mathematics everything is algorithm and nothing is meaning, even when it doesn't look like that because we seem to be using words to talk about mathematical things. Even these words are used to construct an algorithm.

—*Ludwig Wittgenstein: **Remarks on the Foundations of Mathematics**, 1956, 1983 G.E.M. Anscombe & B. Blackwell, tr.*

36.8 Linear Programming

1. Linear programming in essence is a method for considering a number of variables simultaneously and calculating the best possible solution of a given problem within the stated limitations. Any manufacturer will at once appreciate that this is a precise statement of his own problem. In deciding what particular items to manufacture, and in what quantities, he must take into account a great number of factors.... With linear programming ... it becomes possible to locate definitely the optimum solutions among all the available ones....

—*William W. Cooper and Abraham Charnes: "Linear Programming"; **Scientific American**, August, 1954*

2. Linear programming is a technique used to provide a mathematical description (or model) of a real-life problem in which something needs to be maximized (e.g. profits or security) or minimized (e.g. costs or risks). The required optimization is achieved by a suitable choice of values of a number of parameters (or variables).... The linear-programming was—and is—perhaps the single most important real-life problem.

—*Keith Devlin: **Mathematics: The New Golden Age**, 1988*

3. The theory of linear programming that developed in the United States during World War II (in the U.S.S.R. as early as 1939) is regarded as a mathematical model that is more realistically stated in terms of actual business planning and decision making. Its original development in this country was associated with military decision making, but the Soviet examples ... dealt, at an early stage, with production economics.

—*Lawrence R. Klein: "The Role of Mathematics in Economics"; **The Mathematical Sciences: A Collection of Essays**, Edited by the National Research Council's Committee on Support of Research in the Mathematical Sciences, 1969*

36.9 Operations Research

1. A war of a battle, a mission or a sortie, none is repeatable and none is an experiment. Yet the young scientists brought to them the conviction that in them and nowhere else must be found the empirical evidence for which war is made. The passion of these men was to trace in operations involving life and death the total skeleton of experimental truth.

—*Jacob Bronowski: Review of Phillip M. Morse and George E. Kimball: **Methods of Operation Research**, 1951; in **Scientific American**, October, 1951*

2. Charles Babbage previsioned the vast and important field known as operations research. It was his book *Economy of Manufactures and Machinery*, devoted to a study of scientific manufacturing processes of all kinds, and produced as a by-product of his interest in computing machinery, that foreshadowed the concept. Briefly put, operations research is the scientific analysis of business problems aimed at providing executives and management with information leading to more effective operation of their business.

—*Howard W. Eves: **In Mathematical Circles**, 1969*

3. ...Just as with every other field of applied science, the improvement of operations of war by the application of scientific analysis requires a certain flair which comes with practice, but which is difficult to put into words.

—*Phillip M. Morse and George E. Kimball: **Methods of Operation Research**, 1951*

4. Operations research is a general mathematical technology which began in World War II when it was necessary to devise a strategy for damaging the enemy during an attack when very little was known about the disposition of the enemy's forces.

It is a mathematical technology to increase the efficiency of any campaign—whether it is military, sales, political, or advertising—when the target of the campaign is not clearly delineated.

—*Lloyd Motz & Jefferson Hane Weaver: **The Story of Mathematics**, 1993*

5. [Operations research] has been defined as "a scientific method of providing executive departments with a quantitative basis for decisions regarding the operations under their control." The definition is a little inflated but it conveys the general outline of the subject.

—*James R. Newman: **The World of Mathematics**, Vol. 4, 1956*

36.10 Mathematical Models

1. All models are wrong but some are useful.

—*G.E.P. Box: in **Robustness in Statistics**; R.L. Launer & G.N. Wilkinson, eds., 1979*

2. The preeminence of astronomy rests on the peculiarity that it can be treated mathematically; and the progress of physics, and most recently biology, has hinged equally on finding formulations of their laws that can be displayed as mathematical models.

—*Jacob Bronowski: **The Ascent of Man**, 1973*

3. Mathematical modeling is about rules—the rules of reality. What distinguishes a mathematical model from, say a poem, a song, a portrait or any other kind of "model," is that the mathematical model is an image or picture of reality painted with logical symbols instead of with words, sounds or watercolors. These symbols are then strung together in accordance with a set of rules expressed in a special language, the language of mathematics.

—*John Casti: **Reality Rules**, vol. I, "Preface," 1992*

4. Mathematical modeling of natural phenomena is hardly new. Nevertheless, advances in numerical analysis and the development of the computer have made it possible in ways that are much more complex and more realistic than ever before. Mathematical modeling in partnership with the computer is rapidly becoming a third element of the scientific method, coequal with more traditional elements of theory and experiment.

—*E.E. David: Quoted in Harold M. Ness: "Mathematics: an integral part of our culture"; **Essays in Humanistic Mathematics**,*

5. A theory has only the alternative of being right or wrong. A model has a third possibility: it may be right, but irrelevant.

—*Manfred Eigen: in Jagdish Mehra, ed. **The Physicist's Conception of Nature**, 1973*

6. Nature has ... some sort of arithmetical-geometrical coordinate system, because nature has all kinds of models. What we experience of nature is in models, and all of nature's models are so beautiful. It struck me that nature's system must be a real beauty, because in chemistry we find that the associations are always in beautiful whole numbers—there are no fractions.

—*R. Buckminster Fuller: "In the Outlaw Area"; profile by Calvin Tomkins in **The New Yorker**, January 8, 1966*

7. In real life, the mathematician's main task is to formulate problems by building an abstract mathematical model consisting of equations, which will be simple enough to solve without being so crude that they fail to mirror reality. Solving equations is a minor technical matter compared with the this fascinating and sophisticated craft of model-building, which calls for both clear, keen common-sense and the highest qualities of artistic and creative imagination.

—*John Hammersley: in Mina Rees "Mathematics in the Market Place," **The American Mathematical Monthly**, 65, May, 1958*

8. The making of models or pictures to explain mathematical formulae and the phenomena they describe, is not a step towards, but a step away from reality; it is like making graven images of a spirit.

—*Sir James Jeans: **The Mysterious Universe**, 1930*

9. The purpose of models is not to fit the data but to shape the questions.

—*Samuel Karlin: 11th R.A. Fisher Memorial Lecture, Royal Society, April 20, 1983*

10. It is generally recognized that high-speed computers are valuable tools in the development of mathematical models. The normal procedure is somewhat as follows. The social scientist collects a large amount of data. This leads him to some general principles which, when formulated in a mathematical language, provide a theoretical model. It is the task of the mathematician to develop this formulation. Theoretical mathematics reduces problems to routine computations, and the computer is the tool for carrying out the computations.

—*John G. Kemeny: "The Social Sciences Call on Mathematics"; **The Mathematical Sciences: A Collection of Essays**, Edited by the National Research Council's Committee on Support of Research in the Mathematical Sciences, 1969*

11. Thomas Malthus created a mathematical model in which population multiplies in a geometric progression while the food supply increases only arithmetically, precipitating a "struggle for existence." Both Charles Darwin and Alfred Russel Wallace, on reading Malthus, saw in that struggle the mechanism with which to explain natural selection. An essentially mathematical idea, in other words, can be said to have contributed to the development of the central concept of biological evolution.

—*Edward F. Moore: "Mathematics in the Biological Sciences"; **Scientific American**, September, 1964*

12. [Although geometers draw figures as an aid to their investigations] they are not thinking about these figures but of those things the figures represent; thus it is the square in itself and the diameter in itself which are the matter of their arguments, not that which they draw; similarly, when they model or draw objects, which may themselves have images in shadows or in water, they use them in turn as images, endeavoring to see those absolute objects which cannot be seen otherwise than by thought.

—*Plato: in Ivor Thomas: **Greek Mathematical Works**, 1967*

13. No real phenomenon (physical, biological, or social) is perfectly described by any mathematical model. There's usually a choice among several incompatible models, each more or less suitable.

—*Hilary Putnam: "What is Mathematical Truth?"; **Mathematics, Matter and Method**, 1986*

14. It is a paradox in mathematics and physics that we have no good model for the teaching of models.

—*Hartley J. Rogers: in Lynn A. Steen: **Mathematics Tomorrow**, 1981*

15. I am never content until I have constructed a mechanical model of the subject I am studying. If I succeed in making one, I understand; otherwise I do not.

—*William Thomson [Lord Kelvin]: Notes of Lectures on **Molecular Dynamics and Wave Theory of Light**, 1891–94*

16. No good model ever accounted for all the facts, since some data was bound to be misleading if not plain wrong.

—*James Dewey Watson: Quoted in Francis Crick: **Some Mad Pursuit**, 1988*

37
The Theory of Probability

37.1 Calculating Probabilities

1. I believe the Calculation of the Quantity of Probability might be improved to be a very successful and pleasant Speculation, and applied to a great many Events which are accidental, besides those of Games....

—*John Arbuthnot: **Of the Laws of Chance**, 1692; Quoted in Isaac Todhunter: **History of the Theory of Probability**, 1865*

2. It seems that to make a correct conjecture about any event whatever, it is necessary to calculate exactly the number of possible cases and then to determine how much more likely it is that one case will occur than another.

—*Jacob I Bernoulli: **Ars Conjectandi**, 1713*

3. A Bernoulli trial is simply an experiment with a dichotomous outcome. It results in either success or failure, black or white, on or off. There is no middle ground, no room for compromise, no comfort for the wishy-washy.... A single Bernoulli trial is rarely of much interest. The plot thickens, however, when Bernoulli trials are conducted repeatedly, and we observe how many of these trials yield success and how many yield failures. This accumulated record can shed some very useful information on the underlying processes.

—*William Dunham: **The Mathematical Universe**, 1994*

4. All possible "definitions" of probability fall short of the actual practice.

—*William Feller: **An Introduction to Probability Theory and Its Applications**, 1960*

5. The laws of probability, so true in general, so fallacious in particular.

—*Edward Gibbon: **Memoirs of My Life and Writings**, 1794*

6. Gumperson's Law: The probability of anything happening is in inverse ratio to its desirability.

—*R.F. Gumperson: in **Changing Times**, November, 1957*

7. Probability today is a cornerstone of all the sciences, and its daughter, the science of statistics, enters into all human activities.

—*Mark Kac: "Probability"; **Scientific American**, September, 1964*

8. A misunderstanding of Bernoulli's theorem is responsible for one of the commonest fallacies in the estimation of probabilities, the fallacy of the maturity of chances. When a coin has come down heads twice in succession, gamblers sometimes say that it is more likely to come down tails next time because 'by the law of averages' (whatever that may mean) the proportion of tails must be brought right some time.

—*W. C. Kneale: **Probability and Induction**, 1952*

9. We see ... that the theory of probabilities is at bottom only common sense reduced to calculation; it makes us appreciate with exactitude what reasonable minds feel by a sort of instinct, often without being able to account for it.... It is remarkable that [this] science, which originated in the consideration of games of chance, should have become the most important object of human knowledge.

—*Pierre-Simon de Laplace: **Oeuvres, vol. VII, Theorie Analytique des Probabilities**, "Introduction," 1812–1820*

10. The most important questions of life are, for the most part, really only problems of probability. Strictly speaking one may even say that nearly all our knowledge is problematical; and in the small number of things which we are able to know with certainty, even in the mathematical sciences themselves, the principle means for ascertain truth—induction and analogy—are based on probabilities.

—*Pierre-Simon de Laplace: "A Philosophical Essay on Probabilities," 1814*

11. Probability—Each one can employ it; no one can take it away.

—*Blaise Pascal:* ***Pensees****, 1670*

12. The theory of probabilities is simply the science of logic quantitatively treated.

—*Charles Sanders Peirce: "The Red and the Black":* ***The Collected Papers of Charles Sanders Peirce****, Charles Hartshorne & Paul Weiss, eds., 1931–35*

13. The director of a life insurance company does not know when each of the insured will die, but he relies upon the calculus of probabilities and on the law of great numbers, and he is not deceived, since he distributes dividends to his stockholders.

—*Henri Poincare:* ***Science and Method****, 1952*

14. ...the probability curve has a bell-shaped form.

—*J.V. Uspensky:* ***Introduction to Mathematical Probability****, 1937*

37.2 Probability, Ignorance and Certainty

1. Are no probabilities to be accepted merely because they are not certainties?

—*Jane Austen:* ***Sense and Sensibility****, 1811*

2. Probability: An erudite measure of ignorance. Being dimensionless, it is best used with a dimensional measure, especially a grain of salt.

—*Ambrose Bierce:* ***The Devil's Dictionary****, 1909*

3. Probability is expectation founded upon partial knowledge. A perfect acquaintance with all the circumstances affecting the occurrence of an event would change expectation into certainty, and leave neither room nor demand for a theory of probabilities.

—*George Boole:* ***An Investigation of the Law of Thought on Which Are Founded the Mathematical Theories of Logic and Probabilities****, 1854*

4. It is truth very certain that, when it is not in our power to determine what is true, we ought to follow what is most probable.

—*Rene Descartes:* ***Discourse on Method****, 1637*

5. Probability may be described, agreeably to general usage, as importing partial incomplete belief.

—*Francis Y. Edgeworth: "The Philosophy of Chance";* ***Mind****, vol. 9, 1884*

6. Natural selection is a mechanism for generating an exceedingly high degree of improbability.

—*Ronald Aylmer Fisher:* ***Perspectives in Medicine and Biology****, 1973*

7. But if probability measures the importance of our state of ignorance it must change its value whenever we add new knowledge. And so it does.

—*Thornton C. Fry:* ***Probability and Its Engineering Uses****, 1965*

8. A reasonable probability is the only certainty.

—*Edgar W. Howe:* ***Country Time Sayings****, 1911*

9. One of the difficulties arising out of the subjective view of probability results from the principle of insufficient reasons. This principle ... holds that if we are wholly ignorant of the different ways an even can occur and therefore have no reasonable ground for preference, it is likely to occur one way as another.

—*Edward Kasner & James Newman:* ***Mathematics and the Imagination****, 1940*

10. It has been pointed out already that no knowledge of probabilities, less in degree than certainty, helps us know what conclusion are true, and that there is no direct relation between the truth of a proposition and its probability. Probability begins and ends with probability.

—*John Maynard Keynes:* ***A Treatise on Probability****, 1906—1912*

11. Probability has reference partly to our ignorance, partly to out knowledge.

—*Pierre-Simon de Laplace:* ***Theorie analytique des probabilities****, 1820*

12. Is probability probable?

—*Blaise Pascal: Quoted in E.T. Bell:* ***Men of Mathematics****, 1937*

13. The very name calculus of probabilities is a paradox. Probability opposed to certainty is what we do not know, and how can we calculate what we do not know?

—*Henri Poincare:* ***The Foundations of Science****, 1946*

37.3 Miscellaneous Views of Probability

1. Life is a school of probability.

—*Walter Bagehot: Quoted in* ***The World of Mathematics****, James R. Newman, ed., 1956*

2. Events with a sufficiently small probability never occur, or at least we must act, in all circumstances, as if they were impossible.

—*Emile Borel:* ***Probabilities and Life****; "Introduction," 1962*

3. To us probability is the very guide of life.
—Bishop Joseph Butler: ***Analogy of Religion****, "Preface," 1736*

4. Probabilities direct the conduct of the wise man.
—Cicero: ***De Natura Decorum****, 45 B.C.*

5. As for a future life, every man must judge for himself between conflicting vague probabilities.
—Charles Darwin: ***Life and Letters of Charles Darwin****, Francis Darwin, ed., 1887*

6. Less men suspect your tale untrue,
Keep probability in view.
—John Gay: ***Fables****, "The Painter Who Pleased Nobody," 1727 In J.R. Newman, ed.* ***The World of Mathematics****, 1956*

7. Probability must atone for want of truth.
—Matthew Prior: ***Solomon on the Vanity of the World****, "Preface," 1718*

8. In almost everything, we act but upon probabilities; and one exception out of a thousand ought never to determine us.
—Samuel Richardson: ***Sir Charles Grandison****, 1749*

9. When we want something, we always have to reckon with probabilities.
—Jean-Paul Sarte: ***The Philosophy of Existentialism****, 1965*

37.4 Chance

1. Games of chance are probably as old as the human desire to get something for nothing; but their mathematical implications were appreciated only after Fermat and Pascal in 1654 reduced chance to law.
—E.T. Bell: ***The Development of Mathematics*** *1940*

2. Chance, too, which seems to rush along with slack reins, is bridled and governed by law.
—Boethius: ***The Consolation of Philosophy****, ca. 480–525*

3. ...the laws of chance are just as necessary as the casual laws themselves.
—D. Bohm: ***Causality and Chance in Modern Physics****, 1957*

4. Chance is both tempting and troubling. It tempts in that it excuses us from all responsibility: what happens by chance is exempt from rhyme or reason; it is something we can't know and can't control; it falls out of the blue or comes out of nowhere.... And it troubles for all the same reasons.... Things that happen by chance are effects in search of causes. They do not belong in a reasonable world. To some, including Einstein, probable causes were simply unacceptable.
—K.C. Cole: ***The Universe and the Teacup*** *1997*

5. Chance is the only source of true novelty.
—Francis Compton Crick: ***Life Itself, Its Original Nature****, 1981*

6. Chaos umpire sits
And by decision more
embroils the fray
by which he reigns: next
him high arbiter
Chance governs all.
—John Milton: ***Paradise Lost****, 1667*

7. [My aim is] to reduce to an exact art, with the rigor of mathematical demonstration, the incertitude of chance, thus creating a new science which could justly claim the stupefying title: the mathematics of chance.
—Blaise Pascal: ***The Thoughts of Blaise Pascal****, 1975*

8. Chance is only the measure of our ignorance. Fortuitous phenomena are, by definition, those whose laws we do not know.
—Henri Poincare: "Chance" in ***The World of Mathematics****, James R. Newman, ed., 1956*

9. How dare we speak of the laws of chance?
Is not chance the antithesis of all law?
—Bertrand Russell: ***Calculus of Probabilities***

37.5 Gambling

1. The "expectation" in a gamble is the value of the prize multiplied by the probability of winning the prize. According to Pascal the value of eternal happiness is infinite. He reasoned that even if the probability of winning eternal happiness by leading a religious life is very small indeed, nevertheless, since the expectation is infinite (any finite fraction of infinity is itself infinite) it will pay anyone to lead such a life.
—E.T. Bell: ***Men of Mathematics****, 1937*

2. Even if gambling were altogether an evil, still on account of the very large number of people who play, it would seem to be a natural evil. Thus it is not absurd for me to discuss gambling, not in order to practice it, but in order to point out the advantages in it, and, of course, the disadvantages, so they may be reduced to a minimum.
—Girolamo Cardano: ***Liber de ludo aleae****, 1563*

3. It is true that a man who does this is a fool [The best strategy is betting on the first trial for "Gambler's Ruin"]. I have only proved that a man who does anything else is an even bigger fool.
—Julian Lowell Coolidge: In Howard Eves: ***Return to Mathematical Circles****, 1988*

4. Man has probably been speculating on games of chance since antiquity. The earliest indication that there are different probabilities for the various throws that can be made with three dice appears in 1477 in a commentary on Dante's *Divine Comedy.*

—Martin Eisen: ***Introduction to Mathematical Probability Theory****, 1969*

5. In 1654 the Chevalier de Mere, an expert gambler, consulted Pascal on some problems connected with games of chance.... Pascal wrote to Fermat on the matter, and the ensuing correspondence (a set of eight letters, the first of which is lost) can be said to mark the birth of the mathematical theory of probability.

—Stuart Hollingdale: ***Makers of Mathematics****, 1989*

6. In moderation, gambling possesses undeniable virtues. Yet it presents a curious spectacle replete with contradictions. While indulgence in its pleasures has always lain beyond the pale of fear of Hell's fires, the great laboratories and respectable insurance palaces stand as monuments to a science originally born of the dice cup.

—Edward Kasner & James Newman: ***Mathematics and the Imagination****, 1940*

7. The excitement that a gambler feels when making a bet is equal to the amount he might win times the probability of winning it.

—Blaise Pascal: Quoted in N. Rose: ***Mathematical Maxims and Minims****, 1988*

8. It is an indubitable result of the theory of probabilities that every gambler, if he continues long enough, must ultimately be ruined.

—Charles Sanders Peirce: "The Red and the Black": ***The Collected Papers of Charles Sanders Peirce****, Charles Hartshorne & Paul Weiss, eds., 1931–35*

9. Probability theory originated in a supremely practical topic—gambling. Every gambler has an instinctive feeling for "the odds." Gamblers know that there are regular patterns of chance—although not all of their cherished beliefs survive mathematical analysis.

—Ian Stewart: ***Does God Play Dice?****, 1989*

37.6 Permutations and Combinations

1. "The number of all the atoms which make up the world is, although excessive, finite, and as such only capable of a finite [although also excessive] number of permutations. Given an infinite length of time, the number of possible permutations must be exhausted, and the universe must repeat itself. Once again you will be born of the womb, once again this page will reach your same hands, once again you will live all the hours until the hour of your incredible death." Such is the customary order of the argument, from its insipid prelude to the enormous threatening denouement.

—Jorge Luis Borges: "The Doctrine of Cycles," 1934

2. The theory in question [of probability] affords an excellent illustration of the application of the theory of permutation and combinations which is the fundamental part of the algebra of discrete quantity; it forms in the elementary parts an excellent logical exercise in the accurate use of terms and in the nice discrimination of shades of meaning and, above all, it enters into the regulation of some of the most important practical concerns of modern life.

—George Chrystal: ***Algebra****, 1889*

3. Bernoulli was one of the first to point out the importance of the binomial coefficients in calculating the probabilities of competing events—the famous coin-tossing problem. One of Bernoulli's most important contributions to probability theory—which stemmed from his study of combinations—is his formula for the number of permutations of n things taken p at a time.

—Lloyd Motz & Jefferson Hane Weaver: ***The Story of Mathematics****, 1993*

37.7 Discrete Mathematics

1. The notion of the discrete as opposed to the continuous is emphasized by coinage, which goes by standardized units. If the coins are perceived as being too valuable, they may be broken. If the coins are not sufficiently large, the articles in the exchange may be subdivided. This leads to the idea of fractions ("breakings").

—Philip J. Davis and Reuben Hersh: ***The Mathematical Experience****, 1981*

2. ...I've named them [n!] facultes. [Louis Francois Antoine] Arbogast has proposed the denomination factorial, clearer and more French. I've recognized the advantage of this new term, and adopting its philosophy I congratulate myself of paying homage to the memory of my friend.

—Christian Kramp: ***Elements d'arithmetique universelle****, "Preface," 1808*

3. [Discrete mathematics is] a subject of great beauty and depth which has gained enormous importance in applications because of the availability of computers.

—Peter Lax: "The Flowering of Applied Mathematics in America"; in ***A Century of Mathematics in America, Part II****, Peter Duren, ed., 1989*

37.8 Making Predictions

1. ...what mortal, I ask, could ascertain the number of diseases, counting all possible cases, that afflict the human body in every one of its parts and at every age, and say how much more likely one disease is to be fatal than another—plague than dropsy, for instance, or dropsy than fever—and on what basis make a prediction about the relationship between life and death in future generations?

—Jakob Bernoulli: Quoted in ***The World of Mathematics****, Vol. 3, James R. Newman, ed., 1956*

2. Toss a coin, and you cannot predict whether it will come up heads or tails; no matter how many times you toss it, the probability of it coming up heads or tails remains fifty-fifty. However, if you toss a coin a million times, you can be certain it will come up tails roughly 500,000 times. While no gambling establishment can predict which number will come up on a single role of dice, they can predict with some confidence the outcome of a great many rolls—that's how they make their profits.

—K.C. Cole: ***The Universe and the Teacup****, 1997*

3. I consider that I understand an equation when I can predict the properties of its solutions, without actually solving it.

—Paul Dirac: Quoted in F. Wilczek & B. Devine: ***Longing for Harmonies****, 1988*

4. Probability theory helps you to put some kind of pattern on randomness. You can't tell what's going to happen from step to step, but you can predict what's going to happen over the long haul.

—Ed Packel: Quoted in Keith Devlin: ***Life by the Numbers****, 1998*

5. To say that observations of the past are certain, whereas predictions are merely probable, is not the ultimate answer to the question of induction; it is only a sort of intermediate answer, which is incomplete unless a theory of probability is developed that explains what we should mean by "probable" and on what ground we can assert probabilities.

—Hans Reichenbach: ***The Rise of Scientific Philosophy****, 1951*

6. Mathematicians and other scientists, however great they may be, do not know of the future. Their genius may enable them to project their purpose ahead of them; it is as if they had a special lamp, unavailable to lesser men, illuminating their path; but even in the most favorable cases the lamp sends only a very small cone of light into the infinite darkness.

—George A. Sarton: ***The Study of the History of Science****, 1957*

38

Statistics and Statisticians

38.1 STATISTICIANS

1. Don't believe the statistics unless you know the statistician.

—Lynne Alpern & Esther Blumenfeld: ***Oh, Lord. I Sound Just Like Mama****, 1986*

2. A Statistician is a man who draws a mathematically precise line from an unwarranted assumption to a foregone conclusion.

—Anonymous

3. A statistician is a man who comes to the rescue of figures that cannot lie for themselves.

—Anonymous

4. To a statistician, fractions speak louder than words.

—Anonymous

5. Thou shalt not answer questionnaires
Or quizzes upon world affairs,
Nor with compliance
Take any test. Thou shalt not sit
With Statisticians nor commit
A social science.

—W.H. Auden: "Under Which Lyre"; ***Collected Poems of W.H. Auden****, 1976*

6. To call in the statistician after the experiment is done may be no more than asking him to perform a postmortem examination: he may be able to say what the experiment died of.

—Ronald Aylmer Fisher: ***Indian Statistical Congress****, Sankhya, ca. 1938*

7. The statistician cannot evade the responsibility for understanding the process he applies or recommends.

—Sir Ronald A. Fisher: ***The Design of Experiments****, 1937*

8. The statistician's job is to draw general conclusions from fragmentary data. Too often the data supplied to him for analysis are not only fragmentary but positively incoherent, so that he can do next to nothing with them. Even the most kindly statistician swears heartily under his breath whenever this happens.

—M.J. Moroney: ***Facts from Figures****, 1951*

9. A Statistician says a man stands sixteen chances to be killed by lightning to one of being worth a million of money.

—Martin F. Tupper: ***Proverbial Philosophy A Book of Thoughts and Arguments****, 1867*

10. Now we must remember that statistics deals with uncertain inference. We must not expect the statistician to come to an absolutely firm conclusion. We must expect him to give a two-part answer to out question. One part of this reply goes: "My best estimate is...." The inescapable other part of his reply is: "The degree of confidence which you are justified in placing in my estimate is...."

—Warren Weaver: "Statistics"; ***Scientific American****, January, 1952*

38.2 THE SCIENCE OF STATISTICS

1. A knowledge of statistical methods is not only essential for those who present statistical arguments it is also needed by those on the receiving end.

—R.G.D. Allen: ***Statistics for Economists****, 1957*

2. Statistics are the triumph of the quantitative method, and the quantitative method is the victory of sterility and death.

—Hilaire Belloc: ***The Silence of the Sea****, 1941*

3. Statistics, which first secured prestige here by a supposedly impartial utterance of stark fact, have enlarged their domain over the American consciousness by becoming the most powerful

statement of the "ought"—displacers of moral imperatives, personal ideals, and unfulfilled objectives.
*—Daniel J. Boorstin: **The Decline of Radicalism**, 1973*

4. A statistical estimate may be good or bad, accurate or the reverse; but in all cases it is likely to be more accurate than a casual observer's impression, and the nature of things can only be disproved by statistical methods.
*—Arthur L. Bowley: **Elements of Statistics**, 1946*

5. The way statistics are presented, their arrangement in a particular way in tables, the juxtaposition of sets of figures, in itself reflects the judgment of the author about what is significant and what is trivial in the situation which the statistics portray.
*—Ely Devons: **Essays on Economics**, 1961*

6. On the other hand, the methods of statistics are so variable and uncertain, so apt to be influenced by circumstances, that it is never possible to be sure that one is operating with figures of equal weight.
*—Havelock Ellis: **The Dance of Life**, 1923*

7. [Statistics are] the only tools by which an opening can be cut through the formidable thicket of difficulties that bars the path of those who pursue the Science of Man.
*—Sir Francis Galton: **Natural Inheritance**, 1889*

8. The word statistics has at least six different meanings in current use, four in the context of statistical theory alone.
*—Lancelot Hogben: **Science in Authority**, 1957*

9. Statistics is the art of stating in precise terms that which one does not know.
*—William Kruskal: "Statistics, Moliere, and Henry Adams"; **American Scientist** 55, 1967*

10. A statistical analysis, properly conducted, is a delicate dissection of uncertainties, a surgery of suppositions.
*—M.J. Moroney: **Facts from Figures**, 1951*

11. There is something inhuman and vaguely pornographic about statistics.... Pornography, on the other hand, with its loosely bound sequence of storyless sexual couplings (or triplings) often has the feel of a statistical survey.
*—John Allen Paulos: **Once Upon a Number**, 1998*

12. Statistical knowledge, though in some degree searched after in the most early ages of the world, has not till within these last 50 years become a regular object of study.
*—William Playfair: **The Statistical Breviary**, 1801*

13. There is something in statistics that makes it very similar to astrology.
—Gian-Carlo Rota: Attributed

14. Statistics, ideally, are accurate laws about large groups; they differ from other laws only in being about groups, not about individuals.
*—Bertrand Russell: **The Analysis of Matter**, 1954*

15. Statistics is essentially totalitarian because it is not concerned with individual values of even the few characters measured, but only with classes. However much we analyze the data to show the variation between the parts, we still deal with sub-groups and sub-averages; we never get back to the individuals.
*—L.C. Tippett: **Statistics**, 1944*

16. Statistics as a science is to quantify uncertainty, not unknown.
*—Chamont Wang: **Sense and Nonsense of Statistical Inference**, 1993*

38.3 Statistics and Lies

1. Statistics: 1. A form of lying that is neither black, white, nor color. 2. An attempt to analyze data—rare and archaic. 3. A disorderly, but not quite random, progress from datum to datum.
*—David Durand: "A Dictionary for Statismagicians"; **The American Statistician** vol. 24, June, 1970*

2. Statistics is 'hocus-pocus with numbers.
*—Audrey Habera & Richard P. Runyon: **General Statistics**, 1973*

3. A well-wrapped statistic is better than Hitler's "big lie"; it misleads, yet it cannot be pinned on you.
*—Darrell Huff: **How to Lie with Statistics**, 1954*

4. In ancient times they had no statistics so they had to fall back on lies.
*—Stephen Leacock: "A Force of Statistics": **Literary Lapses**, 1914*

5. Statistics is the art of lying by means of figures.
*—Wilhelm Stekel: **Marriage at the Crossroads**, 1931*

6. There are two kinds of statistics, the kind you look up and the kind you make up.
*—Rex Stout: **Death of a Doxy**, 1966*

7. Statistics are mendacious truths.
*—Lionel Strachey: in Michael Holroyd: **Lytton Strachey: A Critical Biography**, 1968*

8. Figures often beguile me, particularly when I have the arranging of them myself; in which case the remark attributed to Disraeli would often apply with justice and force: "There are three kinds of lies: lies, damned lies, and statistics.
*—Mark Twain: **North American Review**, July 5, 1907; **Mark Twain's Own Autobiography: The Chapters from the North American Review**, J. Kiskis, ed., 1990*

38.4 Miscellaneous Views on Statistics

1. Statistics are a group of numbers looking for an argument.
—*Anonymous*

2. Statistics prove that you can prove anything by statistics.
—*Anonymous*

3. Statistics means never having to say your certain.
—*Anonymous*

4. Like dreams, statistics are a form of wish fulfillment.
—*Jean Baudrillard:* ***Cool Memories****, 1987*

5. A knowledge of statistics is like a knowledge of foreign languages or of algebra; it may prove of use at any time under any circumstances.
—*Arthur L. Bowley:* ***Elements of Statistics****, 1946*

6. A judicious man looks at Statistics not to get knowledge but to save himself from having ignorance foisted on him.
—*Thomas Carlyle:* ***On Heroes, Hero-Worship and the Heroic in History****, 1840*

7. Statistics is numbers that are part of a story.
—*George Cobb: Quoted in Keith Devlin:* ***Life by the Numbers****, 1998*

8. The essence of life is statistical improbability on a colossal scale.
—*Richard Dawkins:* ***The Selfish Gene****, 1976*

9. Statistics are like alienists—they will testify for either side.
—*Fiorello H. La Guardia: "The Banking Investigation,"* ***Liberty****, May 13, 1933*

10. Statistics are like a bikini bathing suit. What they reveal is suggestive, but what they conceal is vital.
—*Andrew Lang: Quoted in Howard Eves:* ***Return to Mathematical Circles****, 1988*

11. Politicians use statistics in the same way that a drunk uses a lamppost—for support rather than illumination.
—*Andrew Lang: Speech, 1910: Quoted in Alan L. Mackay:* ***The Harvest of a Quiet Eye****, 1977*

12. If your experiment needs statistics, you ought to have done a better experiment.
—*Lord Ernest Rutherford: In N.T.J. Bailey:* ***The Mathematical Approach to Biology and Medicine****, 1967*

13. A man can't prove anything without statistics; no man can.... Why statistics are more precious and useful than any other one thing in this world, except whisky—I mean hymnbooks.
—*Mark Twain: Speech in Hartford, October 26, 1880*

14. Statistical thinking will one day be as necessary for efficient citizenship as the ability to read and write.
—*H.G. Wells: Quoted by Warren Weaver: "Statistics";* ***Scientific American****, January, 1952*

15. Satan delights equally in statistics and in quoting scripture.
—*H.G. Wells:* ***The Undying Fire****, 1919*

38.5 Samples and Sampling

1. After painstaking and careful analysis of a sample, you are always told that it is the wrong sample and doesn't apply to the problem.
—*Arthur Bloch:* ***Murphy's Law****, 1979*

2. By a small sample we may judge of the whole piece.
—*Miguel de Cervantes:* ***Don Quixote****,*

3. The purely random sample is the only kind that can be examined with entire confidence by means of statistical theory, but there is one thing wrong with it. It is so difficult and expensive to obtain for many uses that sheer cost eliminates it.
—*Darrell Huff:* ***How to Lie with Statistics****, 1954*

4. If it is granted that the ideal random sample can be a reliable instrument of investigation, the questions remain: Can the ideal be attained? Are the actual samples that are used as reliable as random samples?
—*L.C. Tippett: "Sampling and Standard Error"* ***Statistics****, 1944*

5. The problem of drawing inferences concerning a population from a sample is a problem in probability.... It turns out that in general the only good method of sampling is a random method. In a random method the sample is picked in accordance with purely probabilistic criteria, personal choice or prejudice being completely excluded.
—*Warren Weaver: "Statistics";* ***Scientific American****, January, 1952*

38.6 Data

1. Not even the most subtle and skilled analysis can overcome completely the unreliability of basic data.
—*R.G.D. Allen:* ***Statistics for Economists****, 1957*

2. Everything is data. But data isn't everything.
—*Pauline Bart: in Cheris Kramarae and Paul A. Treichler;* ***A Feminist Dictionary****, 1985*

3. It is a capital mistake to theorize before one has data.

—*Arthur Conan Doyle:* ***Scandal in Bohemia,***

4. No human mind is capable of grasping in its entirety the meaning of any considerable quantity of numerical data.

—*Sir Ronald A. Fisher:* ***Statistical Methods for Research Workers,*** *1970*

5. Statistical figures referring to economic events are historical data. They tell us what happened in a nonrepeatable historical case.

—*Ludwig Elder von Mises:* ***Human Action,*** *1949*

6. In general, it is necessary to have some data on which to calculate probabilities.... Statisticians do not evolve probabilities out of their inner consequences, they merely calculate them.

—*L.C. Tippett: "Sampling and the Standard Error";* ***The World of Mathematics,*** *Vol. 3, James R. Newman, ed., 1956*

38.7 Average Values

1. Of itself an arithmetic average is more likely to conceal than to disclose important facts; it is the nature of an abbreviation, and is often an excuse for laziness.

—*Arthur L. Bowley:* ***The Mathematical Gazette,*** *vol. 12; July, 1925*

2. Great numbers and the averages resulting from them, such as we always obtain in measuring social phenomena, have great inertia.

—*Arthur L. Bowley:* ***Elements of Statistics,*** *1946*

3. I abhor averages. I like the individual case. A man may have six meals one day and none the next, making an average of three per day, but that is not a good way to live.

—*Louis D. Brandeis: In Osmond K. Fraenkel, ed.* ***The Curse of Bigness,*** *1934*

4. Comparing groups is also tricky because you can't compare everyone in one group with everyone in another. Therefore, most studies compare averages. And "average" is about the slipperiest mathematical concept ever to slide into popular consciousness.

—*K.C. Cole:* ***The Universe and the Teacup,*** *1997*

5. It is difficult to understand why statisticians commonly limit their inquiries to Averages, and do not revel in more comprehensive views. Their souls seem as dull to the charm of variety as that of the native of one of our flat English counties, whose retrospect of Switzerland was that if its mountains could be thrown into its lakes, two nuisances would be got rid of at once.

—*Francis Galton:* ***Natural Inheritance,*** *1889*

6. The knowledge of an average value is a meager piece of information.

—*Francis Galton:* ***Natural Inheritance,*** *1889*

7. Historically, Statistics is no more than State Arithmetic, a system of computation by which differences between individuals are eliminated by the taking of the average. It has been used—indeed, still is used—to enable rulers to know how far they may safely go in picking the pockets of their subjects.

—*M.J. Moroney:* ***Facts from Figures,*** *1951*

8. A want of the habit of observing and an inveterate habit of taking averages are each of them often equally misleading.

—*Florence Nightingale:* ***Notes on Nursing,*** *1860*

38.8 Decision-Making

1. Years ago a statistician might have claimed that statistics deals with the process of data ... today's statistician will be more likely to say that statistics is concerned with decision making in the face of uncertainty.

—*Herman Chernoff & Lincoln E. Moses:* ***Elementary Decision Making,*** *1959*

2. A statistician is a mathematician who, although he may know exactly what he is talking about and what he says may be mathematically true, may never make a correct decision.

—*W.P. Coole: "Letters to the Editor";* ***The American Statistician,*** *Vol. 23, 1; February, 1969*

3. People generally think of the numbers and less of what is to me the interesting part: using numbers to make decisions about everything under the sun.

—*Hal Stern: Quoted in Keith Devlin:* ***Life by the Numbers,*** *1998*

Bibliography

The following books are sources of many of the quotations found in the collection. Wherever possible the listing refers to the latest edition of the book. If no publisher is listed, it appears that the book is out-of-print, but may be found in libraries. Some titles in the list are provided as sources of additional information on the quotation topics. Periodical, journal or other nonbook sources are cited in the text with their quotations.

Aaboe, Asger, **Episodes from the Early History of Mathematics**, New York: Random House, 1964

Abbott, Edwin A.; **Flatland: A Romance of Many Dimensions**, Boston: Little Brown, 1929; Princeton: Princeton University press, 1991

Abel, Niels, **Oeuvres completes**, 1832; 2 vols., Johnson Reprint Corp., 1964

Abelson, H., and A.A. di Sessa, **Turtle Geometry: The Computer as a Medium for Exploring Mathematics**, paperback, MIT Press, 1986

Adams, Douglas, **The Hitchhiker's Guide to the Galaxy**, 1979, reprint, Ballantine Books, 1995

Adamson, Donald, **Blaise Pascal: Mathematician, Physicist and Thinker About God**, 1995

Adler, Claire Fisher, **Modern Geometry**, New York: McGraw-Hill, 1958, reprint, 1967

Adler, Irving, **A New Look at Geometry**, New York: John Day Co., 1966

Adler, Irving, **Thinking Machines**, New York: John Day, 1961

Aichele, Douglas B., and Robert E. Reys, **Readings in Secondary School Mathematics**, Boston: Prindle, Weber & Schmidt, 1971

Albers, Donald J. and Gerald L. Alexanderson, eds., **Mathematical People**, Boston: Birkhauser, 1985

Albers, Donald J., Gerald L. Alexanderson and Constance Reid, eds. **More Mathematical People**, Boston: Harcourt Brace Jovanovich, 1990

Al-Biruni, **Chronology of Ancient Nations**, E.C. Sachau, tr., London, 1879

Al-Biruni, **The Exhaustive Treatise on Shadows**, E.S. Kennedy, tr., Aleppo: University of Aleppo, 1976

Al-Daffa, A.A., **The Muslim Contribution to Mathematics**, Atlantic Highlands, N.J.: Humanities Press, 1977

Alexandroff, A.D., A.N. Kolmogorov and M.A. Lavrentev, eds. **Mathematics: Its Content, Methods and Meaning**, Cambridge: M.I.T. Press, 1963

Alic, Margaret, **Hypatia's Heritage**, Boston: Beacon Press, 1986

al-Khowarizmi, Musa, **Calculation with the Hindu Numerals**

al-Khowarizmi, Musa, **Hisab, al-jabr w'al-muguabala**

Allen, R.G.D., **Statistics for Economists**, 1957

Allman, G.J., **Greek Geometry from Thales to Euclid**, Dublin: University press, 1889

Andrade, E. N. da C., **Isaac Newton**, New York: Macmillan, 1954

Anglin, W.S., **The Heritage of Thales**, New York: Springer-Verlag, 1995

Anglin, W.S., **Mathematics, A Concise History and Philosophy**, New York: Springer-Verlag, 1994

Anton, F., **The Age of the Maya**, New York: Putnam, 1970

Anzoletti, Luisa, **Maria Gaetana Agnesi**, Milan: L.F. Cogliati, 1900

Apollonius of Perga, **Conics**, 3 vols., R. Catesby Taliaferro, tr., Annapolis MD.: Classics of the St Johns Program, 1939; G.T. Toomer, ed. Springer-Verlag, 1990

Apostle, H.G., **Aristotle's Philosophy of Mathematics**, University of Chicago Press, 1952; Perspective Press, 1992

Apostol, Tom M., **Introduction to Analytic Number Theory**, New York: Springer-Verlag, 1976

Arago, Jean, **Oeuvres**, 1854

Arbuthnot, John, **Of the Laws of Chance**, London: Benj. Matte, 1692

Arbuthnot, John, **The Usefulness of Mathematical Learning**, c. 1690

Archibald, R.C., **Outline of the History of Mathematics**, 6th ed., Mathematical Association of America, 1949

Archibald, R.C., **A Semicentennial History of the American Mathematical Society**, New York: Mathematical Society of America, 1938, 1980

Archimedes, **The Sand-Reckoner**, Gilliam Bradshaw, Forge, 2000

Archimedes, **The Work of Archimedes**, Sir Thomas L. Heath, tr., Cambridge: Cambridge University Press, 1897

Aris, Rutherford, **Mathematical Modelling Techniques**, 1978, reprint, New York: Dover, 1995

Aristotle, **The Oxford Translation of Aristotle**, W.D. Ross, tr. and ed., Oxford: Oxford University Press, 1928

Aristotle, **Writings**, E.M. Edhill, J.L. Stocks, E.W. Webster, and others, tr., Chicago: Encyclopedia Britannica, 1952

Armitage, Angus, **Copernicus: The Founder of Modern Astronomy**, New York: W.W. Norton, 1938; New York: A.S. Barnes, 1957

Armitage, Angus, **Edmond Halley**, Thomas Nelson and Son, 1966

Armitage, Angus, **John Kepler**, London: Faber and Faber, 1966

Arnold, B.H., **Intuitive Concepts in Elementary Topology**, 1962

Artin, E., **Galois Theory**, Notre Dame, Ind.: University of Notre Dame Press, 1944

Asimov, Isaac, **Asimov on Numbers**, New York: Pocket Books, 1978; paperback, Acadia, 1986

Asimov, Isaac, **Asimov's New Guide to Science**, Plaza & James Editors, 1984

Asimov, Isaac, **Foundation and Earth**, Acacia Press, 1986

Asimov, Isaac, **The Genetic Code**, New York: Orion Press, 1962

Asimov, Isaac and J.A. Shulman, eds., **Isaac Asimov's Book of Science and Nature Quotations**, New York: Wiedenfeld & Nicolson, 1988

Augarten, Stan, **State of the Art: A Photographic History of the Integrated Circuit**, 1984

Auster, Paul, **The Music of Chance**, paperback, Penguin, 1993

Ayer, A.J., **Language, Truth and Logic**, 1936, reprint paperback, New York: Dover, 1946

Babbage, Charles, **Charles Babbage and His Calculating Engines**, New York: Dover, 1961

Babbage, Charles, **Passages from the Life of a Philosopher**, 1864; paperback, Martin Campbell-Kelly, ed., Rutgers Union Press, 1995

Babbage, Charles, **The Works of Charles Babbage**, Marti Campbell- Kelly, ed., New York University Press, 1989

Bacon, Francis, **The Advancement of Learning**, 1605; paperback, Kessinger Publishing Co., 1997

Bacon, Francis, **Bacon's Essays**, Chicago: Macmillan, 1952

Bacon, Francis, **Novum Organum**, 1620; paperback, Kessinger Publishing Co., 1997

Bacon, Roger, **The Opus Majus of Roger Bacon**, 1207, Robert Belle Burke, tr., 1928; New York: Russell & Russell, 1962

Bag, A.K., **Mathematics in Ancient and Medieval India**, Chauhambha Orientalia Varanasi, 1979

Bailey, Norman T.J., **The Mathematical Approach to Biology and Medicine**, New York: John Wiley & Sons, 1967

Bain, Alexander, **Education as a Science**, New York, 1898

Bakst, Aaron, **Mathematics Its Magic & Mastery**, New York: D. Van Nostrand, 1952

Ball, W.W. Rouse, **A History of the Study of Mathematics at Cambridge**, Cambridge University Press, 1889

Ball, W.W. Rouse, **Mathematical Recreations and Essays**, University of Toronto press, 1974

Ball, W.W. Rouse, **A Short Account of the History of Mathematics**. New York: MacMillan, 4th ed., 1908: reprint, New York: Dover, 1960

Ball, W.W. Rouse, and H.S.M. Coxeter, **Mathematical Recreations & Essays**, 13th, ed., New York: Dover, 1973

Banchoff, Thomas F., **Beyond the Third Dimension: Geometry, Computer Graphics, and Higher Dimensions**, New York: Scientific American Library, 1990

bar Hiyya, Abraham, **Treatise on Mensuration**

Barker, S.F., **Philosophy of Mathematics**, Englewood Cliffs, N.J.: Prentice-Hall, 1964

Barlow, Peter, **The Theory of Numbers**, 1811

Barnett, Lincoln, **The Universe of Dr. Einstein**, New York: William Sloane Associates, 1948, 1957

Barnett, P.A., **Common Sense in Education and Teaching**, New York: 1905

Barnsley, Michael, **Fractals Everywhere**, paperback, Morgan Kaufman Publishing, 1993

Baron, Margaret E., **The Origins of the Infinitesimal Calculus**, New York: Dover, 1969; paperback, 1987

Barr, Stephen, **Experiments in Topology**, 1964; paperback, New York: Dover, 1989

Barrow, Isaac, **Mathematical Lectures**, 1734, paperback, London: Kessinger Publishing Co., 1936

Barrow, John D., **The Artful Universe**, Oxford: Clarendon Press, 1995

Barrow, John D., **Pi in the Sky**, Oxford: Clarendon Press, 1992

Barrow, John D., **Theories of Everything**, Oxford: Oxford University Press, 1991

Barrow, John D., **The World Within the World**, Oxford: Clarendon Press, 1998

Barrow, J.D., and J. Silk, **The Left Hand of Creation: The Origin and Evolution of the Universe**, New York: Basic Books, 1983

Barry, Frederick, **The Scientific Habit of Thought**, AMS Press, 1927

Bartlett, M.S., **Essays of Probability and Statistics**, 1962

Bass, Hyman: **Introduction to Some Methods of Algebraic K-Theory**, American Mathematical Association, 1982

Baum, Robert J., **Philosophy of Mathematics from Plato to the Present**, San Francisco: Freeman, Cooper, 1973

Baumel, Judith, **The Weight of Numbers**, Middleton, Ct.: Wesleyan University Press, 1988
Baumgardt, Carola, **Johannes Kepler, Life and Letters**, Victor Gollancz, 1952
Beberman, Max, **An Emerging Program of Secondary School Mathematics**, Cambridge: Harvard University Press, 1958
Beck, A., M. Bleicher, and D. Crowe, **Excursions into Mathematics**, New York: Worth Pub., 1969
Beckenbach, Edward and Richard Bellman, **An Introduction to Inequalities**, 1961, paperback, Mathematical Association of America, 1975
Beckmann, Peter, **A History of "π,"** New York: St. Martin's Press, 1971
Belhoste, Bruno, **Augustin-Louis Cauchy: A Biography**, New York: Springer-Verlag, 1991
Bell, A.E., **Christiaan Huygens and the Development of Science in the Seventeenth Century**, Edward Arnold, 1947
Bell, Eric Temple, **Debunking Science**, Seattle: University of Washington, 1930
Bell, Eric Temple, **The Development of Mathematics**, New York: McGraw- Hill, 1949
Bell, Eric Temple, **The Handmaiden of the Sciences**, Baltimore: Williams & Wilkins, 1937
Bell, Eric Temple, **The Magic of Numbers**, New York: Dover, 1946
Bell, Eric Temple, **Mathematics, Queen and Servant of Science**, New York: McGraw-Hill, 1951
Bell, Eric Temple, **Men of Mathematics**. New York: Simon & Schuster, 1937; paperback, 1965
Bell, Eric Temple, **The Search for Truth**, New York: McGraw-Hill, 1949
Bellman, Richard, **A Brief Introduction to Theta Functions**, New York: Holt, Rinehart & Winston, 1961
Bellman, Richard, **A Collection of Modern Mathematical Classics: Analysis**, New York: Dover, 1961
Berge, Claude, **The Theory of Graphs**, Alison Doig, tr., London: Meuthen, 1962
Berggren, J.L., **Episodes in the Mathematics of Medieval Islam**, New York: Springer-Verlag, 1986
Berkeley, George, **The Analyst; or, A Discourse Addressed to an Infidel Mathematician**, 1734, in G. Berkeley, **Works**, 4 volumes, A.C. Fraser, ed., Oxford: Clarendon Press, 1901
Berkeley, George, **The Principles of Human Knowledge**, 1710; Glasgow: Fontana Library, 1962; Gloucester: P. Smith, 1978
Berlinghoff, William, Kerry Grant and Dale Skrien, **A Mathematical Sampler**, 4th ed., New York: Ardsley House, 1996
Berlinski, David, **The Advent of the Algorithm**, New York: Harcourt, 2000
Berlinski, David, **A Tour of the Calculus**, New York: Vintage Books, 1997
Bernal, John Desmond, **The Origin of Life**, London: Weidenfeld & Nicolson, 1967
Bernard, Claude, **Introduction to the Study of Experimental Medicine**, 1865, paperback, Henry Copley Greir, tr., Transaction Pub., 1999
Bernays, Paul and A.A. Fraenkel, **Axiomatic Set Theory**, North- Holland Publishing Co., 1958
Bernoulli, Jakob, **Ars Conjectandi**, Basel: 1713, Bide Jouvenel, tr., as **The Art of Conjecture**, London: Weidenfeld and Nicolson, 1967
Bernoulli, Jakob, **Opera**, 2 vols., 1744; Boston: Birkhauser, 1968
Bernoulli, Johann, **Opera Omnia**, 4 vols., 1742; George Olms, 1968
Beveridge, W.I.B., **The Art of Scientific Investigation**, 1957
Bhaskara, **Lilavati**, A.D., 12th cent.
Biggs, N.C., **Algebraic Graph Theory**, Cambridge: Cambridge University Press, 1994
Biggs, N.C., Gary Chartrand, and Linda Lesniak, **Graph Theory 1736-1936**, Oxford: Oxford University Press, 1976; Clarendon Press, 1999
Billingsley, H., **The Elements of Geometrie of the Most Ancient Philosopher Euclide of Megare**, 1570
Birkhoff, Garrett, **Lattice Theory**, New York: American Mathematical Society, 1948
Birkhoff, Garrett, and Saunders MacLane, **A Survey of Modern Algebra**, New York: McMillan Co., 1965
Birkhoff, Garrett, and Uta C. Merzbach, **A Source book of Classical Analysis**, Cambridge: Harvard University Press, 1973
Birkhoff, George David, **Relativity and Modern Physics**, 1923
Bishop, Errett, **Foundations of Constructive Analysis**, New York: McGraw-Hill, 1967
Black, Max, **The Nature of Mathematics: A Critical Survey**, New York: Harcourt Brace, 1935
Blackwell, David and M.A. Girshick, **Theory of Games and Statistical Decisions**, New York: John Wiley & Sons, 1954
Blatner, David, **The Joy of Pi**, Walker & Co., 1997
Bliss, Gilbert A.: **The Calculus of Variations**, Open Court, 1925
Bloor, David, **Knowledge and Social Imagery**, Chicago: University of Chicago Press, 1991
Blumenthal, Leonard M., **A Modern View of Geometry**, San Francisco: W.H. Freeman, 1961
Boas, Ralph P. Jr., **A Primer of Real Functions**, Mathematical Association of America, 1960
Boas, Ralph P., Jr., **Lion Hunting and Other Mathematical Pursuits**, Washington, D.C.: Mathematical Association of America, 1995
Bochenski, I.M., **A History of Formal Logic**, Ivor Thomas , tr., University of Notre Dame Press, 1961
Bochner, Salomon, **The Role of Mathematics in the Rise of Science**, Princeton: Princeton University Press, 1966
Boden, M. A., ed., **The Philosophy of Artificial Intelligence**, Oxford: Oxford University Press, 1990
Boehm, George A., **The New World of Mathematics**, London: Faber and Faber, 1959
Boethius, **The Consolation of Philosophy**, Peter

Walsh, ed., paperback, Oxford University Press, 2000

Bohn, D., **Causality and Chance in Modern Physics**, 1957

Bollobas, Bela, **Littlewood's Miscellany**, Cambridge: Cambridge University Press, 1986

Bolzano, Bernard, **Paradoxes of the Infinite**, New Haven: Yale University Press, 1960

Bolzano, Bernard, **Schriften**, 5 vols., Koniglichen Bohmischen Gesellschaft der Wissenschaften, 1930-48

Bonola, Roberto, **Non-Euclidean Geometry: A Critical and Historical Study of Its Development**, H.S. Carslaw, tr., New York: Dover, 1955

Boole, George, **Collected Logical Works**, LaSalle: Open Court, 1952

Boole, George, **An Investigation of the Laws of Thought**, 1854; paperback, New York: Dover, 1958, 1973

Boole, George, **The Mathematical Analysis of Logic**, 1847; paperback, St. Augustine Press, 1998

Borel, Emile, **Geometrie, premier et second cycles**, 1908

Borel, Emile, **Probabilities and Life**, M. Baudin, tr., New York: Dover, 1962

Borel, Emile, **Probability and Certainty**, New York: Walker, 1963

Boring, Edwin G., **A History of Experimental Psychology**, 1929

Born, Max, **Einstein's Theory of Relativity**, New York: Dover, 1965

Born, Max, **My Life and Views**, 1968

Born, Max, **Natural Philosophy of Cause and Chance**, New York: Dover, 1964

Boscovich, Roger Joseph, **Theory of Natural Philosophy**, 1763

Bottazzini, W., **The Higher Calculus: A History of Real and Complex Analysis From Euler to Weierstrass**, 1986

Bourbaki, N., **Elements de mathematiques: Algebre**, Paris: Hermann, 1942

Bourbaki, N., **Elements de mathematiques: Groupes et Algebres de Lie**, Fasc. XXXVII, Paris, 1972

Bourbaki, N., **Elements de mathematiques: Topologie generale**, Paris, Hermann, 1940

Bowditch, Charles P., **The Numeration, Calendar Systems and Astronomical Knowledge of the Maya**, Cambridge: Cambridge University Press, 1910

Bowman, M.E., **Romance in Arithmetic: A History of Our Currency, Weights and Measures, and Calendar**, London: London Press, 1950

Box, G.E.P., **Robustness in Statistics**, R.L. Launer and G.N. Wilkinson, eds., John Wiley & Sons, 1979

Boyer, Carl B., **The Concepts of Calculus**, New York: Dover, 1949

Boyer, Carl B., **History of Analytic Geometry**, New York: Scripta Mathematica, 1956

Boyer, Carl B., **The History of Calculus and Its Conceptual Development**, New York: Dover, 1959

Boyer, Carl B., **A History of Mathematics**, New York: John Wiley & Sons, 1968; paperback, Princeton: Princeton University Press, 1985

Boyle, Robert, **The Usefulness of Mathematics to Natural Philosophy**, London: A. Millary, 1772

Boys, C.V., **Soap Bubbles: Their Colors and the Forces Which Mold Them**, New York: Dover, 1959

Braithwaite, R.B., **Theory of Games as a Tool for the Moral Philosopher**, Cambridge: Cambridge University Press, 1955

Branford, Beuchara: **A Study of Mathematical Education**, 1908

Brewster, Sir David, **Memoirs of the Life, Writings, and Discoveries of Sir Isaac Newton**, 1855; Edinburgh: Edmonston, 1860; Johnson Reprint Corp., 1965

Bridgman, Percy W., **The Logic of Modern Physics**, New York: Macmillan, 1927

Broad, Charles Dunbar, **Leibniz: An Introduction**, London: Cambridge University Press, 1975

Bronowski, Jacob, **The Ascent of Man**, Boston: Little, Brown & Co., 1973

Bronowski, Jacob, **Science and Human Values**, paperback, rev. ed., HarperCollins, 1990

Bronowski, Jacob, **The Written Intellectual Tradition**, 1960; paperback, HarperCollins, 1986

Brouwer, L.E.J., **Formal Methods in Mathematics**, 1928

Brouwer, L.E.J., **On the Foundations of Mathematics**, 1907

Brown, Lloyd, **The Story of Mayas**, 1949; paperback, New York: Dover, 1979

Browne, Sir Thomas, **Garden of Cyprus**, 1690; in **Major Works**, C.A. Patrides, ed., paperback, Penguin, 1995

Brumbaugh, Robert S., **The Philosophers of Greece**, paperback, State University of New York Press, 1982

Brumbaugh, Robert S., **Plato's Mathematical Imagination**, Indiana University Press, 1954

Bruner, Jerome S., **The Process of Education**, Cambridge: Harvard University Press, 1960, reprint, 1977

Bruno, Giordano, **On the Infinite Universe and World**, 1584

Buchanan, Scott, **Poetry and Mathematics**, Philadelphia: J.B. Lippincott Co., 1962

Buckingham, Burdette R., **Elementary Arithmetic**, Boston: Ginn, 1947

Budden, F.J., **The Fascination of Groups**, London: Cambridge University Press, 1972

Budler, Justin, ed., **The Philosophy of Charles Sanders Peirce**, 1940; paperback, New York: Dover, 1986

Buffon, Georges, **Historie Naturelle des Mineraux**, Ken B. Serling, ed., Robert Kerr, tr., Ayer Co.: 1978

Buhler, W.K., **Gauss: A Biographical Study**, New York: Springer- Verlag, 1981
Bunch, Bryan H., **Mathematical Fallacies and Paradoxes**, New York: D. Van Nostrand, 1982
Bunt, L.N.H., P.S. Jones, and J.D. Bedient, **The Historical Roots of Elementary Mathematics**, Prentice Hall, 1976
Burde, Gerhard and Heiner Zieschang, **Knots**, Walter De Gruyter, 1985
Burk, Frank: **Lebesque Measure and Integration: An Introduction**, Wiley-Interscience, 1998
Burke, William L., **Spacetime, Geometry, Cosmology**, 1980
Burkert, W., **Lore and Science in Ancient Pythagoreanism**, E.L. Milnar, Jr., tr., Cambridge: Harvard University Press, 1972
Burns, Marilyn, **About Teaching Mathematics: A K-8 Resource**, paperback, Math Solutions Pub., 1992
Burton, David M., **Elementary Number Theory**, 1976; paperback, McGraw- Hill, 1997
Burton, David M., **A History of Mathematics: An Introduction**, Boston: Allyn & Bacon, 1985
Burtt, E.A., **The Metaphysical Foundations of Modern Physical Science**, Routledge, 1932
Bush, Vannevar, **Science is Not Enough**, Ayer Pub., 1967
Butler, Charles H., and F. Lynwood Wren, **The Teaching of Secondary Mathematics**, 1941
Butterfield, Herbert, **The Origins of Modern Science**, Macmillan, 1951
Byerly, W.E., **Integral Calculus**, 1890
Cajori, Florian, **The Early Mathematical Sciences in North and South America**, Boston: Gorham: 1928
Cajori, Florian, **A History of Elementary Mathematics**, New York: MacMillan, 1917
Cajori, Florian, **History of Mathematical Notations**, Chicago: Open Court Publishing, 1928-29
Cajori, Florian, **Sir Isaac Newton's Mathematical Principles of Natural Philosophy and His System of the World**, Berkeley: University of California Press, 1934
Cajori, Florian, **The Teaching and History of Mathematics in the United States**, New York: Chelsea, 1890
Calaprice, Alice, ed., **Albert Einstein, The Expanded Quotable Einstein**, Princeton University Press, 2000
Calinger, Ronald, ed., **Classics of Mathematics**, Oak Park, Ill.: Moore Publishing Co., 1982
Calinger, Ronald, **Gottfried Wilhelm Leibniz**, Troy, N.Y.: Allen Memorial, 1976
Campbell, Douglas, **The Whole Craft of Numbers**, 1976
Campbell, Douglas, and John Higgins, **Mathematics: People, Problems and Results**, paperback, 1984
Campbell, Lewis and William Garnett, **The Life of James Clerk Maxwell**, New York: Macmillan, 1882
Campbell, Norman, **What Is Science**, 1921
Campbell, P., and L. Grinstein, **Women of Mathematics**, New York: Greenwood Press, 1987
Cantor, George, **Contributions to the Founding of the Theory of Transfinite Numbers**, P.E.B. Jourdain, tr., Chicago: Open Court Publishing Co., 1961; paperback, New York: Dover, 1961
Capra, Fritjof, **The Tao of Physics**, 1975; Shambbala Pubns., 1991
Caratheodory, C., **Theory of Functions**, F. Steinhardt, tr.; New York: Chelsea, 2nd. ed., 1958
Cardano, Girolamo, **The Book of Games of Chance**, Holt, Rinehart and Winston, 1961
Cardano, Girolamo, **The Book of My Life**, J. Stoner, tr., London, 1931; New York: Dover, 1962
Cardano, Girolamo, **The Great Art, or The Rules of Algebra**, T. Richard Witmer, tr., Cambridge: The MIT Press, 1968
Cardano, Girolamo, **Opera Omnia**, Johnson Reprint Corp., 1964
Carlyle, Thomas, **Sartor Resartus**, Kerry McSweeney and Peter Saber, eds., Oxford: Oxford University Press, 2000
Carlyle, Thomas, **Selected Writings**, Alain Shelston, ed., Penguin Classics, 1980
Carmichael, R.D., **The Logic of Discovery**, Chicago: Open Court, 1930; Ayer Co. Pub., 1975
Carnap, R., **Introduction to Symbolic Logic and Its Applications**, New York:, Dover, 1958
Carnap, R., **Logical Foundations of Probability**, Chicago: The University of Chicago Press, 1939
Carr, H.W., **Leibniz**, New York: Dover, 1960
Carroll, Lewis, **Alice's Adventures in Wonderland** and **Through the Looking Glass**, New York: Grosset and Dunlap, 1946
Carroll, Lewis, **The Complete Works of Lewis Carroll**, New York: Modern Library, 1936
Carroll, Lewis, **The Hunting of the Snark**, Martin Gardner and Henry Holiday, eds., Penguin Classics, 1998
Carruccio, Ettore, **Mathematics and Logic in History and Contemporary Thought**, Isabel Quigley, tr., London: Faber and Faber, 1964; Chicago: Aldine, 1964
Cartwright, M.L., **The Mathematical Mind**, Oxford: Oxford University Press, 1955
Cassirer, Ernst, **Substance and Function, and Einstein's Theory of Relativity**, New York: Dover Press, 1953
Casti, John: **Five Golden Rules**, New York, John Wiley & Sons, 1996
Casti, John L.: **Paradigms Lost**, New York, Avon: 1989
Casti, John, **Reality Rules**, 1992; paperback, John Wiley & Sons, 1997
Cauchy, Augustin L., **Oeuvres completes**, 26 vols., Paris: Gauthier- Villars, 1882-1938
Cayley, Arthur, **The Collected Mathematical Papers**, 13 vols., Cambridge University Press, 1889-97; Johnson Reprint Corp., 1963
Chace, A.B., L.S. Bull, H.P. Manning and R.C.

Archibald, eds., **The Rhind Mathematical Papyrus**, Oberlin, Ohio: Mathematical Association of America, 1927-1929
Chambers, Robert, **Vestiges of the Natural History of Creation**, 1844; University of Chicago Press, 1994
Charnes, A., W.W. Cooper and A. Henderson, **An Introduction to Linear Programming**, New York: John Wiley & Sons, 1951
Chasles, Michel, **Apercu historique des methodes en geometrie**, Paris, Gauthier-Villars, 1889
Chernoff, Herman, and Lincoln E. Moses, **Elementary Decision Making**, paperback, New York: Dover, 1987
Chiera, E., **They Wrote on Clay**, Chicago University Press, 1938
Child, J.M., **The Early Mathematical Manuscripts of Leibniz**, Open Court, 1920
Child, J.M., **The Geometrical Lectures of Isaac Barrow**, Open Court, 1916
Chinn, W.G., and N.E. Steenrod, **First Concepts of Topology**, Mathematical Association of America, 1966
Chomsky, Noam, **Aspects of the Theory of Syntax**, Cambridge: The MIT Press, 1965
Chomsky, Noam, **Language and Mind**, New York: Harcourt, Brace, and World, 1968
Chomsky, Noam, **Language and the Problems of Knowledge**, MIT Press, 1988
Chomsky, Noam, **Syntactic Structures**, The Hague:, Mouton, 1957; Peter Lang Pub., 1978
Christie, Dan, **Basic Topology**, New York: Macmillan, 1976
Chrystal, George, **Textbook of Algebra**, 7th ed., Chelsea Pub. Co., 1980
Churchill, Ruel V., **Complex Variables and Applications**, New York: McGraw-Hill, 1960
Clagett, Marshall, **Archimedes in the Middle Ages**, Madison, Wisc.: University of Wisconsin Press, 1964
Cladgett, Marshall, **Greek Science in Antiquity**, New York: Abelard Schuman, 1959; 3rd. ed., Collier, 1969
Clairaut, Alexis-Claude, **Elements of Geometry**, 1741
Clarke, Arthur C., **The Nine Billion Names of God**, New York: Harcourt, Brace & World, 1967
Clavius, C., **Euclides Elementorus Libre XV**, 1591
Clawson, Calvin C.: **Mathematical Mysteries**, Cambridge, Mass., Perseus Books, 1996
Clifford, William Kingston, **Collected Mathematical Papers**, 1882; Chelsea, 1968
Clifford, William Kingston, **Common Sense in the Exact Sciences**, New York: Knopf, 1946
Clifford, William Kingston, **Lectures and Essays**, L. Stephen and F. Pollock, eds., London: Macmillan, 1879
Cohen, I. Bernard, **The Birth of the New Physics**, Doubleday, 1960
Cohen, J.B., **The Newtonian Revolution**, Cambridge: Cambridge University Press, 1980
Cohen, J.B., **Revolution in Science**, paperback, Cambridge: Harvard University Press, 1987
Cohen, Paul J., **Set Theory and the Continuum Hypothesis**, W.A. Benjamin, 1966
Cole, K.C., **The Universe and the Teacup**, San Diego: Harcourt Brace & Co., 1997
Coleridge, Samuel Taylor: **Biographia Literana**, 1817; Nigel Leark and George Lawtson,, eds., Evergreen Paperback Classics, 1990
Collatz, L., **Numb. Beh. Diffgl.**, Boston: Birkhauser, 1982; Springer-Verlag, 1987
Comte, Auguste, **Philosophy of Mathematics**, New York: Harper, 1851
Comte, Auguste, **The Positive Philosophy**, Harriet Martineau, tr., 1853; London: Chapman, 1875; paperback, Hackett Pub., 1988
Conant, James B., **Science and Common Sense**, New York: Franklin Watts, 1951
Conant, L.L., **The Number Concept, Its Origin and Development**, NY: Simon & Schuster, 1923
Condorcet, Marie-Jean de, **Sketch for a Historical Pictures of the Human Mind**, 1794; New York, Macmillan, 1961; Hyperion Press, 1980
Connolly, Paul, and Teresa Vilardi, **Writing to Learn Mathematics and Science**, Teachers College Press, 1989
Cook, Cynthia Conwell, **Western Mathematics Comes of Age**, Garden City, N.Y.: Doubleday, 1977
Cook, Theodore Andrea, **The Curves of Life**, 1914
Coolidge, Julian Lowell, **History of the Conic Sections and Quadric Surfaces**, Oxford: Clarendon, 1945
Coolidge, Julian Coolidge, **A History of Geometrical Methods**, Oxford: Oxford University Press, 1940; paperback, New York: Dover, 1963
Coolidge, Julian Lowell, **An Introduction to Mathematical Probability**, Oxford: Clarendon Press, 1925
Coolidge, Julian Lowell, **The Mathematics of Great Amateurs**, New York: Dover, 1949, reprint, 1963
Coolidge, Julian Lowell, **A Treatise on the Circle and the Square**, Oxford: Oxford University Press, 1916
Cooper, Necia Grant, ed., **From Cardinals to Chaos**, 1988
Copernicus, Nicolaus, **On the Revolutions of the Heavenly Spheres**, Charles Glenn Wallis, tr., Encyclopedia Britannica, Inc., 1939; Octavo Corp., 1999
Cornford, F.M., **Plato's Cosmology**, Cambridge: Cambridge University Press, 1937; paperback, Oscar Priest, ed., Macmillan, 1981
Coulson, G.A., **The Spirit of Applied Mathematics**, 1953
Courant, Richard, **Differential and Integral Calculus**, E.J. McShane, tr., 1934; paperback, New York: John Wiley & Sons, 1992
Courant, Richard, and David Hilbert, **Methods of Mathematical Physics**, New York: Interscience, 1953

Courant, Richard and Herbert Robbins, **What Is Mathematics?**, New York: Oxford University Press, 1948

Cournot, Antoine Augustin, **Researches into the Mathematical Theory of the Principles of Wealth**, 1838; N.T. Bacon, tr., New York, 1897; Augustus M. Kelley Pub., 1971

Couturat, L., **Mathematical Infinity**, Paris: Alcan, 1896

Coxeter, H.S.M., **Introduction to Geometry**, New York: John Wiley & Sons, 1961

Coxeter, H.S.M., **Non-Euclidean Geometry**, 4th. rev. ed., Toronto: University of Toronto Press, 1957

Coxeter, H.S.M. **Projective Geometry**, Edinburgh, Oliver & Boyd, 1964

Craig, Thomas, **A Treatise on Projection**, 1901

Crick, Francis Compton, **Life Itself, Its Original Nature**, London: MacDonald, 1981; New York: Basic Books, 1988

Crick, Francis Compton, **What Mad Pursuit**, London: Weidenfeld & Nicolson, 1988

Crombie, A.C., **Augustine to Galileo**, Falcon Press, 1952

Croom, Fred H., **Basic Concepts of Algebraic Topology**, New York: Springer-Verlag, 1941, 1978

Crowe, Michael J., **Historica Mathematica**, 1975

Crowe, Michael J., **A History of Vector Analysis**, University of Notre Dame Press, 1967; paperback, New York: Dover, 1994

Crowell, Richard Henry, and Ralph H. Fox, **Introduction to Knot Theory**, New York: Blaisdell Publishing Co., 1963

Crump, T., **The Anthropology of Numbers**, Cambridge: Cambridge University Press, 1990

Curry, Haskel, **Foundations of Mathematical Logic**, 1963; paperback, New York: Dover, 1977

D'Alembert, Jean Le Rond, **Essai sur les Gens Letters**, 1764; paperback, Chicago: University of Chicago press, 1995

Dampier-Whetham, W.C.D., **A History of Science and Its Relations with Philosophy and Religion**, Cambridge University Press, 1929

Dantzig, Tobias, **The Bequest of the Greeks**, New York, Macmillan, 1955

Dantzig, Tobias, **Number, The Language of Science**, New York: MacMillian, 3rd. ed., 1939; paperback, New York: Doubleday, 1964

Darter, Francis Michael, **The Story of True Pi**, 1962

Datta, B., and A.N. Singh, **History of Hindu Mathematics**, Bombay: Asia Publ. House, 1935, 1938, 1962

Dauben, Joseph Warren, **Georg Cantor: His Mathematics and Philosophy of the Infinite**, Princeton: Princeton University press, 1990

Dauben, Joseph Warren, **The History of Mathematics from Antiquity to the Present: A Selective Bibliography**, New York & London: Garland, 1985

Dauben, Joseph Warren, ed., **Mathematical Perspectives**, New York: Academic Press, 1981

David, F.N., **Games, Gods and Gambling: A History of Probability and Statistical Ideas**, paperback, New York: Dover, 1998

Davies, Charles, **Elements of Algebra: Translated from the French of M. Bourdon**, 1835

Davies, Paul, **About Time**, New York: Simon & Schuster, 1995

Davies, Paul, **God and the New Physics**, New York: Simon and Schuster, 1983

Davies, Paul, **The Mind of God**, New York: Simon & Schuster, 1992

Davies, Paul, **Superforce**, New York: Simon & Schuster, 1984

Davies, P.C.W., and Julian Brown, eds., **Superstrings: A Theory of Everything?**, Cambridge: Cambridge University Press, 1988

Da Vinci, Leonardo, **The Notebooks of Leonardo Da Vinci**, Vol. I & II, Edward MacCurdy, tr., New York: Reynal & Hitchcock, 1938

Da Vinci, Leonardo, **Philosophical Diary**, Philosophical Library, 1959

Da Vinci, Leonardo, **Treatise on Painting**, Princeton: Princeton University Press, 1956

Davis, John, **The Measure of the Circle**, 1854

Davis, Philip J., **The Lore of Large Numbers**, New York: Random House, 1961; Mathematical Association of America, 1975

Davis, Philip J., **Spirals: From Theodorus to Chaos**, Wiley, 1993

Davis, Philip J. and Reuben Hersh, **The Mathematical Experience**, Boston: Birkhauser, 1981; paperback, Boston: Houghton Mifflin Company, 1998

Dawkins, Richard, **The Selfish Gene**, 1976; paperback, Oxford: Oxford University Press, 1990

Day, Jeremiah, **Introduction to Algebra**, 1814; New Haven: Durrie and Peck, 1857

Debus, Allen, **Man and Nature in the Renaissance**, Cambridge: Cambridge University Press, 1978

Decker, R., and S. Hirshfield, **The Analytical Engine**, Belmont, CA:, Wadsworth, 1990

Dedekind, J.W.R., **Gesammelte Mathematische Werke**, 3 vols., F. Viewig und Sohn, 1930-32; Chelsea, 1968

Dedron, P. and J. Itard, **Mathematics and Mathematicians**, London: Transworld Publications, 1973

Delambre, M., **Historie de l'Astronomie Moderne**, 1921

Deming, William Edwards, **Some Theory of Sampling**, New York: John Wiley & Sons, 1960; paperback, 1984

Deming, William Edwards, **Statistical Adjustment of Data**, 1943; New York, Dover, 1984

De Morgan, Augustus, **Budget of Paradoxes**, Chicago: Open Court, 1940

De Morgan, Augustus, **The Encyclopedia of Eccentrics**, 1915

De Morgan, Augustus, **Essays on the Life and Work of Newton**, Chicago: Open Court, 1914

De Morgan, Augustus, **On the Study and Difficul-**

ties of Mathematics, 1831; Chicago: Open Court, 1898, 1902
De Morgan, Augustus, **Trigonometry and Double Algebra**, London, 1849
Desargues, Girard, **Oeuvres**, Leiber, 1864
Descartes, Rene, **Correspondence: Rene Descartes**, C. Adam and G. Milhaud, eds., Presses Universitaire de France, 1936-56
Descartes, Rene, **Descartes' Philosophical Writings**, John Cottingham, tr., Cambridge: Cambridge University Press, 1985
Descartes, Rene, **Discourse on Method and the Meditation**, New York: E.P. Dutton, 1912; paperback, Baltimore: Penguin Books, 1961, 1998
Descartes, Rene, **La Geometrie**, 1637, David Eugene Smith & Marcia L. Latham, tr., New York: Dover, 1954
Descartes, Rene, **Philosophical Essays & Correspondence**, Roger Arian, ed., Hackett Publishers, 2000
Descartes, Rene, **The Philosophical Works of Descartes**, Sylvia Sprigge, tr., French & European Pubns., 1941
Devi, Shakuntala, **Figuring, The Joy of Numbers**, 1977
de Villiers, M., **The Number Words, Their Origin, Meaning, History and Lesson**, London: H.F. & G. Witherby, 1923
Devlin, David, **Microchip Mathematics: Number Theory for Computer Users**, Cheshire, England: Silva Pub., 1984
Devlin, Keith, **Goodbye, Descartes**, New York: John Wiley & Sons, 1997
Devlin, Keith, **Life by the Numbers**, New York: John Wiley & Sons, 1998
Devlin, Keith, **Logic and Information**, Cambridge: Cambridge University Press, 1991
Devlin, Keith, **Mathematics: The New Golden Age**, London: Penguin, 1998
Devlin, Keith, **Mathematics: The Science of Patterns**, New York: Scientific American Library, 1994
Devons, Ely, **Essays in Economics**, 1961; Greenwood Publishing, 1980
Dewdney, A.K., **The Magic Machine**, New York: W.H. Freeman, 1990
Dewdney, A.K., **A Mathematical Mystery Tour**, New York: John Wiley & Sons, 1999
DeWitt, Cecil M., **Relativity, Groups and Topology**, New York: Gordon and Breach Science Pub., 1964
Dick, Auguste, **Emmy Noether (1882-1935)**, Boston: Birkhauser, 1981
Dick, T.P., and C.M. Patton, **Calculus of a Single Variable**, International Thompson Pub., 1994
Dickson, Leonard E., **History of the Theory of Numbers**, New York: G.E. Stechert, 1934; New York: Chelsea, 1966
Dickson, Leonard, E., **Linear Algebras**, Cambridge University Press, 1914
Dickson, Leonard, E., **Modern Algebraic Theories**, Chicago: B.H. Sanborn, 1926
Dickson, Paul, **The Official Explanation**, 1978; Federal Street Press, 1999
Dieudonne, Jean, **Foundations of Modern Analysis**, New York: Academic Press, 1960
Dieudonne, Jean, **History of Algebraic Geometry**, J.D. Sally, tr., Wadsworth Advanced Books, 1985
Dieudonne, Jean, **Mathematics—The Music of Reason**, Berlin: Springer-Verlag, 1987, 1992
Dieudonne, Jean and James B. Carrell, **Invariant Theory, Old and New**, New York: Academic Press, 1971
Dijksterhuis, E.J., **Archimedes**, New York: Humanities Press, 1957
Diogenes Laertius, **Lives of Eminent Philosophers**, Cambridge: Harvard University Press, 1966
Dirac, P.A.M., **Principles of Quantum Mechanics**, 1930; paperback, 4th ed., Oxford: Clarendon, 1982
Dirichlet, P.G.L., **Werke**, 1889-97; Chelsea, 1967
Dodgson, Charles L., **A New Theory of Parallels**, London: Macmillan, 1890
Dorrie, H., **100 Great Problems of Elementary Mathematics: Their History and Solution**, D. Antin, tr., New York: Dover, 1965
Dorn, William S., and Herbert Greenberg, **Mathematics and Computing**, New York: John Wiley & Sons, 1967
Drabkin, I.E., and Stillman Drake, **Galileo Galilei: On Motion and Mechanics**, University Of Wisconsin Press, 1960
Draper, John William, **History of the Conflict Between Science and Religion**, 1890; Gregg Int. Pub., 1975
Dreyer, J.L.E., **A History of Astronomy from Thales to Kepler**, New York: Dover, 1953
Dreyer, J.L.E., **Tycho Brahe: A Picture of Scientific Life and Work in the Sixteenth Century**, New York: Dover, 1963
Dubbey, J.M., **Development of Modern Mathematics**, New York, 1970
Dubbey, J.M., **The Mathematical Work of Charles Babbage**, Cambridge: Cambridge University Press, 1978
Dubisch, Roy, **The Nature of Numbers**, New York: Ronald Press, 1952
Dudley, Underwood, **Elementary Number Theory**, 2nd. ed., New York: W.H. Freeman, 1978
Dugas, H., **A History of Mechanics**, New York: Central Book, 1955
Duher, Pierre, **The Aim and Structure of Physical Theory**, New York: Antheneum, 1977
Dunham, William, **Euler: The Master of Us All**, Mathematical Association of America, 1999
Dunham, William, **Journey Through Genius**, New York; John Wiley & Sons, 1990
Dunham, William, **The Mathematics Universe: An Alphabetical Journey Through the Great Proofs, Problems, and Personalities**, New York: John Wiley & Sons, 1994
Dunnington, G. Waldo, **Carl Friedrich Gauss:**

Titan of Science, New York: Exposition Press, 1955; Stechert-Hafner, 1960
Duren, Peter, Richard A. Askey, and U. Mersham, eds. **A Century of Mathematics in America**, 1988
Durer, Albrecht, **The Art of Measurement**, 1525; Printed Sources of Western Art Series
Durrenratt, Freidrich, **The Physicists**, James Kirkup, tr., New York: Grove Press, 1992
Dyson, Freeman, **Disturbing the Universe**, New York: Harper & Row, 1979
Dyson, Freeman, **Infinite in All Directions**, Gifford Lectures given at Aberdeen, Scotland, April-November, 1985, 1988
Eames, Charles and Ray, **A Computer Perspective**, paperback, Harvard University Press, 1990
Eddington, Sir Arthur S., **The Expanding Universe**, 1933; paperback, Cambridge: Cambridge University Press, 1988
Eddington, Sir Arthur S., **The Mathematical Theory of Relativity**, Cambridge: Cambridge University Press, 1954
Eddington, Sir Arthur S., **The Nature of the Physical World**, Cambridge: Cambridge University Press, 1928; AMS Press, 1995
Eddington, Sir Arthur S., **New Pathways of Science**, New York: MacMillan, 1935; Ann Arbor: University of Michigan Press, 1959
Eddington, Sir Arthur S., **The Philosophy of Physical Science**, 1958
Eddington, Sir Arthur S., **Space, Time, and Gravitation**, Cambridge: Cambridge University Press, 1920; paperback, Cambridge University Press, 1987
Edge, D.O., and M.J. Mulkey, **Astronomy Transformed**, 1976
Edgeworth, Francis Y., **Mathematical Physics**, 1981
Edwards, Charles Henry Jr., **The Historical Development of the Calculus**, New York: Springer-Verlag, 1979; 1994
Edwards, Harold M., **Fermat's Last Theorem**, paperback, New York: Springer-Verlag, 1977, 2000
Eglash, Ron: **African Fractals**, Rutgers University Press, 1999
Einstein, Alfred, **Autobiographical Notes**, Centennial ed., P.G. Schlipp. ed., LaSalle: Open Court Press, 1991
Einstein, Alfred: **German Essays On Science in the 20th Century**, Wolfgang Schirmaker, ed., paperback: Continuum Pub. Grp., 1996
Einstein, Alfred, **Ideas and Opinions**, New York: Bonanza Books, 1954
Einstein, Alfred, **Meaning of Relativity**, Princeton: Princeton University Press, 1956
Einstein, Alfred, **Out of My later Years**, 1950; Outlet, 1993
Einstein, Alfred, **Relativity: The Special and the General Theory: A Popular Exposition**, Methuen; R.W. Lawson, tr., New York: Henry Holt & Co., 1920
Einstein, Alfred, **Sidelights on Reality**, New York: E.P. Dutton, 1922
Einstein, Alfred, **The World as I See It**, 1934; paperback, Citadel Press, 1993
Einstein, Albert, and Leopold Infeld, **The Evolution of Physics**. New York: Simon & Schuster, 1940, 1967
Eisen, Martin, **Introduction to Mathematical Probability Theory**, 1969
Epicteus, **Discourses**, Nicholas C. White, tr., Hackett Press, 1983
Erdos, Paul, **The Art of Counting: Selected Writings**, Joel Spencer, ed., Cambridge: The MIT Press, 1973
Erickson, Martin J., **Introduction to Combinatorics**, John Wiley & Sons, 1996
Ernest, Paul, **The Philosophy of Mathematics Education**, London: Falmer Press, 1991
Ernest, Paul, **Social Constructivism and a Philosophy of Mathematics**, Albany: State University of New York Press, 1998
Euclid, **The Thirteen Books of Euclid's Elements: Introduction and Commentary**, by T.L. Heath, New York: Dover, 1956
Euler, Leonhard, **Algebra**, 1770
Euler, Leonhard, **Analysis of the Infinite**, J.D. Blanton, tr., Springer-Verlag, 1990
Euler, Leonhard, **Institutiones Calculi Differentialis**, Academiae Imperialis Scientiarum Petropolitanae, 1755; John D. Blanton, tr., Springer-Verlag, 2000
Euler, Leonhard, **Opera Omnia**, Berlin: Teubner, Basel: Birkhauser, 1911; Leipzig: 1915-1925
Eves, Howard W.: **An Introduction to the History of Mathematics**, New York, Holt, Rinehart & Winston, 1964; Philadelphia: Saunders, 1983
Eves, Howard W., **In Mathematical Circles**, two volumes, Boston: Prindle, Weber & Schmidt, Inc., 1969
Eves, Howard W., **Mathematical Circles Adieu**, Boston: Prindle, Weber & Schmidt, 1977
Eves, Howard W., **Mathematical Circles Revisited**, Boston: Prindle, Weber & Schmidt, 1971
Eves, Howard W., **Mathematical Circles Squared**, Boston: Prindle, Weber & Schmidt, 1972
Eves, Howard W., **Return to Mathematical Circles**, Boston: Prindle, Weber & Schmidt—Kent Publishing Co., 1988
Eves, Howard W., **A Survey of Geometry**, Boston: Alyn and Bacon, 1963
Eves, Howard E., and Carroll V. Newsom, **An Introduction to the Foundations and Fundamental Concepts of Mathematics**, rev. ed., New York: Holt, Rinehart & Winston, 1965
Ewing, John, ed., **A Century of Mathematics: Through the Eyes of the Monthly**, The Mathematical Association of America, 1994
Fadiman, Clifton, ed., **Fantasia Mathematica**, New York: Simon and Schuster, 1958
Fang, J., **Bourbaki**, New York: Paideia Press, 1970
Faulkner, T. Ewan, **Projective Geometry**, Edinburgh: Oliver and Boyd, 1949

Fauvel, John, and Jeremy Gray, eds., **The History of Mathematics: A Reader**, paperback, Mathematical Association of America, 1997; Kluwer Academic Press, 2000
Feigenbaum, E.A., and J. Feldman, eds., **Computers and Thought**, 1963; paperback, MIT Press, 1995
Felix, Lucienne, **The Modern Aspects of Mathematics**, Julius H. Hlavaty and Fancille H. Hlavaty, tr., New York: Basic Books, 1960
Feller, William, **An Introduction to Probability Theory and Its Applications**, Vol. I, 2nd. ed., New York: John Wiley & Sons, 1957
Fellman, Emil A., **G.W. Leibniz Marginalia in Newton's Principia Mathematica**, Paris, Vrin, 1973
Fennema, Elizabeth, and Gilot Leder, eds., **Mathematics and Gender**, paperback, Teachers College Press, 1990
Fermat, Pierre de, **Oeuvres**, 4 vols., Paris: Gauthier-Villars, 1891-1912
Feynman, Richard P., **The Characteristic of Physical Law**, 1965; paperback, MIT Press, 1967
Feynman, Richard P., **The Feynman Lectures on Physics**, paperback, Addison-Wesley, 1963
Feynman, Richard P., **QED: The Strange Theory of Light and Matter**, Harmondsworth: Penguin Books, 1990
Fibonacci, Leonardo, **Liber abaci**, 1202; in **Book of Squares**, L.E. Sigler, tr., Unknown, 1987
Field, H., **Realism, Mathematics and Modality**, Oxford: Blackwell, 1989
Field, H., **Science Without Numbers**, Oxford: Blackwell, 1980, 1989
Field, Michael J. and Martin Golubitsky, **Symmetry in Chaos**, Oxford: Oxford University press, 1992
Fine, Henry B., **The Number-system of Algebra**, 1890
Fish, Daniel W., **Robinson's Progressive Practical Arithmetic**, 1858
Fishback, W.T., **Projective and Euclidean Geometry**, John Wiley & Sons, 1962
Fisher, Sir Ronald A., **Perspectives in Medicine and Biology**, 1973
Fisher, Sir Ronald A., **Statistical Methods for Research Workers**, 1970; Macmillan, 1973
Fitch, G.D., **The Fourth Dimension Simply Explained**, 1910
Fitch, J.C., **Lectures on Teaching**, 1906
Flammarion, Camille, **Popular Astronomy: A General Description of the Heavens**, Piccadilly: Chatto & Windus, 1894
Flegg, G., **Numbers: Their History and Meaning**, London: Andre Deutsch, 1983
Fletcher, T.J., **Some Lessons in Mathematics**, Cambridge: Cambridge University Press, 1964
Fontenelle, Bernard de, **Elements de la geometrie de l'infini**, 1727
Forder, Henry G., **The Foundations of Euclidean Geometry**, Cambridge: Cambridge University Press, 1927
Forsyth, A.R., **Perry's Teaching of Mathematics**, London, 1902
Fourier, Jean Baptiste Joseph, **Analytical Theory of Heat**, Alexander Freeman, tr., Cambridge: Cambridge University Press, 1878; Chicago: Encyclopedia Britannica, 1952; New York: Dover, 1955
Fraenkel, A.A., **Georg Cantor**, 1932
Fraenkel, A.A. and Y Bar-Hillel, **Foundations of Set Theory**, North-Holland Publishing Co., 1958
Fraleigh, John B., **Abstract Algebra**, Addison-Wesley, 1967, 1999
Frank, Philipp, **Einstein: His Life and Times**, 1947; De Capo Press, 1989
Frankland, W.B., **The Story of Euclid**, Gordon Press, 1986
Fraser, J.T. and N. Lawrence, eds. **The Study of Time**, New York: Springer-Verlag, 1975
Frayn, Michael, **Construction**, 1974
Frege, Gottlob, **The Basic Laws of Arithmetic**, University of California Press, 1965
Frege, Gottlob, **The Foundations of Arithmetic**, 1884; J.L. Austin, tr., Oxford: Blackwell, 1968, 1980
Frege, Gottlob; **The Frege Reader**, Michael Bearing, ed. paperback, Blackwell Pub., 1997
Freiberger, Paul, and Daniel McNeill, **Fuzzy Logic**, New York: Simon and Schuster, 1993
Frend, William, **Principles of Algebra**, 1796
Freudenthal, Hans, **Mathematics as an Educational Task**, Dordrecht, Holland: Reidel, 1973
Friedman, Bernard, **Principles and Techniques of Applied Mathematics**, New York: John Wiley & Sons, 1956
Friedrichs, K.O., **From Pythagoras to Einstein**, L.W. Singer, 1965
Frucht, William, ed., **Imaginary Numbers: An Anthology of Marvelous Mathematical Stories, Diversions, Poems and Musings**, New York: John Wiley & Sons, 1999
Fry, Thornton C., **Probability and Its Engineering Uses**, D. Van Nostrand, 1928
Fuchs, Walter R., **Mathematics for the Modern Mind**, Boston: Little Brown, 1864; H.A. Holstein, tr., New York: Macmillan, 1967
Fuller, R. Buckminster **Synergies**, 1975
Gabor, Denis, **Innovations: Scientific, Technical and Social**, 1970
Gade, John A., **The Life and Times of Tycho Brahe**, Princeton University Press, 1947
Gagne, Robert, **The Conditions of Learning and Theory of Instruction**, 1965; Wordsworth, 1997
Galilei, Galileo, **Dialogue on the Great World Systems**, Chicago: University of Chicago Press, 1953
Galilei, Galileo, **Dialogues Concerning Two New Sciences**, New York: Macmillan, 1914; Henry Crew and Alfonso de Salvio, trs., 1952; paperback, Stillman Drake, tr., University of California Press, 1967
Galilei, Galileo, **Opere**, 20 vols., G. Barbera, 1964-66
Galois, Evariste, **Works and Letters of Galois**, Fauvel and Gray, tr., 1987

Galois, Evariste, **Oeuvres mathematiques**, Paris: Gauthier-Villars, 1897

Galton, Francis, **Natural Inheritance**, 1889; paperback, Genetics Heritage Press, 1996

Gamow, George, **One Two, Three ... Infinity**, New York: Viking Press, 1947

Gamow, George, **A Star Called the Sun**, New York: Viking Press, 1964

Gantmacher, F.R., **The Theory of Matrices**, New York: Chelsea, 1959

Gaposchkin, Cecilia Payne, **Introduction to Astronomy**, Englewood Cliffs, NJ: Prentice-Hall, 1970

Gardiner, A., **Discovering Mathematics: The Art of Investigation**, New York: Oxford University Press, 1987

Gardner, Martin, **Codes, Ciphers and Secret Writing**, New York: Dover, 1972

Gardner, Martin, **Fads and Fallacies**, New York: Dover, 1957

Gardner, Martin, **Ha! Insight!**, paperback, W.H. Freeman, 1978

Gardner, Martin, **Mathematical Circus**, New York: Knopf, 1979

Gardner, Martin, **Mathematical Puzzles and Diversions**, New York: Simon and Schuster, 1959

Gardner, Martin, **Mathematics, Magic and Mystery**, New York: Dover, 1956

Gardner, Martin, **New Mathematical Diversions from Scientific American**, New York: Simon & Schuster, 1966

Gardner, Martin, **No-Sided Professor**, 1946; Prometheus Books, 1987

Gardner, Martin, **Time Travel and Other Mathematical Bewilderments**, New York: W.H. Freeman, 1988

Gauss, Carl Friedrich, **Disquisitiones Arithmeticae**, Arthur A. Clarke, tr., New Haven: Yale University Press, 1966; Springer- Verlag, 1986

Gauss, Carl Friedrich, **Werke**, 1825; Koniglichen Gesellschaft der Wissenschaften zu Gottingen, 1876; 1929

Gelbaum, Bernard R., and James G. March, **Mathematics for the Social and Behavioral Sciences: Probability, Calculus and Statistics**, 1969

Gibbs, Josiah Willard, **Thermodynamics**, 1881; paperback: Ox Bow Press, 1993

Gibbs, Josiah Willard, and E.B. Wilson, **Vector Analysis**, 1901; New York: Dover, 1960

Gillies, Donald, ed., **Revolutions in Mathematics**, 1992; paperback, Oxford: Oxford University Press, 1996

Gillings, R.J., **Mathematics in the Time of the Pharaohs**, Cambridge: The MIT Press, 1972

Gingerich, Owen, ed., **The Nature of Scientific Discovery**, Washington, D.C., The Smithsonian Institution, 1975

Girard, Albert, **New Invention in Algebra**, 1595-1632

Gittleman, Arthur, **History of Mathematics**, Columbus, Ohio: Charles E. Merrill Publishing, 1975

Glaserfeld, Ernst von, **Radical Constructivism: A Way of Knowing and Learning**, Falmer Press, 1996

Gleick, James, **Chaos: Making a New Science**, New York: Penguin Books, 1987

Glickman, A.M., **Linear Programming and the Theory of Games**, New York: John Wiley & Sons, 1963

Goedel, Kurt, **Collected Works**, Solomon Feferman, ed., Oxford University Press, 1995

Goedel, Kurt, **The Consistency of the Axiom of Choice and of the Generalized Continuum Hypothesis with the Axioms of Set Theory**, Princeton: Princeton University Press, 1940

Goedel, Kurt, **On Undecidable Propositions of Formal Mathematical Systems**, Princeton: Princeton University Press, 1943

Goldberg, Samuel, **Introduction to Difference Equations**, New York: John Wiley & Sons, 1958

Goldstine, H.H., **The Computer from Pascal to von Neumann**, Princeton: Princeton University press, 1972; paperback, 1980

Goldstine, H.H., **A History of Numerical Analysis from the 16th Through the 19th Century**, New York: Springer-Verlag, 1977

Golos, Ellery B., **Foundations of Euclidean and non-Euclidean Geometries**, New York: Holt, Rinehart & Winston, 1968

Gompers, Theodor, **Greek Thinkers**, John Murray, 1920

Goodfield, June, **An Imagined World: A Story of Scientific Discovery**, Lansing: University Michigan Press, 1991

Goodstein, R.L., **Essays in the Philosophy of Mathematics**, Leicester: Leicester University Press, 1965

Goodstein, R.L., **Mathematical Logic**, 1957

Gore, George, **The Art of Scientific Discovery or the General Conditions and Methods of research in Physics and Chemistry**, 1878

Gorman, P., **Pythagoras: A Life**, London: Routledge, 1979

Gould, Stephen Jay, **Ever Since Darwin: Reflections on Natural History**, 1977; paperback, W.W. Norton, 1992

Gow, James, **A Short History of Greek Mathematics**, 1884

Grabiner, Judith V., **The Origins of Cauchy's Rigorous Calculus**, Cambridge: The MIT press, 1981

Graham, Ronald L., Donald E. Knuth and Oren Patashnik, **Concrete Mathematics**, Reading, Ma.: Addison-Wesley, 1989

Graham, R.L., and J. Nesetril, eds., **The Mathematics of Paul Erdos**, New York: Springer-Verlag, 1997

Grant, Eugene L., **Statistical Quality Control**, McGraw-Hill, 1952

Grasshoff, Gerd, **The History of Ptolemy's Star Catalogue**, Springer-Verlag, 1990

Grassmann, Hermann G., **Gesammelte Mathematische und physikalische Werke**, 3 vols., Teubner, 1894-1911

Grattan-Guinness, Ivor, **The Development of the Foundations of Mathematical Analysis from Euler to Riemann**, Cambridge: MIT Press, 1970

Grattan-Guinness, Ivor, ed., **From the Calculus to Set Theory, 1630- 1910: An Introductive History**, London: Duckworth, 1980

Grattan-Guinness, Ivor, **The Rainbow of Mathematics**, paperback, New York: W.W. Norton & Co., 2000

Graves, Robert P., **Life of Sir William Rowan Hamilton**, Dublin: Hodges, Figges & Co., 1882-1889; Ayer Co., 1975

Gray, Jeremy, **Ideas of Space: Euclidean, Non-Euclidean, and Relativistic**, Oxford: Clarendon Press, 1979

Gray, Jeremy, **Linear Differential Equations and Group Theory from Riemann to Poincare**, Boston: Birkhauser, 1985

Gregory, Richard, **Mind and Science**, 1981

Griffin, F.L., **Introduction to Mathematical Analysis**, 1936

Grinstein, Louise S., and Paul J. Campbell, eds., **Women of Mathematics**, New York: Greenwood Press, 1987

Groom, A., **How We Weigh and Measure**, London: Routledge, 1960

Grossmann, Hermann, **Werke**, 1904

Grossmann, Israel, and Wilhelm Magnus, **Groups and Their Graphs**, New York: Random House, 1964; paperback, Mathematical Association of America, 1975

Gudder, Stanley, **A Mathematical Journey**, New York: McGraw-Hill, 1976, 1994

Guillen, Michael, **Bridges to Infinity: The Human Side of Mathematics**, Tarcher Inc., 1983

Guliberg, Jan, **Mathematics from the Birth of Numbers**, New York: W.W. Norton, 1997

Guthrie, W.K.C., **A History of Greek Mathematics**, Oxford University press, 1921

Guy, Richard K., **Unsolved Problems in Number Theory**, New York: Springer-Verlag. 1981, 1994

Haack, Susan, **Deviant Logic, Fuzzy Logic: Beyond the Formalism**, paperback, University of Chicago Press, 1996

Haber, Audrey, and Richard P. Runyon, **General Statistics**, 1973

Hacking, Ian, **The Emergence of Probability**, Cambridge: Cambridge University Press, 1975

Hadamard, Jacques, **The Psychology of Invention in the Mathematical Field**, Princeton: Princeton University Press, 1945

Hahn, Hans, **The Collected Works of Hans Hahn**, L. Schmetterer & K. Sigmund, eds., 1995

Hahn, Roger, **The Anatomy of a Scientific Institution: The Paris Academy of Sciences**, Berkeley: University of California Press, 1971

Haldane, John Burdon Sanderson, **Daedalus, or Science and the Future**, New York: Harper & Bros., 1923

Hales, Stephen, **Vegetable Staticks**, 1727; New York: History of Science Library, 1969

Hall, A. Rupert, **From Galileo to Newton**, Collins, 1963

Hall, A. Rupert, **Philosophers at War: The Quarrel Between Newton and Leibniz**, Cambridge: Cambridge University Press, 1980

Hall, A. Rupert, **The Scientific Revolution**, Longmans Green, 1954

Hall, G. Stanley, **Educational Problems**, New York, 1911

Halley, Edmund, **Degrees of Mortality of Mankind**, 1942

Halmos, Paul, **A Hilbert Space Problem Book**, Springer-Verlag, 1967

Halmos, Paul, **I Want to Be a Mathematician: An Autobiography in Three Parts**, Washington, D.C.: Mathematical Association of America, 1985

Halmos, Paul, **Naive Set Theory**, New York: D. Van Nostrand, 1960

Halsted, G.B., **Bolyai's Science of Absolute Space**, 1896

Halsted, G.B., **Science**, 1905

Hamilton, Sir William Rowan, **Elements of Quaternions**, 2 vols., 1866; Chelsea, 1969

Hamilton, Sir William Rowan, **The Mathematical Papers**, 3 vols., Cambridge University Press, 1931, 1940, 1967

Hamming, Richard W., **Coding and Information Theory**, 1980

Hammonds, Nathaniel, **Elements of Algebra**, London, 1742

Hankel, Hermann, **Geschichte der Mathematik im Altertum und im Mittelalter**, Leipzig, 1874

Hankins, Thomas, **Jean d'Alembert: Science and Enlightenment**, Oxford: Clarendon Press, 1970

Hankins, Thomas, **Sir William Rowan Hamilton**, Baltimore: Johns Hopkins University Press, 1980

Hanson, Norwood Russell, **Patterns of Discovery**, Cambridge: Cambridge University Press, 1958

Harary, Frank, **Graph Theory**, Reading, MA: Addison-Wesley, 1972

Hardy, Florence E., **Latter Years of Thomas Hardy, 1892-1928**, Reprint Services, 1992

Hardy, G.H., **Collected Papers of G.H. Hardy**, Oxford: Clarendon, 1966

Hardy, G.H., **Divergent Series**, Oxford University Press, 1949

Hardy, G.H., **A Mathematician's Apology**, London: Cambridge University Press, 1940

Hardy, G.H., **Pure Mathematics**, New York: Cambridge University Press, 1959

Hardy, G.H., **Ramanujan**, New York: Chelsea, 1959

Hardy, G.H., J.E. Littlewood, and G. Polya, **Inequalities**, Cambridge: Cambridge University Press, 1934

Hardy, G.H. and E.M. Wright, **An Introduction to the Theory of Numbers**, Oxford: Clarendon Press, 1945

Harel, D., **Algorithmics: The Spirit of Computing**, New York: Addison-Wesley, 1987

Harris, William Toney, **Psychological Foundations of Education**, New York: 1898
Harrison, Edward, **Cosmology**, London: Cambridge University Press, 1961
Hatcher, Allan, **Algebraic Topology**, Cambridge University Press, 2001
Hausdorff, F., **Set Theory**, New York: Chelsea, 1957
Hawking, Stephen W., **A Brief History of Time**, London: Bantam, 1988
Hawkins, Thomas, **Lebesque's Theory of Integration: Its Origin and Development**, New York: Chelsea, 1975
Hayes, John R., **The Complete Problem Solver**, Hillsdale, NJ: Erlbaum Associates, 1989
Heath, Sir Thomas L., **Apollonius of Perga, Treatise on Conic Sections**, New York: Barnes and Nobel, 1961
Heath, Sir Thomas L., **Diophantus of Alexandria: A Study in the History of Greek Algebra**, Cambridge: Cambridge University Press, 1921; New York: Dover, 1964
Heath, Sir Thomas L., **A History of Greek Mathematics**, Oxford: The Clarendon Press, 1921
Heath, Sir Thomas L., **A Manual of Greek Mathematics**, Oxford: Oxford University Press, 1931
Heath, Sir Thomas L., **Mathematics in Aristotle**, 1949; paperback, Thoemmes Press, 1998
Heath, Sir Thomas L., **The Thirteen Books of Euclid's Elements**, New York: Cambridge University Press, 1926; New York: Dover, 1956
Heath, Sir Thomas L., **The Work of Archimedes**, Cambridge: Cambridge University Press, 1897; reprint, New York: Dover, 1953
Heaviside, Oliver, **Electromagnetic Theory**, 1893; 3rd. ed., Chelsea Publishing, 1970
Hegel, Georg, **Hegel, The Essential Writings**, Frederick G. Weiss, ed., paperback, HarperCollins, 1993
Heisenberg, Werner, **The Physical Principles of the Quantum Theory**, Carl Ekhart and Frank C. Hoyt, tr., Chicago: University of Chicago Press, 1930
Heisenberg, Werner, **Physics and Beyond**, 1958; New York: Harper & Row, 1971
Helmholtz, Herman von, **Academic Discourses**, 1862
Helmholtz, Herman von, **Counting and Measuring**, D. Van Nostrand, 1930
Helmholtz, Herman von, **Epistemological Writings**, Dordrecht, 1977
Helmholtz, Herman von, **Popular Lectures on Scientific Subjects**, New York, Dover, 1962
Henderson, Linda D., **The Fourth Dimension and non-Euclidean Geometry in Art**, Princeton: Princeton University Press, 1983
Henkin, Leon, L.A. Steen, and D.J. Albers, **Teaching Teachers, Teaching Students**, 4th Intl. Congress on Mathematics Education, 1981
Henrion, Claudia, **Women in Mathematics: The Addition of Difference**, Bloomington: Indiana University Press, 1997
Herbart, J.F., **Werke**, 1890
Herivel, John, **Joseph Fourier, The Man and the Physicist**, 1975
Herken, R., ed., **The Universal Turing Machine: A Half-Century Survey**, Oxford: Oxford University Press, 1988
Hermite, Charles, **Comptes Rendus**, 1895
Herodotus, **History**, George Rawlinson, tr., Everyman's Library, 1997
Hersh, Reuben, **What Is Mathematics, Really?**, New York: Oxford University Press, 1997
Herschel, Sir John, **Outlines of Astronomy**, New York: P.F. Collier, 1902
Herschel, Sir John, **A Preliminary Discourse on the Study of Natural Philosophy**, 1839
Herstein, I.N., **Abstract Algebra**, New York: Macmillan, 1986
Herstein, I.N., **Topics in Algebra**, New York: Blaisdell Publishing, 1963
Hesse, H.B., **Models and Analysis in Science**, 1963
Heyer, Paul, ed., **Architects on Architecture**, 1978; paperback, Van Nostrand, 1993
Heywood, Robert B., **The Works of the Mind**, Chicago: University of Chicago Press, 1947
Hilbert, David, **The Foundations of Geometry**, E.J. Townsend, tr., LaSalle, Ill.: Open Court, 1902. Originally published as **Grundlagen der Geometrie**, 1899; B.G. Teubner, 1930
Hilbert, David, **Gesammelte Abhandlungen**, Julius Springer, 1933
Hilbert, David, **Zahlbericht**, 1897
Hilbert, David, and W. Ackermann, **Principles of Mathematical Logic**, New York, Chelsea, 1950-|59
Hilbert, David, and S. Cohn-Vossen, **Geometry and the Imagination**, P. Nemenyi, tr., New York: Chelsea Publishing Co., 1952
Hildebrand, John Henry, **Perspectives in Biology and Medicine**, 1970
Hill, G.F., **Arabic Numerals in Europe**, Oxford: Oxford University Press, 1915
Hillier, F., and G. Liebman, **Introduction to Operations Research**, McGraw-Hill, 1995, 2000
Hintikka, J. and U. Remes, **The Method of Analysis: Its Geometrical Origin and Its General Significance**, Dordrecht: Reidel, 1974
Hobbes, Thomas, **The English Works of Thomas Hobbes**, Sir William Molesworth, ed.,
Hobbes, Thomas, **Leviathan**, paperback, Prometheus Books, 1996
Hobson, E.W., **John Napier and the Invention of Logarithms**, Cambridge University Press, 1914
Hobson, E.W., **Squaring the Circle and Other Monographs**, Oxford: Oxford University Press, 1913; Chelsea, 1953
Hocking, John, and Gail Young, **Topology**, Reading, Ma.: Addison Wesley, 1961
Hodges, Andrew, **Alan Turing—the Enigma**, New York: Simon & Schuster, 1983; paperback: Walker & Co., 2000

Hodges, Wilfred, **Building Models by Games**, London Mathematical Society, 1985
Hodges, Wilfred, **Logic**, London: Penguin Books, 1980
Hodnett, Edward, **The Art of Problem Solving**, New York: Harper and Row. 1955
Hoffman, F.S., **Sphere of Science**, 1898
Hoffman, Paul, **Archimedes' Revenge**, New York: W.W. Norton & Co., 1988
Hoffman, Paul, **The Man Who Loved Only Numbers**, London: Fourth Estate Limited, 1998
Hofmann, J.E., **The History of Mathematics**, Philosophical Library, 1957
Hofstadter, Douglas, **Goedel, Escher, Bach: an Eternal and Golden Braid**, New York: Basic Books, 1980
Hogben, Lancelot, **Mathematics for the Millions**, New York: W.W. Norton & Co., 1937, paperback, New York: Norton, 1983
Hogben, Lancelot, **Mathematics in the Making**, London: Rathbone Books, 1960
Hogben, Lancelot, **Science in Authority**, 1957
Hollingdale, Stuart, **Makers of Mathematics**, London: Penguin Books, 1989
Holt, Michael, **Mathematics in Art**, New York: Van Nostrand Reinhold, 1971
Holt, Michael and D.T.C. Marjoram, **Mathematics in a Changing World**, 1973
Holton, Gerald, **Thematic Origins of Scientific Thought**, 1973; paperback, Harvard University Press, 1988
Honsberger, Ross, **Ingenuity in Mathematics**, Random House, 1970
Honsberger, Ross, **Mathematical Gems**, Washington, D.C.: Mathematical Association of America, 1973
Honsberger, Ross, **Mathematical Morsels**, Washington, D.C.: **Mathematical Association of America**, 1978
Hooper, Alfred, **Makers of Mathematics**, New York, Random House, 1948
Howson, A.G., ed., **Developments in Mathematical Education**, Cambridge: Cambridge University Press, 1973
Howson, A.G., **History of Mathematics Education in England**, Cambridge: Cambridge University Press, 1982
Hoyle, Fred, **The Nature of the Universe**, 1950; New York: Harper Bros., 1960
Hoyle, Fred, **Of Men and Galaxies**, 1964; University of Washington Press, 1966
Hrosvita of Gandersheim, **Sapientia**, 980
Hubble, Edwin Powell, **The Nature of Science and Other Lectures**, San Marino: Huntington Library, 1954
Huff, Darrell, **How to Lie with Statistics**, New York: W.W. Norton & Co., 1954, 1993
Hughes, Barnabas, **Thinking About Problems: A Manual of Mathematical Heuristic**, Palo Alto: Creative Pub., 1976
Hughes, Barnabas, **Regiomontanus on Triangles**, University of Wisconsin Press, 1967
Hume, David, **An Enquiry Concerning Human Understanding**, 1748; P.H. Nidditch, ed., paperback, Cambridge: Clarendon Press, 1975
Hume, David, **A Treatise of Human Nature**, 1739; E.C. Mossnes, ed., Viking Press, 1986
Huntington, E.H., **The Continuum**, Cambridge: Harvard University Press, 1917
Huntley, H.E., **The Divine Proportion**, New York: Dover, 1970
Hutten, Ernest H., **The Language of Modern Physics**, London: George Allen and Unwin, Ltd., 1956
Huxley, Aldous, **Complete Essays**, James D. Sexton, ed., Ivan R. Dee, 2000
Huxley, Aldous, **Young Archimedes and Other Stories**, Transaction, 2000
Huxley, Thomas H., **Collected Essays**, 1893-4; Greenwood Pub., 1970
Huxley, Thomas H., **Major Prose of Thomas H. Huxley**, Alan P. Bauer, ed., University of Georgia Press, 1997
Huygens, Christiaan, **Oeuvres completes**, 22 vols., M. Nyhoff, 1888-1950
Huygens, Christiaan, **Treatise on Light**, 1690; Sylvanus P. Thompson, tr., Chicago: Encyclopedia Britannica, 1952
Hyman, Anthony, **Charles Babbage—Pioneer of the Computer**, New York: Dover, 1961
Iamblichus, Thomas Taylor, tr., **On The Philosophy of the Pythagoreans**, Inner Tradition Intl., 1986; paperback, 1998
Iannelli, Richard, **The Devil's New Dictionary**, Secaucus: Citadel Press, 1983
Ibn Gabriol, Solomon, **Selected Religious Poems of Solomon Ibn Gabriol**, Jewish Pub. Soc., 1974
Ibn Khaldun, **The Mugaddish**, 14th cent. A.D., N.J. Dawood's abridgement of F. Rosenthal, tr., 1967; paperback, Princeton University Press, 1969
Ifrah, George, **From One to Zero**, New York: Viking Press, 1985
Ifrah, George, **The Universal History of Numbers**, New York: John Wiley & Sons, 2000
Infled, Leopold, **Whom the Gods Love: The Story of Evariste Galois**, New York: McGraw-Hill, 1948
Itard, Jean, **Les Livres Arithmetique d'Euclide**, Paris: Hermann, 1961
Itard, Jean and Pierre Dedron, **Mathematics and Mathematicians**, J.V. Field, tr., London: Transworld, 1973
Ivins, William M., Jr., **Art and Geometry**, New York: Dover, 1964
Jacob, Francois, **The Possible and the Actual**, 1982; paperback, University of Washington Press, 1994
Jacobi, C.G.J., **Gesammelte Werke**, 7 vols., G. Riemer, 1881-91; Chelsea, 1968
Jammer, Max, **Concepts of Space**, Harvard University Press, 1954
Jeans, Sir James, H., **Astronomy and Cosmogony**, New York: Dover, 1961

Jeans, Sir James H., **The Growth of Physical Science**, London: Cambridge University Press, 1951
Jeans, Sir James H., **The Mysterious Universe**, New York: Macmillan, 1930; AMS Press, 1933
Jeans, Sir James H., **Physics and Philosophy**, Ann Arbor: University of Michigan Press, 1958
Jeans, Sir James H., **The Universe Around Us**, New York: Macmillan, 1929
Jeffers, Robinson, **The Beginning of the End**, 1954; New York: Random House, 1963
Jeffreys, William H., and R. Robert Robbins, **Discovering Astronomy**, New York: John Wiley & Sons, 1981
Jenner, W.E., **Rudiments of Algebraic Geometry**, 1963
Jevons, W. Stanley, **The Principles of Science**, London: Macmillan, 1887; Clements, 1986
Jevons, W. Stanley, **Theory of Political Economy**, 1871; Augustus M. Kelly, 1965
Johnson-Laird, P., **The Computer and the Mind: An Introduction to Cognitive Science**, Cambridge: Harvard University Press, 1988
Jones, Raymond, **The Non-Statistical Man**, New York: Belmont Prods., 1964
Jones, Samuel I., **Mathematical Wrinkles**, 1912
Jordan, Camille: **Oeuvres**, 4 vols., Paris: Gauthier-Villars, 1961-64
Joseph, C.G., **The Crest of the Peacock**, 1991; paperback, Princeton: Princeton University Press, 2000
de Jouvenel, Bertrand, **The Art of Conjecture**, New York: Basic Books, 1967
Jowett, Benjamin, **Dialogues of Plato**, New York, 1897; Thoemmes Press, 1999
Judson, H., **The Eighth Day of Creation**, 1910; paperback, Cold Springs Harbor Laboratory, 1996
Jung, C.G., **Man and His Symbols**, 1964; paperback, Laureleaf, 1977
Juster, Norton, **The Dot and the Line; a romance in lower mathematics**, New York: Random House, 1963
Kac, Mark, **Enigmas of Chance: An Autobiography**, New York: Harper and Row, 1985
Kac, Mark, **Statistical Independence in Probability Analysis and Number Theory**, New York: John Wiley & Sons, 1959
Kac, Mark, Gian-Carlo Rota and Jacob T. Schwartz, **Discrete Thoughts**, Boston: Birkhauser, 1986
Kac, Mark, and Stanislaw Ulam; **Mathematics and Logic**, New York: Frederick Praeger, 1968
Kahn, C.K., ed., **The Art and Thought of Heraclitus**, Cambridge: Cambridge University Press, 1981
Kahn, David, **The Code Breakers**, New York: Macmillan, 1967
Kaku, Michio, **Hyperspace**, New York: Oxford University Press, 1994
Kanigel, Robert, **The Man Who Knew Infinity: A Life of the Genius Ramanujan**, New York: Washington Square Press, 1991
Kant, Immanuel, **Critique of Judgment**, 1790; J.C. Meredith, tr., Oxford: Oxford University Press, 1997
Kant, Immanuel, **Critique of Pure Reason**, 1890, 2nd. edition, New York, 1900; J.M. Meiklejohn, tr., paperback, Great Books in Philosophy, 1990; paperback, Cambridge: Cambridge University Press, 1999
Kant, Immanuel, **Werke**, Rosenkranz and Schubert, eds., Leipzig, 1838
Kaplan, Abraham, **The Conduct of Inquiry**, 1964; paperback, Transaction Pub., 1998
Kaplan, Robert, **The Nothing That Is: A Natural History of Zero**, Oxford, Oxford University Press, 1999
Karpinski, Louis C., **Bibliography of Mathematical Works Printed in America Through 1850**, Ann Arbor, University of Michigan Press, 1940
Karpinski, Louis C., **The History of Arithmetic**, Chicago: University of Chicago Press, 1925; Russell & Russell, 1965
Karpinski, Louis C., **Robert of Chester's Latin Translation of the Algebra of Al-Khwarizmi**, New York, 1915
Kasner, Edward, and James R. Newman, **Mathematics and the Imagination**, New York: Simon & Schuster, 1940
Kauffman, Stuart, **At Home in the Universe**, paperback, Oxford University Press, 1995
Kaufmann, W.A., and Forest E. Baird, eds., **Philosophical Classics: Thales to St. Thomas**, paperback, Prentice-Hall, 1999
Kelley, J.L. **General Topology**, Princeton: D. Van Nostrand, 1955
Kelvin, Lord (William Thomson), **Popular Lectures and Addresses**, London: Macmillan, 1891-94
Kemeny, John G., **Random Essays on Mathematics: Education and Computers**, Englewood Cliffs, J.J.: Prentice-Hall, 1964
Kemeny, H.G., and J.L. Snell, **Mathematical Models in the Social Sciences**, Cambridge, The MIT Press, 1972
Kendall, M.G., and A. Stuart, **The Advanced Theory of Statistics**, London: C. Griffin, 1947
Kendall, Phoebe Mitchell, ed., **Maria Mitchell, Life, Letters and Journals**, 1896
Kennedy, Hubert C., **Peano: Life and Works of Giuseppe Peano**, Dordrecht: Reidel, 1980
Kennedy, Hubert C., ed., **Selected Works of Giuseppe Peano**, paperback, Kluwer Academic Press, 1980
Kepler, Johannes, **Astronomia Nova**, 1609; W.H. Donahue, tr., Prometheus Books, 1995
Kepler, Johannes, **Concerning the More Certain Foundations of Astrology**, Clancy Pubns., 1942
Kepler, Johannes, **Epitome of Copernican Astronomy**, c. 1600; Charles Glenn Wallis, tr., Prometheus Books, 1995
Kepler, Johannes, **The Harmony of the World**, 1619; E.T. Acton & A.M. Dumas, tr., American Philosophical Society, 1999

Kepler, Johannes, **Mysterious of the Cosmos**, 1596
Kepler, Johannes, **The Six-Cornered Snowflake**, 1611
Keynes, John Maynard, **A Treatise on Probability**, London: Macmillan, 1921; Harper & Row, 1962
Keyser, Cassius J., **The Human Worth of Rigorous Thinking**, New York: Scripta Mathematica, 1940
Keyser, Cassius, J., **Lectures on Science, Philosophy and Art**, New York: Dutton, 1908
Keyser, Cassius J., **Mathematical Philosophy**, New York: Dutton, 1922
Keyser, Cassius, J., **Mole Philosophy and Other Essays**, New York: E.P. Dutton, 1927
Keyser, Cassius J., **The Pastures of Wonder**, New York: University of New York Press, 1929
Khan, Mohammad Abdur Rahman, **A Brief Survey of Moslem Contribution to Science and Culture**, 1946
Khurgin, Ya, **Did You Say Mathematics?**, Moscow: MIR, 1974
Khayyam, Omar, **Algebra of Omar Khayyam**, AMS Press, 1931
Kierkegaard, Soren, **The Universe and the Modern World**, S. Nash, ed., 1943
King, Jerry P., **The Art of Mathematics**, New York: Plenum Press, 1992
Kingsley, Charles, **Hypatia or New Foes with Old Faces**, Chicago: W.B. Conkley, Co., 1853
Kitcher, Philip, **The Nature of Mathematical Knowledge**, Oxford: Oxford University Press, 1984
Kleene, Stephen C., **Introduction to Metamathematics**, Princeton, New Jersey: D. Van Nostrand, 1952
Klein, H. Arthur, **The World of Measurements**, New York: Simon and Schuster, 1974
Klein, Felix, **Development of Mathematics in the 19th Century**, M. Ackerman, tr., Brookline: Math Science Press, 1979
Klein, Felix, **Elementary Mathematics from an Advanced Standpoint**, trans. from the German 3rd. ed., Vols. I,II, New York: Macmillan, 1932; New York: Dover, 1961
Klein, Felix, **Famous Problems of Elementary Geometry**, W.W. Berman and D.E. Smith, tr., New York: Dover, 1956
Klein, Felix, **The Mathematical Theory of the Top**, 1897
Klein, Felix, **Vorlesungen uber die Entwicklung der Mathematik im 19. Jahrhunderten**, 2 vols., Chelsea, 1950
Klein, Jacob, **Greek Mathematical Thought and the Origin of Algebra**, Brann, tr., Cambridge: MIT Press, 1968
Kline, Morris, **Mathematical Thought from Ancient to Modern Times**, Oxford: three volumes, Oxford University Press, 1972
Kline, Morris, **Mathematics—A Cultural Approach**, Reading, Ma.: Addison-Wesley, Publishing Co., 1962
Kline, Morris, **Mathematics and the Physical World**. New York: Dover, 1959
Kline, Morris, **Mathematics and the Search for Knowledge**, New York: Oxford University Press, 1985; paperback, World Bank: 1986
Kline, Morris, **Mathematics for the Nonmathematician**, New York: Dover, 1967
Kline, Morris, **Mathematics in Western Culture**. London: Oxford University Press, 1953; paperback, New York: Doubleday, 1963
Kline, Morris, **Mathematics: The Loss of Certainty**, New York: Oxford University Press, 1980
Kline, Morris, **Why Johnny Can't Add: The Failure of the New Math**; 1974
Kline, Morris, **Why the Professor Can't Teach**, New York: St. Martin's Press, 1977
Kneale, W.C., **Probability and Induction**, Oxford: Clarendon Press, 1952
Kneale, William, and Martha Kneale, **The Development of Logic**, New York: Oxford University Press, 1962
Knoor, Wilbur, **The Ancient Tradition of Geometric Problems**, New York: Dover, 1993
Knoor, Wilbur, **The Evolution of the Euclidean Elements**, Dordrecht and Boston: Reidel, 1975
Knopp, K., **Theory and Application of Infinite Series**, London: Blackie and Son, 1928
Koblitz, Ann, **A Convergence of Lives: Sofia Kovalevskaia—Scientist, Writer, Revolutionary**, Boston: Birkhauser, 1983; paperback, Reprint ed., Rutgers University Press, 1993
Koenderink, J., **Solid Shape**, MIT Press, 1990
Koenigsberger, L., **Carl Gustav Jacob Jacobi**, Leipzig: Teubner, 1904
Koestler, Arthur, **The Act of Creation**, London: Pan Books, 1964; paperback, Arkana, 1990
Koestler, Arthur, **The Watershed: A Biography of Johannes Kepler**, New York: Doubleday, 1959, paperback, Anchor Books, 1960
Koestler, A., and V.R. Smithees, eds., **Beyond Reduction**, 1968
Kolmogoroff, A.N., **Foundations of the Theory of Probability**, New York, Chelsea, 1956; Springer-Verlag, 1992
Kolmogoroff, A.N., and S.V. Fomin, **Measure, Lebesque Integrals, and Hilbert Space**, New York: Academic Press, 1961
Kolmogoroff, A.N., and M.A. Laurentes, eds. **Mathematics: Its Content, Methods and Meaning**, 1963; paperback, New York: Dover, 1999
Kopency, J., **Euclid's Fifth Postulate**, 1933
Korner, Stephan, **The Philosophy of Mathematics**, London: Hutchinson, 1960; New York, Dover, 1986
Kovalevskaya, Sofya, **A Russian Childhood**, New York: Springer-Verlag, 1978
Kramer, Edna E., **The Main Stream of Mathematics**, New York: Oxford University Press, 1955; Fawcett, 1964
Kramer, Edna E., **The Nature and Growth of Mod-**

ern Mathematics, New York: Hawthorn Books, Inc., 1970

Krauss, Lawrence M., **Fear of Physics**, 1993; paperback, Basic Books, 1994

Kronecker, Leopold, **Leopold Kronecker's Werke**, 5 vols., K. Hensel, ed., New York: Chelsea, 1968

Kronecker, Leopold, **Vorlesungen uber Zahlentheorie**, Leipzig: Teubner, 1901; reprint, Springer-Verlag, 1978

Kronecker, Leopold, **Zahlentheorie**, Leipzig, 1901

Kuhn, Thomas S., **The Copernican Revolution**, New York: Vintage Books, 1962

Kuhn, Thomas, **The Structure of Scientific Revolutions**, Chicago: University of Chicago Press, 1970; paperback, 1996

Kummer, E.E., **Berliner Monatsberichte**, 1867

Kuratowski, K. **Introduction to Set Theory and Topology**, 1962

Kuratowski, K., **Topologie**, Warsaw, Matematycne, 1933

Kurschak, Josef, compiler, **Hungarian Problem Book**, Washington, D.C.: Mathematical Association of America, 1963

Lacroix, S.F., **Elements of Algebra**, John Farrar, tr., Cambridge: Hilliard and Metcalf, 1818; Boston: Hilliard, Gray, Little and Wilkins, 1831

Lagrange, Joseph-Louis, **Mecanique analytique**, 2 vols., Paris: Librarie scientifique et technique, Albert Blanchard, 1965; Boston Studies in the Philosophy of Science, Auguste Claude Boissonnade and Victor N. Vagliente, tr., Kluwer Academic Pug., 1997

Lagrange, Joseph-Louis, **Oeuvres de Lagrange**, Paris: Gauthier- Villars, 1868-1873

Laing, R.D., **Knots**, New York: Vintage Books, 1970

Lakatos, Imre, **Mathematics, Science and Epistemology**, Cambridge: Cambridge University press, 1978

Lakatos, Imre, **Philosophical Papers**, New York: Cambridge University Press, 1978

Lakatos, Imre, **Proofs and Refutations: The Logic of Mathematical Discovery**, New York: Cambridge University Press, 1976

Lamb, Harold, **Omar Khayyam, A Life**, New York: Doubleday, 1936

Lancaster, Peter, **Mathematics: Models of the Real World**, Englewood Cliffs, NJ: Prentice-Hall, 1976

Lanczos, Cornelius, **Linear Differential Operators**, paperback, New York: Dover, 1996

Lanczos, Cornelius, **Numbers Without End**, Edinburgh: Oliver & Boyd, 1968

Lanczos, Cornelius, **Space Through the Ages: The Evolution of Geometrical Ideas from Pythagoreas to Hilbert and Einstein**, New York: Academic Press, 1970

Landau, Edmund: **Differential and Integral Calculus**, 3rd. ed., New York: Chelsea, 1981

Landau, Edmund, **Elementary Number Theory**, New York: Chelsea, 1958

Landau, Edmund, **Foundations of Analysis**, New York: Chelsea, 1950

Landau, Rom, **Arab Contribution to Civilization**, 1958

Lang, Serge, **The Beauty of Doing Mathematics**, New York: Springer- Verlag, 1985

Langer, Suzanne K., **Philosophy in a New Key**, 1942; paperback, 3rd. ed., Cambridge: Harvard University Press, 1957

Lao Tze, **Tao Te Ching**, 6th cent. B.C.; Stephen Mitchell, tr., paperback, Harperperrenial, 1992

Lapin, Lawrence, **Statistics for Modern Business Decisions**, New York: Harcourt, Brace Jovanovich, 1973; paperback, Duxbury Press, 1995

Laplace, Pierre Simon, **Celestial Mechanics**, New York: Chelsea, 1966

Laplace, Pierre Simon, **Oeuvres Completes de Laplace**, Paris: Gauthier-Villars, 1886

Laplace, Pierre Simon, **Philosophical Essays on Probabilities**, translated from the 1825 5th ed. by Andrew I. Dale, New York: Springer-Verlag, 1995

Launer, R.L. and G.N. Wilkinson, eds., **Robustness in Statistics**, Academic Press, 1979

Lavine, S., **Understanding the Infinite**, Cambridge: Harvard University Press, 1994

Lavoisier, Antoine Laurent, **Elements of Chemistry**, Robert Kerr, tr., paperback, New York: Dover, 1984

Lawlor, Robert, **Sacred Geometry**, 1982

Leach, Edmund Ronald, **Rethinking Anthropology**, 1961; paperback, Athlone Press, 1966

Leacock, Stephen, **The Penguin Stephen Leacock**, London: Penguin, 1981

Lebesque, Henri, **Measure and the Integral**, San Francisco: Holden- Day, 1966

Lec, Stanislaw J., **More Unkempt Thoughts**, New York: Funk & Wagnalls, 1968

Lec, Stanislaw J., **Unkempt Thoughts**, Jacek Galazka, tr., New York: Funk & Wagnalls, 1962

Lederman, Leon, **The God Particle**, Boston: Houghton Mifflin, 1993

Lefevre, Arthur, **Number and Its Algebra**, Boston, 1903

Lefschetz, Solomon, **Introduction to Topology**, Princeton: Princeton University press, 1949

Legendre, Adrien-Marie, **Elements de geometrie**, 1794; A. Blanchard, 1955

Legendre, Adrien-Marie, **Theorie des nombres**, 2 vols., A. Blanchard, 1955

Lehman, H., **Introduction to the Philosophy of Mathematics**, Oxford: Blackwell, 1979

Lehmer, D.N., **An Elementary Course in Synthetic Projective Geometry**, 1917

Leibniz, G.W.F, **Basic Writings**, George R. Montgomery, tr., LaSalle: Open Court, 1968; paperback, Unknown, 1973

Leibniz, G.W.F, **Leibniz: Discourses on Metaphysics**, George Montgomery, tr., Chicago: Open Court, 1902

Leibniz, G.W.F, **Logical Papers**, G.A.R. Parkinson, ed. & tr., Oxford University press, 1966

Leibniz, G.W.F, **Monadology and Other Philosophical Essays**, Indianapolis: Bobbs-Merrill, 1965

Leibniz, G.W.F., **New Essays Concerning Human Understanding**, LaSalle: Open Court, 1949

Leibniz, G.W.F., **Philosophical Papers and Letters**, L.E. Loemker, ed. and tr., Chicago: University of Chicago Press, 1956

Le Lionnais, Francois, ed., **Great Currents of Mathematics**, French & European Publishers, 1971

Lerner, Eric J., **The Big Bang Never Happened**, New York: Tine Books, 1991

Levinson, Horace, **The Science of Chance**, New York: Holt, Rinehart & Winston, 1950

Levy, Hyman, **Modern Science**, New York: Knopf, 1939

Levy, Hyman, **The Universe of Science**, New York: The Century Co., 1933

Lewes, G.H., **Physiology of Common Life**. 1859

Lewes, G.H., **Problems of Life and Mind**, 1875

Lewis, C.I. and C.H. Langford, **Symbolic Logic**, The Century Co., 1932

l'Hopital, G.F., **Analyse des infiniment petits pour l'intelligence des lignes courbes**, 1696

Libbrecht, Ulrich, **Chinese Mathematics in the Thirteenth Century**, Cambridge: MIT Press, 1973

Lichtenberg, Georg C., **Lichtenberg: Aphorisms and Letters**, Franz Mautner and Henry Hatfield, tr., London: Jonathan Cape, 1969

Lie, Sophus, **Continuous Groups**, 1893; Chelsea, 1970

Lie, Sophus, **Leipziger Perichte** 47, 1895; Chelsea, 1976

Lie, Sophus, **Theorie der Transformationsgruppen**, 3 vols., Leipzig: 1893; Chelsea Pub., 1970

Lind, Douglas A. and Robert J. Mason, **Statistical Techniques in Business and Economics**, 1967; Richard D. Irwin, 1995

Linn, C.F., **The Golden Mean: Mathematics and the Fine Arts**, 1974

Littlewood, J.E., **A Mathematician's Miscellany**, London: Meuthen and Co., 1953

Littlewood, J.E., **The Mathematician's Art of Work**, 1967

Li Yan and Du Shiran, **Chinese Mathematics: A Concise History**, J.N. Crossley and A. W.-C. Lun, trs., Oxford: Oxford University Press, 1987

Lloyd, G.E.R., **Greek Science After Aristotle**, New York: W.W. Norton, 1973

Lloyd, G.E.R., **Magic, Reason and Experience**, Cambridge: Cambridge University Press, 1979

Locke, John, **The Conduct of Understanding**, 1690

Locke, John, **An Essay Concerning Human Understanding**, Oxford: Clarendon Press, 1956

Lodge, Sir Oliver, **Pioneers of Science**, New York: Macmillan, 1930

Lombroso, Cesare, **The Man of Genius**, 1891

Lorentz, H.A., A. Einstein, H. Minkowski and H. Weyl, **The Principle of Relativity**, New York: Dover, 1923

Lotze, Hermann, **Metaphysic**, G. Hirzel, tr., Leipzig, 1879; Oxford: Clarendon Press, 1887

Lovelace, Ada Byron; **Ada: The Enchantress of Numbers**, Cartech Inc., 1998

Lucas, H.N. Bunt, Phillip S. Jones and Jack D. Bedient, **The Historical Roots of Elementary Mathematics**, Englewood Cliffs, N.J.:, Prentice-Hall, 1976

Luminet, Jean-Pierre, **Black Holes**, 1987; Cambridge University Press, 1992

MacDuffee, C.C., **The Theory of Matrices**, New York: Chelsea, 1950

Macfarlane, Alexander, **Lectures on Ten Mathematicians of the Nineteenth Century**, New York: John Wiley & Sons, 1916

Mach, Ernst, **The Economical Nature of Physical Inquiry**, 1882

Mach, Ernst, **Popular Scientific Lectures**, 1910

Mach, Ernst, **The Science of Mechanics**, LaSalle: Open Court, 1942

Mach, Ernst, **Space and Geometry**, T.J. McCormack, tr.; paperback, Unknown, 1988

MacHale, Desmond, **Comic Sections**, 1933

MacHale, Desmond, **George Boole: His Life and Work**, Dublin: Boole Press, 1985

Mackie, G.L., **Truth, Probability and Paradox**, New York: Oxford University Press, 1973

MacLane, Saunders, **Mathematics: Form and Function**, New York: Springer-Verlag, 1986

Maclaurin, Colin, **Collected Letters of Colin Maclaurin**, S. Mills, ed., 1982

Maclaurin, Colin, **A Treatise of Algebra**, 1748

Maclaurin, Colin, **Treatise on Fluxions**, two volumes, Edinburgh: T. Ruddimans, 1742

Macrae, N., **John von Neumann**, New York: Pantheon, 1992

Maddy, Penelope, **Realism in Mathematics**, New York: Oxford University Press, 1992

Mahoney, Michael S., **The Mathematical Career of Pierre de Fermat, 1601-1665**, Princeton: Princeton University Press, 1973

Maimonides, Moses, **The Guide of the Perplexed**, M. Friedlander, tr., London: George Routledge & Sons, 1919

Maldevitch, Joseph, and Walter Meyer, **Graphs, Models, and Finite Mathematics**, Englewood Cliffs, N.J.: Prentice-Hall, 1974

Malthus, Thomas Robert, **An Essay on the Principles of Population**, 1798; paperback, Antony G. Flew, ed., Penguin English Library, 1985

Mandelbrot, Benoit B., **The Fractal Geometry of Nature**, New York: W.H. Freeman, 1983; 1988

Manheim, Jerome J., **The Genesis of Point Set Topology**, New York: Macmillan, 1964

Manin, Yu I., **A Course in Mathematical Logic**, New York: Springer-Verlag, 1977

Mankiewicz, Richard: **The Story of Mathematics**, 2000

Manning, Henry F. **The Fourth Dimension Simply Explained**, New York: Munn & Co., 1910; Peter Smith Pub., 1950

Manning, Henry F., **Geometry of Four Dimensions**, New York: Dover, 1956

Mansfield, M.J., **Introduction to Topology**, 1963
Maor, Eli, **e: The Story of a Number**, Princeton: Princeton University Press, 1994
Maor, Eli, **To Infinity and Beyond: A Cultural History of the Infinite**, Boston: Birkhauser, 1987
Mardsen, J.E., and A.J. Tromba, **Vector Calculus**, 1981
Marr, Richard, **4-Dimensional Geometry**, Boston: Houghton Mifflin, 1970
Maschke, H., **Present Problems of Algebra and Analysis**, 1905
Maseres, Francis, **Dissertation on the Use of the Negative Sign in Algebra**, 1759; London, 1904
Mason, S.F., **A History of the Sciences**, Routledge, 1953
Mathews, G.B., **Theory of Numbers**, Chelsea, Pub. Co., 1982
Maxwell, James Clerk, **The Scientific Letters and Papers of James Clerk Maxwell**, P.M. Harmon, ed., New York: Cambridge University Press, 1995
Mayne, Ethel Colburn, **The Life and Letters of Anne Isabelle, Lady Noel Byron**, Reprint Services Corp., 1929
Maziarz, Edward, and Thomas Greenwood, **The Birth of Mathematics in the Age of Plato**, Washington: American Research Council, 1964
Maziarz, Edward, and Thomas Greenwood, **Greek Mathematical Philosophy**, New York: Ungar, 1968
McCorduck, Pamela, **Machines Who Think**, San Francisco: W.H. Freeman, 1979
McKinsey, J.C.C., **Introduction to the Theory of Games**, McGraw-Hill, 1952
McLeish, John, **Number**, London: Bloomsbury, 1991
McShane, E.J., **Integration**, Princeton: Princeton University Press, 1947
Mehra, Jagdish, ed., **The Physicist's Conception of Nature**, World Scientific Pub., 1973
Mehrtens, Herbert, ed., **Social History of Nineteenth Century Mathematics**, Boston: Birkhauser, 1981
Meier, J., and T. Riskel, **Writing in the Teaching and Learning of Mathematics**, paperback, Mathematical Association of America, 1998
Mellor, J.W., **Higher Mathematics for Students of Chemistry and Physics**, New York: Dover, 1955
Mencius, **The Works of Mencius**, James Legge, tr., New York: Dover, 1990
Mendelsohn, Elliott, ed., **Transformations and Traditions in the Sciences**, Cambridge: Cambridge University Press, 1984
Menninger, K., **Number Words and Number Symbols: A Cultural History of Numbers**, Cambridge, The MIT Press, 1969,
Merriman, Gaylord M., **To Discover Mathematics**, New York: John Wiley & Sons, 1942
Mersenne Marin, **les Questions theologiques physiques, morales et matematiques**, 1634; Henry Guerion tr., 1985
Merz, J.T., **A History of European Thought in the Nineteenth Century**, Edinburgh and London, 1904; New York, Dover, 1965; Thoemmes Press, 2000
Meschkowski, Herbert, **Evolution of Mathematical Thought**, Holden- Day, 1965
Meschkowski, Herbert, **Ways of Thought of Great Mathematicians**, San Francisco: Holden-Day, 1964
Metropolis, N., J. Howlett, and G. Rota, eds., **A History of Computing in the Twentieth Century**, Academic Press, 1980
Mickens, R.E., ed., **Mathematics and Science**, Singapore: World Scientific, 1990
Midonick, H.O., **The Treasury of Mathematics**, New York: Philosophical Library, 1965
Mikami, Yoshio, **The Development of Mathematics in China and Japan**, New York: Hafner, 1913; Chelsea, 1961, 1974
Milhaud, G., **Descartes Savant (The Philosophy of Descartes)**, 1921
Mill, John Stuart, **An Examination of Sir William Hamilton's Philosophy**, London, 1878
Mill, John Stuart, **Systems of Logic**, 1843; London: Longsman, 1868; 8th ed., Classworks, 1986
Miller, Arthur I., **Insights of Genius: Imagery and Creativity**, paperback, MIT Press, 2000
Miller, G.A., **Historical Introduction to Mathematical Literature**, 1921
Minkowski, Hermann, **The Principle of Relativity**, Calcutta: University of Calcutta, 1920
Misner, Charles W., Kip Thorne, and John A. Wheeler; **Gravitation**, paperback, San Francisco, W.H. Freeman, 1973
Moebius, P.J., **Ueber die Anlage zur Mathematik**, Leipzig, 1900
Moffatt, Michael, **The Ages of Mathematics**, Garden City, N.J.: Doubleday, 1977
Moise, E.E., **Elementary Geometry from and Advanced Standpoint**, Reading, Ma.: Addison-Wesley, 1963
Molesworth, William, ed., **Collected Works of Thomas Hobbes**, 1939-45
Montague, H.F., and M.D. Montgomery, **The Significance of Mathematics**, Columbus, Ohio, 1963
Montucla, Jean Etienne, **Histories des mathematiques**, 1757; Paris: A. Blanchard, 1960
Moore, David S., and George P. McCabe, **Introduction to the Practice of Statistics**, Mew York: W.H. Freeman, 1989
Moore, G.H., **Zermelo's Axiom of Choice: Its Origins, Development, and Influence**, New York, 1982
Moore, John, **Arithmetic**, 1660
Morash, Ronald P., **A Bridge to Abstract Mathematics**, 2nd. ed., New York: McGraw-Hill, |1990
Mordell, Louis Joel, **Reflections of a Mathematician**, Montreal: Canadian Mathematical Congress, 1959

Mordell, Louis Joel, **Three Lectures on Fermat's Last Theorem**, Cambridge University press, 1921
More, Louis T. **Isaac Newton**, New York: Dover, 1962
More, Louis T. **The Limitations of Science**, 1915
Moritz, R.E., **Memorabilia Mathematica**, 1914, Mathematical Association of America, 1942
Moritz, R.E., **On Mathematics and Mathematicians**, New York, 1914
Morley, Christopher, **Translations from the Chinese**, 1927
Morley, Sylvanus Morley, **The Ancient Maya**, Palo Alto: Stanford University Press, 1947, 3rd. ed., 1956
Moroney, M.J., **Facts from Figures**, 3rd. ed., Penguin Books, 1956
Morris, Desmond, **The Naked Ape: A Zoologist's Study of the Human of the Human Animal**, 1967; paperback, Dell Pub., 1999
Morrison, Foster, **The Art of Modeling**, John Wiley & Sons, 1991
Morrow, G.R., **Proclus, A Commentary on the First Book of Euclid's Elements**, Princeton: Princeton University Press, 1970
Morse, Philip M. and George E. Kimball, **Methods of Operation Research**, John Wiley & Sons, 1950
Mortimer, Ernest, **Blaise Pascal: The Life and Work of a Realist**, New York: Harper and Brothers, 1959
Moschovakis, Yiannis, **Descriptive Set Theory**, 1980
Mostowski, Andrzej: **Thirty Years of Foundational Studies**, Barnes and Noble, 1966
Motz, Lloyd, and Jefferson Hane Weaver, **The Story of Mathematics**, New York: Avon, 1993
Motz, Lloyd, and Jefferson Hane Weaver, **The Story of Physics**, New York: Avon, 1989
Moulton, F.R., **Introduction to Astronomy**, New York: Macmillan, 1922; as **Introduction to Celestrial Mechanics**, 2nd. rev. ed., paperback, New York: Dover, 1988
Mozans, H.J., **Woman in Science**, New York: Appleton and Co., 1913
Mueller, Ian, **Philosophy of Mathematics and Deductive Structure in Euclid's Elements**, Cambridge, MIT Press, 1981
Muir, Jane, **Of Men and Numbers**, New York: Dover, 1996
Muir, Thomas, **The Theory of Determinants in the Historical Order of Development**, 1906; New York: Dover, 1960
Mumford, David, **Geometric Invariant Theory**, New York: Academic Press, 1965
Naas, J., and H.L. Schmid, **Mathematisches Worterburch**, Berlin: Akademie-Verlag, 1961
Nachbin, Leopoldo; **Topology and Order**, 1965
Nagel, Ernest, **Principles of the Theory of Probability**, Chicago: University of Chicago Press, 1939
Nagel, Ernest, and James R. Newman, **Goedel's Proof**, New York: New York University Press, 1958
Napier, John, **Mirifici logarithmorum canonis constructio (The Construction of the Wonderful Canon of Logarithms**, 1614; W.R. MacDonald, tr., 1889; AMS Press, 1991
Nasr, Seyyed Hossein, **Science and Civilization in Islam**, Cambridge: Harvard University Press, 1968
National Research Council's Committee on Support of Research in the Mathematical Sciences, Cambridge: The MIT Press, 1969
Needham, J., **Science and Civilization in China**, Cambridge: Cambridge University Press, 1970
Nehemiah, **Mishnat ha-Middot**, c. A.D. 150
Neugebauer, Otto, **Astronomy and History, Selected Essays**, paperback, Springer-Verlag, 1983
Neugebauer, Otto, **The Exact Sciences in Antiquity**, Providence: Brown University Press, 1957; New York: Harper & Bros., 1962
Neugebauer, Otto, **A History of Ancient Mathematical Astronomy**, 3 vols., New York: Springer-Verlag, 1975
Newcomb, Simon, **The Reminiscences of an Astronomer**, Reprint Services, 1903
Newell, Virginia K., et al, eds., **Black Mathematicians and Their Works**, Ardmore, Pa: Dorrance, 1980
Newman, James R., **The World of Mathematics**, New York: Simon & Schuster, 1956
Newton, Sir Isaac, **The Correspondence of Isaac Newton**
Newton, Sir Isaac, **Mathematical Principles of Natural Philosophy**, University of California Press, 1946
Newton, Sir Isaac, **Mathematical Works**, D.T. Whiteside, ed., Johnson Reprint Corp., 1967
Newton, Sir Isaac, **Memoirs of Newton**, David Brewster, ed., 1855
Newton, Sir Isaac, **Methodus Fluxioum et Serierum Infintarum**, 1671
Newton, Sir Isaac, **Principia**, A. Motte, tr., 1729; Florian Cajori, ed., University of California Press, 1924; Chicago: Encyclopedia Britannia, 1952
Newton, Sir Isaac, **Universal Arithmetic**, 1707, D.T. Whiteside, tr., 1728
Nicholas of Cusa, **Die Kunst der Vermutung, a Selection from His Works**, paperback, Book Tree, 1999
Nicomachus of Gerasa, **Introduction to Arithmetic**, Martin Luther D'Orge, tr., New York: Macmillan, 1926, 1946
Nidditch, P.H., **The Development of Mathematical Logic**, Glencoe, Ill.: Free Press, 1962
Nietzsche, Friedrick Wilhelm, **Human, All Too Human**, 1886; Lincoln: University of Nebraska Press, 1984
Nietzsche, Friedrick Wilhelm, **The Will to Power**, Walter Kaufman, tr., Random House, 1987
Nightingale, Florence, **Notes on Nursing**, 1860; paperback, New York: Dover, 1969; Lippincott, Williams & Wilkins, 1992
Niven, Ivan, **Irrational Numbers**, (Carus Mono-

graph No. 9). The Mathematical Association of America, New York: John Wiley & Sons, 1950

Niven, Ivan, and H.S. Zuckerman, **An Introduction to the Theory of Numbers**, 4th ed., New York: John Wiley & Sons, 1980

Noether, Max, **Mathematische Annalen**, 1895

Northrup, E.P., **Riddles in Mathematics: A Book of Paradoxes**, D. Van Nostrand, 1944

Novalis (Friedrich Leopold von Hardenberg), **Schriften (Philosophical Writings)**, Berlin, Zweiter Teil, 1901; Margaret M. Stoljar, ed., State University of New York Press, 1997

Novy, Lubos, **Origins of Modern Algebra**, Jaroslav Tauer, tr., Prague: Academiae, 1973

Odum, D.P., **Fundamentals of Ecology**, Philadelphia: W.B. Saunders, 1971

Ogyu, Sorai, **Complete Works on Japan's Philosophical Thought**, 1956

Ohanian, Susan, **Garbage Pizza, Patchwork Quilts and Math Magic**, paperback, W.H. Freeman, 1994

O'Leary, De Lacy, **How Greek Science Passed to the Arabs**, Routledge, 1949

Oman, John, **The Natural and the Supernatural**, New York: Macmillan, 1931

Oppenheimer, J. Robert, **Science and Common Understanding**, New York: Simon and Schuster, 1954

Ore, Oystein, **Cardano: The Gambling Scholar**, Princeton University Press, 1953

Ore, Oystein, **Niels Henrik Abel: Mathematician Extraordinary**, Minneapolis: University of Minnesota Press, 1957

Ore, Oystein, **Number Theory and Its History**, New York: McGraw Hill, 1948

Osen, Lynn M., **Women in Mathematics**, Cambridge: MIT Press, 1974

Osserman, Robert, **Poetry of the Universe**, New York: Anchor Books, 1995

Ostwald, Wilhelm, **Natural Philosophy**, 1910

Ouspensky, P.D. (Peter Demianovich Uspenskii), **Tertium Organum**, 1912; Vintage Books, 1970; paperback: Kessinger Pub., 1998

Overbye, Dennis, **Lonely Hearts of the Cosmos**, 1991; paperback, Little Brown & Co., 1999

Owen, George E., **The Universe of the Mind**, Baltimore: The Johns Hopkins University Press, 1971

Ozanam, Jacques, **Curus Mathematica**, 1712

Pagels, Heinz R., **The Cosmic Code**, New York: Simon and Schuster, 1982

Pagels, Heinz R., **The Dreams of Reason**, New York: Simon and Schuster, 1988

Pagels, Heinz R., **Perfect Symmetry**, New York: Simon and Schuster, 1985

Panichas, George A., **A Simone Weil Reader**, 1977; paperback, Mayer Bell, 1983

Pannekoek, A., **A History of Astronomy**, New York: John Wiley & Sons, 1961

Panofsky, Erwin, **Life and Art of Albrecht Durer**, paperback, Princeton University press, 1971

Papert, Seymour, **Mindstorms**, New York: Basic Books, 1980

Pappas, George S., **Berkeley's Thoughts**, Cornell University Press, 2000

Pappas, Theoni, **The Joy of Mathematics**, San Carlos, Ca.: Wide World Publishing/Tetra, 1993

Pappas, Theoni, **Mathematical Footprints**, San Carlos, Ca.: Wide World Publishing/Tetra, 1999

Pappas, Theoni, **Mathematical Scandals**, San Carlos, Ca.: Wide World Publishing/Tetra, 1997

Pappas, Theoni, **More Joy of Mathematics**, San Carlos, Ca.: Wide World Publishing/Tetra, 1993

Parker, F.W., **Number-system of Algebra**, New York: E.L. Kellogg, 1894

Parker, F.W., **Talks on Pedagogics**, New York: E.L. Kellogg, 1894

Parker, John, **The Quadrature of the Circle**, 1874

Parsons, Edward Alexander, **The Alexandrian Library**, New York: Elsevier, 1952

Pascal, Blaise, **The Essential Pascal**, R.W. Gleason, ed., 1966

Pascal, Blaise, **Oeuvres completes**, Hachette, 1909

Pascal, Blaise, **Pensees**, W.F. Trotter, tr., Chicago: Encyclopedia Britannica, 1952; paperback, A.J. Krailsheimer, tr., Penguin Classics, 1995

Pascal, Blaise, **Scientific Treatises**, Richard Scofield, tr., Chicago: Encyclopedia Britannica, 1952

Patterson, Elizabeth, **Mary Somerville, 1780-1872**, New York: Oxford University Press, 1979

Paul, Charles B., **Science and Immortality: The Eulogies of the Paris Academy of Sciences (1699-1791)**, Berkeley: University of California Press, 1981

Pauli, Wolfgang, **Scientific Correspondence with Bohr, Einstein, Heisenberg and Others**, New York, 1979

Paulos, John Allen, **Beyond Numeracy**, paperback, Vintage Books, 1992

Paulos, John Allen, **Innumeracy**, New York: Hill and Wang, 1988

Paulos, John Allen, **Mathematics and Humor**, Chicago: The University of Chicago Press, 1980

Paulos, John Allen, **Once Upon a Number**, 1998; paperback, Basic Books, 1999

Peacock, George, **A Treatise on Algebra**, 2 vols., 1842; Scripta Mathematica, 1940

Peano, Giuseppe, **Opere scelte**, 3 vols., Edizioni Cremonese, 1957-59

Pearl, Judea, **Probabilistic Reasoning in Intelligent Systems**, San Mateo: Morgan Kaufman Publishing, 1988

Pearson, Karl, **The Grammar of Science**, London: J.M. Dent & Sons, 1937

Pearson, Karl, **The History of Statistics in the 17th and 18th Centuries Against the Changing Background of Intellectual, Scientific, and Religious Thought**, E.S. Pearson, ed., New York: Macmillan, 1978

Pearson, Karl, **The Life Letters and Labors of Francis Galton**, Cambridge: Cambridge University Press, 1914

Pedersen, Olaf, **A Survey of the Almagest**, Copenhagen, 1974

Peebles, P.J.E., **Physical Cosmology**, Princeton University Press, 1971

Peet, T.E., ed., **The Rhind Mathematical Papyrus**, London, 1923

Peirce, Benjamin, **An Elementary Treatise on Algebra: to Which Are Added Exponential Equations and Logarithms**, Boston: James Munroe and Company, 1837

Peirce, Benjamin, **Linear Associative Algebra**, 1870, Reprint Services, 1990

Peirce, Charles Sanders, **The Doctrine of Chance**, 1878

Peirce, Charles Sanders, **Chance, Love, and Logic**, New York: Harcourt, Brace, Inc., 1923

Peirce, Charles Sanders, **Collected Papers of Charles Sanders Peirce**, Charles Hartshorne and Paul Weiss, eds., Cambridge: Harvard University Press, 1933, 1960

Peirce, Charles Sanders, **The New Elements of Mathematics**, The Hague: Mouton, 1976

Peitgen, Heinz-Otto and Peter H. Richter, **The Beauty of Fractals**, New York: Springer-Verlag, 1986

Penrose, Roger, **The Emperor's New Mind: Concerning Computers, Minds, and the Laws of Physics**, Oxford: Oxford University Press, 1989

Penrose, Roger, **Shadows of the Mind**, Oxford: Oxford University Press, 1994

Perry, John, **The Teaching of Mathematics**, London, 1902-4

Pesin, Ivan N., **Classical and Modern Integration Theory**, Academic Press, 1970

Peter, Rozsa, **Playing with Infinity**, New York: Simon and Schuster, 1962

Peterson, Ivars, **Islands of Truth: A Mathematical Mystery Cruise**, New York: W.H. Freeman, 1990

Peterson, Ivars, **The Mathematical Tourist**, New York: W.H. Freeman & Co., 1988

Petsinis, Tom, **The French Mathematician**, 1998; paperback, Berkeley Pub. Grp., 2000

Petty, William, **Political Arithmetick**, 1676, 1690

Phillip, Frank, **Modern Science and Its Philosophy**, 1967

Philip, J.A., **Pythagoras**, Toronto: University of Toronto Press, 1966

Phillips, E.R., ed., **Studies in the History of Mathematics**, Washington, D.C.: Mathematical Association of America, 1987

Phin, John, **The Seven Follies of Science**, 1912

Picard, Emile, **Traite d'Analuse**, Paris: Gauthier-Villars et fils, 1893-1901

Pickover, Clifford A., **Keys to Infinity**, New York: John Wiley & Sons, 1995, 1997

Pinter, Charles, **A Book of Abstract Algebra**, McGraw-Hill, 1990

Pirsig, Robert M., **Zen and the Art of Motorcycle Maintenance**, New York: William Morrow, 1974; paperback, Quill, 1999

Pistorius, P.V., **Plotinus and Neoplatonism**, 1952

Planck, Max, **Scientific Autobiography and Other Papers**, New York: Philosophical Library, 1949; Greenwood Pub. Grp., 1968

Planck, Max, **The Universe in the Light of Modern Physics**, London: George Allen & Unwin, 1931

Planck, Max, **Where Is science Going?**, James Murphy, tr., New York; W.W. Norton, 1977

Plato, **The Collected Dialogues**, E. Hamilton and H. Cairns, eds., Princeton: Princeton University Press, 1961

Playfair, William, **The Statistical Brevity**, London: T. Bensley, 1801

Pliny the Elder, **Natural History**, Cambridge: Harvard University Press, 1962

Plotinus, **The Six Enneads**, paperback, John Dillon, ed., Stephen Mackenna, tr., Penguin, 1991

Plotz, Helen, **Imagination's Other Place**, New York: Thomas T. Crowell, 1955

Plutarch, **The Lives of Nobel Grecians and Romans**, Chicago: Encyclopedia Britannica, Vol. 14, 1952; paperback, Wordsworth, 1999

Poincare, Henri: **The Foundations of Science**, Garrison, N.Y.: The Science Press, 1913, 1929

Poincare, Henri, **Mathematics and Science: Last Essays**, J.W. Bolduc, tr., New York: Dover, 1963

Poincare, Henri, **Oeuvres**, Paris: Gauthier-Villars, 1954

Poincare, Henri, **Science and Hypothesis**, London: Walter Scott Publishing Co., 1905; New York: Dover, 1952

Poincare, Henri, **Science and Method**, New York: Dover, 1952; St. Augustine Press, 2000

Poincare, Henri, **The Value of Science**, New York: Dover, 1958

Poirot, James, and Daniel Groves, **Computers and Mathematics**, Manchaca, Tx.: Sterling Swith, 1979

Polanyi, Michael, **Knowing and Being**, M. Greene, ed., Chicago: Chicago University press, 1969

Polanyi, Michael, **Personal Knowledge**, paperback, Chicago: University of Chicago Press, 1958; 1974

Polkinghorne, John C., **The Faith of a Physicist**, paperback, Fortress Press, 1996

Pollock, F., **Clifford's Lectures and Essays**, 1901

Polya, George, **How to Solve It**, Princeton: Princeton University Press, 1945

Polya, George, **Mathematical Discovery**, two volumes, New York: John Wiley & Co., 1962

Polya, George, **Patterns of Plausible Inference**, two volumes, Princeton: Princeton University Press, 1954

Polya, George, **A Polya Picture Album**, G.L. Alexanderson, ed., 1987

Poncelot, Jean-Victor, **Treatise on the Projective Properties of Figures**, 1822

Ponomarev, L.I., **The Quantum Dice**, paperback, Institute of Physics Publications, 1993

Pontryagin, Lev S., **Foundations of Combinatorial Topology**, 1952; paperback, New York: Dover, 1999

Pontryagin, Lev S., **Topological Groups**, Emma Lehmer, tr., Princeton: Princeton University Press, 1958

Popper, Karl, **Conjectures and Refutations: The Growth of Scientific Knowledge**, New York: Harper and Row, 1965
Popper, Karl, **The Logic of Scientific Discovery**, London: Hutchinson, 1959
Popper, Karl, **The Open Universe**, Totowa: Rowman and Littlefield, 1982
Porter, T.M. , **The Rise of Statistical Thinking: 1820-1900**, Princeton: Princeton University Press, 1986
Poudra, M., ed., **Letters of Desargues**, 1864
Prasad, G., **Some Great Mathematicians of the Nineteenth Century**, Benares: Benares Mathematical Society, 1933-34
Price, B., **Treatise on Infinitesimal Calculus**, Oxford: Oxford University Press, 1868
Price, Derek John de Solla, **Little Science, Big Science**, 1954
Price, Derek John de Solla, **Science Since Babylon**, 1962; paperback, New Haven: Yale University Press, 1975
Priestly, W.M., **Calculus: An Historical Approach**, New York: Springer-Verlag, 1979, 1998
Proclus Diadochus, **Commentary on Euclid**, Paperback, Ares Pub., 1997
Ptacek, Greg, **Mothers of Invention**, 1988
Ptolemy, Claudius, **Almagest**, Gerald J. Toomer, tr., paperback, Princeton: Princeton University Press, 1998
Ptolemy, Claudius, **Geography**, tr. and printed about 1472; Paperback, Edward Luther Stevenson, tr., New York: Dover, 1991
Pullan, P.M., **The History of the Abacus**, New York: Frederick A. Praeger, 1969
Purcell, E., and D. Varberg, **Calculus with Analytic Geometry**, 1991; Prentice Hall, 1999
Purkert, W., **Leopold Kronecker**, Berlin: Biographien bedeutender Mathemamtiker, 1973
Purkert, W. and H-l. Ilgauds, **Georg Cantor**, Basel: Birkhauser, 1987
Putnam, Hilary, **Mathematics, Matter and Method**, paperback, Cambridge University Press, 1985
Quetelet, Adolphe, **De systeme social et des lois qui le regissent**, Paris: Guillaumin, 1848
Quetelet, Adolphe, **A Treatise on Man and the development of His Facilities**, Gainesville: Scholar's facsimiles & Reprints, 1969
Quine, Willard von Orman, **Elementary Logic**, Cambridge: Harvard University Press, 1980
Quine, Willard von Orman, **Mathematical Logic**, paperback, rev. ed., Harvard University press, 1981
Quine, Willard von Orman, **Methods of Logic**, New York: Holt, 1959
Quine, Willard von Orman, **Set Theory and Its Logic**, Cambridge: Harvard University Press, 1963
Quine, Willard von Orman, **The Ways of Paradox and Other Essays**, New York: Random House, 1966
Quintilian, **Institutes Oratoria**, H.E. Butler, tr., Harvard University press, 1970
Rademacher, Hans, and Otto Toeplitz, **The Enjoyment of Mathematics**, H. Zuckerman, tr., Princeton: Princeton University press, 1957
Raisz, E., **General Cartography**, New York: McGraw-Hill, 1948
Raleigh, A.S., **Occult Geometry**, 1932; paperback, reprint ed., Devorss & Co., 1991
Ramsey, Frank Plympton, **The Foundations of Mathematics and Other Logical Essays**, London: Routledge & Kegan Paul, 1954
Ramsey, Frank Plympton, **Philosophical Papers**, D.H. Mellor, ed., 1990
Ramsey, James B., **Economic Forecasting: Models or Markets?**, San Francisco: Sato Institute, 1980
Randall, John Herman, Jr., **Making the Modern Mind**, 1940; paperback, Columbia University Press, 1977
Raphael, Ellen, **Sophie Germain, Mathematician, A Biological Sketch**, Senior Thesis, Brown University, 1978
Rashed, R., **The Development of Arabic Mathematics: Between Arithmetic and Algebra**, Dordrecht, 1994
Rayleigh, Lord [John William Strutt], **The Theory of Sound**, 2 vols., New York: Dover, 1945
Read, Herbert, **Icon and Idea: The Function of Art in the Development of Human Consciousness**, Cambridge: Harvard University Press, 1955
Rebiere, A., **Mathematiques et Mathematicians**, 1898
Recorde, Robert: **The Grounde of Artes: Teachying the Worke and Practise of Arithmetike**, London, 1558
Recorde, Robert: **The Whetstone of Witte**, London, 1557
Reichenbach, Hans, **Elements of Symbolic Logic**, Macmillan, 1947
Reichenbach, Hans, **The Philosophy of Space and Time**, Maria Reichenbach, tr., New York: Dover, 1982
Reichenbach, Hans, **The Rise of Scientific Philosophy**, paperback, University of California Press, 1951
Reicher, Charles-Albert, **A History of Astronomy**, 1963
Reichmann, W.J., **Use and Abuse of Mathematics**, New York: Oxford University Press, 1962
Reid, Alastair, **Ounce, dice, trice**, Gregg Press Children's Literature, 1956
Reid, Constance, **From Zero to Infinity**, Thomas Y. Crowell, 1966
Reid, Constance, **Hilbert**, New York: Springer-Verlag, 1970
Reid, Constance, **Introduction to Higher Mathematics for the General Reader**, New York: Thomas Y. Crowell, 1959
Reid, Constance, **Julia: A Life in Mathematics**, Mathematical Association of America, 1997
Reid, Constance, **A Long Way from Euclid**, Thomas Y. Crowell, 1963
Reid, Thomas, **Essay on the Powers of the Human**

Mind, Edinburgh, 1812; A.D. Woezley, ed., paperback, Lincoln Rembrandt Pub., 1986
Renyi, Alfred, **Dialogues on Mathematics**, San Francisco: Holden-Day, 1967
Renyi, Alfred, **A Diary on Information Theory**, New York: John Wiley & Sons, 1984
Ricardo, David, **On the Principles of Political Economy and Taxation**, Prometheus Books, 1996
Richardson, Lewis Fry, **Collected Papers of Lewis Fry Richardson**, Oliver M. Ashford, ed., Cambridge University Press, 1993
Richardson, Lewis Fry, **The Mathematical Psychology of War**, 1919
Riemann, Bernhard, **Gesammelte Mathematische Werke**, 1876, 1892; New York Dover, 1953
Rindler, Wolfgang, **Essential Relativity**, rev 2nd. ed., paperback, Springer-Verlag, 1980
Ritchie, Robert W., **New Directions in Mathematics**, Englewood Cliffs, N.J.: Prentice-Hall, 1963
Roberts, A. Wayne, and Dale E. Varberg, **Faces of Mathematics**, New York: Harper & Row, 1978
Robinson, Abraham, **Non-Standard Analysis**, 2nd. ed., New York: North-Holland Pub., 1974
Robinson, James Henry, **The Mind in the Making**, 1921
Robinson, E., and J. Wimp, **Against Infinity**, Primary Press, 1979
Rogers, Eric, **Physics for the Inquiring Mind**, 1960
Rogosinski, W.W., **Volume and Integral**, Endinburgh, Oliver and Boyd, 1952
Roscher, Wilhelm, **Principles of Political Economy**, 1854
Rose, N., **Maxims and Minims**, 1988
Rosenbloom, P., **The Elements of Mathematical Logic**, 1950
Rosenbloom, Paul C. and George E. Forsythe, **Numerical Analysis and Partial Differential Equations**, 1958
Rosenbluth, A., **Philosophy of Science**, 1945
Rosenfeld, B.A., **A History of Non-Euclidean Geometry: Evolution of the Concept of Geometric Space**, New York: Springer-Verlag, 1988
Ross, W.D., ed. and tr., **Aristotle Selections**, 1st edition, 1928, reprint, Oxford: Oxford University Press, 1955
Rota, G.-C., **Indiscrete Thoughts**, Cambridge: Birkhauser, 1996
Rothman, Tony and George Sudarshan: **Doubt and Certainty**, Reading, mass., Perseus Books, 1998
Rotman, B., **Ad Infinitum—The Ghost in Turing's Machine**, Stanford, 1993
Rowan-Robinson, Michael, **Our Universe: An Armchair Guide**, New York: W.H. Freeman, 1990
Rowe, David E., and John McCleary: **The History of Modern Mathematics**, Vol. I, Boston: Academic Press, 1989
Rucker, Rudy, **The Fourth Dimension: A Guided Tour of the Higher Universes**, reprint ed., paperback, Boston: Houghton Mifflin, 1985
Rucker, Rudy, **Geometry, Relativity and the Fourth Dimension**, New York: Dover, 1977
Rucker, Rudy, **Infinity and the Mind**, Boston: Birkhauser, 1982; paperback, Princeton: Princeton University press, 1995
Rucker, Rudy, **Mind Tools: The Five Levels of Mathematical Reality**, paperback, New York: Houghton Mifflin, 1987
Rudin, W., **Principles of Mathematical Analysis**, New York: McGraw- Hill, 1953
Russell, Bertrand, **The ABC of Relativity**, New York: Harper Bros., 1925
Russell, Bertrand, **The Analysis of Matter**, London, George Allen & Unwin, 1921, 1954
Russell, Bertrand, **The Autobiography of Bertrand Russell**, Boston: Little, Brown, 1967; reissue ed., Routledge, 1998
Russell, Bertrand, **An Essay on the Foundations of Geometry**, New York: Dover, 1956; Routledge, 1996
Russell, Bertrand, **A Free Man's Worship and Other Essays**, 1923
Russell, Bertrand, **A History of Western Philosophy**, New York: Simon & Schuster, 1945; paperback, Simon and Schuster, 1975
Russell, Bertrand, **Human Knowledge: Its Scope and Limits**, 1948; paperback, Routledge, 1994
Russell, Bertrand, **The Impact of Science on Society**, 1952; paperback, Routledge, 1985
Russell, Bertrand, **In Praise of Idleness and Other Essays**, paperback, Routledge, 1994
Russell, Bertrand, **Introduction to Mathematical Philosophy**, London: Allen and Unwin, 1919; paperback, New York: Dover, 1997
Russell, Bertrand, **Mathematics and the Metaphysicians**, 1903
Russell, Bertrand, **My Philosophical Development**, revised ed., Unwin Hyman, 1995
Russell, Bertrand, **Mysticism and Logic**, New York: Longmans Green, 1919
Russell, Bertrand, **Portraits from Memory**, 1956
Russell, Bertrand, **The Principles of Mathematics**, Cambridge: Cambridge University Press, 1903; London: G. Allen & Unwin, 1937; paperback, W.W. Norton, 1996
Russell, Bertrand, **The Problems of Philosophy**, 1912; paperback, New York: Dover, 1999
Russell, Bertrand, **Religion and Science**, London: Oxford University Press, 1960
Russell, Bertrand, **The Scientific Outlook**, 1931
Russell, Bertrand, **The Study of Mathematics; Philosophical Essays**, London, 1910; paperback, Routledge, 1994
Russell, Bertrand, and Alfred North Whitehead, **Principia Mathematica**, Cambridge: Cambridge University Press, 1910
Ryser, H.J., **Combinatorial Mathematics**, Mathematical Association of America, 1963
Ryabov, Y., **An Elementary Survey of Celestial Mechanics**, New York, Dover, 1961

Ryser, H.J., **Combinatorial Mathematics**, Carus Mathematical Monographs, American Mathematical Association, 1967
Saaty, T.L., **The Four-Color Problem: Assaults and Conquest**, New York: McGraw-Hill, 1977
Saaty, T.L., ed. **Lectures on Modern Mathematics**, Vol. I, II, III, New York: John Wiley & Sons, 1963
Saaty, Thomas L. and F. Joachim Weyl, eds., **The Spirit and Uses of the Mathematical Sciences**, 1969
Saccheri, Gerolamo, **Euclides ab Omni Naevo Vindicatus**, G.B. Halsted, tr., Open Court, 1920; Chelsea, 1970
Safford, T., **Mathematical Teaching**, 1907
Sagan, Carl, **Broca's Brain**, 1979; Ballantine, 1993
Sagan, Carl, **Contact**, 1985; Pocket Books, 1997
Sagan, Carl, **Cosmos**, New York: Random House, 1980; paperback, 1983; Ballantine, 1999
Salmon, George, **A Treatise on the Analytical Geometry of Three Dimensions**, Dublin, 1882; Chelsea Pub., 1960
Sambursky, S., **The Physical World of the Greeks**, Routledge, 1956
Santillana, G. de, **The Crime of Galileo**, University of Chicago Press, 1955
Sarton, George, **A History of Science**, Harvard University Press, 1952
Sarton, George, **The Study of the History of Mathematics and the History of Science**, New York: Dover, 1936, 1954, 1957
Savage, L.J., **The Foundations of Statistics**, New York: John Wiley & Sons, 1954
Sawyer, W.W., **A First Look at Numerical Functional Analysis**, Oxford: Clarendon Press, 1978
Sawyer, W.W., **Mathematician's Delight**, 1967; paperback, Penguin Books, 1991
Sawyer, W.W., **Prelude to Mathematics**, Middlesex: Penguin Books, 1960
Schaaf, William L., **A Bibliography of Mathematics Education**, Forest Hills, N.Y.: Stevinus Press, 1941
Schaaf, William L., **A Bibliography of Recreational Mathematics, A Guide to the Literature**, Washington, D.C.: National Council of Teachers of Mathematics, 1970
Schaaf, William L., **Mathematics: Our Great Heritage**, New York: Harper, 1948
Schattschneider, Doris, **M.C. Escher: Visions of Symmetry**, San Francisco, W.H. Freeman, 1990
Schattschneider, Doris, **Notebooks, Periodic Drawings, and Related Works of M.C. Escher**, paperback, W.H. Freeman, 1992
Schechter, Bruce, **My Brain Is Open: The Mathematical Journeys of Paul Erdos**, New York: Simon and Schuster, 1998
Schimmel, Annemarie, **The Mystery of Numbers**, Oxford University Press, 1993
Schlipp, Paul A., **Albert Einstein, Philosopher-Scientist**, New York: Tudor Pub., 1951; paperback, LaSalle, Open Court, 1988
Schlipp, Paul A., ed., **The Philosophy of Rudolf Carnap**, Library of Living Philosophers, 1963
Schmalz, Rosemary, **Out of the Mouths of Mathematicians**, Mathematical Association of America, 1993
Schneider Hans,, and George Philip Baker, **Matrices and Linear Algebra**, New York: Dover, 1993
Schoenberg, Arnold, **Structural Function of Harmony**, 1911; paperback, W.W. Norton, 1969
Schoenfeld, Alan H., **Mathematical Problem Solving**, Orlando, FL: Academic Press, 1985
Scholfield, P.H., **The Theory of Proportion in Architecture**, Cambridge University Press, 1958
Schonland, Davis S., **Molecular Symmetry**, London: D. Van Nostrand, 1965
Schopenhauer, Arthur, **The World as Will and Representation**, 1844; E.F.J. Payne, tr., paperback, New York: Dover, 1966
Schroder, Manfred, **Fractals, Chaos, Power Lines: Minutes from an Infinite Paradise**, 1992
Schrodinger, Erwin, **From Mind and Matter**, Cambridge University Press, 1992
Schrodinger, Erwin, **Nature and the Greeks**, New York: Cambridge University Press, 1954
Schrodinger, Erwin, **Science and Human Temperament**, 1935; paperback, Roger Penrose, tr., Cambridge University Press, 1996
Schrodinger, Erwin, **Science Theory and Man**, London: G. Allen and Unwin, 1935
Schrodinger, Erwin, **What Is Life: The Physical Aspect of the Living Cell and Mind and Matter**, 1944; paperback, Cambridge University Press, 1992
Schubert, Hermann, **Mathematical Essays and Recreations**, Thomas McCormack, tr., Chicago: Open Court, 1903
Schwartzmann, Steven, **The Words of Mathematics: An Etymological Dictionary of Mathematical Terms Used in English**, paperback, Mathematical Association of America. 1994
Scientific American, **Mathematics in the Modern World: Readings from the Scientific American**, San Francisco: W.H. Freeman, 1968
Sciama, D.W., **The Unity of the Universe**, Garden City, NJ: Doubleday, 1959
Scott, Charlotte Angus, **Modern Analytical Geometry**, New York: G.E. Stechert, 1924
Scott, Charlotte Angus, **Projective Methods in Plane Analytical Geometry**, 1894
Scott, Dana, ed., **Axiomatic Set Theory**, American Mathematical Association, 1976
Scott, Joseph Frederick, **A History of Mathematics; From Antiquity to the Beginning of the Nineteenth Century**, London: Taylor and Francis, 1960, 1969
Scott, Joseph Frederick, **The Scientific Work of Rene Descartes**, Taylor & Francis, 1952
Scott, Walter, **Sonja Kovalevsky, Biography and Autobiography**, London, Ward & Downey, 1895
Seidenberg, A., **Lectures in Projective Geometry**, 1962

Selberg, Arte, **Collected Papers**, 1989; Springer-Verlag, 1991
Sentilles, D., **A Bridge to Advanced Mathematics**, Baltimore: Williams & Wilkins, 1975
Shanker, S.G., **Goedel's Theorem in Focus**, London: Routledge, 1988
Shannon, C., and W. Weaver, **A Mathematical Theory of Communication**, Urbana: University of Illinois Press, 1949
Shaw, James Byrnie, **Lectures on the Philosophy of Mathematics**, Chicago: Open Court, 1918
Shaw, James Byrnie, **Synopsis of Linear Associative Algebra**, Carnegie Institution of Washington, 1907
Shenker, Israel, **Words and Their Masters**, 1974
Shirer, Hampton N., ed., **Nonlinear Hydrodynamic Modeling: A Mathematical Introduction**, Lecture Notes on Physics, Vol. 27, 1985
Shotwell, James T., **The History of History**, 1923
Silk, Joseph, **The Big Bang**, San Francisco: W.H. Freeman, 1980
Simmons, George F., **Calculus Gems**, New York: McGraw-Hill, 1992
Simplicius, **Commentaries**, A.D. Heilberg, ed., 1884; Cornell University Press, 2000
Singh, Jagit, **Great Ideas in Information Theory, Language and Cybernetics**, New York: Dover, 1966
Singh, Jagjit, **Great Ideas of Modern Mathematics: Their Nature and Use**, New York: Dover, 1959
Singh, Simon, **Fermat's Enigma**, New York: Walter & Co., 1997
Singmaster, David, **Chronology of Computing Version 4**, 1994
Skinner, B.F., **Contingencies of Reinforcement: A Theoretical Analysis**, 1965
Skinner, B.F., **Walden Two**, paperback, Allyn & Bacon, 1976
Slonin, Morris James, **Sampling**, New York: Simon and Schuster, 1960
Smith, Adam, **The Wealth of Nations**, 1776; Modern Library, 1994
Smith, David Eugene, **History of Mathematics**: two volumes, Dover, 1951, 1958
Smith, David Eugene, **The Poetry of Mathematics and Other Essays**, New York, Scripta Mathematica, 1934
Smith, David Eugene, **The Progress of Arithmetic**, New York: Ginn, 1923
Smith, David Eugene, **A Source Book in Mathematics**, New York: McGraw- Hill, 1929, New York: Dover, 1959
Smith, David Eugene, **The Teaching of Elementary Mathematics**, New York, 1902
Smith, David Eugene, **The Teaching Of Geometry**, Boston: Ginn, 1911
Smith, D.E., and Jekuthiel Ginsburg, **Numbers and Numerals**, 1937
Smith, David Eugene, and L.C. Karpinski, **The Hindu-Arabic Numerals**, Boston and London, 1911
Smith, D.E. and M.L. Latham, **The Geometry of Rene Descartes**, Chicago: Open Court, 1925
Smith, D.E., and Y. Mikami, **A History of Japanese Mathematics**, Chicago: Open Court, 1914
Smith, H.W., **Art Matrix**. 1993
Smith, J. Maynard, **Mathematical Ideas in Biology**, Cambridge: Cambridge University Press, 1968
Smith, James, **The Quadrature and Geometry of the Circle Demonstrated**, 1872
Smith, Norman Kemp, **New Studies in the Philosophy of Descartes**, Macmillan, 1952
Smith, Preserved, **A History of Modern Culture**, Holt, Rinehart and Winston, 1940
Smith, W.B., **Introduction to Modern Geometry**, 1893
Sommerville, D.M.Y., **The Elements of Non-Euclidean Geometry**, New York: Dover, 1958
Somerville, Mary, **Personal Reflections from Early Life to Old Age of Mary Somerville with Selections from Her Correspondence**, Martha Somerville, ed., London: John Murray, 1873
Spencer, Herbert, **Essays on Education**, 1861; J.M. Dent & Sons, 1977
Spencer-Brown, George, **The Laws of Form**, 1969; paperback, Cognizer Co., 1994
Spiers, D., **Leonhard Euler**, 1929
Springer, T.A., **Invariant Theory**, New York: Springer-Verlag, 1977
Srinivasiengar, C.N., **The History of Ancient Indian Mathematics**, Calcutta, 1967
Stafford, T.H., **Mathematical Teaching**, Boston, 1907
Stahl, W.H., **Roman Science**, Madison: University of Wisconsin Press, 1962
Steen, Lynn A., ed. **For All Practical Purposes**, New York: W.H. Freeman, 1988
Steen, Lynn A., ed. **Mathematics Today**, New York: Springer-Verlag, 1978
Steen, Lynn A., ed. **Mathematics Tomorrow**, New York: Springer-Verlag, 1981
Steen, Lynn A., ed., **On the Shoulder of Giants: New Approaches to Numeracy**, National Academy Press, 1990
Steen, Lynn A., and D.J. Albers, ed., **Teaching Teachers, Teaching Students**, 4th Int. Congress on Mathematics Education, 1981
Steen, Lynn A., and J. Arthur Seebach, Jr., **Counterexamples in Topology**, New York: Holt, Rinehart and Winston, 1970
Stein, Dorothy, **Ada [Ada Byron Lovelace]: A Life and a Legacy**, Cambridge: MIT Press, 1985
Stein, Sherman K., **Mathematics: The Man-made Universe**, San Francisco: W.H. Freeman, 1963
Stein, Sherman K., **Strength in Numbers**, John Wiley & Sons, 1996
Steiner, Jacob, **Werke**, 1881; Chelsea Pub. Co., 1971
Steinhaus, Hugo, **Mathematical Snapshots**, 2nd. ed., New York: Oxford University press, 1960; paperback, New York: Dover, 1995
Stevens, Peter S., **Patterns in Numbers**, Boston: Little, Brown and Co., 1974

Stevin, Simon, **Die Thiende**, and **La Disme**, 1585
Stewart, Dugald, **The Complete Works of Dugald Stewart**, Sir William Hamilton, ed., Edinburgh: Thomas Constable & Co., 1854; Thoemmes Press, 1997
Stewart, Dugald, **Elements of the Philosophy of the Human Mind**, New York: Garland Pub., 1971
Stewart, Ian, **Concepts of Modern Mathematics**, Penguin, 1975; paperback, New York: Dover, 1995
Stewart, Ian, **Does God Play Dice?**, Oxford: Basil Blackwell, 1989
Stewart, Ian, **From Here to Infinity: A Guide to Today's Mathematics**, New York: Oxford University press, 1996
Stewart, Ian, **Galois Theory**, Chapman & Hall, 1973
Stewart, Ian, **Life's Other Secret**, New York: John Wiley & Sons, 1998
Stewart, Ian, **The Magical Maze**, New York: John Wiley & Sons, 1997
Stewart, Ian, **Nature's Numbers**, London: Weidenfeld and Nicolson, 1995
Stewart, Ian, **The Problems of Mathematics**, Oxford: Oxford University Press, 1987
Stewart Ian, and Martin Golubitsky, **Fearful Symmetry**, Oxford: Blackwell, 1992
Stewart, James, **Single Variable Calculus**, Brooks/Cole, 1999
Stibitz, G.R., **Mathematics in Medicine and the Life Sciences**, Year Book Medical Publishers, 1966
Stifel, Michael, **Arithmetica integra**, 1544
Stigler, Stephen M., **The History of Statistics**, paperback, Harvard University press, 1990
Storr, Anthony, **The Dynamics of Creation**, 1976; paperback, Unknown, 1993
Strong, Edward W., **Procedures and Metaphysics**, George Olms, 1966
Struik, Dirk, **A Concise History of Mathematics**, New York, 1987
Struik, Dirk, **Lectures on Analytic and Projective Geometry**, 1953; paperback, New York: Dover, 1988
Struik, Dirk, **A Source Book of Mathematics**, New York: Dover, 1967; Princeton University press, 1986
Styles, Stephen M., **The History of Statistics: The Measurement of Uncertainty Before 1900**, 1986
Sullivan, J.W.N., **Aspects of Science**, New York: Jonathan Cape & Harrison Smith, 1923
Sullivan, J.W.N., **The Bases of Modern Science**, Garden City, NJ: Doubleday, 1929
Sullivan, J.W.N., **Contemporary Mind, Some Modern Answers**, 1934
Sullivan, J.W.N., **The History of Mathematics in Europe**, London: Oxford University press, 1924
Sun Tze, **Gallery of Chinese Immortals**, AMS Press, 1975
Sun Tze, **The Illustrated Art of War**, Thomas Cleary tr., Shambbala Pubns., 1990
Sutton, O.G., **Mathematics in Action**, G. Bell, 1957
Swann, W.F.G., **The Architecture of the Universe**, New York: Macmillan, 1934
Swetz, F., **Learn from the Masters**, paperback, Mathematical Association of America, 1995
Sylvester, James Joseph, **The Collected Mathematical Papers of James Joseph Sylvester**, Cambridge: Cambridge University Press, 1908
Synge, J.L. **Relativity: The Special Theory**, Amsterdam: North-Holland Pub., 1956
Synge, J.L., and B.A. Griffith, **Principles of Mechanics**, New York: McGraw-Hill, 1959
Szent-Gyorgyi, Albert, **Perspective in Biology and Medicine**, 1971
Tagore, Rabindranath, **Our Universe**, Bombay: Jaico Pub., 1969
Tanur, J.M., et al, **Statistics: A Guide to the Unknown**, 1978
Tarnas, R., **The Passion of the Western World**, 1991; paperback, Ballantine, 1993
Tarski, Alfred, **Introduction to Logic and to the Methodology of Deductive Sciences**, 2nd. ed., New York: Oxford University Press, 1946
Tarski, Alfred, **Logic, Semantics, Metamathematics**, New York: Oxford University Press, 1956
Taton, Rene, ed., **The Beginnings of Modern Science**, Basic Books, 1964
Taylor, E.G.R., **The Mathematical Practitioners of Hanoverian England**, Cambridge: Cambridge University Press, 1966
Taylor, E.G.R., **The Mathematical Practitioners of Tudor and Stuart England**, Cambridge: Cambridge University Press, 1954
Taylor, Henry Osborn, **Thought and Expression in the Sixteenth Century**, Crowell-Collier, 1962
Teller, Edmund, **The Pursuit of Simplicity**, Malibu: Pepperdine University press, 1981
Temple, George, **The Structure of Lebesque Integration Theory**, 1971
Thayer, H.S., **Newton's Philosophy of Nature**, 1953
Thomas, Ivor, **Greek Mathematical Works**, Cambridge: Loeb Classical Library, 1967
Thomas, Ivor, tr., **Selections Illustrating the History of Greek Mathematics**, 1941, reprint, Cambridge: Harvard University Press, 1968
Thomas, J.M., **Theory of Equations**, New York: McGraw-Hill, 1938
Thompson, D'Arcy Wentworth, **On Growth and Form**, two volumes, Cambridge: Cambridge University Press, 1942
Thompson, Sylvanus P., **Calculus Made Easy**, New York: Macmillan, 1929
Thompson, Sylvanus P., **Life of William Thomson, Baron Kelvin of Largs**, London: 1910
Thompson, William P., **Science and Common Sense**, London: Longsman, Green Co., 1937
Thomson, William, **Popular Lectures and Addresses**, London: Macmillan, 1891
Thomson, William, and P.G. Tait, **Treatises on Natural Philosophy**, 1891
Thurston, William P., **Three-Dimension Geometry and Topology**, Silvio Levy, ed., Princeton University Press, 1997

Tietze, Heinrich, **Famous Problems of Mathematics**, New York: Graylock Press, 1965

Tikhomirov, V.M., **Stories About Maxima and Minima**, Abe Schenitzer, tr., Springer-Verlag, 1990

Tiles, Mary, **Mathematics and the Image of Reason**, Routledge, 1991

Tillich, Paul: **The Courage to Be**, paperback, New Haven: Yale Tippert. L.C., **Statistics**, 1944

Titchmarsh, E.C., **Mathematics for the General Reader**, 1950; New York: Dover, 1981

Titchmarsh, E.C., **The Theory of Functions**, Oxford: Oxford University Press, 1953

Tobias, R., **Felix Klein**, Leipzig: Teubner, 1981

Todhunter, Isaac, **The Conflict of Studies and Other Essays**, London, 1873

Todhunter, I., **History of the Calculus of Variations During the Nineteenth Century**, New York, 1861; New York: Chelsea, n.d.

Todhunter, I., **A History of the Mathematical Theory of Probability from the Time of Pascal to that of Laplace**, New York: Chelsea, 1949

Todhunter, I., **Private Study of Mathematics: Conflict of Studies and Other Essays**, 1873

Toeplitz, O., **The Calculus: A Genetic Approach**, Chicago: University of Chicago Press, 1963

Torrey, J., **The Philosophy of Descartes**, 1892

Toulouse, E., **Henri Poincare**, Paris: Flammarion, 1910

Trigg. C.W., ed., **Mathematical Quickies**, 1985

Trudeau, Richard J.: **Dots and Lines**, The Kent State University Press, 1976

Trudeau, Richard J., **The Non-Euclidean Revolution**, Boston: Birkhauser, 1987

Truesdell, Clifford, **Essays in the History of Mechanics**, New York: Springer-Verlag, 1968

Truesdell, Clifford, **Six Lectures on Modern Natural Philosophy**, Berlin: Springer-Verlag, 1966

Tuller, Annita, **A Modern Introduction to Geometries**, Toronto: D. Van Nostrand, 1967

Tupper, Martin, **Proverbial Philosophy: A Book of Thoughts and Arguments**, Philadelphia: E.H. Butler, 1867

Turnbull, Herbert W., **The Great Mathematicians**, New York: New York University Press, 1961, 1969

Turnbull, Herbert W., **The Mathematical Discoveries of Newton**, Glasgow, 1934; Blackie and Sons, 1945

Turnbull, H.W., and J.F. Scott, **The Correspondence of Isaac Newton**, 4 vols., Cambridge University Press, 1959-1967

Tutte, W.T., **Graph Theory**, Menlo Park, Ca.: Addison-Wesley, 1984

Tymoczko, Thomas, ed., **New Directions in the Philosophy of Mathematics**, Boston: Birkhauser, 1986; paperback, Princeton University Press, 1998

Ulam, Stanislaw, **Adventures of a Mathematician**, New York: Charles Scribners' Sons, 1976

Ulam, Stanislaw, **A Collection of Mathematical Problems**, John Wiley & Sons, 1960

Untermeyer, Jean, **Albert Einstein: Creator or Rebel**, 1973: New American Library, 1988

Urton, Gary, **The Social Life of Numbers: A Quechua Ontology of Numbers and Philosophy of Arithmetic**, paperback, Austin: University of Texas Press, 1997

Uspensky, J.V., **Introduction to Mathematical Probability**, 1977

Uspensky, J.V., **Theory of Equations**, New York: McGraw-Hill, 1948

Valery, Paul, **Collected Works**, J. Matthews, ed., 1970; William M. Stewart tr., Unknown, 1989

Van de Walle, John A., **Elementary School Mathematics: Teaching Developmentally**, paperback, Addison-Wesley, 1977

Van der Poorten, Alf, **Notes on Fermat's Last Theorem**, New York: John Wiley & Sons, 1996

Van Der Waerden, Bartel L., **Geometry and Algebra in Ancient Civilizations**, New York: Springer-Verlag, 1983

Van Der Waerden, Bartel L., **Modern Algebra**, New York: Ungar, 1949

Van Der Waerden, Bartel L., **Science Awakening**, Groningen: P. Noordhoff, 1954

Varberg, Dale, and Edwin I. Purcell, **Calculus with Analytical Geometry**, 1987; Prentice-Hall, 1996

Varenius, Bernhard, **Geographica Generalis**, 1650

Veblen, Oswald, and J.H.C. Whitehead, **The Foundations of Differential Geometry**, Cambridge: Cambridge University Press, 1932

Veblen, Oswald and John Wesley Young, **Projective Geometry**, Ginn, 1910-18

Veblen, Thorstein, **The Place of Science in Modern Civilization and Other Essays**, 1919; paperback, Transaction Pub., 1989

Venn, John, **The Logic of Chance**, London: Macmillan, 1888

Venn, John, **Symbolic Logic**, 1894; Chelsea, 1979

Vieta, Francois, **Introduction to the Analytical Art**, 1591

Vieta, Francois, **De numerosa poestatus resolutions**, 1600

Vieta, Francois, **Opera mathematica**, 1646, George Olms, 1970

Vitruvius Pollio, **The Ten Books of Architecture**, Frank Granger, tr., Cambridge: Loeb Classical Library, 1962; Harvard University Press, 1986

Von Clausewitz, Karl, **On War**, M. Howard and P. Paret, eds. & trs., 1976; Viking Press, 1983

Von Mies, Richard, **Mathematical Theory of Probability and Statistics**, New York: Academic Press, 1964

Von Mies, Richard, **Probability, Statistics and Truth**, Macmillan, 1957; Academic Press, 1964

von Mises, Ludwig Elder, **Human Action: A Treatise on Economics**, paperback, Fenn & Wilkins, 1997

von Mises, Ludwig Elder, **Positivism: A Study in Human Understanding**, 1957

Von Neumann, John, **Collected Works**, New York: Pergamon Press, 1961

Von Neumann, John, **The Computer and the Brain**, New Haven, Ct.: Yale University Press, 1959

Von Neumann, John and Oskar Morgenstern, **The Theory of Games and Economic Behavior**, Princeton: Princeton University Press, 1955

Vrooman, Jack V., **Descartes, A Biography**, New York: Putnam, 1970

Waddington, C.H., **Behind Appearances: A Study of Relations Between Painting and the Natural Sciences in the Century**, 1969

Waismann, Friedrich, **Introduction to Mathematical Thinking**, Frederick Unger Publishing, 1951

Walcott, C.D., **Smithsonian Mathematical Tables**, Smithsonian, 1909

Walker, F.A., **Discussions in Education**, New York, 189

Walker, Marshall, **The Nature of Scientific Thought**, Prentice-Hall, 1963

Wallas, May, ed. **The Art of Thought**, 1945

Wallis, John, **Algebra**, 1685; George Olms, 1968

Wallis, John, **Opera**, 3 vols., 1693-99; George Olms, 1968

Walls, H.S., **Creative Mathematics**, Austin: University of Texas Press, 1963

Walterhausen, Sartorius von, **Biography of Carl Gauss**, 1860; Springer-Verlag, 1965

Wang, Chamont, **Sense and Nonsense of Statistical Inference**, Marcel Dekker, 1993

Wang, H., **Reflections on Kurt Goedel**, Cambridge: MIT Press, 1988

Warren, Sir Charles, **The Ancient Cubit**, London: The Committee of the Palestine Exploration Fund, 1903

Wassen, Henry: **The Ancient Peruvian Abacus**, 1931

Watson, C.M., **British Weights and Measures**, London: John Murray, 1910

Weaver, Jefferson Hane: **The World of Physics**, New York: Simon and Schuster, 1987

Weaver, Warren, **Lady Luck**, Garden City, NY: Doubleday, 1963

Weber, Renee, **Dialogues with Scientists and Sages**, 1986

Weber, Renee, compiler, **A Random Walk in Science**, Adam Hilger, 1974

Wedberg, A., **Plato's Philosophy of Mathematics**, Westport, Ct.: Greenwood, 1955, 1977

Weeks, Jeffery R., **The Shape of Space**, New York: Michael Dekker, 1985

Weil, Andre, **Apprenticeship of a Mathematician**, Boston: Birkhauser, 1992; Jennifer Gags, tr., Springer-Verlag, 1992

Weil, Andre, **Number Theory: An Approach Through History**, Boston: Birkhauser, 1984

Weil, Simone, **The Need for Roots**, 1949; Routledge, 1996

Weil, Simone, **Notebooks**, 1952-55; Arthur Walls tr., Wonderbooks, 1970

Weil, Simone, **On Science, necessity, and the Love of God**, 1968

Weinberg, Gerald M., **An Introduction to General Systems Thinking**, paperback, John Wiley & Sons, 1975

Weinberg, Steven, **The First Three Minutes**, New York: Basic Books, 1977

Weinstein, Michael, **Examples of Groups**, paperback, Polygonal Pub., 1977

Weierstrass, Karl, **Mathematische Werke**, 7 vols., Mayer and Muller, 1895-1924

Weissglass, Julian, **Exploring Elementary Mathematics**, paperback, Kendall/Hunt, 1990

Weissmann-Chajes, Marcus, **Hokma UMusar**, 1875

Wells, David, **Curious and Interesting Mathematics**, London: Penguin Books, 1997

Wells, David, **Curious and Interesting Numbers**, London: Penguin Books, 1986

Wells, David, **You Are a Mathematician**, New York: John Wiley & Sons, 1995

Wells, R.O., and H.L. Resnikoff, **Mathematics in Civilization**, 1973; New York: Dover, 1985

Westfall, Richard S., **The Construction of Modern Science**, Cambridge: Cambridge University Press, 1980

Westfall, Richard S., **Never at Rest: A Biography of Isaac Newton**, Cambridge: Cambridge University Press, 1980, 1983

Weyl, Hermann, **Algebraic Theory of Numbers**, Princeton: Princeton University Press, 1940

Weyl, Hermann, **The Classical Groups: Their Invariants and Representations**, Princeton: Princeton University Press, 1939

Weyl, Hermann, **The Concept of a Riemann Surface**, Reading, Ma.: Addison-Wesley, 3rd. ed., 1955

Weyl, Hermann, **The Continuum: A Critical Examination of the Foundations of Analysis**, Thomas Bole, tr., New York: Dover, 1994

Weyl, Hermann, **Gesammelte Abhandlungen**, 4 vols., Springer-Verlag, 1968

Weyl, Hermann, **God and the Universe: The Open World**, New Haven: Yale University Press, 1932

Weyl, Hermann, **Mind and Nature**, Philadelphia: University of Pennsylvania Press, 1934

Weyl, Hermann, **Philosophy of Mathematics and Natural Science**, Princeton: Princeton University Press, 1947

Weyl, Hermann, **Space—Time—Matter**, New York: Dover, 1951; paperback, 1985

Weyl, Hermann, **Symmetry**, Princeton: Princeton University Press, 1952

Weyl, Hermann, **The Theory of Groups and Quantum Mechanics**, London: Methuen, 1931

Whatley, R., **Annotations to Bacon's Essays**, 1873

Wheeler, John Archibald, **Gravitation**, paperback, W.H. Freeman, 1973

Whetham, W.C.D., **Recent Development of Physical Science**, Philadelphia; P. Blackston's, 1904

Whewell, William, **Astronomy and General Physics**, London: Pickering, 1833

Whewell, William, **Elementary Treatise on Mechanics**, 1819

Whewell, William, **History of Inductive Sciences**, New York: Appleton, 1890; Specialized Book Services, 1967

Whewell, William, **History of Scientific Ideas**, 1860
Whewell, William, **The Philosophy of the Inductive Sciences**, London: 1858
Whewell, William, **Thoughts on the Study of Mathematics**, London: 1838
Whimbey, Arthur, **Problem Solving and Comprehension**, Philadelphia: Franklin Institute Press, 1982
White, Leslie, **The Science of Culture: A Study of Man and Civilization**, 1949
White, W.F., **A Scrapbook of Elementary Mathematics**, Chicago, 1908
Whitehead, Alfred North, **Adventures of Ideas**, New York: Macmillan, 1933; paperback, Mentor Book, 1955
Whitehead, Alfred North, **The Aims of Education**, New York: Macmillan, 1929; paperback, Free Press, 1985
Whitehead, Alfred North, **The Concept of Nature**, Cambridge: Cambridge University Press, 1920; paperback, Cambridge University Press, 1994
Whitehead, Alfred North, **An Introduction to Mathematics**, paperback, New York: Oxford University Press, 1959
Whitehead, Alfred North, **Modes of Thought**, New York: Macmillan, 1938
Whitehead, Alfred North, **The Principles of Relativity**, Cambridge: Cambridge University press, 1922
Whitehead, Alfred North, **Science and the Modern World**, New York: MacMillian, 1925; paperback, New York: New American Library, 1948
Whitehead, Alfred North, **Universal Algebra**, Cambridge: Cambridge University Press, 1898
Whitrow, Gerald J., **The Natural Philosophy of Time**, New York: Oxford University Press, 2nd. ed., 1980
Whitworth, William Allen, **Modern Analytic Geometry**: Cambridge: Cambridge University Press, 1866
Whitworth, William Allen, **Choice and Chance**, Hafner Publishing, 1951
Whyburn, G.T., **Analytical Topology**, American Mathematical Society, 1942
Wickelgren, Wayne A., **How to Solve Problems**, San Francisco: W.H. Freeman, 1974
Wiener, Norbert, **Cybernetics**, New York: John Wiley & Sons, 1948
Wiener, Norbert, **Ex-Prodigy**, Cambridge: The MIT Press, 1953
Wiener, Norbert, **The Human Use of Human Beings: Cybernetics and Society**, 1950; paperback De Capo, 1988
Wiener, Norbert, **I Am a Mathematician**, Garden City, N.J.: Doubleday, 1956
Wiener, P.P., ed., **Leibniz Selections**, Macmillan, 1982
Wigner, Eugene P., **Evolution of Mathematical Concepts**, London: Transworld Books, 1974
Wigner, Eugene P., **Mathematics as a Cultural System**, Oxford: Pergamon Press, 1981
Wigner, Eugene, **Symmetries and Reflections**, Westport, CT.: Greenwood Press, 1967
Wilder, Raymond L., **The Evolution of Mathematical Concepts**, New York: John Wiley & Sons, 1968, 1974
Wilder, Raymond L., **The Foundations of Mathematics**, New York: John Wiley & Sons, 1965
Wilder, Raymond L., **Mathematics as a Cultural System**, New York: Pergamon Press, 1981
Wilf, Herbert S., **Mathematics for the Physical Sciences**, John Wiley & Sons, 1962
Wilhelm, R., tr., **The I Ching or Book of Changes**, New York, 1950; Dover reprint, 1963
Wilks, Samuel S., **Elementary Statistical Analysis**, Princeton: Princeton University Press, 1948
Willerding, Margaret, **A Probability Primer**, Boston: Prindle, Weber & Schmidt, 1968
Williams, John Davis, **The Complete Strategist**, New York: McGraw- Hill, 1954
Wilson, J.C., **On the Tracing of Geometrical Figures**, Oxford University Press, 1905
Wimbish, G. Joseph, ed., **Readings for Mathematics: A Humanistic Approach**, Belmont, Ca.: Wadsworth Publishing, 1972
Winger, R.M., **An Introduction to Projective Geometry**, 1962
Wittgenstein, Ludwig, **On Certainty**, New York: Harper Torchbooks, 1969
Wittgenstein, Ludwig, **Philosophical Grammar**, 1974; A.J. Kenny, tr., University of California Press, 1978
Wittgenstein, Ludwig, **Philosophical Investigations**, G.E.M. Anscombe, tr., 1953; Oxford: Blackwell; Prentice-Hall, 1973
Wittgenstein, Ludwig, **Remarks of the Foundations of Mathematics**, New York: MacMillan, 1958; paperback, MIT Press, 1983
Wittgenstein, Ludwig, **Tractatus Logico-Philosophicus**, London: Routledge and Kegan Paul, 1922, 1933; Prentice-Hall, 1973
Wolf, Alan, **Parallel Universes**, New York: Simon and Schuster, 1988
Wolfe, H.E., **Non-Euclidean Geometry**, Holt, Rinehart and Winston, 1945
Woodville, Anthony, **Dictes and Sayeings of the Philosophus**, 1477
Woodward, Robert S., **Probability and Theory of Errors**, New York: John Wiley & Sons, 1906
Wordsworth, William, **The Prelude**, New York: D. Appleton & Co., 1850
Wright, Frank Lloyd, **The Works of the Mind**, Robert B. Heywood, ed., 1947
Wright, Harry N., **First Course in Theory of Numbers**, New York: John Wiley & Sons, 1939
Wylde, D.J., **Optimum Seeking Methods**, Englewood Cliffs, NJ: Prentice-Hall, 1964
Wylie, Clarence Raymond, Jr., **101 Puzzles in Thought and Logic**, New York: Dover, 1957
Xenophon, **A History of My Time**, Rex Warner, tr., Viking Press, 1985

Xenophon, **Memorabilia**, Amy L. Bonnette, tr., Cornell University Press, 1996

Yang, C.N., **Elementary Particles**, Princeton University Press, 1961

Yanin, Y., **Mathematics and Physics**, Boston: Birkhauser, 1983

Yates, Robert C., **The Trisection Problem**, Washington D.C., National Council of Teachers of Mathematics, 1971

Yedlham, F.A., **The Story of Reckoning in the Middle Ages**, London: Harrap, 1926

Youden, W.J., **Experimentation and Measurement**, Washington, D.C.: NCTM, 1962

Young, Charles Wesley, **Fundamental Concepts of Algebra and Geometry**, New York, 1910

Young, John W., **Projective Geometry**, Chicago : Open Court, 1930

Young, John W., **The Teaching of Mathematics**, London, 1907

Young, Robert M., **Excursion in Calculus**, paperback, Mathematical Association of America, 1992

Young, William H. and Grace C. Young, **The Theory of Sets of Points**, Cambridge: Cambridge University Press, 1906

Yule, George U., **An Introduction to the Theory of Statistics**, New York: Hafner Pub., 1950

Yushkevich, A., **A History of Mathematics in the Middle Ages**, Cambridge: Cambridge University Press, 1985

Zariski, O., **Algebraic Surfaces**, 2nd. ed., New York: Springer- Verlag, 1971

Zassenhaus, Hans, **The Theory of Groups**, Saul Kravetz, tr., New York: Chelsea, 1949

Zasvlasky, C., **Africa Counts: Number and Pattern in African Culture**, Boston: Prindle, Weber & Schmidt, 1973

Zee, A., **Fearful Symmetry**, New York: Macmillan, 1986

Zeeman, E. Christopher, **Catastrophe Theory**, 1977; Addison- Wesley, 1980

Zeiger, Monte, **The Magic of Pi**, 1979

Zeilik, Michael, **Astronomy: The Evolving Universe**, New York: Harper & Row, 1982

Zeller, M.C., **The Development of Trigonometry from Regiomontanus to Pitiscus**, Ann Arbor: Edwards, 1946

Zukav, Gary, **The Dancing Wu Li Masters**, New York: William Morrow, 1979

Author Index

References are to chapter number, decimal point, section number, decimal point, and the item in that section. For instance. 23.5.8 refers to quotation number 8 of section 5 in chapter 23.

Keyword Index

Certain words such as mathematics, mathematicians, number, science *and* scientists *occur so frequently they are not included in this index. References are to chapter number, decimal point, section number, decimal point, and the item in that section. For instance. 23.5.8 refers to quotation number 8 of section 5 in chapter 23.*